MEDICO-LEGAL ASPECTS OF REPRODUCTION AND PARENTHOOD

ADDENDUM

Some of the discussion of the Human Fertilisation and Embryology Act 1990 in Chapters 8 and 10 is unclear as to the distinction between the precise wording and the spirit of the Act. For the avoidance of doubt:

Section 4(1)(b) admits the possibility of donor insemination in private without the cover of a licence although the probable intention of the Act was to encourage the use of licensed clinics. Thus, while surrogacy is indirectly under the control of the Human Fertilisation and Embryology Authority insofar as it requires donor insemination, such control is only partial (page 260).

Section 28(2) is unconditional as to the status of the operator. Thus, the results of privately arranged inseminations are included in the section but, reading the section as a whole, HFEA would probably perceive it as requiring licensed treatment to be fully effective (page 215).

Titles in the Series:

All titles are provisional

MEDICO-LEGAL ASPECTS OF REPRODUCTION AND PARENTHOOD

SECOND EDITION

J.K. MASON
CBE, MD, LLD, FRCPath, FRSE
Regius Professor (Emeritus) of Forensic Medicine;
Honorary Fellow in the Faculty of Law
in the University of Edinburgh

DARTMOUTH

Aldershot • Brookfield USA • Singapore • Sydney

Published by
Dartmouth Publishing Company Limited
Ashgate Publishing Limited
Gower House
Croft Road
Aldershot
Hants GU11 3HR
England

Ashgate Publishing Company
Old Post Road
Brookfield
Vermont 05036
USA

British Library Cataloguing in Publication Data
Mason, J. K. (John Kenyon), 1919–
    Medico-legal aspects of reproduction and parenthood. – 2nd
    ed. – (Medico-legal series)
    1.Human reproduction – Law and legislation – Great Britain
    I.Title
    344.4'1'04194

Library of Congress Cataloging-in-Publication Data
Mason, J. K. (John Kenyon)
    Medico-legal aspects of reproduction and parenthood / J.K. Mason.
    –2nd ed.
        p. cm. — (Medico-legal series)
        Includes bibliographical references and index.
        ISBN 1-84014-065-8 (hbk.). – ISBN 1-85521-816-X (pbk.)
        1. Human reproduction–Law and legislation.   2. Husband and wife.
    3. Parent and child (Law)   I. Title.   II. Series.
    K2000.M37   1998
    346.01'63–dc21   97-38226
                                                                CIP

ISBN 1 84014 065 8 (Hbk)
ISBN 1 85521 816 X (Pbk)

Typeset by Manton Typesetters, 5–7 Eastfield Road, Louth, LN11 7AJ, UK.

Printed and bound by Athenaeum Press. Ltd.,
Gateshead. Tyne & Wear.

Contents

List of Cases

Australian cases

Battersby v. Tottman and State of South Australia (1985) 37 SASR 524; 92
Chamberlain v. The Queen (1983) 46 ALR 493; [No 2] (1983) 153 CLR 521 (HC); 382 n.30
Doodeward v. Spence (1908) 6 CLR 406; 177
Elizabeth, Re (1989) 13 Fam LR 47; 78 n.40, n.42
Ellis v. Wallsend District Hospital (1990) 2 Med LR 103; 91 n.105
F, F v. F, Re (1986) Unreported, Supreme Court of Victoria, 2 July; 311
F v. R (1983) 33 SASR 189, SC; 95
Jane, Re (1989) 13 Fam LR 47; 78
K v. Minister for Youth and Community Service and another [1982] 1 NSWLR 311; 53 n.52
L and M, Re (1993) 17 Fam LR 357; 79 n.46
Marion, Re (1992) 17 Fam LR 336; 79 n.45
R. v. Cogley [1989] VR 799; 9, 29 n.52
R. v. Davidson [1969] VR 667; 113
R. v. Harris (1989) 35 A Crim R 146; 9
R. v. Hutty [1953] VR 338; 388
R. v. McGuiness (1989) 35 A Crim R 146; 9
R v. Wald and others (1972) 3 DCR (NSW)25; 113 n.23
Rogers v. Whitaker (1992) 109 ALR 625, [1993] 4 Med LR 79; 91 n.100, 92
Secretary, Department of Health and Community Services (N.T.) v. J.W.B. and S.M.B. (1992) 66 ALJR 300; 78 n.43,n.44
Teenager, Re a (1988) 13 Fam LR 85; 78, 83 n.63
Watt v. Rama [1972] VR 353; 146 n.17,n.18

Canadian cases

Baby R, Re (1989) 53 DLR (4th) 69; 174 n.166
Borowski v. Attorney General of Canada et al. (1987) 39 DLR (4th) 731; 121 n.54, 144 n.3

United States cases

Table of Statutes

Preface

Seven years in medical law and ethics is comparable to the seven ages of man. So much has happened since the first edition was published that this product has felt, throughout, more like a new book than a new edition.

The greater part of the field covered here has been transformed by the passing of the Human Fertilisation and Embryology Act 1990, the Children Acts have come into force and a single section of the Criminal Justice and Public Order Act has revolutionised the criminal aspects of sexuality. Case law governing the treatment of children has been dominated by Lord Donaldson in his role of Master of the Rolls but, while the clinical autonomy of the medical profession has been increasingly acknowledged, the forced retreat from *Bolam* gathers speed. And, just as you are beginning to think that there is no more room in which new situations can develop, Mrs Blood is refused access to posthumous insemination by her husband and P wins the right to change sex between classes. A major problem has been to decide when to lower the portcullis and allow no more new material through.

But that is what makes medical law such a fascinating subject and none of us teaching and researching in the field would have it otherwise. It does, however, make single authorship a hazardous occupation and I am, again, particularly grateful to my colleagues both in and beyond the Faculty of law in the University of Edinburgh for their unfailing willingness to help me with the intricacies of the law – for another problem of medical law is that it crosses all recognised legal boundaries.

I also record my gratitude to Ashgate Publishing for smoothing out a voyage of publication that has been characterised by a degree of turbulence beyond that which they normally experience.

Edinburgh   JKM
October 1997

1   Sex and Marriage

This book is concerned, in the main, with reproduction – for which marriage is not an essential prerequisite. Nevertheless, much of sexuality and the greater part of parenthood still subsist within the marital relationship. Sex and marriage are interdependent; indeed, the definition of the latter depends upon that of the former. A short introductory note on marriage and sex is not, therefore, out of place.

Marriage

Considering the fact that some one in three marriages end in divorce,[1] it is surprising to find that marriage is still defined in the purely civil ceremony conducted in the Registrar's Office as the union of one man and one woman, voluntarily entered into, for life, to the exclusion of all others.[2] The general principles, however, remain intact despite the erosion of permanence. Thus, although there has been a marked increase of ethnic minorities within the British population in the late 20th century, it is still impossible to contract a lawful polygamous marriage while a resident of or domiciled in the United Kingdom.[3] The official status of a marriage is ensured by the legal need to accept a number of associated preliminaries and ceremonies. While it is still possible to marry in Scotland by way of cohabitation with repute, marriage throughout the United Kingdom must otherwise take place before a Superintendent Registrar of Marriages, according to the rites of the Anglican Church, according to the customs and rites of the Quakers or Jews (in which case, the marriage need not be public) or before a person who is authorized to celebrate marriage, generally a minister of a particular religious group.[4] It is difficult to judge how long this situation will prevail. An increasing amount of statute law gives equal rights to both a cohabiter and an officially married spouse,[5] and in some areas of the Commonwealth the position of the de facto spouse has even greater recognition;[6]

1

very large numbers of couples now cohabit as a matter of preference and virtually all the disadvantages of illegitimacy to any offspring have now been eliminated. The British are, however, inately opposed to change and the number of couples who resort to marriage following often long periods of living together is notable; moreover, the state has a continuing interest in keeping records of marriages for purposes such as the payment of welfare benefits. It is probable that the existing order will be maintained for the foreseeable future – certainly as to the general requirements.

Valid marriage

The following are the essentials for a valid marriage.

a   It must be monogamous. This is a legal matter which has no medical connotations.
b   It must be voluntary, a matter which raises both legal and medical issues. Firstly, the parties must be legally capable of consenting and this is essentially a question of age. Parental consent is required in England and Wales (but not in Scotland) if either person is aged less than 18 years.[7] It is not needed when the proposed marriage has been announced by means of ecclesiastical banns or in the seemingly unlikely event that the minor is a widow or widower; in any event, an application can be made to the court – generally the magistrates' – if consent is withheld and, further, the fact that a minor has married without parental consent will not invalidate the marriage. Secondly, the parties must also be medically able to consent; this is mainly a problem of mental capacity.
c   The marriage must be heterosexual, a matter which may be of profound medical interest and importance.

Void marriage

A void marriage is one which never was – it is a matter of fact and the parties concerned have no option of rejection; no decree of nullity is called for of necessity. It may, however, be in the interests of one or other party to obtain such a decree as the court could then apply the same powers to make financial and other orders as it has when dissolving a valid marriage. A marriage is void in England and Wales because:

a   it is not a valid marriage under the provisions of the Marriage Acts 1949 to 1983, that is to say where:
   i   the parties are within the prohibited degrees of relationship;[8]

ii either party is under the age of 16; or

iii the parties have intermarried in disregard of certain requirements as to the formation of marriage;[9]

b at the time of the marriage either party was already lawfully
married;

c the parties are not, respectively, male or female;

d in the case of a polygamous marriage entered into outside England and Wales, either party was at the time of the marriage
domiciled in England and Wales.[10]

The reasons are slightly different in Scotland and are categorised
in the Marriage (Scotland) Act 1977 as either rendering the marriage
specifically void – by virtue of a party being under the age of 16 or
the parties being within the forbidden degrees of kinship (ss.1 & 2[11])
– or as constituting a legal impediment to marriage. The latter may
operate prospectively or retrospectively (s.5(4)) and include age,
bigamy, forbidden degrees of relationship, the fact that both parties
were of the same sex or that one or both parties was incapable of
understanding the nature of the marriage ceremony or of consenting
to marriage. Purely administrative reasons for a marriage being void
have been removed by the Law Reform (Miscellaneous Provisions)
(Scotland) Act 1980, s.22.

Voidable marriage

Voidable marriages, by contrast, are those marriages which are valid
unless they are annulled. The list of grounds in England and Wales is
long but is quite specific:[12]

a that the marriage has not been consummated owing to the incapacity of either party to consummate it;

b that the marriage has not been consummated owing to the wilful
refusal of the respondent to consummate it;

c that either party to the marriage did not validly consent to it,
whether in consequence of duress, mistake, unsoundness of mind
or otherwise;

d that at the time of the marriage either party, though capable of
giving a valid consent, was suffering (whether continuously or
intermittently) from mental disorder within the meaning of the
Mental Health Act 1983 of such a kind or to such an extent as to
be unfitted for marriage;

e that at the time of the marriage the respondent was suffering
from venereal disease in a communicable form;[13]

f that at the time of the marriage the respondent was pregnant by
some person other than the petitioner.[14]

In Scotland, impotency constitutes the only ground for regarding a marriage as voidable; the other reasons cited in England may or may not, depending on the circumstances, provide grounds for divorce.

It is clear that the medico-legal interests in the validity of marriage relate to the mental health and the sex of the parties. Consummation of marriage is more a matter of sexual intercourse and reproduction and will be considered as a separate issue.

Mental disorder and marriage   The definition of what constitutes mental disorder of sufficient severity to render a marriage voidable in England or void in Scotland is not absolutely clear. The English law has moved further than that in Scotland insofar as the Scots criteria are far more difficult to satisfy; this difficulty was, in fact, a main reason for the introduction of the English statutory wording now found in the Matrimonial Causes Act 1973, s.12 (*d*).

It will be apparent that a considerable degree of mental disorder is required to invalidate consent to marriage. It has been said that, to ascertain the nature of the contract of marriage, a man must be mentally capable of appreciating that it involves the responsibilities normally attaching to marriage,[15] and that this is not a severe test – a point which was made in the Scottish case of *Long* v. *Long*.[16] Moreover, a person with severe mental disorder may be sufficiently lucid at the time of the ceremony to satisfy the requirements for a valid consent. There is also considerable doubt as to who is to draw attention prospectively to the legal impairment of a lack of understanding of the marriage ceremony. It seems to be asking for a considerable degree of diagnostic skill on the part of the minister or registrar to recognise such a defect at the time of the ceremony if no-one has previously contested the marriage and if a medical certificate of mental incompetence, as is required by statute, has not been provided. All in all, it appears that it is considerably harder to have a marriage declared void on the grounds of mental illness in Scotland, where there are no provisions comparable to those in the Matrimonial Causes Act 1973, s.12, than it is to have a similar marriage assessed as voidable in England.

On the other hand, the English term 'unfitted for marriage', apart from having unfortunate paternalistic overtones, is so vague as to leave much room for uncertainty: it is hard to see the limits of what constitutes an inability to carry on a normal married life or, indeed, quite what physical or behavioural shortcomings render one unfitted for marriage that would not, at the same time, constitute grounds for divorce. The situation is not made any easier by the fact that, in contradistinction to the grounds relating to venereal disease and pregnancy, knowledge of mental disorder at the time of marriage is not a bar to a petition for annulment. The most apposite case still appears to be *Bennett* v. *Bennett*,[17] despite the fact that the judgment related to the wording of the then extant Matrimonial Causes Act 1965. ORMROD J was critical of the drafting. 'I am quite unable,' he said, 'to suggest any meaning that can be given to the phrase "unfitted for the procreation of children" ' (at 542) and, again: 'What attacks of insanity are, I do not know' (at 542); and there can be no doubt that his strictures were mainly responsible for the altered phraseology of the Nullity of Marriage Act 1971.[18] Nevertheless, the judge was clearly reluctant to extend the grounds for voiding a marriage any further than could be helped: 'It can only be those unfortunate people who suffer from a really serious mental disorder who can positively be stated in humane terms to be incapable of marriage'; and he expanded on this in relation to Mrs Bennett herself: 'That she was going to be a rather difficult person to be married to ... is a very different matter.'

The case of *Re B*[19] demonstrates another aspect of uncertainty in that, if it is unlawful to have sexual intercourse with a mentally ill person,[20] and if the marriage of one who is mentally disordered is subject to being held voidable, then it would appear that no mentally disordered woman may have sexual intercourse lawfully,[21] and this raises a strong suspicion of unreasonable discrimination against the handicapped. Despite the number of modifications that have been made over recent years, there still seems to be a need to tidy up the relationship between mental disorder, nullity and divorce.

Sex

Ormrod pointed out in 1972 that the law was largely indifferent to sex,[22] and this may well be so; the observation certainly applies, say, in relation to social security and insurance,[23] passports, driving licences and the like. We, however, are concerned here only with sex as it applies to family law through marriage and, in that context, it is highly significant. As we will see later, British law has always been adamant that the sex entered on one's birth certificate records a historic fact which can be altered only in the event that there was a genuine error at the time. The possible ways of making a mistake at birth thus merit description.

The common way of diagnosing the sex of a baby is to look at the *genitalia* which are normally differentiated after the fourth month of gestation. The testes are present in the male scrotum and the female vulva is formed by the time of birth. Developmental abnormalities include hypospadias in the male; in its extreme form, the open urethra and minute penis may be mistaken for female genitalia. There are a number of congenital conditions in which there is failure to 'masculinise', detailed discussion of which is beyond the scope of this book. They are mainly associated with failure to produce or utilise the 'male' hormone testosterone, the general rule being that female differentiation is, in the main, a negative process – feminisation occurs when there are no male factors operating. The majority of such hormonal conditions are determined genetically. Simulated male genital organs may occur in the female in the condition of congenital adrenal hyperplasia, in which an excess of adrenal hormones may cause enlargement of the clitoris to penile size. This may be due to ingestion of maternal androgens or to a genetic abnormality; in the latter circumstance, signs and symptoms are more likely to arise in childhood or later and this may account for a proportion of those cases in which a genuine change of sex has been suspected.

The *gonadal* sex is likely to be difficult to ascertain in those cases in which the true sex is in doubt because, almost by definition, the male testes will be undescended and retained either within the abdominal cavity or in the inguinal canal. An abdominal operation might therefore be needed to distinguish between testes and ovaries or to determine whether both were present – as occurs in the very rare condition of true hermaphroditism; such an intrusion would be almost impossible to justify *per se* and sex determination on these grounds would only be made as part of a surgical treatment. The extreme accompaniment of maldescent of the testes is the testicular feminisation syndrome in which the tissues do not respond to the elaboration of male hormones and masculinisation does not occur: the term is, therefore, a misnomer. The typical result is the slim type of female beauty with female breasts and normal external genitalia; the subject, nevertheless, remains chromosomally male (see below), is sterile and has an inadequately developed internal female sexual anatomy, in particular, and most importantly in the present context, often having an atretic vagina. In an 'incomplete' form of the condition, maleness increases at puberty, a situation which may again suggest a natural change of sex.

The paired sex chromosomes are designated X and Y – the Y chromosome being needed for the development of testes. The normal female therefore has the genetic constitution XX and the male XY. There are various ways in which this *chromosomal* sex can be demonstrated. The most specific method is to culture the white cells of the blood and to isolate the nuclear chromosomes which can then be observed and counted; this, however, dictates the use of a specialist laboratory. More simply, the second X in the female can be seen as a 'Barr body' – a condensation of chromosomal material which lies at the periphery of the nucleus of up to half the cells in the female body.[24] Alternatively, the 'Davidson body', a drumstick-like nuclear appendage, can be found in 2–3 per cent of the polymorphonuclear white cells in the blood of a female. Maleness is only diagnosed negatively by these means. The Y chromosome can be identified positively and with greater difficulty by using a fluorescence technique. Numerical abnormalities of the sex chromosomes occur in up to 1:1000 live births. Thus there may be an excess of X chromosomes in the male (XXY or XXXY, Klinefelter's syndrome) or a deficiency in the female (XO, Turner's syndrome);[25] although there is a tendency to appearances of the opposite sex in these persons, the diagnosis is rarely in doubt.

The result of an error in sexing a neonate may be seen in the social sexual status or *gender* of the developing child. It has been shown above that several types of apparent sex change – and others which have not been included – will manifest themselves only at puberty when anomalies as to, say, menstruation, may appear. By this time, the child may have become psychiatrically attuned to his or her 'wrong' sex and the management of the case may thus present serious problems. It may well seem that the kindest course is to maintain the status quo and, if necessary, to support this with any surgical or hormonal treatment indicated. To do so, however, would probably involve some deception of the child and would be, at the least, deontologically suspect. Moreover, what may have seemed at the time to be a good utilitarian decision may turn out, in the end, to have been misjudged. The nature of any condition which gives rise to doubt as to sex must, almost certainly, result in later difficulties as to sexual intercourse and procreation; the wrongly sexed child is likely to be doomed to an unsatisfactory sex life and to a miserable marriage which may terminate in the emotional arena of the family court. In any case, there are bound to be severe psychiatric disturbances which may, ultimately, lead to rejection of the sex assigned.

Some examples of the gender dysphoria syndrome – or transsexualism – may develop in this way, but they must be a minority. Most cases arise in persons whose anatomical sex is undisputed but who are diametrically opposed to its psychiatric acceptance. Some of these attitudes may be stimulated by the environment in which the person lives but, on the whole, it is more probable that one's psychological sex, or personal gender, is predetermined at birth.[26] In any event, the conviction of being of the wrong sex tends to grow from puberty and may be accompanied by actual physical changes.[27] In the end, there may be recourse to reassignment surgery and it is the surgically converted transsexual who poses the greatest dilemma in respect of marriage – for successful treatment, at least in the case of the originally male transsexual, results in a person who is able to provide affection and sexual satisfaction in the role with which the subject is socially and emotionally compatible.[28] Apposite cases which come to be adjudicated before the courts are rare; it may be that transsexual 'marriages' occur more commonly than is supposed and that it is only those running into difficulty which achieve public notice.[29] In such circumstances, the British transsexual seems to be received less sympathetically than is his or her counterpart in Europe or the United States, a situation which is sustained by continued reliance on the judgment in *Corbett*.[30]

Transsexual 'marriage'

The essential issue in *Corbett* was to decide whether or not a man who had undergone reassignment surgery was a woman for the purposes of marriage, and the trial judge was at pains to emphasise the relatively restricted nature of the case. In the event, the judgment was to the effect that the answer must be reached on the basis of biological criteria: 'Marriage is a relationship,' said ORMROD J, 'which depends on sex and not on gender' (at 107). Having thus decided, it was then relatively easy to establish three main biological findings – the chromosomal pattern, the original gonadal status and the pre-operative genitalia – which were congruent in determining male-ness; accordingly, and notwithstanding the effect of any plastic surgery, the 'marriage' was seen as one between two biological males and one which was, therefore, void.

The *Corbett* case set a precedent and the judgment has stood the test of 25 years' scrutiny – at least within the United Kingdom. Yet there are several aspects of the judgment which leave loose ends. The foremost of these centres on the fortunate fact that there was no real argument as to the congruence of the biological criteria of sex. ORMROD J gave it as his opinion obiter that, given a discrepancy between them, the pre-operative condition of the genitalia would take pre-cedence over the other two, but the law report gives no indication of what genital conditions would be invoked. The presence of a penis pierced by a urethra may be adequate in man, but what of a woman: a vulva, a vagina of given length, a palpable cervix? Secondly, the biological criteria were held to be paramount because no others would define a person who is 'naturally capable of performing the essential role of the woman in marriage'. But whether this is regarded as giving sexual satisfaction or as procreating children makes a great deal of difference and is unstated. There is also the comparatively unimportant implication that the decision might have been influenced had the respondent been an example of Klinefelter's syndrome, as was suggested at the time. Were that condition to obtain, the overriding importance of the Y chromosome as an indicator of male-ness would be called into question.

The facts that such criticisms can be raised and that the answers are so uncertain serve to explain why the *Corbett* decision is widely thought to have concentrated on the chromosomal constitution as representing the ultimate arbiter of sex. This parameter has the values of permanence and of certainty but, otherwise, it must be the least satisfactory measure; of all the criteria available for consideration, whether they be biological, hormonal or psychological, the one thing that ordinary persons do not know about themselves, nor care about, is the appearance of their karyotype. But, no matter what may be the impression that has gained ground, it is by no means certain that ORMROD J intended his judgment to be so interpreted. That can only be inferred from his words:

> The biological sexual constitution of an individual is fixed at birth (at the latest), and cannot be changed, either by the natural development of organs of the opposite sex, or by medical or surgical means ... The only cases where the term 'change of sex' is appropriate are those in which a mistake as to sex is made at birth and subsequently revealed by further medical investigation (at 104).

But, on analysis, it is seen that the genital appearances can certainly be changed by hormonal treatment and that, equally, the gonadal constitution can be affected either by disease or by surgery. One is then left, as a matter of exclusion, with the chromosomal state as being the only criterion which is clearly immutable. Thus *Corbett* was interpreted in *R v. Tan*[31] as holding that a person who was born a man and *remained biologically a man* (my emphasis) was a man for the purposes of marriage and it was considered that the rule should also apply to the Sexual Offences Acts of 1956 and 1967. But, in *Tan*, the appellant's gonadal and genital biological constitution *had* been altered – so, again, only the chromosomes can be said to be 'remaining'. Such inevitable complications that result from extrapolating family law to the criminal field have been addressed in the Australian cases of *R v. Cogley* and *R v. Harris, R v. McGuiness*,[33] where the practical irrelevance of a person's chromosomes to his or her gender was stressed.

The *Corbett* doctrine has, however, been criticised on less academic grounds as showing a lack of sympathy for and understanding of those who are suffering from a recognized medical abnormality; it has even been described as 'infamous'.[34] Thus it is suggested that a marriage should not be declared legally never to have existed unless it can be shown never to have existed in the minds of the parties themselves. The test of validity should be that of 'apparent sex' and the marriage should be valid if the transsexual is found to be capable of fulfilling the role of the sex he or she has assumed, including the ability to give and to attract love and understanding.[35] 'What pride can there be,' it has been asked, 'for a law which vetoes the attitudes dictated by ordinary humanity?'[36] Samuels has summed up these attitudes:[37] 'A person should be entitled to choose his or her own destiny, identity, gender, and sex, provided that he or she conforms to the usual social norms and is socially acceptable. Society ought not to deny these human rights'.[38]

The law itself has moved in that direction in the United States, where the test of sex appears to be based, in the main, on function. Thus, in *B* v. *B*,[39] which was a case involving female-to-male reassignment, a marriage was annulled on the grounds that the 'man' could never function sexually as a man. A very different conclusion was reached, however, in the New Jersey case *M T* v. *J T*,[40] concerning the more common male to female transition, in which the sex of the transsexual was founded on the post-operative state; 'she' was found to be capable of acting within marriage as a female and the reasoning in *Corbett* was specifically rejected. HANDLER J felt: 'impelled to the conclusion that, for marital purposes, if the anatomical or genital features of a genuine transsexual are made to conform to the person's gender, psyche or psychological sex, then identity by sex must be given by the congruence of these standards'; and he could perceive 'no legal barrier, cognisable social taboo, or reason grounded in public policy, to prevent that person's identification, at least for the purposes of marriage, to the sex generally indicated'. The fact that there was little acrimony associated with the case may have had a mellowing effect on the judge. Nonetheless, faced with a difficult and uncommon situation, the approach in *M T* v. *J T* appears preferable to that taken in *Corbett*. The problem is, however, surely one which must be solved through legislation rather than by way of judicial opinion.

The difficulties associated with the *Corbett* test are demonstrated most clearly when confronted with the testicular feminisation syndrome. It is a familial X-linked condition which exists in about 1:25 000 'women'. No-one would doubt the 'femininity' of the vast majority of instances and there must be a very considerable number of undisclosed cases, many of whom are happily married. Ormrod[41] has written that, confronted with such a case in the family court, the genital sex would probably take precedence over the other criteria. This is inconsistent on at least two grounds. Firstly, given the persistence of the *Corbett* decision, it is almost bizarre to classify someone who has no ovaries but who has recognisable testes[42] and XY chromosomes as not being of male sex. Secondly, since most cases have an atretic vagina and, at best, a vestigial uterus, the biological test ceases to be genital and becomes, rather, vulval. It is argued later (p.31) that this may, in fact, be a reasonable interpretation, but it would be more honest and more generally acceptable to admit that cases of the testicular feminisation syndrome are female by virtue of their personal and societal gender. The wheel has then turned full circle, because consistency would direct that converted transsexuals should be subject to a similar test. There is, of course, a difference in that the feminisation case has never been regarded as being anything other than female, whereas the transsexual's gender has changed. It follows that each disputed case of transsexualism would have to be judged on its own facts but that, amongst those, it would be proper to include the extent and acceptability of the 'sex change', including, in the *Corbett* phraseology, how convincing was the 'pastiche of femininity'; in short, there is nothing to prevent society perceiving a person to be a man or a woman on the basis of his or her compliance with the superficial characteristics of one sex rather than those of the other. Moreover, the *Corbett* test leads to the incongruous, though logical, conclusion that a marriage between a converted male to female transsexual and a biological woman would be perfectly legal despite the fact that the ceremony would have all the trappings of a lesbian 'marriage'.[43] In fact, it seems that at least one such marriage has been officially registered since this chapter was rewritten.[44]

There can be little doubt that legal opinion, at least, is being swept in the tide of liberal pan-Europeanism towards a gender-based definition of sex. This is well seen in the recent opinion of TESAURO A-G in *P v. S and Cornwall County Council*.[45] This case was, admittedly, unconnected with marriage and was concerned with the relationship between the Council of Europe Directive 76/2207/EEC[46] and the Sex Discrimination Act 1975. The question put was, in essence, whether the directive was breached by the dismissal of an employee who was appointed as a man but who wished to remain in the same post as a surgically reassigned woman. The learned Advocate General, rightly, ignored *Corbett* – for, as we have seen, *Corbett* concerned marriage only – but also cast aside the principles of anatomy, physiology and genetics and concentrated entirely on the question of personal rights. The Advocate General asked the Court to make a courageous decision 'in the profound conviction that what is at stake is a universal fundamental value ... : *the irrelevance of a person's sex with regard to the rules regulating relations in society*' (emphasis in the original), which they duly did, holding that 'to tolerate such discrimination would be tantamount, in regard to such a person, to a failure to respect the dignity and freedom to which he or she was entitled, and which the court had a duty to safeguard'.[47]

But can we adopt this approach and apply it to marriage? The question is already partially answered in that a transsexual's post-operative sex is recognised in at least 11 European countries[48] – and possibly more, depending on the definition of recognition, which is subject to varying legal and administrative requirements. The requirements for lawful change of sex in Germany provide an example of the restrictions imposed. They include that: the medical condition of transsexualism has been present for at least three years, the subject is aged over 25 years, is unmarried, has been sterilised and has undergone adequate reassignment surgery.[49] Such legislation may be distasteful to many, but others could regard it as being preferable to relying on case law, particularly when the case law is likely to be made by a court composed of judges from disparate jurisdictions.[50] There are eight countries in the European Union in which the legal definition of sex is sufficiently wide to include transsexual marriage;[51] this liberal attitude extends beyond Europe and now includes South Australia, New Zealand and many of the states of the USA and provinces of Canada.[52] The United Kingdom, however, has resolutely defended the concept of the inviolate birth certificate, and continues to do so.[53] While, as we have seen, this is of remarkably little significance in the great majority of daily life situations, it is of critical importance to marriage where misstatement of one's sex by way of a false declaration[54] may constitute an offence under the Perjury Act, 1911, s.3. This dichotomy could, in fact, lead to practical as well as theoretical difficulties within the European Union, in that the capacity to marry is determined by the antenuptial domicile of the parties concerned; a British transsexual would, therefore, be barred from marriage in Germany where the ceremony would be legal.[55] The resulting paradoxical situation has already been addressed twice in the European Court of Human Rights where appellants have contended that the United Kingdom legislation transgresses the individual's basic rights to privacy and to marriage.[56]

The first of these, *Rees v. United Kingdom*,[57] concerned a female-to-male conversion, a change which is, admittedly, often difficult to support on physiological grounds. The court had little difficulty in dismissing the appeal on the largely technical grounds that the relatively relaxed attitude to sex in the United Kingdom precluded an interference with a person's privacy – a 12:3 decision as to article 8;[58] the judges were unanimous that, since marriage was clearly a matter of union between two persons of opposite biological sex, there was no infringement of article 12. Five years later, the court was asked, effectively, to overturn *Rees* in *Cossey v. United Kingdom*.[59] This they refused to do but, on this occasion, by the slender majority of 10:8 as to article 8 and by 14:4 in respect of article 12. The main arguments were, again, largely technical and the greatest interest in *Cossey* lies, perhaps, in the dissenting judgment of MARTENS J, who based his opinion largely on the changing societal attitudes to activities that are essentially private. He drew attention to the fact that the court in *Rees* had left the door open to a reassessment in the event of later scientific and societal developments,[60] and suggested that full legal acceptance of the change in status was an integral part of the 'treatment' of gender dysphoria. There can be little doubt of a general shift of mood in the European Court and it would be difficult to predict the result were a similar case to be brought against the United Kingdom today.[61]

Humane decisions taken within the liberal ambience of continental Europe are one thing, but the question remains open as to whether or not intrasex marriages would be regarded as desirable in the United Kingdom on grounds of public policy. Some might hold that the increase in cohabitation resulting from both custom and legislation, coupled with the current ease and acceptability of divorce, have so undermined the status of marriage that a further invasion is irrelevant.[62] Thomson has also suggested that the way to intrasex marriage may be found in the wording of the relevant legislation; thus, while *Corbett* was decided on the basis of the ceremonial definition of marriage – the union of one man and one woman – the later Matrimonial Causes Act 1973, whether or not by express intention, uses the terms 'male' and 'female' in similar context. Reverting to the testicular feminisation syndrome, it is, as we have seen, nearly impossible to avoid the logical conclusion that the subject is a 'man'; but, at the same time, it is pragmatic and acceptable good sense to see 'him' as being female – and it is not a big step to extrapolate such reasoning to the transsexual. Similar observations are to be found in the academic textbooks.[63]

Public opinion might be willing to approve a change in the law to allow for a genuine medical need within an acceptable, albeit potentially hypocritical, 'pastiche' of marriage as it is generally understood. The practical difficulty which is foreseen is that those promoting such a change would be unable to resist extending it. Thus, some years ago, Kennedy[64] pursued his argument in favour of transsexual marriage so as to include blatantly homosexual marriages: 'I have no doubt [they] will occur,' he wrote, 'later if not sooner'. The analogy is, however, at least suspect. While marriage is defined as the union between man and woman, the parties do not have to be *complete* men or women. A man with undescended testes or a woman with no uterus or a surgically enlarged vagina would, rightly, expect to be regarded as being of their relevant sexes for the purposes of marriage. The gap between such a person and a converted transsexual is not unbridgeable. A homosexual marriage, by contrast, would be unequivocally a marriage of like with like where no such continuum is sustainable. It is suspected that public policy would stop short at such a point and would, accordingly, resist *any* legislative interference with traditional heterosexual marriage: the opportunity for constructive change might thereby be lost.

Transsexual marriage is, however, a continuing saga and, since this chapter was completed, the United Kingdom position has been attacked from a relatively novel angle. In *X, Y and Z* v. *United King-dom*,[65] a female-to-male transsexual had enjoyed a stable relationship with a woman for 15 years. During that time, the couple had had three children by way of artificial insemination by donor (see Chapter 8); X applied not to have his birth certificate altered but, rather, to be recognised as the father of the eldest child for the purposes of registration of her birth. Somewhat surprisingly, the application was turned down, but this was largely on the grounds that the law is, currently, in too uncertain a state for a decision to be made, particularly when the welfare of a child is in issue. The significance of the Human Fertilisation and Embryology Act 1990, s.28(3) was considered only in the dissenting opinions. The effect of the section is to allow that, when a man and a woman have lived in a stable relationship and the woman conceives as a result of mutually consensual artificial insemination by donor, that man – her partner – shall be regarded as the father of the child. Clearly, then, X was unable to rely on the 1990 Act once the pure *Corbett* principles were applied – and this despite the fact that the male 'pastiche' was particularly good in his case.[66] Thus, the dissenting opinion that, as a result, this constituted discrimination on the grounds of sex has some force. It may be that the European Court of Human Rights is prepared to slow down what has been suggested above as a relentless march to 'liberalism'. But there are still more British cases in the European legal pipeline – not to mention in–house problems.[67]

Notes

1   A total of 154 873 decrees absolute were granted in England and Wales in 1994; somewhat surprisingly, this constituted a fall of 4.7 per cent on the 1993 figure: Judicial Statistics 1994 (1995) (Cm 2891) London: HMSO.

2   Following Lord Penzance in *Hyde* v. *Hyde* (1866) LR 1 P & D 130 at 133.

3   See *Dryden* v. *Dryden* [1973] Fam 217; Matrimonial Causes Act 1973, s.11(*d*); Marriage (Scotland) Act 1977, s.2(3) and s.5(4).

4   Marriage Act, 1949, Parts II and III. In Scotland, an 'approved celebrant' includes anyone who is recognized as entitled to solemnize marriage by a religious body prescribed by the Secretary of State. By virtue of the Marriage Act 1994, a civil marriage may now be celebrated in premises approved for the purpose by the local authority.

5   For example, Domestic Violence and Matrimonial Proceedings Act 1976; Matrimonial Homes (Family Protection) (Scotland) Act 1981.

6   For example, De Facto Relationships Act 1984 (NSW).

7   Marriage Act 1949, sch. 2. The consent of the local authority is needed if the minor is subject to a care order. Similarly, the consent of the person with whom the minor is living is needed in the event that he or she is subject to a residence order (Children Act 1989, s.8).

8   Marriage Act, 1949, sch. 1 as amended by the Marriage (Prohibited Degrees of Relationship) Act 1986, sch. 1). As a result, relationships by affinity are now

excluded provided both parties are aged 21 and the younger party has not at any time before attaining the age of 18 lived in the same household as the other party and been treated by the other party as a child of the family.

9   Marriage Act 1949, s.25 as amended by Marriage Act 1983, sch. 1.

10 Matrimonial Causes Act 1973, s.ll(a)–(d).

11 The Marriage (Prohibited Degrees of Relationship) Act 1986 runs to Scotland.

12 Matrimonial Causes Act 1973, s.12

13 The term 'venereal disease' is to be taken as including any disease that is sexually transmitted and would, therefore, include HIV infection or AIDS. One wonders what would be the position as to conditions which *can* be transmitted through sexual intercourse but in which that is not the main method.

14 The number of decrees absolute of nullity granted in 1994 in England and Wales was 1017 – a dramatic increase over 1993, when the comparable figure was 410. The majority of decrees relate to non-consummation (Judicial Statistics 1994 (1995)(Cm 2891) London: HMSO). Note that petitions under items (c), (e) and (f) are subject to a three-year time bar.

15 *In the estate of Park, decd. Park* v. *Park* [1954] P 112 per SINGLETON LJ at 127.

16 1950 SLT (Notes) 32.

17 [1969] 1 All ER 539. Prior to 1971, lack of consent rendered a marriage void as opposed to voidable as it now is. This has practical effects, particularly as to the invalidation of wills by marriage: *Re Roberts (deceased), Roberts* v. *Roberts* [1978] 3 All ER 225. The general principles of what constitutes consent are, however, unlikely to be disturbed.

18 Now incorporated in Matrimonial Causes Act 1973, s.12(d).

19 *Re B (a minor) (wardship: sterilisation)* [1988] AC 199.

20 Sexual Offences Act, 1956, s.7; Mental Health (Scotland) Act 1984, s.106.

21 D. Brahams, 'Legal dilemma on handicapped girl' (1987), *The Times*, 27 March, p.13.

22 R. Ormrod, 'The medico-legal aspects of sex determination' (1972) 40 Med-Leg J 78.

23 See, for example, *White* v. *British Sugar Corporation* [1977] IRLR 171.

24 The 'buccal smear' of cells taken by scraping the inside of the cheek is a good preparation for examination.

25 The fact that such anomalies cast doubt on the absoluteness of the concept of chromosomal sex was noted by the European Court of Human Rights especially in *B* v. *France*, see n.58 below.

26 C.N. Armstrong, 'Transsexualism: a medical perspective' (1980) 6 J Med Ethics 90.

27 See the remarkable clinical history in *X-Petitioner* 1957 SLT (Sh Ct) 61. Although this case was described as one of transsexualism, there were anatomical changes and it may well have been an unusual case of partial androgen receptor deficiency in which feminisation usually occurs in adolescence.

28 J.M. Thomson, 'Transsexualism: a legal perspective' (1980) 6 J Med Ethics 92, puts the transsexual's case very persuasively. Note that reassignment surgery is no 'hole in corner' affair – it has been widely performed under NHS auspices for many years; see J.B. Randell, in discussion of M. Roth, 'Transsexualism and the sex change operation: a contemporary medico-legal and social problem' (1981) 49 Med-Leg J 5. At the same time, the severity and complexity of the operation are considerable: J.J. Hage, 'Medical requirements and consequences of sex reassignment surgery' (1995) 35 Med Sci Law 17. Moreover, the results are not always satisfactory. In one study of seven surgical reassignments, only three end-points were described as 'good', although another 3 were 'reasonable': J. Costa-Santos, and R. Madeira, 'Transsexualism in Portugal: the legal

framework and procedure, and its consequences for transsexuals' (1996) 36 Med Sci Law 221.

29 A remarkable case has come to notice recently where a woman and a female-to-male transsexual who had not undergone genital surgery were 'married' for 17 years; not even the woman's parents realised that her children were born by artificial insemination. The woman actually claimed to have been unaware of the anomaly: C. Dyer, 'The sex factor' (1996) *The Guardian*, 10 February, p.29.

30 *Corbett* v. *Corbett* (orse. *Ashley*) [1971] P 83.

31 *R* v. *Tan and others* [1983] 2 All ER 12. The accused, who was a converted male-to-female transsexual, was found guilty under Sexual Offences Act 1956, s.30 of being a man knowingly living on the earnings of prostitution.

32 [1989] VR 799: a case of assault with intent to insert a man's penis into the vagina of a converted transsexual.

33 (1989) 35 A Crim R 146, in which a converted male-to-female transsexual was deemed to be female while a person with similar gender dysphoria but who had not undergone surgery was held to be male for the purposes of the Crimes Act 1900 (NSW); discussed in J.L. Taitz, 'Confronting transsexualism, sexual identity and the criminal law' (1992) 60 Med-Leg J 60.

34 S. Whittle, 'An association for as noble a purpose as any' (1996) 146 NLJ 366.

35 H.A. Finlay, 'Sexual identity and the law of nullity' (1980) 54 ALJ 115. See a further Australian view: R.J. Bailey, 'Family law – decree of nullity of marriage of true hermaphrodite who has undergone sex change surgery' (1979) 53 ALJ 659, which recognises a potential conflict between the medical and legal professions in this field.

36 D.A.R. Green, 'Transsexualism and marriage' (1970) 120 NLJ 210, 301. For a similar European view, see P. Petit, 'L'ambigüité de droit face au syndrome transsexuel' (1976) 74 Rev Dr Civ 263. See also the *cri de coeur* from Advocate General Tesauro, n. 45 below.

37 A. Samuels, 'Once a man, always a man; once a woman, always a woman – sex change and the law' (1984) 24 Med Sci Law 163. But this must be a difficult counsel to follow when the subject is originally a Roman Catholic priest! See G. Armstrong, 'Sister Paola poses papal problem' (1987), *The Guardian*, 30 September, p.1.

38 But it might not be as simple as that. Indeed, the Council of Europe directive on equal treatment (see n. 46 below) specifically allows for its non-application in occupational activities where the sex of the worker constitutes a determining factor (Art. 2.2). See *M* v. *Chief Constable*, n. 47 below.

39 355 NYS 2d 712 (1974).

40 355 A 2d 204 (1976).

41 Note 22 above.

42 In practice, such testes would almost always be removed by way of good medical practice as they are very liable to malignant disease in the future.

43 One wonders why, in fact, the dissenting opinions in *Cossey* v. *United Kingdom* (1991) 13 EHRR 622 thought that there would be doubts as to the legality of a marriage of this kind (at 665).

44 See Whittle, n. 34 above. In practice, the great majority of transsexuals are psychiatrically heterosexual.

45 Court of Justice of the European Communities Case C-13/94.

46 Directive of 9 February 1976 dealing with the implementation of the principle of equal treatment for men and women as regards access to employment … and working conditions.

47 *P* v. *S and another (Case C-13/94)* [1996] ICR 975; *P* v. *S* [1996] 2 CMLR 247. The ruling of the Court of Justice of the European Communities was followed in a later industrial tribunal case in which a transsexual wished to become a police-

woman; the Chief Constable was, however able to produce special reasons – mainly under the Police and Criminal Evidence Act 1984 and the codes made under the Act – why she could not be employed in that status: *M* v. *Chief Constable of West Midlands Police* (1996) IT case 08964/96.

48 The Czech and Slovak Republics, Finland, Greece, the Netherlands, Italy, Sweden, Switzerland, Germany, Norway, Poland and Portugal; quoting from J.L. Taitz, 'Confronting transsexualism, sexual identity and the criminal law' (1992) 60 Med-Leg J 60.

49 From A. Cremona-Barbaro, 'Medicolegal aspects of transsexualism in Western Europe' (1986) 5 Med Law 89. The requirement as to age has since been lowered to 18 years.

50 Since British case law is relatively firm, any changes are likely to be imposed by the European Court of Human Rights. The British position is not alone in being under attack; see, for example, *Van Oosterwijck* v. *Belgium* (1980) 3 EHRR 557 where, by a majority of seven to three, the ECHR found that Belgium's refusal to alter a female birth certificate prevented 'him' from marrying and founding a family, contrary to the European Convention on Human Rights, art. 12. The European Court of Justice declined to take cognisance of the case on technical grounds.

51 Denmark, Finland, Germany, Italy, Luxemburg, the Netherlands, Spain and Turkey. See the dissenting opinion of MARTENS J in *Cossey* v. *United Kingdom* (1991) 13 EHRR 622 at 661.

52 See Whittle, n. 34 above.

53 *R* v. *Registrar General for England and Wales, ex parte P, Same* v. *Same, ex parte G* [1996] 2 FCR 588, in which applications for judicial review of the registrar's decision not to amend their birth certificates was dismissed. There was a faint suggestion, however, that modern research might be taken into consideration in order to justify a reassessment.

54 See Marriage Act 1949, s.44 as amended by Marriage Ceremony (Prescribed Words) Act 1996.

55 K.McK. Norrie, 'Reproductive technology, transsexualism and homosexuality: new problems for international private law' (1994) 43 ICLQ 757. Norrie argues that, by contrast, such an intrasex marriage between two Germans would be legal if performed in Britain.

56 European Convention on Human Rights, arts 8 and 12.

57 (1986) 9 EHRR 56; [1987] 2 FLR 111.

58 An opposing decision was reached in the case of *B* v. *France* [1992] 2 FLR 249, (1993) 16 EHRR 1 on the grounds that the birth certificate in France was a widely used document which exerted a profound effect on a person's right to privacy.

59 [1991] 2 FLR 492, (1991) 13 EHRR 622.

60 At para. 47.

61 In fact, there is even less doubt now that the plaintiff would win his/her case following a recommendation by the European Commission on Human Rights. See F. Gibb, 'Transsexuals win European backing in battle for legal recognition' (1997), *The Times*, 20 March, p.4.

62 See Thomson, n. 28 above.

63 S.M. Cretney and J.M. Masson, *Principles of Family Law* (5th edn, 1990), London: Sweet & Maxwell, p.48.

64 I.M. Kennedy, 'Transsexualism and single sex marriage' (1973) 2 Anglo-Amer L Rev 112.

65 (1997) Times, 23 April; ECHR case no. 75/1995/581/667.

66 While the Act speaks of a 'man and a woman', the *X* v. *United Kingdom* judg-

ment translated this as the 'male partner'. Thomson, n. 28 above, might argue
that this is a misconception.

67   What is the converted transsexual's position in a single sex educational establishment? (Sex Discrimination Act 1975, s.7(2)). See E. Wilkins 'All–Women
Newnham split on don who had sex change' (1997), *The Times*, 24 June, p.1.

2 Sexual Intercourse

It sometimes seems to the non-lawyer that the law has an obsession with sexual intercourse and its definition. But, so far as family law is concerned, this is no more than a legacy of ecclesiastical law which regarded sexual intercourse as the crowning expression of marriage, particularly in the Middle Ages when marriages could be contracted validly without either religious or civil ceremonial.[1] The criminal law related to sexual intercourse is, however, unconcerned with satisfactory union – it is there to protect women, and especially young women, against sexual harassment; thus the definition of what constitutes sexual intercourse in the criminal field is far less exacting than is that in family law. The two extremes meet in the definition of adultery, which is an ecclesiastical offence but which is a matter of aggrievement only in secular law. These various conditions will be discussed separately.

Sexual intercourse and the criminal law

There have been major changes in the criminal law relating to sexual intercourse since the first edition of this book in which considerable space was devoted to the statutory distinction between lawful and unlawful sexual intercourse. Much of the confusion has now been removed, although some remains. It is worth taking a look at the way these changes have evolved.

The words 'unlawful sexual intercourse' appear in United Kingdom legislation, *inter alia*, in the Sexual Offences Act, 1956, s.5 (having unlawful intercourse with a girl under the age of 13), s.6 (unlawful sexual intercourse with a girl aged between 13 and 16) and s.7 (having unlawful intercourse with a mentally defective person, as amended by the Mental Health Act 1959, s.127). In general, the relevant wording runs: 'It is an offence for a man to have unlawful sexual intercourse with a girl [woman]'. The word 'unlawful' is not used in s.1 in relation to impersonating a woman's husband,[2] nor does it appear in ss. 10 and 11 (incest), where the offence is simply that of a man and a woman having sexual intercourse. It was introduced in relation to rape by the Sexual Offences (Amendment) Act 1976, s.1, but it has now been deleted from the definition.[3] Generally similar wording, other than that relating to rape, which is a common law offence in Scotland, is now to be found in the Criminal Law (Consolidation) (Scotland) Act 1995.[4]

One reasonable reaction is to assume that there is an essential legalistic difference between, on the one hand, rape and incest – which are always offences – and, on the other, those offences related to age and mental capacity which, it would seem, may or may not be proscribed, depending upon whether the intercourse is lawful or unlawful. That proposition is, however, scarcely tenable insofar as the latter offences cannot be rendered lawful by consent on the part of the girl. Since non-consensual intercourse must always be an offence, the use of the word 'unlawful' in the criminal context must either be tautologous, which is an unusual error for a parliamentary draughtsman, or it must have a specific meaning. The problem has been addressed by the courts with a surprising diffidence and, often, in an indirect way. A most useful approach was that developed in *R v. Chapman*[5] where the possibility of surplusage in the use of 'unlawful' was considered specifically. DONOVAN J thought that those drawing up the early sex legislation may have been influenced by the canon law and were, therefore, likely to regard any sexual intercourse outside the bonds of matrimony as being unlawful. Their successors, it was suggested, had simply repeated the wording 'without a close consideration of its necessity or precise meaning' (at 104). The court was clearly reluctant to ascribe any deeper intentions to the draughtsmen of the mid-20th century and concluded that 'unlawful' simply meant illicit: that is, outside marriage.

The court in *Chapman* was, admittedly, concerned with the Sexual Offences Act, 1956, s.19, a matter of abduction of minor females. Nevertheless, it seems only rational to extrapolate what is meant by unlawful sexual intercourse in one section of the Act to other sections where the wording is similar. This was the attitude adopted, rather hesitantly, by LORD PARKER CJ 10 years later, in *Mohamed v. Knott*.[6] Once again, the case was not concerned directly with 'unlawful sexual intercourse' but was, rather, dealing with the welfare in the United Kingdom of a young girl who was legally married under Nigerian law. Even so, the Lord Chief Justice was prepared to extend *Chapman* to an interpretation of s.6 of the 1956 Act and to accept that sexual intercourse between the man and the girl, who was aged below 16 years, was lawful insofar as it was undertaken within a valid marriage. There is, then, general agreement that 'unlawful', as used in the 1956 Act and retained in the Criminal Law (Consolidation) (Scotland) Act 1995, means extramarital and, accordingly, that lawful implies within the marriage bonds – and this was the uncomplicated view adopted by the Criminal Law Revision Committee in 1980.[7] The apparent contradiction in terms that unlawful sexual intercourse can be legalized by a 'marriage' which is, itself, void if one party is aged less than 16 years is dispelled to some extent by the provision of a statutory defence to charges under s.6; the man would not be guilty of an offence if he could show that he honestly believed that his under-age 'wife' was, in fact, aged over 16 at the time of the ceremony. No such defence is available, however, when the charge is that of having sexual intercourse with a girl below the age of 13 years,[8] and it is almost impossible to conceive of an occasion when intercourse in such circumstances could be lawful;[9] the word must surely be surplus, at least in connection with s.5 of the 1956 Act and s.5(1) of the Scottish Act. The problem of unlawfulness has, however, been addressed directly in relation to intramarital rape.

Intramarital 'rape'

The acceptance of an irrevocable commitment to sexual intercourse on marriage by a woman was a matter of common law which was expressed in the 18th century by Sir Matthew Hale: 'The husband cannot be guilty of rape committed by himself upon his lawful wife for, by their mutual matrimonial consent and contract, the wife hath given herself in this kind unto her husband which she cannot retract.'[10] A more rational view was summarised some 200 years later by Gordon:

> The idea of an 'irrevocable consent' to intercourse is similar to the idea that the husband has 'an irrevocable privilege to have sexual intercourse' during the marriage ... and the latter concept has only to be stated to be seen to be archaic. The common law must take contemporary attitudes and *mores* into account and contemporary *mores* manifestly do not recognise any such privilege.[11]

The gulf between the two philosophies was bridged more rapidly in jurisdictions other than that of England where, as recently as 1976, the opportunity was taken to incorporate the ancient common law into statute.[12] Apart from those which have abandoned the crime of rape as such, for example Canada, New Zealand and New South Wales,[13] many states in the United States have, for some time, had legislation in place which protects women from their husbands, albeit often with limitations.[14] The extent of such limitations in favour of the husband which are likely to be imposed is indicated in the pioneering legislation of South Australia which runs:

a person shall not be convicted of rape or indecent assault upon his spouse ... (except as an accessory) unless the alleged offence consisted of, was preceded or accompanied by, or was associated with

- (a) assault occasioning actual bodily harm, or threat of such an assault upon the spouse;
- (b) an act of gross indecency, or threat of such an act, against the spouse;
- (c) an act calculated seriously and substantially to humiliate the spouse, or threat of such an act; or
- (d) threat of the commission of a criminal act against any person.[15]

In the absence of legislation, the United Kingdom courts limped towards modernisation by slowly contracting the status within which the marital privilege could be claimed – and, even within this narrow envelope, England lagged behind Scotland. The process is now a matter of history and scarcely deserving of repetition. It is, however, worth recalling the seminal cases by which the United Kingdom law was changed.

The prosecution of several cases of rape between married couples who were either separated or living apart suggested that the writing was on the wall in Scotland when the first case alleging rape between a husband and wife who were still cohabiting at the time of the incident came to be heard.[16] At the trial, the charge was held to be relevant on the grounds that whether or not a woman consented to sexual intercourse was a matter of fact and that it did not matter if this was inside or outside marriage. LORD MAYFIELD adopted the approach of the Canadian and New South Wales' legislatures and declined to differentiate between rape and any other form of assault: 'It is clear on the authorities that rape is an aggravated form of assault and equally clear that it is a criminal offence to assault a wife. Accordingly, I am not impressed by the apparent distinction between assault and rape.'[17]

It is interesting to contrast this reasoning with that in the South African case, *S* v. *H.*[18] Each achieved its object of exposing an offender to punishment but, in the latter case, it did so by dissociating sexual intercourse and violence. It was argued that, to claim that assault within marriage is not unlawful because rape is not unlawful is only possible if the crime of rape involves sexual intercourse obtained by force. Rape, however, is now conceived as sexual intercourse obtained without consent and force or violence is not an essential element of the crime. It follows, therefore, that the immunity conferred on the husband in relation to rape does not logically carry within it an exemption from liability for assault.[19] It will be seen, however, that, while this reasoning is both logical and ingenious, it still allows only for a conviction for assault within marriage –

a possibility which also exists in England.[20] By firmly associating rape and violence, however, the Scottish direction opened the door to a conviction for rape. It is arguable that this approach is particularly compatible with the law in Scotland, where the definition of rape is in terms of sexual intercourse obtained by overcoming a woman's will rather than of having intercourse with a woman who does not consent to it. Significantly in this respect, the conviction in *Stallard* was firmly upheld on appeal: 'The reason [given by Lord Hume[21] for the existence of a marital exemption to rape] affords no justification for his statement of the law because rape has always been essentially a crime of violence and, indeed, no more than an aggravated assault';[22] and the court went on to say: 'Whether or not the reason for the husband's immunity given by Hume was a good one in the eighteenth or early nineteenth centuries, it has since disappeared altogether' (at 254).

Meantime, the English criminal law was placed in equal confusion by a plethora of conflicting judicial directions[23] and an apathetic Parliament; the problems were, however, resolved by the House of Lords in *R v. R.*[24] In this case, the parties were considering divorce and were living apart when the husband attempted intercourse with his wife without her consent. The trial judge considered that the verbal agreement to live apart, accompanied by a clear indication that consent to sexual intercourse had been withdrawn, was sufficient to terminate any marital immunity that existed; however, the Court of Appeal and, later, the House of Lords, addressed the meaning of 'unlawful sexual intercourse' directly. In the former, LORD LANE LCJ dismissed the word 'unlawful' in the 1976 Act as mere surplusage:[25] 'This is not the creation of a new offence, it is the removal of a common law fiction which has become anachronistic and offensive' (at 266).

In the House of Lords, Lord Keith, employing not a little semantic juggling, found that 'unlawful' simply defined sexual intercourse with *any* woman without her consent and that the supposed marital exemption in rape formed no part of modern English law.[26] By reinterpreting the wording of the 1976 Act, the House avoided the charge that they were interfering with statutory legislation;[27] in any event, s.1 of the Sexual Offences Act 1956, already amended by the Sexual Offences (Amendment) Act 1976, was replaced by virtue of the Criminal Justice and Public Order Act 1994, s.142, in which the word 'unlawful' is omitted.

Some persons, including this writer, looked upon the conviction in *R v. R* as unfair by way of being based on retrospective law and, thus, contravening the European Convention on Human Rights, art. 7.1. Nonetheless, the European Court of Human Rights has, itself, found that there was no such injustice in that the decisions on appeal did no more than continue a perceptible line of developing case law. At the time of the trial, the law had evolved to a stage where judicial recognition of the absence of any marital immunity had become reasonably foreseeable.[28]

Thus the problems associated with unlawful sexual intercourse have been solved in relation to rape. In that circumstance, however, the issue was bound up with the relationship between unlawfulness and the marital state, the close association being something of a historical accident. We have seen that there can be no such marital connection in the other relevant sexual offences. The reason for retention of the word 'unlawful' is, at least to this writer, obscure; it may, indeed, be meaningless.

Indecent assault within marriage

Although it is quite clear that no husband has any right to inflict unreasonable harm on his wife,[29] non-consensual indecency may cause no recognisable physical harm and is not necessarily proscribed. The question has been put beyond doubt in England by *Kowalski*.[30] In that unpleasant case, a husband frightened his wife into committing fellatio. Even if consent had once been given and, even, long practised, said KENNEDY J, it could not run backwards to attach to the marriage vows; consent to an act of fellatio had to be shown to be a particular consent if it was not to be an assault. Even if a wife found oral sex to be other than indecent, circumstances could alter to the point where she was entitled to say that she now found it abhorrent. It is, therefore, clear that no marital privilege attaches to acts of indecency.

The definition of sexual intercourse in the criminal law

As mentioned above, the criminal law in the field of sexual offences is designed, in the main, for the protection of women and children. Such is the importance attached to the fact of actual intercourse that whether or not it has occurred may suffice to change the offence of indecent assault, which attracts a relatively light penalty, to one which carries the potential of imprisonment for life. Moreover, the conditions for defining sexual intercourse in the context of the criminal law are deliberately reduced to a minimum.

These are well known in respect of vaginal intercourse. In brief, in the United Kingdom, only simple penetration of the vulva is needed to establish criminal sexual intercourse; Williams[31] regards this as a common law definition. Thus there is no requirement for the hymen to be ruptured and the irrelevance of emission is a matter of statute law.[32] For criminal legal purposes, sexual intercourse is 'completed' upon vulval penetration, but the act continues until withdrawal of the male penis.[33] This apparently simple and restricted interpretation is now complicated by the revised Sexual Offences Act, 1956, s.1(2)(*a*) which refers to having 'sexual intercourse with a person (whether vaginal or anal)'. There is no positive indication that this is confined to the rape situation and it is arguable – and has been so interpreted by at least one annotator – that the legal definition of sexual intercourse is, thereby, extended to include anal intercourse in any circumstance;[34] in this writer's opinion, however, the section redefines rape rather than sexual intercourse. Had the latter been the intention, it would have had to be done in a general definition section and not in a section devoted to one specific, nominate offence. Unfortunately, s.44 of the 1956 Act, which is undisturbed by the Criminal Justice and Public Order Act 1994, sows seeds of doubt in speaking of 'sexual intercourse (whether natural or unnatural)'. In dealing with offences against women, the 1956 Act refers throughout to 'sexual intercourse' not to 'natural sexual intercourse': can it be that sexual intercourse has *always* included intercourse *per anum* for the purposes of the criminal law?[35] Certainly rape, prior to 1994, could only be *per vaginam* but it is arguable that the Sexual Offences (Amendment) Act 1976, s.7(2) distinguished rape from other sexual offences by specifically delineating the major offence. The commentator to *R* v. *O'Sullivan*,[36] in which the concept of anal rape was, at the time, rejected, dismissed the wording of s.44 as merely defining a characteristic of sexual intercourse: namely, that it required penetration but not emission. This is almost certainly the correct approach; where 'sexual intercourse' is used in a section relating to a crime, it means normal, heterosexual intercourse. As to the post-1994 definition of rape in England and Wales, there is no definition of the concept of 'anal sexual intercourse'. It can be assumed, however, that the conditions for this offence would be the same as for that of buggery – anal penetration by the penis, but not seminal emission, would be essential and, by analogy with vulval rape, this would not have to be complete; in short, Sexual Offences Act 1956, s.44 would apply to the altered terminology.

The reasons underlying the overriding importance previously attached to 'natural' sexual intercourse in British criminal law are difficult to unravel; they are probably associated with the long-established property rights over a wife which were traditionally vested in the husband. Until comparatively recently, virginity was a state which carried very great significance both for the prospective husband and for the woman concerned; loss of her virginity represented loss of her prospects of marriage and, with them, deprivation of a status to be prized above all others. No other sexual assault carried the same potential stigmatic consequences and, hence, intercourse *per vulvam* was determined to be of exclusive significance. Looked at in this way, the extension of rape to include anal penetration is a logical step in the elimination of sexism from modern sociological thinking and is, at the same time, additionally protective of women and young men.

English sex law has undergone one further important change since the first edition of this book. The patently absurd irrebuttable presumption that a boy below the age of 14 is incapable of an offence involving sexual intercourse has been abolished by the Sexual Offences Act 1993. There has never been a similar rule in Scotland.[37]

Consummation of marriage

The definition of sexual intercourse within marriage is a very different matter. The relationship between intercourse and marriage was well expressed three centuries ago by the Scottish institutional writer, Viscount Stair:[38]

> So then it is not the consent to marriage, as it relateth to the procreation of children, that is requisite, for it may consist though the woman be far beyond that date: but it is the consent, whereby ariseth that conjugal society, which may have the conjunction of bodies as well as of minds; as the general end of the institution of marriage is the solace and satisfaction of man, for the Lord saw that it was not fit for him to be alone, and therefore made him an help meet for him.

Stair was clearly referring to the satisfaction of the male rather than of mankind and, to that extent, he is certainly outmoded. Nevertheless, the concept that intramarital intercourse is a pleasurable matter and one which is essential to the emotional bonding of the couple is one with which most would agree today; it forms the basis of the law relating to consummation of marriage.

The seminal English case lies in the old report *D-e* v. *A-g*[39] which, being concerned with vaginal atresia, has several interesting medical aspects and will be referred to again later. For the present, some of the observations of Dr Lushington serve to illustrate the attitudes to lawful sexual intercourse which were prevalent in the 19th century. The following speak for themselves:

> Without that power [of sexual intercourse] neither of the two principal ends of matrimony can be attained, namely, a lawful indulgence of the passions to prevent licentiousness and the procreation of children (at 1045 [298]).

> [To retain an imperfect sexual relationship] would not tend to the prevention of adulterous intercourse, one of the greatest evils to be avoided. (1045 [298])

When the coitus itself is absolutely imperfect ... there is not a natural indulgence of natural desire; almost of necessity disgust is generated, and the probable consequences of other connexions with men of ordinary self control become almost certain. I am of opinion that no man ought to be reduced to this state of quasi unnatural connexion and consequent temptation. (1045 [299]).

By today's standards, this judgment contains some remarkable implications as to the functions of a wife. Nonetheless, Dr Lushington has been quoted with approval in the post-Second World War era[40] and, with modification, his observations on *vera copula* provide the basis for the current family law on the subject; that is, that there must be an element of satisfaction in the sexual act: 'I do not think there is any authority which binds me to find that any penetration, however transient, amounts to consummation of a marriage.'[41] On a more positive note, it has been said that there must be erection and penetration for a reasonable length of time, but neither orgasm nor emission is essential.[42] The essential element appears to be that of physical union of the bodies and it has been extrapolated that some form of sexual motion is also necessary.[43] Even so, the definition of *vera copula* remains imprecise and may confuse the judiciary itself: 'It seems to me that it is impossible to determine exactly where normal sexual intercourse begins and ends'.[44]

More certainly, it has been confirmed repeatedly that the procreation of children is irrelevant to the consummation of marriage – a proposition which was expressly addressed by the Lord Chancellor in *Baxter*.[45] This important case concerned the use of condoms and, specifically, whether their use constituted a wilful refusal to consummate the marriage. The opinion of the House of Lords was clear:

In any view of Christian marriage the essence of the matter ... is that the children, if there be any, should be born into a family ... but this is not the same thing as saying that a marriage is not consummated unless children are procreated or that procreation of children is the principal end of marriage. (per LORD JOWITT LC at 286)

Other pretences such as the possibility of pregnancy through *fecundatio ab extra* have been invoked in comparable circumstances, for example in declaring that *coitus interruptus* does not constitute refusal to consummate,[46] but they seem, now, to be quite unnecessary. From the other aspect, the fact that a couple have conceived a child does not, of itself, prove that intercourse within its socially acceptable meaning has occurred.[47]

The general impression remains that family law in this area is directed to contentment and that Dr Lushington was not so wide of the mark as might appear at first reading. Detailed discussion of consummation is, in fact, probably anachronistic, in that a sexually unhappy couple will find it easier to obtain a divorce than to engage in a nullity suit: even as long ago as 1950, a wife obtained a divorce on the grounds of cruelty from a husband who persisted in *coitus interruptus*.[48]

An approach to defining *vera copula* that has greater medico-legal significance in the modern world is to study the law's response to attempts to improve the degree of happiness achieved: in essence, to seek to answer the question, what is the attitude of the civil law to the surgical operation of colpoplasty or vaginoplasty – the fashioning of a new or improved vagina? The United Kingdom law in this area is inconsistent and this is largely because much of the argument is ill-founded. It now seems almost certain that the 'females' involved in the two major nullity cases concerned with imperfect vaginas, *D-e* and *SY*,[49] were, in fact, examples of the testicular feminisation syndrome and were, therefore, chromosomal males. Nevertheless, this could not be appreciated at the relevant times and, for practical purposes, the cases can still be looked upon as expressing the courts' attitudes to consummation by the anatomically imperfect woman. On the other side of the coin, we have the legal reactions to the fashioning of an admittedly wholly false vagina which are to be found in, first, *B* v. *B*[50] and, later, *Corbett* v. *Corbett*.[51] The outcomes in *D-e* and *SY* were opposed, despite the remarkable similarity of the facts. This is, however, no more than a reflection of a century's progress – both in medical technology and in the social status of women – and does not indicate any violent change in legal principle.

The unfortunate Maria A-g had a vagina some one and a half inches in depth. It was not disputed that sexual intercourse had taken place on numerous occasions and that, in addition to incorporating a therapeutic element, it had provided her with some sexual satisfaction; moreover, it had allowed the husband 'ordinary excitement'. There had also been an appreciable increase in the size of her vagina during the time that she was 'married'. It is, however, clear that her impatient husband was increasingly at risk of adulterous intercourse and contemporary medical opinion was that the condition was untreatable. Accordingly, said the judge: 'The condition of the lady is greatly to be pitied, but on no principle of justice can her calamity be thrown upon another.' In declaring the marriage void, Dr Lushington did, however, emphasise that his decision would have been different had the condition been amenable to medical or surgical treatment.

Precisely the same situation presented over one hundred years later in *SY*. The face of medicine was, by now, different and there was no doubt that the vaginal atresia could be treated surgically. The altered circumstances were fully appreciated by the court, which said that: if [Dr Lushington were sitting to-day], 'he would in the light of modern medical science have held himself bound to refuse a decree. I am content to follow the same reasoning' (WILLMER J at 58); a petition for nullity was refused. In the course of the judgment, however, WILLMER J made some interesting observations which serve to link the two relevant types of vaginal abnormality. The problem of whether there was *any* vagina or whether the case concerned a vestigial organ was raised but, although such evidence as there was indicated that the latter was correct, the court was inclined to dismiss the matter as being irrelevant: 'For myself', said WILLMER J, 'I find it difficult to see why the enlargement of a vestigial vagina should be regarded as producing something different in kind from a vagina artificially created from nothing.'

He went on to discuss the court's reasons for minimising any possible distinction and affirmed that, even if the wife had *no* natural vagina and she was given an artificial organ, coitus by artificial vagina constituted *vera copula*. Were the contrary to be held:

> it would seem to follow that she would be incapable in law of being the victim of a rape ... [and] would be incapable in law of committing adultery. Consequently, the wife of a man engaging in intercourse with such a woman would be left wholly without remedy. I should regard such a result as bordering on the fantastic (at 60–61).[52]

Later,[53] ORMROD J was to declare himself not bound by this decision of the Court of Appeal, regarding the remarks as obiter and, in respect of adultery, not very important. We have seen in Chapter 1 that the *Corbett* decision has been criticised widely and this was an additional reason for so doing; it is, however, possible to argue that there are significant differences between the two cases, and these will be discussed later. Meantime, it is clear that WILLMER J's observations, whether or not they form part of the ratio of the case, were diametrically opposed to the pre-existing decision in *B* v. *B*,[54] a case which may be closest either to *SY* or to *Corbett*.

The circumstances in *B* v. *B* were unusual, to say the least. The 'wife' in this case was born with certain male organs which were removed at the age of 17; the nature of these organs is unspecified, but they were almost certainly testes. There were some general appearances which were thought to be inconsistent with a normal female, no vagina was present and she had never menstruated. She underwent vaginoplasty and an organ of some four to six inches was formed; but, in what seems to have been a chapter of accidents, this was not used biologically until it had become stenotic as a result of fibrosis. As with all the early cases of doubtful sex, it is interesting to speculate on what was Mrs B's sexual karyotype. She may have been a case of sex reversal, in which case she was probably XX; equally, she could have been another example of the testicular feminisation syndrome, when she would have been XY; and there are several other possibilities. Whatever the true state of affairs, the case was, again, discussed at two levels. Commissioner Grazebrook was, first, satisfied that the marriage was not consummated by virtue of the surgical contracture. But he went on to say that:

> Even if the wife had satisfied me that there was connexion ... I do not consider that it could be held to be consummation in the circum-stances having regard to the artificiality of her organ ... It would be impossible in this case ... to cure the defect in the wife to the extent of making her in the real sense of the term capable of having sexual relations with her husband (at 47).

Thus, once again, the definition of the legal status of an artificial vagina was not essential to the decision and could be regarded as obiter; nevertheless, it is surprising that this opinion was not referred to in *Corbett.*

Even there, the conclusions as to the nature of sexual intercourse came as something of an aside. ORMROD J – who, one suspects, had little affection for transsexuals – was, however, quite prepared to hold that the respondent, April Ashley, was physically incapable of consummating a marriage:

> I do not think that sexual intercourse using the completely artificial cavity ... can possibly be described ... as 'ordinary and complete intercourse' or as *'vera copula* – or the natural sort of coitus'. In my judgment, it is the reverse of ordinary, and in no sense natural. When such a cavity has been constructed in a male, the difference between sexual intercourse using it and anal or intracrural [*sic*] intercourse is, in my judgment, to be measured in centimetres (at 107).

This analysis of the cases strongly suggests that, while there is little in the way of judicial unanimity on the subject, there have been none in which the quality of an artificial vagina formed the ratio of the decision. The obiter remarks have inevitably been made with the precise circumstances of each case very much to the forefront of the judges' minds; hints of policy considerations as to future develop-ments are, however, sometimes, apparent. Thus ORMROD J was wor-ried that, 'by over-refining and over-defining the meaning of "normal" one may, in the end, produce a situation in which consummation may come to mean something altogether different from normal sexual intercourse' (at 108).

Such reasoning as this may have influenced the court in *SY* who considered the argument that *any* artificial opening, no matter where it was placed, could be said to represent a vagina; the court emphasised that there was no question of such a situation arising: the passage would be located precisely in the position where a normal vagina would be. Thus, so long as this is agreed as being a prerequisite to acceptable vaginoplasty, ORMROD J's observations on the location of the artificial passage actually plead its case for recognition: it has been pointed out that the difference between two *hetero*sexuals indulging in vaginal or anal intercourse can also be measured in centimetres.[55]

Judicial attitudes to intercourse via an artificial vagina follow two lines of thought. On the one hand, the artefact is judged on strict anatomico-physiological terms; on the other, consideration is given only to its functional value. Whichever approach is accepted, it is difficult to see any meaningful difference between a vagina which is fashioned *ab initio* and one which, using precisely the same technique, is grafted onto a vestigial organ. Function, insofar as it is limited to reception of the erect penis during a normal sexual embrace, is the same and the two have similar anatomical and physiological flaws. To hold otherwise and to admit to *degrees* of artifice would involve the courts in absurd discussion as to measurement which would, in any event, ignore the fact that the functional efficiency of a vagina is related to the size of the ingressive penis. There is much to be said for the argument advanced in *B* v. *B* that there is no conceptual difference between a vagina formed by plastic surgery and an apparatus strapped to the groin of an impotent man so long as only anatomy and *anatomical* function are considered.

But it seems to go relatively unnoticed that, if *vera copula* involves some satisfaction of the male sex urge, then it ought also to give some sexual pleasure – or special pleasure beyond that of mere bodily contact – to the female. Once this is accepted, a fundamental difference between partial and total vaginoplasty can be seen. Absent some particularly effective plastic surgery, the totally false female passage cannot achieve orgasm: the necessary discriminatory innervation is not there; the woman with an enlarged vagina, however, is at least liable to clitoral stimulation and satisfaction. In short, the essential difference between the two states rests on the presence or absence of a vulva.

Concentration on the vulva, rather than on the vagina, as the hallmark of female genitalia simultaneously solves a number of the medico-legal problems that arise in the interwoven fields of sex and intersex. The difference between curability of an existing condition and the creation of a new status becomes clear and the distinction made between, say *SY* and *B* is explained; the apparent contradiction between *SY* and *Corbett* falls neatly into place; and the extent of Ormrod's genital test (see p. 8) is simply defined as was there or was there not a vulva? Finally, WILMER J's concerns expressed in *SY* v. *SY* are also disposed of fairly comfortably. Admittedly, the converted transsexual could, then, be raped only anally in England,[56] but this would not be because he/she had an artificial vagina but because there never was a vulva. S.W. in *SY* v. *SY*, whose *gender* was never in doubt, could, however, have been raped because she had a vulva and vulval penetration is all that is required for the *actus reus* of the offence: the state of the vagina is immaterial. The resolution of what may appear to be unfairness to the genuine transsexual depends on changing the law rather than on setting up another anatomical and physiological fiction.

Adultery

WILLMER J was also concerned with the relationship of the artificial vagina to adultery; the problem, perhaps, deserves more attention than it was given in *Corbett* but, even so, it may have been over-stated. It is generally assumed that some form of 'natural' sexual intercourse is essential to adultery, but the question of the *degree* of necessary intercourse still seems to be inadequately resolved. Thus, in 1954, KARMINSKI J thought that 'nobody has ... yet attempted to define adultery'.[57] He then went on to make some negative defini-tions. Firstly, he considered that acts such as manual satisfaction could not, by themselves, amount to adultery, and this view was certainly accepted, and used, by ORMROD J in *Corbett*. KARMINSKI J con-tinued: 'On the other hand, it has been said many times that an act of adultery need not be such a complete act of intercourse as is required to consummate a marriage ... there can be adultery without *vera copula*' (at 399). The difficulty with this statement is that it fails to define the *nature* of the difference: does it involve the emotional bonding in intercourse, as has been discussed above, or is it a simple matter of an anatomical distinction implying, for example, that the definition of adulterous intercourse is similar to that applied in the British concept of rape?[58] A third possibility has been mooted: that is, that adultery consists of little more than a state of mind or of an intention to behave as if within the marriage bed. The basis for this last proposition is to be found in the speech of Viscount Birkenhead in *Rutherford* v. *Richardson*[59] in which he said: 'If there was evidence [inconsistent with penetration but not inconsistent with some lesser act of sexual gratification] it cannot be doubted that, whatever view may have been taken in past ages in the Ecclesiastical Courts, a decree based on adultery might issue.'

The case was clearly one in which all sympathy lay with the wife. Moreover, a decree by reason of adultery was refused on the particular facts of the case; the remarks of the Lord Chancellor may, there-fore, be regarded as obiter only. Nevertheless, they must open the door to, say, regarding attempted sexual intercourse as adultery. But, for completion of the circle of argument, one may revert to KARMINSKI J in *Sapsford*: 'Mutual intercourse, in my view, means that there has to be intercourse in which both the man and the woman play what may be described as their normal roles' (at 400).

The two cases, taken together, indicate that, at the very least, the intention to penetrate the vulva with the penis is essential to adul-tery; alternatives such as manual masturbation or fellatio would not qualify – this being another expression of the husband's anachronis-tic property rights over his wife's sexual organs. There is, however, a suspicion that mutual masturbation through penile/clitoral friction would be sufficient to constitute adultery: the man and the woman would be playing at, albeit not actually playing, their normal roles. For a contrary view, one can look at the opinions expressed in *Dennis* v. *Dennis*, where it was said:[60]

> I think that all the authorities ... when they speak of adultery are
> speaking of the physical act, understood as carrying with it a concep-
> tion of natural copulation between the sexes. I think the word has not
> been extended to include such a form of what may be described as a
> lesser sexual gratification (per HODSON LJ at 160).

SINGLETON LJ, in the same case, was even more precise: 'In my view there is no distinction to be drawn between the words "sexual inter-course" in the definition of "adultery' and "carnal knowledge' in the criminal law. [In the latter] it must be shown that there is some penetration' (at 160). This equation of the ecclesiastical offence of adultery with the secular concept of unlawful carnal knowledge is very persuasive and, whatever may be the minima, it certainly seems that penetration of the vulva is the most that is absolutely required for adulterous intercourse.[61] In *Thompson* v. *Thompson*,[62] the wife con-cerned was diagnosed medically as being a virgin. She had, however, stayed in a hotel with the corespondent and LANGTON J was, regret-fully, 'forced to the conclusion that the respondent and the intervener in this case have had mutual intercourse amounting to adultery in law' (at 173).

The greater part of the confusion stems from the absurd conditions attached to divorce prior to the passage of the Divorce Reform Act 1969 and the Divorce (Scotland) Act 1976. Proof of adultery, which was so important to a successful action, was then, very largely, a matter of circumstantial, and often contrived, evidence. Medical proof or disproof of intercourse, the adequacy of reports by private investi-gators and judicial interpretation of 'evidence' became intermingled;

precise definitions thus tended to take second place to the needs of natural justice. Those days are past and there is little practical value in reviving outmoded academic debate; behaviour which renders cohabitation intolerable does not depend upon niceties of sexual anatomy.

In conclusion, it is to be noted that adulterous intercourse, whatever may be its true nature, must be consensual. There is, for example, no adultery by a woman who is raped.[63]

Non-consummation of marriage

The nature of sexual intercourse which is considered necessary to constitute consummation of marriage has been discussed above. It is, however, appropriate to look at non-consummation as a separate aspect of sexual intercourse because interest then centres not so much on the quality of the sex act but, rather, on the reasons for its non-occurrence in the appropriate circumstances.

Non-consummation may be rendered inevitable by 'disease', which may be disease as it is commonly understood in the form, say, of inflammation or tumour, but which may also result from congenital malformation; examples of the latter have been described above. Disease may also be of a psychiatric type and may be of such severity that erection is impossible or, more dramatically, that the vaginal muscles are forced into spasm – the condition of vaginismus. The proposition that such psychological inability to consummate represents a true impotency within the terms of existing legislation[64] has been confirmed in G v. G.[65]

Whatever may be the reason for impotency, there are certain features of the condition which must be met before it can form the base on which a marriage is voidable. In particular, it must exist at the time of marriage – impotence developing within a marriage does not provide such grounds – and it must be incurable. The definition of incurability may cause some difficulties, most of which are beyond the compass of this chapter. The problems are mainly related to the duties and attitudes of the impotent party. Refusal of treatment is clearly likely to be a bar to a declarator of nullity if the petitioner is the affected person; the same would not apply, however, were he or she the defendant – indeed, in that case, an action might also be available in England on the basis of wilful refusal to consummate.[66] On the other hand, the court would not expect a person to undergo hazardous or otherwise unreasonable treatment to effect a cure,[67] and the condition would be deemed incurable if such therapy was refused; late attempts at cure are, however, not discouraged even when these are undertaken in order to forestall proceedings.[68]

Clearly, then, it may be difficult to distinguish psychological impotency from wilful refusal to consummate a marriage. This is of no great import in England, where either condition would serve for voidance of a marriage.[69] In Scotland, however, wilful refusal is a reason only for divorce, and this is based on behavioural grounds. There might, therefore, be some need to differentiate the two conditions if there is an element of doubt.[70] The consequences of divorce and nullity are, however, now so similar – for example, as regards financial provision, social security legislation and the like – that the distinction has lessening significance; moreover, in view of the increasing importance attached to dissolving broken marriages with as little disturbance as possible, it seems unlikely that the courts would now wish to complicate matters unnecessarily. It is, however, noteworthy that Scottish courts would be unlikely to order a diagnostic medical examination in order to assess the presence or absence of true impotency; the English courts, by contrast, may – and do – order such examinations and they may draw adverse inferences against a party who refuses to cooperate.

None of which is to say that couples *must* have sexual intercourse in order to be properly married; such a suggestion would militate very strongly against, say, second marriages after the death of a spouse. It is perfectly reasonable for a marriage to take place between two persons who have no intention of adopting sexual practices or between a couple, one of whom is known to be incapable of consummation. Agreement or shared knowledge will, however, be a bar to any subsequent petition for nullity. *Morgan*, in which case two elderly persons married on the basis of companionship, is a classic example;[71] the husband later petitioned for nullity on the grounds of his own impotence, but this was refused because of the manifest injustice to his wife were it to be allowed. Approbation of such type is now defined by statute:[72] a decree of nullity on the ground that a marriage is voidable shall not be granted if the respondent satisfies the court (a) that the petitioner, with knowledge that it was open to him to have the marriage avoided, so conducted himself in relation to the respondent as to lead the respondent reasonably to believe that he would not seek to do so; and (b) that it would be unjust to the respondent to grant the decree.

Such provisions have, however, no counterpart in Scots law. It has been said to be unwise to try to lay down rules as to what will and what will not amount to a personal bar to a declarator of nullity in Scotland;[73] the matter will turn on the particular facts and on the justice or injustice of the result. This was expressed by LORD SELBORNE:[74]

I think I can perceive that ... there may be conduct on the part of the person seeking this remedy which may estop that person from having it, as, for instance, any act from which the inference ought to be drawn that during the antecedent time the party has, with a knowledge of the facts and of the law, approbated the marriage which he or she afterwards seeks to get rid of, or has taken advantages and denied benefits from the matrimonial relation which it would be unfair and inequitable to permit him or her, after having received them, to treat as if no such relation had ever existed.

LORD WATSON, after spelling out much the same criteria, said: 'If that be ... the rule of the law of England, I have no hesitation in saying that it is a rule which prevails in Scotland also' (at 45).

These opinions were quoted with approval in a more recent case which concerned a couple who, having discovered the wife's impotency, resorted, first, to successful artificial insemination with the husband's semen and, secondly, to adoption of a further child; the pursuer was held to have approbated the marriage and to have adopted it as valid on both counts; the action was, accordingly, dismissed.[75] It is uncertain whether or not approbation is more difficult to prove in England than in Scotland, but it will bar a petition for nullity on the ground of non-consummation in both jurisdictions if it was expressed either as foreknowledge or as later condonation of an unfortunate state of affairs.

Notes

1   S.M. Cretney and J.M. Masson, *Principles of Family Law* (5th edn, 1990), London: Sweet & Maxwell state that this relied on Genesis 2. 24: 'Therefore shall a man ... cleave unto his wife: and they shall be one flesh' (p. 5).
2   As substituted by Criminal Justice and Public Order Act 1994, s.142.
3   Criminal Justice and Public Order Act 1994, s.142.
4   Although, interestingly, where the English legislation has specifically removed the word (Sexual Offences Act, 1956, ss.2(1) and 3(1) as amended by Criminal Justice and Public Order Act 1994, sch. 11 (procurement of a woman)), the comparable Scottish statute retains it (Criminal Law (Consolidation) (Scotland) Act 1995, ss. 7(1)(*a*) and (2)(*a*), (*b*) and (*c*)). The 1995 Act, however, making no new law of itself, did not receive extensive parliamentary scrutiny.
5   [1959] 1 QB 100, CCA.
6   [1969] 1 QB 1, CCA.
7   Working Paper on Sexual Offences, October 1980, where 'extra-marital' was inserted by way of explanation of the use of the term 'unlawful' in the Sexual Offences (Amendment) Act 1976.
8   The defence of error as to age might be available in respect of the Scottish common law crime of having intercourse with a girl below the age of puberty. See G.H. Gordon, *The Criminal Law of Scotland* (2nd edn, 1978), para. 33-15.
9   Although it would appear from *Mohamed*, n. 6 above, that intramarital intercourse with a 'wife' who was showing signs of puberty could be lawful if an Islamic marriage had been contracted outwith the United Kingdom.
10   *Historia Placitorum Coronae* (1736), p. 636. The proposition was also supported

by the great Scottish institutional writers: see, for example, Hume *Commentaries on the Law of Scotland Respecting Crimes* (4 edn, 1844), vol. 1, p. 306.
11   Gordon, n. 8 above, p. 889.
12   Sexual Offences (Amendment) Act 1976, s.1.
13   Criminal Code, ss. 246.1, 246.2, 246.2 (Canada); Crimes Amendment (No 3) Act 1985 (New Zealand); Crimes (Sexual Assaults) Amendment Act 1981 (NSW). It has never been suggested that a wife consents to assault; thus a man who 'rapes' his wife is as guilty as is the stranger who does so.
14   See M.D.A. Freeman, '"But if you can't rape your wife who(m) can you rape?" – the marital rape exemption re-examined' (1981) 15 Fam LQ 1; A.F. Schiff, 'Rape: wife vs husband' (1982) 22 J Forens Sci Soc 235; 'Husband versus wife: rape' (1987) 27 J Forens Sci Soc 193.
15   Criminal Law Consolidation Act 1930–1980, s. 73(5).
16   *Stallard* v. *HM Advocate* 1989 SCCR 248. The status of the couple was emphasised by the Crown in the indictment.
17   At 250.
18   *S* v. *H* (1985) (2) SA 750 (N), discussed in J.R.L. Milton, 'Rape in marriage and assault in rape' (1985) 102 SALJ 367.
19   Per NIENABER J at 755.
20   *R* v. *Miller* [1954] 2 QB 282; *R* v. *Kowalski* (1988) 86 Crim App Rep 339.
21   Note 10 above.
22   Per LORD EMSLIE L J-G at 253.
23   See, for example, *R* v. *J* [1991] 1 All ER 759; *R* v. *C* [1991] 1 All ER 755.
24   *R* v. *R* – *(rape: marital exemption)* [1991] 1 All ER 747, Crown Ct; [1991] 2 All ER 257, CA; [1991] 4 All ER 481, HL.
25   [1991] 2 All ER 257 at 265.
26   [1991] 4 All ER 481 at 489.
27   This is difficult to do but not impossible. For further discussion, see M. Giles, 'Judicial law-making in the criminal courts: the case of marital rape' (1992) Crim LR 407.
28   *S W* v. *United Kingdom, C R* v. *United Kingdom* (1995) Times, 5 December.
29   *R* v. *Miller* [1954] 2 QB 282.
30   Note 20 above.
31   G. Williams, *Textbook of Criminal Law* (2nd edn, 1983), London: Stevens, p. 236. See also *R* v. *Hughes* (1841) 9 C & P 752.
32   Sexual Offences Act, 1956, s.44
33   *Kaitamaki* v. *The Queen* [1985] AC 147.
34   Although, strictly speaking, it is irrelevant to this chapter, s.142 of the 1994 Act extends the definition of rape to include anal intercourse with a man without his consent. It does not go so far as those Commonwealth jurisdictions which include any bodily orifice and also penetration by an instrument; for example, Crimes (Sexual Assaults) Amendment Act 1981, s.61A (New South Wales). By contrast, s. 142 of the 1994 Act does not run to Scotland; there thus seems to be a marked dichotomy in the criminal law of the United Kingdom.
35   Speaking in terms of homosexual activity, Honoré pointed out that the term 'unnatural' is too vague to describe anal intercourse and that 'the concept, even if it were clear, is too debatable for a legislator': T. Honoré, *Sex Law* (1978), London: Duckworth, p. 109.
36   [1981] Crim LR 406.
37   Or in several other Commonwealth jurisdictions; see, for example, New Zealand Crimes Act 1961, s. 127.
38   Viscount, Stair, *The Institutions of the Law of Scotland* (2nd edn, 1693), Book 1, Tit. 4, para. 6; ed. D.M. Walker (1981), Edinburgh and Glasgow: University Presses, p. 108.

39   *D-e* v. *A-g (falsely calling herself D-e)* (1919) 163 ER 1039 editing (1845) 1 Rob Ecc 279.
40   For example, in *Baxter* v. *Baxter* [1948] AC 247; *W (orse K)* v. *W* [1967] 3 All ER 178.
41   *W* v. *W*, n. 40 above, per BRANDON J at 178.
42   *R* v. *R (orse F)* [1952] 1 All ER 1194; *W (orse W)* v. *W*, n. 40 above. See also *SY* v. *SY* [1963] P 37.
43   J. Taitz, 'The law relating to consummation of marriage when one of the spouses is a post-operative transsexual' (1986) 15 Anglo-Amer L Rev 141. I suggest that this is overstretching the judicial opinion in *W* v. *W*.
44   *Cackett (orse Trice)* v. *Cackett* [1950] 1 All ER 677 per HODSON J at 680.
45   Note 40 above.
46   *White* v. *White* [1948] P 330; *Cackett (orse Trice)* v. *Cackett* n. 44 above.
47   *Clarke* v. *Clarke* [1943] 2 All ER 540. The problems of artificial insemination are dealt with separately in Chapter 8.
48   *Cackett* n. 44 above.
49   *D-e* v. *A-g*, n. 39 above; *SY* v. *SY (orse W)*, n. 42 above.
50   [1955] P 42.
51   *Corbett* v. *Corbett (orse Ashley)* [1971] P 83.
52   This proposition was tested quite recently in the Australian case, *R* v. *Cogley* [1989] VR 799, where a man was accused of assault with intent to insert his penis into a woman's vagina without her consent. The complainant was a post-operative transsexual; the trial judge found her to be a woman and to have a vagina. On appeal, it was held that the charge was one of 'intent' and the court declined to say what would have happened had the charge been one of vaginal rape. See A. Dickey, 'Family law' (1990) 64 ALJ 85 for criticism.
53   In *Corbett*, n. 51 above.
54   Note 50 above.
55   Taitz, n. 43 above.
56   And, currently, not at all in Scotland. But, in those anglophone jurisdictions which have legislated further, the situation would be covered by 'any other bodily orifice'. Moreover, in the unreported case of *R* v. *Matthews*, the trial judge thought that it was possible to rape a converted transsexual *per vaginam* in England. The case and its significance are discussed in M. Hicks and G. Branston 'Transsexual rape – a loophole closed?' [1997] Crim LR 565 who also raise the interesting question as to whether intercourse with an artificial vagina is sexual intercourse or buggery.
57   *Sapsford* v. *Sapsford and Furtado* [1954] P 394.
58   'Penetration for however short a period suffices for the definition of sexual intercourse for adultery and rape': S.M. Cretney and J.M. Masson, *Principles of Family Law* (5th edn, 1990), p. 51 at fn. 20.
59   [1923] AC 1.
60   [1955] P 153.
61   From this it follows that artificial insemination cannot be regarded as adultery. See *MacLennan* v. *MacLennan* 1958 SC 105, discussed in detail in Chapter 8.
62   *Thompson (orse Hulton)* v. *Thompson* [1938] P 162.
63   *Redpath* v. *Redpath* [1950] 1 All ER 600.
64   Matrimonial Causes Act 1973, s. 12(*a*). The voidability of marriage on the ground of non-consummation in Scotland depends on *CB* v. *AB* (1885) 12 R (HL) 36.
65   [1924] AC 349.
66   *D* v. *D (Nullity: Statutory Bar)* [1979] Fam 70. For Scotland, see *WY* v. *AY* 1946 SC 27.

67 For a very old case, see *C* v. *M* (1876) 3 R 693. In England, see *S* v. *S* [1956] P 1 (indecision rather than refusal).
68 *S* v. *S* [1963] P 162; *WY* v. *AY*, n. 66 above.
69 Matrimonial Causes Act 1973, s.12(*b*); and, in fact, many actions are brought on both grounds.
70 *Paterson* v. *Paterson* 1958 SC 27.
71 *Morgan* v. *Morgan* [1959] P 92.
72 Matrimonial Causes Act 1973, s.13(1).
73 E.M. Clive, *The Law of Husband and Wife in Scotland* (3rd edn, 1992), Edinburgh: W Green/Sweet & Maxwell, p.104.
74 In *CB* v. *AB*, n. 64 above at 38.
75 *AB* v. *CD* 1961 SC 347 *sub nom G* v. *G* 1961 SLT (Reps) 324.

3 Contraception

Family planning is an integral part of modern existence. Couples may, of course, restrict their capacity to procreate for purely selfish reasons and few would deny them the right to choose for themselves. The majority of family planning within marriage is, however, more likely to be directed towards the good of the children, whose individual prospects must decline as the number of siblings increases. Thus there is very little moral objection to contraception; indeed, it may be positively applauded in societies faced with an expanding population and finite resources. The firmest, and most articulate, objection to fertility control comes, in practice, from the official teaching of the Roman Catholic church;[1] there are also academic philosophical criticisms which deserve mention.

The official teaching of the Roman Catholic church is founded on the simple and unequivocal premise that the two major objectives of sexual intercourse – unitive and procreative – are inseparable and that the connection, which is willed by God, cannot be broken on man's own initiative. To destroy the responsibility, even if only partially, to transmit life is contradictory to the design of marriage and to the nature of a man and woman's most intimate relationship.[2] No-one would doubt the sincerity of those who have propounded this belief over the years in the face of mounting opposition, but it is here, surely, that conservative Roman Catholicism loses contact with a proportion of the Church's followers, many of whom are unconvinced of the essential unity of 'making love' and determinedly 'having a baby'.[3] Reasons other than those based purely on hedonism can be adduced in support of this attitude. For example, it could well be held that a couple who abstain from sexual intercourse are preventing the transmission of life in just the same way as they are when they employ some means of contraception; moreover, in adopting the former policy they are, at the same time, excluding what most people, including the Church, would regard as an integral part of a successful marriage: contraceptives may be supporting, albeit paradoxically, the institution of marriage. The argument that contraceptives encourage adultery or extramarital intercourse is also scarcely tenable; neither needs encouragement in the modern world and, as was said in a well-known American case, to adopt that view is: 'as though the state decided to dramatize its disapproval of motorcycles by forbidding the use of safety helmets.'[4] Finally, as will be discussed later, successful contraception obviates the need for, and is greatly preferable to, the alternative of abortion.

It is, indeed, very difficult to see rejection of contraception as being compatible with the economics of modern life. In present circumstances, 'open' sexual intercourse imposes a duty on society to care for many children whose upbringing must, at some point, become an impossible burden for an individual couple; it could be argued that it is irresponsible and positively immoral to abuse the beneficence of the state in this way. To which the Church's riposte would be that one should either refrain from sexual intercourse, which we have already dismissed as an unsatisfactory answer, or intercourse should be limited to infecund phases of the female cycle. The latter is acceptable to the theologians, on the grounds that the couple are making use of a natural disposition; positive contraceptive methods, by contrast, impede the development of natural processes. Ignoring the essentially practical concern that these presumptions leave the morality of *coitus interruptus* in something of a grey area, they also raise wider theoretical grounds for doubt. It is, for example, difficult to see why it should be admissible to alter the physiological function of the body in, say, the treatment of hormone-dependent malignant disease if it is wrong to alter the tissue levels of hormones which naturally inhibit further conception and implantation; arguments against contraception which depend upon 'unnaturalness' must be confined to 'barrier' methods.[5]

Having said which, it is also strongly suggested that the argument that all forms of inhibition of new life are similar should be resisted. There is a strong move to go further than we have already done and to attempt to justify abortion – and even neonaticide – on the grounds that, since their objectives, the prevention of life, are similar, they are on the same moral plane as chastity and contraception.[6] This concept will be readdressed later, but for present purposes it is regarded as unacceptable. Both abortion and, certainly, neonaticide involve the destruction of living human tissue; there is no such destructive element in either abstinence or contraception which are, accordingly, to be clearly distinguished – and which may be properly considered to be on a par with each other. Indeed, as already intimated above, it is difficult to escape the conclusion that the escalation of abortion, and the consequent bitter moral divisions that have followed, would have been avoided had contraceptive instructions and materials been available through the National Health Service before the passage of the Abortion Act 1967.

Thus, while accepting – as one is bound to do – the right of anyone to refuse to limit his or her progeny, the remainder of this chapter will be based on the assumption that family planning by means of contraception is morally, medically and legally acceptable in modern society.[7] The limits, if any, to that acceptability need to be determined.

Medical aspects of contraception

Contraceptive methods should not, however, be regarded lightly. Virtually none is foolproof and most have some complicating effects. These factors must be considered before issuing contraceptives to those who cannot appreciate their significance and, particularly, before ordering compulsory pregnancy planning for those who are regarded as unsuited to child begetting and rearing.

An effectiveness in the region of 90 per cent can be achieved through the use of the so-called 'rhythm method' or 'safe period'. This involves a careful evaluation of menstrual dates, of genital symptoms in the woman and of her body temperature; these 'natural methods' can be combined with others that are used during the estimated fertile period. The methods call for considerable intelligence and mutual cooperation, which some might regard as protective of a marriage; the alternative view is that the state of chronic anxiety induced can hardly contribute to marital stability. Natural methods do not interfere with a woman's physiology and are the method of choice for the orthodox Roman Catholic. But, in the end, the chances of conception can only be looked on as being relatively less than those following unprotected intercourse.[8]

The oldest and, perhaps, best known of artificial contraceptives are of 'barrier' type and are represented by condoms in the male and diaphragms or sponges in the female. No barrier is ever likely to be perfect and even condoms may be inadvertently perforated or displaced. Nevertheless, an effectiveness rate of up to 98 per cent is probable given intelligent use. Condoms are virtually without danger: one can imagine the possibility of a man being sensitive to the rubber or other manufacturing constituents, but the author can remember no reported case. Condoms are not available through the National Health Service, although there is a tenable argument that they ought to be, in that they protect against some forms of sexually transmitted disease, including infection by the human immunodeficiency virus. The political importance attached to this condition has led to a greatly increased availability of free condoms, but this is by way of the social services' care for special at-risk groups. The diaphragm represents the corresponding barrier in the female and its use has declined markedly since the introduction of hormonal methods. The diaphragm has its in-built contraindications: a number of women are sensitive to the chemical spermicides which must be used in combination and their continued use may lead to infection which can spread to the urinary tract. The major objection to barrier contraceptives is, however, psychological, in that they dictate some premeditation in respect of sexual intercourse while the condom, at least, introduces an element of artificiality into what should be a wholly natural act. Contrariwise, perhaps the main advantage of barrier methods lies in the protection they provide against specific infections and, in the case of the woman, against malignancy in the uterine cervix. There is also evidence that some of the spermicides used with them are viricidal to the human immunodeficiency virus.[9] The diaphragm is probably the contraceptive of choice for the older woman and certainly for those women in whom hormonal contraception is contraindicated (see below).[10]

We come to more significant potential troubles when considering the use of the intrauterine device. The function of an intrauterine device (IUD) is, in the main, to prevent implantation of the fertilised ovum; the legality of that procedure is discussed later. For the present, we are concerned only with the medical aspects, and these can be serious. It is a characteristic defence mechanism of the body to react to the presence of a foreign body by way of inflammation; inflammation, in turn, results in repair which may involve fibrosis. The use of an IUD, which is, essentially, a foreign body that remains in place for five years or more, sometimes results in inflammation which has both acute and chronic effects.

Modern IUDs must be fitted by a specially trained physician; they then have an effectiveness rate of up to 99 per cent, the greatest improvement resulting from the incorporation of a copper wire with a substantial surface area.[11] Their presence is not felt and there is no interference with natural intercourse. Older patterns of IUD were associated with excess menstrual loss but this can be substantially alleviated by incorporating long-acting hormonal preparations in the device.[12] Thus there is every reason to suppose that the IUD could be a contraceptive of choice and this is particularly true, not only for the older woman, but also for women in societies in which continued medical treatment might be difficult for economic reasons; it has, for example, been estimated that some 40 million Chinese women use IUDs.[13] Nonetheless, the problem of complications exists and this came to light, particularly, in the litigious ambience of the United States where a particular device – the Dalkon shield – has been described as 'one of the most litigated products in pharmaceutical history'.[14]

It is extremely difficult for an outsider to follow the outcomes of the litigation which has surrounded this particular issue: a search of data bases, in fact, yielded more cases associated with legal professional ethics than with the actual medico-legal issue. It appears, however, that more than two million American women used the shield and, of these, 17 died and a large number either contracted pelvic inflammation and were, as a consequence, rendered sterile, or sustained a septic abortion;[15] in addition, it was said that some 3700 British women claimed damages for resultant infertility.[16] Actions were brought against the manufacturers on the grounds of negligence, warranty and strict liability but, while some were successful, many fell foul of some legal limitation and it was found very difficult to surmount the hurdle of causation in negligence actions: it is not easy to exclude other causes of pelvic inflammation and, indeed, it may well be that the main factor determining its presence is the number of sexual partners involved with a woman or with her principal partner.[17] Strict liability actions were also struck down on the grounds that an IUD is an unavoidably unsafe product.[18] Nonetheless, the company concerned was bankrupted and there was a massive retreat from this form of contraception as a whole in the United States. Whether all this was necessary will probably never be known for certain; it can be said, however, with some assurance that there are no grounds for extrapolating the results of using the Dalkon shield to other modern IUDs. Any danger from these is generally transient and is probably related to the actual process of insertion;[19] it is for this reason that IUDs are best left undisturbed so long as the device is working effectively and the need for contraception remains.[20]

Oral contraceptives are, in general, based on the two female hormones, oestrogen and progesterone or its synthetic analogues, the progestogens; progestogen-only pills have been introduced and are valuable when oestrogens are, for whatever reason, contraindicated. When taken by mouth, the preparations must be taken regularly each day. They act either by preventing ovulation or by altering the secretions within the female genital canal in such a way that the vagina becomes a hostile environment for the sperm. Almost from the time of its introduction, there had been controversy as to whether or not 'the pill' induces dangerous blood clotting in women.[21] Based on personal autopsy experience, the present author has no doubts that the early formulations were dangerously thrombotic – at least on the arterial side of the circulation. This was due mainly to the oestrogen content, which has been steadily reduced as contraceptive expertise has improved; as a consequence, dangerous reactions have been very greatly reduced.[22] Considerable concern was raised, therefore, when the Committee on the Safety of Medicines reported something of a twofold increased risk of venous thromboembolism in women taking pills containing the very latest – or 'third generation' – progestogens.[23] This episode exemplifies the difficulties facing the authorities in these days of litigious (or even political) medicine. Although the difference may sound considerable, it is, in practical terms, relatively slight (it has been pointed out that the issue boils down to whether 9998 or 9997 out of 100 000 'pill users' will remain free of venous thrombosis)[24] yet failure to warn of such a risk would attract major criticism from consumers. Scientists, on the other hand, might well regard the announcement as premature, particularly bearing in mind that a specific contraindication may be balanced by other, as yet, hidden advantages. In the context of oral contraceptives, this is illustrated by the fact that the 'third generation' progestogens were introduced in the hopes that they would cut down the incidence of *arterial* thrombosis which, in the form of myocardial infarction or stroke, is far more dangerous than is clot formation on the venous side of the circulation. Leaving aside the general proposition that pregnancy carries far more risks than does contraception, the choice of 'pill' is probably best considered from the viewpoint of risk factors. Thus hormones which predispose to venous thromboembolism should not be used in those who are obese, have varicose veins or who have a history of thrombosis from any cause. Those which are associated with arterial disease are contraindicated with increasing age and, most particularly, in smokers. Indeed, it is probable that the greatest risk from hormonal contraception stems from smoking while taking the pill, rather than from the type of pill being used.[25] Even when using low oestrogen dosage, there are many who feel that the increased thrombotic activity following surgery, particularly that related to venous thrombosis, dictates that oral contraceptives should be discontinued for at least a month before undergoing a major operation.[26]

The provision of hormonal contraception for men must be regarded as being, at present, in the experimental stage.[27] To be effective, the hormone – testosterone – must be injected, which seriously limits the acceptability of the method. More importantly, while contraception in the female can be seen as little more than manipulation of the reproductive cycle, suppression of sperm formation in the male represents serious physiological intervention. Adverse side-effects may, therefore, be of a wholly different order from those found in women. Moreover, the moral, albeit paralogistic, justifications of the use of the pill in women cannot be applied in the case of men.

A word might also be interpolated concerning the possible association of oral contraception with carcinoma in general and, particularly, with carcinoma of the breast. This has been a matter of fierce controversy which is probably not yet resolvable since women who have been regularly exposed to contraceptive medication are only now reaching the age at which the risk of cancer of the breast is greatest. Many malignant tumours are hormone-dependent and it would not be surprising if long-term administration of hormones had some effect on their occurrence. Suffice it to say that no major augmentative effect of contraceptive medicines on breast cancer has yet been demonstrated. The most recent study indicates that there is a small increase in the relative risk of having breast cancer when women are taking combined oral contraceptives and in the 10 years after stopping doing so. There is no apparent excess of breast cancers in women more than 10 years after stopping medication; moreover, the cancers discovered in those who have taken long-term contraception are less advanced clinically than are those found in women who have not done so.[28] The variability in patters of use are, however, so diverse and the additional potentially important factors are so many that any such studies must be looked at cautiously.[29] It is to be noted that any supposed relationship is not all one-way. There is good evidence that contraceptives actually protect against ovarian and endometrial cancer;[30] the net balance of 'cancer risk' may, in fact, be favourable to those 'on the pill'.

It is probable that this general uncertainty as to what constitutes correct medical practice is responsible for the dearth of reported negligence actions related to contraceptive prescription; for reasons which are discussed in greater detail in the next chapter, it is difficult to succeed in a medical negligence suit when the medical profession is, itself, in doubt as to what constitutes proper medical care.[31] Indeed, the most apposite British case discovered concerned not the normal contraceptive regime but the use of long-term or depot hormonal contraceptives. These may be given by injection and have a failure rate of something less than 0.5 per 100 woman years. The hormones, which are of progestogen type and are oestrogen-free, are released slowly over a period of two to three months. They therefore have a special place in covering danger times of short duration, such as when a patient is awaiting admission for elective surgery,[32] or following anti-viral immunization. They often cause the menstrual periods to become irregular, although they may also reduce the menstrual flow – and a number of other, largely psychosomatic, side-effects have been described following the use of the most widely used preparation, Depo Provera. With far less certainty of ethical propriety, they can also be used for population control or in other circumstances when regular oral dosage might be difficult to maintain, for example in the control of pregnancy in the mentally handicapped. An alternative and far more sophisticated application is by way of subcutaneous implants which, mainly in the form of Norplant, will give one of the most effective methods of contraception currently available.[33] The main difficulty arising from the procedure is that it depends on the expertise of the health carers, whose experience of removal of implanted capsules is less than that of their insertion. Almost inevitably, a large number of lawsuits are pending in the United States alleging pain and disfigurement following premature removal;[34] the outcome of the class action is not known at the time of writing.

The British case referred to relates to the irregular bleeding which is a fairly frequent feature of depot contraception. A Mrs Blyth brought such an action for negligence related to the prescription of Depo Provera.[35] She did not, however, pursue any claim for negligence on the part of the manufacturer or on the part of the doctor who prescribed her 'cover' for an anti-rubella vaccination. Her complaint was, rather, that she would not have had the injection had she been informed of the unpleasant side-effects. The action was, therefore, one of consent-based negligence, the nature of which is described in the more important context of sterilisation in Chapter 4. Somewhat surprisingly in the circumstances of the case, general damages and minimalised special damages were awarded by the trial judge on the grounds that

> the defendants were negligent in not advising the plaintiff as fully as they ought to have done in the light of her manifest and reasonable request to be advised ... the evidence does not enable [the Court] to say where the fault occurred, but merely to conclude that it occurred somewhere. Most probably it was simply a matter of communication.

As was to be expected, the Court of Appeal reversed this decision but, in doing so, it clarified the interpretation of one aspect of the law relating to so-called 'informed consent' to medical treatment (see Chapter 4). It has long been the general belief that something of a strict liability to answer truthfully and fully rests on a doctor who is asked a specific question relating to proposed treatment.[36] This view appeared to be confirmed in the House of Lords in the landmark case of *Sidaway*,[37] in which it was said: 'when questioned specifically by a patient of apparently sound mind about risks involved in a particular treatment proposed, a doctor's duty must, in my opinion, be to answer both truthfully and as fully as the questioner requires' (per LORD BRIDGE at 898). This observation, and others in the same vein, was quoted by the trial judge in *Blyth* and certainly influenced his finding of negligence. In effect, the judge was one of the first to attempt to set a limit to the *Bolam* test of medical negligence, which holds that negligence will be decided by whether or not a doctor has acted in accordance with a practice accepted as proper by a body of responsible and skilled medical opinion.[38] LEONARD J placed a limit to such a test when it came to questioning on specific points, as opposed to general enquiry, by the patient: no professional 'privilege', or prevarication on the grounds of what the doctor considers to be in the best interests of the patient, was available in the former case. This reasoning was, however, rejected in the Court of Appeal:

> I am not convinced that the *Bolam* test is irrelevant even in relation to the question of what answers are properly to be given to specific enquiries or that ... Lord Bridge intended to hold otherwise. It seems to me that there may always be grey areas, with differences of opinion, as to what are the proper answers to be given to any enquiry, even a specific one, in the particular circumstances of any case. (Per KERR LJ)

Blyth, therefore, has general interest in the field of negligence and has considerable importance in extending protection of the doctor's judgment[39] but, despite the facts, the case has no particular relevance to contraception. British pharmaceutical companies and physicians however, have been, more fortunate than have been their American counterparts even before the Norplant actions. In *MacDonald v. Ortho Pharmaceutical Corp*,[40] the plaintiff was prescribed contraceptive pills, the container for which – and a booklet prepared and presented by her gynaecologist – warned of the risk of abnormal blood clotting which might damage the brain or other organs; no specific mention was made within that envelope of the possibility of sustaining a 'stroke'. After three years' use of the pills, the patient suffered a stroke and contended that she would not have used them had she been warned of the risk. The jury found the defendant to have been negligent despite the fact that the warnings given on the label conformed to the requirements laid down by the federal Food and Drugs Administration. Interestingly, however, the lower court's ruling that a manufacturer of a prescription drug was relieved of any duty to warn the patient once the patient's physician had been warned was reversed in the Supreme Court of Massachusetts; the rationale was that the participation of the doctor was limited in matters such as the provision of contraceptives: the decision to use oral contraceptives was essentially a matter between the manufacturer and the woman concerned.

The main purpose of this brief review has been to demonstrate that the use of contraceptives may raise many medico-legal issues – in particular, those related to medical negligence and to pharmaceutical liability and its nature. These arise because contraceptive appliances and drugs all have their dangers, limitations and contraindications. They cannot be fitted or prescribed without adequate consideration of those factors and this applies particularly when consent to their use is either inadequate, as may be the case in the mentally handicapped, or of doubtful legal validity, as in the case of children. The position of these special groups is discussed in the following paragraphs.

Contraception and the mentally handicapped

The legality and morality of depriving a person of his or her capacity to reproduce is discussed in greater detail in Chapter 4. The subject is addressed there because sterilisation is, and is intended to be, a permanent contraceptive measure and it is the element of permanence that is important. By contrast, all the methods of contraception described above can be abandoned at will and fertility can be established in a reasonably short time. Thus the use of such contraceptive measures in non-consensual but *bona fide* medically controlled conditions may be less difficult to justify than is the case with sterilisation.

This would certainly seem to be so in practice. Very little has been written on contraception in the mentally handicapped and there have been no court decisions, although the remarks of Lord Brandon in *Gillick*[41] as to the application of the criminal law are to be noted and are mentioned below (p. 54). Rather, the majority of decisions related to non-consensual sterilisation of the mentally handicapped have either resulted in refusal of permission for surgical intervention on the grounds that other means of contraception were available or leave to sterilise has been granted on the understanding that medical contraception was not a viable alternative.[42] The decision to institute a contraceptive regime for a mentally handicapped woman is, therefore, one which the courts are, in general, content to leave to good medical practice.

There can be little doubt that hormonal contraceptives *are* given to mental patients without their appreciation of their purpose, often through the medium of injected long-acting preparations. There are some who might see this as rampant medical paternalism and as an infringement of the individual's fundamental right to procreate. The nature of this right is discussed below (p. 84). For the present, it need only be noted that the 'right' itself derives from other 'rights', including those to have sexual intercourse, to gestate and to parent – and an individual who is incapable of exercising one of these procreative rights is not, thereby, deprived of the general right,[43] particularly if the deprivation is temporary and subject to readjustment. Moreover, medical care involves treatment of the whole person rather than of a single pathological condition; it would be absurd to advocate extensive therapy for mental handicap and, at the same time, to insist that no attempt should be made to prevent any good effects being nullified by a pregnancy which was not intended or, indeed, understood by the woman concerned. The medical alternative would be segregation and this, in itself, is an interference with another right – that of free societal association.

The stronger argument would therefore seem to be that contraceptive protection of the mentally handicapped is justified both by medico-legal necessity and by the moral doctrine of double effect: in this case, that the comparative evil of non-consensual treatment is justified by the resultant benefit of personal liberty.[44] This, however, is subject to two major provisos. First, it applies only in the context of the treatment of an individual in good faith; no such justification would be available were contraceptive hormones to be dispensed on a general scale, say, for the supervisory benefit of the health carers themselves. Secondly, there is no statutory basis for the proposition. The Mental Health Act 1983 and the Mental Health (Scotland) Act 1984 authorise non-consensual treatment of compulsorily detained persons only insofar as the treatment is directed to the condition giving rise to detention and, in the present state of the law, no-one has power to consent to extraneous treatment on behalf of an incompetent adult.[45] The doctor must, therefore, depend upon the common law, expressed by LORD GRIFFITHS in the words:

> In a civilised society, the mentally incompetent must be provided with medical and nursing care and those who look after them must do their best for them. Stated in legal terms, the doctor who undertakes responsibility for the treatment of a mental patient who is incapable of giving consent to treatment must give the treatment that he considers to be in the best interests of his patient.[46]

Contraception for minors

We are on rather more litigious ground when we come to the supply of contraceptives to minors. Perhaps this is because, by contrast with the relatively closed world of the mental hospital, the control – or lack of control – of teenage sexuality is something society cannot look away from; there were 1358 live births and 3437 abortions involving girls below the age of 16 in England and Wales in 1994, and a proportion of the 3666 live births to girls aged 16 must have derived from unlawful intercourse. The problem is one which intimately affects the rights of what the Americans identify as the mature minor, of parents and of society as a whole. Subject to the limitation set by the legislation (see below), consent to contraception is to be regarded as one aspect, albeit an emotive aspect, of consent to medical treatment; as Norrie has said: 'There is no ground in logic or in principle for distinguishing contraceptive advice [and abortion advice] from all other types of medical treatment ... [to do so] is to introduce an arbitrary distinction as a new rule of law'.[47] Logically, therefore, we should look at the general law relating to consent by minors before considering the specific conditions of contraception, although to do so is to pre-empt discussion which might be better placed in Chapter 12.

Somewhat surprisingly, there was no firm precedent available in England and Wales prior to 1985 on which to assess the legality of treating a child in the absence of parental consent. The Family Law Reform Act 1969, s.8 undoubtedly allows a minor over the age of 16 to consent to medical or surgical treatment, but it is silent either way in regard to the child below the age of 16 – and, parenthetically, it is to be noted that, although it is widely assumed to be covered, the prophylaxis of pregnancy does not seem to be included in medical treatment. In 1983, Samuels wrote: 'The law is as it ought to be, that a minor, under 16, cannot give lawful consent to an operation or medical treatment. Only the parents, or those exercising parental powers, can give lawful consent'.[48] This is a clear rule but it is one which makes no allowance for the overriding justification of necessity. Put in medical terms, this implies a primary concern for the well-being of the minor patient and, if it is necessary, taking a decision to provide treatment in defiance of parental instructions that are detrimental to the patient – the sort of problem which is frequently met and overcome in the case of, for example, the families of Jehovah's Witnesses (see Chapter 12). Moreover, it takes no cognisance of the gradual emergence of an autonomous human being with increasing age. Many years ago, LORD DENNING put it: 'Parents have a dwindling right which the courts will hesitate to enforce against the wishes of the child, and the more so the older he [or she] is. It starts with the right of control and ends with little more than advice.'[49]

Clearly, parental authority diminishes *pari passu* with the increasing intelligence and decision-making capacity of the child and it was this test of understanding which Samuels found uncertain and unsatisfactory. Nevertheless, it represented the common law as it was interpreted, for example, in Scotland and it expressed a principle which the courts were increasingly willing to apply, starting with the seminal Canadian case of *Johnston v. Wellesley Hospital*.[50] It was firmly held in that case that a minor's capacity to give a legally effective consent to a medical procedure depends upon whether he or she can understand the nature and the consequences of the procedure in question. The emergence of a classic British case was, however, delayed until 1982,[51] when BUTLER-SLOSS J was asked to decide on the propriety of an abortion for a girl aged 15 years against the wishes of her parents who were prepared to support their grandchild. In authorising the operation, the judge said: 'I am satisfied [the girl] wants this abortion; she understands the implications of it. Indeed, she went so far as to say she will feel guilty about it later after it happened but that she will live with the guilt of it and she is very anxious that it will happen.'

Nevertheless, this trend was not accepted without question. *Johnston* was met in 1982 by another influential Commonwealth decision,[52] concerned with the extent to which parents may overrule requests for treatment by children. *Johnston*, it was held, was no authority for any proposition at common law that there is no right in a guardian to prevent treatment in a minor who has consented; 'might,' said the court (per HELSHAM CJ) 'is another matter'. Taken all in all, then, doctors concerned with the treatment of intelligent minors were forced to work in something of a legal vacuum. Moreover, whatever the law might be, there was internal professional discipline to contend with in the form of possible breaches of confidentiality of the doctor/patient relationship, a matter which has always been regarded extremely seriously in the United Kingdom by the General Medical Council. Only one apposite disciplinary case appears to have been reported[53] in which a doctor who informed the parents of a girl that she was taking contraceptive medication was exonerated on the grounds that he was acting in the best interests of his patient. Although this seems clear-cut, the decision caused consternation in legal circles at the time and it is almost inconceivable that the Council would have taken a similar view a decade later. Such, then, was the somewhat unsatisfactory situation which faced the doctor in England and Wales – though probably not in Scotland – before Mrs Gillick brought her case against the Department of Health and Social Security.[54]

The Gillick case

Gillick has become such an important medico-legal case and has been applied so widely that a full discussion is, now, probably unwarranted. In summary, the action derived from instructions issued by the DHSS (HN (80) 44 as revised in HSC (IS) 32) to the effect that, in certain exceptional circumstances, a doctor might counsel and prescribe contraception for a girl under the age of 16 years; the decision whether or not to do so was a matter for the doctor's clinical judgment. Mrs Gillick sought a declaration that the advice was unlawful and that no doctor or other professional person employed by the Area Health Authority might give advice or treatment as to contraception or abortion to any of her female children under the age of 16 without her prior knowledge and consent.

The judge at first instance was, in large part, concerned with the criminal law and, in particular, with the suggestion that a doctor prescribing contraceptives to a minor female would be abetting an offence under the Sexual Offences Act, 1956, s.6 (having sexual intercourse with a girl under the age of 16) or with actually offending against s.28 (*inter alia* encouraging intercourse with a girl under 16).[55] This aspect of the case is outside the scope, of this book although it may be said that, as anticipated, the suggestion received minimal support in the long history of the case; only Lord Brandon in the House of Lords agreed with the proposition.[56] Lord Brandon, indeed, went so far as to suggest that, because of the criminal connotations, not only could doctors not prescribe contraceptives but parents could not consent to contraception for a girl under the age of 16 and neither could the court in wardship.[57] Were this so, it would also be impossible to give contraceptive treatment to the mentally handicapped for fear of transgressing the Sexual Offences Act, 1956, s.7, or the Mental Health (Scotland) Act 1984, s.106; fortunately, however, the definitive *Gillick* decision is quite clear that there is no substance to the suggestion.

WOOLF J also distinguished between non-medical treatment, such as giving a pill, and conduct which would amount to a trespass such, it is supposed, as fitting an IUD; the implication is that the latter would always require parental consent. This distinction seems to me to be unnecessary. Parental consent to *treatment* may or may not be necessary, but any dividing line must be placed by reason of the severity and/or permanence of that treatment. A vaginal examination may certainly be a trespass, but it can scarcely be regarded as hazardous – and the potential dangers of the IUD and of hormonal prophylaxis, discussed above, are of very similar degree. In essence, WOOLF J's judgment was that whether or not a child is capable of giving the necessary consent to treatment will depend upon the child's maturity and understanding and the nature of the consent which is required. He found nothing unlawful in the DHSS recognising that, in the exceptional case, there remains a discretion for the doctor, based on clinical judgment, as to whether or not to prescribe contraception.

This judgment was overturned unanimously in the Court of Appeal.[58] The major thrust of the reversal lay in that, whereas WOOLF J had regarded a parent's interest in his or her child as a responsibility or duty, the Court of Appeal, per PARKER LJ at 137–8, considered that a parent or guardian has a parcel of rights in relation to children in his or her custody and that these rights, which include the right to control the manner in which and the place at which the child spends his or her time, can neither be abandoned nor transferred. It is clearly recognised, said the court, that there is some age below which a child is incapable as a matter of law of giving any valid consent or making any valid objection for itself in regard to its custody or upbringing and that age for girls is at present 16.

Such misgivings were not, however, shared by the House of Lords, who reversed the Court of Appeal decision by a majority of 3 to 2. The main speech was given by LORD FRASER, who based his opinion on the assumption that a child does not, on attaining a given age, suddenly acquire independence. Rather, most wise parents relax their control gradually as the child develops and encourage him or her to become increasingly independent. LORD FRASER went on to say: 'The only practicable course is, in my opinion, to entrust the doctor with a discretion to act in accordance with his view of what is best in the interests of the girl who is his patient' (at 174). But – and this is most significant – he then laid down the criteria which had to be met before the doctor could exercise this discretion. These were that the doctor must be satisfied:

i.   That the girl will understand his advice.
ii.   That he cannot persuade the girl to inform her parents or allow him to inform them that she is seeking contraceptive advice.
iii. That she is likely to have sexual intercourse with or without contraceptive treatment.
iv.   That, unless she receives the treatment, her physical or mental health or both are likely to suffer.
v.   That her best interests require him to give her contraceptive advice, treatment or both without parental consent.

As a final warning, LORD FRASER said that the result ought not to be regarded as a licence for doctors to disregard the wishes of parents on this matter whenever they find it convenient to do so: 'Any doctor who behaves in such a way would, in my opinion, be failing to discharge his professional responsibilities, and I would expect him to be disciplined by his own professional body accordingly.'

LORD SCARMAN, in a concurring opinion, admitted the legal right and duty of parents to determine whether or not to seek medical advice in respect of their child and, having received advice, to give or withhold consent to medical treatment. Moreover, he thought that certainty was always an advantage in the law. Nevertheless, certainty carries with it an inflexibility and rigidity: 'If the law should impose on the process of "growing up" fixed limits where nature knows only a continuous process, the price would be artificiality and a lack of realism in an area where the law must be sensitive to human development and social change.' Ultimately, while holding that the parental right to determine the medical treatment of a child under the age of 16 terminates as and when the child achieves a sufficient understanding and intelligence to enable him or her to understand fully what is proposed, he emphasised that it is not enough that the girl should understand the nature of the advice being given to her; she must also have a sufficient maturity to understand what is involved.

This, then, is the current position which LORD SCARMAN himself described as resulting in uncertainty – an uncertainty which was the price to be paid to keep the law in line with social experience.[59] 'I accept,' he said, 'that great responsibilities will lie on the medical profession ... [but] it is a learned and highly trained profession regulated by statute and governed by a strict ethical code which is vigorously enforced.' These words are significant, in that *Gillick* has been extrapolated to include all medical treatment and would probably cover research involving children (see Chapter 12). Williams[60] went so far as to suggest that the rule laid down by LORD SCARMAN made the law a trap for doctors and that it had a potentially disturbing effect upon the notion of consent in general. Indeed, the doctors themselves were not slow to cover their tracks and the General Medical Council issued guidelines which, while protective of the doctor, introduced concepts which were frankly detrimental to the young patient's expectations of privacy. Even a decade later, the relevant advice from the GMC reads:

Problems may arise if you consider that a patient is incapable of giving consent to treatment because of immaturity, illness, or mental incapacity, and you have tried unsuccessfully to persuade the patient to allow an appropriate person to be involved in the consultation. If you are convinced that it is essential in the patient's medical interests, you may disclose relevant information to an appropriate person or authority. You must tell the patient before disclosing any information. You should remember that the judgment of whether patients are capable of giving or withholding consent to treatment or disclosure must be based on an assessment of their ability to appreciate what the treatment or advice being sought may involve, and not solely on their age.[61]

While this probably represents as good a *general* compromise as is likely to be obtained, it still puts the young person in an unenviable position. Essentially, the girl seeking contraceptive advice must prove her intelligence and understanding; only when she has done so is she guaranteed the confidentiality of the doctor/patient relationship – and this is no atmosphere in which to embark on a most private consultation.[62]

The ruling in *Gillick*, with its emphasis on the conflict between 'growing up' and fixed age limits, calls into question those age limits which are already laid down by statutes. As a correspondent to *The Times* put it at the time:

Perhaps someone could explain to [me] why my daughters will be unable to buy cigarettes, alcohol or fireworks under the age of 16 (presumably because they are not yet considered mature enough to make decisions about such health hazards) yet at the same time they will be regarded as mentally and physically mature enough to make decisions about the health hazards resulting from sexual intercourse; and that, while I will have redress in law against those who sell my children harmful substances, I will not against doctors who prescribe possibly damaging chemicals, thereby encouraging them to risk their health and break the law?[63]

Put another way, modern parents have difficulty enough in bringing up their children without doctors taking upon themselves the role of those who are most closely affected by the law relating to contraception in young persons.[64]

Time has not stood still since this legal epic was concluded. We have already noted that the *Gillick* principles have been extended to cover medical and surgical treatment in general and we now have an established legal entity in the '*Gillick*-competent' child – a term coined by LORD DONALDSON MR in *Re R (a Minor)*[65] – and that status is now recognised in statute in Scotland;[66] on the other side of the coin, there have been two important cases which have clearly put something of a brake on the process to which we will return in the discussion of 'Consent' in Chapter 12. Perhaps the major controversy, however, surrounds the issue of the minor's right to *refuse* treatment.

It has been widely assumed that the right to consent to treatment carries with it a parallel right to refuse treatment; it has, indeed, been suggested that to hold otherwise is bordering on the perverse.[67] I suggest that this is not strictly so – there may well be a parallel right, but it need not be an equal right. I return to the subject in Chapter 12. For present purposes, it need only be said that, while I do not deny that both consent and refusal are aspects of self-determination, it does seem that passing the 'Fraser test' (see p. 55) requires a different *quality* of understanding in respect of refusal of treatment than is needed for valid consent. But we are straying some way from the specific problems of contraception.

Interceptive methods

Norrie[68] has pointed out that there is a world of difference in the legal response to family planning, on the one hand, by way of contraception and sterilisation and, on the other, by abortion: 'we must be aware of when conception is completed and when pregnancy has commenced for, after the completion of conception there can be no contraception, and before the commencement of pregnancy there can be no abortion'. Certain forms of family planning act, in the main, by preventing implantation of the fertilised ovum rather than by inhibiting conception; the two most important are intrauterine devices and post-coital anti-pregnancy medication, commonly, albeit wrongly, known as the 'morning after pill'. Since it is the 'conceptus' which implants, they cannot logically be regarded as contraceptive methods; and if, as will be argued later in Chapter 5, we conclude that pregnancy begins with implantation, they cannot be said to terminate a pregnancy. At this point, therefore, the reproductive cycle is in something of a state of limbo in which the law finds itself ill-equipped; there are also obvious semantic difficulties which have been solved, in part by the use of the neologism 'contragestation' to describe the process of post-coital birth control.

The intrauterine device has been described above under the heading of medical aspects of contraception. From what has been said in the foregoing paragraph, it is clear that this is, strictly speaking, a misplacement, but it follows common usage. In practice, I prefer to limit the contragestational use of IUDs to their deliberate insertion during the interval between sexual intercourse and potential implantation of the zygote; it then becomes the most effective method of 'emergency contraception' but is clearly not ideal.[69] Post-coital anti-pregnancy medication generally consists of large doses of oestrogen and progestogen repeated at 12 hours – the so-called 'Yuzpe regime'; their action is complex but certainly includes an element of alteration of the receptivity of the endometrium. The treatment can be given effectively within 72 hours after hazardous intercourse: the use of the term 'morning after pill' is, therefore, misleading.[70] The current failure rate is of the order of 2.5 per cent, which is higher than can be regarded as wholly satisfactory; alternative preparations are on trial.[71]

In my view, any legal problems associated with the use of interceptive contragestational methods are of an academic nature only and the issues are, in practice, solved. They turn on the precise interpretation of the working of the Offences Against the Person Act, 1861 and of the Abortion Act 1967. As to the first, the question arises as to whether preventing implantation is or is not 'procuring a miscarriage'. A legal argument can be developed to show that the two processes are similar,[72] in which case an attempt to prevent implantation would constitute an offence under s.58 of the 1861 Act. Medically speaking, however, there is a wealth of difference, the most particular being that the contents of the body's passages which are open to the exterior are, themselves, 'external' to the body. A simple example is to be seen in the ingestion of a toxic substance; an analysis of the stomach or bowel contents may indicate the fact of ingestion but cannot demonstrate poisoning: the substance has not been absorbed and is, accordingly, still 'external' in nature. Something which is external is carried only in the loosest sense – it can be dropped either intentionally, accidentally or naturally. There can be little or no doubt that bodily 'carriage' implies some form of integration with the body or, as Kennedy has said: 'there can be no miscarriage without carriage'.[73] This being so, there can, equally, be no offence against the Abortion Act 1967, s.5(2). In practice, it is almost impossible to conceive of the law risking ridicule by prosecuting for the prescription of a post-coital contraceptive pill, and a prosecution would certainly be incompetent in Scotland where proof of pregnancy is needed before an offence relating to abortion can be committed at common law. Even if it *were* an offence in England – and there is reason to suppose that *intention* to procure a miscarriage must include a *belief* that the woman is pregnant[74] – it would be, surely, that form of abortion which created the least emotional disturbance in both the public and the private mind. The Attorney General has expressed this view in saying: 'It is clear that, used in its ordinary sense, the word 'miscarriage' is not apt to describe a failure to implant, whether spontaneous or not ... Likewise, the phrase 'procure a miscarriage' cannot be construed to include the prevention of implantation.'[75] At the same time, he said that no action would be taken in cases which were referred to the Director of Public Prosecutions. It is to be noted that the relevant law relates to procuring a miscarriage or to termination of pregnancy; there is no offence in the United Kingdom of feticide *per se* – still less of embryocide. Finally, and, perhaps, of greatest significance, the legality of emergency contraception is so assured that there are calls for contragestational preparations to be made available as 'over the counter' medicines.[76]

The ground is slightly less sure when discussing the use of intrauterine devices, particularly when these are inserted *after* sexual intercourse as defined above; there is an intuitive, even if illogical, distinction to be made between using an instrument and prescribing a pill. Tunkel[77] described the situation in a clinic where the insertion of IUDs up to 10 days after intercourse was an openly advertised service and argued that, since any person to whom an IUD is fitted *might* be a few days pregnant, the logical conclusion was that IUDs were illegal in all circumstances. This seems to overstate the case as it ignores the significance of the phrase in the Offences Against the Person Act s.58: 'whosoever with intent to procure [a] miscarriage'; a distinction is thus to be made between the doctor who fits an IUD because the patient has *had* sexual intercourse and one who does so because she *may* do so. Even if we ignore the latter practitioner – and, in practice, we *must* do so since some 6 per cent of women in the United Kingdom use IUDs which are fitted without qualm in Family Planning Clinics – we are still faced with the problems of belief in a pregnancy and, equally importantly, of the definition of pregnancy.

There is, therefore, a potential distinction to be made between fitting an IUD within 10 days of intercourse, during which time implantation is improbable, and fitting one later, when the scenarios run from the possibility of implantation, through laboratory proof of pregnancy to its clinical diagnosis. There is some rather unsatisfactory case law to support this view. In *R v. Price*,[78] a case which was heard just before the Abortion Act 1967 came into force, a doctor was prosecuted under the Offences Against the Person Act, s.58, for inserting an IUD in a woman who was between 10 and 14 weeks pregnant. Dr Price was convicted but the conviction was quashed on appeal, on the grounds that the jury was misdirected as to corroboration of evidence given by an accomplice; nevertheless, the charge was still held to be relevant. By contrast, we have the unfortunately unreported case of *R v. Dhingra*.[79] In this instance, the doctor fitted the IUD 11 days after intercourse and was, again, charged under s.58. The judge, however, withdrew the case after hearing gynaecological evidence. He is reported as saying: 'It is highly unlikely any ovum became implanted and only at the completion of implantation does the embryo become a fetus. At this stage she can be regarded as pregnant.'[80] WRIGHT J appears also to have invoked the 'state of the art' interpretation of statutes in saying: 'In 1861, the mechanics of a woman's reproductive organs were not as well understood as they are to-day. Nor were the modern techniques of interference available.'[81] It goes without saying that such a charge would be unsound in Scotland, where a woman must be shown to be pregnant before an abortion-associated offence can be proved.

Displanting methods

A displanting method of contraception – that is, one which is designed to remove an implanted embryo – is clearly a contradiction in terms; but so, also, is a displanting method of contragestation for, by definition, the woman must have gestated for a short time. This confusion demonstrates that displantation is in a different class of birth control and, at the same time, carries its own legal difficulties. Once implantation has occurred, it is impossible to plead 'non-carriage' in a legal sense; it will be argued later (see p. 110) that the moral ambience has also been transformed. The classic displanting method of contraception is euphemistically termed 'menstrual extraction' or 'menstrual regulation'. In this procedure, the endometrium is evacuated at about the time the woman is missing a period. This is incontrovertibly either an actual or an attempted abortion and has been described as such by the Director of Public Prosecutions.[82] Whether it could be prosecuted as such under either the Offences Against the Person Act, 1861 or the Abortion Act 1967 – or whether it would be desirable to do so – would depend very much on the definition of 'good faith' and on the knowledge or beliefs of the operator, as already discussed. It might, indeed, be difficult to disso-ciate action in good faith from a genuine effort to discover whether or not the patient was pregnant and, as Norrie has put it, 'wilful ignorance equals knowledge, and the dislodging of an implanted egg with knowledge equals abortion'.[83] Thus, although there are many who would see menstrual extraction as a form of contracep-tion, the implications are better discussed under the heading of abor-tion.

Summary

The subject of contraception has been discussed mainly in the context of the English law and it would seem that any extant problems are associated with that jurisdiction. The prosecution of a Scottish doctor for contraceptive practices is almost inconceivable in the absence of evil intent on his or her part. It will also be seen in Chapter 5 that a woman's right to privacy would legalize any contraceptive method, including menstrual extraction, in America[84] – and there is no doubt that the concept of the mature minor is deeply entrenched in that country. There has been no judgment against an American physician who provided contraceptive services to a minor of any age.[85]

Notes

1   Though this is a Western view; there is strong opposition to birth control in Moslem countries. See D.A.A. Verkuyl, 'Two world religions and family plan-ning' (1993) 342 Lancet 473.

2   Pope Paul VI, encyclical letter, *On the Regulation of Birth* (1968), Boston: St Paul edn, p. 10.

3   It has been said that 83 per cent of Catholic young adults believe they can disagree with the Church's teaching on the subject yet remain good Catholics: leading article, 'Unholy struggle with third-world genie' (1993) 342 Lancet 447.

4   *Carey v. Population Services International* 431 US 678 (1977) per STEVENS J at 715.

5   This might not be so, however, in respect of the male 'pill', as men have no natural cycles of hormonally controlled infertility.

6   See, for example, J. Glover, *Causing Death and Saving Lives* (reprinted 1986), Harmondsworth: Penguin Books, pp. 137 ff.

7   This chapter, which is essentially concerned with the family, will not address such wide-ranging topics as population control. Suffice it to say that, in some circumstances, family limitation might be seen as a moral imperative: see H.E. Emson, 'A right to reproduce?' (1992) 340 Lancet 1083.

8   Interestingly, a Catholic doctor, struggling with the moral issues involved, finds that she is far more often consulted on the rhythm method by those anxious to achieve pregnancy than by those trying to avoid it: J. Poole, *The Cross of Unknowing* (1989), London: Sheed and Ward, p.18.

9 C.A.M. Reitmeijer, J.W. Krebs, P.M. Feorino and F.N. Judson, 'Condoms as physical and chemical barriers against human immunodeficiency virus' (1988) 259 J Amer Med Ass 1851.

10 See P. Stott, 'Rediscovering the diaphragm' (1988) 296 Brit Med J 377.

11 J. Newton, 'IUD safety and acceptability: recent advances' (1993) 3 Current Obstet Gynaecol 28.

12 J.K. Anderson and G. Rybo, 'Levonorgestrel-releasing intrauterine device in the treatment of menorrhagia' (1990) 97 Brit J Obstet Gynaecol 690.

13 J. Bamford, 'Dalkon shield starts losing in court' (1980) 2 Amer Lawyer 31.

14 P. Pendergast and H.L. Hirsh 'The Dalkon shield in perspective' (1986) 5 Med Law 35. See, in general, G.R. Thornton 'Intrauterine devices: malpractice and product liability' (1986) 14 Law Med Hlth Care 4.

15 'Notes and News' (1987) 1 Lancet 1504. See, in general, H. Buchan, L. Villard-Mackintosh, M. Vessey *et al.*, 'Epidemiology of pelvic inflammatory disease in women with special reference to intrauterine devices' (1990) 97 Brit J Obstet Gynaecol 780.

16 *Wagmeister* v. *A H Robins* 382 NE 2d 23 (Ill, 1978).

17 N.C. Lee, G.L. Rubin, H.W. Ory and R.T. Burkman, 'The intrauterine device and pelvic inflammatory disease: new results from the Women's Health Study' (1988) 72 Obstet Gynecol 1.

18 *Terhune* v. *A H Robins* Co 577 P 2d 975 (Wash, 1978).

19 T.M.M. Farley, M.J. Rosenberg, P.J. Rowe *et al.*, 'Intrauterine devices and pelvic inflammatory disease: an international perspective' (1992) 339 Lancet 785.

20 Editorial comment, 'Does infection occur with modern intrauterine devices?' (1992) 339 Lancet 783.

21 The early papers include V. Beral, 'Cardiovascular-disease mortality trends and oral-contraceptive use in young women' [1976] 2 Lancet 1047; S. Shapiro, L. Rosenberg, D. Slone *et al.*, 'Oral-contraceptive use in relation to myocardial infarction' [1979] 1 Lancet 743; J. Bonnar, 'Coagulation effects of oral contraception' (1987) 157 Amer J Obstet Gynecol 1042.

22 The number of cases of venous thromboembolism (or local clotting followed by passage of the clot to the lungs) in women taking low oestrogen pills containing so-called 'second generation' progestogens is said to be about 15 per 100 000 users, as compared with 5 per 100 000 non-users, giving a mortality of two to three per million users: J. Guillebaud, 'Advising women on which pill to take' (1995) 311 Brit Med J 1111. Note that the rate for thromboembolism in pregnancy is about 60 per 100 000 pregnant women.

23 'Combined oral contraceptives and thromboembolism', 18 October 1995.

24 E. Johannisson, 'Safety of modern oral contraceptives' (1996) 347 Lancet 258.

25 K. McPherson, 'Third generation oral contraception and venous thromboembolism' (1996) 312 Brit Med J 68; A.L. Lewis, W.O. Spitzer, L.A.J. Heinemann *et al.* 'Third generation oral contraceptives and risk of myocardial infarction: an international case-control study' (1996) 312 Brit Med J 88.

26 J. Guillebaud, 'Surgery and the pill' (1985) 291 Brit Med J 498. For a contrary opinion, see H. Sue-Ling and L.E. Hughes, 'Should the pill be stopped preoperatively?' (1988) 296 Brit Med J 447.

27 D. Bonn, 'What prospects for hormonal contraceptives for men?' (1996) 347 Lancet 316.

28 Collaborative Group on Hormonal Factors in Breast Cancer, 'Breast cancer and hormonal contraceptives: Collaborative reanalysis of individual data on 53 297 women with breast cancer and 100 239 women without breast cancer from 54 epidemiological studies' (1996) 347 Lancet 1713. For a critique, see E. Hemminki, 'Oral contraceptives and breast cancer' (1996) 313 Brit Med J 63.

29 Compare, for example, C. La Vecchia, 'Oral contraceptives and breast cancer'

(1992) 1 Breast 76. An increased incidence of the very rare tumour, adenocarci-
noma of the cervix, is also said to result from the use of hormonal contraceptives.

30 See A. Szarewski and J. Guillebaud, 'Contraception' (1991) 302 Brit Med J 1224.

31 A probable association between cerebral thrombosis and oral contraceptives
was admitted in *Coker* v. *Richmond, Twickenham and Roehampton AHA* [1996] 7
Med L R 58. An action in negligence failed because the plaintiff had been
properly informed of the risks and complications.

32 J. Guillebaud, 'Should the pill be stopped preoperatively?' (1988) 296 Brit Med
J 786.

33 L. Mascarenhas, 'Long acting methods of contraception' (1994) 308 Brit Med J
991.

34 J. Roberts, 'Women in US sue makers of Norplant' (1994) 309 Brit Med J 145.

35 *Blyth* v. *Bloomsbury Health Authority and another* (1985) Times, 24 May, QBD;
(1987) Times, 11 February, CA; [1993] 4 Med LR 151, CA.

36 A well-developed concept particularly in Canada, starting with *Lepp* v. *Hopp*
(1979) 98 DLR (3d) 464.

37 *Sidaway* v. *Board of Governors of the Bethlem Royal Hospital and the Maudsley
Hospital* [1985] 1 AC 871, HL.

38 *Bolam* v. *Friern Hospital Management Committee* [1957] 2 All ER 118. For fuller
consideration, see Chapter 4.

39 It has, however, been suggested that this is a simplification, in that, rather than
withholding information, the doctor was simply unaware that the information
existed: see I. Kennedy and A. Grubb, *Medical Law: Text with Materials* (2nd edn,
1994), London: Butterworths, p. 210.

40 475 NE 2d 65 (Mass, 1985).

41 *Gillick* v. *West Norfolk and Wisbech Area Health Authority* [1986] AC 112, HL.

42 For example, *Re B (a minor) (Wardship: Sterilisation)* [1988] AC 199; *Re F (Mental
patient: Sterilisation)* [1990] 2 AC 1; *Re W (a Patient)* [1993] 1 FLR 381.

43 J.A. Robertson, 'Procreative liberty and the control of conception, pregnancy,
and childbirth' (1983) Virginia L Rev 405. See also C. Heginbotham, 'Sterilizing
people with mental handicaps', in S.A.M. McLean (ed.), *Legal Issues in Human
Reproduction* (1988), Aldershot: Gower.

44 This presupposes that contraception is not, *in itself*, an evil – as it would not be
if it was prescribed, as suggested, for the medical benefit of the handicapped
person.

45 This lacuna in the law is under scrutiny at the time of writing. See Law Commission, *Mental Incapacity* (1995), Law Com No. 231, London: HMSO; Incapable Adults (Scotland) Bill 1995.

46 In *Re F (Mental patient: Sterilisation)* n. 42 above at 69. In other words, contraceptive treatment might be subsumed under the umbrella of treatments ancillary to the core treatment: cf. *B* v. *Croydon District Health Authority* (1994) 22
BMLR 13.

47 K. McK. Norrie, 'The Gillick case and parental rights in Scots law' 1985 SLT 157.

48 A. Samuels, 'Can a minor (under 16) consent to a medical operation?' (1983) 13
Fam Law 30.

49 In *Hewer* v. *Bryant* [1970] 1 QB 357 at 369.

50 (1970) 17 DLR (3d) 139.

51 *Re P (a Minor)* (1982) 80 LGR 301, [1986] 1 FLR 272.

52 *K* v. *Minister for Youth and Community Service and another* [1982] 1 NSWLR 311.

53 *General Medical Council* v. *Browne* (1971) *The Times*, 6 March, pp 1 and 2; 8
March, p. 2.

54 *Gillick* v. *West Norfolk and Wisbech Area Health Authority* [1984] QB 581.

55   Similar provisions are now to be found in the Criminal Law (Consolidation) (Scotland) Act 1995, ss.5 & 10.

56   *Gillick*, n. 41 above at 198.

57   *Gillick* n. 41 above at 198.

58   *Gillick* v. *West Norfolk and Wisbech AHA* [1986] AC 112, CA.

59   For criticism, see P.N. Parkinson, 'The Gillick case – just what has it decided?' (1986) 16 Fam Law 11.

60   G. Williams, 'The Gillick saga' (1985) 135 NLJ 1156, 1179.

61   General Medical Council, *Duties of a Doctor: Confidentiality* (1995) para. 10.

62   The situation has, however, been further clarified. See G. Scally, 'Confidentiality, contraception, and young people' (1993) 307 Brit Med J 1157.

63   D. McKinley, 'Implications of the Gillick ruling', Correspondence (1985), *The Times*, 22 October.

64   As suggested in editorial comment, 'Legislation and teenage sex' (1983) 287 Brit Med J 1826. See also P. Gerber, 'Law and family planning' (1984) 140 Med J Aust 320.

65   *Re R (a Minor) (Wardship: medical treatment)* [1992] Fam 11 at 23.

66   Age of Legal Capacity (Scotland) Act 1991, s.2(4). Interestingly, this 'medical' right forms an exception to the general rule that a person below the age of 16 cannot make a valid contract in Scotland.

67   I. Kennedy, 'Consent to treatment: the capable person', in C. Dyer (ed.), *Doctors, Patients and the Law* (1992) Oxford: Blackwell Scientific. For a rather similar Scottish view, see L. Edwards, 'The right to consent and the right to refuse: more problems with minors and medical consent' [1993] Juridical Rev 52.

68   For a particularly good review of this subject, see K. McK. Norrie, *Family Planning Practice and the Law* (1991), Aldershot: Dartmouth, ch. 4.

69   J.O. Drife, 'Deregulating emergency contraception' (1993) 307 Brit Med J 695.

70   R. Burton, W. Savage and F. Reader, 'The "morning-after" pill is the wrong name for it' (1990) 15 Brit J Fam Plan 119.

71   Such as progestogens alone or the medical abortifacient mifepristone. See D. Baird, 'Post coital contraception and menstrual induction' in A.A. Templeton and D.J. Cusine (eds), *Reproductive Medicine and the Law* (1990), Edinburgh: Churchill Livingstone.

72   I.J. Keown, '"Miscarriage": a medico-legal analysis' [1984] Crim LR 604.

73   I. Kennedy, quoted by Legal Correspondent 'The postcoital pill: lawful or not?' (1983) 287 Brit Med J 64. See also the reasoning of G. Williams, 'Human life and post-coital pill' (1983), *The Times*, 13 April, p. 11.

74   Well argued by Norrie, n. 68 above, on the basis of the successful appeal in *R* v. *Price* [1968] 2 All ER 282.

75   P. Henley, 'Use of post-coital pill "not illegal"' (1983), *The Times*, 11 May, p. 1. The words used in a statute should be given the meaning they had at the time the Act was passed – emergency contraception cannot have been considered in 1861.

76   Though, generally, only as an adjunct to wider sex education. See Drife, n. 69 above; Editorial Comment, 'After the morning after and the morning after that' (1995) 345 Lancet 1381.

77   V. Tunkel, 'Abortion: how early, how late, and how legal?' [1979] 2 Brit Med J 253.

78   Note 74 above.

79   See T. Shaw, 'GP cleared of procuring his secretary's miscarriage' (1991), *Daily Telegraph*, 25 January, p. 5.

80   WRIGHT J may well have been fortified by the Human Fertilisation and Embryology Act 1990, s.2(3), which states: 'For the purposes of this Act, a woman is not to be treated as carrying a child until the embryo has become implanted.'

Despite the qualifying phrase, the words would be very persuasive of official policy in other branches of the law.

81 Although, it is problematic whether such an interpretation is valid, see, for example, *Barker* v. *Wilson* [1980] 1 WLR 884 (duties laid down in the Bankers' Books Evidence Act 1879 held to extend to microfilm). In general, D.J. Hurst 'The problem of the elderly statute' [1983] LS 21.

82 For an analysis of the case of Mr Goldthorp, who published his practice in this field ([1977] 2 Brit Med J 562), see Tunkel, n. 77 above.

83 K. Norrie, 'Post coital anti-pregnancy techniques and the law', in A.A. Templeton and D.J. Cusine (eds), *Reproductive Medicine and the Law* (1990), Edinburgh: Churchill Livingstone, at 15.

84 *Griswold* v. *Connecticut* 381 US 479 (1965); *Eisenstadt* v. *Baird* 405 US 438 (1972).

85 H.L. Hirsh, 'The law protecting children in the United States', in J.K. Mason (ed.), *Paediatric Forensic Medicine and Pathology* (1989), London: Chapman & Hall, ch. 29.

4 Sterilisation

A person who is sterilised is unable to conceive naturally unless the process is reversed. The process of sterilisation may be voluntary or involuntary, the latter being generally associated with acquired or congenital disease, the proximate causes being more varied in women than in men. It is also convenient to consider sterility as being of functional or biological type. Thus there are many reasons why a woman could require a hysterectomy. Having lost her womb, she will be functionally sterile, in that she cannot implant an embryo or carry a fetus; she will still, however, be able to produce ova and cannot be said to be biologically sterile; indeed, the woman who is hysterectomised or who has a congenitally defective uterus is one of the group for whom womb leasing as a means of reproduction would be justifiable on medical grounds (see Chapter 10). Ascending infection in the female genital tract is likely to spread bilaterally. The consequent blockage of both Fallopian tubes is one of the commoner causes of involuntary sterility; a proportion of such cases is attributable to sexually transmitted disease, but this is by no means always so. Natural disease in the male must, with few exceptions, affect the testes bilaterally in order to cause sterility. Bilateral malignant disease necessitating removal of both testes can occur – and testicular neoplasms tend to arise in comparatively young men – but, most often, primary malignant testicular disease is unilateral; the commonest pathological cause of involuntary male sterility will be a generalised disease such as mumps, the effects of which include involvement of the gonads – of both men and women. Similarly, exposure to ionising radiation will sterilise both sexes.

Involuntary sterility following surgical – or, rarely, medical – procedures aimed at the treatment of disease has legal and ethical implications only insofar as procedures which will inevitably prohibit further procreation are particularly subject to rational, or 'informed', consent. Considering the many medical programmes which appear in the entertainment media, it is often a source of astonishment how

patients can fail to appreciate what are apparently obvious concomitant effects of a treatment. It has been held that a patient who wishes
to be informed of something which would be obvious to a reasonable
man or woman must ask about it,[1] but there is no reason to suppose
that the courts will always maintain such professionally oriented
attitudes. It is, however, clear that a married patient can, if he or she
so desires, give valid uncorroborated consent to a sterilising operation so long as sterility is a secondary effect of otherwise necessary
therapy. A surgeon would do well to attempt to persuade the patient
to involve his or her spouse and, if necessary, to record the fact of
refusal; but he is fully justified in proceeding – and must do so in
strict confidence if he is so instructed. Whether or not the same
applies following a request for voluntary, non-therapeutic or contraceptive sterilisation is discussed at p 87.

A matter of rather greater medico-legal concern is whether sterilisation is ever permissible in the absence of consent by the patient;
this is a situation which sharply focuses on the question of ability to
consent to medical intervention and, in the event of such inability, on
the legality and morality of consent by proxy. For the purpose of
discussion, it is convenient to distinguish two forms of non-consensual surgery. These can be defined, firstly, as involuntary sterilisation
– in which either the operation is carried out in the face of competent
objection by the subject, or the subject is capable of consenting to the
procedure and is not asked – and, secondly, non-voluntary sterilisation where the subject is incapable of giving valid consent. In practice, the latter is generally a matter of mental incompetence although,
occasionally, the evaluation of '*Gillick*-competence' in a mentally normal adolescent may be in issue.

Non-consensual sterilisation

Involuntary sterilisation

At its worst, non-consensual sterilisation can be used as a concealed
method of genocide, something which arose in the 20th century out
of a policy of racial improvement instigated by a European government.[2] It is reasonable to suppose that this extreme example of involuntary sterilisation is a matter of history only; although efforts at
population control have been tried and may yet become essential for
ecological reasons,[3] an attempt to eliminate human imperfections on
a national scale is not something which we are likely to see again in
the foreseeable future.[4] Its occurrence within living memory needs to
be recorded, however, because the evidence suggests that its acceptance by some cultures started as a eugenic exercise which was sup-

ported by competent doctors, and this is of significance to the eugenic debate in general. Pfafflin[5] has quoted a Swiss psychologist as including among the sort of people who should not be allowed to procreate all criminals, the mentally deranged, the evil-minded and the quarrelsome – and other individuals incapable of producing a healthy race on account of a pathological constitution. The ease with which such categories can be expanded to include whole ethnic groups scarcely needs emphasis. It is salutary to remember that the indications are that the impetus to eugenic sterilisation derived, in part, from the free society of America.

Eugenic sterilisation   The belief that mental capacity and behaviour are genetically determined, and that such disadvantages can be eliminated by selective sterilisation, certainly had a vogue in the United States at the turn of the century. Only 25 years ago,[6] 26 states of the United States had sterilisation laws, 23 of which allowed for a compulsory operation, particularly in respect of those who were institutionalised. Some remarkable, and relatively unrecognised, campaigns were being waged even before the relevant statutes were enacted. Meyers, for example, records that 600–700 reform school boys were sterilised by a pioneer vasectomist before 1907.[7] The great majority of statutes designated the feeble-minded, the mentally retarded and the mentally ill, together with epileptics, as falling within their ambit of compulsion; 12 states included sterilisation – but not castration – as a recognisable treatment of recidivist criminals. As a result, some 64 000 persons were sterilised in the United States up to 1964. A few states[8] still have sterilisation statutes extant, but the provisions are now invoked only rarely, if at all. Judicial attitudes to the provisions are, therefore, of little more than historic interest, but are worth recapitulating in summarised form – if only for the opinion of HOLMES CJ, which was delivered in *Buck* v. *Bell* and which shows the changes in attitude which have occurred in 70 years.

In that case, the state of Virginia sought to sterilise an 18-year-old mentally subnormal girl who was the daughter of a defective mother and who had, herself, given birth to a mentally impaired child. HOLMES CJ concluded:

We have seen more than once that the public welfare may call upon the best citizens for their lives. It would be strange if it could not call upon those who already sap the strength of the state for these lesser sacrifices, often not felt to be such by those concerned, in order to prevent our being swamped with incompetence. It is better for all the world, if instead of waiting to execute degenerate offspring for crime, or to let them starve for their imbecility, society can prevent those who are manifestly unfit from continuing their kind. The principle that sustains compulsory vaccination is broad enough to cover cutting the Fallopian tubes ... . Three generations of imbeciles are enough.[10]

Meyers criticised this opinion on several grounds, the most generally applicable of which was that vaccination has a beneficial effect on the subject and on society without depriving the former of any capabilities – this being in direct contradiction to the result of compulsory sterilisation. Nevertheless, the ruling – which, by today's standards, is almost incredibly indifferent to the privacy entitlements of the individual – was widely followed until the case of *Skinner* v. *Oklahoma*.[11] Here the conditions were, admittedly, dissimilar, but the rights of the individual were still at stake. The essential issue was whether or not crimes – and criminals – could be distinguished on the basis of their intrinsic 'moral turpitude' despite the fact that they were subject to the same penalties; the relevant Oklahoma statute did so, in that it provided for sterilisation of recidivist criminals whose offences were designated 'immoral'. At this point, the Supreme Court of the USA took a stance which is more in line with contemporary thinking:

> We are dealing here with legislation which involves one of the most basic civil rights of man. Marriage and procreation are fundamental to the very existence and survival of the race. The power to sterilize, if exercised, may have subtle, far-reaching and devastating effects. In evil or reckless hands it can cause races or types which are inimical to the dominant group to wither and disappear.[12]

As something of an envoi, we might note that the ghosts of the eugenists still survive; moreover, they are not all those of citizens of the United States. The Sexual Sterilization Act 1928 of the Canadian province of Alberta was not repealed until 1972, during which time 2832 men and women were sterilised. It is reported as recently as 1966 that a woman who was sterilised under the Act in 1959 at the age of 14 has been awarded exemplary damages against the government for wrongful sterilisation; she had been classified as a moron and told that the operation was for an appendicectomy.[13] Even so, such conditions are things of the past – at least in the Western world.[14] The emphasis as to the control of procreation by those who are mentally impaired has shifted dramatically from the general to the particular and is discussed below under the title of non-voluntary sterilisation.

Punitive sterilisation   The proposition that excess sexuality can be controlled by castration was once strongly held but now has minimal support; the subject, therefore, hardly merits discussion. Nevertheless, some relatively powerful voices are still heard advocating castration of the sexual offender – and of the paedophile tourist. Castration as a form of punishment or as a therapy of sexual recidivism must, therefore, be looked at briefly.

Castration as a punishment in itself can surely be relegated to the history books. Even if no other reason for its exclusion as a punitive option existed, it would be, *par excellence*, a cruel and unusual punishment such as is prohibited specifically in the Eighth Amendment to the United States Constitution, in Article 3 of the European Convention on Human Rights or, generally as to medical participation, in the Declaration of Tokyo.[15] The situation as regards recidivism is, however, less clear-cut: there is ample opportunity, for all but the principal, to make distinctions between what 'is good for one' and what is punishment. The question does not seem to have arisen in Britain, but it is one with which the American courts and legislatures have grappled over the last 20 years, particularly following *Skinner* v. *Oklahoma*.[16]

The issue is not quite dead and still has interesting ramifications. Thus, in the last decade, the parents of a child who died apparently as a result of malnutrition were charged with intentional child abuse, later reduced by agreement to the lesser charge of criminal recklessness. The accused were sentenced to imprisonment for two and a half years with the option that this would be reduced to one and a half years if they agreed to voluntary sterilisation.[17] The issue turned on the trial judge's authority to offer such an option in the absence of any statutory indications; the State Supreme Court distinguished the need to protect any future children from abuse from any other accepted reasons for imposed sterilisation[18] and found that the court should not require such a serious and far-reaching procedure in the absence of specific statutory authorisation.

Somewhat surprisingly, the statutes that are extant in Mississippi, North Carolina and West Virginia are still effective. In a case which I am unable to trace, a South Carolinan rapist was offered – and accepted – castration as an alternative to 30 years' imprisonment, but it was not possible to find a surgeon who was willing to carry out the operation.[19] This is further evidence that there is little or no modern medical support for the concept that castration reduces the recidivism rate of sexual offenders. Meyers was probably right when he said: 'The cause and answer to the sexual psychopath's abnormal urges lie in his cranium not his scrotum.'[20] Which is not to say that there are not other approaches available for the treatment of the sex offender. This book is, however, concerned with reproduction, not recidivism, and enough has been said already on an aspect of reproduction which is no more than marginal to the main theme.

Non-voluntary sterilisation

Sterilisation of the mentally impaired Soskin[21] was one of the first to identify the problem which is inherent in the care and control of sexuality in those who are apparently incapable of controlling their own reproductive capacity by virtue of their mental condition. It is simple, on the one hand, to hold that a person, incompetent or not, has a right to protection against invasion of his or her bodily privacy; since the incompetent is, by definition, incapable of consent – and since the likelihood of an improvement in understanding is an unknown quantity – there must be a strong presumption that non-voluntary sterilisation at the instigation of a parent, guardian or other carer is an unacceptable violation of that privacy. So-called 'reproductive rights' which are vested in both normal adults and in the 'mature minor' are, however, not necessarily only positive in nature; rights to contraception, abortion and sterilisation run concurrently with any that are attached to procreation. It follows that a refusal to authorise sterilisation of an incompetent is, simultaneously, a denial of that incompetent's right to choose a form of contraception which would be desired were he or she capable of self-expression. The dilemma thus resolves itself into balancing the exercise of this choice by proxy against the possibility of abuse of the powers of 'substituted judgment'. Inevitably, because of the several jurisdictions involved and because of the sheer size of the population, the solution of the question has been addressed most actively in the United States of America.

Many states of the United States repealed their statutes upholding eugenic sterilisation between 1960 and 1980 but, in doing so, left a legal vacuum in which the courts found themselves unable to accede to petitions for sterilisation of incompetents on the grounds that there was no statutory authority to do so. This hurdle was first crossed in 1978,[22] when the Supreme Court protected the immunity of a state court which had authorised the sterilisation of a girl despite the fact that the judge 'might have erred in exceeding his authority'. This was quickly followed up in New Jersey where, relying largely on the important case of Karen Quinlan,[23] the court's right to exercise jurisdiction over a sterilisation petition in the absence of statute was upheld; discretion was placed in the hands of the parents, provided that they demonstrated their genuine good faith and that the best interests of the incompetent, rather than their own or the public's convenience, were their primary concern; final approval, however, remained the prerogative of the court.[24] Effectively, *Grady* introduced a 'substituted judgment' test which allowed for full consideration of the incompetent's right to choose through the medium of his or her parents acting in concert with the court. The majority of states in which the jurisdiction of the court is recognised have, by contrast, opted for a substantive 'best interests' form of adjudication in which paternalism – or, in legal terms, the *direct* rather than monitory use of the of *parens patriae* power – is the prevailing influence.

Each case has, therefore, to be judged on its particular facts and, inevitably, there appear to be conflicting decisions. Thus some courts have been concerned above all to preserve the 'right to procreation'[25] – and decisions along these lines have shown a marked wariness of appearing to support the now discredited eugenic precepts. Others have supported the 'right to choose',[26] while yet others have taken into consideration factors such as the potential quality of parenthood in determining whether or not to authorise the non-consensual sterilisation of incompetents.[27] To a very large extent, this may be due to difficulty in defining 'best interests' – are these to be confined to the best medical interests or can the best social interests be included?[28]

The conflicts were demonstrated most vividly in the Californian case of *Valerie N*.[29] Here the majority of the Supreme Court of California went so far as to hold that a statute prohibiting the sterilisation of a developmentally disabled person was invalid insofar as it denied such persons rights which were available to all other groups – and that this was in violation of the guarantees of privacy and of equal protection which were given at both state and constitutional level. BIRD CJ, however, delivered a forthright dissenting opinion in which he said:

> Today's holding will permit the State, through the legal fiction of substituted consent, to deprive many women prematurely of the right to conceive and bear children ... It is a misguided attempt to guarantee a right of procreative choice for one they assume has never been capable of choice and never will be.

United States courts have, therefore, been struggling with the several constitutional issues involved, in particular, firstly, as to the extent of the *parens patriae* doctrine in default of legislation and, secondly, as to the balance of the individual's opposing contraceptive and procreative rights. The shadow of the discredited eugenic programme has been pervasive and has, to an extent, dictated a policy which must be *seen* to be non-coercive while, at the same time, paying due regard to the inbuilt rights of parents to control their children's upbringing; it has been said: 'Since the State should normally defer to the wishes of the parents, it has a serious burden of justification before abridging parental autonomy by substituting its judgment for that of the parents'.[30] Understandably, therefore, the courts have been laying down stringent conditions which must be met before they will accept jurisdiction to order sterilisation of an incompetent. These can be summarised as: (a) the incompetent is represented by a disinterested guardian *ad litem*; (b) there has been independent assessment of the individual who is (c) incapable of forming a judgment; and (d) the incompetent is physically capable of procreation, is likely to engage in sexual activity and there is no reasonable alternative to sterilisation.[31]

Criteria such as these make no distinction between therapeutic and non-therapeutic procedures, a distinction which lies at the heart of the ethical debate which has developed in the countries of the Commonwealth. Because of their rather more uniform jurisdictions, the courts of Canada, Australia and the United Kingdom have been able to evolve a relatively coherent policy as to the legality of non-consensual sterilisation and as to the role of the courts and the guardians in applying that policy. It will be seen that the same conclusions have not always been reached and a brief review of the decisions in all three jurisdictions is instructive.

The Canadian approach   It is convenient to consider, first, the Canadian case of *Eve*,[32] because the matter was considered over a period of five years and the intervention of a number of *amici curiae* allowed the court to take note of a wide expression of views. The facts were relatively simple. Mrs E applied to the supreme provincial court for permission to consent to the sterilisation of Eve, her adult daughter, who was mentally retarded. It is central to the analysis of the case to appreciate that a major ground for the application was that, in the event of Eve becoming innocently pregnant, the burden of caring for the child would fall upon her ageing mother.

The judge at first instance laid down several fundamentals. He thought that a parent or a Mental Health Committee could give a valid consent for any strictly therapeutic operation on behalf of a retarded person, but distinguished this from a contraceptive, and specifically sterilising, procedure; he further considered that the court should intervene on behalf of Eve under its *parens patriae* jurisdiction and that it could authorise a surgical procedure which was necessary to her health even though sterilisation might be a side effect – and that this could, in certain circumstances, apply when such an authorisation was required in the public interest. On the other hand, he concluded that the right to inviolability of the person superseded any right to be protected from pregnancy; the protection of the higher right was an obligation of the law and the fact that such protection might result in inconvenience or even hardship to others was irrelevant. He then distinguished between a clinically therapeutic procedure and one which was purely contraceptive – and dismissed the application.

The Supreme Court of Prince Edward Island then allowed an appeal,[33] this being based on the unanimous opinion that:

the Court has, in proper circumstances, the authority and jurisdiction to authorize the sterilization of a mentally incompetent person for non-therapeutic reasons. The jurisdiction of the Court originates from its *parens patriae* powers towards individuals who are unable to look after themselves and gives the Court authority to make the individual a ward of the Court.

Again the therapeutic/non-therapeutic distinction was brought into play and the very strict limitation of the *parens patriae* jurisdiction was emphasised: 'it must,' said CAMPBELL J (at 317), 'be exercised solely to serve the general welfare of a mentally retarded person'. Nonetheless, the Appeal Court was clearly minded to interpret 'welfare' liberally. Thus CAMPBELL J, again, considered that:

Without the protection of a permanent sterilization, the protected environment Eve enjoyed will become a guarded environment and the loss to Eve in terms of her social options and her relative freedom would cause substantial injury of sufficient degree to meet the test [that there is a likelihood of substantial injury in the absence of sterilization].

In effect, by the time the case came to the Supreme Court of Canada, virtually every view within the ethical spectrum of non-consensual sterilisation had been both expressed and supported.

The opinion of the Supreme Court, delivered by LA FOREST J, was particularly comprehensive and it is proposed to limit discussion here, in the main, to those aspects which are relevant to the later British cases. The problem of the scope of the *parens patriae* jurisdiction was, however, addressed in detail; numerous cases were cited which indicated that the extent of the jurisdiction was undefined and undefinable and, in particular, that the absence of precedent was no bar to the court assuming such powers in, say, a matter of medical treatment.[34]

The Supreme Court was thus in no doubt that the court had jurisdiction to authorise a surgical operation that was necessary to the health of a person who could not give personal consent, the term 'health' being defined as including mental as well as physical well-being. The fundamental issue was that discretion to exercise that jurisdiction was limited by the principle of benefit for the person concerned, not for others. Even then, the analysis of 'benefit' must take into account the seriousness and the permanence of the procedure. In Eve's case, there was nothing to indicate that failure to perform the operation would have any detrimental effect on her health; any benefit to her was in the form of protection against possible mental or physical trauma in the future – and the scientific bases for regarding menstruation, childbirth and the like as being more stressful to the mentally handicapped than to the mentally normal were regarded as being demonstrably weak. 'How are we to weigh the best interests of a person in this troublesome area,' asked LA FOREST J, 'keeping in mind that an error is irreversible? Unlike other cases involving the use of the *parens patriae* jurisdiction, an error cannot be corrected by the subsequent exercise of judicial discretion.' *In fine*, the procedure should never be authorised for non-therapeutic purposes under the *parens patriae* jurisdiction: 'If sterilization of the mentally incompetent is to be adopted as desirable for general social purposes, the legislature is the appropriate body to do so.' In so saying, LA FOREST J was in clear accord with the American Appeal Court in *Eberhardy*,[35] where HEFFERNAN J, speaking for the court, considered that 'a properly thought out public policy on sterilization ... is a problem that ought to be addressed by the legislature on the basis of factfinding and the opinions of experts' (at 895).

Turning to the contention that the court should follow a 'substituted judgment' test rather than one of 'best interests', the judge succinctly expressed a view which is widely supported.[36] Choice, it was pointed out, presupposes that the person has the mental competence to make a choice. What an incompetent would do if he or she could choose is simply a matter of speculation and it is obviously a fiction to suggest that a decision made by a court, on whatever basis, is that of the mentally incompetent person. LA FOREST J's summary deserves quotation in full:

> The court undoubtedly has the right and duty to protect those who are unable to take care of themselves and, in doing so, it has a wide discretion to do what it considers to be in their best interests. But this function should not, in my view, be transformed so as to create a duty obliging the court, at the behest of a third party, to make a choice between two alleged constitutional rights – the right to procreate or not to procreate – simply because the individual is unable to make that choice. All the more so since, in the case of non-therapeutic sterilization as we saw, the choice is one the courts cannot safely exercise.

The appeal was, of course, allowed and the wording of the opinion was so strong that it seems likely that it will represent the law in Canada for the foreseeable future. The only time at which it is likely that a court there will be induced to authorise non-consensual sterilisation of a mentally incompetent is when it can be shown that the procedure is therapeutic and, in that context, the Supreme Court was rather more reticent. It was summarised that, in order to avoid an allegation of battery, the onus of proving the need for the procedure lies on those who seek to have it performed; that burden, although a civil one, must be commensurate with the seriousness of the measure proposed. In reaching the rather bland conclusion that a court must proceed with extreme caution in such circumstances, LA FOREST J had explained that, while sterilisation may be an inevitable accompaniment of treatment for a serious illness, this does not allow for subterfuge or for the weighing of marginal justifications against what is a grave intrusion on the physical and mental integrity of the person. In so saying, he was clearly influenced by what was, effectively, the only apposite Canadian precedent of *Re K and Public Trustee*.[37]

In that case, the sterilisation by hysterectomy of a severely retarded 10-year-old child was ordered, this being mainly on the grounds that the child was said to have a phobic aversion to blood which, it was feared, would affect her when her menses began. A comparison of *Eve* and *K* provides a fascinating insight as to the difficulties involved in the therapeutic/non-therapeutic discussion. On the one hand, we have LA FOREST J regarding the decision in *K* as being, at best, dangerously close to the limits of the permissible. On the other, ANDERSON JA believed that *K* was a case which should never have been before the courts:

> Once it was determined that infant K would not suffer a loss of a right to reproduce in any realistic sense, the issue was no different from that in other cases where parents ... have authorized surgical operations in the best interests of the child. ... If the course followed here becomes normal practice, the fate of children like infant K may well be prejudiced. (At 278)

The court in *K*, through ANDERSON JA, considered that the fact of sterilisation was irrelevant and agreed with the Attorney General, who submitted that hysterectomy was not proposed to sterilise the child for the benefit of society but, rather, to spare her a little further anguish. In essence, while the *Eve* court considered the matter from the objective stance of the mentally handicapped in general, ANDERSON JA and his colleagues thought the correct test to be purely subjective: were the anticipated benefits of the operation such that they exceeded the harm or the risk of harm to infant K? It is clear that the problems of menstruation stand mid-way between the concepts of sterilisation for the benefit of the carers and sterilisation which is an inevitable result of surgical treatment of disease and can, accordingly, be used in argument by either protagonist in the therapeutic/non-therapeutic ethical debate.[38]

The Australian experience　Rather more cases have been reviewed in the Australian courts and these, taken in sequence, bring the problems of jurisdiction and management of the mentally handicapped adolescent or woman into sharp focus. The cases exemplify the important contribution made by Australia to all aspects of medical jurisprudence.

The issue most carefully addressed in that jurisdiction has been the need for the involvement of the courts in such matters; specifically, is the sterilisation of a mentally handicapped minor a matter competent to be decided within the family? Again the basic problem has been seen in terms of a therapeutic/non-therapeutic distinction and this, in large measure, depends on judicial attitudes to the medical profession. Thus, in *Re a Teenager*,[39] COOK J said: 'It is not conceivable to this Court that medical advisers would prostitute their Hippocratic Oath to perform unnecessary or ill-advised and untimely operations, particularly of a major kind' and held that it was within parental power to authorise the operation. The *Teenager* was regarded as a 'menstrual' case (see below) rather than a true sterilisation but, even so, it is unsurprising that, in *Re Jane*,[40] a case heard only shortly after the *Teenager*, NICHOLSON CJ was unable to accept this somewhat optimistic evaluation of the medical profession as a whole. Leaving aside the inevitable professional maverick, it is also possible, he said, 'that members of that profession may form sincere but misguided views about the appropriate steps to be taken'[41] and concluded that the approval of the court was essential when a medical procedure involved interference with a basic human right and had a non-therapeutic purpose as a major aim.[42]

There was, therefore, considerable confusion until the matter was considered for the first time by the High Court of Australia.[43] This case, concerning a 14-year-old girl suffering from epilepsy and severe intellectual disabilty, resulted in perhaps the deepest judicial analysis of the problem that is available. All seven judges addressed the distinction between therapeutic and non-therapeutic sterilisation and the majority concluded that it had to be made despite the uncertainty of definition and the haziness of any dividing line. Space does not admit of a full discussion of this case.[44] Suffice it, for the present, to say that the court concluded that recourse to the courts was unnecessary if the procedure was clearly therapeutic. The Australian approach, however, differed from that of the Canadians, in that the Australian judges did not accept that non-therapeutic non-consensual sterilisation should never be authorised. Faced with such a situation, the Australian court would apply a 'best interests' test: that is, sterilisation would be approved if it was 'necessary to enable [the girl] to lead a life in keeping with her needs and capacities'. Different definitions of 'therapeutic' were given in the several opinions, but it is clear that, as emphasised by Cica, 'there is always a danger that a procedure will be described as therapeutic, or in the patient's best medical interests, when it is really being performed for the non-therapeutic purpose of furthering what some perceive to be her best social interests'. An indication of the difficulties involved is provided by the fact that the court in *J.W.B.* were happy to see themselves as dealing with a non-therapeutic situation; when the case was remitted to the Family Court, however, NICHOLSON CJ considered that it probably fell into 'the category where the court's consent is unnecessary since, on the facts as I have found them, the procedure was required for medical and therapeutic reasons'.[45]

There has been a further case which, to an extent, demonstrated the application of the 'best interests' rule in harshly real terms. In this, three doctors favoured the sterilisation of a 17-year-old victim of birth trauma who could never be expected to care for a child. WARNICK J, however, regarded the application as being one brought on social grounds and found that such risk of pregnancy as there was did not justify interference with her bodily privacy. In refusing to authorise hysterectomy, he said: 'To make a decision in favour of sterilisation would be virtually equivalent to establishing that all females, with profound disabilities resembling those inflicting Sarah, should be sterilised.'[46] Thus the Australian position lies somewhere between the rigid 'rights' stance of the Canadian Supreme Court and, as we will see, the determined 'welfare'-oriented attitude of the British courts.

The English decisions   The precedential British case was very similar to *Eve*, both in fact and in disposal, and the evidence suggests that it was very persuasive to the Supreme Court of Canada. In *Re D (a minor)*,[47] the authority of the court was sought for sterilisation of an 11-year-old girl suffering from Sotos' syndrome – as a result of which she had aggressive behavioural problems and an IQ of about 80; this did not necessarily make it impossible for her to cope reasonably well in everyday life, or even to marry and raise a child. D's doctor, however, accepted that there was a risk that she might give birth to an abnormal baby, that her epilepsy might cause her to harm the baby and that sterilisation was the only satisfactory method of birth control. He also thought that she would be unable to manage a family and would only be able to survive in a sheltered environment. His intention to arrange for sterilisation was resisted and wardship was granted; the matter came before HEILBRON J.

Her opinion was strongly influenced by the expert medical evidence to the effect that the child's condition was not static and might be improved. She was, in consequence, concerned as to the irreversibility of sterilisation and as to the significance of carrying it out on so young a person who was, in any case, unlikely to become pregnant:

A review of the whole evidence leads me to the conclusion that in the case of a child of 11 years of age, where the evidence shows that her mental and physical condition and attainments have already improved, and where her future prospects are as yet unpredictable, where the evidence also shows that she is unable as yet to understand and appreciate the implications of the operation and could not give valid or informed consent, that the likelihood is that in later years she will be able to make her own choice where, I believe, the frustration and resentment of realising (as she would one day) what happened could be devastating, an operation of this nature is, in my view, contra-indicated (at 196).

The judge also referred firmly to 'the basic human right of a woman to reproduce' and considered that it would be a violation of that right if sterilisation were performed for non-therapeutic reasons in the absence of her consent. Since the child was a ward of court, it was 'of course, beyond dispute that the welfare of the child is the paramount consideration and the court must act in her best interests'. Accordingly, leave to perform the operation was refused.

It has been pointed out that *Re D* was essentially concerned with the instant case and HEILBRON J has been criticised for her failure to address the broad principles.[48] At the same time, it must not be forgotten that, at least in this writer's opinion, *Re D* was a unique case, in that it is the only example in the wide range of reported judicial appraisals in which the medical evidence pointed to a hopeful prognosis; an appreciation of this is essential to the understanding of the later English cases. Nevertheless, the sentiments expressed had not been challenged and the case represented the English authority – the matter not having been publicised in Scotland – until the case of *In re B (a minor) (sterilisation)*[49] came to the courts and, ultimately, to the House of Lords.

Re B concerned the treatment of a 17-year-old girl who was in the care of the local authority. B was said to have a moderate degree of mental handicap which did not require protection under the Mental Health Act, but she could not be let out because she did not understand either the dangers of traffic or the use of money; she might, it was thought, attain the mental age of a child of five or six years in some skills. Nevertheless, she was showing signs of sexual awareness and of a sexual drive, which introduced a risk of pregnancy. These problems were to be balanced against the emerging policy of returning mentally handicapped persons to the community so far as is possible; as a result, medical opinion was that she should be placed on long-term contraception or be sterilised. The Court of Appeal,[50] although clearly influenced by the opinion in *Re D*, took the view that B would never appreciate the 'right to reproduce' and that she would be unable to associate sexual activity with the birth of a baby; the only appropriate result of a pregnancy would be a legal termination. The court, per DILLON LJ, concluded that it had jurisdiction to authorise sterilisation of a ward and did so on the understanding that it was a jurisdiction which should be exercised only in the last resort.

In confirming this order, the House of Lords, per LORD HAILSHAM LC, emphasised that the decision was based purely on the well-being and interests of the ward; no element of public policy was involved and, in particular, there was no question of a eugenic motive. LORD HAILSHAM noted that recognition of a pregnancy might be delayed until it was too late to terminate; delivery would then be by Caesarean section, carrying with it the possibility that she might tear open her operation wound. Sterilisation was a preferable alternative to incarceration and constant contraceptive medication was impracticable; his Lordship concurred with the Court of Appeal that occlusion of the Fallopian tubes was the only viable option.

Both LORD HAILSHAM and LORD OLIVER rejected the reasoning in *Eve* which had led to the conclusion that sterilisation for a non-therapeutic purpose should never be authorised, the former contending that such a holding was in stark contrast to the welfare principle. LORD OLIVER, in addition, objected to the suggestion that to classify a sterilisation as 'non-therapeutic' would be to exclude the taking of measures intended for protection from future harm; the implication contradicted the basis of the case, which was to further the best interests of the girl and to decide how best she could be given the protection which would enable her to live the fullest life possible within the limits of her intellectual capacity.[51]

This approach, which attracted severe criticism at the time, seems reasonable, at least to a medical person. Preventive medicine is a legitimate aspect of therapy, and the fact that concepts of preventive medicine, public health and social medicine may overlap or intermingle may not be, as Lord Hailsham said, irrelevant and, at least, deserve serious consideration. Granted this wide view of treatment, the various decisions on both sides of the Atlantic begin to fall into place, the definitive test being the *medical* interests of the person concerned. Thus *Eve* can be distinguished from *Re B* on the grounds that the court could find no *medical* indications in the former. The American decisions can be distilled into the proposition that sterilisation can be authorised without consent if it is 'medically ... clearly necessary ... to preserve the life or physical or mental health of the incompetent minor';[52] since this would include 'the possibility of pregnancy threatening the physical or mental health of the person', it is clearly in line with *Re B* and with the less publicised case of *T* v. *T*.[53]

T was a 19-year-old, severely mentally handicapped girl who was found to be pregnant; court wardship being impossible after the age of 18, her mother sought a declaration under the terms of the Rules of the Supreme Court (Order 15, rule 16) that a termination of pregnancy accompanied by sterilisation would not be illegal in the absence of valid consent from the person. The judge made the declaration on the grounds that a medical adviser had to consider what decision would be in the best interests of the person's health; the problem was to decide what good medical practice demanded, and the court was convinced that it was in the girl's interests that the procedures be performed.

This somewhat pragmatic decision was later endorsed in the House of Lords in *Re F*,[54] in which the House of Lords' primary concerns were jurisdictional. The, perhaps, unfortunate speed with which the House of Lords had to decide *Re B* was dictated by the subject's approaching 18th birthday; F, however, was an adult who, in contradistinction to T, was not pregnant. The problem facing the court in *Re F* was, therefore, not so much whether or not the sterilisation was indicated as by what mechanism it could be authorised. Their Lordships concluded that the *parens patriae* jurisdiction of the English courts had lapsed since the passage of the Mental Health Act, 1959 and the consequent withdrawal of the Sign Manual under which the sovereign's powers were delegated to the courts;[55] no-one, then, not even the court, could consent to treatment on behalf of an incompetent adult unless that treatment was directed to treatment of the underlying mental condition. In the event, the court again had recourse to the Rules of the Supreme Court and ruled by way of a declaration that sterilisation would not be an unlawful act by reason only of the patient's lack of capacity to consent to the operation. It was, however, clear that there was a gap in the law which called for urgent legislative attention.[56]

The House in *Re F*, however, made some important practical observations. In particular, per LORD BRANDON, it concluded that, at common law, a doctor could lawfully operate on, or give other treatment to, adult patients incapable of consenting, but that the legality depended upon that treatment being in the best interests of the incompetent, best interests being tested in *Bolam* terms (see p. 90);[57] it might, then, be the *duty* of the doctor to provide treatment. Thus, while involvement of the court in a question of sterilisation of a mentally disabled woman was not strictly necessary as a matter of law, it was, nevertheless, highly desirable as a matter of good practice.[58] The House set out six reasons for particularly distinguishing a sterilisation operation from other surgery. These included the deprivation of the right to bear children which was 'widely, and rightly, regarded as one of the fundamental rights of a woman' and the risk of the matter being decided, or being thought to have been decided, wrongly at the clinical level. In effect, the court was providing a 'third opinion' (although the present author cannot easily see why a judge's *clinical* opinion should be any more or less valuable than, say, a doctor's *judicial* opinion); the more important aspect is highlighted by the words '*thought* to have been decided': that is, that a major function is to reassure the public that their rights are being protected. There was, in fact, only one dissenting opinion, LORD GRIFFITHS taking the view that sterilising a woman should be brought into the category of inflicted harms which cannot be legalised by consent (see Chapter 12); he would have preferred to make new law and to have held that non-voluntary sterilisation was unlawful if performed without the consent of the High Court.

Lord Griffiths' approach would, at least, leave no room for doubt; one unsatisfactory outcome of *Re F* is that it still leaves the medical profession in something of a quandary as to whether or not a given case should be referred to the courts. The probability is that any case concerning a minor should be referred;[59] the conditions of the Children Act 1989, s.8(1) suggest that this may be done by seeking a specific order or by appeal to the inherent jurisdiction of the court, the latter being the preferred route.[60] There is, however, no doubt that, despite the protestations of the House of Lords in *Re B*, a therapeutic/non-therapeutic distinction *is* being made in the British courts. At one extreme, the need for sterilisation may be obvious and scarcely open to criticism, as in a case of severe menstrual dysfunction where hysterectomy would be the treatment of choice in any case.[61] In one such instance, SIR STEPHEN BROWN P declined to grant a declaration of lawfulness on the grounds that it was unnecessary and that to do so would cause confusion for the doctors.[62] He did, however, lay down useful guidelines for the benefit of the profession. These were that no application to the courts would be necessary if two doctors agreed that the operation was (a) necessary for therapeutic purposes, (b) in the patient's best interests, and that (c) no less intrusive treatment was practicable.

Such cases are clear-cut, but the profession is on less firm ground when it turns to such 'medical reasons' as 'a phobic aversion to blood', an indication which has been advanced in a number of the reported cases.[63] No-one would deny that physical and psychiatric disease should be regarded as being equivalently significant, but there is a world of difference between a true psychosis and a simple distaste. The danger is that here, as elsewhere, a disease can be generated by giving it a name.[64] This is to be resisted particularly in the context of sterilisation as the prophylaxis of haemophobia – hysterectomy – involves a far more serious operation than does the prophylaxis of pregnancy – tubal ligation.

Other English cases

In fact, there is some evidence that the English courts, at least, are prepared to extend the concept of therapeutic non-consensual sterilisation to an extent which tends to confirm the existence of a jurisprudential gap between *Eve* and *Re B*. In *Re M*, for example, it is difficult to exclude an element of eugenics from a decision to sterilise a girl suffering from the genetically controlled fragile X syndrome; in *Re P*, the social interests of the minor were certainly more important to the decision than were her medical interests.[65] The implications of a more recent case, *Re W*,[66] deserve particular attention.

Re W concerned a 20-year-old woman with severe epilepsy and a mental age of seven. Medical evidence was to the effect that pregnancy would make the epilepsy worse, but the social evidence was that the risk of pregnancy was very small, a point which was stressed by the Official Solicitor who, nevertheless, did not actually oppose the application for authority to sterilise. In the course of granting the application, HOLLIS J said: 'If worry affected Mrs W [the mother], then it would be likely to affect the care of W. This is not a factor that has been dwelt upon by counsel before me but it is nevertheless a factor that I take into account' (at 383). While the rest of the learned judge's reasons were clearly to the point, it is difficult to see this as other than admitting the interests of others through the back door of the patient's 'best interests'; it must represent a suspect encroachment.

In point of fact, the present writer does not share to the hilt the general antagonism to medicalisation of non-consensual sterilisation decisions. It is difficult to apply broad-brush philosophical concepts to medicine where every case has its own particular features; it follows that every case must be judged on its own facts, and many of the apparently anomalous decisions in the courts can probably be explained on the relative severity of the subjects' mental handicap. Nonetheless, it remains desirable that doctors should not extrapolate from the treatment of the patient to the treatment of society without some supervision from those whose duty it is to protect society – but it is still reasonable to question whether the adversarial arena is the correct place to exercise that restraint.

The right to procreate

It is clear that the foregoing discussion centres on a conflict between, on the one hand, the essentially paternalistic concept of the patient's best interests and, on the other, the patient's rights as an autonomous individual. It would be inadequate to close without addressing the issue of the so-called 'right to procreate'.

The concept in law of a 'right to procreate' seems to have originated in the judgment in *Skinner* v. *Oklahoma*. Since then, the phrase has often been repeated in the United States – a fundamental right to bear or beget offspring.[67] It has been strongly upheld in the Canadian case of *Eve*[68] and, in Britain, HEILBRON J's now famous allusion to the 'basic human right of a woman to reproduce'[69] has been repeated with approval both in the Court of Appeal and in the House of Lords.[70] Lord Hailsham, in the latter, was not, however, prepared to see such a basic right as being absolute, and it remains to be considered whether this was no more than a matter of special pleading in a particular case.

It is, in fact, quite possible to adduce general reasons for doubting the existence of a 'right to procreate', the most fundamental being that there can be no *right* to something which necessarily involves a second party who has an equal right to withhold co-operation.[71] A naturally infertile woman has no such right which, taken to its logical conclusion, carries a 'right' of access to modern reproductive techniques, including *in vitro* fertilisation and womb leasing; the proposition then becomes untenable. As the deontological moralist Paul Ramsey said many years ago, 'Not everyone, simply by being, has a right to procreate',[72] or, from a more modern philosopher, 'obviously, there is no general right to reproduce'.[73] What, then, is the true 'right'? The answer to this question can be approached in two ways. Firstly, the right could be modified to being one to choose to procreate or not, which is no more than a specific expression of the right of control over one's own body.[74] Alternatively, as suggested by McLean and Campbell,[75] it is better stated as a right to retain the capacity to procreate.

Given the first proposition, it is not difficult to justify a court's authorisation of non-voluntary sterilisation on the grounds of an individual's inability to make a choice. As LORD HAILSHAM said in *Re B*: 'The right [of a woman to reproduce] is only such when reproduction is the result of informed choice of which the ward in the present case is incapable'; and later, 'To talk of the "basic right" to reproduce of an individual who is not capable of knowing the causal connection between intercourse and childbirth [or who] is unable to form any maternal instincts or to care for a child, appears to me wholly to part company with reality'[76] and this reasoning applies whether a substituted judgment or a best interests test is being applied to the welfare of the ward. There seems no overriding reason why, once the need for a clinical assessment of each case is accepted, the principle cannot be generalised.

Sterilisation, however, is less easy to justify in the face of McLean and Campbell's claim. It depends upon the definition of procreation. It is impossible to believe that any of the learned judges who have referred to the 'right to procreate' intended this in an amphibian-like sense of the impersonal production of offspring. The state has a clear duty to protect its children, and parents cannot simply abandon their responsibilities;[77] no state could be expected to tolerate a 'right' of its subjects to insist on institutional care for their progeny – to do so would, *inter alia*, strike at the whole concept of the family as the basic societal unit. Procreation must, therefore, involve bringing up the child during its vulnerable state of development and, while it is in no sense denied that many who are mentally handicapped can appreciate parentage and do, in fact, make successful family relationships, it would be flying in the face of experience to deny that there are some who cannot. Indeed, this concept of procreation would be equally violated in the vast majority of cases such as those under consideration when the neonate had to be removed from its mother.

Some support for this definition of procreation is to be derived from the European Convention for the Protection of Human Rights, art. 12, which speaks only in terms of a right to marry and found a family; there is no mention of a right to procreation *per se* and the inclusion of the word 'marry' might, indeed, be taken as an explicit expression of concern for the welfare of the children of a sexual union.

There thus seems no reason to reject the leading decision in *Re B* as being one which contravenes a basic moral right. Rather, particular attention should be paid to that part of the opinion of the court which emphasises the safeguards to be applied when considering the biological needs of the mentally handicapped. Thus, in the Court of Appeal in *Re B*, DILLON LJ emphasised that the power to authorise a non-consensual sterilisation was one which should be exercised only in the last resort, while, in the House of Lords, LORD TEMPLEMAN, albeit obiter, considered that a court exercising the wardship jurisdiction was the only authority empowered to authorise such a drastic step as sterilisation of a mentally handicapped minor. There is no need to fear that the United Kingdom will drift back towards an era of legal eugenics,[78] yet there are no grounds for complacency. We already have the House of Lords in *Re F* backing away from *Re B* in intimating that not all cases that are not clearly therapeutic need to be brought to the courts; there is a suggestion from *Re W* that the Official Solicitor is looking at cases in a more relaxed fashion; the impression remains, as in *L, Petitioner*, that the courts are requiring less stringent reasons for authorising comparatively serious operations; and some of the reasoning in, say, *Re M* and *Re W* provokes a slight raising of the eyebrows.

And yet, again, looked at from the purely practical viewpoint, can we firmly believe that any of the British decisions have been *wrong*? As Norrie has pointed out,[79] we must be careful to define what rights are at risk and, having done so, we must decide if they are, in fact, infringed in the circumstances envisaged. Are there rights that are superior to the rather tenuous right of retaining an unuseable capacity to procreate – such as the right to free association – which are actually enhanced by sterilisation of the mentally handicapped? We might do well to remember 'the importance of not erecting such legal barriers against the provision of medical treatment for incompetents that they are deprived of treatment which competent persons would expect to receive in similar circumstances'.[80]

Consensual non-therapeutic sterilisation

Attitudes evolve in all aspects of sexual life. Times have changed since Lord Denning described sterilisation in the male as 'degrading to the man himself and injurious to his wife and to any woman whom he may marry'.[81] Less than 20 years later, contraceptive sterilisation was made available under the National Health Service,[82] and this approach to family planning now has worldwide acceptance.[83] The major outstanding medico-legal problem, albeit one that is now largely resolved, concerns the need for spousal consent to the procedure.

On general principles, it is reasonable to hold that an adult person has jurisdiction over his or her body and that this is true no matter what the specific decision; the only limiting factor is based on the public interest which, clearly, is now unaffected by individual options for sterilisation – indeed, population control may be very much *in* the public interest. The main argument against the practice is that found in the orthodox Roman Catholic teaching that non-therapeutic sterilisation is a permanent mutilation which deprives the subject of a natural function and, as such, is morally unacceptable. This view, which has its secular counterpart in the concept of maim, is one which can be sincerely held, particularly in the light of the importance attached by the Catholic Church to procreation as a moral absolute. Given the current sexual mores of the Western world, however, the majority in a pluralistic society would base any argument against sterilisation as a method of contraception only on its permanence.[84] Even so, other decisions which alter the future irrevocably are commonly made by adults and, provided the operation results from free, unfettered and rational choice, there are relatively few who would deny the right of individuals to autonomy in their choice; it is also difficult to raise any substantial ethical argument against medical effectuation of that choice; in the extreme case, the individual doctor is under no obligation to apply his expertise to a non-therapeutic measure of which he or she disapproves.

It would not necessarily be the same in the case of a married person. The mere use of the phrase 'family planning' implies that any planning decision has stopped being a matter for the individual and is, rather, one for a procreative couple; in short, a good case can be made out for insistence on spousal consent to sterilisation within the ambience of the family. Any basis for such a suggestion must be ethical; certainly, it has no legal justification: it has, for example, been said that no court would ever grant an injunction to stop sterilisation or vasectomy.[85] Any suggestion that a husband has a right to veto his wife's decision to forgo childbearing flies in the face of modern concepts of a woman's status and there are practical difficulties in the application of such a rule in these days of permanent partnerships and other extramarital family arrangements. Moreover, professional pressures would probably operate, in that the obligation of confidentiality to the individual would outweigh any supposed obligation to the family as a whole.

On the other hand, as in the case of a single person, no doctor is compelled to undertake treatment simply because he is medically qualified and it is doubtful whether, when a non-therapeutic operation is intended, he is even required to arrange an alternative source for the 'treatment' which he is unwilling to provide. The doctor is certainly not obliged to court deliberately an involvement in litigation and, although there is no case law *directly* to the point, there is no reason why *Bravery*,[86] which was an action for divorce on the grounds of cruelty, should not be re-enacted on the modern grounds that the respondent (or defender), in undergoing sterilisation in secret, had behaved in such a way that the petitioner (or pursuer) could not reasonably be expected to cohabit with him or her.[87] As LORD EVERSHED MR said in that case: 'It would not be difficult ... to construct in imagination a case of grave cruelty on a wife founded on the progressive hurt to her health caused by an operation for sterilization undergone by her husband in disregard of, or contrary to, the wife's wishes or natural instincts' (at 62).

In summary, therefore, there is no legal duty to obtain spousal consent to sterilisation, but there are good reasons, both ethical and pragmatic, why a doctor might be reluctant to perform the operation in such circumstances. The General Medical Council is silent on the specific point; the British Medical Association has, however, said that, while spousal consent is clearly unnecessary, it is good medical practice to encourage patients to discuss such procedures with their partners.[88]

Non-therapeutic sterilisation is a relatively simple operation in both the male and the female and involves obliteration of the lumina of the tubes through which the sex cells pass to the exterior in the man (vasectomy) or to the uterus in the female (tubal ligation or excision). It is thus arguable that the main objection to sterilisation – that is, its permanence – could be obviated by using methods which were readily reversible. This may be attainable in the female. In *Re M*,[89] it was said that the operation was 50–75 per cent reversible – so much so that it was regarded as contraception rather than sterilisation – and in *Re P*,[90] the somewhat surprising expert evidence was given that 'The situation to-day is that the operation is not irreversible although it is still the current ethical practice to tell patients that it is an irreversible operation' (at 189).

The same cannot be said of the operation in the male.[91] Nevertheless, the immediate object of the operation is to insure against parentage and the more 'reversible' is the technique used, the less certain is that insurance. Indeed, for many years now, the major medico-legal interest in sterilisation has centred on failure of the operation, and it is to that aspect that we will shortly turn. Before doing so, however, it is necessary to outline briefly the concept of consent to treatment and its relationship to medical negligence.

The doctrine of 'informed consent'

Touching a person without his or her consent is an assault and may be actionable in either the civil or criminal jurisdictions. Leaving aside the possibility that, as a matter of public policy, some assaults will always be illegal – 'when the infliction of bodily harm is a probable consequence, and when such an act is proved, consent is immaterial'[92] – liability is elided by consent. But true consent can only be given on the basis of understanding and that, in turn, derives from information – from which it follows that consent given without being adequately informed is flawed consent. There are, then, two possible views of the nature of the flaw. The first is that flawed consent is no consent, from which it would follow that any treatment given on the basis of such consent is an assault and whether or not harm results is of *post hoc* consequence only. To make such an accusation because counselling was inadequate is, however, an unattractive jurisprudential proposition in the absence of misrepresentation or fraud[93] and, as a consequence, patients who feel they have suffered because they have not been properly advised will now argue: 'But for the lack of information as to the risks involved, I would not have had the treatment and I would not be suffering the effects of a recognised risk of that treatment.' The action thus becomes one of negligence: the patient has suffered harm because the doctor has failed in his duty of care which, for present purposes, can be defined as: 'A duty to disclose in a reasonable manner all significant medical information that the physician possesses ... that is material to an intelligent decision by the patient whether to undergo the proposed treatment.'[94] This is an American statement but, despite the volume of literature which suggests the opposite, there is much common ground between British and American thinking in this area. Current English law is probably best described by LORD TEMPLEMAN: 'The patient is free to decide whether or not to submit to treatment recommended by the doctor and therefore the doctor impliedly contracts to provide information which is adequate to enable the patient to reach a balanced judgment.'[95] Any differences which exist centre on the words 'reasonable manner' and 'adequate' and how they are to be determined: is the decision to be that of the doctor or the patient and, if it is to be the latter, is the view to be based on the reasonable patient (the objective standard) or on the particular patient (the subjective standard)? The position in the United States is, inevitably, complex and does not add a great deal to the understanding of medical negligence law in the United Kingdom, which is based on the *Bolam* principle.[96]

In précis, *Bolam* states that a doctor is not negligent if he acts in accordance with a practice accepted at the time as proper by a responsible body of medical opinion. The problem of whether this blatantly professional, or doctor-oriented, standard applies to warning and advice has been tested and approved in the lower courts but its imprimatur derives from *Sidaway*.[97] The bare bones of this seminal case were that Mrs Sidaway underwent an operation to her neck which was associated with a risk of damage to the spinal cord of something less than 1 per cent; the risk materialised and the plaintiff, who was not told of the risk, brought a classic consent-based action for negligence: that she would not have consented to the procedure had she known of the risk and that, accordingly, her surgeon, in failing to inform her, had failed in the duty of care he owed her. In the event, Mrs Sidaway lost her case at first instance, in the Court of Appeal and in the House of Lords. The *Bolam* principle was applied to counselling and, once it was established that a body of responsible practitioners would not have informed her of the risk, there was no negligence.

Sporadic attempts to undermine the all-pervading influence of *Bolam* have originated in the lower courts and it is, perhaps, ironic that the first cracks in its defences are to be seen in *Sidaway* which, one imagines, was expected to consolidate the law. Although the House of Lords accepted *Bolam* as the benchmark, only one Law Lord (LORD DIPLOCK) can be seen as applying the unadulterated principle to the provision of information. We have noted LORD TEMPLEMAN above, in addition, LORD BRIDGE was of the opinion that 'the judge might in certain circumstances come to the conclusion that disclosure of a particular risk was so obviously necessary to an informed choice on the part of the patient that no reasonably prudent medical man would fail to make it' (at 900). But perhaps the most significant warning shot was fired by LORD SCARMAN, who said, in what was, effectively though not in practice, a dissenting opinion:

> It would be a strange conclusion if the courts should be led to conclude that our law, which undoubtedly recognises a right in the patient to decide whether he will accept or reject the treatment proposed, should permit the doctors to determine whether and in what circumstances a duty arises requiring the doctor to warn his patient of the risks inherent in the treatment which he proposes (at 882).

This approach was, as already noted, a minority opinion, but *Sidaway* certainly established, firstly, that there is a duty to inform the patient of material risks; secondly, that a doctor is under a duty to answer specific questions; and, thirdly, that the court may conclude that the need for information is so obvious that, irrespective of conflicting medical opinion, the doctor who fails to provide it is negligent.

The significance of this last conclusion is not only that it nibbles at *Bolam* but that it is edging towards the compromise position reached in the landmark Canadian case of *Reibl v. Hughes*,[98] where it was made clear that, whether or not an opinion was held by a body of doctors, it was ultimately a matter for the court to decide whether that opinion was *rightly* held.[99] The main attack on *Bolam* as a test for the measure of disclosure has, indeed, come from the Commonwealth and it has now been wholly rejected by the Australian High Court.[100] By contrast, attempts in the United Kingdom to avoid the rule have foundered when confronted by the superior courts,[101] although there have been some recent spirited incursions which may yet go to appeal.[102]

This, then, represents the current status of consent-based negligence in England; a similar approach has been adopted in Scotland.[103] It is important to note that an obligation to inform a patient of the inherent risks of a procedure exists on both sides of the Atlantic; the difference lies in the test applied to distinguish acceptable from negligent practice. Thus the strong tendency in the United States is to adopt the objective patient test: what would a reasonable patient have expected to be told in the circumstances?[104] There is pressure to go further and consider the subjective patient – what would that *particular* patient have expected or needed – a test which is clearly at the mercy of hindsight.[105] In the United Kingdom, the professional standard set by *Bolam* effectively asks the question, what would the reasonable doctor have disclosed? Thus there is no denial of the need for doctor/patient communication when, for example, DUNN LJ says: 'The concept of informed consent forms no part of English law',[106] or when LORD DONALDSON MR says: 'English law does not accept the transatlantic concept of informed consent'.[107] All that the Lords of Appeal are saying is that the adequacy of information disclosure is judged differently.

The outstanding question then becomes, what degree of risk is to be regarded as so substantial or material as to require disclosure? This must be a matter of conjecture, especially because materiality is a question not only of incidence but, also, of severity. Inevitably, the answers will appear capricious but may be dictated by special circumstances. For example, a well recognised risk of blindness was considered insufficient to dictate disclosure in the South Australian case of *Battersby*, but the patient was severely depressed and the case illustrates the use, albeit justified only with difficulty, of the 'therapeutic privilege' (see below); in *Rogers*, a New South Wales case, it was found, by contrast, that failure to disclose a risk of blindness of 1: 14 000 was negligent – here, the patient exhibited particular anxiety as to the possibility.[108] It is everywhere agreed that the 10 per cent risk of a stroke in the case of *Reibl* warranted disclosure, but the risk of severe complications of about 1 per cent in *Sidaway* apparently did not; but such comparisons are meaningless and do not take into account such factors as the potential reversibility of the outcome. It has to be noted, however, that all these considerations, in the United Kingdom at least, are subject to 'therapeutic privilege': the doctor is entitled to withhold information if he feels it would be detrimental to patient care – a decision which would be subject to an unadulterated *Bolam* test, and probably rightly so.

Failed sterilisation or wrongful pregnancy

As the records of the various medical defence societies show, actions in negligence for wrongful pregnancy following an operation for sterilisation in either the male or female partner are common – and certainly only a minority of cases are officially reported. At the same time, very few suits are based on the *performance* of the operation which, certainly in the case of vasectomy, is a relatively simple affair. Rather, the difficulty in this area is that of communication and, in particular, of failure to explain that no operation can be regarded as 100 per cent effective. This is due to the fact that natural recanalisation of ligated or resected ducts occurs in a very small proportion of cases.[109] The plaintiff is, then, effectively pleading: 'Had you informed me of this risk, I would have continued with contraceptive methods even after the operation. You did not inform me and, as a result, I have sustained damage in the form of unwanted pregnancy.' The action is, therefore, of classic 'consent-based' type, as discussed above.

The problem is often compounded by the fact that, since the woman does not *expect* to become pregnant, diagnosis may be so delayed that therapeutic termination becomes an unacceptable option. Once again, this is an area which has been greatly clarified since the first edition of this book. Nevertheless, the three complementary English cases – *Thake* v. *Maurice*,[110] *Eyre* v. *Measday*,[111] and *Gold* v. *Haringey Health Authority*[112] – still merit recapitulation.

The case of Mr Thake exemplifies many of the problems and is distinct, in that the action, which was brought in both breach of contract and in negligence, turned on the nature of contractual negligence. The plaintiff had undergone a successful vasectomy; nevertheless, the operation reversed itself and Mrs Thake conceived her sixth child. The surgeon had, however, given no warning that there was a small risk of natural reversal and, in the absence of such a warning, PETER PAIN J held that a contract to make the plaintiff irreversibly sterile had been made and had been breached: even if there had been no guarantee in the contract, there had been a collateral warranty that the man would become permanently sterile and the plaintiffs had relied on that contract (at 521). The judge was of the opinion that the doctrine of 'informed consent' did not bear on the case because the risk involved was one of nature reversing an operation which had, itself, been entirely satisfactory.

The majority of the Court of Appeal, however, took a different view. A contract to perform a vasectomy operation was subject to the duty to carry it out with reasonable skill and care. It was the common experience of mankind that the results of medical treatment were, to some extent, unpredictable and any treatment might be affected by the special characteristics of the particular patient: 'A reasonable person would have left the consulting room thinking that Mr Thake would be sterilised by the vasectomy operation [but] such a person would not have left thinking the defendant to have given a *guarantee* that Mr Thake would be absolutely sterile' (per NEILL LJ at 510). On the other hand, the unanimous view was that, in failing to give a warning of the risk of recanalisation, the surgeon was negligent as regards the duty of care owed to a patient – it must have been in his reasonable contemplation that there was a risk that the wife of a sterilised man would not appreciate that she was pregnant until it was too late for her to have an abortion. The Court of Appeal, therefore, took a diametrically opposed view to the trial judge, a matter which was of practical significance in the next case, concerning Mrs Eyre.

Mrs Eyre was an unfortunate victim of the legal system insofar as her case came to appeal between the trial and appeal stages of *Thake*. The circumstances of her case were broadly comparable in that, having been 'sterilised' through a laparoscopy incision, she subsequently became pregnant; she, similarly, sued her surgeon both in contract and in negligence. The case provides a classic example of semantic misinterpretation, in this instance of the word 'irreversible'. Thus the trial judge, FRENCH J, in finding for the defendant said:

> The highest that the plaintiff can put her case is that the use of the word 'irreversible' together with the absence of any mention of the minute risk of the procedure being unsuccessful amount to such a contractual undertaking [of 100 per cent success in preventing such pregnancy] or collateral warranty. ... I am sure the defendant did not knowingly give ... such a guarantee ... No informed and officious bystander who heard the defendant telling the plaintiff ... that the procedure was intended to be irreversible and must be regarded as irreversible could have supposed that he was thereby guaranteeing that the plaintiff would never become pregnant again. (Repeated per SLADE LJ at 491)

Mrs Eyre subsequently withdrew her action in negligence on the advice of her counsel who relied on the decision of PETER PAIN J in *Thake* – which is doubly unfortunate, as the Court of Appeal, per SLADE LJ, considered that 'the less we say about that decision the better' (at 492). As to contract, Mrs Eyre said she had been told that 'once I had it done it was irreversible' and the trial judge was sure that she believed that she had a guarantee of permanent sterility. Nevertheless, the Court of Appeal took the view that the reference to irreversibility simply meant that the operative procedure in question was incapable of being reversed, that what was about to be done could not be undone – and it did so despite the fact that it had been admitted that, at the relevant time, there was a 10 per cent chance that fertility might be restored, should it be so desired. FRENCH J thought that few would doubt that it would be quite wrong, with a prospect of irreversibility nine to one, for the defendant to hold out any real hope that, had the plaintiff changed her mind, he could restore her prospects of conceiving a further child, which seems an unusual analysis – racecourses would surely be less entertaining were any horse which was given odds against winning of 10:1 or greater to go unsupported.

Mrs Eyre also lost her case on the grounds of implied warranty. Her belief that the operation would render her absolutely sterile was of no assistance to her as a matter of law. 'I am afraid,' said SLADE LJ, 'that, in my view, if [she and her husband] had wanted a guarantee of the nature which they now assert, they should have specifically asked for it.' Which seems to put patients in something of a Catch 22 position; it is asking a lot of a person who is unable to understand the nature of a contract to be so intelligent as to perceive the need to question it.

It is appropriate to interpolate at this point the important Australian case of *F* v. *R*,[113] where, again, the issue of specific questioning was raised. There it was held (per KING CJ) that, while the duty to inform a patient – not only of the risks inherent in a surgical operation but also of any real chance that the treatment may prove ineffective – was said to extend only to matters which might influence the decisions of a reasonable person in the position of the patient (the objective standard), an explicit request for information placed a doctor under an obligation which he should think long and hard before not assuming fully (a subjective standard). Not to mention the failure rate of the operation – 0.5 per cent, the same as in the case of Mrs Eyre – might not have been the best practice, but that did not mean to say that the appellant was in breach of a duty of care. The situation would, have been different however, had the respondent asked a specific question, said KING CJ and, in this, he was supported strongly by LEGOE J, who, as a corollary, considered that to impose a duty to divulge very small risks while *offering* voluntary information was to set too high a standard.

F v. *R* had it in common with the British case of *Gold* that the alternative, and generally more successful, possibility of vasectomy in the husband was ignored in both. The two benches did, however, differ in their approaches to the test of an adequate standard of professional care. The Australian court approved the relatively innovative attitude adopted in Canada, in *Reibl* v. *Hughes*,[114] in holding that medical evidence as to accepted practice cannot be decisive in all circumstances (KING CJ at 193); the ultimate test of conduct was whether it conformed to the standard of reasonable care demanded by the law. *Gold*, by contrast, is instructive in demonstrating the innate conservatism of the British courts in their assessment of medical negligence.

The story is virtually standard. Mrs Gold was sterilised following the birth of her third child and gave birth to a fourth just over three years later. The action was taken in negligence, which was accepted by the trial judge only in respect of a failure to warn that the operation might not succeed and of failure to mention the alternative of vasectomy. To all intents, the action was based on the former averment; *Gold* is, therefore, a precedental British case.

The trial judge was confronted with a strongly held view that there would have been a substantial body of responsible doctors who, in 1979, would not have given a warning of a failure rate of between 0.2 and 0.6 per cent. However, SCHIEMANN J adopted a position somewhat like that taken in *F* v. *R* and decided that the degree of disclosure to a woman who was *seeking advice* was not to be determined solely by a professional standard but depended on the court's view as to whether the person giving the advice acted negligently.

The Court of Appeal, however, refused to depart from the principle on which the *Bolam* test is founded, which relates to *any* person professing to have a particular skill beyond that of the now legendary man on the top of the Clapham omnibus. Given that the provision of contraceptive advice involved a measure of skill, the *Bolam* test applied and the doctor's duty of care was not to be dissected into component parts (per LLOYD LJ at 490). The Court of Appeal considered that only one finding was open on the evidence: that there was a body of responsible opinion which would not have given any warning as to the failure of female sterilisation and the possible alternatives. And, as a final nail in the coffin containing Mrs Gold's action, SLADE LJ's interpretation in *Eyre* of the word 'irreversible' was accepted without comment.

There have been a number of reported decisions – and, in addition, several which have appeared as news items only – since these leading cases. In general, they have done little other than to emphasise the difficulties faced by plaintiffs in wrongful pregnancy suits. There are two formidable hurdles. First, the plaintiffs must prove that they were inadequately warned of the vagaries of nature – and here their problem lies in the inherent improbability of experienced men failing to do so in modern circumstances: 'It is clear that if [the professor] expressed himself in the terms described by either plaintiff he was not merely negligent, he would have been plainly mischievous and irresponsible.'[115] Secondly, they must convince the court that they would have continued contraceptive methods had they been warned – and, again, it is inherently difficult to do so. Thus, in *Newell* v. *Goldenberg*,[116] the couple received damages for the anxiety and distress of a pregnancy resulting from an admitted failure to warn, but were refused damages for the child's upkeep, MANTELL J having ruled that they would not have taken further precautions even if they had been warned. This, in itself, raises an interesting question, currently not completely resolved, as to whether a wrongful pregnancy constitutes a single injury including both the pain and suffering associated with gestation *and* the costs involved in rearing the resultant child, or whether there are two separate foreseeable heads of loss. The latter was approved at first instance in *Allen* v. *Bloomsbury Health Authority*;[117] subsequently, however, the Court of Appeal has taken the opposing view: that a wrongful pregnancy is a personal injury which cannot be separated from its inevitable consequence.[118] One practical result of this is that actions for economic loss following the birth of a child conceived as a result of another's negligence are subject to the same three-year time bar as are actions for any personal injury.[119]

Otherwise, it seems that actions for unwanted pregnancy are now so commonplace that they are reported only if there is a specific point of interest. Thus *Scobie*[120] is interesting in that a husband provided negative sperm tests *after* his wife was found to be pregnant: the principals' rights to a paternity test in the event of dispute were, thereby, illustrated. It has been established that a surgeon carrying out a vasectomy has no duty of care to an unspecified woman who may, at some time in the future, rely upon his expertise[121] and, in one of the more unusual actions in this field, it has been held that the government is under no duty to keep the general public informed of relevant research.[122] On the other hand, there is some evidence that the balance in favour of the defendants is being slightly redressed. In *Gowton* v. *Wolverhampton Health Authority*,[123] it was held that adequate initial warning of a risk of recanalisation following vasectomy in the region of 1:2000–1:3000 had not been given. A more recent case is of considerable importance in that, while it was possible that a warning had been given, there was evidence that 'a sufficiently clear and comprehensible warning was never given',[124] indicating that so-called 'informed consent' must be 'understood informed consent'; the circumstances of this case were such that the inherent improbability of post-operative contraception being continued once a warning had been given was tilted the other way.

In the end, however, the reported cases do little to satisfy the distress of those whose sterilisation operations have failed by virtue of the vagaries of nature. The most tangible result from the cases has been the strong advocation by the medical defence organisations that the consent form related to sterilisation should be reworded to include a statement to the effect that: 'I understand that there is a possibility that I may not become or remain sterile',[125] a practice which has become standard in the last decade.

Many cases have been largely concerned with the quantum of damages for wrongful pregnancy and there is no place for detailed discussion of such a specialised subject in this book. The matter of compensation for the birth of a normal, albeit unplanned, child is, however, one of medico-legal significance and merits consideration as a separate issue. The underlying ethical dilemma was well expressed in *Jones* v. *Berkshire Area Health Authority*:

> It remains a matter of surprise to me that the law acknowledges an entitlement in a mother to claim damages for the blessing of a healthy child. Certain it is that those who are afflicted with a handicapped child or who long desperately to have a child at all and are denied that good fortune would regard an award for this sort of contingency with a measure of astonishment. But there it is: that is the law.[126]

The issue has been debated for some time in the United States, where it has had a chequered history, as might be expected in a country which combines 51 different jurisdictions. As a result, an analysis of the United States cases seems to have little relevance to the position in the United Kingdom; moreover, although the problem has not been addressed by the House of Lords, United Kingdom policy has stabilised following a rather hesitant start. In brief, the US court decisions vary from, at one extreme, rejecting any claims for the upkeep of a normal, but unexpected, child on the general grounds: 'To allow damages for the normal birth of a normal child is foreign to the universal public sentiment of the people'.[127] This policy is said to operate in 29 of the states.[128] At the other extreme, only New Mexico allows full recovery[129] and, in doing so, has rejected the variation that recovery is appropriate *only* if the request for sterilisation stemmed from economic reasons.[130] A number of jurisdictions have opted for something of a halfway house in which the benefits of parenthood are offset against the economic loss imposed by the birth of a child.[131] The unfair aspect of this approach is clearly that those parents who come to love their new baby will be penalised for so doing.[132] A final approach involves a retreat to public policy: 'Our courts have simply determined that public sentiment recognizes that these benefits to the parents [including some security in their old age] outweigh their economic loss in rearing and educating a healthy, normal child.'[133] Under this rule, damages would be allowed for the expenses of pregnancy and birth, but not for upkeep of the child which would, among other things, place an intolerable burden on the physician.

The British scene has developed by fits and starts, but reasonably steadily along its somewhat independent line, since 1980, when the case of *Sciuraga* v. *Powell* – a matter of a failed abortion – was heard.[134] The comments of the trial judge, WATKINS J, were, in the circumstances, obiter but, nevertheless, indicated a possible trend:

> Surely no one in these days would argue [that damages were irrecoverable] if the child was born defective or diseased. The fact that the child born is healthy cannot give rise to a different conclusion save as to a measure of damages. So I hold that the plaintiff is entitled to receive such damages as have by the evidence been proved to flow from the defendant's breach of contract.

The appeal court, per WALLER LJ, looked further ahead and to the possibility of public policy considerations defining the award of damages: 'In [ignoring policy considerations] I must not be taken as assenting to the view that they would be irrelevant in every case … once a woman has given birth to a healthy child without harm to her … I would not regard it as unarguable in another case that thereafter no more damages would arise.[135]

The question of whether the birth of a healthy child was fortunate or unfortunate was, however, first squarely addressed in *Udale*.[136]

The plaintiff in this case had, admittedly, wanted a sterilisation operation which was surgically reversible but, even as such, it was performed negligently. Damages were sought for pain, discomfort and distress caused by the unsuccessful operation, for loss of earnings during pregnancy, birth and early rearing of the child, for the cost of enlarging the home and for the cost of the child's upbringing until the age of 16. The trial judge was easily persuaded that, on the grounds of public policy, a plaintiff's claims, insofar as they were based on negligence which allowed the child to come into the world, should not be allowed. His reasons were forthright: it is highly undesirable and disruptive of family life and of society that a child should learn that he or she was unwanted; a parent who gave love and care to an unexpected child would be disadvantaged as compared with the bitter woman because her ultimate joy at the child's birth might be set off against the natural disadvantages of parenthood; doctors would be under subconscious pressure to encourage abortions in order to avoid claims for negligence; and 'it has been the assumption of our culture for time immemorial that a child coming into the world, even if, as some say, "the world is a vale of tears", is a blessing and an occasion for rejoicing' – and, in so saying, he followed the majority of the American jurisdictions.

JUPP J, in *Udale*, may have been influenced by the trial phase of *Emeh*,[137] where, by virtue of the plaintiff's refusal to have an unexpected pregnancy terminated (see p. 100), the issue of public policy was avoided but was not entirely dismissed. *Emeh*, as will be seen below, was overturned but, meantime, it was held in *Thake* that there was no general rule of public policy to the effect that damages cannot be awarded in respect of the birth of a healthy child. PETER PAIN J said: 'I can well understand the reasons of one who asks: "how could [the birth of a baby] possibly give rise to an action for damages?" But every baby has a belly to be filled and a body to be clothed. The law relating to damage is concerned with reparation in monetary terms and this is what is needed for the maintenance of a baby.'[138]

The current English law is, however, now to be found in the appeal stage of *Emeh*,[139] where it was firmly established that there was no reason in public policy why damages should not be recovered for a negligent failure to perform the necessary operation whether or not the child which was born thereafter was healthy (per SLADE LJ at 1054). And further: 'I see no reason for the court to introduce into the perfectly ordinary, straightforward rule of recovery of damages ... some qualification to reflect special social provisions' (per PURCHAS LJ at 1056). This decision was accepted without demur in the Court of Appeal in *Gold*.

Relevant cases in Scotland have, in general, been surprisingly poorly reported, but the position appeared to have been clarified – albeit in the Outer House only – in *Allan* v. *Greater Glasgow Health Board*.[140] This action in negligence failed on its merits. Nonetheless, in discussing the potential quantum in damages, the court explicitly accepted that there were no grounds to prevent the award of damages for the upbringing of a normal child born in such circumstances – and the judge discarded the notion of an 'offset' for the benefits derived from the birth. The situation was, however, destabilised by the decision in *McFarlane* v. *Tayside Health Board*.[141] Here, Lord Gill was of the view that the question of compensation was to be decided on the principle that the privilege of being a parent was immeasurable in monetary terms and that the benefits of parenthood transcended any putative patrimonial loss. No damages were, therefore, obligatory following the unexpected birth of a healthy and normal child. The opinion in *McFarlane* was most ably argued, but is very likely to be appealed. Meantime, pending a decision in the House of Lords, the United Kingdom as a whole – and, certainly, England – seems to favour the unmodified concept of full recovery for the upbringing of a normal child born as a result of negligent sterilisation.[142]

Only the relationship between 'wrongful pregnancy' and abortion remain to be briefly noted: why, in fact, do failed sterilisations ever come to a live birth when there are often multiple reasons for a legal termination of pregnancy which are accepted in the Abortion Act 1967? Leaving aside, for the present, the morality of using abortion as a socio-legal tool, many would have some sympathy with the court of first instance trying the case of Mrs Emeh, who refused to have an abortion. PARK J said: 'I hold there was such a [breach in the chain of causation] as the plaintiff's act in failing to obtain an abortion was ... so unreasonable as to eclipse the defendant's wrongdoing'.[143]

Most would, equally, agree that a woman must be free to consent to an abortion and that the courts must not be seen to be encouraging the practice.[144] Against this, it could be argued that a woman is not denied the choice by being informed that a failure to rectify a wrong will elide the wrong itself; all that has happened is that the conditions governing the decision have altered. Secondly, not everyone would agree with WALLER LJ that a refusal to rectify the mistake by abortion does not come up to the standard required for a *novus actus interveniens* – that is, an action which is so unreasonable that no ordinary person would be so foolish as to take it.[145] The fact that righting the wrong entailed two or three days in hospital could be regarded as merely another head under which damages could be assessed,[146] and the avoidance of an abortion could be regarded as a benefit offsetting the award of damages. Thirdly, while taking into account all the factors particular to the individual case, a refusal to have a pregnancy terminated could be regarded as an objective measure of the woman's assessment of the wrong done to her: by and large, a person who is deeply injured will go to considerable lengths to avoid the consequences of that injury.

In general, the English courts have about them an aura of distaste for abortion. Success in an action for 'wrongful life' would be against public policy (see Chapter 6, p. 163); Mrs Eyre was commended for her 'great good sense' in refusing termination; SLADE LJ, again, in *Emeh*, was in 'profound disagreement' with the trial judge's attitude to abortion; and JUPP J found Mrs Udale's condition remindful of the Gospel of St John. But, given that an unexpected pregnancy is subject to a delay in diagnosis, the essential plea in the advice- or warning-based case, and a possible supplementary plea in a negligent operation case, is that the negligence deprived the woman of the chance of an early, and safe, abortion. Such a claim would, however, be impossible were the pregnancy, in fact, to be discovered early; in such circumstances, it would at least be arguable that damages for the upkeep for the resultant child were no longer available in the face of a refused termination[147] – and this despite the fact that the quick-witted woman who decided to keep her fetus would then be penalised, by contrast with her less astute counterpart.[148]

Whatever may be the merits of such speculation, the English law as it currently stands is summed up in the words of SLADE LJ: 'Save in the most exceptional circumstances [it cannot be right] that the court should ever declare it unreasonable for a woman to decline to have an abortion in a case where there is no evidence that there [are] any medical or psychiatric grounds for terminating that particular pregnancy.'[149] Which is a good continuity line to take us to the next chapter.

Notes

1 *Eyre* v. *Measday* [1986] 1 All ER 488.
2 The law on the 'Prevention of Hereditary Disease in Future Generations' was passed by the Reichstag on 14 July 1933.
3 In 1976, the Indian government tried to introduce compulsory sterilisation by vasectomy in some states, accompanying this with minor forms of enticement. The resentment caused is said to have lost the next election for the party in power.
4 This may, of course, be a particularly Western view. One is reminded of a news item, 'Parenthood banned for mentally retarded', in which it was suggested that China was drafting countrywide legislation to bar mentally retarded people from having children, including the use of compulsory sterilisation and abortion: *The Scotsman*, 26 November, 1988, p. 7.
5 F. Pfafflin, 'The connections between eugenics, sterilization and mass murder in Germany from 1933 to 1945' (1986) 5 Med Law 1.
6 The greater part of the information on early American practice is derived

from the classic monograph by D.W. Meyers, *The Human Body and the Law* (1970), Edinburgh: Edinburgh University Press, ch. 2. See also P.R. Reilly, 'Eugenic sterilization in the United States' in A. Milunsky and G. Annas, *Genetics and the Law – III* (1985), New York: Plenum.

7   Quoting E.Z. Ferster, 'Eliminating the unfit – is sterilization the answer?' (1966) 27 Ohio St LJ 591.

8   Including Mississippi, North Carolina and West Virginia.

9   274 US 200 (1927).

10   At p. 207.

11   316 US 535 (1942).

12   Per DOUGLAS J at 541.

13   O. Dyer, 'Canadian women compensated for sterilisation' (1996) 312 Brit Med J 330.

14   G. Nandan 'Women in India forced to have hysterectomies' (1994) 308 Brit Med J 558.

15   J.K. Mason, and R.A. McCall Smith, *Law and Medical Ethics* (4th edn, 1994), London: Butterworths, Appendix D.

16   Note 11 above.

17   *Smith and Smith* v. *Superior Court of Arizona* 725 P 2d 1101 (Ariz, 1986). Meyers, n. 6 above, at p. 37, quoted a rather similar older case, *In the Matter of Hernandez*, No 76757 Santa Barbara Superior Court, 8 June 1966.

18   For example, *People* v. *Blankenship* 265 P 2d 352 (Cal, 1936) (rapist affected by syphilis). But this was impliedly overruled in *People* v. *Dominguez* 64 Cal Rptr 290 (1967).

19   G. Dunea, 'Sense and senselessness' (1985) 290 Brit Med J 776.

20   Note 6 above, p. 46.

21   R.M. Soskin, 'Sterilization of the mentally retarded' (1983) 2 Med Law 267. For a thoroughgoing update of the issues, see C. Heginbotham, 'Sterilizing people with mental handicaps' in S.A.M. McLean (ed.), *Legal Issues in Human Reproduction* (1989), Aldershot: Gower, ch. 6.

22   *Stump* v. *Sparkman* 435 US 349 (1978). My interpretation may, however, be an oversimplification. See D. Lachance, 'In re *Grady*: the mentally retarded individual's right to choose sterilization' (1981) 6 Am J Law Med 559.

23   *Re Quinlan* 355 A 2d 664 (NJ, 1976). The court empowered the parents of a girl who was in the persistent vegetative state as a result of drug-induced brain damage to authorise her removal from ventilator support.

24   *In the matter of Lee Ann Grady* 426 A 2d 467 (NJ, 1981). *Grady* is discussed at length in K.McK. Norrie, *Family Planning Practice and the Law* (1991), Aldershot: Dartmouth, ch. 7.

25   *Matter of A W* 637 P 2d 361 (Colo, 1981).

26   *Matter of Moe* 432 NE 2d 712 (Mass, 1982).

27   *Matter of Johnson* 263 SE 2d 805 (NC, 1980).

28   For a UK analysis, see A. Grubb and D. Pearl, 'Sterilisation and the courts' (1987) 46 Cambridge LJ 439.

29   *Conservatorship of the person of Valerie N* 707 P 2d 760 (Cal, 1985).

30   *Re Phillip B* App 156 Cal Rptr 48 (1979) per CALDECOTT PJ. See also, for example, *Wisconsin* v. *Yoder* 406 US 205 (1972).

31   *In the Matter of Edith Hayes* 608 P 2d 635 (Wash, 1980).

32   *Re Eve* (1987) 31 DLR (4th) 1.

33   *Re Eve* (1981) 115 DLR (3d) 283.

34   See, in particular, *Re X (a minor)* [1975] 1 All ER 697 in both the trial and appeal stages.

35   *Matter of Eberhardy's Guardianship* 294 NW 2d 540 (Wis, 1980). The proposition

was supported in the State Supreme Court, *In the matter of the Guardianship of Joan I Eberhardy* 307 NW 2d 881 (Wis, 1981).

36 I believe that there are many occasions on which it is possible to base a decision on 'substituted judgment', as in withdrawal of treatment from the brain-damaged patient. This, however, presupposes that one can make an objective assessment as to what the 'reasonable person' would decide: see J.K. Mason and G.T. Laurie, 'The management of the persistent vegetative state in the British Isles' [1996] Juridical Rev 263. It is, however, hard to conceptualise an objective standard in the circumstances now under discussion.

37 (1985) 19 DLR (4th) 255.

38 See, for example, the New Zealand case *Re X* [1991] 2 NZLR 365 and the Scottish case *L, Petitioner* 1996 SCLR 538, Outer House see n. 55 below.

39 (1988) 13 Fam LR 85.

40 *Re Jane, Re Elizabeth* (1989) 13 Fam LR 47.

41 It is, of course, always possible that judges may err in their views on appropriate medical steps to be taken!

42 A similar result was reached in *Re Elizabeth*. The Australian cases have been critically reviewed by K. Petersen, 'Private decisions and public scrutiny: sterilisation and minors in Australia and England' in S.A.M. McLean (ed.), *Contemporary Issues in Law, Medicine and Ethics* (1996), Aldershot: Dartmouth, ch. 4.

43 *Secretary, Department of Health and Community Services (N.T.)* v. *J.W.B. and S.M.B.* (1992) 66 ALJR 300.

44 For an exhaustive review of this case, see N. Cica, 'Sterilising the intellectually disabled: the approach of the High Court of Australia in *Department of Health* v. *J.W.B. and S.M.B.*' (1993) 1 Med L Rev 186.

45 *Re Marion (No 2)* (1992) 17 Fam LR 336.

46 *Re L and M* (1993) 17 Fam LR 357 at 374.

47 [1976] Fam 185.

48 See, for example, A. Bainham, 'Handicapped girls and judicial parents' (1987) 103 LQR 334.

49 [1988] AC 199.

50 (1992) 2 BMLR 126.

51 Norrie, in particular, suggests that there is nothing in the Canadian Supreme Court's judgment which precludes such measures: K.McK. Norrie, *Family Planning Practice and the Law* (1991), Aldershot: Dartmouth, ch. 7, p. 121.

52 *Wentzel* v. *Montgomery General Hospital* 447 A 2d 1244 (Md, 1982).

53 *In re T, T* v. *T and another* [1988] Fam 52.

54 *Re F (mental patient; sterilisation)* [1990] 2 AC 1.

55 The *parens patriae* jurisdiction does, however, survive in Scotland: *Law Hospital NHS Trust* v. *Lord Advocate and others* 1996 SLT 848. The opportunity also exists to appoint a tutor dative who can authorise medical treatment for those who are unable to consent. There have been at least three cases in which such decisions have involved sterilisation of incompetents – and the ease with which such decisions can be reached is in sharp contrast to the English prcedures. See A. Ward 'Tutors to adults: developments' 1992 SLT (Notes) 325. *L., petitioner* was the first case in which the petition was opposed – albeit unsuccessfully.

56 See WOOD J in *T* v. *T*, n. 53 above.

57 The application of this test outside the frontiers of medical negligence is certainly open to criticism. See, for example, D. Ogbourne and R. Ward, 'Sterilization, the mentally incompetent and the courts' (1989) 18 Anglo-Amer L Rev 230.

58 But whose practice – medical or legal – is unclear.

59   Though, perhaps, even here, the courts are inclined to less soul-searching. See
      Re HG (specific issue: sterilisation) [1993] 1 FLR 587.
60   *Practice Note (Official Solicitor: sterilisation)* [1993] 3 All ER 222.
61   In *Re E (a minor) (medical treatment)* [1991] 2 FLR 585, SIR STEPHEN BROWN P said
      that the operation was necessary for therapeutic reasons and that the parents
      were in a position to give a valid consent.
62   *Re GF* [1992] 1 FLR 293.
63   Amongst others, of those already cited, *Re a Teenager* (Australia), *Re K* (Canada),
      L, Petitioner (Scotland), *Re E* and *Re GF* (England). It may also be a major
      factor justifying mass hysterectomies in India: Z. Imam, 'Mass hysterectomies
      in India' (1994) 343 Lancet 592.
64   A concept derived from T.S. Szasz, 'Diagnoses are not diseases' (1991) 338
      Lancet 1574.
65   *Re M (a minor) (wardship: sterilisation)* [1988] 2 FLR 497; *Re P (a minor) (ward-
      ship: sterilisation)* [1989] 1 FLR 182.
66   *Re W (mental patient) (sterilisation)* [1993] 1 FLR 381.
67   *Guardianship of Tulley* 146 Cal Reptr 266 (1978).
68   Note 32 above.
69   Note 47 above.
70   *In re B*, nn. 49 and 50 above, per LORD HAILSHAM CJ, DILLON LJ.
71   A right to procreate, as such, should be gender-free but it is obvious from the
      same argument that men could not claim such a right.
72   P. Ramsey, 'Freedom and responsibility in medical and sex ethics: a protestant
      view' (1956) 31 New York Univ LR 1189.
73   R. Gillon, 'On sterilising severely mentally handicapped people' (1987) 13 J
      Med Ethics 59.
74   As argued most plausibly by Grubb and Pearl, n. 28 above. See also S.A.M.
      McLean, 'The Right to Reproduce', in T. Campbell, D. Godberg, S.A.M. McLean
      and T. Mullen, *Human Rights. From Rhetoric to Reality* (1986), Oxford: Basil
      Blackwell.
75   S.A.M. McLean and T.D. Campbell, 'Sterilisation' in S.A.M. McLean (ed.),
      Legal Issues in Medicine (1981), Aldershot: Gower, pp. 178 ff.
76   [1988] AC 199 at 204.
77   Children Act 1989, s.2(9)–(11).
78   M.J. Freeman, 'For her own good' (1987) 84 LSG 949, had such a fear.
79   Note 51 above.
80   In *Re F* [1990] 2 AC per LORD JAUNCEY at 83.
81   In *Bravery* v. *Bravery* [1954] 3 All ER 59 at 67–8.
82   National Health Service (Family Planning) Amendment Act 1972.
83   Some countries have age limits below which contraceptive sterilisation is
      illegal; for example, federal regulations in the United States require a mini-
      mum age of 21.
84   This is a matter of considerable moment when dealing with the incompetent
      patient. See, for example, the long arguments in *Re M*, n. 65 above.
85   *Paton* v. *British Pregnancy Advisory Service Trustees* [1979] QB 276 per SIR JOHN
      BAKER P at 280.
86   *Bravery* v. *Bravery* [1954] 3 All ER 59.
87   Matrimonial Causes Act 1973, s.1(2)(*b*); Divorce (Scotland) Act 1976, s.1(2)(*b*).
88   A. Sommerville (on behalf of the Working Party), *Medical Ethics Today: Its
      Practice and Philosophy* (1993), London: BMJ Publishing Group, p. 110.
89   Note 65 above.
90   Note 65 above.
91   In passing, it may be reiterated that physiological interference should not be
      undertaken lightly. There has long been a suspicion that vasectomy *per se*

might predispose to disease; there is, however, no evidence that the operation predisposes to arteriosclerosis or prostatic cancer – at least for the first eight years: L.M. Schuman (ed.), 'Health status of American men – a study of post-vasectomy sequelae' (1993) 46 J Clin Epidemiol 697.

92 *R* v. *Donovan* [1934] 2 KB 498 per SWIFT J at 507; confirmed in *R* v. *Brown* [1993] 2 All ER 75, HL.

93 See LASKIN CJC in *Reibl* v. *Hughes* (1980) 114 DLR (3d) 1 at 10–11.

94 *Harnish* v. *Children's Hospital Medical Center* 387 Mass 152 (1982).

95 In *Sidaway* v. *Board of Governors of the Bethlem Royal Hospital and the Maudsley Hospital* [1985] AC 871, HL at 904.

96 *Bolam* v. *Friern Hospital Management Committee* [1957] 2 All ER 118. In Scotland, see *Hunter* v. *Hanley* 1955 SC 200 for, if anything, an even stricter test.

97 *Sidaway* v. *Board of Governors of the Bethlem Royal Hospital and the Maudsley Hospital* [1984] QB 493, CA; [1985] AC 871, HL.

98 (1980) 114 DLR (3d) 1.

99 But, as things stand, an English judge cannot choose between two conflicting opinions: *Maynard* v. *West Midlands Regional Health Authority* [1985] 1 All ER 635.

100 *Rogers* v. *Whitaker* (1992) 109 ALR 625, [1993] 4 Med LR 79. For full discussion, see D. Chalmers and R. Schwartz, '*Rogers* v. *Whitaker* and informed consent in Australia: a fair dinkum duty of disclosure' (1993) 1 Med L Rev 139. For the logical devastation of *Bolam* as a whole, see H. Teff, *Reasonable Care* (1994), Oxford: Clarendon Press.

101 For example, *Gold* v. *Haringey Health Authority* [1988] QB 481, CA.

102 *McAllister* v *Lewisham and North Southwark Health Authority* [1994] 5 Med LR 343; *Smith* v. *Tunbridge Wells Health Authority* [1994] 5 Med LR 334.

103 *Moyes* v. *Lothian Health Board* 1990 SLT 444.

104 *Canterbury* v. *Spence* 464 F 2d 772 (DC, 1972). For a review of the basis, see *Largey* v. *Rothman* 540A 2d 504 (NJ, 1988).

105 The subjective patient may be becoming the model in Australia: *Ellis* v. *Wallsend District Hospital* [1990] 2 Med LR 103. See discussion of the options in M. Brazier, 'Patient autonomy and consent to treatment: the role of the law?' (1987) 7 LS 169.

106 In *Sidaway* [1984] QB 493 at 517.

107 In *Re T (adult) (refusal of medical treatment)* [1992] 4 All ER 649 at 663.

108 *Battersby* v. *Tottman and State of South Australia* (1985) 37 SASR 524; *Rogers* v. *Whitaker*, n. 100 above. The difference, in fact, lay in the attitudes of the patients, which must also be a factor to be considered.

109 This is about 1:2000 cases of vasectomy. The incidence in the female is higher (said to be 2 to 6:1000 in *Eyre* v. *Measday*, n. 111 below) but it is difficult to provide a precise figure as the operative techniques for occluding the Fallopian tubes are far more variable.

110 *Thake and another* v. *Maurice* [1984] 2 All ER 513, QBD; [1986] 1 All ER 497, CA.

111 *Eyre* v. *Measday* [1986] 1 All ER 488, CA.

112 *Gold* v. *Haringey Health Authority* [1986] 1 FLR 125; [1988] QB 481, CA.

113 (1983) 33 SASR 189, SC.

114 (1981) 114 DLR (3d) 1.

115 TURNER J in *Scobie* v. *Central Birmingham Health Authority* (1994) 22 BMLR 135.

116 *Newell and Newell* v. *Goldenberg* [1995] 6 Med LR 371.

117 [1993] 1 All ER 651. For discussion, see A. Stewart, 'Damages for the birth of a child' (1995) J Law Soc Scot 298.

118 *Walkin* v. *South Manchester Health Authority* (1995) 25 BMLR 108.

119 Limitation Act 1980, s.11(1).

120   Note 115 above. But the phenomenon is not so rare as might be supposed: possibly about 1:80 000 cases; see J.C. Smith, D. Cranston, T. O'Brien *et al.*, 'Fatherhood without apparent spermatozoa after vasectomy' (1994) 344 Lancet 30.

121   *Goodwill* v. *British Pregnancy Advisory Service* (1996) 31 BMLR 83.

122   *Danns* v. *Department of Health* (1995) 25 BMLR 121. It is surprising that this case was directed against the Department alone; there was no corresponding claim against either the surgeon or the Health Authority for failure to warn of the risks of failure.

123   [1994] 5 Med LR 432, QBD. Note that it was the initial warning that was deficient. The fact that, in 1986, a responsible body of medical opinion would not have informed of a risk after two negative sperm tests was irrelevant.

124   *Lybert* v. *Warrington Health Authority* [1996] 7 Med LR 71, CA per OTTON LJ.

125   Annual Report of the Medical Defence Union (1987), p. 37.

126   Per OGNALL J, 2 July 1986, unreported. Quoted in *Gold*, CA per LLOYD LJ at 890.

127   *Shaheen* v. *Knight* 11 Pa D & C 2d (1957) at 41–2. See also *Sutkin* v. *Beck* 629 SW 2d 131 (Tex, 1982).

128   *Lovelace Medical Center* v. *Mendez* 805 P 2d 603 (NM, 1991) per ALARID J.

129   In *Lovelace*, n. 128 above.

130   *Burke* v. *Rivo* 551 NE 2d 1 (Mass, 1990).

131   *Sherlock* v. *Stillwater Clinic* 260 NW 2d 169 (Minn, 1977); *Ochs* v. *Borelli* 445 A 2d 883 (Conn, 1982).

132   This possibility was specifically addressed in *Public Health Trust* v. *Brown* 388 So 2d 1084 (Fla, 1980).

133   *Terrell* v. *Garcia* 496 SW 2d 124 (Tex, 1973) at 128.

134   (1979) 123 SJ 406.

135   Also quoted in *Udale* v. *Bloomsbury Health Authority* [1983] 2 All ER 522 at 530.

136   Note 135 above.

137   *Emeh* v. *Kensington, Chelsea and Fulham Area Health Authority* (1983) Times, 3 January, QBD.

138   [1984] 2 All ER 513 at 526.

139   *Emeh* v. *Kensington and Chelsea and Westminster Area Health Authority* [1984] 3 All ER 1044.

140   (1993) 17 BMLR 135. A somewhat similar result was obtained in *Cameron* v. *Greater Glasgow Health Board* 1993 GWD 6-433.

141   1997 SLT 211. Relying, in particular, on *Brown*, n. 132 above.

142   This is not quite a unique stance – a similar policy has evolved in South Africa. See *Administrator, Natal* v. *Edouard* 1990 (3) SA 581 (A).

143   Note 137 above; quoted in *Emeh*, n. 139 above, at 1049.

144   K.McK. Norrie, 'Damages for the birth of a child' 1985 SLT 69; A. Mullis, 'Wrongful conception unravelled' (1993) 1 Med L Rev 320.

145   Quoting *McKew* v. *Holland & Hannen & Cubitts (Scotland) Ltd* [1969] 3 All ER 1621 at 1624.

146   The possibility that the refusal of an *early* abortion might be regarded as unreasonable still remains open.

147   For further discussion, see K.McK. Norrie, 'Liability for failed sterilisation' 1986 SLT 145.

148   In *Crouchman* v. *Burke* (as yet unreported), damages were awarded for the birth of a healthy child which was *in utero* before the operation for sterilisation. The plaintiff would have had an early abortion but, as LANGLEY J. put it, 'understandably' declined one at 16 weeks. The case seems to raise a number of interesting points. See F. Gibb 'Sterilised mother who had baby wins £100,000' (1997) *The Times*, 10 July, p. 10.

149   In *Emeh*, n. 139 above, at 1053.

5 Abortion

'This is a deadly game.'[1] It is difficult to believe that a leading article in a major medical journal would so describe family planning in 1993. Yet the scenario described is one in which clinics are vandalised, attacked, bombed and burned and doctors are murdered – and this in the United States, where abortion was legalised more than 25 years ago. Moreover, this is not only a transatlantic phenomenon. On the other side of the English Channel, the French government has had to introduce a law making it a criminal offence to obstruct abortions,[2] while it is a matter of history that the reunification of West and East Germany very nearly foundered on the rocks of abortion law.[3]

In short, it cannot be said that abortion is a dead issue consequent upon the acceptance by many jurisdictions of relatively liberal laws. On the contrary, it still generates intense emotion and it is not difficult to see the reasons for this. In the two previous chapters, we have discussed the prevention of an unwanted pregnancy, and there are many who would regard abortion as doing no more than extending this concept to the prevention of an unwanted birth. As has already been intimated, it is possible to establish a philosophical argument to the effect that contraception, sterilisation and abortion are of the same moral order, in that the result of all is to prevent the development of a new human life,[4] but to do so is to ignore the introduction of a new dimension. There is a clear distinction to be made in that, of these three procedures, only abortion prevents the future development of a life which is already developing; and since the state has an interest in protecting human life, the law must see abortion as being different from other forms of fertility control. The critical point is, then, to decide what form of human life is at stake and what degree of protection it should be afforded. My own guiding medico-legal principle rests on the statement by Lord Chief Justice Coleridge over a century ago: 'every legal duty is founded on a moral obligation'.[5] If this be accepted, it follows that we must look briefly at the moral

107

bases on which the abortion debate – or conflict – is founded before considering the legal 'solutions' that have evolved.

Fundamentally, and platitudinous though it may now sound, all the problems hark back to the question, when does human life begin? This single question is by no means open to a single answer because, in Socratic tradition, it merely leads to a further question: what do we mean by human life? We can speak in genetic terms: that is, by making a molecular distinction between the species *homo sapiens* and that of any other primate; one can look to humanness or the likeness to an adult human being – something which is of major significance in orthodox Jewish teaching;[6] or one can look further and think in terms of what is now often referred to as 'personhood' – a quality which is measured by intellect and the power to make decisions.[7] But whatever definition is being used, there are several points in human development which could be said to represent that moment at which 'human life' begins.

At one practical extreme, we have birth, which is, legally speaking, an ideal marker. It is at that instant that the fetus becomes a 'reasonable creature in being' and is clearly entitled to that degree of protection which the state owes to all its citizens; as a consequence, it is the point at which many fetal rights mature (see Chapter 6 for discussion). Medically speaking, however, the *fact* of birth is not especially material. Certainly, the fetus *in utero* depends upon its mother but, had it been born, say, two days earlier, its chances of survival would, in normal circumstances, have been no different; it is, therefore, illogical to make an absolute distinction between the potential for life of a mature fetus and a neonate.

It is mainly for this reason that the concept of viability, or the capacity to exist independently of the mother, has been tied so strongly to the definition of fetal status. Viability is, however, very much a product of the legal mind – and, particularly, of the American legal mind – and, as things stand, is effectively defined in England as the capacity to breathe by the use of one's own lungs, with or without the use of a ventilator.[8] Proof or disproof of such a state is, however, unsatisfactory: it arises either *de facto* when the neonate proves his or her viability by suviving or as a *post hoc* morbid anatomical diagnosis in the event of stillbirth or neonatal death. But the very inclusion of the words 'with or without the use of a ventilator' indicates that, both medically and morally speaking, viability is an imprecise determinant of 'human' life, in that it depends not only on the maturity of the fetus but also on the technology that is available to support its extrauterine life – and on the motivation with which that technology is put to use. Thus a premature fetus may survive in a hospital neonatal intensive care unit while one of similar or greater maturity and health will die if born under a hedgerow; it is clearly illogical to suggest that the former was technically and morally 'alive', while the latter was not. We will see later, however, that the concept of viability now forms little or no part of English law.

In former centuries, when medical intervention was less effective, a similar significance was attributed to 'quickening', or appreciation of fetal movements by the pregnant woman. But, although movement indicates some form of 'life', this point in time, again, suffers from being one which is measured subjectively and, at the same time, is largely independent of fetal maturity: there is no reason to suppose that a lazy fetus is any less alive than is one which is hyperactive.

At the other extreme, there are many who would hold that life begins at conception; that is, at the formation of the zygote by fusion of male and female gametes. It is generally supposed that this is, particularly, the teaching of the Roman Catholic Church – which is true – and that this has always been the case, which is untrue.[9] Up to 1869, Catholic philosophy was dominated by Aquinian theories of animation or ensoulment which was thought to be associated with quickening; prior to this, the fetus was accorded what Aristotle described as a vegetative existence 'informed by a nutritive soul'.[10] It was only in the 19th century that the Roman Catholics adopted the stance that human life and the sanctity of that life exist from conception. It may well be that this was, as Dunstan has suggested, a pragmatic move to counter the increasing ease and availability of abortion which were apparent at the time. An alternative, and perhaps better, view is that it coincided with the scientific appreciation of the formation of the zygote; the difficulty of defining the point at which human life begins was exposed and conception was chosen as the significant moment with the object, so to speak, of 'giving the fetus every benefit of the doubt'.[11] Whatever may have been the fundamental reason for change, the current attitude is one which is firmly adopted and fully supported by conservative Roman Catholic opinion. The 'case for conception' was well argued by Iglesias,[12] and may be summarised from two of the points she makes:

> To be a human being is to be a person. There are no stages in our existence at which this identity does not hold ... If we are to make sense of our existence *now* as human personal beings we must admit that whatever capacities we have now have developed from what we were in the beginning.

Nevertheless, it is not easy to accept the Vatican's absolutist view. The facile, but most practical, reason for doubt is that untold numbers of zygotes are lost daily on a worldwide basis; if we honestly believe that each represents a dead human being, we should, logically, regard each menstrual period as a potential for mourning – and such a conclusion is ludicrous.

On a more theoretical plane, we must consider what we mean by humanity or what it is that distinguishes humans from the rest of the animal kingdom. There are those who believe that to hold that there is such a distinction is to fall into the moral trap of speciesism;[13] by and large, however, the great majority of us have no difficulty in differentiating between *homo sapiens* and *macaca rhesus*, despite the fact that we share a common blood group antigen. The definition of this distinction is, admittedly, difficult but it can be summarised as being that man is capable of reacting to an intellectual stimulus rather than solely to instinct or intuition. The human being can make and act upon decisions and he or she can assess the moral value of what he or she does. It is possible to translate this capacity to distinguish moral right from moral wrong into the 'soul of man' and, going one step further, to equate the philosophical concept of humanity with the spiritual belief in ensoulment.

Two conclusions follow from this argument. The first is negative: that is, that genetic material of *homo sapiens* which has had no human contact cannot be seen as having acquired a spiritual soul; this means that a free zygote has no humanity. But it also follows that, once contact is made and once there is an infusion of humanity from mother to fetus, the fact of the latter's humanity is unarguable. In short, there is a persuasive argument for supposing that implantation is the point at which one should attribute humanity to the human embryo. This reasoning does not, however, take into account the possibility of technology advancing to the point where extrauterine development of full-term fetuses is possible. We do not *know* whether such beings would or would not possess intellectual morality or what we perceive as humanity and we would, of course, be confronted with the contradiction in spiritual terms of a soulless human being. One can only say that, fortunately, that problem is one for the relatively distant future and, at the same time, plead that the argument is tenable within the confines of current legal and technical expertise: for, although a different judgment may be shown later to be correct, 'a particular contingent judgment can still be the only correct one in its situation'.[14]

It is for reasons which are all too apparent from the foregoing that many reject the idea of a moment at which humanity is acquired and advocate, in preference, a gradualist approach to the problem. On this theory, humanity is a quality which evolves with time and which is only expressed to the full at the time of birth. Thus no time is set at which the embryo achieves human status, but the rights to humanness increase with maturity.[15] It is, however, quite possible to see the positivist and gradualist approaches as being compatible with one another. A being can have rights and yet be incapable of expressing or exercising them. Such rights may well appear to be overriding when viewed in isolation; once they conflict with similar rights of another party, however, they become relative. A fetus and a pregnant woman may have equal humanity, but to hold that they have equal access to the rights attaching to a human being would border on the absurd. Nonetheless, the fetus has the potential for the full autonomy of a human being and the respect due to that autonomy depends upon the strength of the potential. The subject of fetal rights is discussed in greater detail in Chapter 6. For present purposes, we can see, at one extreme, the recently implanted embryo which will disimplant naturally in some 40 per cent of cases – clearly, the potential for human autonomy is very low; at the other end of the scale, we have the fetus within the pregnant woman in the second stage of labour; the fetus' potential is now maximal and the mother's own life would have to be in jeopardy to the fetus before we could justify its destruction in deference to the mother's needs.[16] This analysis is obviously applicable only when there is a maternal/fetal connection; once this is broken at birth, the neonate attains full human autonomy as of right.

In summary, this diversion into the abstract has tried to show that the implanted embryo has acquired humanity and is entitled to protection; feticide for its own sake *must* be immoral. However, in the event of a conflict between mother and fetus, the rights of the contenders should be regarded as relative; in such circumstances, a case can be made out for the morality of abortion which will, essentially, turn on the twin problems of fetal maturity and of the health of mother and fetus. We must next consider the legal response to this conclusion.

The law in the United Kingdom

The recognition of variable fetal rights has fluctuated in English law. The influence of mediaeval teaching was still apparent in 1803,[17] when procuring the miscarriage of a woman who was 'quick with child' was a statutory offence subject to capital punishment. Abortion at an earlier state of gestation carried a lesser penalty, albeit a sentence of up to 14 years' transportation. The law remained the same until 1861, when the Offences Against the Person Act came into being. This introduced two major changes: firstly, the death penalty was replaced by potential penal servitude for life and, secondly, any distinction as to fetal age was abolished. The 1861 Act remains the definitive law in England, Wales and Northern Ireland and s.58 reads:

> Every woman, being with child, who, with intent to procure her own miscarriage, shall unlawfully administer to herself any poison or other noxious thing, or shall unlawfully use any instrument or other means whatsoever with like intent, and whosoever with intent to procure the miscarriage of any woman, whether she be or be not with child, shall unlawfully administer to her or cause to be taken by her any poison or other noxious thing, or shall unlawfully use any instrument or other means whatsoever with the like intent, shall be guilty of an offence, and being convicted thereof shall be liable ... to be kept in penal servitude for life.

One suspects that the United Kingdom Parliament of the time was mainly concerned at the number of abortions which were being carried out and that this may also explain the similar penalty attached to the offence and the attempted offence by an outside party. Be that as it may, the pendulum swung again in 1929, with the passing of the Infant Life (Preservation) Act.[18] This short Act included two innovations, one of which will be discussed later. For the present, s.1(1) reads:

> any person who, with intent to destroy the life of a child capable of being born alive, by any wilful act causes a child to die before it has an existence independent of its mother, shall be guilty of an offence, to wit, of child destruction ...
> Provided that no person shall be found guilty of an offence under this section unless it is proved that the act which caused the death of the child was not done in good faith for the purpose only of preserving the life of the mother.

This sub-section had two purposes. Firstly, it closed a gap in the criminal law, albeit a rare one, which made it impossible to penalise a person for killing a child *in the process* of being born naturally.[19] Secondly, it was particularly designed to legalise, beyond doubt, the operation of craniotomy – or the crushing of an impacted fetal head, inevitably causing fetal death – which was widely practised before Caesarian section became commonplace.

Thus it will be seen that, until 1929, there was no specific exclusion of therapeutic abortion from the criminal law, although, with the benefit of hindsight and of later Australian judgments (see p. 113), it seems probable that a defence of good medical practice always existed. Even after the passing of the 1929 Act, however, its specifically restrictive terms added to the uncertainty of the doctor's position and this was clearly an unsatisfactory situation. It was not until the historic case of *R* v. *Bourne*, in 1938,[20] that it can be said to have been clarified.

The facts of the case are now well known and need only be summarised. An eminent gynaecologist announced that he intended to abort the fetus of a 15-year-old victim of rape. He did so and was indicted for transgressing the Offences Against the Person Act, 1861, s.58. The judge, in his charge to the jury, chose to link the 1861 and 1929 statutes and ruled that, in a case brought under the former Act, the burden rested on the Crown to satisfy the jury that the defendant did not procure the miscarriage of the girl in good faith for the purpose only of preserving her life, this being on the grounds that the terms of the later Act defined the meaning of the word 'unlawful' in the Act of 1861. Having crossed that hurdle, MCNAGHTEN J skipped over the second in holding: 'if the doctor is of the opinion ... that the probable consequence of the continuance of the pregnancy would be to make the woman a physical or mental wreck, the jury are quite entitled to hold that the doctor who ... operates is operating for the purpose of preserving the life of the woman'.[21]

Mr Bourne was acquitted; the way was thus cleared for doctors to use their clinical judgment in dealing with pregnancies which were detrimental to the health of the pregnant woman and the case also became the authority in many parts of the Commonwealth. In Australia, where legislation comparable to the Offences Against the Person Act, 1861 remains the unqualified statutory law in several states,[22] the Act has been considered from the slightly different angle that, given that it is an offence to procure a miscarriage unlawfully, there must, by definition, be a lawful means of doing so.[23] Thus, in *R* v. *Davidson*, it was said:

> to establish that the use of an instrument with intent to procure a miscarriage was unlawful, the Crown must establish either:
> a) that the accused did not honestly believe on reasonable grounds that the act done by him was necessary to preserve the woman from a serious danger to her life or her physical or mental health ... which the continuance of the pregnancy would entail; or
> b) that the accused did not honestly believe on reasonable grounds that the act done by him was in the circumstances proportionate to the need to preserve the woman from. (Per MENHENNITT J at 672)

With some exceptions, this remains the law in Australia. There have been no prosecutions of doctors since 1972 and it appears that attitudes to abortion in, at least, New South Wales and Victoria are now amongst the most liberal in the world. Petersen, in a major study of contemporary abortion attitudes in anglophone jurisdictions, has noted, albeit with some surprise, that the abortion controversy is most settled in those countries where regulation remains by way of archaic statutes which are, nevertheless, modified by an adaptive medical profession working in concert with developing public opinion.[24]

Scots law on abortion is a matter of common law. The subject has never been of as great interest in Scotland as it has been in England, occupying less than three pages in Gordon.[25] This is because, in general, criminality in Scotland results only from evil intent and the good faith of doctors has always been supposed; there can be no Scottish *Bourne* because it is almost impossible to envisage the Crown Office instituting proceedings in such circumstances. Even in England, the concept of a medically supervised abortion being acceptable only on the grounds that pregnancy and childbirth would result in the mental or physical wreckage of a woman was soon abandoned in favour of damage to her physical or mental health.[26]

All the law so far discussed relates to the early fetus. The Infant Life (Preservation) Act, 1929 remains in force in England and Wales and clearly protects the fetus which is 'capable of being born alive' – indeed, the status of such a fetus and its mother are equal save only in circumstances where a choice must be made between the death of one or other. In the hope of avoiding confusion, s.1(2) goes on to say: 'For the purposes of this Act, evidence that a woman had at any material time been pregnant for a period of twenty-eight weeks or more shall be prima facie proof that she was at that time pregnant of a child capable of being born alive.'[27]

The Act is thus clear in that there is no denying that a fetus of 28 weeks' gestation or more is capable of being born alive. What it does *not* clarify is the age below which a fetus can be said without doubt *not* to be capable of being born alive. Moreover, the Act does not define what it means by being born alive. These issues were, however, virtually eliminated by the ruling in *C* v. *S*,[28] a case which also did away with any academic distinctions between a viable fetus and one capable of being born alive.[29] It is also to be noted that the potential conflict between the Infant Life (Preservation) Act, 1929 and the Abortion Act 1967 in relation to the therapeutic termination of late pregnancy has now been avoided by the Human Fertilisation and Embryology Act 1990, s.37(4), which protects the doctor who is working within the terms of the 1967 Act from prosecution under the 1929 Act.

It would seem, then, that abortion has for some time – and probably always – been available in Great Britain for therapeutic purposes. It is, therefore, not inappropriate to ask if there ever was a need for further legislation to protect the medical profession from the sanctions of the Offences Against the Person Act, 1861. The reasons which can be adduced are varied. Firstly, the medical profession was still uncertain of the position even after *R* v. *Bourne*: any abortion performed was still subject to attack in Menhennitt terms as being 'disproportionate treatment in relation to the need'. Secondly, such stated grounds for a lawful termination of pregnancy as existed were fairly stringently confined. Thirdly, the number of illegitimate and socially disastrous pregnancies after the Second World War was considerable and, as a result, the backstreet abortionist supposedly flourished. The precise extent of the trade is unknown and unknowable; a typical estimate is that there were between 10 000 and 100 000 unlawful abortions each year in the United Kingdom in the early 1960s, but the breadth of the bracket testifies to its lack of authority. It is interesting to note that the largest annual number of deaths attributable to abortion in that era was given as 185 in the statistics of the Register General for England and Wales; in 1966, 62 persons were sent for jury trial under the Offences Against the Person Act, 1861, s.58 and, of these, 28 received sentences of imprisonment.[30] Nevertheless, a serious potential mortality and morbidity existed and a need was perceived for regulation and documentation of practice in an area of what is, essentially, social medicine or public health. The result was the Abortion Act 1967.

The Abortion Act 1967

The Abortion Act 1967, which began its life with the far more appropriate title of the Medical Termination of Pregnancy Bill, has been under attack since it came into force. On the one hand, criticism has come from what has become known as the 'pro-life' movement, on the grounds that its terms are too liberal; on the other, it is said by the 'pro-choice' group to pay too little regard to the rights of women to control their own bodies and to place too much social power in the hands of the medical profession. The debate has, however, been conducted in a relatively calm atmosphere and the Act stood unmodified until 1990, when a number of significant amendments were introduced by the Human Fertilisation and Embryology Act. Several of these will be discussed in the text below. For present purposes, it is merely noted that the most important are, firstly, the general removal of the restrictions on late terminations previously imposed by the Infant Life (Preservation) Act, 1929[31] and, secondly, their replacement by a 24-week gestation limit in relation to s.1(1)(a) – see below.

It is important to appreciate that the 1967 Act is not the definitive law on abortion in Great Britain. It does no more than specify the circumstances in which it will not be unlawful for an abortion to be performed. From this point of view, the important part of the Act is contained in s.1(1)(*a*)–(*d*) which runs:

> a person shall not be guilty of an offence under the law relating to abortion when a pregnancy is terminated by a registered medical

practitioner if two registered medical practitioners are of the opinion, formed in good faith –

(a)   that the pregnancy has not exceeded the twenty-fourth week and that the continuance of the pregnancy would involve risk, greater than if the pregnancy were terminated, of injury to the physical or mental health of the pregnant woman or any existing children of her family; or

(b)   that the termination is necessary to prevent grave permanent injury to the physical or mental health of the pregnant woman; or

(c)   that the continuance of the pregnancy would involve risk to the life of the pregnant woman, greater than if the pregnancy were terminated;[32] or

(d)   that there is a substantial risk that if the child were born it would suffer from such physical or mental abnormalities as to be seriously handicapped.

There are, therefore, four grounds for a lawful abortion which can be summarised in convenient shorthand: to save the life of the pregnant woman – the life-saving ground; to avoid serious permanent damage to the health of the pregnant woman – the preventive ground; to obviate adverse affects of relatively minor severity on the woman or on the existing family – the social ground; or to forestall the birth of a defective infant – the eugenic ground. These are often divided into what are described as the maternal grounds (the first three) and the fetal ground (the last), but this is a misconception. The 'fetal' ground is directed to the effects on the mother resulting from the birth of a defective child; fetal rights are not involved and the importance of this distinction will be apparent at many points in the discussion which follows. At the same time, it has to be emphasised that, in British law, the decision to terminate a pregnancy is a *medical* one; the pregnant woman may, of course, give or withhold consent to the operation, but nowhere does the Act empower her to authorise the termination of pregnancy. In this respect, the British indications for therapeutic termination are certainly less liberal than are those, say, in the United States. It has, in fact, been pointed out that, were the United Kingdom to be part of the United States, the restrictions of the 1967 Act would be sufficient to render it unconstitutional.[33]

Nonetheless, a moment's reflection reveals that the terms are, in fact, extremely wide, particularly in relation to s.1(1)(*a*) where there is no indication of 'serious' risk such as has been suggested in the Australian courts as being a desirable criterion. The test is simply one of comparison with non-termination. Given that she is actively seeking termination, it is difficult to see how the fact of motherhood could not have a *relatively* adverse mental effect on the woman concerned; and, in the absence of a cornucopian supply of plenty, it is inconceivable that the arrival of a sibling would not have a greater effect on the existing family than would its non-arrival. Such academic considerations surface at their most acute in respect of termination on the grounds of fetal sex, of which a spokesman of the British Medical Association is reported as saying: 'To terminate a pregnancy solely on the grounds of the sex of the foetus is an abuse of medical skills. It is unethical and I believe the GMC should take a serious view ... [of] a doctor who undertakes that sort of work.'[34] But consider the woman of several ethnic minorities who is expected to produce a male child but is pregnant with a third female; there can be no doubt that both her physical and mental health are at risk – and particularly when it is remembered that s.1(2) of the 1967 Act states: 'In determining whether the continuance of a pregnancy would involve such risk of injury to health ... account may be taken of the pregnant woman's actual or reasonably foreseeable environment.'

Even the Caucasian Englishwoman may be happy, say, to produce a first daughter, but will be unwilling to jeopardise the family finances by the birth of a fourth son. Abortion on the grounds of sex may well be unethical, and ecologically unsound, but it is certainly not illegal. On strictly medical grounds, the dangers of pregnancy and those of termination depend to an extent on the age and parity of the pregnant woman and the length of the gestation. Nevertheless, there would be few obstetricians who would deny that, *in general*, the risks to the health of a woman who carries a baby to full term and undergoes labour are greater than are those of an early termination; from which it follows that the mere *fact* of pregnancy is sufficient justification for its legal termination on social grounds.

Extrapolating one step further, it is difficult to see how it is possible now to perform an unlawful abortion in Great Britain provided the administrative conditions of the Act and its associated regulations are observed. Within that envelope, the sole restraints on termination of early pregnancy lie in the words 'in good faith'. But even this term is surprisingly devoid of meaning. In the first place, a decision can be taken in good faith notwithstanding that it is unreasonable. More significantly, if the reasoning in the preceding paragraphs is accepted, it follows that a decision under the Act cannot be taken in bad faith: it is a refusal to terminate which requires explanation and this lends special importance to the 'conscience clause' (s.4) which is discussed further below.

Thus, since there is, in effect, now no legal objection to abortion when performed by registered medical practitioners, opposition must be based on the presumption that the morality of the law is flawed and that the balance between maternal and fetal rights has been distorted. This presumption needs to be examined but, first, it is useful to consider the parallel evolution of the law elsewhere.

The Comparative Scene

Northern Ireland   The situation in Northern Ireland requires explanation as the Offences Against the Person Act, 1861 applies to, but the Abortion Act 1967 does not run to, that part of the United Kingdom; s.37 of the Human Fertilisation and Embryology Act 1990 is also excluded. On the other hand, the terms of the Infant Life (Preservation) Act, 1929 are repeated in the Criminal Justice Act (Northern Ireland), 1945, s.25. The position is, therefore, still governed by *R v. Bourne* as modified by the liberalising influences of the last half-century. The situation has been criticised as being unclear.[35] This is exemplified in the comparatively recent case of *Re K (a minor)*.[36] Here the High Court of Justice held that the law of Northern Ireland lay in the Offences Against the Person Act, 1861 and in the charge to the jury in *Bourne*. Termination of a 13 weeks' pregnancy in a ward of court was authorised; nevertheless, the patient was referred to England for the operation. Further clarification was provided by a second case,[37] in which a declaration was granted that it would be lawful to terminate the pregnancy of a severely mentally handicapped 24-year-old woman, the ratio lying in the patient's best interests. It was said that:

> For the purposes only of preserving the life of the mother, the Criminal Justice (N.I.) Act, 1945, s.25 does not relate to some life threatening situation only. Life in this context means the physical or mental health or well-being of the mother. Termination would not be unlawful if continued pregnancy would adversely affect the health of the mother. (Per MCDERMOTT LJ)

It is to be noted that the circumstances in this case were markedly less severe than they were in *Re K*. Thus the situation is broadly comparable to that pertaining in New South Wales. The proximity to the Republic of Ireland imposes an element of particular sensitivity on the issue.

The Republic of Ireland   Therapeutic termination is legal in the Republic of Ireland only in the strictest circumstances involving the life of the pregnant woman and it is said that a large number of Irishwomen travel to Great Britain for the purpose. The legality of such travel has been questioned and it has been held that no general right exists, despite the fact that a majority of the Irish people support the right to both travel and information as to the availability of termination. The state's right to prohibit the dissemination of such information was at first upheld by the Court of Justice of the European Communities,[38] but this was later countered by the European Court of Human Rights.[39] The Supreme Court of Ireland has now extended the grounds for a legal termination to include instances where it is probable that there is a real and substantial risk to the life of the mother.[40] It seems likely that Irish law will become rather more inclined to acknowledge the rights of the pregnant woman at the expense of those of the fetus but improbable that it will approach that of Britain in the foreseeable future.

Germany　The history of abortion legislation in Germany is singled out for mention not as an example of European Community law but, rather, as an example of the way constitutional and common law can conflict on the issue. Abortion law was isolated as the only exception to the general rule that western institutional and legislative experience should be applied to East Germany on reunification of the country in 1990. At that time, abortion was effectively at the demand of the pregnant woman in the first 12 weeks of pregnancy in East Germany; by contrast, the operation was illegal in the Federal Republic, save in conditions which depended, in large part, on the 'stage of the fetus'; interestingly, however, the termination rates in the two jurisdictions were very much the same. Even so, the seeds of conflict were sown and germinated in an atmosphere increasingly dominated by the concept of abortion as a means of social engineering rather than as a matter of women's rights.[41]

Two years later, the federal parliament legislated for abortion by choice during the first three months of pregnancy subject to social counselling, but the Constitutional Court ruled this to be contrary to German basic law insofar as it failed to meet the minimum standards for the protection of unborn human life as set out in the Constitution. It was then proposed that consensual abortion within the first trimester would remain illegal but that no prosecution would follow its being carried out provided the woman had been counselled independently.[42] This remarkable example of pragmatic prevaricaton – which appears to be a relatively common feature of Continental European jurisdictions[43] – has only recently been approved by the Bundestag but, even today, attempts are being made to limit its effect.[44] Perhaps the most interesting feature of this controversy has been the recognition in the German Constitution of a fetal right to life in the very early stages of development.

The American approach　The American experience still merits consideration as its evolution dominates the rhetoric of abortion. Prior to 1973, the states of America had various laws as regards abortion. Some, for example those of California, were restrictive; others, including those in New York, were extremely liberal. The majority essentially represented variations on the theme of the English Infant

Life (Preservation) Act, 1929 which allowed for some fetal rights even when these clashed with those of the pregnant woman. Citizens' rights in the United States are, however, enshrined in the Constitution, which is silent as to the position of the fetus and it was on constitutional grounds that restrictive abortion laws were attacked. This resulted in the historic twin decisions in *Roe* v. *Wade* and *Doe* v. *Bolton*,[45] the effect of which was to concentrate on the woman's constitutional right to privacy, one aspect of which is a right of access to termination of pregnancy. In essence, the Supreme Court held that a woman had an unfettered right to abortion in the first trimester of pregnancy; the state could intervene in decision making in the second trimester, but only on behalf of the pregnant woman: the state could, for example, stipulate that a termination was carried out in 'hospital' conditions; intervention on behalf of the fetus was permissible only in the third trimester and this, in turn, depended upon its 'viability'. The Supreme Court was not prepared to define viability but placed it at between 24 and 28 weeks' gestation; the definition, it was said, was essentially a medical one, to be made in individual cases, although it will be argued later that this can hardly be more than a reasonable guess which must be conditioned by the intentions of the physicians involved.

The most obvious feature of the *Roe* v. *Wade* decision is the virtual dismissal of fetal rights. As an immediate commentator put it, 'the Constitution does not confer legal personality on the unborn'.[46] The judicial opinion pays no regard to the quite distinct problems surrounding fetal defect, which seems to be a universal failing of courts and legislatures. The court's concentration on the 'privacy' doctrine has also been persistently attacked by those who see the fetus as a right-possessing human being. Nevertheless, the Supreme Court reaffirmed its decision in 1986:

> The Constitution embodies a promise that a certain private sphere of individual liberty will be kept largely beyond the reach of government. That promise extends to women as well as to men ... A woman's right to make that choice [to end her pregnancy] freely is fundamental. Any other result, in our view, would protect inadequately a central part of the sphere of liberty that our law guarantees to all.[47]

As we have seen, however, the abortion issue in the United States is very highly charged and, consequent upon a change in the personnel of the Supreme Court, the status quo was challenged yet again, this time by the state of Missouri, where the relevant but unimplemented law, in addition to declaring that life begins at conception, sought, *inter alia*, to emphasise the state's interest in the well-being of the fetus. The result of the hearing satisfied neither party insofar as the court was unwilling to overturn the principles laid down in *Roe* but, nevertheless, held that a state statute which limited the availability of abortion was constitutionally valid.[48] The long-running battle continues and the Supreme Court was again invited to consider the legality of a state statute in 1992,[49] this time in Pennsylvania, where the Abortion Control Act 1982 attempted to limit the trend towards abortion at the demand of the pregnant woman. The contrasting principles here were, on the one hand, a woman's right to bodily privacy and, on the other, the state's interest in the protection of life and a preference for childbirth over abortion. The compromise adopted was to empower the state to erect barriers to abortion provided these did not impose a substantial obstacle to, or an undue burden on, a woman choosing to terminate her pregnancy. In this way, the woman's right to freedom of conscience and bodily integrity were maintained while, at the same time, some fetal rights – especially those in respect of the viable fetus – were protected. Once again, the decision, by a bare majority, pleased no-one,[50] and the American debate is likely to continue in an atmosphere of increasing politicisation of what is, essentially, a moral issue.

Other jurisdictions It would be impossible in a book of this type to undertake an exhaustive review of national abortion laws throughout the world. Knoppers[51] has set out the various judicial and other restrictions placed on available abortion facilities; she has also considered the constraints imposed by way of medical qualification, the place of abortion, methods of approval and imposed delays. It is probably fair to say, however, that the practice of abortion is ultimately decided by the religious and social attitudes of the particular medical profession which is responsible for the implementation of the law. The potentiality for conflict has been demonstrated in Canada, where control of abortion was, at one time, vested in hospital abortion committees.[52] The Supreme Court, however, ultimately ruled that this violated the security and liberty of the pregnant woman: 'Forcing a woman, by threat of criminal sanction, to carry a fetus to term unless she meets certain criteria unrelated to her own priorities and aspirations, is a profound interference with a woman's body and thus a violation of security of the person.'[53] To eliminate any possible doubt, it was held, at much the same time, that the fetus was not protected by the Canadian Charter of Rights and Freedom[54] and, although it was held that the provincial Charter of Rights of Quebec did provide such protection to a 20-week fetus, that interpretation was rapidly reversed by the Supreme Court of Canada.[55]

Thus it seems that the 'pro-choice' lobby, inspired by the concept of women's rights, is dominant across the Atlantic despite being subject to relentless attack; in Europe, access to termination of pregnancy is, in practice, relatively open in the first 12 weeks of gestation but later is constrained by regulations of varying severity; very few apposite cases come to the courts in the United Kingdom but, when they do, the judiciary adopts a pro-fetus view, and it is suggested that this tendency is increasing. The validity of this belief is considered in the next chapter.

The conflict of interests

It is glaringly apparent that abortion develops parallel and conflicting interests. Those who maintain that fetal life is human life will hold that abortion is basically immoral and is to be equated with legitimised murder on the grand scale; at the other end of the spectrum stand those who hold that the autonomous woman has a right to dispose of her own body as she chooses and that this right extends to choosing whether or not to procreate. There are very few who would attempt to deny this proposition as it relates to sexual abstinence or contraception – or, come to that, the right to homosexual relationships. To extend the right to abortion is, however, to include a right to the destruction of what is, at a minimum, living cellular tissue of the genus *homo sapiens*. Proponents of the two extremes are unlikely to agree. The Vatican position is intransigent as, indeed, it *must* be once the philosophy of the sanctity of human life from the time of conception is adopted: it is illogical to think of liberalising abortion *within* the envelope of existing Roman Catholic faith.[56] As to the other side, Callahan has pointed out that 'the prochoice movement in its most political manifestation … has never made sufficient room in its public stance for a serious consideration of the fetus.'[57] Yet, try as one may, the difficulties of reaching a middle position which is *morally* defensible are almost overwhelming. Given the premise that the implanted fetus has humanity, it is impossible to maintain that one of 12 weeks' age is any less human than is one of 20 weeks' gestation: 'the progress from the basic skeletal structure and emergence of internal organs at around 8 weeks to viability about 20 weeks later is a smooth and steady maturation process'.[58] Equally, once one assumes that abortion is acceptable on the grounds that pregnancy may be injurious to a woman's health, it is hard to see why an adverse effect on her social conditions is any less of a justification; indeed, the two conditions are hardly separable. Any attempt to reconcile the 'pro-life' and 'pro-choice' pressure groups must rest on a pragmatic rather than a deontological basis.[59] Such a pragmatic argument could be based on an increase in fetal rights which may arise with maturity – an application of the 'gradualist' theory of humanity. This is the route which will be taken here but, first, we must look at the alternative, maternally based view.

The rights of the pregnant woman

In its extreme form, the 'pro-choice' ethos is founded on the concept of self-defence: that is, that a woman is entitled to defend herself against an intruder who threatens her in some way. This is a thoroughly acceptable position when the pregnant woman's life is at stake, but it needs deeper analysis when the 'threat' is refined further so as to include one aimed at an undefined state of health or social security.

There can be no doubting that the extent of a self-defensive action is, in law, restricted by the extent of the aggressive action. It is a well-established legal principle that violence used in self-defence must be commensurate with the danger of the situation. It seems to follow that, since feticide is an inevitable accompaniment of early abortion, it cannot be justified, say, on the basis of a threat to one's convenience. This argument depends, however, on accepting that the fetus has rights of its own and the ambivalence of the law in this area will be discussed in Chapter 6. Equally importantly, the use of force in self-defence can only be *morally* justified on the grounds of evil intent on the part of the assailant,[60] and it is difficult to see how such an accusation can be levied against the fetus – save, perhaps, in the context of the fetus being derived from, say, rape.[61] If it is so raised, it is a self-defeating contention, in that it implies a will and a personality in the fetus which *must*, then, be accorded rights.

A rather less robust variation on the theme is that, irrespective of the 'rape' scenario, the fetus may be occupying an unwilling host; if the woman has a right to ownership of her body, she then has a right to reject an occupant of her body irrespective of its own right to personhood.[62] This approach has the merit of defining the fetal status in basic terms of invitation. A fetus which has been willingly conceived can be said to be neither aggressive nor unwanted and, accordingly, has a right of occupation. By contrast, given the fact that the couple have used adequate contraceptive methods, they may reasonably reject an unwanted result. A further attraction of this proposition is that it introduces the concept of responsibility and disallows the assumption that an intention to seek abortion, should the need eventuate, is an acceptable routine method of family planning. Unfortunately, and paradoxically, it not only places contraception and abortion on the same moral plane but also fails to answer the problem of the woman who takes no precaution against conception; the logical corollary would be to punish the reckless woman with gestation and motherhood – and this is clearly unacceptable.

The difficulty with the 'pro-choice' stance is that, rather than concentrate on the woman's right not to become pregnant – with which only the ultra-conservative moralist would disagree – it insists on the right not to remain pregnant, or, effectively, on the right to feticide. This is the potentially offensive aspect of abortion which carries with it some worrying extrapolations. It has been pointed out, for example, that there is not a massive difference between being inconvenienced by a fetus and being inconvenienced by a child.[63]

Nevertheless, the overriding rights of the pregnant woman are widely accepted and are particularly guarded by the American courts. In the United States, the Supreme Court, among other decisions, has held statutes to be unconstitutional which mandate that a pregnant woman should be advised of the alternatives to abortion; this was on the grounds that it is a poorly disguised attempt to discourage the abortion decision and that such instructions pose an unacceptable danger of deterring the exercise of a woman's right to end a pregnancy.[64] There is no evidence that the British courts would go, or, indeed, have the power to go, to such lengths. It will, however, be seen in the next section that, despite some evidence of distaste for the operation, there is no legal movement to interfere with the increasingly liberal provision of abortion services.

At the same time, the courts on both sides of the Atlantic strongly uphold the right of a woman to refuse abortion. Thus, in England, it was held that the courts 'should never have to declare that a woman ought to have an abortion,'[65] while, in the United States, it has been said that: 'the right to have an abortion may not be automatically converted into an obligation to have one'.[66]

Abortion in practice

It is probable that the original drafters of what was finally called the Abortion Bill intended to do no more than to contain the number of illegal abortions which were being performed at the time and, simultaneously, to provide relief for those who were apparently precluded from a termination of a pregnancy which was manifestly undesirable. We have seen that, by 1967, the latter were largely protected under the *Bourne* doctrine; published figures indicate that, by 1963, some 2 per cent of women in a middle-of-the-road Scottish city were provided with abortion facilities.[67] The probable expectation was, therefore, that there would be a sharp increase in the number of *notified* terminations but that this would achieve a generally acceptable plateau within a few years.

If this be so, the facts belie the expectations. The number of legal terminations increased annually and reached a peak in 1990, when nearly 187 000 terminations were performed in England and Wales. The first fall since 1967 occurred in 1991, when the total number of legal terminations was 179 522, giving a rate for resident women of

13.06:1000 women in the age group 14–49.[68] The similar figures for 1993 were 168 714, giving a rate of 12.3:1000, in England and Wales, and 11 069 with a rate of 10:1000 women aged 15–44 for Scotland, where there has been no comparable fall in either the number or rate of legal terminations. The greatest concentration of terminations has always lain in the age group 16–24 years, followed closely by those aged 25–29.

Whatever status is allotted to the fetus – and *some* degree of humanness must be conceded even by the most dedicated supporter of women's rights – this represents a remarkable toll of living human tissue. The figures, coupled with the noticeably low-key objections in the United Kingdom, indicate a general public acceptance of abortion as part of the natural way of life. It is the shift in attitudes of the medical profession, however, that is of greater interest to one who practised before 1967. All attempts made by politicians of a 'pro-life' persuasion to stem the increase in terminations have been firmly resisted by the medical establishment. Indeed, the major medical criticism these days is to the effect that terminations are unduly restricted and should be available on demand – at least in the first trimester.[69]

Even if facilities for abortion are inadequate, which is an unusual criticism coming from a body of professionals which adheres, at least by implication, to the principle of 'maintaining the utmost respect for human life from the time of conception',[70] room is, nevertheless found for a substantial number of abortions to be performed on foreign women in England and Wales.[71] Admittedly, all but a handful of these are performed in private clinics and it is in this area that abuses of the Act, if there are any, are likely to be found. Proof of abuse is almost impossible to adduce and, indeed, it has been suggested that any dubious practices in the private sector could not be controlled legally without, at the same time, imposing crippling restrictions on *bona fide* clinical decisions.

Whether or not there are contraventions of the Act, there is certainly very little evidence of them to be found in the criminal courts. As far as can be seen, there has been only one successful prosecution of a doctor for contravening the 1967 Act,[72] and this was on the basis of how, rather than why, the operation was performed. Relatively recently, a doctor who removed a uterus containing an 11-week fetus during an exploratory laparotomy was charged under the Offences Against the Person Act, 1861, s.58; his defence rested on the provisions of the Abortion Act 1967, s.1(4) which allow for a termination on the recommendation of a single doctor when it is immediately necessary in order to save the life of or to prevent grave permanent injury to the physical or mental health of the pregnant woman; he was acquitted.[73] Actions through the General Medical Council are also very few. Only two apposite cases have been discovered: in one,[74] a finding of serious professional misconduct on account of advertising abortion services was quashed by the Privy Council; the other resulted in suspension from the register for 12 months but was more a matter of industrial relations than of medical ethics.[75] There have been no cases reported in the Council's annual reports since 1981.

Parliamentary evidence of dissatisfaction with the Abortion Act 1967 has been largely concentrated on its wide terms. Nevertheless, despite repeated attack, the Act remained unamended until 1990, when some changes were admitted in order to ensure the passage of the Human Fertilisation and Embryology Act. The main concession to the 'pro-life' supporters, introduced in s.37 of the 1990 Act, was to reduce the fetal age beyond which a termination would not be legal on what we have called the social ground from 28 to 24 weeks' gestation – this, in itself, being a compromise with the original demand for a limit of 18 weeks. At the same time, all timeous limit was removed in the case of termination on the eugenic ground. The result can therefore be seen as a Pyrrhic victory for both 'sides' – or, better, as a victory for common sense in the face of rapidly improving therapeutic and diagnostic expertise. It is currently possible for fetuses of 24 or even fewer weeks' gestation to be born alive and to be 'viable' given adequate intensive care facilities, while several techniques capable of demonstrating fetal handicap may not, in practice, be completed within a specified timescale (see Chapter 6).

Other people's rights

The father

Many would think that the father, who contributes half the genetic foundation of the fetus and who is, surely, entitled to paternal ambitions, would have some rights over the abortion of his child. This has, however, been consistently denied in the great majority of English-speaking jurisdictions.

In the United States, a long series of decisions was consolidated in *Casey*,[76] in which notification of the husband was the only one of a list of fairly restrictive conditions which was found to be unacceptable to the Supreme Court. In England, an attempt by a father to prevent an abortion in 1979 was firmly rejected by the Family Court.[77] A second, and inevitably doomed, attempt was made in 1987[78] in which the father could not even claim to be the 'legitimate' parent; indeed, the decision against the father was not even appealed. This may have been due mainly to the force of the European decision which followed an appeal in *Paton*.[79] The European Court was in no doubt that the rights of the pregnant woman were supreme, at least insofar as the pre-viable fetus was concerned. The court was undecided, and was clearly relieved not to be called upon to decide, what the position might be in relation to a viable fetus. This question has still not been addressed in England as, in *C* v. *S*, the fetus was concurrently declared to be non-viable. Even so, it is unlikely that the gestatitional age of the fetus would influence a decision based only on the wishes of the father; logically, the rights of the pregnant woman are subject to modification only by the increasing rights of the fetus as it ages.

The supremacy of the woman's rights appears to have been challenged least unsuccessfully in Canada, where a guardian, albeit not the father, has been appointed to represent the fetus in an abortion situation.[80] A husband was given standing to seek an injunction against his wife having an abortion in *Medhurst* v. *Medhurst*;[81] despite manifest sympathy on the part of the court, he was found to have no capacity to act as the next friend of the fetus. The nearest a father has come to recognised 'rights' in respect of a fetus was in *Tremblay* v. *Daigle*, when the Quebec Court of Appeal granted the father an interlocutory injunction to prevent an abortion. The arguments were, however, largely constitutional in respect of Federal and Provincial Charters of Human Rights and, as already noted, the decision was struck down forcefully by the Supreme Court of Canada.[82]

It is difficult not to feel sympathy for the father of the child in these circumstances. As it was said in *Medhurst*, 'The husband could suffer real injury of a particularly agonising kind.'[83] At first glance, it is also difficult to understand the legal contrast between the father's rights as regards his developing child – which are nil – and those in respect of his cryopreserved embryo – which are co-equal with those of its mother (see p. 236). It cannot, however, be denied that it is the woman who carries the child for nine months and who risks her health in so doing and it is, no doubt, this factor which carries the greatest weight with those who make the rules. Even so, some allowance should surely be made for the *reason* for the abortion. There is a world of difference between, on the one hand, grave danger to a woman's health and, on the other, some of the relatively trivial reasons for termination which will still satisfy the conditions of the Abortion Act 1967. It is suggested that more consideration might well be given to the hurt done to a man whose fatherhood is denied in the latter circumstances.

The professionals

It is surprising that so much attention has been paid to the religious and moral aspects of abortion yet so little has focused on the medical ethos. Both the Hippocratic Oath and the Declaration of Geneva specifically proscribe the destruction of life after conception and it is, therefore, essential that some exemption is available to the doctor who maintains a Hippocratic conscience. This is to be found in s4 of the 1967 Act, which allows for conscientious objection to taking part in the procedure.[84]

The privilege is, however, tightly circumscribed. In the first place, the doctor or nurse in England and Wales must prove his or her conscientious status.[85] Secondly, the exception does not apply if the life of the pregnant women is in issue or if there is a grave danger to her health (s.4(2)). Thirdly, the section does not absolve the doctor from his duty of care to the patient. Other than in the circumstances noted above, the doctor need not carry out or certify a termination but, in the event that a woman wants the operation and that there is a reasonable expectation that the legal grounds are satisfied, the doctor cannot give advice which is contrary to the patient's benefit; the normal rules concerning medical negligence pertain. There is no legitimate alternative to referring the patient to a colleague in the event that she wishes to proceed. Paradoxically, therefore, the doctor who has such an objection is at some professional disadvantage. He or she may be shunned in general practice and, inevitably, will not now be able to specialise in obstetrics and gynaecology. The disadvantage is, perhaps, even more apparent in the case of nurses who, as Lord Denning pointed out,[86] are expected to be mobile throughout the hospital system. Moreover, in modern conditions of termination, the nursing staff are particularly exposed to the more disturbing aspects of abortion.[87] It could well be that this was a major underlying cause of the action *Royal College of Nursing of the United Kingdom v. Department of Health and Social Security.*[88]

Essentially, this action turned on whether or not a nurse carrying out the procedure for a prostaglandin termination – or abortion by means of intravenous or intrauterine infusion of abortifacient hormones – was acting legally as had been intimated in the instructions from the Department of Health and Social Security;[89] the alternative view was that the nurses who were carrying out the procedure were not registered medical practitioners and were, accordingly, in breach of the Abortion Act 1967, s.1(1). The Royal College sought to have the question clarified by inviting the court to declare the Department's instructions to be wrong in law. The judge at first instance saw the procedure as being similar to that involved in a normal birth in which the nurse was fully qualified to carry out the doctor's instructions. Provided that a registered medical practitioner initiated and was responsible for the conduct of the termination, it was he who carried out the *treatment*, despite the fact that the nurses played the major part in the process. The judgment included a positive statement that the 'conscience clause' extended to nurses, and also looked to the future where abortion might be initiated by taking a pill[90] – such an action would result from a doctor's opinion and prescription and would, therefore, not contravene the law.

The Court of Appeal rejected this unanimously, but was then overruled in a 3:2 majority decision in the House of Lords. The dissenting view followed that expressed by BRIGHTMAN LJ in the Court of Appeal, that the true analysis was that the doctor provided the nurse with the means to terminate the pregnancy, not that the doctor terminated the pregnancy. The majority, however, took the broader view that the doctor

> should carry out any physical acts, forming part of the treatment, that in accordance with accepted medical practice are done only by qualified medical practitioners and should give specific instructions as to the carrying out of such parts of the treatment as ... are carried out by nurses or other members of the hospital staff. ... The requirements of the subsection are satisfied when the ... medical practitioner remains in charge throughout. (Per LORD DIPLOCK at 829)

Termination of pregnancy is, therefore, a team effort, but the extent of that team has yet to be defined. Thus, in the case of Mrs Janaway,[91] both the Court of Appeal and the House of Lords upheld the decision that a general practitioner's secretary, who was required by her employment to type a letter of referral to a specialist for a possible termination of pregnancy, was not excused from her contract of work by virtue of her conscientious objection to abortion. The decision in the Court of Appeal was based on the complementary nature of ss.1(1) and 4(1) from which it was inferred that the 'conscience clause' was there for the protection only of those whose actions would have been criminal prior to the enforcement of the 1967 Act. The House of Lords, however, reverted to principle in holding that 'treatment', which is the subject of the conscience clause, is something which occurs in a hospital environment; it was further considered that the parliamentary insertion of the word 'treatment' was intentional. Even so, *Janaway* does not end the matter. A secretary is clearly not part of the treatment team, but what of the hospital porter? What is the position of the pharmacist, either within the hospital or in general practice, in the not improbable event that medical abortion becomes available on a doctor's prescription?[92] This is not the only area in which it is possible to agree with Lord Diplock's comment on the 1967 Act, which resulted from a Private Member's Bill: 'It lacks that style and consistency of draftsmanship both internal to the Act itself and in relation to other statutes which one would expect to find in legislation that had its origin in the office of parliamentary counsel.'[93]

Abortion and minors

While an abortion may now have a minimal physical morbidity, the psychological effects can be profound; an abortion involving a minor is, therefore, a very serious matter. The decision whether to terminate or not is one which must be taken relatively often: there were 3437 legal terminations in England and Wales involving resident girls below the age of 16 in 1994. All but 114 were justified on the 'social' ground, but the ethico-legal basis for such decision making merits consideration.

There is no reason to suppose that consent to abortion by minors below the age of 16 lies outside the general umbrella provided by the *Gillick* decision (see p. 53).[94] That being so, considerable maturity will be required of a minor before such a decision can be taken without parental consent. The number of 'schoolgirl' abortions is such as to suggest that the criteria laid down in *Gillick* cannot always be fulfilled. But this is not to suggest that these operations are either criminal, tortious or professionally unethical. Termination of pregnancy is unusual insofar as it is one of the very few 'therapies' which are controlled by statute. The Abortion Act 1967 is silent as to age and all case law points to the inviolate rights of the pregnant woman as to her relationship with her physician. Confidentiality in the doctor/ patient relationship must be particularly imperative in this situation and there seems to be no overwhelming reason why a doctor *should* have to obtain consent to termination from anyone other than the pregnant girl herself, so long as the conditions of the 1967 Act, s.1(1) and Lord Fraser's criteria, suitably modified, are met (see p. 55).[95]

It is, however, very difficult in practice to diagnose pregnancy and to perform a legal abortion on a schoolgirl without parental knowledge and it must be that the pregnancy is terminated at the request of both the pregnant girl and her parents in the great majority of cases. Difficulties arise only when there is a difference of opinion between them and, here, the English law has to be considered in two parts, according to whether the minor is aged above or below 16 years. Consent to medical treatment of the former is governed by the Family Law Reform Act 1969, s.8, which has been discussed briefly in Chapter 3. Insofar as s.8(1) refers to consent to 'treatment', its application to abortion depends upon the recognition of abortion as a medical treatment. It is incontestably so in respect of ss.1(1)(*b*) and (*c*) but that holds less certainly as to ss.1(1)(*a*) and (*d*). The matter is probably settled by the fact that, whatever the reason for the termination, its legality rests on the opinion of two *medical* practitioners and is, accordingly, something to which the 16-year-old can legally consent; the issue is, in practice, almost certainly a matter of pedantry only but it is, nevertheless, suggested as deserving of note by those who campaign for the demedicalisation of abortion.[96]

The position when there is conflict between parents and a mature child below the age of 16 has been clouded to an extent by the Court of Appeal decision in *Re R*,[97] which was the first case to test the general application of the *Gillick* principles. The cases are discussed in Chapter 12; for the present, it need only be said that the Master of the Rolls held that, while the mature minor could legally consent to medical and surgical treatment, the parallel parental right to consent remained: it was only the parental right to determine, and, with it, the right to veto, treatment of the minor that was extinguished by *Gillick*. Thus, assuming, again, that termination of pregnancy is medical treatment, a parent *could* consent to an abortion were a so-called '*Gillick*-competent' minor refusing to do so. This, however, would do no more than protect a doctor against a later accusation of assault; there is no concurrent obligation on him or her to act on that consent and, save in truly life-threatening conditions, it is difficult to imagine him or her doing so or of the court imposing an abortion on a child who wished to keep her fetus: the opinion given in the adult case of *Emeh*[98] would surely be adopted.

The opposite situation – where the prospective grandparents wish to keep the baby alive – is far more probable, but the same principles would apply. Thus, in theory, the mature minor's decision would empower the doctor to proceed with a termination; in practice, he or she would probably be rash to do so without the sanction of the court.[99] Having done so, the court would almost certainly support the pregnant minor once it was satisfied as to her maturity. The established English precedent is *Re P*.[100] In that case, a 15-year-old girl was pregnant for the second time and her parents were prepared to care for the baby when it was born. In authorising the termination, BUTLER-SLOSS J said: 'I am satisfied she wants this abortion; she understands the implications of it. Indeed she went so far as to say she will feel guilty about it later – after it happens – but that she will live with the guilt of it as she is very anxious it should happen.'

In effect, therefore, the judge pre-empted the *Gillick* decision by several years. Her ruling as to the termination has not been challenged in the courts and has been followed more recently. The 12-year-old girl who was the subject of *Re B*[101] was of normal intelligence and sought a termination of pregnancy which was opposed by her mother. The local authority caused her to be made a ward of court and applied to the court for a termination on grounds of health; the court was, thus, bound to approach the matter on the basis of the ward's best interests. In the course of allowing the application, HOLLIS J had this to say:

The court ... has been called in in this case to make the decision on the principle that the interests of the ward are first and paramount. Thus, it seems to me that the ward's wishes are not decisions but are, in my view, a part of the evidence which it is important to take into consideration ... [The expert for the mother] was clearly putting the interests of the foetus, and not the ward, as first and paramount. (At 429 and 431)

Thus, although *Re P* and *Re B* were decided on different bases, the cases together make it clear that the courts are unlikely to support the concept of childhood maternity without very good reason. Some idea of the depth of feeling is given by the fact that termination was authorised in the case of *Re B* on medical grounds despite the fact that the girl was 20 weeks' pregnant – at which time the hazards of termination could be considerable.

Abortion and the mentally handicapped

Very similar problems arise in the case of the pregnant and mentally handicapped woman, but this situation is more complicated in at least two ways. Firstly, judicial powers to intervene on behalf of a handicapped person aged more than 18 years are severely limited in the absence of a clear *parens patriae* jurisdiction in England and Wales.[102] Secondly, the statutory licence to treat a person who is compulsorily detained under the Mental Health Act 1983 or the Mental Health (Scotland) Act 1984 without the consent of the patient is confined to treatment of the mental condition which has led to detention. Not only is this therapeutically restrictive, but it is also difficult at times to distinguish between physical treatment and treatment which is directed to alleviation of the mental state.[103] This dilemma is well illustrated in the context of abortion. Thus there are many, including the present writer, who would see an unsought and possibly uncomprehended pregnancy as being inevitably harmful to an existing abnormal mental state; termination of the pregnancy could, thus, be fully justified as *preventive* mental therapy. On the other hand, it has been said that the argument that abortion could be looked on as *treatment* for the woman's mental disorder is one which would be 'alarming to most people and clearly not within the contemplation of the legislation'.[104]

The moral difficulties are similar in quality to those which have already been discussed in respect of sterilisation (Chapter 4). They are different in degree insofar as abortion should not deprive a woman permanently of her ability to procreate. Generalisations are, however, inappropriate to the topic. Whether or not a particular mentally handicapped woman will benefit from a non-consensual termination of pregnancy and whether or not such a procedure is an unacceptable infringement of her bodily privacy must depend upon the facts of the *individual* case, including, most importantly, the degree and the effect of the mental handicap which is present.

One suspects that many such non-consensual terminations have been carried out in the past by doctors who have depended upon the support of the twin pillars of clinical good faith and the legal doctrine of necessity – and, indeed, this is probably the preferred option.[105] Equally, judicial decisions may have been taken in privacy; it is, perhaps, significant that, in an early case involving an adult, the judge is reported as saying he did not know how the details of the application had become known.[106] This case concerned a mentally handicapped woman, aged 25, who was 20 weeks pregnant. Faced with an urgent decision, LATEY J was not concerned to investigate the residuum of his *parens patriae* powers – which are now known not to exist[107] – but, rather, made a simple declaration that an abortion would not be an unlawful act on the doctor's part; it is interesting that the case was considered to be of such urgency that the judge was willing to ignore the fact that the application was wrongly brought under the wardship jurisdiction.

Two further cases followed hard upon this. In the first of these,[108] REEVE J made a declaration[109] that it would not be unlawful to carry out an operation for the termination of a defendant's pregnancy by reason only of her lack of capacity to give informed consent for the operation. The limited nature of the decision is emphasised by the specific exclusion of the terms of the Infant Life (Preservation) Act, 1929 and the Abortion Act 1967 from the ratio: meeting the statutory requirements was considered to be a matter for clinical judgment. The second case, *T* v. *T*,[110] also illustrated the judicial dilemma posed by the repeal of the *parens patriae* powers and has already been discussed in Chapter 4.

The English law in this area, however, has now been relatively clarified. In *Re SG (adult mental patient: abortion)*,[111] SIR STEPHEN BROWN P discussed, particularly, whether abortion was a procedure of a 'special category' which always required court approval when the patient was unable to consent to or refuse treatment. He pointed out that abortion differed from sterilisation in that the former is closely regulated by statute; thus the doctor does not require any further safeguards. So long as the conditions of the Abortion Act 1967, s.1 are complied with, a formal declaration is not required for this particular treatment (at 331). The general concern of the courts to distance themselves so far as is possible from 'good medical practice' is, therefore, confirmed. The problem has not been addressed specifically in Scotland, where it would be difficult to bring a case against a practitioner performing an abortion in such circumstances; in general, a lack of evil intent on the part of the doctor would be presumed.

Reduction of multiple pregnancy and selective reduction

It will be seen in Chapter 9 that modern treatments for infertility or childlessness often result in numerically undesirable multiple pregnancies and their management is probably best discussed under the heading of the infertile woman. For some time, there was doubt as to whether the deliberate reduction of the pregnancy was legal, the main reason being that feticide for this purpose leaves the woman still pregnant, whereas the Abortion Act speaks of the 'termination of pregnancy'.[112] The doubt has now been removed by the Human Fertilisation and Embryology Act 1990, s.37(5) which amends the Abortion Act 1967, s.5(2) so that, provided the grounds for abortion are present and can be applied to the individual fetus, the termination applies to that fetus rather than to the pregnancy as a whole. It is not difficult to interpret s.1 in this way. A woman's mental health or her foreseeable environment may well accommodate the arrival of twins, but is likely to suffer in the event of quintuplets being born; the same applies to her existing family in the rather unlikely event of there being any other children in the circumstances envisaged – and s.1(1)(*a*) is very certainly satisfied if the fetuses themselves are regarded as existing children of the family. Selective reduction, in which abnormal fetuses are removed as a matter of deliberate preference, now comes clearly under the umbrella of s.1(1)(*d*).

The downside of the legislation is that, given the very wide interpretation that can be applied to s.1(1)(*a*), it is now lawful to reduce, say, a twin pregnancy which has occurred naturally and without any medical intervention; while it is, perhaps, illogical to distinguish between abortion and selective abortion, it seems unlikely that the latter was included in Parliament's intentions.[113]

'Preventive' abortion

The legal position in respect of very early terminations of a prophylactic nature remains to be considered. The procedure of menstrual extraction or menstrual regulation has been mentioned above, on p. 60, from which it will be seen that it must be illegal unless it is performed within the terms of the Abortion Act 1967 and the Abortion Regulations 1991.[114] Even then, the legality is suspect firstly because, as the Director of Public Prosecutions pointed out, it is impossible to hold a prognostic opinion as to the effect of a pregnancy in good faith if one is uncertain as to whether a pregnancy exists. Secondly, the Abortion Act refers to 'a termination of pregnancy', not to a termination of 'possible pregnancy' and there is no prospective way of being certain that a pregnancy exists at the time menstrual extractions are usually performed. The extracter might, therefore, still be guilty of intending to procure the miscarriage of a woman 'whether or not she be with child'.[115]

This situation has to be regarded as most unsatisfactory: nothing has happened to help resolve the doubts since the Lane Committee[116] recommended, over 20 years ago, that the Act should be amended so as to include as not being unlawful 'acts done with intent to terminate a pregnancy if such exists'. As things stand, menstrual extraction, which does little more than ensure what is the natural end point of some 40 per cent of implantations, has to be regarded as being unlawful when, given precisely the same risks to health or family conditions, a second trimester termination, with all its attendant physical and psychological trauma, could be perfectly legal. In practice, however, menstrual extraction must be used with rapidly decreasing frequency as the use of medical abortifacients becomes more widespread.

Revision of the law

It is nearly a decade since Freeman wrote: 'The law [on abortion] is in an unholy mess and should be thought out again from scratch. This is not the province of the Private Member's Bill',[117] yet the changes to the law have been relatively few and piecemeal in nature; Parliament has shown a remarkable reluctance to undertake a comprehensive review of the last 30 years' experience.

Abortion remains an emotive issue and, whatever is done or not done, it will never be possible to accommodate the views of the extreme 'pro-life' protagonists and, at the same time, those of the radical feminist movement. Within these limits, it is accepted that the public as a whole wants access to legal termination of pregnancy and that an Abortion Act is going to remain on the statute book. We have noted that the United Kingdom is singularly free from violent confrontation and it may be that our legislators are wise to let well alone.

In my view, we would do well to eliminate the evident hypocrisy of the present situation and admit to abortion on request – including prophylactic treatment – up to the twelfth week of pregnancy. This should be accompanied by vigorous campaigning for acceptable contraceptive advice and treatment, not excluding contraception by abstinence. As a *quid pro quo*, but also on the basis of moral principle, I believe that terminations between the twelfth and twenty-fourth weeks of pregnancy should be legally available only on the grounds of a *grave* effect on the health of the mother or by reason of the likelihood of severe fetal defect. Termination after the twenty-fourth week should be limited by the acceptance of equality of fetal and maternal rights to life, subject only to the need to destroy the fetus in order to save the life of the mother or, again, by reason of the likelihood of severe fetal defect. It is essential in my view that 'fetal indications' for termination are clearly oriented towards the autonomy of the fetus rather than of the mother and, indeed, it is apparent that these proposals incorporate an increased appreciation of fetal rights in general. These will be discussed in the following chapters.

Notes

1   Editorial comment (1993) 342 Lancet 939.
2   And apparently the government has difficulty in enforcement: A. Dorozynski, 'Paris court attacks abortion law' (1995) 311 Brit Med J 149.
3   For an interesting history, see M. Prützel-Thomas, 'The abortion issue and the Federal Constitutional Court' (1993) 2 German Politics 467. Even then, the law has only recently been finalised: H.L. Karcher, 'New German abortion law agreed' (1995) 311 Brit Med J 149.
4   J. Glover, *Causing Death and Saving Lives* (reprinted 1986) Harmondsworth: Penguin, p. 139.
5   *R* v. *Instan* (1893) 1 QB 450 per LORD COLERIDGE LCJ at 453.
6   A. Steinberg, 'Induced abortion in Jewish law' (1980) 1 Int J Law Med 187.
7   This is a proposition strongly advanced by H. Kuhse and P. Singer, *Should the Baby Live?* (1985), Oxford: Oxford University Press, ch. 6. For a general overview with special reference to US law, see S. Bok, 'Who shall count as a human being?' in M.F. Goodman (ed.), *What is a Person?* (1988) Totowa, NJ: Humana Press.
8   *C* v. *S* [1988] QB 135. See also *Rance* v. *Mid-Downs Health Authority and Storr* [1991] 1 QB 587, in which BROOKE J held that the word 'viable' is convenient shorthand for 'capable of being born alive'.
9   J.T. Noonan, 'An almost absolute value in history' in J.T. Noonan (ed.), *The Morality of Abortion* (1970), Harvard: Harvard University Press.
10 I am indebted to G.R. Dunstan, 'The moral status of the human embryo: a tradition recalled' (1984) 10 J Med Ethics 38 for this analysis. Professor Dunstan also introduces the interesting theory that the Greek Orthodox Church may have been the true upholder of humanity arising at conception, see St Basil, writing about 370: 'any fine distinction as to [the fetus] being completely formed or unformed is not admissible among us'.
11 A.V. Campbell, *Moral Dilemmas in Medicine* (3rd edn, 1984), Edinburgh: Churchill Livingstone, p. 124.
12 T. Iglesias, '*In vitro* fertilisation: the major issues' (1984) 10 J Med Ethics 32.
13 See P. Singer, *Practical Ethics* (2nd edn, 1993), Cambridge: Cambridge University Press.
14 K. Rahner, *Theological Investigations* (1972), London: Darton Longman and Todd, p. 239; quoted by K. Boyd, B. Callaghan and E. Shotter, *Life Before Birth* (1986), London: SPCK, p. 146.
15 See, for example, R.N. Wennberg, *Life in the Balance* (1985), Grand Rapids:

Eerdmans, pp. 112 ff. The proposition lies at the heart of nearly all legislation on abortion.

16 But the recent tendency has been to save the mature fetus in the face of the mother's objection to treatment, starting with *Re S (adult: refusal of medical treatment)* (1992) 9 BMLR 69 (see Ch. 6).

17 43 George III, ch. 58, 1803.

18 It is difficult to refer accurately to the United Kingdom law in this area without confusing the non-British reader. The Offences Against the Person Act 1861 runs to Northern Ireland but not to Scotland; the Infant Life (Preservation) Act 1929 is not applicable in Scotland but is repeated in the Criminal Justice (Northern Ireland) Act, 1945, s.25; the Abortion Act 1967 does not apply to Northern Ireland.

19 The Scottish equivalent is to be found in *HMAdv.* v. *M'Allum* (1858) 3 Irv. 187. The Canadian criminal case of *R* v. *Sullivan* (1991) 63 CCC (3d) 97 is instructive. Two midwives were charged with causing the death of a baby as a result of criminal negligence; they could not be convicted because a child in the process of being born is not a person.

20 [1939] 1 KB 687.

21 At 1 KB 694.

22 Eg. Crimes Act 1900 (NSW), ss.82-84; Crimes Act 1958 (Vict), ss.65,66; Criminal Code Act, 1899 (Qd), ss.224-6.

23 *R* v. *Wald and others* (1972) 3 DCR (NSW) 25; *R* v. *Davidson* [1969] VR 667.

24 K. Petersen, 'Abortion laws: comparative and feminist perspectives in Australia, England and the United States' (1996) 2 Med Law Internat 77.

25 G.H. Gordon, *The Criminal Law of Scotland* (2nd edn, 1978), Edinburgh: W. Green, Chap. 28. There is no offence of attempted abortion in Scotland.

26 *R* v. *Newton and Stungo* (1958) Crim LR 469.

27 Note that the 1929 Act has not been modified in the light of the Still-Birth (Definition) Act 1992.

28 Note 8 above. The meaning of being born alive remains the same as it was defined over a century ago: *R* v. *Handley* (1874) 13 Cox CC 79.

29 For discussion of the case, see S.P. de Cruz, 'Abortion, C v. S and the law' (1987) 17 Fam Law 319. It is probably true to say that viability is not a concept known to English law: K.McK. Norrie, 'Abortion in Great Britain: one Act, two laws' [1985] Crim LR 475.

30 Registrar General's Statistical Review of England and Wales for 1967, Part III (1971), London: HMSO.

31 S.5(1) of the 1967 Act amended by s.37(4) of the 1990 Act.

32 Note that the two doctor requirement may be waived in respect of subsections (b) and (c).

33 P.T. O'Neill and I. Watson, 'The father and the unborn child' (1975) 38 MLR 174.

34 'Babies of wrong sex aborted, claims report' (1988), *The Scotsman*, 4 January, p. 2.

35 C. Francome, 'Abortion in Ireland' (1992) 305 Brit Med J 436; S. Kingman, 'Northern Ireland's abortion law criticised as unclear' (1993) 307 Brit Med J 284.

36 *Re K (a minor) (Northern Health and Social Services Board* v. *F and G)* [1994] 2 Med L Rev 371.

37 *Re A (Northern Health and Social Services Board* v. *AMNH)* [1994] 2 Med L Rev 374.

38 *SPUC* v. *Grogan* (1991) 9 BMLR 100.

39 *Open Door Counselling and Dublin Well Woman* v. *Ireland* (1992) 18 BMLR 1.

40 *Attorney-General* v. *X* (1992) 15 BMLR 104. A relatively full but slightly out-

dated description of the European scene is to be found in R. Boland, 'Abortion law in Europe in 1991-1992' (1993) 21 J Law Med & Ethics 72.

41   Kolinsky, E., 'Women in the new Germany' in G. Smith, *et al* (eds) *Developments in German Politics* (1992), ch. 14, Basingstoke: Macmillan Press.

42   M. Prutzel-Thomas, 'The abortion issue and the Federal Constitutional Court' (1993) 2 German Politics 467.

43   See, for example, the control of euthanasia in the Netherlands.

44   S. Goldbeck-Wood, 'Bavaria threatens to reduce abortion access' (1996) 312 Brit Med J 1118.

45   *Roe* v. *Wade* 93 S Ct 705 (1973); *Doe* v. *Bolton* 93 S Ct 739 (1973).

46   S.R. Shapiro, 'Validity, under Federal Constitution, of abortion laws' (1973) 35 L Ed 2d 735.

47   *Thornburgh et al.* v. *American College of Obstetricians and Gynecologists et al.* 476 US 747 (1986) at 772.

48   *Webster* v. *Reproductive Health Services* 109 S Ct 3040 (1989). For critical discussion, see W. Dellinger and G.B. Sperling, 'Abortion and the Supreme Court: the retreat from *Roe* v. *Wade'* (1989) 138 U Penn LR 83 and associated papers.

49   *Planned Parenthood of Southeastern Pennsylvania* v. *Casey* 112 S Ct 2791 (1992).

50   I. Loveland, 'Abortion and the U.S. Supreme Court' (1992) 142 NLJ 974.

51   B.M. Knoppers, 'Comparative abortion law; The living abortus' in J.K. Mason, (ed), *Paediatric Forensic Medicine and Pathology* (1989), London: Chapman and Hall.

52   Criminal Code 1971, s.251.

53   *R* v. *Morgentaler* [1988] 1 SCR 30 per DICKSON CJ at 56.

54   *Borowski* v. *A-G of Canada* (1987) 39 DLR (4th) 731.

55   *Tremblay* v. *Daigle* (1989) 62 DLR (4th) 634.

56   Although many Catholic doctors will question the scientific accuracy of equating the fertilised ovum with 'human life'. See, for example, J. Poole, 'Time for the Vatican to bend' (1992) 339 *Lancet* 1340.

57   D. Callahan, 'How technology is reframing the abortion debate' (1986) 16 Hastings Center Report (1). 33.

58   Note 11 above, p. 125.

59   S.A.M. McLean, 'Abortion law: is consensual reform possible?' (1990) 17 J Law & Soc 106 floated the interesting suggestion that women requesting a termination should be encouraged and given the opportunity to carry the fetus until it is viable and available for adoption – subject, she insists, to accepting the woman's right to abortion at any time.

60   S. McLean and G. Maher, *Medicine, Morals and the Law* (1983), Aldershot: Gower, p. 26.

61   Interestingly, the UK legislation is in the minority in not specifically legalising abortion in such cases – though they are, of course, well covered in the general terms of the 1967 Act.

62   E.F. Paul and J. Paul, 'Self-ownership, abortion and infanticide' (1979) 5 J Med Ethics 133.

63   J.H. Ely, 'The wages of crying wolf: a comment on *Roe* v. *Wade'* (1973) 82 Yale LJ 920.

64   *Colautti* v. *Franklin* 439 US 379 (1979). But the American courts are increasingly sympathetic to the States' interest in the preservation of life: see *Casey*, note 49 above.

65   *Emeh* v. *Kensington and Chelsea and Westminster Area Health Authority* [1984] 3 All ER 1044, per SLADE LJ at 1053.

66   *Ziemba* v. *Sternberg* 45 A 2d 230 (NY, 1974). See also *Fassoulas* v. *Ramey* 450 So 2d 822 (Fla, 1984).

67 D. Baird, 'Induced abortion: epidemiological aspects' (1975) 1 J Med Ethics 122.

68 Even so, this is not a high rate as compared with most jurisdictions. See D. Munday, C. Francome and W. Savage, 'Twenty one years of legal abortion' (1989) 298 Brit Med J 1231. A major exception is in the 'liberal' ambience of the Netherlands where the abortion rate is about half that of England and Wales. The downward trend in the numbers of abortions performed in England and Wales which has been noted since 1991 may now have been halted. 177 225 operations were carried out in 1996 with a 15 per cent rise over the previous year among teenagers: I. Murray, 'Abortions rise for first time in 5 years' (1997), *The Times*, 23 July, p. 7.

69 D. Paintin, 'Abortion in the first trimester' (1992) 305 Brit Med J 967. Interestingly, the government of Bavaria is attempting to limit abortions by limiting the amount of money a practitioner can earn from the procedure: S. Goldbeck-Wood, 'Bavaria threatens to reduce abortion access' (1996) 312 Brit Med J 1118.

70 Declaration of Geneva, as amended at Sydney, 1968. The Declaration of Oslo 1970 circumvents this by considering the possible conflict between the vital interests of a mother and her unborn child and states at para 3: 'Diversity of response to this situation results from the diversity of attitudes towards life of the unborn child. This is a matter of individual conviction and conscience which must be respected'.

71 The number is steadily dropping as more and more jurisdictions ratify their own Abortion Acts.

72 *R v. Smith (John)* [1974] 1 All ER 376. For a rather similar US example, see *People v. Franklin* 683 P 2d 775 (Colo, 1984).

73 *R v. Dixon* (unreported, Nottingham Crown Court, 21 December 1995). See C. Dyer, 'Gynaecologist acquitted in hysterectomy case' (1996) 312 Brit Med J 11. The case had considerable civil overtones.

74 *Faridian v. General Medical Council* [1970] 3 WLR 1065.

75 *Tarnesby v. Kensington, Chelsea and Westminster Area Health Authority* [1980] ICR 475, CA; [1981] IRLR 369, HL. A doctor was struck off the register in 1981 after being sentenced to 9 months' imprisonment for using an instrument with intent to procure a miscarriage in a 16-year-old girl (1981), *The Times*, 6 March, p. 21.

76 Note 49 above.

77 *Paton v. British Pregnancy Advisory Service Trustees* [1979] QB 276. The possibility that the custody of an unborn child might be given to the father was raised but not pursued; see C.M. Lyon and G.J. Bennett, 'Abortion – whose decision?' (1979) 9 Fam Law 35.

78 *C v. S* [1988] QB 135. A similar claim has now been rejected in Scotland: *Kelly v. Kelly* 1997 SLT 896.

79 *Paton v. United Kingdom* (1981) 3 EHRR 408.

80 *Re Simms and H* (1980) 106 DLR (3d) 435; the case does, however, seem to have minimal precedental importance.

81 (1984) 9 DLR (4th) 252.

82 *Tremblay v. Daigle*, note 55 above.

83 Note 81 above per REID J at 259.

84 In what may be seen as a back-door attack by the 'pro-life' lobby in the United States, attempts are being made to apply a 'conscience clause' to both trainees and trainers in undergraduate medical education: Editorial Comment 'A de-facto end to abortion in the USA?' (1996) 347 Lancet 1055.

85 In Scotland, a simple statement of objection – on oath if in court proceedings [s.4(3)] – would be accepted as satisfying the conditions.

86   In *Royal College of Nursing of the United Kingdom* v. *Department of Health and Social Security* [1981] AC 800 at 804-5.
87   Glover emphasises the effect on outside parties when arguing that there is a moral difference between abortion and, say, contraception: J. Glover, *Causing Death and Saving Lives* (reprinted 1986), Harmondsworth: Penguin Books at 142. The controversy over the technique of intact dilatation and evacuation in the US culminating in the Presidential veto of the Partial-Birth Abortion Ban Act is to be noted: J. Rovner (1995) 346 Lancet 1287, 1618, (1996) 347 Lancet 1107.
88   Note 86 above, CA and HL.
89   CMO (30) (2)-90
90   Medical termination of pregnancy of less than 9 weeks' duration is, of course, now a well-established practice: M. Heard and J. Guillebaud, 'Medical abortion' (1992) 304 Brit Med J 195. At the same time, it raises many specific ethical and practical problems and is subject to considerable opposition above and beyond that reserved for abortion as a whole. It is reported that a major pharmaceutical company has been forced to withdraw from the production and distribution of mifepristone: A. Dorozynski, 'Boycott threat forces French company to abandon RU486' (1997) 314 Brit Med J 1150. The Abortion Act 1967, s.3A amends the method of approval of abortion clinics so as to accommodate medical terminations.
91   *R* v. *Salford Health Authoritty, ex p Janaway* [1988] 2 WLR 442, CA; *sub nom Janaway* v. *Salford Area Health Aurhority* [1989] AC 537, HL.
92   Argued, within the context of a US statute, by B.D. Weinstein, 'Do pharmacists have a right to refuse to fill prescriptions for abortifacient drugs?' (1992) 20 Law Med Hlth Care 220.
93   Note 86 above at AC 824.
94   *Gillick* v. *West Norfolk and Wisbech Area Health Authority* [1986] AC 112, HL. See also Age of Legal Capacity (Scotland) Act, 1991, s.2(4).
95   Although the comparative law is of decreasing importance, it is worth noting that the position in the United States is uncertain following the Supreme Court decision in *Casey* (n. 49 above). Here, the provisions in the State statute requiring a minor to have parental or court authorisation for abortion were not found to be unconstitutional. As a result of the Supreme Court's generally negative attitude, increases in the States' regulatory powers have accumulated: I. Loveland, 'Abortion and the U.S. Supreme Court' (1992) 142 NLJ 974.
96   The problem does not arise in Scotland where, by virtue of the Age of Legal Capacity (Scotland) Act, 1991, s.2(4), a mature minor of any age can consent to a medical or surgical *procedure*.
97   *Re R (a minor) (wardship: medical treatment)* [1992] Fam 11.
98   Note 65 above.
99   Either by way of the inherent jurisdiction of the court or by a specific order under the Children Act 1989, s.8(1).
100 *Re P (a Minor)* (1982) 80 LGR 301; [1986] 1 FLR 272.
101 *Re B (wardship: abortion)* [1991] 2 FLR 426.
102 Such a power still exists in Scotland. See *Law Hospital NHS Trust* v. *Lord Advocate* 1996 SLT 848.
103 The courts do, however, adopt something of a liberal interpretation of s.63. See, for example, *B* v. *Croydon Health Authority* [1995] Fam 133; *Tameside and Glossop Acute Services Trust* v. *CH* [1996] 1 FLR 762.
104 M.J. Gunn, 'Sex and the mentally handicapped: a lawyer's view' (1986) 5 Med Law 255.
105 In *CH*, note 103 above, for example, it was said that an induction of birth and,

possibly, a Caesarian section would have been lawfully performed without court intervention had the woman been compliant.

106 F. Gibb, 'Judge orders abortion on woman, aged 25' (1987) *The Times*, 28 May, p. 1.

107 *Airedale NHS Trust* v. *Bland* [1993] AC 789 per LORD BROWNE-WILKINSON at 883.

108 *In re X* (1987) Times, 4 June.

109 Rules of the Supreme Court, Order 15, Rule 16.

110 *In re T, T* v. *T and another* [1988] Fam 52.

111 [1991] 2 FLR 329.

112 For opposing views, see J. Keown, 'Selective reduction of multiple pregnancy' (1987) 137 NLJ 165 and D.P.T. Price, 'Selective reduction and feticide: The parameters of abortion' [1988] Crim LR 199.

113 See R.L. Berkowitz, 'From twin to singleton' (1996) 313 Brit Med J 373.

114 Abortion Regulations 1991, S.I.1991/499; Abortion (Scotland) Regulations 1991, S.I.1991/460.

115 There is no offence in Scotland unless it can be shown that the woman was pregnant – which raises an intriguing doubt as to the effects of a histological (microscopic) examination of the products of extraction on the culpability of the doctor.

116 *Report of the Committee on the Working of the Abortion Act* (Chairman, Mrs Justice Lane) (1974) Cmnd. 5538, London: HMSO. It is true that the Attorney General and the Solicitor General considered the process to be lawful in 1979. The powers of such officers are, however, limited and their interpretation of the law is not binding.

117 M. Freeman, 'Abortion – what do other countries do?' (1988) 138 NLJ 233.

6 Protection of the Fetus

The previous chapter looked at the termination of pregnancy almost entirely from the point of view of the pregnant woman and her immediate circle of advisers. The position of the fetus has been deliberately isolated for special consideration, firstly, in the general sense that the condemned man is a principal in a hanging and deserves individual attention but, also, because the status of the fetus is being greatly changed by developments in medical expertise. In addition, the last few years have shown what appears to be a legal groundswell in the United Kingdom in favour of fetal rights, which are being recognised in the United States to an even greater extent. With something of the order of 40–60 million abortions being performed annually on a worldwide basis,[1] the interaction between the legal and the moral aspects of injury and death of *homo sapiens in utero* merits examination.

The legal rights of the fetus

The moral position of the fetus is defined by the answer to the question, 'when does life begin?' and this has been discussed in detail in the previous chapter. Here we are concerned with the acquisition of a legal personality and, although the position has been modified, often with confusing implications, we must start from the premise that, *fundamentally*, the common law sees no personality in the unborn fetus: any personal rights as do exist can mature only at birth.

There have been judgments in all the common law countries supporting this view. Such judicial conflict as there is has been most acute in the United States, where the basic opinion is that set out by HOLMES J in the rhetorical question:

if we should assume ... that a man might ... incur a conditional prospective liability in tort to one not yet in being ... we should then

143

be confronted by the question ... whether an infant dying before it may be able to live separated from its mother could be said to have become a person recognized by the law as capable of having a *locus standi*.[2]

The result of the case indicated that this should not be so. A century later, it was stated in Canada:

Although rapid advances in medical science may make it generally desirable that some legal status be extended to foetuses, irrespective of ultimate viability, it is the prerogative of Parliament, not the courts, to enact whatever legislation may be considered appropriate to extend to the unborn any or all legal rights possessed by living persons ... there is no existing basis in law which justifies the conclusion that foetuses are legal persons.[3]

The position has been stated equally clearly in England, where the President of the Family Division has said: 'There can be no doubt, in my view, that in England and Wales the foetus has no right of action, no right at all, until birth',[7] and this opinion was fully endorsed in the important case of *C* v. *S*.[5] Birth is, therefore, essential to any supposed fetal rights – at least in respect of compensation for negligence.[6] The rationale here is that, while the fetus may well *sustain* injury *in utero*, it can only *suffer* damage and be compensated on birth, the latter always assuming that the damage ought reasonably to have been foreseen by the alleged wrongdoer. When we speak of fetal rights, therefore, we must distinguish between the rights of the fetus *per se* and the rights of the fetus which devolve on the neonate. As to the former, there is strong precedent derived from many branches of the law that the fetus is not a person and has no rights *pro tempore*.[7] The latter rights are, however, more controversial and it is helpful to look, first, at the possibilities from the viewpoint of Scots law. Scots law is heavily influenced by that of the Romans which, as modified by modern civil code law, developed the concept of what has been termed 'birth for benefit' or the *nasciturus* rule.[8] We can go back to the mid-18th century for authority: 'By our law, rights may be granted in favour of children *nascituri* of any particular person, tho' not begotten at the time, and upon their existence they are intitled thereto, in the same manner as if they had been born at the date of the rights'.[9]

Thus the fetus is deemed never to have existed if it is not born alive; prior to birth, however, an unborn child is taken care of just as much as if it were in existence in any case when to do so is in the child's own advantage.[10] This principle has always been applied in common law countries to the law of property and succession but, prior to the passing of the Congenital Disabilities (Civil Liability) Act

1976, it was by no means certain that it applied to English tort law. Thus the victims of the thalidomide disaster settled for substantially less than would have been their due following a successful action for negligence and this was at least partly due to fear as to the precise state of the law;[11] an action brought in Scotland would have been free of such doubt – indeed, the 1976 Act does not run to Scotland, on the grounds that it would be superfluous.[12]

The evolution of the fetus' legal rights not to be damaged *in utero* are best evidenced in the United States and in Canada, which was one of the first countries to take the view that it was no more than natural justice that a child injured *in utero* should be allowed to maintain an action in the courts if born alive and viable.[13] Although that particular case arose in the civil law jurisdiction of Quebec, it came to be followed in the United States, particularly in the landmark case of *Bonbrest* v. *Kotz*.[14] Judicial opinion on the point in the United States has, however, been strongly influenced by the concept of 'independence' of the fetus as a prerequisite to legal personhood and this state was generally equated with 'viability' or an ability to survive. The definition of viability and its dependence on environmental factors has been discussed in Chapter 5. It has no legal merit because of its uncertainty and, if it is accepted that humanity is conferred, at least, at implantation, it becomes also a morally indefensible cut-off point. Moreover, the fetus is at its most susceptible to non-violent outside influences during the first trimester. The complicating factor here is that the earlier in pregnancy that a fetus is insulted, the more difficult it may be to prove a causative link between the incident and later disability – but that is no reason for denying the opportunity to do so. It did not take long for the American courts to appreciate this; in the instructive case of *Smith* v. *Brennan* it was said:

> the viability distinction has no relevance to the importance of denying recovery for harm which can be proved to have resulted from the wrongful act of another. Whether viable or not at the time of the injury, the child sustains the same harm after birth, and therefore should be given the same opportunity for redress.[15]

In other words, there is no conceptual difficulty in attributing a 'legal personality' to the unborn baby and society can place the point at which a legal entity exists wherever it chooses; all that is needed is to recognise that life is a continuum from conception to death and that birth is no more than an event in that process.

English statute law has responded to the challenge with the passing of the somewhat arcane Congenital Disabilities (Civil Liability) Act 1976, which pays no regard to the gestational age of the fetus.

Under the Act, anyone responsible for an occurrence affecting the parent of a child which causes that child to be born disabled will be liable in tort to the child if he would have been liable to the parent (s.1(3)). Section 1(2)(*b*) defines such an occurrence as one which 'affected the mother during her pregnancy, or affected her or the child in the course of its birth, so that the child is born with disabilities which would not otherwise have been present'. Thus it is clear that English law still does not recognise a specific and independent liability to the child, but it now accepts that there is such a liability to be derived from that owed to the parents.[16] The insistence on a live birth before such liability arises is maintained and, indeed, the Act of 1976 specifies not only a live birth but also survival for 48 hours.[17]

Can we say the fetus is a person?

The foregoing relates, essentially, to the rights of the neonate in tort or delict rather than to any truly fetal rights. Thus the status of the fetus *per se* is not greatly advanced; any such advance depends upon the attribution of some form of personality and it is here that one begins to detect a softening of judicial attitudes. Perhaps the main nudge in this direction has come from road traffic injuries *in utero*; indeed, such an incident formed the basis of what has become a seminal decision in this area.[18] Here again, however, the importance of survival following birth is exemplified: once this is established, the courts will now have little difficulty in regarding the fetus as a person who can be injured or killed.[19] The opinion in an Australian case is significant: 'I would hold that an injury suffered during ... its journey through life between conception and parturition is not injury to a person devoid of personality other than that of the mother-to-be. N's personality was identifiable and recognisable.'[20]

The fundamental jurisprudential arguments are, however, best seen in the contrasting Scottish cases of *Cohen* v. *Shaw*,[21] *McWilliams* v. *Lord Advocate*[22] and *Hamilton* v. *Fife Health Board*.[23] All three concerned the application of the Damages (Scotland) Act 1976, s.1 to the fetus. The section makes a person who negligently causes bereavement liable to pay damages to any relative of the deceased and schedule 1 includes any person who was a parent or child of the deceased under the definition of 'relative'. The question to be decided arises in two different contexts, but requiring the same answer: first, can a fetus *in utero* be a person having a right to sue and, conversely, can the same fetus be regarded as a person capable of sustaining personal injuries leading to his or her death?

The first question was answered in *Cohen*, a case involving the death of a father in a road traffic accident, using the ploy of applying the *nasciturus* principle. The probability was that this was unnecessary since such a right existed at common law.[24] The second, and more complex, question had something of a chequered course. *Hamilton* concerned a child who died three days after a negligently performed forceps delivery. When the case was heard in the Outer House, it was argued on behalf of the pursuers that the common law would have no trouble in affording a right of action in such a case and that, in passing the 1976 Act, Parliament had not intended to diminish such rights as already existed; nonetheless, LORD PROSSER concluded that the word 'person' did not include an unborn child who could not, therefore, sustain personal injuries; the words in the statute did not cover the situation where an injury is sustained by a fetus rather than a person. *McWilliams*, concerning a child who was born brain-damaged as a result of obstetric negligence, was heard some six months later. Here, LORD MORTON discarded the *nasciturus* principle in favour of the view of the Scottish Law Commission that, if a child is born with defects resulting from harm sustained antenatally, liability could be tested by ascertaining the cause of the defects from the succession of events and by considering whether that succession of events ought reasonably to have been foreseen by the alleged wrong-doer. Any breach of duty must persist after the act or neglect until the damage is suffered: 'From the point of view of the child the wrong is complete, injury is sustained and damage is suffered when it is born alive ... . When the defect emerges only some time after birth, the wrong is complete at that time.'[25]

The situation clearly needed urgent review and *Hamilton* was appealed in 1993.[26] In LORD MCCLUSKEY's opinion, which was the only judgment reported, injuries with which a child is born that were inflicted *in utero* are injuries to his person although not to his legal persona. It was clear that the phrase 'personal injuries sustained by him' was perfectly apt to include injuries inflicted to the person of a child immediately before his birth and continuing to impair his condition after his birth: 'It is perfectly common in ordinary speech to refer to the child in utero as 'he', 'she', 'him' or 'her' ... . It was this child who sustained injuries to his person and who died in consequence of personal injuries sustained by him' (at BMLR, 164–5) and the Outer House decision was firmly rejected.

It is possible to hold that, insofar as the Inner House decision is apparently no more than a further example of fetal rights devolving on the neonate, *Hamilton* is a relatively unimportant case which may, in the end, do no more than clarify the interpretation of a statute. It is also possible to see the case as significant in that, although there may be no consequences in the absence of a live birth, the fact that there can be *any* consequences depends on the fundamental attribution of contemporaneous personhood to the fetus *in utero*. Having said which, it has to be admitted that the rule that legal personality commences at birth, and not before birth, was not subject to challenge in *Hamilton* – and any such foray would have been doomed to failure.

Wrongful death of the fetus

Despite the persisting insistence on live birth as a prerequisite to 'fetal' rights, it might, at this point, be useful to interpolate a note on the current position of the fetus that dies as a result of negligence or criminal activity.

It could reasonably be supposed that killing would be the ultimate negligent injury. Nonetheless, it follows from what has been said that, since there can never be any benefit to a stillbirth, no right of action for negligence is vested in a stillborn child and, as a result, a fetal suit for 'wrongful death' is not available at civil law in the United Kingdom.[27] Despite the manifest inequity of this situation as regards the deterrence of sub-standard practice, the conclusion seems only just in terms of compensation, because the fetus has suffered no compensatable injury and can in no way be said to have an estate which has suffered financially from its death. However, a new form of tort is developing in this area in the United States and this appears to result, very largely, from a punitive motivation. Thus we have judicial opinion: 'To require his birth [for compensation for injury in utero] would mean the greater the harm, the better the chance of the [tortfeasor's] immunity';[28] and, again: 'To deny a stillborn child recovery for fatal injuries during gestation while allowing such recovery for a child born alive would make it more profitable for the defendant to kill the plaintiff than to scratch him.'[29]

Several actions for wrongful death have now been accepted in the United States but, in general, success depends upon viability, the rationale being that a viable fetus could survive outside the mother's body and could have a separate existence and should, therefore, have a cause of action; the same cannot be said of the non-viable fetus.[30] The time of the injury can be immaterial so long as the fetus is viable at the time the injury becomes apparent,[31] and the current position in the United States is probably best expressed in *Thibert*,[32] in which it was held that recovery for pre-natal injuries is available to (a) a child who is born alive – regardless of viability at the time of injury; and (b) a viable fetus even if it is not born alive.

Inevitably, in the light of *Roe* v. *Wade*,[33] the courts have found difficulty in going further and crossing the viability barrier in respect of deaths *in utero*. Thus the New Hampshire Supreme Court reasoned that, if a mother had a constitutional right to abort a pre-viable fetus, a third party should not be held liable for unintentionally harming such a fetus; viability either before or after the time of prenatal injury was considered to be an essential prerequisite to recovery.[34] Other courts, however, have been able to distinguish fetal rights which do not exist under the 14th amendment, as was made clear in *Roe* v. *Wade*, from those which are definitely available – and which would include the right to personhood as defined in statute;[35] it has even been argued that to allow recovery by a pre-viable fetus is merely to 'join the modern trend' and is not barred by the rule in *Roe* v. *Wade*.[36] On the face of things, the argument that the wrong lying in being deprived of life is the same irrespective of fetal age is very strong;[37] if there is to be a variable assessment of the wrong, such an apparent inequality can only be justified on the grounds that the pre-viable fetus is relatively less likely to survive to maturity than is the mature fetus.[38] Thus, so long as it is agreed that the law of tort embodies an element of deterrence,[39] an action for 'wrongful death' is not only acceptable but is a logical consequence of an acceptance of fetal rights; as Pace put it in a seminal analysis: 'There is paradox enough in the present position; liability is incurred for negligent injury to the fetus but not – or at least not necessarily – for its deliberate destruction'[40] and similarly oriented judicial observations have been made.[41]

At least two hurdles must be crossed, however, before the immature fetus can be allowed to recover damages following its death. Firstly, some accommodation must be reached with the current abortion law. It has been possible in the United States to achieve this by the denial of personhood to the fetus only within the specific confines of the 14th amendment to the Constitution, which states that no person may be deprived of life, liberty or property without due process of law, nor shall any person be denied the equal protection of the laws;[42] such an escape route would not be available in Great Britain. In addition, several states of the United States incorporate specific exclusion clauses in respect of therapeutic abortion in their child abuse statutes.

Secondly, whether we are considering the viable or non-viable fetus, some way must be found to apportion any damages allowed. The American courts have circumvented the problem of compensating the estateless fetus in several ways, depending upon the precise wording of the various 'wrongful death' state statutes. They include consideration for loss of aid, advice, comfort and protection which the child would have given had it lived and the sorrow and bereavement experienced by the relatives of the dead fetus.[43] Similar reasoning has recently been applied to the parents while, at the same time, denying the stillborn fetus the status of a person under a wrongful death statute.[44] One's impression is that the success of 'wrongful death of the fetus' suits in the United States depends on two policy factors. Firstly, they satisfy the not unreasonable public demand for deterrence of medical negligence.[45] Secondly, any such compensation is clearly for the benefit of the parents and, indeed, the actions are brought by the parents. There is no reason why justifiable compensation of this nature should not also be available in the United Kingdom.[46]

Wrongful death actions on behalf of the fetus may well become the norm in the United States, where they are supported by statute; one wonders if they would ever be allowed at common law in the United Kingdom. On the face of things, this seems an unlikely development as, currently, there are at least two major barriers in their path. Firstly, an entity that has never become a person cannot be said to have lived and, therefore, cannot be said to have died; secondly, while there may have been a breach of duty which caused death, there can be no *actionable* breach of duty to those born dead – for the stillbirth cannot sue and has no executor to do so.[47] Nevertheless, one feels intuitively that this retreat behind a legal rampart is less than satisfactory and there is a sense of some erosion of its foundations. For example, albeit somewhat surprisingly, DILLON LJ linked together claims outstanding in respect of 'children stillborn before 22 July 1976 or any children born before that date', thus suggesting that an action for wrongful death was not out of the question.[48] Additionally, the possibility has been mooted above that the decision in *Hamilton*[49] improves the fetus' legal position; there seems nothing to stop the progress of actions, at least, along the line of *Bagley*.[50] We can, however, look to the criminal law for further indications of a trend towards fetal protection against wrongful death.

The effect of the Abortion Act 1967 on the protection afforded the fetus by the Offences Against the Person Act, 1861 has been discussed in Chapter 5 and is referred to briefly below. Outside these two statutes, the one safeguard granted the fetus by Act of Parliament lies in the rule that it is the offence of child destruction to intentionally destroy the life of a fetus that is capable of being born alive, subject only to the overriding need to preserve the life of the mother.[51] In practice, this is a poor protection as it is difficult to prove, first, intent and, second, that a dead fetus of less than 28 weeks' gestation – above which point a presumption is imposed – was capable of being born alive. Moreover, there is clearly no protection for the non-viable fetus outside the law relating to abortion: no statutory offence of feticide exists in the United Kingdom.[52]

Very recently, however , the common law position has been defined. *Attorney-General's Reference (No 3 of 1994)*[53] concerned a case in which a woman who was stabbed gave birth to a grossly premature infant which was found to have been injured in the assault; the child died 120 days later, the cause of death being unconnected with the injury but resulting directly from premature birth. In essence, the answers to the Attorney General's questions included, firstly, that, subject to the requirements of causation being met, the fatal injuring of a fetus *in utero* can be charged as either murder or manslaughter irrespective of whether the injury is directed to the mother or to the fetus, provided that the fetus is subsequently born alive; and, secondly, that the doctrine of transferred malice can operate either way as between mother and fetus, the fact that the fetus was not, at the time, an existing person being immaterial.[54] The ruling was described in the media as the latest in a series strengthening the legal status of the fetus;[55] this, however, may well be a misinterpretation. In the first place, the requirement for post-natal survival persists; the concept of a criminal offence of feticide was specifically rejected. Secondly, the basis for the decision was not that the fetus is an entity in itself but that it is an integral part of the mother: an intention to cause serious bodily injury to the fetus satisfies the *mens rea* of murder only by way of causing severe injury to the mother. The court went so far as to describe the status of the fetus as comparable to that of the mother's arm or leg, which is a difficult proposition to accept, insofar as you could not charge murder for the death of a leg.[56]

The case is also unsatisfactory from the point of view of those seeking increased fetal rights, insofar as the reasoning behind the decisions is essentially negative. Thus no positive basis for regarding the fetus as a recognisable recipient of transferred malice is provided; the court was content to observe: 'We can see no reason to hold that malice can only be transferred where the person to whom it is transferred was in existence at the time of the act causing death' (at 19), and a similar negative attitude is to be found in the comparable Scottish case: 'There is no authority in the law of Scotland to the effect that a relevant charge of culpable homicide would not lie' following the death of a person born alive caused by injuries inflicted before birth.[57] Thus the additional recognition of the fetus as a person provided by the criminal law is not great, but it is rather more than insignificant, and the questions posed by the Attorney General may yet go to the House of Lords.

Even so, the resistance to the concept of feticide is deeply entrenched – as evidenced in the, albeit minor, case of *HM Adv.* v. *McDougall*.[58] This concerned a road traffic accident involving the death *in utero* of a 30-week-old fetus: 'viable' by any standards. The Sheriff held very firmly that liability for injuries sustained by the fetus arose only with the live birth of the injured child and that it was the latter condition that lay at the heart of the otherwise similar case of *McCluskey*.[59] There is certainly no anxiety in either Scotland or the United Kingdom as a whole to follow the American track.[60]

Fetal rights to treatment

It may well be, however, that we should look to the therapeutic arena if we are to discover an increasing awareness that the fetus has *some* recognisable rights as a person. Undoubtedly, the major impetus along these lines springs from the increasing feasibility and availability of treatments for, or other interventions on behalf of, the fetus *in utero*, and it is in this area that conflict between fetal and women's rights is most likely to develop. Thus, on the one hand, 'The increasing tendency to view the fetus as an independent patient or person occurs at the cost of reducing the woman to the status of little more than a maternal environment.'[61] On the other, the view is expressed that the extent of the obligation to the unborn child should be expanded and that, because of the continuum which exists between the two states, there should be the same legal protections for and interventions on behalf of the fetus as are attributable to children. On this analysis, the need to wait until birth to establish a legal personality – and its associated rights to protection – is no longer a tenable fiction.[62]

The emergence of fetal medicine and surgery has obvious implications in the abortion debate: how can you justify saving imperilled premature newborns while accepting abortion of perfectly healthy fetuses of the same age? asked Callahan.[63] Indeed, the 'pro-life' appeal to the Hippocratic conscience is greatly reinforced by the technical developments in this field; not only is the paradox of similarly qualified doctors working in the abortion clinic and the neonatal intensive care unit highlighted, but physicians must increasingly see the fetus as a patient in its own right and, as such, entitled to the protection of individual care. This is not to deny that doctors' dilemmas are, at times, self-imposed. There is no doubt that some of the more bizarre examples of fetal treatment can be criticised as being, at worst, little other than experimental and, at best, premature, in that they could have been postponed until birth.[64] The fact remains, however, that the concept of organic unity between fetus and the mother – with its concomitant denial of fetal independence – is being eroded.[65] All of which is of academic concern only, so long as there is no maternal/fetal conflict of interests. This will be the position in the great majority of cases, in that, since most treatments can be given only to the relatively mature fetus, a question of fetal therapy will, in general, only arise when the pregnant woman has chosen to accept her obligations towards her child – an acceptance that is reinforced by the fact that termination of pregnancy on the grounds of serious fetal abnormality is now lawful at any stage of fetal maturity. Nonetheless, opposing interests can and do materialise and may do so consciously, as when a considered decision has to be made as to medical management of the fetus, or unwittingly, when the mother's general conduct or way of life is such as to be regarded by others as being contrary to the fetal interest. Both these situations merit analysis.

Interventional treatment of the fetus

It is one thing to postulate on the continuum theory that the fetus and the child have similar rights to protection; it is quite another to conclude that the exercise of such rights is equivalent. There is a clear distinction to be made on the grounds that treatment of the fetus requires gynaecological invasion of the woman's body. Thus, while the mother may have, at best, a doubtful right to assert her parental authority in refusing treatment for her child, the extent of any right to do so in the case of the fetus will depend upon balancing the degree of maternal risk against the needs of the fetus. No-one can rightly be compelled to accept treatment which is to one's disadvantage, but that generalisation may have to be modified once a second 'person' is also affected; we have seen that English law accepts this principle through the Infant Life (Preservation) Act, 1929 while, in the United States, the state accepts a compelling interest in protecting the life of the viable fetus subject only to preservation of the mother's life or health.[66] The viable fetus – and, indeed, the pre-viable fetus – may also be protected by statute as, for example, in California.[67]

The presumption in favour of the woman's health is, however, very strong – at least in the United States.[68] Reported cases tending to override the woman's wishes have been very rare,[69] but the researches of Kolder and her colleagues[70] indicated that attempts to obtain court orders for compulsory treatment in favour of the fetus, including several instances of the incontrovertibly invasive process of Caesarean section, are by no means uncommon, and many have been successful. A slightly surprising feature of their survey was the widespread approval of compulsory intervention by the physicians concerned, which may reflect an instinctive sympathy for the plight of the treatable fetus. Those who share such concern have suggested guidelines to the effect that non-consensual intervention would be permissible if the risks to the fetus were minimal as compared with a substantial benefit to be expected and if the risks to the woman were such as she should reasonably accept on behalf of her child.[71] Such an approach has not been rejected by the American courts. In *Taft* v. *Taft*,[72] the Massachusetts Supreme Court reversed an order of the lower court that a woman undergo surgical treatment so as to insure against a likely miscarriage. Nonetheless, the court reserved judgment on whether or not there might be a justification for ordering *medical* treatment in order to assist in carrying a child to term: 'The state's interest in some circumstances might be sufficiently compelling to justify such a restriction on a person's constitutional right of privacy.'

The majority of commentators do, however, come down against the legal enforcement of any fetal rights to treatment in the face of maternal opposition. In general, this view stems from the impossibility of defining significant harm or benefit to the fetus or of reasonableness in relation to refusal, from the uncertainty of diagnosis and prognosis, from the inequity of singling out pregnant women as being properly compellable to provide altruistic treatment for others, from the inevitable impairment of the doctor/patient relationship and from the near impossibility of achieving equal standards of enforcement. Such reasoning may not provide a good moral basis for the conclusion, but it makes excellent pragmatic sense.

This submission to 'reality' is not regarded as a confession of inability to reach a tenable conclusion. The subject, on analysis, seems to be one which is of major interest only in the context of academic argument or for use as a socio-political platform. As has already been intimated, the vast majority of women who have progressed to late pregnancy are anxious to complete their term and will go to very considerable lengths to preserve their infants. It is, of course, impossible to check all the cases which were unearthed by Kolder, but there is a definite impression that at least a majority of instances in which the courts have compelled treatment have been associated with strongly held religious views – and this is an area in which judicial intervention on behalf of the fetus or child, who can have no expressed beliefs, is widely practised. There is, however, much to be said for the view that attempts to enforce a possible ethical obligation by legal means will create more harm than they can prevent, an attitude which appeared to be clearly supported by the remarkable case of *Re AC*.[73]

Here a Caesarian section was ordered against the wishes of a moribund woman suffering from malignant disease who was 26 weeks' pregnant. In the event, the mother survived only long enough to see her baby die within a few hours of delivery. This scarcely credible decision was, in fact, overturned *post facto* by the Appeal Court,[74] which held that a right to informed refusal of medical treatment exists and that a fetus cannot have rights that are superior to those of a person who has already been born. The court was not, however, prepared to foreclose the possibility completely, holding: 'We do not quite foreclose the possibility that a conflicting State interest may be so compelling that the patient's interest must yield but we anticipate that such cases will be extremely rare and truly exceptional' (per TERRY J).

The treatment of the fetus *in utero* seems hardly to have become a jurisprudential issue in the United Kingdom; by contrast, the enforced Caesarian delivery has caused something of a stir in medico-legal circles. The origin of this lies in the obiter remarks of LORD DONALDSON MR in *Re T.*[75] In this case, the court repeatedly emphasised the rights of the competent adult to refuse medical or surgical treatment. In the course of his opinion, however, the Master of the Rolls said: 'The only possible qualification is a case in which the choice may lead to the death of a viable foetus ... and, if and when it arises, the courts will be faced with a novel problem of considerable legal and ethical complexity' (at 653). The eventuality materialised some three months later, when a 30-year-old born-again Christian refused Caesarian delivery of a full term fetus impacted in a transverse lie.[76] Clearly, SIR STEPHEN BROWN P had no time in which to consider the complexities and a declaration that non-consensual Caesarian section could be performed lawfully was granted in an 18-minute hearing. The President acknowledged that there were no English authorities directly in point and, while citing *Re AC*, presumably relied on Justice Terry's caveat quoted above when he suggested that a similar declaration would have been granted in such circumstances in the United States. The decision in *Re S* raised a storm of protest.[77] Some of this was, in my view, unmerited. The fact, for example, that the decision was taken in haste was an inevitable concomitant of an impacted labour of two days' duration – there seems little point in prolonged judicial consideration of treatment for a woman who died during the process. On the other hand, the decision ran contrary to the increasingly widely held rule that the disposition of one's own body is a fundamental human right and the reported reasoning behind it was certainly inadequate to support a new legal precedent.[78] The judge might, though it is not so stated, have regarded Mrs S's refusal of treatment, which was supported by her husband, as being vitiated by reason of undue outside influence: both LORD DONALDSON (in *Re T* at 662) and BUTLER-SLOSS LJ (in *Re T* at 667) were deeply suspicious of the combined pressure of a close relationship and religious belief. The effect of all such arguments is, however, only to demonstrate the sophistic depths that are currently plumbed by the law in this area. At the end of the day, Sir Stephen Brown probably relied on no more than intuition to tell him that the avoidable loss of *two* lives was something the law and the state should not support and, in doing so, he is likely to have attracted general, if not academic, approval.

An echo of *Re S* is to be found in *Tameside and Glossop Acute Services Trust* v. *CH.*[79] Here a paranoid schizophrenic detained compulsorily under the Mental Health Act 1983, s.3 was considered likely to resist treatment of her pregnancy. The obstetrician was of the opinion that her fetus' life was in danger; he accordingly sought a declaration that it would be lawful to perform a Caesarian section, and to apply the force necessary to do so, despite the woman's inability to consent. In the event, WALL J granted the declaration on the grounds that an ancillary reason for induction and, if necessary, section was to prevent a deterioration of the woman's mental state; that the birth of a live child was a prerequisite of successful treatment for her schizophrenia; and that her anti-psychotic medication could be resumed once her pregnancy was ended. The proposed induction of labour was, therefore, treatment of her mental condition and could be undertaken within the terms of the Mental Health Act 1983, s.63 and which, thus, did not require consent.[79a]

That, however, was not the end of the saga. In two cases, decided rapidly and almost simultaneously, JOHNSON J held that the women, although not suffering from a mental disorder, lacked the mental competence to make a decision as to surgical intervention because the highly emotional conditions of prolonged labour rendered them incapable of weighing up the considerations that were involved.[80] The judge was of the opinion that the lives of the women, in addition to those of the fetuses, were at risk in both cases and he, effectively, justified his action on the principle that, where there is a necessity to act: 'the action taken must be such as a reasonable person would in all the circumstances take, acting in the best interest of the assisted person'.[81] No matter how one may agree – or disagree – with this sentiment, the fact remains that these decisions were made rapidly and, of major jurisprudential importance, the women were not represented at the hearing. It was imperative that the position received more thorough judicial investigation and this was provided by the Court of Appeal in *In re MB*.[82] In this case, non-consensual Caesarian section was authorised on the grounds that a phobia of needles was sufficient to render a woman temporarily incompetent and incapable of making a decision. The Court of Appeal upheld this decision but, at the same time, made it clear that the court would have no power to intervene if a competent woman decided against medical intervention – and this despite the fact that the decision might be irrational or taken for no reason at all and was one that might result in the death of or serious handicap to the child or in the death of the woman herself.

Thus it is now difficult to see these cases as anything approaching victories for fetal rights. As things stand, the accolade rests on the principle of personal autonomy; as BUTLER-SLOSS LJ put it: 'If the competent mother refuses to have the medical intervention, doctors may not lawfully do more than attempt to persuade her. If that persuasion is unsuccessful, there are no further steps towards medical intervention to be taken.' Which may be impeccable jurisprudence – and which also attracts considerable academic support; the logical conclusion is, however, that health carers are forced to stand by while a patient dies in severe pain. This being the case, it seems paradoxical that the Royal College of Obstetricians and Gynaecologists supports the policy without qualification. Generals do not, however, commonly serve in the trenches; one wonders how many nurses have been consulted as to their opinions.

Interest in the potential rights of the viable fetus has not, however, been extinguished entirely and further consideration may be reserved for Parliament – where it really belongs. Clause 40 of the Incapable Adults (Scotland) Bill 1995 is intended to regularise the binding effect of an advanced statement as to the rejection of treatment in the event of mental incapacity. Sub-clause 7(*d*), however, goes on to say:

(7) An advance statement shall not have effect –
...
(d) in the case of a female adult, where compliance with it would endanger the development of a foetus being carried by her where the pregnancy has exceeded its twenty-fourth week

The argument as to whether this exception represents, on the one hand, a movement in favour of the fetal status or, on the other, an unacceptable restriction of personal autonomy on the grounds of mental incapacity should make interesting listening.

Fetal rights and abortion

Strictly speaking, the fetus has no *rights* vis-à-vis its mother until it is capable of being born alive. At that time, the Infant Life (Preservation) Act provides it with a partial right to life which is subject only to the mother's superior right to life; comparable protection is given in the United States by way of the viability provisions of *Roe v. Wade*.[83] In the United Kingdom, the 24-week-old fetus is, again, partially protected by the specific limitation on termination of pregnancy provided by the Abortion Act 1967, s.1(1)(*a*). Prior to that, we have seen that there are few, if any, legal concessions to fetal autonomy and this is, perhaps, expressed most vividly in the fact that the fetus is even denied the basic right to prefer death to an unacceptable form of life – a right which accrues to the neonate at the moment of birth and which is discussed in detail in Chapter 11.

At the heart of this injustice lies the wording of the Abortion Act 1967, s.1(1)(*b*) which clearly implies that the legality of an abortion on the grounds of severe fetal abnormality is determined by the effect such a child would have on the mother[84] – no distinction is made between abortion and what Ramsey called, many years ago, 'fetal euthanasia'.[85] Ramsey rightly pointed out that arguments in favour of abortion in the interests of the mother are, effectively, also arguments in favour of infanticide in order to preserve her well-being, and very few would accept the latter as being morally justifiable; the post-natal analogue of fetal euthanasia, however, is selective non-treatment of the new born which, being premised on the interests of the infant, is a far less unacceptable concept. It seems to me that the situation could be both rectified and clarified by adding the words: 'and that, as a result, its life would be intolerable' to s.1(1)(*d*) of the 1967 Act, which authorises termination on the grounds of fetal handicap. At the same time, however, the admission of a fetal *right to* abortion would have important implications for the 'wrongful life' action, a matter which is discussed in greater detail below.

Any indications for fetal euthanasia will result from the use of antenatal diagnostic methods; applying the results obtained is a matter of genetic counselling. It is impossible within the title of this book to consider the subject of genetic counselling in detail.[86] There are serious specific ethical and legal problems surrounding, say, the establishment of genetic registers,[87] profound difficulties as to concepts of medical confidentiality arise,[88] while the general basis of counselling is not, itself, free from moral criticism. It is not difficult to visualise a transition from a genuine concern for an individual family to a return of 'eugenics' or the elimination of the less than perfect, should the principles be misapplied. A brief overview of these is attempted below.[89]

Genetic counselling may be undertaken either pre- or post-conception. In the former, a partnership or a couple intending to enter into a partnership may be alerted to a possible genetic defect in their families and seek advice as to procreation. One option is then for a controlled pregnancy, in which case the couple join the second group, which is composed of those who are concerned for the outcome of a pregnancy already in being, and it is this situation which is relevant to the current discussion. In either case, genetic disease may be of three types. Firstly, it may be unifactorial, caused by a single abnormal gene, the transmission of which can be traced and the occurrence of which is mathematically predictable;[90] a well-defined variant is responsible for what is known as X-linked disease, when the abnormal gene exists on the X sex chromosome and, in general, is transmitted by the female but causes disease only in the male. Alternatively, the condition may be multifactorial in origin. Here the manifestation of an underlying genetic defect depends on the environmental circumstances; the condition of neural tube defect – spina bifida or anencephaly – is the most important in the reproductive phase although, in general terms, conditions such as coronary artery disease and several forms of carcinoma are of far greater significance. The occurrence of such disease can only be predicted empirically in the light of previous experience. Thirdly, genetic disease may be due to chromosomal abnormality. The commonest abnormality is the possession of a trio, rather than the normal pair, of similar chromosomes – so-called 'trisomy'. Although it is theoretically possible for a trisomal female to pass on the defect to half her children, it is, in practice, easier to regard the condition as one that appears sporadically; its occurrence is, however, heavily dependent on environmental factors, maternal age being the most important. Some degree of mental handicap is a common feature of chromosomal disease, of which Down's syndrome (or, technically, trisomy 21) is the best known example. Some 5 per cent of cases of Down's syndrome are, however, due to what is known as translocation of a gene fragment; this will arise sporadically but, once it has done so, a carrier state develops and the involvement of future generations can be predicted mathematically; it will also be independent of maternal age.[91] Finally, one has to mention congenital disease which results entirely from environmental factors. For reasons which are largely of administrative origin, often within a laboratory, it is this type of disease which gives rise to the majority of tort actions; the prime example is the congenital rubella, or German measles, syndrome.

The function of the genetic counsellor is then to assess the likelihood of there being an abnormality in the fetus and to provide the parents with sufficient information so that they can decide what is best for them *and* for the fetus in the circumstances of that individual family.[92] He or she has several technological aids in addition to empirical knowledge. Thus the presence of certain abnormalities – including, in particular, neural tube defect – may be inferred from an examination of the mother's blood; X-ray examination of the fetus is contraindicated, but the use of ultrasound imaging is, so far as is known, harmless and has a high diagnostic efficiency;[93] given the fact that the fetus is sufficiently mature, fetal blood sampling may also be available.[94] But probably the most useful procedure currently available is that of amniocentesis, whereby samples of the fluid medium surrounding the fetus are removed. These contain both active fetal cells and fetal excretions; it is thus possible to evaluate the chromosomal component of the cells, the metabolism of such cells, abnormalities associated with open lesions and, with the advent of DNA recombinant technology, the intimate genetic constitution of the fetus.[95]

There are, however, difficulties associated with many of these procedures. Firstly, they are not without danger to the fetus: thus, amniocentesis results in miscarriage in some 0.5 per cent of investigations; secondly, they are demanding of resources; thirdly, they all take time. It is, for example, virtually impossible to obtain an adequate amniotic sample before the fourteenth week of pregnancy and, using the best expertise, it may take up to three weeks to obtain an analysable chromosomal culture; as things stand at present, therefore, the vast majority of terminations for fetal abnormality are likely to be undertaken in the mid-trimester. The time involved may be shortened appreciably by the advance on amniocentesis that is known as chorion villus sampling, in which fetal cells are obtained from the developing placenta. The use of this technique, however, involves a trade-off in terms of safety: the miscarriage rate following chorion villus sampling, at the time of writing, is of the order of 2–5 per cent, and there are other practical and ethical considerations.[96] Genetic counselling involving invasive techniques is thus not something to be undertaken lightly and certainly not as a routine; there must be some indication, such as maternal age or a significant family history, before patients are accepted.

Given that there is a chance that the fetus will be defective, there are several possibilities which may be put to the parents; these include termination of pregnancy, a controlled pregnancy during which the progress of the mother and the fetus can be assessed, or continuation of the pregnancy and acceptance of the infant. In providing the care of an advisory service, the counsellor, like any other contractor, is liable in tort to the parents and the standard rules of medical negligence will apply. There can be no doubt that negligent advice to the effect that an abnormal fetus is normal can, and does, give grounds for an action by the pregnant woman who was, thereby, deprived of the chance to have the pregnancy terminated: what is popularly known as a 'wrongful birth' action.[97]

As things stand, the fetus, itself, appears to have no right of action against a counsellor unless his or her action was such as to be positively to its detriment. Thus the 1976 Act states specifically that there will be no liability to the child for treatment or advice given to the parent if the counsellor took reasonable care, having due regard to then received professional opinion applicable to the particular class of case (s.1(5)). The ambiguous rider to the effect that 'this does not mean that he is answerable only because he departed from received opinion' is, then, of no relevance to the fetus unless, say, the counsellor negligently prescribes a teratogenic drug to the pregnant woman – which is highly improbable – or fails to detect a *treatable* condition in the fetus. The more likely scenario is that negligent and incorrect advice is given to the effect that the fetus is normal and that the fetus is subsequently born defective. The affected fetus may then argue that it has been brought into existence in a defective state and that it would not have been were it not for someone's negligence; it has, thereby, been wronged. This is the basis of the so-called and hotly debated 'wrongful life' action.

The 'wrongful life' action

The difference between the 'wrongful birth' and the 'wrongful life' action is that the former is brought by the parents, as described above, while the latter is brought by the infant who is, effectively, saying: 'But for your negligence, I would not be living in a deprived condition; I am disadvantaged and, therefore, I am entitled to compensation.' For his part, the counsellor will argue: 'But for my action you would not be alive; hence my action, even if negligent, gives you a positive attribute and I owe you nothing in damages.'[98] The conceptual difficulty of the wrongful life action is thus to be found in two areas. Firstly, there is the problem of causation: only in the most exceptional circumstances would the counsellor have *caused* the defect. He is responsible only for the consequences which, secondly, can be compared only to non-existence which is the single available alternative, and it is this latter problem which has so exercised the minds of the courts. Once again, the history and development of the wrongful life action is best traced through the American legal system.

The wrongful life action seems to have been born in Illinois, with a case in which the issue was that of being born illegitimate.[99] The seminal case is, however, generally considered to be *Gleitman* v. *Cosgrove*.[100] Despite the fact that, allegedly as a result of negligent counselling, the mother gave birth to a deaf mute who was nearly blind, the court, in dismissing the action on the part of the child, wrote:

> If [the plaintiff] could have been asked as to whether his life should be snuffed out before his full term of gestation could run its course, our felt intuition of human nature tells us he would almost surely choose life with defects against no life at all. 'For the living there is hope, but for the dead there is none.'

The court considered it impossible to weigh the value of a handicapped life against non-existence. A year later, a similar case was rejected on the grounds that the law of tort was directed to protection against wrongs – and the greatest wrong was to cause a person's death.[101] The classical approach, however, still comes from the New York Court of Appeals:

> Whether it is better never to have been born at all than to have been born with even gross deficiencies is a mystery more properly to be left to the philosophers and the theologians. Surely the law can assert no competence to resolve the issue, particularly in view of the very nearly uniform high value which the law and mankind has placed on human life, rather than its absence.[102]

In 1980, however, a dichotomy arose, particularly contrasting the legal attitudes on the Pacific and Atlantic coasts of the United States, when the California Court of Appeals awarded damages to a child born with Tay-Sachs disease whose parents had been wrongly assured they did not carry the abnormal gene.[103] This was followed by the important decision in *Turpin* v. *Sortini*,[104] in which it was stated that it cannot be held as a matter of law that an impaired life is preferable to non-life in all situations; the law, it was thought, permits parents to make this determination in the interest of the unborn child. Nevertheless, the court was not prepared to go the whole way and, while admitting special damages, refused general damages largely because of the technical difficulty of comparing an impaired life with not being born at all; a similar restrictive line of reasoning was followed in the state of Washington.[105] Following this, it appeared that the west had influenced the east when the New Jersey Supreme Court allowed a wrongful life suit.[106] That action, however, was complicated by the fact that the parents were time-barred as to litigation and there was obvious concern that the child would have no other means of recovery. Even so, the court recoiled at the possible escalation of awards, particularly if recovery for general damages was allowed: 'Such a claim would stir the passions of jurors about the nature and value of life, the fear of non-existence, and about abortion. That mix is more than the judicial system can digest.'

Thus what seemed, at one time, to be a definite trend towards the acceptance of the wrongful life suit has been checked and later claims have been specifically rejected.[107] The New Hampshire case of *Smith* was particularly instructive. The reasons for rejection included an inability to declare a life not worthwhile, a fear of characterising congenital disabled persons as 'injured' and the practical likelihood that juries would never agree as to the proper extent of compensation. In general, the court considered that the small benefit of damages being awarded in the rare cases where 'wrongful life' was the only route to compensation was outweighed by the symbolic harmful effect of judicial recognition of the suit. Indeed, the American courts seem, now, to be settling these cases on the pragmatic grounds that the child does not *need* a wrongful life action so long as a wrongful birth action is available to the parents;[108] the possibility of a successful claim for wrongful life in the event that the parents cannot bring an action is not excluded – nor is the possibility of the defendants' liability for the child's care in the event of the parents' death. The tendency once shown by the American courts to demonstrate a judicial preference for childbirth over abortion, and thereby to reject not only actions for wrongful life but also those for wrongful birth,[109] seems to have been reversed.

A judicial antipathy to abortion is also to be seen in the only apposite English case,[110] a case which, taken in conjunction with the terms of the Congenital Disabilities (Civil Liability) Act 1976, s.1(2)(*b*), may well have closed the door on a wrongful life action throughout the United Kingdom.[111] *McKay* arose from the relatively common situation of an infant being born suffering from the congenital rubella syndrome, the allegation being that the mother's routine blood specimen was negligently tested. The wrongful life issue derived from a claim by the infant that the doctor's negligence in failing to treat her mother caused the injury with which she was born. This claim was struck out but, on appeal by the child, LAWSON J reversed the order, holding that there was a cause of action, in that the grounds for the child's complaint were not that she had been born but, rather, that she was born disabled. The matter accordingly went to the Court of Appeal.

In addressing the question of negligence, the Court of Appeal concluded that the child's disabilities were due to a viral infection and not to any failure in duty by the physician. The only 'duty' which might have been infringed would be one to take away life and the court could not see that any such duty could possibly exist. An obligation to abort would mean

> regarding the life of a handicapped child as not only less valuable than the life of a normal child, but so much less valuable that it was not worth preserving, and it would even mean that a doctor would be obliged to pay damages to a child infected with rubella before birth who was in fact born with some mercifully trivial abnormality. These are the consequences of the necessary basic assumption that a child has a right to be born whole or not at all, not to be born unless it can be born perfect or 'normal', whatever that may mean.[112]

The court followed the existing American pattern and questioned the possibility of comparing the value of a flawed life with non-existence or with a potential afterlife. STEPHENSON LJ also took the early American view that it was better to be born maimed than not at all, but can be reasonably criticised for adding: 'except, possibly, in the most extreme cases of mental and physical disability' – a concession which clearly admits of a subjective value judgment. The most interesting part of the opinion in the present context, however, was: 'To impose [a duty to take away life by means of abortion] would be to make a further inroad – in addition to that created by the Abortion Act 1967 – into the sanctity of human life which would be contrary to public policy.'

McKay may well be of no current significance, in that the Congenital Disabilities (Civil Liability) Act 1976, which postdated the case, is said, now, to exclude the possibility of a wrongful life action. Nevertheless, this may not be the case[113] and, certainly, not every jurisdiction meeting the matter for the first time will agree that it is right that it should be so.[114] Many would feel that it was unfortunate that the action in *McKay* was disallowed rather than tried; moreover, the remaining differences were settled out of court, so that we can only assume that the mother was successful in the concurrent 'wrongful birth' action which she was allowed to bring.

The present position is unsatisfactory from the point of view of the child born defective as a result of negligent counselling and there is a considerable body of academic opinion which opposes the present rigid stance.[115] I suggest that many of the difficulties would disappear if, firstly – and as already intimated – the decision to abort on fetal grounds was regarded as a matter for the fetus and, secondly, if the comparison was drawn in the light of the *prevailing* circumstances: that is, between the degree of impaired life and normality. The physician would then be seen to have a clear duty to the fetus while problems of causation could be overcome by accepting that the physician's negligence consisted of depriving the parents of the right to determine *on the child's behalf* whether it should be forced to exist in a defective state;[116] in short, if one stops thinking in terms of wrongful life and considers, instead, diminished life, an action in tort becomes the logical outcome. There is, moreover, no overpowering difficulty in assessing the effect of impairment in monetary terms: the courts undertake similar tasks in respect of other forms of personal injury without qualm. It is, admittedly, true that little practical injustice is caused by denying the wrongful life action; damages attached in the simultaneous wrongful birth suit, which will always be available in the absence of a technical contraindication, will protect the child until majority and the survival of a severely defective child beyond that age is problematic. But that is no reason for negating a principle.

All the foregoing discussion depends, of course, on the assumption that the defective fetus does not *want* to be born and it would be facile to attempt to avoid the obvious difficulty – that the 'fetal' decision must be taken in surrogate fashion. The dilemma is summed up in the sentence, 'We have never heard that in order to protect the fetus from injury, one deprives it of its life.'[117] At the end of the day, the fetus must be allowed to make its own decision, which it can only do by acting on the combined advice of doctor and parents. The concept of 'unexpressed autonomy' is, admittedly, a difficult one, but it has to be accepted; in practice, it reaches its apogee in relation to selective treatment of the newborn; the subject will be reverted to in Chapter 11.

The Preconception Tort

While there is little likelihood of the fetus being able to recover for negligent counselling which affects its future directly, there is very little doubt as to its rights when indirect injury results from negligent advice or treatment given to the mother before conception. English statute law to the point is established within the Congenital Disabilities (Civil Liability) Act 1976, which allows an action in respect of an occurrence which affected either parent of a child in his or her ability to have a normal, healthy child (s.1(2)(a)); such an action is subject to parental ignorance of the risk.

The principle has also come to be accepted in the United States, although its application has been fairly closely circumscribed.[118] The classic situation is provided by the occurrence of haemolytic disease in a child as a result of failure to protect a woman against rhesus sensitisation in a previous pregnancy[119] but there are several other examples.[120] There are no similar British cases, but an action closely related to one for 'preconception tort' has succeeded in England. The case involved a woman who was not informed that her miscarried fetus was anencephalic and, as a result, she had no investigations prior to the birth of a later child born with spina bifida;[121] the action was, however, brought by the mother, essentially as a 'wrongful birth': there was no action by the child and, perhaps significantly, it was said that no such claim *could* be mounted.

The suit brought by the child in preconception tort is to be distinguished from that for wrongful life, in that the injury in the former can clearly be *attributed* to a negligent action or omission on someone's part. The result of any litigation would, however, still depend upon *proof* of causation, and this might be difficult in the light of the inevitable time intervals between cause and effect. The two circumstances can be further distinguished in that preconception negligence, being unappreciated at the time of conception, deprives the parents of options other than abortion – for example, adoption, artificial insemination or not having children – but this, again, is a distinction to be made more in the context of 'wrongful birth'.

The living abortus

The Court of Appeal in *Attorney General's Reference (No 3 of 1994)*[122] emphasised that the decision had no bearing on lawful abortion. It is not easy to see how this can obtain in practice. The Abortion Act 1967, s.5(1) protects the obstetrician against a charge of child destruction – it says nothing about murder or manslaughter. A child that is born alive is a person *in rerum natura* and it is immaterial whether that life results from a lawful or an unlawful act. It follows that one cannot lawfully kill such a child intentionally and the Lord Chief Justice in *Attorney General's Reference* stated that 'such questions have no relevance to the issues which are raised by this reference and we make clear that we have given no consideration to them' (at 17).[123] Thus the problems surrounding the living abortus are by no means closed and, essentially, can be distilled into a discussion of the doctor's duty to keep such a child alive insofar as he or she is able.

'Viability' has been described in the preceding chapters as an uncertain state which depends upon many variables, and particularly upon the available neonatal expertise. It was notably O'CONNOR J in the American case of *Akron*[124] who emphasised the ever-increasing overlap which is occurring at the interface between prematurity and viability. The legality of late abortion in England and Wales is constrained, on the one hand, by the statutory protection of the fetus which is capable of being born alive and, on the other, by the Abortion Act 1967, s.1(1)(*a*) under which an abortion beyond the twenty-fourth week of pregnancy remains a criminal offence other than when performed in order to prevent the death of or grave injury to the mother or by reason of fetal abnormality. The important case of C v. S[125] cleared much of the confusion in English law by virtually equating the qualification 'capable of being born alive' with 'viable' but, in directing that the capacity to be born alive was defined by an ability to survive in the extramaternal environment *with or without* the use of a ventilator, the court still bound the law to the state of the art of intensive care.

It is generally agreed that, although exceptional cases can and do occur, the chances of extrauterine survival for a fetus of less than 23 weeks' gestation are, currently, remote; fetuses older than this *could*, however, be saved, depending upon their maturity and on the effort expended. It is clear, however, that the practical significance of the living abortus cannot, now be great: in Scotland, for example, only four abortions at 25 weeks' gestation and above were performed in 1993.[126] Moreover, as we have already considered, the majority of terminations for severe maternal reasons would pose no ethical dilemma as the woman would be anxious for her baby to survive if possible. The *frequency* with which a problem arises cannot, however, affect its *moral* and *legal* significance, which still merit some consideration.

It is useful, first, to consider the abortion techniques which are likely to be used in this particular age group and which will not result in destruction of the fetus – when, effectively, the conditions are those surrounding a premature birth. The more common methods are those which induce the pregnant woman to expel the fetus and this is done by way of the intra-amniotic infusion of fluids which may operate physically, such as concentrated saline solutions or solutions of urea, or physiologically, such as through the use of the hormone prostaglandin. Those methods that act by altering the physical conditions will be the most specifically feticidal but, at the same time, they are not entirely free of adverse effects on the pregnant woman herself; thus those methods which are least aggressive to the woman are those which are more likely to result in a living abortus. This dilemma can be met by deliberately injecting the fetus with a cardiotoxic drug.

Alternatively, the fetus may be delivered by hysterotomy, in which case, the obstetrician is carrying out a premature Caesarian section. In this situation, the maternal/fetal interests are distorted in favour of the latter: on the one hand, the method involves maximal maternal invasion but, on the other, it is that which is least likely to damage a fetus teetering on the brink of viability. In point of fact, hysterotomy is rarely undertaken; there were only 18 instances in England and Wales in 1995 out of almost 2000 abortions involving fetuses of 20 weeks' gestation or more.[127]

There are two distinct aspects of the living abortus phenomenon to be considered. First, on the ethical plane, we have the incongruity of doctors becoming actively involved in feticide as an objective, rather than as an inevitable component, of abortion. There is, however, little or no point in pursuing such discussion further. As has already been agreed, the Abortion Act is here to stay and the political leaders of the medical profession are committed to its current provisions; it is unlikely in the extreme that a profession of abortionist would ever be established and it follows that the medical profession must continue to face both ways in this particular situation. It is, however, certain that the attitude of many obstetricians to the living abortus is conditioned in major part by the second aspect: that is, by the legal considerations.

The practical difficulty confronting the doctor who produces a living abortus lies in the certainty of the law which holds that an infant who has 'breathed or shown any other sign of life after full expulsion from the mother' is not a stillbirth and is, therefore, entitled to a birth certificate and, if necessary, a certificate as to the cause of death'.[128] This might be regarded as little more than an administrative inconvenience but there are, of course, more serious implications. These are summed up in the words of the Director of Public Prosecutions (DPP), who is reported[129] as having said, albeit in a slightly different context: 'There will certainly have to be consideration whether the public interest requires a prosecution in cases where the doctor has deliberately ended the life of a baby.' There are several platforms from which a prosecution could be launched. Firstly, the obstetrician has certainly injured the fetus *in utero* and, save in the hysterotomy case, has clearly intended to do so; thus, given the death of a living abortus, the conditions for a charge of murder are established and, as we have seen, the particular point has not yet been addressed by the Court of Appeal.[130] The far less unlikely scenario would be based on the fact that deliberate non-treatment of the dying viable fetus could amount to causing death by omission and, accordingly, to manslaughter – and, depending upon the strength of a duty of care, that omission might even amount to murder.[131] Less dramatically, a charge could be brought under the Offences Against the Person Act, 1861, s.2[132] or under the Children and Young Persons Act, 1933, s.1, deriving from a failure to provide adequate care for a child in one's care. Finally, and in parallel, there is no reason why the General Medical Council should not be concerned at the standard of professional conduct which allows a recently delivered and breathing child to die without providing attention.

It is, perhaps, surprising how little legal precedent there is in the United Kingdom where apposite reports are almost entirely anecdotal. I know of only one instance in which a coroner considered that the death of a living abortus was due to want of attention at birth to a premature infant[133] and no further action was taken by the authorities. The precedents are no less unsatisfactory when one turns to the criminal courts. Only the case of Dr Hamilton appears relevant. Here an aborted infant was found to be considerably more mature than had been anticipated – 33 as opposed to 23 weeks' gestation – and was clearly alive after delivery; it is reported that it was then left in the sluice-room for some 15 minutes before being transferred to the intensive care unit, where it survived.[134] Dr Hamilton was charged with attempted murder on the instructions of the Director of Public Prosecutions; the Magistrates' Court then took the apparently unprecedented action in a case initiated by the DPP of deciding that there was no case to answer. Experience has been similar across the Atlantic.[135] Thus it seems – and, it is suggested, rightly so – that no prosecution of a doctor as to the murder or manslaughter of a living abortus is likely to succeed and, as we have seen, a doctor who acts within the terms of the Abortion Act 1967 cannot be prosecuted for the offence of child destruction under the Infant Life (Preservation) Act, 1929.

What, then, is to be done in practice? In ordinary circumstances, the clinician has contracted with the pregnant woman to relieve her of her fetus, and it must be remembered that abortion is justified by *maternal* benefit both by British statute and by American case law. He cannot, in reality, simply record and apologise for his failure in this respect but, at the same time, it would be absurd to suggest that he should be held in any way *responsible* for the live birth. It is suggested that the public as a whole seek *some* protection for the mature fetus and that the medical profession see the current state of the law as unsatisfactory, albeit far easier than it was before 1990.

Granted that the situation is now relatively inconsequential, provision must still be made for the occasional living abortus which is bound to appear, if for no other reason than that an error has been made as to gestational age. There is no policy that is fully consonant with a Hippocratic conscience other than one which ensures that efforts are made to salvage a living human neonate, *always provided* that it is in that neonate's best interests to do so, a matter which is discussed briefly below. I see no reason to alter my previously expressed view that the law should be framed so that an abortion undertaken at a time when the production of a living abortus is possible should be performed in such a way as to provide the maximum opportunity for the preservation of neonatal life.[136] It is, of course, true that such a statutory provision has been struck down in the United States as being an unconstitutional invasion of the relationship between a woman and her physician in that it limits the choice of methods of termination of pregnancy,[137] but American law is not entirely consistent in this area[138] and there is no reason why such a ruling should be followed in the United Kingdom.

The problem remains as to what is to be done with such a salvaged infant. Again, there seems little reason why legislation should not accept the abortus as an abandoned child which could be offered for adoption, subject, of course, to a maternal right of reclaim. This would not be a wholly novel departure; it would be consistent with McLean's interesting proposal that, subject to a woman's overriding right to control her own body, women seeking a termination could be positively encouraged – and given the opportunity – to carry their infants to viability with the intention that they be available for adoption.[139]

Fetal advantage?

The foregoing has assumed that survival is to the advantage of the aborted fetus, but this, of course, may not be true. Thus, as has already been discussed, a high proportion of late abortions are performed because there is a fetal abnormality. In 1995, 1828 or 1.2 per cent of all abortions were performed by reason of the fetal condition; this proportion rose to 31.5 per cent when abortions involving fetuses aged over 20 weeks were considered alone. It follows that obstetricians and/or neonatologists have no simple 'salvage in all circumstances' rule on which to rely. Moreover, the abortus is, by definition, premature and the technical difficulties and resource requirements are, correspondingly, great. Secondly, the best ultimate disposal of the infant *must* be through adoption (only in exceptional cases would the mother wish to recover her defective child) and it is inevitable that such infants would be more difficult to place. Whether or not an abortus is advantaged by aggressive perinatal care is, therefore, a matter of delicate balance.

The doctor still has a further hurdle to overcome. Whereas it is possible to see or otherwise diagnose congenital defects due to chromosomal disease or anatomical malformation, there is no way of assessing immediately the degree of neurological impairment which may result from prematurity *per se*, and this is a very real problem from which the continuing medical, financial and social costs involved cannot be divorced. Thus a major follow-up study of 356 extremely pre-term infants born at 23–8 weeks' gestation revealed that 19 per cent of the *long-term* survivors were impaired and 12 per cent demonstrated a major disability.[140] Yu concluded that all very premature live births should be resuscitated and given curative treatment until these were shown to be futile or lacking in compensating benefit.[141] But it is to be noted that his ethos derived from treatment of the wanted child, not the disowned abortus; further aspects of this most complex area will be discussed in Chapter 11.

Comatose or post-mortem gestation

There is one further development in the cause of fetal survival which is unrelated to abortion but which is associated with the living abortus through the common thread of 'viability': that is, the possibility of continuing ventilation of a comatose or dead woman in order that her fetus may be given a chance of life by increasing its maturity. Medical intervention of this type raises a number of serious moral problems for which it is difficult to find an answer. The practical, and, perhaps, logical, argument would run that, if we are prepared to expend considerable effort and resources to support the premature infant in an incubator, it is only right to use a natural incubator if one is available and offers the optimum treatment mode. More generally, it could be held that there is a duty to preserve life when the opportunity presents, and particularly so if the good (life) can be rescued from the bad (death).

The situation is not, however, uniform and scenarios will differ. At its ethically simplest extreme, the possibility of recovering a fetus by means of emergency Caesarian section of a woman, say, killed outright in an accident has always existed and gives rise to little, if any, moral conflict. The evolution of intensive care has, however, opened up new possibilities. There can be equally little doubt as to the correct course when a pregnant woman, who is being provided with intensive care in her own interests, either gives birth naturally or is induced as part of her treatment; the infant must be provided with the chance to survive and the only problems are those of a social nature.[142] In the middle road, a woman may be maintained alive, despite the futility of treatment, solely in order to bring the infant to viability; the argument between, on the one hand, the saving of fetal life and, on the other, respect for the right of a woman to a natural death may then be finely balanced.[143] The end of the line is the deliberate 'vivification' of the mother's cadaver purely for the benefit of the fetus. This development depends not only on improvements in 'life support' technology but also on the concept of 'brain-stem death', which is to say that, despite the artificial maintenance of the cardiorespiratory system, the body can be said to be dead if the brain-stem is dead.[144]

There have been a number of instances in which women said to be 'brain-stem dead' have been ventilated for more than 50 days in the hope that the fetuses they were carrying could be delivered safely,[145] and there must be many more others in which the period has been shorter. The number is likely to escalate as the intensive care units become increasingly able and willing to undertake such tasks; at the same time, public awareness and public concern grow with every incident reported in the press. There can be little doubt that such women are being 'used' as means to an end; the human female body is converted into what is, essentially, a physiological preparation and this must attract criticism, not least from the feminist movement. Whether the procedure is justified depends, it is suggested, on the stage of gestation at the time of the woman's death: a short period of ventilation may be acceptable, while a long incubation introduces additional practical and moral complications of its own. This seems to have been at the heart of the intense debate surrounding a German case in 1992 involving the death of a woman who was 15 weeks' pregnant; an attempt to salvage her baby was described as 'near the borderline of what is medically feasible and ethically allowable'.[146]

Inevitably, concern must be felt for the psychological status of any resulting child,[147] though it appears that such children as have been followed up show no abnormality. My own main concern, however, is conceptual and, although it is peripheral to the present discussion, I believe it is sufficiently important to merit mention. Jennett[148] has stated that, irrespective of ventilation, cardiac function can be maintained for a few days at most after death of the brain-stem. If this be so, 'ventilation of the brain dead woman for seven and a half weeks' is a contradiction in terms which raises the strong possibility of a misdiagnosis. Attempts to continue gestation in a brain-damaged woman may, therefore, not only represent a final insult to the woman's autonomy but may also be adding to the confusion and distrust which, even today, cloud the concept of brain-stem death.

Fetal neglect

The concept of fetal neglect has gained in importance as a result of increasing evidence of the effects of transplacental transfer of drugs. This phenomenon has been known since pre-Christian times as one which can cause fetal distress[149] and was very apparent – as an inadequately appreciated fetal alcohol syndrome – in the 19th century; the conjunction of a massive increase in drug addiction and the rapidly developing scientific basis of medicine has now forced the problem into a more searching light.

The effect of intrauterine intoxication on the fetus may be morphological, in which case, well-marked physical abnormalities can develop, or behavioural, when evidence of intoxication or of drug withdrawal becomes apparent only upon birth. Such effects may not, however, be the same as those which are to be seen in the affected mother. Thus, while the mother may metabolise and eliminate alcohol from her body fairly readily, the fetus cannot do so to the same extent. The pregnant woman may, therefore, go through bouts of alcoholism from which she recovers relatively rapidly; her fetus, by contrast, lies permanently in an alcoholic environment, and the effects may be equally permanent.[150] The effects of cocaine, the narcotic drugs and the hallucinogens on the fetus are now equally well documented.[151] It is to be noted that these can extend beyond the immediate condition. Thus an abnormally high proportion of affected neonates will die from the sudden infant death syndrome[152] and, as might be expected, infants born to drug-addicted parents are particularly liable to suffer further abuse and neglect in childhood.

Here, however, we are concerned more with the prevention of fetal injury than its diagnosis and the authorities are clearly in great difficulty in this field. All the arguments which are raised against non-consensual treatment of a pregnant woman in the interests of the fetus apply with even greater force in respect of behaviour control to the same end. The American authorities have attempted to apply criminal sanctions against abusing mothers, these being based in the main on existing child abuse legislation. Problems then arise, firstly, as to whether this is justifiable and, if so, secondly, whether the conditions are enforceable.

Myers, in the United States, emphasised that the state has not only a right but also a duty to protect children under its *parens patriae* powers, and was in no doubt that this extends to unborn children in whose welfare the state has a compelling interest.[153] Whether or not the concomitant state statutes prohibiting child abuse and neglect apply to the fetus is problematical. Myers points to the fact that excessive state intervention in parental activity is incompatible with constitutional principle; it follows that, while a delicate balancing operation might be undertaken when extrapolating the concept of child neglect to include maternal behaviour, intervention in such cases should be the rare exception and not the rule. Needless to say, the alternative view has been expressed,[154] and the tenor of the current analysis is to the effect that the authorities are inclining towards increasing acceptance of fetal rights – in which case, the logical extension would be for actions in tort to be available to the affected neonate against its mother. There is some evidence that this might have been possible in the United States at one time. In *Grodin* v. *Grodin*,[155] it was held that an injured child's mother would bear the same liability as a third party for negligent conduct that interfered with the child's legal right to begin life with a sound mind and body; the focal question in a particular case would be whether the woman's decision to continue taking drugs during pregnancy was a reasonable exercise of parental discretion, or, as Bross and Meredyth[156] put it, was there wanton or wilful conduct which dictated protection of the child? It seems, however, that the earlier cases have now been overruled and that the fetus does not fall under child abuse reporting laws.[157]

So far as is known, the United States is the only anglophone jurisdiction in which the question of maternal feticide resulting from behaviour during pregnancy has come before the criminal courts. The most relevant – and very unsatisfactory – case has been poorly reported,[158] but it appears that the mother's pregnancy was complicated by placenta praevia and that she ignored advice to abstain from drugs or sexual intercourse while still pregnant. She sustained an antepartum haemorrhage; the baby was born brain-damaged and was said to have shown toxicological evidence of amphetamine and cannabis ingestion; the mother was charged with wilfully omitting to furnish necessary medical attendance or other remedial care. Not surprisingly, the case was dismissed, but it is significant that the dismissal was on the grounds that there was no statutory basis for the charge.[159] American prosecutors are, however, tenacious. It is reported that a Wisconsin woman is being charged with attempted murder on the grounds that she drank alcohol throughout her pregnancy and was delivered of a child suffering from a mild fetal alcohol syndrome; the prosecution, the result of which seems not to be available, was subject to severe criticism.[160]

The problem has also been addressed by the family courts in Canada, where it has been suggested that statutory abuse reporting could be extended to abuse in the womb: 'It would be incredible to come to any other conclusion than that a drug addicted baby is born abused. The abuse has occurred during the gestation period';[161] and, in a case of maternal chronic alcoholism, it was held that the child *in utero* was a child in need of protection prior to birth by reason of its physical abuse by the mother in her excessive consumption of alcohol.[162]

Irrespective of how one feels about such maternal behaviour – and it is a very arguable view that drug addiction, including alcoholism, rather than being criminal is a medical condition deserving of increased antenatal support – the practical difficulties of enforcing protection for the fetus are almost insuperable, even if 'abuse' is definable in this context. The legal complications have also been highlighted in the English case of *Re F (in utero)*.[163] Here the local authority was concerned at the behaviour of a pregnant woman and its likely effect on her child and, innovatively, sought to have the fetus made a ward of court. In the Family Division, HOLLINGS J first distinguished the fetus as being capable of being born alive and concluded that the fact that the child could not be a party to proceedings did not, in itself, constitute a reason why wardship proceedings could not apply to the unborn child. Nonetheless, the paramount principle in the wardship court was the welfare of the child. There might well be conflict between the welfare of the child and that of the mother and there would be 'repugnance on the part of any right-thinking person to think of applying the principle of paramountcy in favour of the child's welfare at the expense of the mother's'. This opinion was upheld by the Court of Appeal who, further, pointed to possible conflicting legal interests: 'There would be insuperable difficulties if one sought to enforce the order against the mother who refused to comply with the order' (per MAY LJ at 138). Interestingly, MAY LJ concluded that the wording of existing statutes indicated that a 'minor' could only be a person in the sense that he or she had been born;[164] BALCOMBE LJ found no assistance in the statutes but, nevertheless, concluded that an unborn child had no existence independent of the mother and the only purpose of extending the jurisdiction to include a fetus would be to enable the mother's actions to be controlled.[165] Both were agreed that it was for Parliament, not the courts, to say whether a fetus *in utero* was to be regarded as a 'minor'. Until then, the indications are that the law of England sees no way of protecting a fetus against the behaviour of its mother, and the court in *Re F* clearly doubted the desirability of such interference with the liberty of the individual.[166]

The court will, however, ensure protection of the child the moment it feels able to do so. This was demonstrated conclusively in *re D (a Minor)*[167] which, effectively, was concerned as to whether or not the terms of the Children and Young Persons Act 1969, s.1(2) could apply to the fetus *in utero*. The relevant section provides:

If the court before which a child ... is brought ... is of opinion that any of the following conditions is satisfied ...

(a)   his proper development is being avoidably prevented or neglected or his health is being avoidably impaired or neglected or he is being ill-treated ...

and also that he is in need of care or control ... then ... the court may if it thinks fit make such an order.

The case concerned a mother who was a registered drug addict and who gave birth to a child suffering from withdrawal from narcotic uptake. The magistrates approved a place of safety order for the neonate following a period of intensive care and this was reinforced by a succession of interim care orders. The point at issue was not whether the infant was in need of care and control but, rather, whether the order was premature since the child had never been in the care of its parents. The argument thus devolved on the interpretation of the words 'in being' and, to some extent, the semantic niceties are irrelevant to the present discussion. Suffice it to say that both the Court of Appeal and the House of Lords agreed that, when the child was still in hospital, her proper development was being avoidably prevented and that that situation would not have arisen if the mother had not persisted in taking excessive narcotic drugs throughout her pregnancy. It followed that the fact that the cause of the child's actual situation dated to the time before she was born was immaterial, and the legislative purpose of s.1(2)(a) was being furthered by allowing such matters, in such cases, to be taken into account. It was, at the same time, emphasised (per LORD GOFF) that a continuum had to be in existence at the relevant time in order to establish that an antenatal affliction was related to conditions after birth.

The *Re D* decision caused some surprise, in that it not only established a *post hoc* control of the mother's liberty but also accepted that she could be deprived of an opportunity to prove herself to be an efficient mother – something which is not impossible within the drug-dependent sub-culture. The generally accepted proposition that the ideal result of care proceedings is the re-establishment of the family unit was, therefore, being opposed. The correct interpretation of *Re D* must be that the outcome was decided on the particular facts and that it would not necessarily be followed in every instance. What it does do, however, in general, is to make it clear that, when the occasion demands, the family court – and perhaps, but by no means necessarily, the criminal court – can take the prenatal, neonatal and hypothetical future periods as a continuous whole when making its decisions.

It will, in fact, do so. Thus, in *Re re P*,[168] the Court of Appeal authorised the removal of an infant from his parents on the day he was born on the basis of the past and potential future history of sexual abuse within the family. In so doing, it reversed the order of the High Court judge who had said: 'The chilling remedy asked for by the plaintiff invites attention to the fearful possibility that one could possibly be doing one of the worst imaginable things in taking a child from its parents for no proper reason.' This, if it does nothing else, emphasises how disparate and complicated may be the positions adopted in the field of childcare. The dilemma was highlighted in a further case where the local authority announced their attention of making an infant a ward of court and denying the natural parents access immediately after its birth,[169] this being on the grounds that three previous children died within weeks after birth having, apparently, developed virus infections. The measure was described as Draconian and, on the face of things, seems difficult to justify; the action was, however, heard in private and is unreported. These cases are, perhaps, at some distance from the subject of fetal rights; nevertheless, they demonstrate the increasing attention that intragestational behaviour of all types will be accorded when the best interests of the neonate are considered.

Fetal disposal

There remains for brief discussion what may be regarded as the last fetal right: the right to be disposed of decently after death. This is rather more than a matter of emotion and has several medico-legal connotations. One method of disposal of fetal remains is to utilise them for research and experimentation. This, however, is a specialised subject which will be considered in Chapter 7; for the present, we will consider only the broader issues.

There are no regulations as to the disposal of a dead fetus in the United Kingdom, where a marked distinction is made between the product of miscarriage or abortion and a stillbirth. The latter is defined by statute as a fetus which has issued forth from its mother after the twenty-fourth week of pregnancy and which did not at any time after being completely expelled from its mother breathe or show any other sign of life.[170] A stillbirth must be registered, the certificate of cause being signed by a registered medical practitioner or by a registered midwife;[171] alternatively, any qualified informant may complete the certificate in the absence of a suitably qualified professional. The occurrence should be notified to the coroner or procurator fiscal if there is doubt as to whether or not the infant achieved a separate existence. The Human Tissue Act, 1961 does not cover stillbirths. They must be either buried or cremated following much the same pattern as applies to deaths; apart from the adaptation of the necessary cremation forms, the main difference is that the superintendent of the burial ground or the crematorium does not have to notify the registrar of the fact of disposal of a stillbirth.

By contrast, the only limitations as to disposal of the dead fetus are those associated with decency and the requirements of the various Public Health Acts and regulations; there is thus no statutory impediment to the use of fetal materials for research or therapeutic purposes.[172] Increasingly, however, women are becoming concerned as to the fate of what they understandably see as their dead babies; this movement may well be associated with the newer techniques, including, in particular, ultrasonography, which tend to bring pregnant women even closer emotionally to the child *in utero*. As a consequence, it is not uncommon for parents to seek a normal burial and memorial for their 'child'. The superintendent of the burial ground is then in something of a dilemma; there is no objection to parts of the plot being used for such a purpose, but he cannot know that he is not, in fact, disposing of an unregistered stillbirth and is, thus, in breach of the law. There being no official way round this impasse, doctors, in support of the best interests of their patients, are tending to issue certificates of fetal birth which the superintendent may, if he feels able to, accept. Although the practice seems wholly commendable, such certificates are quite unofficial and carry no authority. They may, however, serve a most useful purpose in the management of bereavement and I would like to see a statutory acknowledgement of their use.

The general laxity of fetal disposal regulation has led to some bizarre litigation on a worldwide basis. An Australian case of 1908 is of interest in demonstrating the changes in public standards which have occurred in the last century. In *Doodeward* v. *Spence*,[173] a showman preserved a monstrous stillbirth for display. The High Court held that 'There is no law forbidding the mere possession of a human body, whether born alive or dead, for purposes other than immediate burial if [the preservation of the body] may afford valuable or interesting information or instruction', and the rest of the judgment made it clear that the requirements of public decency had not been infringed! In more recent times, the American courts have dealt with actions in tort associated with preservation of fetal remains for teaching purposes. Thus a suit has been allowed seeking compensation for the emotional pain and injury said to have been sustained when a mother was told her fetus had been retained in cold storage,[174] and damages in negligence and in breach of contract have been awarded when a fetus was preserved in formalin and shown to the mother.[175] A number of cases deriving from Louisiana are of greater interest in the present context. There a statute imposing a duty that the products of abortion be disposed of in a manner consistent with the disposal of other human remains has been struck down on the grounds that it imposed two impermissible psychological burdens on the pregnant woman concerning her abortion: firstly, the statute equated the disposal of a fetus with that of the person and, secondly, it forced the woman to consider whether her abortus should be cremated or buried.[176] The amended statute was then, again, struck down in that it constituted a direct burden on a pregnant woman's abortion rights because the information as to how the abortus was to be disposed of could cause her psychological harm.[177] Certainly, the disposal of fetal remains seems to cause considerable anxiety even to the Supreme Court of the United States,[178] but, while the Louisiana decisions may be regarded as further support for the rights of women, they can equally be seen as insulting to women in questioning their ability to make rational decisions without the need for paternalistic intervention by the courts.

This attitude expressed in *City of Akron*, above, may be contrasted with that in other jurisdictions, for example, Sweden, where there is increasing appreciation of the unique character of the developing fetus. As a result, aborted fetuses – whether natural or therapeutic – of more than 12 weeks' gestation are retained for up to one month pending an expression of the mother's or the couple's wishes and certification by a doctor. Not everyone approves these new regulations – an adverse effect on some women is admitted; they are, however, the logical result of the expressed Swedish view that the developing human life cannot be viewed purely as part of the woman's body.[179]

Notes

1   Medical News, 'Global perspectives on abortion' (1987) 294 Brit Med J 1102.
2   *Deitrich v. Inhabitants of Northampton* 138 Mass 14 (1884) at 16.
3   *Borowski v. Attorney-General of Canada et al.* (1984) 4 DLR (4th) 121 per MATHESON J at 131.
4   *Paton v. British Pregnancy Advisory Services Trustees* [1979] QB 276.
5   *C v. S* [1988] QB 135. Now confirmed in Scotland: *Kelly v. Kelly* 1997 SLT 896. Permission was granted to appeal to the House of Lords but there were no further proceedings.
6   For modern overviews of the situation, see A. Whitfield, 'Common law duties to unborn children' (1993) 1 Med Law Rev 28 and, for Scotland, K.McK. Norrie, 'Liability for injuries caused before birth' 1992 SLT 65.
7   *R v. Tait* [1989] 3 All ER 682 (fetus not 'another person' who could be threatened under the Offences Against the Person Act, 1861, s.16); *R v. Newham London Borough Council, ex p Dada* (1995) Times, 3 February (fetus not a person who might cohabit with the mother for the purposes of the Housing Act 1985, s.75); *R v. Wenham* (1990) unreported, Liverpool Crown Court (stillborn fetus of 8 months' gestation not 'killed by reckless driving' when mother run down).
8   *Nasciturus pro iam nato habetur quotiens de eius commodo agitur.* For discussion,

see J.M. Thomson, *Family Law in Scotland* (2nd edn, 1991) Edinburgh: Butterworths, p. 149.

9   Bankton, *Institute* (1751–3), I, ii, 7.

10 *Elliot* v. *Joicey* 1935 SC 57. See the rather old but authoritative paper, D.M. Yorke, 'The legal personality of the unborn child' 1979 SLT 158. Note that the 'fiction' exists for the benefit of the child alone, not for that of third parties.

11 *S* v. *Distillers Company (Biochemicals) Ltd* [1969] 3 All ER 1412. It transpires that such doubts were ill-founded: *Burton* v. *Islington Health Authority; de Martell* v. *Merton and Sutton Health Authority* [1992] 3 All ER 833, CA.

12 See Scottish Law Commission, *Liability for Ante-natal Injury* (1973), Scot Law Com no. 30.

13 *Montreal Tramways* v. *Leveille* (1933) 4 DLR 337. Followed in *Duval* v. *Seguin* (1973) 40 DLR (3d) 666.

14 65 F Supp 138 (DC, 1946).

15 157 A 2d 497 (NJ, 1960) per PROCTOR J at 504.

16 Direct liability to the child may arise from negligent infertility treatments: Congenital Disabilities (Civil Liability) Act 1976, s.1A, inserted by Human Fertilisation and Embryology Act 1990, s.44.

17 At s.4(4). See also the very specific opinion to that effect in the important Australian case of *Watt* v. *Rama* [1972] VR 353, discussed in P.F. Cane, 'Injuries to unborn children' (1977) 51 ALJ 704.

18 *Watt* v. *Rama* [1972] VR 353.

19 See, in particular, *McCluskey* v. *HM Adv* 1989 SLT 175. Compare *Williams* v. *Luff* (1978) 122 Sol Jo 164 (survival – out of court settlement) with *R* v. *Wenham*, n. 7 above (no suvival – no road traffic offence).

20 Reported by D. Brahams, 'Australian mother sued by child injured in utero' (1991) 338 Lancet 687. A similar case, taken under the Congenital Disabilities (Civil Liability) Act 1976, s.2 (which allows a child to sue its mother in the event of injury *in utero* due to negligent driving) has been settled in Northern Ireland: *McLaughlin* v. *McLaughlin*, reported by C. Dyer, 'Boy wins damages after injury in utero' (1992) 304 Brit Med J 1400.

21 1992 SCLR 182 ; (1991) Times, 17 September.

22 1992 SLT 1045; (1992) Times, 6 November.

23 (1991) 10 BMLR 41, OH.

24 See *Hamilton* v. *Fife Health Board* (1993) 13 BMLR 156 per LORD MCCLUSKEY at 159–60 for confirmation.

25 Note 12 above.

26 1993 SLT 624; (1993) 13 BMLR 156, IH.

27 While an executor might raise an action in negligence, there can be no executor if no *person* has died.

28 *Vaillancourt* v. *Medical Center Hospital of Vermont Inc* No 4-80 (Me, 5 November 1980).

29 *Amadio* v. *Levin* 501 A 2d 1085 (Pa, 1985).

30 *Thibert* v. *Milka* 646 NE 2d 1025 (Mass, 1995). For a review of the viability standard, see A. Peterfy, 'Fetal viability as a threshold to personhood' (1995) 16 J Leg Med 607.

31 *Jarvis* v. *Providence Hospital* 444 NW 2d 235 (Mich, 1989).

32 Note 30 above.

33 410 US 113 (1973).

34 *Wallace* v. *Wallace* 421 A 2d 134 (NH, 1980). See also *Chrisafogeorgis* v. *Brandenberg* 304 NE 2d 88 (Ill, 1973).

35 *O'Grady* v. *Brown* 654 SW 2d 904 (Mo, 1983).

36 *Group Health Association Inc* v. *Blumenthal* 453 A 2d 1198 (Md, 1983).

37 Originally propounded in *Smith* v. *Brennan* 157 A 2d 497 (NJ, 1960).

38 See *Miccolis* v. *AMICA Mutual Ins Co* 587 A 2d 67 (RI, 1991) in which it was held that a non-viable fetus (5 weeks old in this case) could not maintain a cause of action under the state's wrongful death statute. The court noted, however, that the problem of speculative damages could be solved by the state setting standard damages.

39 See B.R. Furrow, 'Actions for wrongful life', in J.K. Mason (ed.), *Paediatric Forensic Medicine and Pathology* (1989), London: Chapman & Hall.

40 P.J. Pace, 'Civil liability for pre-natal injuries' (1977) 40 MLR 141.

41 For example, in *Amadio* v. *Levin*, n. 29 above.

42 In *Roe* v. *Wade* 410 US 113 (1973) at 158. For exhaustive discussion, see J.E.B. Myers, 'Abuse and neglect of the unborn: can the State intervene?' (1984) 23 Duquesne L Rev 1.

43 *Pehrson* v. *Kistner* 222 NW 2d 634 (Minn, 1974); *Panagopoulous* v. *Martin* 295 F Supp 220 (W Va, 1969).

44 *Milton* v. *Cary Medical Center* 538 A 2d 252 (Me, 1988).

45 Positively stated in *Summerfield* v. *Supreme Court* 698 P 2d 712 (Ariz, 1985); *Eich* v. *Town of Gulf Shores* 300 So 2d 354 (Ala, 1974). For a good discussion of wrongful death of the fetus in general, see H. Brown, M. Dent, L.M. Dyer, *et al.*, 'Legal rights and issues surrounding conception, pregnancy, and birth' (1986) 39 Vand L Rev 597.

46 *Bagley* v. *North Hertfordshire Health Authority* (1986) 136 NLJ 1014.

47 See Whitfield, n. 6 above.

48 In *Burton*, n. 11 above at 843.

49 Note 26 above. Unfortunately, Whitfield's authoritative article pre-dated the Inner House decision.

50 Note 46 above. See also *Grieve* v. *Salford Health Authority* [1991] 2 Med LR 295.

51 Infant Life (Preservation) Act, 1929. The offence of child destruction also covers the killing of a child in the process of birth: the fetus is not being aborted, nor can it be murdered as it is not a 'creature in being'. The importance of such a lacuna is shown in the Canadian case of *R* v. *Sullivan* (1991) 63 CCC (3d) 97, in which a child in the course of being born was held not to be a person subject to criminal negligence.

52 By contrast, such an offence exists at least in the state of California where it has been decided in the Supreme Court that viability is not a required element of fetal murder: see *People* v. *Davis* 30 Cal Rptr 2d 30 (1994). It is to be noted that some of the apparent differences between UK and USA law lie in semantics. In general, a fetal death certificate is required in the USA when a potentially viable fetus dies; there is no such thing as a fetal death certificate in the UK, where the death of a potentially viable fetus – above the age of 24 weeks – is recorded as a stillbirth.

53 [1996] 2 All ER 10, CA.

54 See also the widely quoted case *R* v. *Kwok Chak Ming* [1963] HKLR 349, in which very much the same reasoning was applied.

55 F. Gibb, 'Judges strengthen laws protecting unborn children' (1995), *The Times*, 25 November, p. 7.

56 For a rightly critical review of the judgment, see M. Seneviratne, 'Post-natal injury and transferred malice: the invented other' (1996) 59 MLR 884.

57 *McCluskey* v. *HM Advocate* 1989 SLT 175 at 176.

58 1994 Crim LB 12-3. It is to be noted that this was a decision in the Sheriff Court only.

59 Note 57 above. Here the fetus injured in a road traffic accident was delivered by Caesarian section but died the next day. The driver was convicted of killing by dangerous driving.

60 In *Langford* v. *Blackman* 790 SW 2d 127 (Tex, 1990) it was held that a viable

fetus which died *in utero* as a result of a road traffic accident was a person for the purposes of the state's wrongful death Act.

61 J. Benschof, 'Reasserting women's rights', in 'Late abortion and technological advances in fetal viability' (1985) 17 Fam Plan Perspect 162; quoted by D. Callahan, 'How technology is reframing the abortion debate' (1986) Hastings Center Rep (February) 33.

62 For a powerful expression of this approach, albeit somewhat dated, see E.W. Keyserlingk, 'A right of the unborn child to pre-natal care – the civil law perspective' (1982) 13 Rev de Droit 49.

63 Note 61 above.

64 See N.S. Adzick and M.R. Harrison, 'Fetal surgical therapy' (1994) 343 Lancet 897 for the current state of the art.

65 The subject is addressed in general by C. Wells and D. Morgan, 'Whose foetus is it ?' (1991) J Law & Soc 431.

66 *Roe* v. *Wade*, n. 33 above. See L.J. Nelson, B.P. Buggy and C.J. Weil, 'Forced medical treatment of pregnant women: "Compelling each to live as seems good to the rest"' (1986) 37 Hastings L J 703, for discussion of the relatively limited powers of the state.

67 *Justus* v. *Atchison* 565 P 2d 122 (Cal, 1977); *People* v. *Smith* (1976) 59 Cal App 3d 751. See also n. 52 above.

68 N. Rhoden, 'The judge in the delivery room: the emergence of court-ordered cesareans' (1986) 74 Calif Law Rev 1951. For an evaluation within the confines of a relatively short article, see L.J. Nelson and N. Milliken, 'Compelled medical treatment of pregnant women: life, liberty and law in conflict' (1988) 259 J Amer Med Ass 1060. See also Supreme Court decisions such as *Colautti* v. *Franklin* 439 US 379 (1979); *Thornburgh et al.* v. *American College of Obstetricians and Gynecologists et al.* 106 S Ct 2169 (1986).

69 The classic cases are *Raleigh Fitkin-Paul Morgan Memorial Hospital* v. *Anderson* 201 A 2d 537 (NJ, 1964); *Jefferson* v. *Griffin Spalding County Hospital Authority* 274 SE 2d 457 (Ga, 1981).

70 V.E.B. Kolder, J. Gallagher and M.T. Parsons, 'Court-ordered obstetrical interventions' (1987) 316 New Engl J Med 1192.

71 F.A. Chervenak and L.B. McCullough, 'Perinatal ethics: a practical analysis of obligations to mother and fetus' (1985) 66 Obstet Gynecol 442. A similar argument can be developed on the lines of rights to life versus rights to quality of life. See E.-H.W. Kluge, 'When caesarian section operations imposed by a court are justified' (1988) 14 J Med Ethics 206. The views of F.H. Miller, 'Maternal–fetal ethical dilemmas: a guideline for physicians' (1991) 10 Seminars Anesthet 157 are particularly attractive.

72 446 NE 2d 395 (Mass, 1983).

73 533 A 2d 611 (DC, 1987).

74 *Re AC* 573 A 2d 1235 (DC, 1990).

75 *Re T (adult) (refusal of medical treatment)* [1992] 4 All ER 649.

76 *Re S (adult: refusal of medical treatment)* [1992] 4 All ER 671.

77 Though not universally in medical quarters: 'It would be difficult to argue against the obvious good sense of this finding', said the Editorial comment, 'Court orders a caesarian section' (1992) 82 Bull Med Ethics 3.

78 For a withering criticism, see A. Grubb, 'Commentary on *Re S*' [1993] 1 Med L Rev 92.

79 [1996] 1FLR 762. A very interesting selection of views on the case, almost all critical of the decision, is to be found under the general heading 'Caesarian section: a treatment for mental disorder?' (1997) 314 Brit Med J 1183.

79a This strategem is about to be challenged in the Court of Appeal, permission being granted even though the action was time barred. See C. Dyer 'Woman can challenge hospital over forced caesarean' (1997) 315 Brit Med J 78.

80 *Norfolk and Norwich (NHS) Trust* v. *W* [1996] 2 FLR 613. My other current citation is *Rochdale Healthcare (NHS) Trust* v. *C* [1996] 3 *Hempson's Lawyer* 505.

81 Per LORD GOFF in *In Re F (mental patient: sterilisation)* [1990] 2 AC 1 at 75. While emphasising that the focus of attention was on the patient herself, JOHNSON J commented in *W* that the fetus was a fully formed child, capable of normal life if only it could be delivered from the mother.

82 *In re MB (Caesarian section)* [1997] 2 FCR 541. See also earlier, very similar case: *Re L (patient: non-consensual treatment)* (1996) 35 BMLR 44, FD.

83 Note 33 above.

84 An implication which was confirmed in *McKay* v. *Essex Area Health Authority* [1982] QB 1166, discussed later.

85 P. Ramsey, 'Reference points in deciding about abortion', in J.T. Noonan (ed.), *The Morality of Abortion* (1970), Harvard: Harvard University Press.

86 A useful modern account, with considerable technical detail, is to be found in J.A. Raeburn, 'Genetic counselling and pre-natal diagnosis' in J.K. Mason, (ed.), *Paediatric Forensic Medicine and Pathology* (1989), London: Chapman & Hall.

87 See I.M. Pullen, 'Patients, families and genetic information', in E. Sutherland and R.A. McCall Smith (eds), *Family Rights* (1990), Edinburgh: Edinburgh University Press. A very updated review is G.T. Laurie, 'The most personal information of all: an appraisal of genetic privacy in the shadow of the human genome project' (1996) 10 Int J Law Policy Fam 74.

88 Discussed in particular by C. Ngwena and R. Chadwick, 'Genetic diagnostic information and the duty of confidentiality: ethics and law' (1993) 1 Med Law Internat 73.

89 For a very thorough overview of the whole subject, see Nuffield Council on Bioethics, *Genetic Screening: Ethical Issues* (1993), London: The Nuffield Foundation.

90 This is a convenient way of looking at the situation, but it is probably an oversimplification: J. Alper, 'Genetic complexity in single gene diseases' (1996) 312 Brit Med J 196.

91 The significance of this form of disease was noted in *Gregory* v. *Pembrokeshire Health Authority* (1989) 1 Med LR 81.

92 The counsellor has to distinguish between advice given on the grounds of public health and that designed for the individual family, and impartiality may be very difficult to achieve: A. Clarke, 'Is non-directive genetic counselling possible?' (1991) 338 Lancet 998.

93 It might, however, be expected that there could be a dose effect and that repeated exposure should be avoided: J.P. Newnham, S.F. Evans, C.A. Michael *et al.*, 'Effects of ultrasound during pregnancy: a randomised controlled trial' (1993) 342 Lancet 887.

94 Again, there is a risk/benefit analysis to be made: N.M. Fisk and S. Bower, 'Fetal blood sampling in retreat' (1993) 307 Brit Med J 143.

95 For a review of the conditions for which tests are available, see J.R.W. Yates, 'Medical genetics' (1996) 312 Brit Med J 1021.

96 R.J. Lilford, 'The rise and fall of chorionic villus sampling' (1991) 303 Brit Med J 936; J.A. Boss, 'First trimester prenatal diagnosis: earlier is not necessarily better' (1994) 20 J Med Ethics 146.

97 The 'wrongful birth' action is now well recognised in the United States. For full analysis, see J.R. Botkin and M.J. Mehlman, 'Wrongful birth: medical, legal and philosophical issues' (1994) 22 J Law Med & Ethics 21. This is also true in the United Kingdom, at least by implication: *Salih* v. *Enfield Health*

Authority [1990] 1 Med LR 333. There is, however, no obligation on a woman to have a termination: *Emeh* v. *Kensington and Chelsea and Westminster Area Health Authority* [1984] 3 All ER 1044.

98 For an extensive review, see Furrow, n. 39 above. See also K.McK. Norrie, 'Wrongful life in Scots law: no right, no remedy' [1990] Juridical Rev 205.

99 *Zepeda* v. *Zepeda* 190 NE 2d 849 (Ill, 1963). See also *Williams* v. *State of New York* 18 NY 2d 481 (1966).

100 296 NYS 2d 689 (1967). But note that, at that time, the legality of an abortion would have been very questionable.

101 *Stewart* v. *Long Island College Hospital* 296 NYS 2d 41 (1968). Other well-known early cases include *Dumer* v. *St Michael's Hospital* 233 NW 2d 372 (1975); *Speck* v. *Finegold* 438 A 2d 110 (Pa, 1979); *Blake* v. *Cruz* 698 P 2d 315 (Idaho, 1984).

102 *Becker* v. *Schwartz, Park* v. *Chessin* 386 NE 2d 807 (NY, 1978).

103 *Curlender* v. *Bio-Science Laboratories* 165 Cal Rptr 477 (1980).

104 643 P 2d 954 (Cal, 1982).

105 *Harbeson* v. *Parke-Davis Inc* 656 P 2d 483 (Wash, 1983).

106 *Procanik* v. *Cillo* 478 A 2d 755 (NJ, 1984).

107 *Smith* v. *Cote* 513 A 2d 341 (NH, 1986); *Ellis* v. *Sherman* 515 A 2d 1327 (Pa, 1986).

108 *Proffitt* v. *Bartolo* 412 NW 2d 232 (Mich, 1987); *Viccaro* v. *Milunsky* 551 NE 2d 8 (Mass, 1990). See also the South African case of *Friedman* v. *Glicksman* 1996 (1) SA 1134, an instance of spina bifida in which the wrongful life action failed but the wrongful birth action was accepted.

109 For example, *Azzolino* v. *Dingfelder* 337 SE 2d 582 (NC, 1985); *Siemieniec* v. *Lutheran General Hospital* 512 NE 2d 691 (Ill, 1987).

110 *McKay* v. *Essex Area Health Authority* [1982] QB 1166.

111 Scots law would probably follow *McKay*, n. 110 above: K.McK. Norrie, 'The actionability of birth' 1983 SLT 121.

112 Per STEPHENSON LJ at QB 1180.

113 See, for example, J.E.S. Fortin, 'Is the "wrongful life" action really dead?' [1987] J Soc Welfare L 306.

114 J. Levi, 'Wrongful life decision in Israel' (1987) 6 Med Law 373, where the Supreme Court allowed a wrongful life action by a majority of 4:1.

115 For example, M. Slade, 'The death of wrongful life: a case for resuscitation?' (1982) 132 NLJ 874; G.E. Jones and C. Perry, 'Can claims for "wrongful life" be justified?' (1983) 9 J Med Ethics 162; A.N.C. Liu, 'Wrongful life: some of the problems' (1987) 13 J Med Ethics 69. See also I. Kennedy and A. Grubb, *Medical Law* (2nd edn, 1994), London: Butterworths, p. 976, where it is suggested that, in inserting the Congenital Disabilities (Civil Liability) Act 1976, s.1A by way of the Human Fertilisation and Embryology Act 1990, s.44 (see p.213), Parliament has, in fact, recognised a 'wrongful life' claim.

116 Something of a similar nature was suggested by H. Teff, 'The action for "wrongful life" in England and the United States' (1985) 34 ICLQ 423. For extended discussion, see Norrie, n. 111 above.

117 A. Unterman, quoted by A. Steinberg, 'Induced abortion in Jewish law' (1980) 1 Int J Law Med 187.

118 It was, for example, refused in *Albala* v. *City of New York* 434 NYS 2d 400 (1981) and, more recently, *Hegyes* v. *Unjican Enterprises Inc.* 286 Cal Rptr 85 (1991) – both injury cases.

119 *Renslow* v. *Mennonite Hospital* 367 NE 2d 1250 (Ill, 1977); *Lazevnick* v. *General Hospital of Monro County Inc* 499 F Supp 146 (Md, 1980); *Yeager* v. *Bloomington Obstetrics and Gynecology Inc* 585 NE 2d 696 (Ind, 1992).

120 For example, *Jorgensen* v. *Meade-Johnson Laboratories* 483 F 2d 237 (1973) (drug causing chromosomal abnormality in later twins).

121   *Fish* v. *Wilcox and Gwent Health Authority* (1993) 13 BMLR 134.
122   Note 53 above.
123   Presumably, however, the decision would deny the right to a civil action as in the Canadian case, *Cherry* v. *Borsman* (1991) 75 DLR (4th) 668. Here a mother and child sued for injuries caused by a failed abortion: 'Had the abortion been successfully completed the infant plaintiff would have had no rights. Her rights arose only when and because she was born alive' (per SKIPP J at 667)
124   *City of Akron* v. *Akron Center for Reproductive Health* 462 US 416 (1983).
125   Note 5 above.
126   Interestingly, the numbers were as low or lower even before the passage of the Human Fertilisation and Embryology Act 1990, s.37, which introduced the 24-week limit for lesser indications.
127   Which makes one question the assertion during the parliamentary discussion of the 1990 Act that delivery is usually by Caesarian section if the fetus is mature enough to have a reasonable chance of survival with intensive care (522 HL Official Report (5th series) col. 1052, 18 October 1990 per LORD ENNALS).
128   335 H L Official Report (5th series) col. 776 , 2 December 1974 per LORD WELLS-PESTELL.
129   J.D.J. Havard, 'The legal threat to medicine' (1982) 284 Brit Med J 612.
130   Intention would still have to be proved even were the conditions of the Abortion Act 1967 not observed and if the operation came within the Offences Against the Person Act, 1861, s.58 (Homicide Act, 1957, s.1).
131   Compare *R* v. *Gibbins and Proctor* (1918) 13 Cr App R 134; *R* v. *Stone, R* v. *Dobinson* [1977] QB 354.
132   Abandoning or exposing a child under the age of two years.
133   Inquest on Infant Campbell, Stoke-on-Trent, 19 October 1983.
134   *The Times*, 16 September (1983), p. 1.
135   The Californian case of Dr Waddill is the most sensational. See B. Towers, 'The trials of Dr Waddill' (1979) 5 J Med Ethics 205; 'The Waddill case: treating or not treating the abortus' (1980) *New Physician* 39.
136   J.K. Mason, ,'Abortion and the law', in S.A.M. McLean (ed.), *Legal Issues in Human Reproduction* (1989), Aldershot: Gower.
137   *Colautti* v. *Franklin* 439 US 379 (1979).
138   The same Supreme Court found nothing objectionable in the statutory involvement of a second physician to protect any fetus unexpectedly born alive following late abortion: *Planned Parenthood Association of Kansas City* v. *Ashcroft* 462 US 476 (1983).
139   S.A.M. McLean, 'Abortion law: is consensual reform possible?' (1990) 17 J Law & Soc 106.
140   V.Y.H. Yu, H.L. Loke, B. Bajuk *et al.* 'Prognosis for infants born at 23 to 28 weeks' gestation' (1986) 293 Brit Med J 1200.
141   V.Y.H. Yu, 'The extremely low birthweight infant: ethical issues in treatment' (1987) 23 Aust Paediatr J 97.
142   The question of interim custody arose in a recent Scottish case: J. Robertson, 'Coma woman's baby is taken into care' (1996), *The Scotsman*, 18 April, p. 3.
143   In a current English case, it is reported that an unmarried father may actually sue the hospital for providing intensive care against his wishes; it is difficult to see any way in which he could do so successfully: D. Kennedy, 'Father may sue over coma baby' (1996), *The Times*, 4 July, p. 5.
144   Conference of the Medical Royal Colleges and their Faculties in the United Kingdom on 15 January 1979, 'Diagnosis of death' [1979] 1 Brit Med J 332.
145   Institute of Medical Ethics Bulletin No. 17, August 1986, p. 15.
146   H.L. Karcher, 'German doctors struggle to keep 15 week fetus viable' (1992)

305 Brit Med J 1047. In the event, the baby was stillborn after six weeks of intensive effort.

147 A very good newspaper article on the subject is to be found in C. Toomey and G. Lees, 'Baby row divides Germany' (1992), *The Sunday Times*, 1 November, p. 1.16.

148 B. Jennett, 'Brain death 1981' (1981) 28 Scott Med J 191. See also C. Pallis, *ABC of Brain Stem Death* (1983), London: BMA, pp. 22–3.

149 For an overview, see E.J. Larson, 'Intoxication *in utero*' in Mason, n. 39 above.

150 For full review, see G.C. Briggs, R.K. Freeman and S.J. Yaffe, *Drugs in Pregnancy and Lactation* (3rd edn, 1990) Baltimore: Williams and Wilkins, pp. 245–55.

151 It would be futile to attempt any form of bibliography on the subject. See, for example, J.E.M. Gregg, D.C. Davidson and A.M. Weindling, 'Inhaling heroin during pregnancy: effects on the baby' (1988) 296 Brit Med J 754; P. Caviston, 'Pregnancy and opiate addiction' (1987) 295 Brit Med J 285; N.L. Day, C.M. Cottreau and G.A. Richardson, 'The epidemiology of alcohol, marijuana and cocaine use among women of childbearing age and pregnant women' (1990) 36 Clin Obstet Gynecol 232.

152 C.J. Chaves, E.M. Ostrea, J.C. Stryker, *et al.*, 'Sudden infant death syndrome among infants of drug-dependent mothers' (1979) 95 J Pediat 407. For the effects of smoking on the SIDS death rate, see J. Golding, 'The epidemiology and sociology of the sudden infant death syndrome' in Mason, n. 39 above. Very surprisingly, occasional apparently beneficial effects are noted: see, for example, S. Ioffe and V. Chernick, 'Maternal alcohol ingestion and the incidence of respiratory disease syndrome' (1987) 156 Amer J Obstet Gynecol 1231.

153 J.E.B. Myers, 'Abuse and neglect of the unborn: can the State intervene?' (1984) 23 Duquesne L Rev 1.

154 J. Landwirth, 'Fetal abuse and neglect: an emerging controversy' (1987) 79 *Pediatrics* 508.

155 301 NW 2d 869 (Mich, 1981). See also *Re Vanessa F* 351 NYS 2d 337 (1974).

156 D.C. Bross and A. Meredyth, 'Neglect of the unborn child: an analysis based on law in the United States' (1974) 3 Child Abuse Negl 643.

157 See, for example, *Reyes* v. *Superior Court* 75 Cal App 3d 214 (1977). Larson, n. 149 above, states that the matter has been resolved in the Federal Court of Appeal.

158 'Sources' include (1986), *The Guardian*, 2 October, p. 8; (1986), *New York Times*, 16 November. See also M.A. Field, 'Controlling the woman to protect the fetus' (1989) 17 Law Med Hlth Care 114.

159 The situation in the United States is, however, inevitably complex. Mandatory treatment policies for pregnant drug abusers exist in South Carolina and several other states: J.H. Tanne, 'Jail for pregnant cocaine users in US' (1991) 303 Brit Med J 873. It also appears that a pregnant woman can be prosecuted in South Carolina for endangering her fetus through drug addiction: MacReady, n. 160 below.

160 N. MacReady, 'Fetal homicide charge for drinking while pregnant' (1996) 313 Brit Med J 645.

161 *Superintendent of Family and Child Service and McDonald* (1982) 135 DLR (3d) 330.

162 *Re Children's Aid Society of Kenora and J L* (1982) 134 DLR (3d) 249.

163 *Re F (in utero)* [1988] Fam 122.

164 Relying on the combination of Supreme Court Act 1981, s.41 and the Family Law Reform Act 1969, s.1(1).

165 BALCOMBE LJ also could find no logical basis for distinguishing a viable fetus from one pre-viable if the protection of wardship was allowed.

166 Note the very similar reasoning in the Canadian case, *Re Baby R* (1989) 53 DLR (4th) 69: powers to interfere with the rights of women must be given by specific legislation and nothing less would do (per MACDONNELL J at 80). The situation in Canada remains as it always was: an unborn child is not a child and the power of the Superintendent is restricted to living children.

167 [1987] AC 317.

168 *Re P (a minor) (child abuse: evidence)* [1987] 2 FLR 467.

169 My only source for this case is a leading article, 'Parents tried in their absence' (1987), *The Independent*, 12 November, p. 22.

170 Births and Deaths Registration Act 1953, s.41; Registration of Births, Deaths and Marriages (Scotland) Act 1965, s.56 as amended by Still-Birth (Definition) Act 1992.

171 Nurses, Midwives and Health Visitors Act 1979, s.10.

172 There are, however, serious ethical problems which have been reviewed by the Polkinghorne Committee, for which see Chapter 7 below.

173 (1908) 6 CLR 406.

174 *McCoy v. Georgia Baptist Hospital* 306 SE 2d 746 (Ga, 1983).

175 *Johnson v. Women's Hospital* 627 SW 2d 133 (Tenn, 1975).

176 *Margaret S v. Edwards* 488 F Supp 181 (E D La, 1980).

177 *Margaret S v. Treen* 597 F Supp 636 (E D La, 1984).

178 *City of Akron v. Akron Center for Reproductive Health Inc* 462 US 416 (1983): to impose a choice of methods of disposal of a fetus on a woman is to influence her unduly in her choice of abortion.

179 K. Kallenberg, L. Forslin, and O. Westerborn, 'The disposal of the aborted fetus – new guidelines: ethical considerations in the debate in Sweden' (1993) 19 J Med Ethics 32.

7   Fetal Experimentation

Terminology in this field is not uniform and it may be helpful to define some of the terms used in this chapter – and, in particular, to distinguish between experimental treatment, research and experimentation. Dickens[1] has defined an experimental treatment as a deliberate departure from orthodox therapy; given that medical orthodoxy itself is definable as a rule or procedure supported by an identifiable body of contemporary medical knowledge, this is as apt a description as any that could be formulated. The same author, however, points to the corollary: that a treatment cannot be experimental when there is no standard of orthodoxy; this must still apply to the majority of fetal treatments *in utero*. This chapter, however, is not concerned with treatment, which has been considered briefly already, but, rather, with research and experimentation – procedures which are not necessarily directed to the well-being of the individual subject. The distinction between research and experimentation is frequently blurred and, to some, may be non-existent. For present purposes, a research procedure is defined as one which is undertaken in the pursuit of knowledge or understanding within a defined prospective protocol or programme. An experiment, by contrast, can be regarded as designed to provide information of itself: it need not be preplanned and a useful experimental situation may arise fortuitously. Much the same ethical rules will cover both procedures but nuances of difference may arise: for example, the quality of informed consent, discussed in Chapter 4, may be more exacting if the subject is asked to take part in a research programme which involves rigid schedules.

The moral framework

There have been surprisingly few authoritative reviews of the moral aspects of fetal research. The first effective British consideration, the

Peel Report,[2] dates back to 1972. Four years later, the Department of Health, Education and Welfare in the United States published an exhaustive review of controversial research practices, including those on the fetus.[3] These two review bodies reached much the same conclusions which, at least so far as the United Kingdom was concerned, held the field until overtaken by the Polkinghorne Report in 1989,[4] which will be taken as the benchmark for this chapter.

'Fetal research', however, must be looked at in parallel with fetal existence which has no uniform pattern but is, rather, a matter of phases, each of which differs as to philosophical and ethical evaluation. Thus we can consider the fetus *in utero* and whether it is, at the time, wanted or rejected; in its extrauterine existence, it may be viable or pre-viable and, in either case, it may be alive, dying or dead; the fetus may have been aborted spontaneously or by intervention; and research and experimentation may be directed to the whole organism, to fetal parts or tissues or to the materials ancillary to the fetal environment including the placenta, the umbilical cord and the fetal membranes.

There can be no doubt as to the value of fetal research; the Peel Report listed almost 60 acceptable projects.[5] Equally, there is no doubt of the public concern which exists in relation to the potential for abuse and as to the need to establish a status for the fetus on which to base an ethical code. The US National Commission concluded, irrespective of the legal position, 'that moral concern should extend to all who share human genetic heritage, and that the fetus, regardless of life prospects, should be treated respectfully and with dignity'. The Polkinghorne Committee was equally sincere but, at the same time, hardly more precise. The committee accepted 'a special status for the living human fetus at every stage of its development which we characterise as a profound respect based upon its potential for development into a fully formed human being' (at para. 2.4). As a result, the committee rejected any distinction between the pre-viable and viable fetus and, with it, the Peel Report's conclusion that the former could be used experimentally without the requirement that it lacked the signs of life: 'the category of pre-viable,' it was said, 'is not of ethical relevance' (at para. 3.1). Following this line of thought, it was also held that the body of the dead fetus commanded respect and that, accordingly, any research involving the dead fetus should be subject to review by a research ethics committee (at para. 7.3).

Attitudes to intrauterine research are bound to differ according to whether or not the individual fetus is destined for abortion.[6] This is an area in which it is almost impossible to be wholly objective. Those who see the fetus as something which is disposable at will will see no objection to what might, undoubtedly, be valuable research, and even those who object in principle to abortion might well approve of good coming from an unfortunate evil. Others would contend that a good end cannot be justified if it is achieved by unethical means.[7] Polkinghorne rejected this last argument and held that the respect due to the fetus was not abrogated by a declared intention to abort that fetus.

The Committee thus concluded that interventions on *any* living fetus are acceptable only if they are, on balance, to the benefit of the individual fetus[8] or if there is minimal or no risk attached to the procedure (at para. 3.2). The latter involves a medical evaluation which may shift according to the state of knowledge. Thus it would be quite improper nowadays to expose a fetus to X-irradiation for research purposes. Ultrasonographic investigations, by contrast, appear to pose no threat to the developing organism and would, therefore, be permissible; but the technique is so new that observations, say, on the health of the middle-aged who have been exposed are only recently becoming possible. Our attitudes could, therefore, change and, while no unimpeachable results suggestive of significant ill-effects have yet been obtained, the current view is that it is prudent to limit ultrasonographic examinations to circumstances in which the information is likely to be useful.[9] The same may well apply to other innovations including, for example, nuclear magnetic resonance imaging. Few would, however, disagree with the statement that: 'It is unethical to administer drugs or carry out any procedures during pregnancy with the deliberate intent of ascertaining whether or not they might harm the fetus.'[10]

As we have seen, any statutory protection given to the proposed abortus by the Infant Life (Preservation) Act, 1929 has been abrogated by the Human Fertilisation and Embryology Act 1990, s.37(4). Clearly, however, the late gestation abortus is living *in utero* – albeit probably in a defective state – and is, therefore, covered by the Code of Practice irrespective of its intended destruction. However, should the abortus be born alive, it becomes a creature in being and is, effectively, entitled to the same protection as is a neonate. While, as we will see in Chapter 11, there may be no obligation on the doctor to strive to keep it alive, there can be no doubt that it would be an offence to subject the abortus to procedures which had no personal benefit and which knowingly contributed to its death. Experimental treatments specifically intended to benefit the living abortus would, of course, be another matter; their morality and legality would be governed by the principles that are discussed in Chapter 12.

A somewhat similar situation may arise following the normal birth of a fetus which, while being born alive in the sense that its heart beats and it is able to aerate its lungs, is, nevertheless, so deformed that its life span will be strictly limited. Gross abnormalities resulting from chromosomal trisomy or from maldevelopments of individual parts or organs will place the fetus in this category which is, perhaps, best typified by the anencephalic.[11] The status of such a being remains in some doubt. Any genetic human that is breathing or showing other signs of life must be alive in legal terms – and, therefore, 'in being' – irrespective of the medical interpretation of its quality of life. The problem then arises as to whether it is a 'reasonable creature' in being and whether it is then subject to or lies beyond the protection of the law of homicide.[12] Any such differentiation is of very doubtful morality and is equally unlikely to find legal support. It is difficult to establish what was in the minds of institutional writers of the 16th and 17th centuries, but I have always assumed that the phrase 'reasonable being'[13] was intended to do no more than distinguish *homo sapiens* from the rest of the animal kingdom. The late gestation anencephalic fetus is a rarity today and, perhaps for that very reason, is of particular importance to the current debates on personhood and on the concept of death; these are, however, more related to the issue of therapeutic organ donation than to academic research; further discussion follows at p. 196.

We are left with the moral position of the pre-viable fetus which miscarries or is aborted intentionally. Here a distinction must be drawn between a fetus which is still physiologically maintained through a persisting maternal connection and one whose lifeline has been severed. This distinction may seem artificial to some. Nonetheless, it seems that, for a short period, the extruded fetus with a placental connection has the same status as the fetus *in utero*;[14] admittedly, in our present state of technology, it has no chance of survival, but it is logical to see it as having the same rights to protection as it had in the womb – these 'rights' have already been discussed.

Conditions are, however, changed dramatically once the umbilical cord is severed. Death is now inevitable however it is defined, but we are in that twilight zone which exists between somatic death as an organism and cellular death, which awaits exhaustion of the oxygen supply at tissue level. Once we accept this analogy with adult death, it remains only to ensure that 'brain death' has occurred before those tissues may be made available. Since this assessment is impossible in the circumstances envisaged, we must fall back on an assurance that 'brain *life*' has *not* been established, and it is significant that the Polkinghorne Committee's refused to condone the Peel Committee's concept of the pre-viable fetus and considered that only the categories of 'dead' and 'alive' were ethically significant in relation to fetal research (at para 3.1). The importance of further safeguards has been recognised in both the United States and Britain. Thus, in both, it has been stipulated that the anticipated results should be unobtainable by other means – in particular, as noted by the National Commission, by the use of animal models; both insist on the supervision of research programmes by ethical committees, and the Polkinghorne Committee has specifically included research using dead fetal tissue in the remit of the research ethics committee (at para 7.3). The committee did this in the light of the high level of public concern while, at the same time, recognising that the recommendation was, in many ways, anomalous. Various other recommendations arose, none of which is thought likely to be controversial. Both the American and British bodies have been concerned that the decision as to and the method of therapeutic abortion should not be influenced by an anticipation of research. The Polkinghorne Committee has laid down strict guidelines ensuring that the medical attendants and the researchers are independent of each other; these include the desirability of using an intermediary body to separate the source from the user of fetal tissue (at ch. 5). In addition, there has been wide agreement that no inducements, whether monetary or otherwise, should be offered to procure an abortion for research purposes; the Polkinghorne Committee considered that no monetary exchanges whatsoever should be involved in fetal research, including those that might be regarded as needed to meet the necessary administrative costs. The committee went further and extended the ban to include other contents of the uterus, such as the placenta.

The problems associated with research in the dead fetus are also related to consent and it is here, perhaps, that the Polkinghorne Committee was at its most radical.

Consent and fetal research and experimentation

Legal constraints

Several statutes constrain fetal research in the United Kingdom. These include the Offences Against the Person Act, 1861, the Infant Life (Preservation) Act, 1929, the Human Tissue Act, 1961 and the Abortion Act, 1967.

The Offences Against the Person Act, 1861, ss.58 and 59, proscribes the procuring of a miscarriage or the attempt to do so, subject now, of course, to the enabling provisions of the Abortion Act 1967. The offence is, however, specific to procuring a miscarriage and this may well not be the intention of the researcher. In the absence of a live birth, there is no crime of feticide in England, the problem being, as always, that the pre-viable fetus has no personhood in law.[15] Rather surprisingly, the position may be different in Scotland. Quite apart from the declaratory powers retained by the Scottish courts, it has been stated that 'You can destroy a foetus *in utero* ... you can destroy it on the eve of its birth; or you can kill it in the process of being born.

All these are serious offences which are recognized in law. But they are not murder.'[16] This suggests that feticide and the English offence of child destruction might be looked upon as being of the same order in Scotland. The nature of the 'serious offences' was not, however, specified and, although the matter has never been tested,[17] there is no reason to suppose that the opinion of a trial judge in the middle of the last century would be followed today. Whether or not injury to a pre-viable fetus which caused its death after being born would constitute either murder or manslaughter is also uncertain,[18] but, since the combination of live birth followed by death due to injury sustained before viability is scarcely likely, the proposition is something of a contradiction in terms. In any event, proof both of causation and of the necessary *mens rea* of murder would be very difficult. The Peel Committee thought that deliberate or reckless injury to the fetus caused at any time between conception and delivery – save under the provisions of the Abortion Act 1967 – could be taken to be criminal throughout the United Kingdom, but it is difficult to see the rationale for this.[19] Many would feel that there *should* be such a criminal offence and the Scottish courts might well use their powers if a flagrant case arose, but it would be a matter of general application rather than one confined to research and experimentation. In passing, the relatively obvious point should be noted that, even if the conditions for a legal abortion existed, an abortion resulting from research would be unlawful unless the relevant regulations under the 1967 Act as to certification, location and the like had been followed.

Protection of the fetus capable of being born alive is improved as compared with that accorded to its pre-viable counterpart, but is still incomplete because the crime of child destruction is committed only if there is *intent* to cause death; since this would be very unlikely in the circumstances under discussion, the researcher would be criminally liable only if he were reckless as to the outcome – and this only doubtfully. At this advanced gestational age, however, the fetus might have some protection under the rules governing consent to assault. Consent, which is discussed further below, is vested in the mother but severe injury to a fetus capable of being born alive may be among those assaults which consent does not decriminalise[20] (discussed in rather greater detail in Chapter 12). But, again, this is a derived constraint; it is not easy to accept the Peel Committee's view (at para. 21) that an offence of injuring a fetus capable of being born alive exists *per se*.[21] It scarcely needs recording that the fetus which is born alive is entitled to the same *legal* protection as is any other 'creature in being'.[22]

Legal restrictions as to experimentation on the dead fetus are founded on the Human Tissue Act, 1961 and, here again, the situation is neither uniform nor entirely clear. Certainly, since there are no regulations as to the disposal of the dead pre-viable fetus, the Act does not apply in such an instance and the only legal requirements as to disposal are those relating to public decency. The position of the stillbirth is, however, debatable. On one view, the stillbirth, having never been alive, cannot come within the scope of the 1961 Act; it must, therefore, be registered and disposed of either by burial or by cremation.[23] This, one feels, cannot be correct; amongst other contradictions, it would imply that a post-mortem examination, the authority for which lies in s.2(2) of the Act, would be illegal in the case of a stillbirth, and such a contention is plainly wrong. The better view is that the 1961 Act is irrelevant as to the stillbirth; any use of the stillbirth's tissues is governed only by ethical medical practice.

Civil liability

The civil liability of the fetal researcher in the United Kingdom is daunting when his activities are directed to the infant who will live. The major complication lies in the still unresolved question of whether parental consent to research involving an immature minor is ever possible. Certainly, a parent may give consent to the medical treatment of a child but it is generally accepted that this privilege does not necessarily extend to medical intervention which is not to the child's individual advantage.[24]

Arguments to the contrary are discussed in greater detail in Chapter 12. Those that are founded on a minor's right to his or her autonomy and, perhaps, on a social advantage through participation in research, clearly have no place in a discussion of fetal interests. Nonetheless, given the fact that some fetal research is needed, it seems retrograde to deny its advantages to medical progress on the grounds that consent is impossible.[25] What is undeniable is that the less is the actual subject's capacity to share in the responsibility, so the slighter must the acceptable risks bocame[26] and, since the fetus' contribution to decision making is nil, the risks must either be nil or, at most, minimal: defined by the Institute of Medical Ethics as carrying a risk of a minor complication of less than one in a thousand.[27] The researcher who goes beyond this limit will be liable for injury irrespective of maternal consent; the only possibility of mitigation might lie in the Congenital Disabilities (Civil Liability) Act 1976, s.1(7), through which a degree of contributory negligence might be attributable to the consenting mother. This would undoubtedly depend upon the quality of consent.

Maternal consent to fetal research

It is apparent that the issue of consent is central to the legality and morality of fetal research and it is the latter which has been greatly modified by the Polkinghorne Committee. In the first edition of this book, I expressed the view that the extent to which maternal consent to research on the pre-viable fetus was required depended to a large extent on whether the research subject derived from spontaneous or induced abortion. The victim of a spontaneous miscarriage has undoubtedly lost something precious and there is no doubt that an action in tort related to emotional distress would be available were such a woman to discover that her infant had been used as a research subject without her consent. Whether such certainty attached to a planned abortion was, however, open to argument. In the event, the Polkinghorne Committee followed the United States National Commission in firmly holding that the informed consent of the mother should be obtained for non-therapeutic research directed towards the non-viable fetus *ex utero*, irrespective of its provenance. The Polkinghorne Committee justified this, firstly, on the general ground that purely legal considerations were inadequate and that ethics should dictate practice; thus the mother's consent should always be obtained. As to the particular point, the committee thought it too harsh a judgment of the mother's relation to her fetus to suppose that she was no longer in a special position with regard to it following an abortion; accordingly, maternal consent was required equally, whether the fetal tissue derived from natural or therapeutic abortion. Moreover, the process of consent requires the mother to be counselled and given all the information needed to enable her to make a proper judgment. Interestingly, the committee recommended that, while explicit consent to research, transplantation and teaching should be obtained on all occasions when consent was sought, the mother should not be able to specify the way in which the tissue was to be used and, indeed, she should not know whether or not the fetus was, in fact, used.

In determining that fetal tissue which has become available through spontaneous miscarriage should be dealt with in the same way as that derived from therapeutic abortion, the committee did not, in my opinion, take sufficient note of the additional strain placed upon the woman who is in a state of emotional shock following a miscarriage. On this view, research or experimentation on the natural, spontaneous abortus is something which would be best avoided save in exceptional circumstances. In my opinion, the emotional status of the father is also inadequately considered. His relationship with the fetus may well be, as the report says, less intimate than that of the mother, but that is not to say it is negligible – and once the fetus is *ex utero*, the distinction becomes less impressive. The committee (at para. 6.7) recognised that his involvement might be desirable, but it is hard to see why he should be denied the power of veto of research on the abortus which may well have genetic implications – and he has contributed 50 per cent of the fetal genes.

The Polkinghorne Committee recommended that consent to the use of fetal tissue should be distinct from, and subsequent to, consent to termination of pregnancy although both consents could be obtained on the same occasion – a process which, one feels, would impose minimal further stress on the woman. The further suggestion that the mother should be offered the opportunity to declare any special directions about the disposal of the fetus might, however, be impossible to fulfil (see p. 176). The final recommendation to be considered here was that the pregnant woman should disclaim any property rights in the fetus which would, effectively, become abandoned once it was separated from its mother. Excluding discussion as to whether there are such rights to be disclaimed,[28] experience over the last decade has shown the potential commercial value of human cells;[29] whether such a precondition is now acceptable is a matter for argument[30] – the present writer believes that it would be inequitable.

The use of uterine contents other than the fetus

The Polkinghorne Committee preferred the term 'contents of the uterus' to the Peel Committee's 'fetal materials'; both terms include the placenta, umbilical cord, fluids and membranes.[31] Such materials, although biological, are inanimate and are of no proprietary value to the mother; they will normally be destroyed without compunction and certainly without reference to the recently delivered woman. They are classic examples of *res nullius*.

Nonetheless, they can be of very great value both in academic research and in repair and replacement therapy. They are in no way covered by the Human Tissue Act, 1961 and can be harvested quite properly by any appropriate person; to seek consent to do so – other than for the purpose of identifying transmissible disease when consent would apply as in the case of the fetus – would be superfluous. The possibility of a commercial market in such materials might arise. Since the possible use of uterine contents might affect the decision to terminate a pregnancy, the buying and selling of such materials should be proscribed; the Polkinghorne Committee went so far as to disapprove of, albeit not to veto, allowing a reasonable recompense for the work involved in the collection and distribution of the remains.

The fetus or the neonate as an organ transplant donor

The Polkinghorne Committe was established primarily to consider the far more contentious issue of the use of the fetus as a transplant donor. The reasons for added concern are unrelated to transplantation as a procedure – that is now an established part of the medical armamentarium. Rather, we are, here, in a unique area in which the organ donor can have no part whatever in the decision making and one in which the dividing line between living and cadaver donation is blurred. It has to be appreciated that the fetal *organ* donor *must* be 'viable', using the term in the extended sense that its organs are so mature that they can function independently of a placental connection at cellular level; accordingly, such a fetus is entitled to the full protection of the law, subject only to the superior claims of the life of its mother. It follows that the fetal organ donor must be 'born alive': only exceptionally could a stillbirth be regarded as a suitable donor; strictly speaking, the fetal donor is a neonate. However, it is only very rarely that a wholly normal fetal organ donor will be available; the least unlikely occasion is when its life has to be extinguished as a maternal life-saving measure. Otherwise, fetuses which are abnormal will be available for selective organ donation only when their abnormality results from a defect in a specific organ which is incompatible with survival. It is, therefore, convenient to retain the term 'fetal donors' to distinguish them from neonates who die unexpectedly and whose management as donors parallels that of adults.

Thus we might look, say, for a liver or kidney donation from a fetus with an inoperable cardiac condition;[32] the more likely scenario, however, involves the search for a heart/lung transplant from an anencephalic fetus. Either example demonstrates the major ethical and practical difficulties: not only must the donor be born alive and its life be declared unsalvageable, but it also must be maintained with adequate oxygenation of the tissues until a recipient is available. The surgeon must then be satisfied that the fetus is 'dead' before he removes its organs for, given the first premise of being alive, the conditions of the Human Tissue Act, 1961 must be met.

The fears associated with the process can be illustrated by way of these requirements. First, there must be a fetus. I suggest that the misgivings expressed under this head,[33] which relate mainly to the production of fetuses for use as donors, are probably misplaced in the present context. On first principles, it is unlikely that women would be anxious to embark on the long pregnancy which would be needed to provide organs; fetuses *might* be bred in order to provide cellular tissue (see below) but not, it is felt, to provide spare parts. Moreover, since 'viability' is a prerequisite to organ donation, abortion of a fetal donor would only be legal in order to protect the life or major health of the mother or on account of severe defect in the fetus itself, possibilities which could not be presupposed at the time of conception. Further, in the great majority of cases, transplantation would only be practicable if ventilator support was available, and the chances of finding an obstetrician willing to flout the law flagrantly would not be great. The possibility that a defective fetus would be held in gestation *in order* to provide suitably mature organs is a more important and more likely concern. Such an attempt has been made, apparently wholly altruistically, by a Californian woman carrying an anencephalic child.[34] The attempt failed, but this was not so much because of the ethical difficulties in prolonging the gestation as because of problems associated with ascertaining death in a way that is compatible with successful transplant therapy.

Here there are very obvious difficulties, possibly the most important being the relationship between anencephaly and death. The classic anencephalic fetus has no forebrain but has a functioning brain-stem – the result being very similar to the adult equivalent of the persistent vegetative state.[35] By definition, therefore, the anencephalic is not brain-stem dead; moreover, in the event that the neonate is maintained on a ventilator, there is no way in which the diagnosis of brain-stem death can be made by the standard criteria.[36] As things stand, death in an anencephalic must be made on cardio-respiratory criteria,[37] which means that the infants must be reanimated – in itself, a process of doubtful morality – if they are to be used as donors. Fetal tissues are very sensitive to oxygen lack and it is possible that serious deterioration has occurred meantime; better results have been reported from donors who were used without regard to the persistence of brain-stem activity.[38] As a result, the definition of death is again being questioned in the light of fetal donation and it has, indeed, been suggested that anencephaly should be regarded as a distinct condition to which the normal criteria do not apply.[39] A less extreme movement attempts to redefine brain death in terms of brain absence – a form of semantic juggling which makes no difference to the practical dilemma. To revert to using terms such as 'not really alive' as being synonymous with 'dead' is to reopen the whole issue of 'brain death' and to cast doubt again on what has come to be accepted as a most valuable therapeutic principle.

Theoretically, five lives or more could be saved by one anencephalic fetus,[40] but, in practice, the end results are not so encouraging. In the first place, the number of suitable donors is small[41] and, secondly, the therapeutic success rate is depressingly low.[42] These and other matters were discussed in the only apposite case discovered in the literature, *Re TACP*.[43] In this case, the parents of an anencephalic neonate sought to have her declared dead so that her organs could benefit others. In the event, the court of first instance held that she was not dead, yet, at the same time, gave permission for the removal of a kidney on the grounds that to do so did not harm the infant. The case was later heard by the Supreme Court of Florida, despite the fact that the infant had already died, and the court's determination is significant:

> We acknowledge the possibility that some infants' lives might be saved by using organs from anencephalics who do not meet the traditional definition of 'death' we affirm to-day. But weighted against this is the utter lack of consensus, and the questions about the overall utility of such organ donations. The scales clearly tip in favor of not extending the common law in this instance.

I have concluded that, as things stand, the moral cost of using anencephalic infants as organ donors is too great when related to the practical benefits derived, an opinion which is almost diametrically opposed to that expressed in the first edition of this book. Even so, the scales could be tipped the other way, were there to be a real improvement in the therapeutic benefits. It seems to be an area that is dominated by utilitarian ethics.

The donation of fetal cellular material

Fetal tissues tend to set up an immune reaction less readily than do their adult counterparts and fetal cells of several types – such as bone marrow cells or those of the thymus – may be valuable in the therapy of diseased infants. Few would argue with their use, provided they have been obtained within an ethical framework. We are, however, on a different moral level when considering the use of fetal brain cells. Here fetal tissue is not being applied to the salvage of other young persons but, rather, to replacement for and rejuvenation of the ageing body – currently for the treatment of Parkinsonism but, prospectively, for the amelioration of several other degenerative cerebral conditions, including Alzheimer's disease and senile dementia. There can be few persons of middle or later age who could deny *some* affinity with Dr Faustus in his search for eternal youth; moral concern with this new development results, one suspects, from the concomitant fear that the neurosurgeon is being asked, or is seeking, to assume the role of Mephistopheles. Is such instinctive recoil justified, or is it simply the fact that rejuvenation of the ageing brain is a new and uncharted application of accepted underlying principles that gives rise to such controversy? Surely, every person is entitled to a share of whatever treatment, and for whatever diseases, is available, so long as its provision is both legally and morally acceptable; the fundamental issue is, therefore, whether fetal brain tissue should be harvested at all – not whether it should be supplied for the treatment of conditions which, generally, manifest themselves in old age.

As matters stand, the only brain tissue which is required for therapy is that from very young fetuses – at approximately 10–14 weeks' maturity. It is apparent, therefore, that, in contrast to organ transplantation, the use of fetal brain tissue is intrinsically, perhaps absolutely, tied to abortion; almost inevitably, therefore, opinions on the matter will be polarised. Some (and, in particular, those who see widespread abortion as an unfortunate *fait accompli*) – will look upon an attempt to relieve suffering in this way as a potential good deriving from a necessary evil.[44] Others will see that argument as being morally indefensible insofar as it attempts to justify – and, perhaps, encourage – an action which is fundamentally wrong; in other words, a good end cannot justify unjustifiable means.[45] For present purposes, however, these differences will be ignored; the more useful attitude is simply to assume that the necessary material is available – and that, as a corollary, it could not be provided adequately by way of natural miscarriage – and to approach the problem with that premise established.

General guidelines on the use of fetal tissue in transplantation therapy were issued by the British Medical Association in 1988.[46] The important stipulation in respect of this specific discussion is that which states that nervous tissue should only be used for transplantation in the form of isolated neurones or tissue fragments. This recommendation is clearly designed to settle disquiet at the thought of implanting an intelligent, working brain from one person to another; there is, of course, no current suggestion of such a development.

It is seldom that the identification of ethical parameters for a procedure has preceded its practical application as effectively as in this instance. Only a handful of operations were reported before public opinion asserted itself.[47] As a result, funding by the National Institutes of Health for such operations was withdrawn in the United States and, in the United Kingdom, *The Lancet* called for a halt pending a long-term appraisal of the results obtained thus far.[48] It is arguable whether such constraints are justified. True, the concept of foreign cells seeding and flourishing within a person's brain causes anxiety but, given that adequate animal research has been undertaken to ensure that the process is not fundamentally dangerous, and provided patients are made fully aware of the complications of neurosurgery of any sort, it seems almost unreasonable to prohibit consensual therapy for sufferers who may, otherwise, have to wait several years for completion of the observations which are called for. On one view, it is a matter which can be left to good medical practice undertaken beneath the vigilant eye of properly constituted ethical research committees, for, although brain implantation is therapeutic, it is, at the same time, clearly experimental. The alternative attitude is that the drive to innovation is so strong in the modern medical profession that patients – and especially those who are mentally disabled – must be protected from untried and dangerous techniques at least by way of codes of practice, if not by specific legislation. In the event, conservative counsels have prevailed, for very little has been heard of fetal brain implantation in the ensuing years.

But what of the position of the fetus, given that the potential for experimental activity remains? The conditions of brain tissue implantation require fetal immaturity. Thus, unless there is a marked sociological change, a supply of transplantable material will be readily available through routine legal abortions; a market in fetuses is unlikely to arise in practice and the most urgent fetal consideration rests on the definitions of life and death as they are applied to the pre-viable fetus. The Polkinghorne Committee, however, rejected the concept of a difference in attitude to the fetus according to its stage of development and, in making a distinction only between the live and the dead, sought to define death by reference to the absence of vital functions such as a beating heart or the presence of spontaneous respiration. But such signs are not available in the 10-week fetus who must, in addition, be 'brain alive' if his or her central neural tissue is to be used therapeutically. The problem seems to be one which must be resolved semantically, the argument running that, by definition, the non-viable fetus is incapable of being born alive, and if it is not born alive, it can only be dead. Pragmatically, it is relatively certain that those parts of the brain which are responsible for consciousness and the appreciation of pain are not developed at the gestational age under consideration.[49] Moreover, the vast majority of fetuses used as donors will have been delivered *per vaginam*, and the methods used are incompatible with life as an organism. Having said which, it has to be admitted that the question of 'brain death' raises what are, perhaps, the most intensely held objections to the process.

The Polkinghorne Committee, as we have seen, firmly recommended that maternal consent to use of the fetus should be obtained, irrespective of its provenance. At the same time, the mother was to be denied a voice in choosing the method of use and a blanket consent covering research, transplantation and teaching was to be obtained on all occasions; a nagging doubt remains that a process which involves such controversy and public disquiet should be subject to specific consent. The widely agreed stipulation that the intention to transplant should not interfere with the timing or the method of performing an abortion is, perhaps, more important. There are two specific administrative safeguards which must, of themselves, do much to ensure the ethical limits. These are, firstly, that those terminating the pregnancy should be dissociated from the neurosurgical unit[50] and, secondly, that no inducements of any sort to provide tissues should be imposed on the mother. It follows that the generation or termination of pregnancy in order to produce material for therapy is unethical and contrary to the Code of Practice. With this in mind, I would suggest that close, intrafamilial donations of neural tissue should be discouraged, if not banned: the pressures on women who look after elderly relatives are great enough without adding an inducement to pregnancy and abortion by way of a conscientious obligation to provide them with biological therapeutic material.

Fetal ovaries and ova

It has been suggested that the shortage of ova for the treatment of infertile women (see Chapter 9) could be met, at least in part, by the use of fetal ovaries or ova which could either be brought to maturity in the laboratory or used as implants within the patient's body. The suggestion, however, raises a number of specific problems additional to those of assisted reproduction and transplantation in general.[51]

Amongst these may be cited, firstly, the imposed interference with the natural process whereby defective ova are probably eliminated during the process of maturation; the persistence of such ova could be actively encouraged by the artificial process. Secondly, there is the unknown effect on a resulting child of discovering the facts of his or her unusual ancestry, though whether the child need ever know is discussed in more detail at p. 221. Thirdly, the morality of associating a treatment of infertility with abortion is, at least, questionable. Finally, there are the very special concerns in passing on genetic material – which will be equally that of the fetus' mother and father – for generations to come.

The majority of these problems have either been discussed already or are addressed in greater detail in Chapter 9. Here it need only be said that it is the first which gives rise to greatest concern. Doubtless, the major hazards could be overcome by adequate genetic study of the fetus and its parents, a matter which would give rise to special and specific needs as to consent, coupled with careful embryo selection. The potential dangers are, however, sufficient to indicate that fetal ova should not be used for gamete intrafallopian transfer – a method of assisted reproduction which eliminates embryo selection; there are also good reasons for rejecting the use of fetal female germ cells[52] derived from natural miscarriages, a high proportion of which are associated with fetal abnormality. The close relationship between the procedure and elective termination of pregnancy is, thereby, emphasised.

In the event, further discussion has, at least for the present, been pre-empted by statute. The Human Fertilisation and Embryology

Act 1990, s.3A(1)[53] states: 'No person shall, for the purpose of providing fertility services for any woman, use female germ cells taken or derived from an embryo or a foetus or use embryos created by using such cells.' Research using such cells is not prohibited, but the resulting temptation to use such cells to create embryos for research purposes only would probably be frustrated by refusal of a licence to do so (see Chapters 8 and 9).

Research ethics committees

One theme permeates all recommendations and guidelines related to fetal research: that any research programme should be approved and monitored by an ethics committee. The composition and remit of these committees are, however, relatively undefined and merit brief consideration.

The establishment of British research ethical committees springs from a memorandum issued by the Ministry of Health in 1968;[54] the recommendations have been further refined by committees of the Royal College of Physicians in 1990.[55] The function of the committees has always been very firmly tied to the supervision of *research*; there is no inclination to follow the American trend and to establish bodies that include therapeutic and prognostic decisions among their responsibilities.[56] Emphasis has been laid on the need for special consideration of research programmes involving those who either cannot understand or cannot speak for themselves. Experiments or structured research protocols involving the fetus and neonate are, therefore, pre-eminently suitable for this form of control and this is a matter which was addressed in detail by the Polkinghorne Committee.

The committee was firmly of the opinion that ethics committees should examine all proposals for work with fetuses or fetal tissue whether classified as research or therapy and whether the fetus is alive or dead, this last requirement being considered to be an extension of such committees' normal remits (Report, para. 7.3).[57] The committee was clearly unwilling to limit the responsibilities of the ethics committees and recommended that they should be satisfied of the validity of the research, that the required information could not be obtained in any other way and that the researchers were adequately skilled and resourced. Further power was to be vested in the ethics committee to scrutinise the actual performance of the project, a task which was to be delegated to 'local ethics committees'.

The level at which the committees operate can vary between the extremes of a departmental committee and one based on a District Health Authority, as is the case in England, or on a Health Board in Scotland.[58] The 'official' concept of the local research ethics committee is one established at district level; it is not to be regarded as a management arm of the authority but is, rather, established to 'advise the NHS body under the auspices of which the research is intended to take place'.[59] Thus, while there is nothing to prevent a hospital or hospital trust setting up its own ethics committee[60] – with, perhaps, a different or extended remit – it is the local committee which must be consulted before the responsible NHS body can give permission for research to be carried out on patients within the health service.

There is no established composition of British ethical committees, although it is advised that persons of both sexes should be drawn from hospital medical and nursing staff, general practitioners and at least two lay members who should not be seen as representing their own group.[61] The Polkinghorne Committee clearly envisaged the involvement of ethics research committees which could be said to be 'geographically' local when they recommended that members of LRECs should not be drawn predominantly from people working in the same discipline or institution as the researcher, but this now seems contrary to NHS policy. Since the authority to set up research ethics committees lies in a circular rather than in legislation, the individual committee has no legal standing, although it takes on legal duties and its actions are subject to scrutiny, as are those of any other public body.[62] By the same token, no researcher has a legal obligation to involve the LREC, but he or she could not use NHS patients or resources without so doing and, equally importantly, it is now difficult to publish one's results in a reputable journal without the *imprimatur* of an ethics committee.

Notes

1   B.M. Dickens, 'What is a medical experiment?' (1975) 113 Canad Med Ass J 635.
2   J. Peel, (Chairman), *Report of the Advisory Group on the Use of Fetuses and Fetal Material for Research* (1972), London: HMSO.
3   National Commission for the Protection of Human Subjects of Biomedical and Behavioral Research, *Research on the Fetus*, Appendix B.
4   *Review of the Guidance on the Research Use of Fetuses and Fetal Material* (Cmd 762, 1989).
5   See also the Polkinghorne Report, n. 4 above, Appendix 1.
6   But such distinction is irrational if the fetus can feel pain. It has been said that fetuses as young as six weeks' gestation can do so: S. Leonard, 'Foetuses "feel pain", as young as six weeks' (1996), *Scotland on Sunday*, 3 October, p. 3.
7   These views are likely to be unreconcilable and, as a consequence, it was recommended that no member of the medical or nursing staff should be under any duty to participate in research or therapy using the fetus or fetal tissue if he or she has a conscientious objection to so doing (at para. 2.11).
8   The ethical issues involved in the use of procedures carrying a greater than

minimal risk to the individual but which could be of great potential benefit to the group to which the subject belongs must be considered in a manner 'broadly similar to the way such issues are considered for children and adults': a vague term specifically criticised, among many other aspects of the Report, by J. Keown, 'The Polkinghorne Report on Fetal Research: nice recommendations, shame about the reasoning' (1993) 19 J Med Ethics 114.

9   M.J.N.C. Keirse, 'Frequent prenatal ultrasound: time to think again' (1993) 342 Lancet 878.

10 Polkinghorne Report, para. 3.3, repeated in the *Code of Practice on the Use of Fetuses and Fetal Material in Research and Treatment*, para. 1.2. The Code of Practice, reproduced in the Report, now represents government policy.

11 Strictly speaking, this is a misnomer as the complete absence of a brain is incompatible with life. By popular usage, the term has come to mean the absence of a forebrain while the brain-stem is still preserved.

12 For early appraisals, see Legal Correspondent 'Dr Leonard Arthur: his trial and its implications' (1981) 283 Brit Med J 1340; D. Brahams, 'Transplantation, the fetus and the law' (1988) 138 NLJ 91.

13 3 Co Inst 47.

14 It seems anomalous to speak of a living pre-viable fetus, but much depends on how one defines life and death. Thus a heartbeat might be regarded as signifying life. The Polkinghorne Committee, however, defined death in terms of absence of spontaneous respiration *and* heartbeat (my emphasis); a fetus can neither be viable nor capable of being born alive without physiologically active lungs.

15 Coke's *Institutes of the Laws of England* (3 Co Inst (1680) 50). For recent confirmation, see *Attorney General's Reference (No 3 of 1994)* [1996] 2 All ER 10.

16 Per LORD JUSTICE-CLERK INGLIS in *HMAdv* v. *M'Allum* (1858) 3 Irv 187 at 200.

17 The contrary opinion in *HMAdv* v. *Scott* (1892) 3 White 240 concerned only the relationship between child destruction and murder.

18 Insofar as the concept of transferred malice, which was relied upon in *Attorney General's Reference (No. 3 of 1994)*, n. 15 above, would be difficult to apply in the circumstances, and might not be applied at all in Scotland.

19 Civil liability would lie under both common law and statute law: *Burton* v. *Islington Health Authority; de Martell* v. *Merton and Sutton Health Authority* [1992] 3 All ER 833; Congenital Disabilities (Civil Liability) Act 1976.

20 See *Attorney General's Reference (No 6 of 1980)* [1981] QB 715.

21 *R* v. *Tait* [1990] 1 QB 290 might well apply. For general discussion, see A. Whitfield, 'Common law duties to unborn children' (1993) 1 Med L Rev 28.

22 Note, however, that so far as murder is concerned, the felony–murder rule has been abolished since the Homicide Act, 1957, s.1. For discussion, see J. Temkin, 'Pre-natal injury, homicide and the draft Criminal Code' [1986] CLJ 414.

23 See, for example, A barrister, 'Research investigations and the fetus' [1973] 2 Brit Med J 465.

24 For an old, but still valid, analysis, see G. Dworkin, 'Legality of consent to non-therapeutic research on infants and young children' (1978) 53 Arch Dis Child 443.

25 For discussion, see G. Dworkin, 'Law and medical experimentation: Of embryos, children and others with limited legal capacity' (1987) 13 Monash U LR 189.

26 P.D.G. Skegg, 'English law relating to experimentation on children' [1977] 2 Lancet 754; the concept is fully considered in R.A. McCall Smith, 'Research and experimentation involving children', in J.K. Mason (ed.), *Paediatric Forensic Medicine and Pathology* (1989), London: Chapman & Hall.

27 Institute of Medical Ethics, 'Medical research with children: Ethics, law and practice' (1986) Bulletin no. 14, p. 8.

28 For discussion, see P.D.G. Skegg, 'Medical uses of corpses and the "no property" rule' (1992) 32 Med Sci Law 311; S.R. Munzer, 'An uneasy case against property rights in body parts' (1994) 11 Soc Philos & Pol 259.

29 See, in particular, *Moore* v. *Regents of the University of California* 793 P 2d 479 (Cal, 1990).

30 G. Dworkin and I. Kennedy, 'Human tissue: Rights in the body and its parts' (1993) 1 Med L Rev 291.

31 Peel Report, para. 6; Polkinghorne Report, para. 3.12.

32 I am not, here, considering such techniques as auxiliary or 'assist' transplants, for which the conditions, other than cellular viability, may be different.

33 A. McCall Smith, 'Danger: foetus farming' (1988), *The Times*, 18 April, p. 16; Brahams, n. 12 above.

34 Mrs Winner's case seems to have attracted commercial media coverage only. My information comes from C. Krauthammer, 'Whose life is it anyway?' (1987), *The Scotsman*, 12 December, supp., p. III.

35 B. Jennett and F. Plum, 'Persistent vegetative state after brain damage' [1972] 1 Lancet 734.

36 Conference of Medical Royal Colleges and their Faculties in the United Kingdom, 'Diagnosis of brain death' [1976] 2 Brit Med J 1187.

37 'Organs for transplantation can be removed from anencephalic infants when two doctors who are not members of the transplant team agree that spontaneous respiration has ceased': Report of the Working Party of the Conference of Medical Royal Faculties in the United Kingdom on Organ Transplantation in Neonates (1988).

38 The Medical Task Force on Anencephaly, 'The infant with anencephaly' (1990) 322 New Engl J Med 669.

39 For review, see W.F. May, 'Brain death: Anencephalics and aborted fetuses' (1990) 22 Transplant Proc 885.

40 See M. Harrison, 'Organ procurement for children: the anencephalic fetus as donor' [1986] 2 Lancet 1383.

41 About 20 per year in the United Kingdom: J.R. Salaman, 'Anencephalic organ donors' (1989) 298 Brit Med J 622.

42 D.A. Shewmon, A.M. Capron, W.J. Peacock and B.L. Schulman, 'The use of anencephalic infants as organ sources' (1989) 261 J Amer Med Ass 1773.

43 609 So 2d 588 (Fla, 1992).

44 J.A. Robertson, 'The ethical acceptability of fetal tissue transplants' (1990) 22 Transplant Proc 1025.

45 A short but very useful analysis of expressed views is to be found in R. Gillon, 'Ethics of fetal brain cell transplants' (1988) 296 Brit Med J 1212. The Polkinghorne Committee also rejected the 'moral taint' approach. For further analysis, see D.G. Jones, 'Fetal neural transplantation: Placing the ethical debate within the context of society's use of human material' (1991) 5 Bioethics 23.

46 Medical Ethics, 'Transplantation of fetal material' (1988) 296 Brit Med J 1410.

47 I. Madrazo, V. Leon, C. Torres *et al.*, 'Transplantation of fetal substantia nigra and adrenal medulla to the caudate nucleus in two patients with Parkinson's disease' (1988) 318 New Engl J Med 51. Case reports in the United Kingdom were confined to media activity; see, for example, T. Stuttaford, 'Early days for brain cell implants' (1988), *The Times*, 21 April, p. 13; Leading article, 'Brain to brain' (1988), *The Times*, 18 April, p. 17; O. Gillie, 'The dilemma of brain tissue transplants' (1988), *The Independent*, 20 April, p. 17.

48 Leading article, 'Embryos and Parkinson's disease' [1988] 1 Lancet 1087. For an overview of the US position at that time, see C. Marwick, 'Use of fetal tissue in the United States' (1989) 297 Brit Med J 1357. Implantations were also per-

formed in Spain: M. Ruiz, 'Little opposition to fetal transplants in Spain' (1988) 297 Brit Med J 1358.

49   Though it appears that the 'jury is still out': see Z. Kmietowicz, 'Antiabortionists hijack fetal pain argument' (1996) 313 Brit Med J 188. See also n. 6 above.

50   The Polkinghorne Committee have, in fact, opted for an intermediary to ensure such separation of functions and for careful recording of what was done by the source, the intermediary and the user (Report, ch. 5).

51   See, in particular, Human Fertilisation and Embryology Authority, *Donated Ovarian Tissue in Embryo Research and Assisted Conception – Report* (1994).

52   This is a statutory phrase which unarguably includes primitive as well as mature ova: see A. Grubb, 'Use of fetal eggs and infertility treatment' (1995) 3 Med L Rev 203.

53   Inserted by Criminal Justice and Public Order Act 1994, s.156.

54   HM(68)33.

55   Royal College of Physicians of London, *Guidelines on the Practice of Ethics Committees in Medical Research Involving Human Subjects* (3rd edn, 1996) London: Royal College of Physicians. For a very full review of the formation and function of the LREC, see T. Mander, 'The legal standing of Local Research Ethics Committees' (1996) 2 Med Law Internat 149.

56   See, for example, the judicial decision in *Re Quinlan* 355 A 2d 647 (NJ, 1976): 'subject to concurrence by the hospital ethical committee'.

57   Though, in fact, a local research ethics committee should be involved in any research conducted on those who have died recently in National Health Service premises.

58   The Nuffield Council on Bioethics has been established on a relatively unofficial basis to look into major ethical concerns nationwide. There have been further calls for official centralisation: J. Wise, 'Royal College calls for central research ethics committee' (1996) 313 Brit Med J 251.

59   National Health Service Management Executive, *Local Research Ethics Committees*, HSG(91) 5 (1991).

60   'UK's First Hospital Ethics Committee' (1993) Bull Med Ethics No 90, 5.

61   A very good case can be made out for the invariable inclusion, or cooption, of a lawyer with an interest in medical jurisprudence in the assessment of any project involving work which impinges on statutory or case law. This might apply particularly to fetal research, which is so bound up with abortion legislation. It is to be noted that the professional bioethicist, who is so much a part of the American scene, is a very rare specimen in the United Kingdom.

62   See *R v. Ethical Committee of St Mary's Hospital (Manchester), ex p H* [1988] 1 FLR 512.

8 The Infertile Man

Infertility in general

It is widely held that some 10 per cent of married couples who wish to have children are unable to do so by reason of infertility; the reasons for the condition are divided roughly equally between husband and wife. This morbidity is a source of considerable distress and it is not surprising that it promotes a great deal of research in academic departments of reproductive biology. This results in the development of techniques which are designed, in the main, to do no more than circumvent – or bypass – the fundamental defect which is the cause of the infertility.

It is important to bear in mind that such ruses constitute no more than a secondary extension of a standard therapeutic plan. Ideally, therapy restores a disease state to normal. The process of diagnosis may reveal a medical cause – often, in the case of infertility, in the form of a hormonal deficiency; substitution therapy would then be the first preferred treatment. Alternatively, the cause may be amenable to surgical correction, as, for example, when part of the genital tract has become blocked owing to an inflammatory reaction; another example would be attempted surgical reversal of a previous vasectomy or tubal ligation if so required when a patient's reproductive status changes. It is only when the aptness of such routine treatments has been excluded, or when they have failed, that recourse will be made to 'social' treatments involving, *inter alia*, gamete substitution and, hence, the involvement of parties outside the immediate therapeutic circle. Such social treatments will inevitably impinge upon social policies and, by extension, on legal principles; the extent of this encroachment will be addressed in detail in this and the following chapter. The purpose of this preamble has been no more than to emphasise that they are treatments of a recognisable uninvited condition: childlessness due either to physiological or to pathological abnormality.[1]

Separation of medical and social treatments has two main consequences. First, it raises the question of whether the latter should be provided by a health service – or, put another way, can health purchasers justify the exclusion of treatments for childlessness from what they are prepared to provide?[2] Secondly, the concept of social treatment immediately suggests that this is a matter which is beyond the exclusive control of the medical profession and is one which should be regulated by Parliament. As to the first, a good case can be made out that there is no distinction to be made as to need and, indeed that modern medical technology has, of itself, transformed an unfortunate social disability into a clinical need.[3] Intervention in medical treatment by way of statute represents the careful balancing of the benefits to individual patients against the possible disadvantages to the social order: first, there must *be* a need to do so and, second, the public, through its legislators, must *perceive* the need to do so. The treatment of childlessness, or assisted reproduction, involves gross intrusion into personal privacy and the institution of marriage; by definition, it also results in the production of children by unnatural means. By any standards, it is a technique which cries out for regulation and, after long deliberations by the Warnock Committee and on its report,[4] the United Kingdom Parliament responded with the Human Fertilisation and Embryology Act 1990,[5] which forms the backbone of this and the following chapter.

Some forms of treatment of childlessness which involve gamete manipulation or donation depend for their success on sophisticated and expensive medical technology; others are comparatively simple and scarcely involve professional expertise. With one major exception – surrogate motherhood – treatments for the childless woman fall into the former category; substitution of sperm by donation is, by contrast, easily accomplished. The treatment of childlessness due to infertility in the male is therefore that form which is most open to unsupervised use; indeed, it goes without saying that it *can* be achieved by substitution of the male person; it also illustrates very clearly the potential legal pitfalls that are intrinsic to these processes. At the same time, it will be seen that the 1990 Act is mainly concerned with those techniques designed to assist the childless woman; major discussion of the Act will, therefore, be postponed until Chapter 9. For the present, it need only be said that the Act establishes a Human Fertilisation and Embryology Authority (HFEA) a major function of which is to control, through the appropriate committee, the provision of treatment services for the purpose of assisting women to carry children; these include treatments which involve the use of gametes derived from persons outside the duo of the woman and her husband or partner.

Childlessness due to non-consummation and related reasons

Before considering the main causes of intramarital infertility, it will be convenient to deal with the occasional circumstance when both husband and wife may be fertile, as measured by the production of spermatozoa and ova, but conception is impossible because of impotence in one or other partner. The answer to non-parenthood may then lie in artificial insemination by the husband's or partner's sperm (AIH or AIP).[6]

Artificial insemination by husband or partner

In this simple manoeuvre, the husband's or partner's semen is collected – and, possibly, treated physically so as to improve the likelihood of success – and is injected into the wife's vagina. A resultant child is thus indistinguishable from one which is conceived naturally. There are no immediate matters of legal concern and there is no suggestion that the process should be subject to control. Moral objections will scarcely arise: the male specimen can even be obtained during the course of acceptable love-play rather than by masturbation, which would be disapproved by some; any who condemn the process will do so on the grounds that they object to *any* interference with natural reproduction. A later petition for a decree of nullity might or might not be eliminated on the ground of approbation (see Chapter 2): 'So far as approbation of the marriage is concerned, it must be a question of degree, what acts done, with what intention [AIH is effected, that] constitute approbation.'[7] A child so conceived would never be illegitimate as, irrespective of the outcome of any petition, the parents would have been married at the time of conception.

Posthumous AIH Posthumous AIH has considerable legal significance in its own right and, although the subject is, strictly speaking, beyond the ambit of the treatment of infertility, it merits brief consideration in a book of this type.[8] Semen may be preserved for various reasons (see below) and may then be used after death, but the most immediately apposite scenario involves a wife, currently childless but not wishing necessarily to remain so, arranging for the cryopreservation, or 'banking', of her husband's semen as a deliberate insurance against his dying or being killed before a child is conceived; it is, for example, a practice which is said to be not uncommon in the armed forces.

There is nothing inherently illegal in a woman having a child by any man she chooses; nor is there any legal bar to her choosing a man who is dead: the practical limitation is then simply one of scientific technology. It scarcely needs emphasis, however, that a subsequent claim to paternity on behalf of any child born as a result of posthumous AIH would cause untold difficulties, *inter alia*, in the legal fields of inheritance and succession: the mere possibility of a claim eventuating at some time in the future would effectively proscribe the granting of probate; clearly, therefore, the *outcome* of the practice must be subject to legal rules. Primary supervision would not be as difficult, as posthumous AIH requires a technical expertise, almost certainly involving cryopreservation, which is available only to specialist clinics; the practice could, therefore, be closely supervised and any legislation would be enforceable.

The 1990 statute solves this problem only partially. Section 28(6)(*b*) merely states that, where the sperm of a man, or any embryo the creation of which was brought about with his sperm, is used after his death, he is not to be treated as the father of the child – which deals, at least, with the problems of succession and inheritance. It is clear, however, that there is no intent to deprive a woman of her right to bear her partner's child and the process is not prohibited.[9] We are left, then, with the ethical issues and it is interesting to find that attitudes and practices vary very considerably among the clinics licensed to store gametes. Thus it has been said that more than one-third of such centres are opposed to their posthumous use.[10] Almost half of those who *would* use the gametes or embryos would do so only subject to qualifying restrictions, including such value-laden conditions as only doing so in order to produce a sibling for an existing child. The dichotomy results from conflicting principles in the Act and its associated code of practice. Thus, on the one hand, we have the code saying, 'Centres should avoid adopting any policy or criteria which may appear arbitrary or discriminatory',[11] and, on the other, the Act states: 'A woman shall not be provided with treatment services unless account has been taken of the welfare of any child who may be born as a result of that treatment (including the need of that child for a father)'.[12]

Failure to abide by the wishes or instructions of the gamete donor is, of course, justified under the conscientious objection section 38 (see p. 219 for further discussion) but this scarcely provides ethical cover for the 22 per cent of centres who, as Corrigan and her colleagues discovered, would not transfer the sperm to a centre willing to impregnate the widow; there is certainly no statutory obligation on them to do so but, by analogy with the Abortion Act 1967 (see p. 128), one would have thought there was, at least, a compelling moral duty. This appears to be the view of the Human Fertilisation and Embryology Authority,[13] but it is arguable that the law requires clarification.[14]

The legal position following the somewhat bizarre possible variation of the specimen being *taken* after brain stem death – or, at least, while in terminal coma – has now been aired in *R* v. *Human Fertilis-ation and Embryology Authority, ex parte Blood*.[15] In this case, a woman succeeded in obtaining seminal fluid from her comatose husband who died shortly afterwards;[16] she wished to use this to have their child. There are at least three attitudes that could be adopted when assessing the legality of the procedure. Firstly, it could be looked upon as a simple matter of AIH – or treatment of a man and woman together – and, therefore, beyond the need for a licence and the governance of HFEA. A second, and more pragmatic, solution would be to accept the consent of the husband as implied in view of his intention to have a child which was apparently well-known before his sudden fatal illness. In the alternative, once the husband was dead, it could no longer be a matter of treatment for a man and woman together and, therefore, the use of the male gametes was subject to the consent requirements of the 1990 Act, sch. 3, which include written consent to the *storage* of *all* gametes together with, in particular, instructions as to their disposal in the event of the donor's death. Such consent was not obtained – and, indeed, was unobtain-able;[17] accordingly, the Authority maintained that the treatment must be illegal; Mrs Blood applied for judicial review. The President of the Family Division rejected the first scenario on the grounds that a dead man cannot be a 'party' to treatment and that the taking of the sperm was a unilateral act on the part of his wife. He also held that the second possibility was precluded by the wording of the statute and that written consent was of fundamental importance. In the event, therefore, the court found that the Authority had acted properly and the application failed. Public opinion almost universally condemned the attitude of the Authority and the decision of the court as being narrowly legalistic.

The trial court had, however, also refused to sanction the export of Mr Blood's gametes so that she could be treated overseas – specifi-cally, in Belgium. When the case went to appeal, the court upheld the ruling that the storage of sperm in the absence of consent was unlaw-ful; Mrs Blood could not, therefore, receive treatment within the United Kingdom. The Court of Appeal then noted that she could not, in addition, be treated *outside* the United Kingdom unless the sperm was exported. Failure to sanction the export of the male gametes to a country within the European Community therefore resulted in a direct contravention of Community law which establishes the right of an EC citizen to seek medical treatment in any country of the Community.[18] The appeal was, therefore, allowed to that extent and a very difficult situation was resolved in a somewhat devious way. It is, however, clear that *Blood* does nothing to alter domestic United Kingdom law; indeed, the court pointed out that it was a unique case which should never recur (at 23).

Other reasons for AIH Various other technical reasons for AIH deserve mention, in particular possible laboratory treatment designed to improve the quality of the ejaculate when the husband is infertile by reason of a paucity of spermatozoa (oligospermia)[19] or to eliminate the offending substances when infertility is due to the wife forming antibodies against – or developing an immunity to – the husband's semen. Men who undergo vasectomy may preserve seminal specimens as an insurance against the death of an existing child or remarriage and those undergoing testicular ablation for malignant disease may also do so; the preserved ejaculate may, then, be inserted artificially.

A less worthy reason for replacement of natural intercourse would arise if the couple believed that the sex of the subsequent child could be predetermined by manipulation of the ejaculate.[20] When undertaken purely for reasons of personal preference, the underlying ethical analysis of such primary sex selection is similar to that already outlined in relation to gender-based abortion (see p. 117). But, whether or not one approves of pre-conception sex selection, it can hardly be denied that it is *preferable* to selection by abortion – and this applies whether the procedure is seen as a potential new dimension in family planning or as a legitimate way of eliminating X-linked genetic disease (see p. 158). The difficulty lies in the current inaccuracy of the process which appears to result in a successful selection rate of, at best, 70 per cent, which is not a marked improvement on the 50 per cent success rate of normal sexual intercourse. Since the couple will have gone to considerable expense and discomfort, the procedure will result in 30 per cent of patients being seriously disappointed. This, in turn, can only lead either to a thoroughly unsatisfactory ambience for the resulting child or to abortion – and the first of these clearly indicates the need for regulation and licensing of so-called 'gender clinics'. It is to be noted that, insofar as the process involves the gametes of no third party, it is beyond the official remit of the Human Fertilisation and Embryology Authority.[21]

The infertile husband or partner: artificial insemination by donor (AID)[22]

Infertility in the male may be due to a blockage of the vasa deferentia, in which case, the defect may be reversible by appropriate surgery. More commonly, it results from failure to produce adequate semen, which includes secretions from the seminal vesicles and prostate gland as well as spermatozoa derived from the testes. A reduction in the number of spermatozoa may be partial (oligozoospermia) or complete (azoospermia). Infertility resulting from the former may sometimes be surmounted by multiple emissions or, as we have seen above, by manipulation of the ejaculate; the latter, whether it is due to developmental defects or to previous disease – mumps in childhood is not an uncommon cause – is generally irreparable. In such circumstances, the answer to childlessness may lie in artificial insemination by donor (AID);[23] in this process, the woman is impregnated with semen derived from a man other than her husband. By contrast with AIH, AID could be a minefield of legal hazards in the absence of legislation.

Even then, it bristles with ethical problems. The process involves masturbation, which is a degrading exercise in the eyes of many; there is no element of marital love such as exists in AIH; and the sanctity of marriage is disturbed.[24] It has been well said that the process requires emotional maturity and good understanding of each other's needs on the part of both husband and wife. There are additional medical reasons for disapproving AID, at least in an uncontrolled system: the avid donor of semen may not be the ideal parent from the viewpoint of both the geneticist and the clinical pathologist, and this may be particularly so if donation attracts a monetary inducement. It must also be remembered that, although both AIH and AID may be *technically* very simple operations, a successful outcome is not attained easily.[25] But this depends on several features, including the age and social class of the woman and, above all, on a well organised service which can provide the specimens for the multiple inseminations which are often needed. A strong organisation is also needed if the various medical, ethical, legal and social complexities are to be overcome. It is convenient to look at these from the points of view of the various parties involved.

The role of the medical adviser

There are several reasons why AID should be supervised medically rather than be undertaken on a purely personal basis. Perhaps the major concern is that of counselling: as discussed already, the process is emotionally traumatic and, once successfully embarked upon, reversal is difficult, if not impossible; the relative merits of alternative procedures such as adoption, which is, admittedly, a dwindling option, must certainly be put to the couple.[26] Secondly, there must be some control over the choice of donor insofar as his genetic characteristics should, so far as is reasonable, correspond to those of the infertile husband; he must be free from sexually transmissible disease and he must, himself, be free from significant genetic abnormality. The doctor's responsibility as to selection is, therefore, heavy and, having undertaken a duty of care, his discharge of that responsibility is subject to the normal rules of professional negligence, as amplified by statute.[27] The situation is now reasonably clear. The 1976 Act now states that, in a case where the woman was receiving infertility treatment and the child was born disabled, then, if the disability results from the act or omission in the course of the selection, keeping or use of the gametes or resulting embryo by a person who is answerable to the child in respect of the act or omission, the child's disabilities are to be regarded as damage resulting from the wrongful act of that person and actionable accordingly at the suit of that child. Section 1(5) of the 1976 Act does, however, also confirm the common law defence to medical negligence:[28]

> The defendant is not answerable to the child for anything he did or omitted to do ... when treating or advising the parent, if he took reasonable care having due regard to the then received professional opinion applicable to the particular class of case; but this does not mean that he is answerable only because he departed from received opinion.[29]

Effectively, therefore, the door is opened to a 'diminished life' action, but the hurdle of causation would still have to be surmounted. Many children are born with congenital defects and the majority are either random occurrences or, if genetically controlled, are multifactorial in origin; the attribution of blame to the doctor may, therefore, be very difficult. It is easy to wonder why the 1990 Act includes among its treatments requiring a licence, a procedure such as AID which is, in practice, virtually impossible to control. Difficulties such as those described above serve to emphasise, however, not so much the importance of medical supervision of AID but, rather, the need for *expert* medical supervision. The inclusion of AID under the umbrella of the Human Fertilisation and Embryology Authority is, thereby, justified.

The donor

The problem of unrecognisable disease prompts many AID clinics to seek known fathers – often fathers of children in the post-natal ward – as donors. At least they have been *shown* to produce healthy offspring; only exceptionally should a donor be used who is aged more than 55 years.[30] The majority of therapeutic donors in the United Kingdom are, however, generally drawn from the student population, subject to a minimum age of 18 years. It is, therefore, essential that the normal rules of paternal responsibility by way of aliment and the like are circumvented in the practice of AID; in purely practical terms, there would be no donors were the possibility of such responsibility to exist. The answer to the problem lies, firstly, in the statutory limitation of such responsibility and, secondly, in a guarantee of confidentiality.

As to the former, the United Kingdom has, somewhat haltingly, now followed the lead given by the United States and the Commonwealth.[31] The matter was first addressed in the Family Law Reform Act 1987, s.27 which ran:

> unless it is proved to the satisfaction of any court by which the matter has to be determined that the other party to that marriage did not consent to the insemination, the child [conceived by AID] shall be treated in law as the child of the parties to that marriage and shall not be treated as the child of any person other than the parties to that marriage.

It will be seen that s.27 operated only when the natural mother was party to a marriage which had neither been dissolved nor annulled at the time of insemination. Later legislation amends this but still does not go as far as, say, the law in New South Wales. The Human Fertilisation and Embryology Act 1990, s.28 discusses the meaning of 'father', to which we will revert under the heading of 'the prospective parents'. For present purposes, it is to be noted that s.28(4) dictates that, where a husband or a stable partner is to be treated as the father of a child to whom he is not genetically related, *no other person* is to be treated as the father of the child. This position is bolstered in s.28(6), which states: 'Where the sperm of a man [who has given valid consent to its use for the purpose] was used for a purpose for which such consent was required ... he is not to be treated as the father of the child', thus covering the donor who consents to the impregnation of a woman whose husband has *not* consented to her insemination, and by s.29(2): 'Where, by virtue of ... s.28 of this Act, a person is not to be treated as ... the father of a child, that person is to be treated in law as not being ... the father of the child for any purpose.' All of which may appear sufficiently clear, the overriding condition being, of course, that the insemination is *artificial* and is performed by a person who is *licensed* to do so. The fact that the Act refers only to women with a consenting partner is of no concern to the *donor*, who is protected from irregularities in that context by s.28(6),[32] – save in the unlikely event of his sperm being used *without* his consent.

As to confidentiality, it is implicit from the foregoing section that the medical supervisor must be aware of the origin of the donor sperm. This is dictated not only by the immediate need to assess the suitability of the specimen but also as insurance against the possibilities of mischance in the future. For the latter reason, it would, for example, be important that the origins of any congenital defects in the fetus could be properly investigated, and a record, and limitation, of donations by an individual is also needed so as to minimise the possibility of future incestuous matings. The more general genetic implications of incestuous matings are discussed in Chapter 13. It has been estimated that 25 donations by one man in a population such as that of Scotland would give rise to a recognisable risk of later marriages within the prohibited degrees,[32] and HFEA states that an empirical limit of 10 children fathered by any one donor may be exceeded only in exceptional cases.[34]

The legislative answer to the competing needs of secrecy and openness is to be found in the 1990 Act, ss.31–5. The essentials for present purposes are that the authority must keep a register which contains information related to the keeping or use of the gametes of any identifiable individual. Such information is regarded as highly confidential but, apart from such breaches as are necessary for the efficient running of the centre, disclosure is authorised to the Registrar General when a claim is being made that a man is or is not the father of a child,[35] to the courts following a court order for the purposes of instituting proceedings under the Congenital Disabilities (Civil Liability) Act 1976,[36] and to an applicant aged over 18 years who is seeking to know whether the register indicates that a person other than his or her apparent parent might be his or her parent but for the provisions of the Act. As regards the last, any regulations made cannot require the authority to give any information as to the identity of the person whose gametes have been used. No regulations have been promulgated, but it is assumed that, following the recommendations of the Warnock Committee,[37] the available information would be limited to basic information about the donor's ethnic origin and genetic health. The effect of donor anonymity on the child is discussed below. For present purposes, it may seem that the donor's privacy is protected and, as things stand, the regulations in force at the time of donation cannot be altered retrospectively. Nonetheless, the existence of a register means that the information exists and, such is the trend in today's thinking, that, sooner or later, it is almost inevitable that the proposition that *because* it exists, it *should* be available will prevail. An Act of Parliament can always be repealed and sperm donors may, yet, be confronted by children with whom they have no parental empathy.

A final observation on donor anonymity and selection relates to deliberate attempts at eugenic advancement. There have been reports that this objective is not uncommon in the United States and, so far as can be seen, there is nothing in either United States or United Kingdom law which would make a preferential choice of donors illegal. One's immediate antipathy to such a course is difficult to justify; *some* choice is inherent in the preference for a donor of similar characteristics to the husband with which no-one would disagree, and there is no reason why rejection of an 'inferior' image should be any more acceptable than a preference for a 'superior' version of oneself. It can only be supposed that most doctors would not wish to be associated with eugenic selection. Somewhat strangely, HFEA's *Code of Practice* is silent on the topic[38]; while admitting that the argument was finely balanced, the Warnock Committee was content to remark that, as a matter of principle, they did not wish 'to encourage the possibility of prospective parents seeking donors with specific characteristics by the use of whose semen they hope to give birth to a particular type of child'.

The prospective parents

Many of the legal hurdles of AID which once had to be overcome by the prospective parents have now been lowered – indeed, the process was begun some time before the 1990 Act. The bogey of adultery was laid to rest early in the Scottish courts on the grounds that, as discussed in Chapter 2, adultery must include *some* element of sexual interplay including, almost certainly, some degree of vulval penetration.[39] The issue has also been addressed with the same result in the United States,[40] but not, so far as is known, in the courts of England, where there is no reason to suppose that the decision would be different. In the event of deterioration in marital relationships, there would, accordingly, be no factual evidence by reason of adultery on the part of the artificially inseminated wife on which to ground a petition for divorce. This, of course, assumes that the AID was mutually consensual; non-consensual insemination, by contrast, would almost certainly represent behaviour by reason of which the husband could not reasonably be expected to live with his wife and, as such, a reason for the irretrievable breakdown of the marriage.

The legal position of the husband or male partner of the inseminated woman is now relatively clear and has been partially addressed when considering that of the donor. Effectively, s.28(2) rules that, if a married woman is inseminated by someone other than her husband, the husband will be treated as the father of the child unless it can be shown that he did not consent to the insemination. The section also covers the placing in her of an embryo derived from another man or of sperm and eggs – the process of gamete intrafallopian transfer (GIFT); the position of the unmarried partner is covered in the same way in s.28(3). The absolute nature of the provision has been confirmed in the courts and may, in fact, operate to the advantage of the man if there is any subsequent dispute.[41] The difficulty arises in allowing for the husband or partner who seeks to evade his consent given at the time of the treatment. To circumvent this, s.28(5) retains, *inter alia*, the presumption of *pater est quem nuptiae demonstrant* – or that, at common law, a child is a child of a married couple unless the husband can show otherwise. The unfortunate result of protecting the mother and child against a reneging husband is that it simultaneously penalises the man who never did consent; the latter may still have to exclude his paternity by way of standard blood or DNA tests.[42] Hereditary titles, honours and the like are excluded from the general principles attaching to the AID family by s.29(4); it is unclear how the proof or disproof of patrilinearity is to be discharged.

So far as can be seen, the legal problems associated with the registration of the child's birth have been eliminated. Although the certificate of birth is not mentioned, the 1990 Act states, at s.29(1), that a husband consenting to AID is to be treated in law as the father of the resultant child *for all purposes*; since registration of birth is nowhere excluded, it must come within the ambit of the section which, we have noted, also applies to a consenting partner. Moreover, an attempt to ensure that the fact that a child was born as a result of 'treatment services' was endorsed on his or her certificate of birth was defeated in the House of Commons.[43] One would have thought that the 'father's name' on a birth certificate ought to mean the genetic father – otherwise, the entry is relatively meaningless and is certainly of no use for the purpose of tracing ancestry. The inevitable conclusion is that Parliament has deliberately authorized the falsification of a legal document and there must be some sympathy for Lord Denning who asked: 'is it right to tell a lie on the birth certificate?'.[44] The whole tenor of the debate on the original clause in the Family Law Reform Act 1987 was strongly child-oriented and the impression is that the legislators were, in fact, happy to accept the commission of an offence so long as it spared a child later embarrassment. The major purpose of modern family law is to promote legal equality for children irrespective of the status of their parents and to do this, so far is possible, within a stable family relationship; it seems that falsifying the records is the lesser of two evils, but it would surely be better for the law to admit to the fact and to do so by statute positively rather than by implication.

There have also been suggestions that couples requesting treatment by AID should be subjected to a screening mechanism similar to that which is obligatory in the process of adoption. Such an imposition would be illogical, on at least three counts. Firstly, there is no absolute reason, save on the grounds of aesthetics and of the possible implications in divorce proceedings, why couples should not resort to natural insemination by donor or to unsupervised AID should they wish to avoid such scrutiny – and, in practice, many actual inseminations are performed on a 'do-it-yourself' basis as a matter of clinical policy or personal preference. Secondly, there is no test of suitability for marriage in general; it follows that there is no reason to isolate 10 per cent of couples on the grounds of their infertility when the other 90 per cent of parents would be unscreened. Finally, the two processes are fundamentally different. In adoption, a choice between competing prospective parents is being made for an *existing* child; no such competition is involved in assisted reproduction: the choice lies between being born into a specific family or non-existence and, if any criteria are to be applied, they must be of a different order in the two conditions.[45]

The child conceived by AID

At the end of the day, the major justification for such legal interference with procreation must be the welfare of the subsequent child. Here it is important to remember that we are discussing AID; it may well be that the ethical principles differ from those which apply when the 'treatment' process involves active cooperation by the medical profession and an expensive call upon general resources – a situation that is discussed further at p. 241. Effectively, we have got to disapprove of a given group of women *becoming pregnant* – and, logically, legislate to prevent them doing so – before we can rule that they should be denied AID. The question of whether or not AID should be available to single women or, more especially, to lesbian women who would be more likely to have a psychiatric aversion to natural procreation, thus seems to me to be less urgent than is generally supposed.

Certainly, the Warnock Committee (at para. 2.11) concluded that it is, as a general rule, better for children to be born into a two-parent family and, certainly, the Human Fertilisation and Embryology Act 1990, s.13(5) calls upon the therapist to take account of the resultant child's need for a father.[46] Neither statement can be regarded as being dogmatic and s.13(5) is so imprecise as to be either all-embracing or meaningless.[47] On the other hand, any arguments which seek to demonstrate the advantages of controlled AID over an unsupervised operation in the married state must apply equally, if not more so, to the unmarried. In the event, there is no legal prohibition of AID in the latter situation in the United Kingdom and the acceptance or exclusion of applicants is a matter for individual centres.[48] Many – perhaps fearful for their licences or because of the personal moral stance of the 'person responsible', backed up by the 'conscience clause' (1990 Act, s.38) – will refuse treatment to single women.[49] The prohibition is, however, difficult to justify, and the present writer admits to having changed his attitude since the first edition of this book.

It is customary to consider the lesbian couple as a distinct group in this connection, presumably on the grounds that the child born into such an environment is likely to be particularly exposed to gender pressure; it has been pointed out repeatedly that the legislation is designed not so much to seek a 'father' for the child as to provide a 'man about the house'. The psychological effects of being born into a lesbian household are notoriously difficult to assess: even if an adverse effect is present, it is almost impossible to separate primary from secondary causes. By and large, the most respected studies have failed to demonstrate any adverse effects simply *because* the child has been deprived of a masculine influence in early life;[50] Douglas,[51] for example, has pointed out that the results of planned unmarried parenthood are likely to be better than those of a broken conventional marriage.[52] In practical terms, there seems to be no overpowering ethical argument for the medical profession to seek to withhold parenthood from a group who, by dint of the difficulties involved, are likely to provide a loving maternal environment, but our legislators are clearly anxious not to be seen to be encouraging the process. Perhaps the lesson to be learned is that homosexuals are not a homogeneous group but, rather, a collection of individuals; as with any procedure involving the welfare of children, each case must be decided on its own merits – none can be a precedent for the others.[53]

Recent discussion has focused on the provision of infertility treatment services for older women and, in particular, post-menopausal women; the major bone of ethical contention has related to the effect on the child who is produced in this way. Insofar as the process could involve the use of an embryo derived from ovum and sperm donors, it could be seen as an aspect of artificial insemination. The subject is, however, very much more aligned with *in vitro* fertilisation and ovum donation and will be discussed in the following chapter.

The question of the legitimacy of the child conceived by AID in the United Kingdom has now certainly been solved by the Human Fertilisation and Embryology Act 1990, ss.28(2) and 29(1), whereby the consenting husband is to be regarded as the father of the child for all purposes – excluding the succession to any dignity or title of honour.[54] The proposition is rebuttable only by proof that consent was not given at the time of insemination; a husband who has so consented cannot, later, prove illegitimacy of the child by way of blood group or DNA testing. Conversely, this process *is* open to the non-consenting husband who is the father of the child, by virtue of s.25(5). In other situations, including consensual *natural* insemination by a third party,[55] the stigma, such as it is, could be imposed by the woman's husband, although the legal impediments are now very slight as a result of the Family Law Reform Act 1987 and the Law Reform (Parent and Child) (Scotland) Act 1986.

It will become apparent in the next chapter that the 1990 Act represents an advance in United Kingdom legislation in that, unlike the

Family Law Reform Act 1987, s.27, it addresses the comparable exercise of ovum donation; any anomalies between the laws of England and Scotland as to the status of AID children have also been ironed out.

A matter of far greater concern for such children lies in the problem of their identity, the essential question being whether or not they are entitled, or should be allowed, to know their conceptual origins. The motion for disclosure is based on two main lines of argument. The first is the general moral convention that all persons have a right (and want) to know their family history. This would seem to be overimposing theoretical values on a very practical situation. Few of us would wish to question our paternity: very few loving mothers are suspected of being adulteresses, a condition which is, in practice, less improbable than her being an AID recipient. In general, the AID child can only know his true origin if he is told of it and it is to no-one's advantage to do so; one feels that the child's strong position under the 1990 Act can only be undermined by disclosure if it is changed at all. Moreover, should there ever be a rule that the AID child *must* be told of his origin, it would follow in fairness that every child should, at some time, be assured of the integrity of his parenthood; clearly, such a policy would lead to considerable unease in the family: the theoretical rights of a small minority should give way to the well-being of the majority. It will be argued that information may leak out during a family dispute, but so may other unwelcome news and, in practice, properly counselled husbands and wives who undertake AID tend to have more stable relationships than are found in the average marriage. The difficulty is that there are some situations where the anomaly between 'father' and child *must* come to light, for example in relation to *in vivo* transplantation of organs, in respect of which ss.27–9 of the 1990 Act do not apply for the purposes of the Human Organ Transplants Act, s.2,[56] but such rare possibilities should be met as they arise and should not be allowed to overshadow the wider situation. It is a matter of opinion as to whether or not the compromise reached in the 1990 Act is likely to prove more disruptive and unsatisfying than would be a complete ban on information.

The second argument in favour of 'disclosure' is based on an analogy between AID and adoption; it is said that the right of the adopted child to counselling and information[57] should be available equally to one conceived by AID. But adoption and AID are more dissimilar than alike. In the first place, the adopted child has no genetic association with his 'parents', whereas the AID child shares at least half his genes with his mother. Secondly, while the adoptee can often discover his full parentage, the product of AID cannot: the anonymity of the donor is fully preserved in the legislation; the question of whether partial information is likely to be beneficial to anyone has been raised above. Thirdly, any maternal bonding is *within* the family in AID, whereas adoption involves some suggestion of separation. Finally, and perhaps of the most pragmatic importance, AID is a confidential matter between husband and wife, whereas adoption can scarcely be disguised; the chances of an adopted child hearing of his origins from an extraneous source are high, whereas they are negligible in well-conducted AID.

The English Law Commission thought that compulsory disclosure of non-paternity would serve no useful purpose.[58] The Warnock Committee advised that the AID child should have access to basic information about the donor's ethnic origin and genetic health at the age of 18 (at para. 4.21), a compromise which has been adopted in the 1990 Act, with an extension to the age of 16 in the event of a proposed marriage. I have to admit to a preference for a voluntary code of practice for 'parents' over any form of statutory obligation.

Evading the issue: AIHD

No man likes to be labelled as infertile; every loving wife will prefer a child through her husband rather than as a result of a clinical insemination from an anonymous man. As a result, many couples who are childless by virtue of the husband's infertility attempt to evade the issue and to erect a barricade of doubt as to the true paternity of the AID child. One route to this is to continue intramarital sexual intercourse while, at the same time, practising AID; an alternative is the admixture of the husband's and the donor's semen prior to insemination, a process which is abbreviated to AIHD.

AIHD may be emotionally satisfying, but actual conception by the husband's sperm is statistically contingent on a number of factors. Much depends on the number of motile spermatozoa which are contained in the husband's semen. It is said that the fecundity rate ranges from 0.2 per cent for wives with apparently azoospermic husbands to a maximum of 5.3 per cent when the husband has an oligozoospermia of less than 10 million motile sperm per millilitre of semen,[59] the normal sperm count being in the range of 30–200 million per millilitre in an ejaculate which averages some 3–4 millilitres in total. Much depends, however, on factors such as emotional stress and the effects of continence; indeed, the total fecundity of a couple may be affected by such apparently dissociated features as the wife's capacity to achieve orgasm. A combination of such psychiatric influences may, in fact, explain the rather common phenomenon of conception occurring in an apparently infertile marriage shortly after arranging for adoption. Be that as it may, it is generally held that the minimum concentration of sperm in a fertile semen is of the order of 60 million per millilitre.

It is said that AIHD carries the additional advantage that it salves the conscience of those couples who register the resultant child as their own. The whole exercise, however, then takes on something of the philosophy of the ostrich and is designed for those who find security in uncertainty. And, while it may have been an attractive proposition in the past, it must be wondered whether it is now a good exercise in psychiatric management. The spectre can be foreseen of nagging and increasing doubt and consequent stress until the issue is settled by the now widely available facilities for paternity testing; the probably unwelcome result would then be unlikely to contribute to family stability.

Notes

1 The distinction between the treatment of infertility and of childlessness has been likened to the treatment of defective eyesight by the provision of spectacles: P. Singer, 'Response' (1983) 9 J Med Ethics 198.
2 S. Redmayne and R. Klein, 'Rationing in practice: The case of in vitro fertilisation' (1993) 306 Brit Med J 1521.
3 See D. Evans, 'Infertility and the NHS' (1995) 311 Brit Med J 1586.
4 M. Warnock (Chairman), *Report of the Committee of Inquiry into Human Fertilisation and Embryology* (1984) (Cmnd 9314). (Hereafter referred to as the Warnock Committee or Report.)
5 Hereafter referred to as the 1990 Act. The 1990 Act appears to have become something of a template for other jurisdictions; for Canada, see W. Kondro, 'Canada gets tough with reproductive technologies' (1996) 347 Lancet 1758.
6 Very unusual questions such as a male prisoner's right to AIH while in custody are not addressed here, although the issue involved is of considerable penological interest. For an instance, see D. Fernand, 'Prisoner calls for right to father a child' (1989), *The Sunday Times*, 5 March, p. A9.
7 *REL (orse R)* v. *E L* [1949] P 211 per PEARCE J at 217. In this case, AIH was regarded only as an unsuccessful attempt to 'normalise' the marriage. Compare *G* v. *G*, 1961 SLT (Reps) 324.
8 For earlier discussion, see D.J. Cusine, 'Artificial insemination with the husband's semen after the husband's death' (1977) 3 J Med Ethics 163.
9 The terms of Schedule 3, para. 2(2)(b) apparently allow for such a contingency.
10 E. Corrigan, S.E. Mumford and M.G.R. Hull, 'Posthumous storage and use of sperm and embryos: Survey of opinion of treatment centres' (1996) 313 Brit Med J 24.
11 Human Fertilisation and Embryology Authority, *Code of Practice* (1993), London: HFEA.
12 1990 Act, s.13(5). And it is to be noted that, according to the terms of the Act, any child so born *must* be legally fatherless.
13 CH/94/9 of September 1994, quoted by Corrigan *et al.*, n. 10 above.
14 In my opinion, the problem of the 'missing' husband who may be presumed, but is not known, to be dead also needs to be addressed.
15 (1997) 35 BMLR I, FD and CA.
16 There is some doubt as to whether the man was or was not 'brain stem dead' when the specimen was obtained. He could still be the legal father of any resultant child if the woman was directly inseminated before he was declared

dead; in practice, however, such rapid action would be very unlikely, in which case paternity would be excluded by virtue of the 1990 Act, s.28(6)(*b*). The case report indicates (at 5) that the patient was, in fact, brain dead at the time the procedure was mooted.

17   The fact that, therefore, some form of assault was involved was glossed over.

18   Treaty to Establish the European Community (1957), Arts. 59 and 60.

19   Very sophisticated techniques such as intracytoplasmic sperm injection – or the injection of a single selected spermatozoon into an ovum – may also be used, but should be strictly regulated. The propriety of using sperm extracted from the tissues, that is, directly from the testis or epididymis, is also questioned as the sperm may be immature: S. Mayor, 'Technique for treating infertility may be risky' (1996) 313 Brit Med J 248.

20   See V. Choo 'Sex selection' (1993) 341 Lancet 298.

21   But the Authority is campaigning actively for a change in the law and recommends that licensed infertility treatment centres should not use sperm-sorting techniques in sex selection (HFEA, *Code of Practice* (2nd revision, 1995), para 7.21). The practice, when undertaken for non-medical reasons, is already unlawful in Canada: Human Reproductive and Genetics Technologies Act 1996.

22   There is a movement to use the abbreviation AI (artificial insemination) in order to avoid confusion with the acquired immune deficiency syndrome. This is improbable in the circumstances and I prefer the more accurate format.

23   AID may also be considered if the husband is a carrier of a deleterious gene, especially if this is dominant. But, when possible, a controlled intramarital pregnancy would be preferable (see Chapter 6).

24   I am well aware that many lasting relationships which do not depend upon a civil or religious ceremony are as meaningful as the marital state and may be more so. Unless there is a distinction to be made or a point to be illustrated, the terms marriage, husband, wife and so on should be read as including a stable heterosexual partnership.

25   In exceptional circumstances, licensed treatment centres may even offer home insemination. Overall, the live birth rate is some 8 per cent per treatment cycle, with about three cycles being administered per patient.

26   The Human Fertilisation and Embryology Authority, *Code of Practice* (2nd revision, 1995), Part 6 recognises three types of counselling: implications, support and therapeutic. Implications counselling *must* be offered to all those seeking treatment before they give consent: 1990 Act, s1.3(6), sch. 3, para. 3(1)(*a*).

27   Congenital Disabilities (Civil Liability) Act 1976, s.1A inserted by the 1990 Act, s.44.

28   See *Bolam* v. *Friern Hospital Management Committee* [1957] 2 All ER 118.

29   Admittedly, the present writer finds it difficult to decide whether this means that there must be another indication in order to prove negligence or that the departure from received practice merely provides a rebuttable presumption of negligence, but the point is probably inconsequential.

30   At the time of writing, the Authority is considering lowering the maximum age of donors to 40 years, relying on B.L. Bordson and V.S. Leornardo, 'The appropriate upper age limit for semen donors: a review of the genetic effects of paternal age' (1991) 56 Fertil Steril 397.

31   Legislation in the various states is based on the Uniform Parentage Act 1974. For the pioneering Commonwealth statutes in Australia, see the Artificial Conception Act 1984, s. 6(1) of New South Wales, Status of Children (Amendment) Act 1984 of Victoria, Artificial Conception Act 1985 of Western Australia.

32   But, at the same time, a category of 'fatherless' children is produced: R. Lee and D. Morgan, 'Children of the reproductive revolution' (1990) 87 Law Soc Gaz 2.

33 Marriage Act, 1949; Marriage (Scotland) Act 1977, as amended by Marriage (Prohibited Degrees of Relationship) Act 1986.

34 HFEA, *Code of Practice* (2nd revision, 1995), paras 7.18, 7.19. However, their expectation of how this is to be enforced reads as being somewhat naive.

35 Information as to the identity of the donor is specifically excluded when similar information is required by the courts for the same purpose (s.34(1)). Section 33(6A)(*a*), inserted by the Human Fertilisation and Embryology (Disclosure of Information) Act 1992, places a similar embargo as regards disclosure for the purposes of, or in connection with, any proceedings.

36 The 1990 Act inserts s.4(4A) into the 1976 Act whereby, in the event of an infertility treatment having been given, references to a parent in the latter include references to persons who would be parents were it not for the provisions of the former. (1990 Act, s.35(4)).

37 M. Warnock (Chairman), *Report of the Committee of Inquiry into Human Fertilisation and Embryology* ((1984), Cmnd 9314, para. 4.21.

38 Note 34 above.

39 *MacLennan* v. *MacLennan (or Shortland)* 1958 SC 105. The obiter remarks to the contrary in the Canadian case *Orford* v. *Orford* (1921) 58 DLR 251 can be discounted as being hopelessly outdated.

40 *People* v. *Sorensen* 437 P 2d 495 (Calif, 1968).

41 See, for example, *Re CH (contact: parentage)* [1996] 1 FLR 569, where a remarried woman sought to exclude her previous husband from contact with her (and his) AID child.

42 Family Law Reform Act 1987, ss.20–23; Law Reform (Miscellaneous Provisions) (Scotland) Act 1990, s.70. For paternity testing in general, see J.K. Mason, *Forensic Medicine for Lawyers* (3rd edn, 1995), London: Butterworths.

43 D. Morgan and R.G. Lee, *Blackstone's Guide to the Human Fertilisation and Embryology Act 1990* (1991), London: Blackstone Press, p. 156. This publication is an invaluable aid to the understanding of the Act.

44 Official Reports, HL, Vol 482, col 1282, 11 December 1986.

45 T. Hope, G. Lockwood and M. Lockwood, 'The interests of the potential child' (1995) 310 Brit Med J 1455.

46 The 1990 Act makes provision for the unmarried partnership, but the United Kingdom has not gone so far as to recognise a legal status for *de facto* marriages, as is the case in Australia. Even so, the Infertility (Medical Procedures) Act 1984 of Victoria precludes *single* women from treatment services.

47 For a scathing criticism, see Morgan and Lee, n. 43 above at 145.

48 *Code of Practice*, Part 3.

49 It has been estimated that as few as six out of 60 centres offering insemination will treat single women. See G. Douglas, *Law, Fertility and Reproduction* (1991), London: Sweet & Maxwell, p. 122.

50 See, for example, G. Hanscombe, 'The right to lesbian parenthood' (1983) 9 J Med Ethics 133; S. Golombok, A. Spencer and M. Rutter, 'Children in lesbian and single parent households: Psychosexual and psychiatric appraisal' (1983) 24 Child Psychol Psychiat 551. It has been said that 1.5 million children live with homosexuals in the USA: M. McGuire and N.J. Alexander, 'Artificial insemination of single women' (1985) 43 Fertil Steril 182.

51 Note 49 above.

52 It might also be noted that the courts see no objection in principle to adoption by homosexual couples: *T, Petitioner* (1996) Times, 20 August. The process of assisted reproduction is often compared to adoption.

53 M.B. King and P. Pattison, 'Homosexuality and parenthood' (1991) 303 Brit Med J 295.

54   Section 29(4). In Scotland this would include the right to a coat of arms (s.29(5)).
     It is not thought to be a matter which will overtax the workload of the courts.
55   Note that the wording of s.28(2) is such as to indicate that it applies to *all* AIDs
     in the case of a married woman. The conditions, thus, would apply in the case
     of an insemination undertaken outside the provisions of the Act, though whether
     this was the intention of Parliament is uncertain. The same does *not* apply to
     the 'partnership' in which only licensed insemination is covered by s.28(3).
56   1990 Act, sch. 4, para. 8.
57   Adoption Agencies Regulations 1976 (SI. 1976/1796).
58   *Family Law: Illegitimacy*, Law Commission Report No 118, 1982, at para. 12.23.
59   T.B. Hargreave, 'Artificial insemination by donor' (1985) 291 Brit Med J 613.

9   The Infertile Woman

The previous chapter has described the relative ease with which childlessness by reason of infertility in the male may be addressed. Conditions are far less simple in respect of infertility in the female. The only contribution of the male to reproduction is the provision of his gametes and, in this, he is normally profligate: hundreds of millions of spermatozoa can be provided, to all intents, at will. By contrast, the female will be responsible for the reception of sperm, for conception, for implantation and for the carriage of any resulting embryo to the point of its viability and beyond – all of which is to be accomplished by the extrusion of some 13 ova annually, and this being under physiological control rather than wilful. It follows that there may be many reasons for infertility in the female and that, as discussed in the introduction to Chapter 8, these may be treatable at the basic level or they may be circumvented by treatment for childlessness. Both forms of therapy will depend upon sophisticated methods to overcome the pathological and physiological barriers but they are distinguished, as in the case of male infertility, by the fact that, whereas treatment of infertility is a medical matter between physician and patient, the treatment of childlessness poses a threat to the established social and legal order of society.[1] The treatment of childlessness due to male and female abnormalities differs, however, in that the latter requires the interposition of considerable professional and technical expertise. This chapter is concerned, in the main, with society's response to that intrusion.

Causes of female infertility

As in the case of the male, the correct treatment of female infertility depends upon a correct diagnosis.[2] The primary cause may lie in the woman's inability to ovulate. This may be untreatable; on the other hand, it may result from hormonal deficiencies which can be re-

227

stored by substitution. The legal and ethical problems are minor unless, as often occurs, treatment results in a multiple pregnancy of severe degree: quintuplets are not uncommon and even octuplets have been reported.[3] This problem also arises in connection with embryo transfer; its management is discussed from this aspect at p. 232.

Some women appear to develop antibodies to their husband's semen. Such cases may be amenable either to artificial insemination (by husband or by donor) or to *in vitro* fertilisation (see below for major discussion). There is a proportion of cases in which no reason for infertility in the female can be discovered; conversely, abnormalities can be discovered in both the husband and the wife in some 15 per cent of infertilities, a situation which can give rise to intricate therapeutic problems and solutions. A further group to be isolated are those women who are fertile but are yet incapable of carrying an infant. Many such women present as cases of repetitive natural miscarriage; they can sometimes be treated by careful management combined with specific hormonal therapy, but often there is an associated anatomical abnormality of the uterus. A sub-group of this type of patient consists of women whose physical health would be jeopardised by pregnancy, such as severe diabetics or those with the now relatively uncommon condition of valvular heart disease. This sub-group is particularly important to the current debate in justifying the practices of surrogate motherhood or of 'womb leasing'; the associated problems will be discussed in greater detail under those headings in Chapter 10.

Some 30 per cent of involuntarily childless women are in that state by virtue of abnormalities in the Fallopian tubes which inhibit the ovum's journey from the ovary to the uterine cavity. Generally speaking, such abnormalities also bar the progress of the sperm; penetration of the sperm may, however, result in the condition of ectopic pregnancy, with which we are not at present concerned. Tubal insufficiency which cannot be treated medically or surgically can be circumvented through the dual processes of *in vitro* fertilisation (IVF) and embryo transfer (ET) which are basic to many of the assisted reproductive techniques. It is, therefore, appropriate to address this condition first.

The problem of tubal insufficiency

Tubal blockage may be deliberate (as resulting from elective sterilisation) but is commonly the result of inflammation within the pelvis. This may be of a sexually transmitted nature, but there are many other causes; abdominal tuberculosis, although, for the present, very rare, was once probably the commonest cause of infertility in women. There is no justification for the view which is sometimes aired that money and expertise should not be expended on the treatment of a condition which is self-induced through sexual activity – probably only a minority of cases are so caused.

Strictly speaking, the terms '*in vitro* fertilisation' (IVF) and 'embryo transfer' (ET) refer to two basic *technical* manoeuvres. IVF consists of no more than allowing a spermatozoon to penetrate an ovum within a laboratory environment. Similarly, ET is simply a matter of moving a zygote or embryo from one place to another: an embryo is *transferred* if it is moved only between pieces of equipment. The techniques were, however, developed essentially for the purpose of enabling a husband and wife to overcome infertility of tubal origin while still using their own gametes, or sex cells. It has therefore become customary to refer to this particular treatment as IVF; any deviations are then recognised by specific terminology. In the same way, ET has been recognised in practice to mean the transfer of an embryo from a position *in vitro* to an *in vivo* situation in the womb. Thus, unless specified otherwise, the term 'IVF' will be used in this chapter to describe the treatment of tubal infertility by the *in vitro* production of embryos derived from a husband and wife; the transfer to the womb, which is essential to successful treatment, will be assumed to be no more than part of that process.

In vitro *fertilisation*

The basic pattern of IVF thus defined involves three stages. Firstly, multiple ovulation is induced in the woman by hormonal treatment and the ova are harvested, generally through a laparoscope; clearly, this stage involves considerable medical and surgical skill – not to mention some discomfort for the patient. Secondly, the ova are incubated with the husband's sperm. Although this is popularly known as a 'test-tube baby' technique, the process is carried out in a Petri dish; fertilisation of the ova by spermatozoa is the least complicated part of the technique. Finally, the fertilised ova, or pre-embryos, are transferred to the woman's uterine cavity in the hope that they will implant and develop into viable fetuses. This is unquestionably the hardest part of the therapeutic cycle; the hormonal preparation of the subject and the timing of the operation are complex, but are vital to success. This third stage of embryo transfer, which involves manipulation of the pre-embryo from Petri dish to uterus, occurs in nearly all treatments of childlessness which is due to female abnormalities. The concept of a mechanical process is important medico-legally, insofar as manipulation of any sort exposes the tissue which is manipulated to the risk of damage. There is, in fact, no evidence that children derived from processes involving embryo transfer are any more liable to congenital defects than are those produced naturally but, nonetheless, accusations of negligent injury in this area remain possible. In practice, up to 23 per cent of embryo transfer cycles result in the birth of one or more live children,[4] but the incidence of miscarriage is disproportionately high – up to 28 per cent. There is no reason to suppose that this is due to damage to the cells which will form either the fetus or the placenta. Admittedly, it has been noted that gamete intrafallopian transfer (GIFT) which involves carrying out the fertilisation process within the tube itself produces better results as regards both pregnancy and miscarriage, but GIFT is used in the treatment of idiopathic infertility – or infertility for which there is no obvious cause – and is obviously an unsatisfactory treatment in the presence of tubal disease; great caution should therefore be exercised before assuming that the *process* is responsible for any difference in results.

The term 'pre-embryo' was introduced simultaneously in the United Kingdom and the United States[5] to distinguish that period of human development which occurred before the differentiation of placental from fetal tissues – the period during which all embryo transfer activities take place. While this distinction may be useful semantically and for ease of understanding, it also has the effect of calming the debate surrounding the moral status of the conceptus, or zygote, and its use for experimental or research purposes: there is a considerable emotional divide between reference to the 'human embryo', which has clear connotations with human life, and to the 'pre-embryo', which has not. Nevertheless, the use of the term 'pre-embryo' by supervisory authorities should not be taken as predicating any moral judgment.

Medico-legal complications of IVF   IVF gives rise to no medico-legal problems of itself; the situation is comparable to artificial insemination by the husband's semen (AIH). It is apparent that the process is time-consuming and extravagant in man-hours; it is therefore possible to raise an economic argument against an IVF programme, but this is merely one aspect of the overall debate on the allocation of scarce resources, one which is particularly relevant within a health system which is mainly financed by the state. The moral assessment of any IVF programme thus depends to a large extent on the balance which the individual observer sees as lying between the economic expenditure involved and the societal benefits of treating childlessness.[6] The Warnock Committee[7] recognised the difficulty, but considered the priorities argument to be one in favour of the *controlled* development of the treatment rather than one to be directed against the technique itself.[8]

The subject of resource allocation is academically complex and is also emotionally charged, particularly when parents and their children are involved.[9] In the case of treatments for childlessness, there are a number of specific problems in addition to the generalisations already indicated. As is so often the case, the treatment cannot be regarded as a single, homogeneous entity. IVF can, on the one hand, be used to treat childlessness due to tubal disease (and is probably no less cost-effective than attempts at extensive surgical repair); alternatively – and, particularly, when combined with embryo biopsy[10] – it may be the optimal treatment for fertile couples at risk of producing genetically compromised offspring. The justification for providing or refusing treatment will be different in the two circumstances but, if it is available in one, should it not be available in the other?[11] It is, in fact, difficult to discover how many health authorities provide such treatments as an integral part of the National Health Service (the *Patients' Guide* is silent on the subject); it is said that there were only three such clinics open in 1991, one being in Scotland;[12] while the number may have increased since then, the fact will remain that it is relatively few.

Resource allocation is inevitably bound up with ageism and IVF is no exception: there is considerable debate as to whether older women should be excluded from any programme offered. The unique problem of the post-menopausal woman is discussed at p. 241; here we are concerned only with the older woman who, absent her disability, might have been able to have a child by natural means. Exclusion of such women from a treatment service can, then, only be validated on clinical grounds. In general, the risks of pregnancy increase dramatically with maternal age: maternal mortality in women aged 20–24 is of the order of 5.3 per 100 000 pregnancies; it rises to 53.9 in those aged 40 or more.[13] In particular, the chances of successful implantation decrease with age, falling from the acceptable rate of 18.2 per cent per embryo inserted in first treatments of women aged 25–29 to 6.1 per cent in those aged 40–44;[14] more embryos are therefore required for older women which, apart from contravening the existing limits (see below), might well increase the hazards of ovulatory stimulation.[15] The policy of excluding older women has, in fact, been tested in the English courts, where it was held that a policy to restrict IVF to women below the age of 35, on the grounds of using a limited budget in a way thought to provide the greatest societal benefit, was not illegal; it was not irrational for the authority to take age into account as an appropriate criterion when balancing the need for such a provision against the ability to provide it.[16] The HFEA has no objection to gametes being obtained from women over 35 for their own use; no upper limit is specified.[17]

Age considerations aside, can the assisted reproduction clinic take into account the *suitability* of the recipients when allocating its resources? The subject has been touched upon in the preceding chapter, but the technical and financial differences between insemination and *in vitro* fertilisation are so considerable that the same principles may not apply to each. There can be no doubt that a clinic has the right to select from those who seek licensed treatment; indeed, it is probably an unavoidable duty. We have already seen that account must be taken of the welfare of any child who may be born as a result of the treatment (1990 Act, s.13(5)). In addition, the Authority's Code of Practice lays down a number of factors which the centre should bear in mind; these include some which are frankly social rather than medical, such as the ability of the patients to provide a stable and supportive environment for the prospective child and their likely future ability to look after or provide for a child's needs. One's concern is that such evaluations are bound to be subjective and, given the resource problem, an element of 'competitive' suitability is likely to be introduced. The only precedent – and it is, for many reasons, an unsatisfactory one – arose before the 1990 Act came into force.[18] In this, a former prostitute, who had previously been refused permission to foster or adopt a child, sought IVF treatment through the National Health Service. This was refused, ultimately, on the grounds that the clinic operated the same selection criteria as did the adoption agency. In the circumstances, the court found no evidence of unreasonableness although this was something of a side issue, the major thrust of the determination being related to the function and accountability of hospital ethical committees.[19] There is no doubt that, with the added support of statute, a similar result as to the fairness of the exclusion of the applicant would be reached today; the irony of the situation is that another clinic would be perfectly entitled to regard the family milieu as acceptable.

A further resource-associated problem in the treatment of infertility – that is, the paradox of superfertility – has already been mentioned in relation to hormonal treatment. Much the same difficulty applies to IVF. In this process, not only is it necessary to produce more embryos *in vitro* than will be used – for some will be unuseable – but, also, the success rate will be greatly improved if an excess of embryos are transferred and implanted *in vivo*.[20] Occasionally, the result may be embarrassingly successful and a multiple pregnancy results; even when the number of insertions is limited to three, nearly 7 per cent of clinical pregnancies result in triplets, with occasional quadruplets added as a result of natural identical twinning. Insertion of more than three embryos can, of course, result in even more fetuses although, for unexplained reasons, the overall clinical pregnancy rate is not, thereby, significantly improved. The consequences of, say, sextuplets being born are not only serious for the parents but also provoke a drain on the resources in neonatal intensive care which some would regard as being unjustified; the inherent dangers of pregnancy for the mother are increased with multiplicity and, consequent upon their extreme prematurity, very few sextuplet siblings are likely to survive, despite the most devoted neonatal care; moreover, any survivors may well exhibit some evidence of brain damage. Multiple pregnancies beyond triplets – or even, perhaps, beyond twins – are, therefore, occasions to be avoided and current United Kingdom policy is that no more than three embryos or eggs should be implanted in a woman at any one time, regardless of the precise procedure used.[21] There are those who would object to such a limitation on the grounds that the treatment is a matter of clinical care. Nevertheless, it is relatively clear that the inevitable consequence of a successful high-multiple pregnancy is reduction of that pregnancy.

In this procedure, the excess early fetuses are given a toxic injection and die within the uterus; the results are satisfactory in capable hands.[22] The legal acceptability of selective feticide was, at one time, in doubt, the main argument being centred on the fact that, although the operator was not procuring a miscarriage, the pregnancy was not being terminated, which is all that the Abortion Act 1967 authorises. Thus, while there would probably be no offence under the Offences Against the Person Act, 1861, s.58, the 1967 Act might well be infringed.[23] The problem has now been resolved, however, by the Human Fertilisation and Embryology Act 1990, s.37(5) which, effectively, ensures that, when a woman is carrying more than one fetus, anything done with intent to procure her miscarriage of any fetus is authorised by the Abortion Act 1967, s.1 if any of the grounds for termination of the pregnancy specified in that section apply.[24] It has been argued in Chapter 5 that the terms of the 1967 Act are such that it is virtually impossible to perform an illegal abortion in the United Kingdom provided the administrative regulations are observed; it follows that a reduction of such a pregnancy must be legal and this is irrespective of any additional grounds which can be adduced in respect of multiple pregnancy – and there are several, including, for example, the fact that a multiple birth could undoubtedly be potentially damaging to the health of the pregnant woman and that it could be held that the surviving fetuses were 'existing members of the family' whose health was promoted by the elimination of others. This would apply even if the woman wished to do no more than avoid the burden of twins.[25]

The moral justification of this last procedure depends upon acceptance of the right of a woman to dispose of her body as she wishes (see p. 123). There are, however, more positive grounds for accepting reduction of significantly multifetal pregnancy. Foremost among these is the illogicality, in the extreme case, of virtually ensuring the death of *all* the fetuses by refusing to eliminate some; clearly, a different attitude might well be adopted as between, say, triple and sextuple pregnancies.[26] This is, an area in which the medical profession must put its own house in order. It is also one which might well cause a health worker to invoke the conscience clause in the 1990 Act.

Equally significant medico-legal problems stemming from the practice of superovulation relate to the *in vitro* phase of the process. The overproduction of *in vitro* embryos (or pre-embryos) is an essential and inherent part of the treatment; their disposal poses very considerable moral and legal complications which have exercised the minds of legislatures throughout the world. Fundamentally, a decision has to be taken as to the precise moral status of the *in vitro* embryo. The word 'precise' is used here advisedly: vacillation introduces yet more confusion. This is exemplified in the widely quoted analysis of Dr Walters,[27] who regarded the status of the human embryo as 'more than that of a mouse embryo but less than that of a full human fetus'. A similar ambivalence was shown by the Warnock Committee, which recommended that 'the embryo of the human species should be afforded *some* protection in law' (at para. 11.17, my emphasis). By contrast, I have suggested elsewhere[28] that the *in vitro* embryo should be regarded *either* as an early human being which attracts the rights and privileges of a human being *or* as a creation of the laboratory which has no human attributes.

There is little point in a lengthy recapitulation of the reasons for adopting the latter view which has been referred to already in Chapter 5. It is sufficient to repeat here that I see the difference between the human being and the rest of the animal kingdom as being attributable to the possession of 'human nature', which can be translated as the 'human soul'. It seems absurd to attribute 'ensoulment' to an organism which has had no human contact. Rather, it is natural to suppose that humanity derives from humanity and that 'ensoulment' can follow only from implantation.[29] The antithesis of this proposition is to be found in the current doctrine of the Roman Catholic Church: that is, that an embryo is a human being from the moment of its existence as a single diploid cell[30] and that, as such, it has an inalienable right to life. The embryo cannot be brought into existence in order to be disposed of and, if it dies, it should be accorded the respect due to any human corpse. The choice between these extremes will greatly influence attitudes to the use of surplus embryos for research or experimentation, matters which have generated, perhaps, the greatest dissension amongst those interested.

It is fair to say that, by and large, society – at least in the form of the authorities – leans towards the latter approach; the current legislative control of IVF is discussed later (see p. 238). The policy behind the exaggerated concern of the authorities for the *in vitro* embryo merits analysis, given their cavalier attitude to abortion. One reason must lie in the intuitive suspicion with which the public view the unfettered scientist. As Lady Warnock, herself, has said, society's corporate reaction 'is one of fear. People generally believe that science may be up to no good, and must not be allowed to proceed without scrutiny, both of its objectives and of its methods';[31] and, elsewhere, 'The fears people express about knowledge are mostly fears of the uses to which knowledge may be put.'[32]

Perhaps a more cogent reason is that the embryo *in vitro* stands on its own and is entitled to the protection due to the most vulnerable; the fetus, by contrast, is a dependent being whose interests must be secondary to those of the woman who is carrying him or her. What is very clear is that, in the absence of some regulation, the ethical development of IVF and its associated techniques depends wholly on the good faith and the good sense of the medical and scientific professions.

Irrespective of the moral status of the embryo, further problems remain relating to its material standing. The embryo has been produced only with the consent of two parties, each of whom has contributed a gamete; at the same time, its very existence depends upon the care and the expertise of the professional team responsible for the IVF programme. Who, then, is responsible for its future or, put another way, who, if anyone, has property rights over the embryo *in vitro*? This is, of course, of relatively limited consequence within the immediate practice of IVF as, currently, the embryo cannot be maintained as a living entity in the laboratory setting for more than a few weeks.[33] Cryopreservation, or 'freezing', of both gametes and embryos changes the whole picture, as there seems to be no limit of time for which spermatozoa and embryos can be preserved in a freezing medium while still remaining fit for resuscitation.[34] It is to be noted that embryos are not preserved solely for research purposes. It is clearly to the advantage of a woman to retain a 'back-up' of the surplus embryos rendered inevitable by the procedure against the possibility of her treatment cycle ending in failure. Some women might wish to insure against the death of an existing child while others might want, simply, to delay having a family but would, at the same time, want to avoid the genetic risks of ovulation in later life. Moreover, the pool of surplus embryos maintains a source for donation (see p. 244 below). On the other hand, irrespective of clinical concerns, some limit must be placed on storage with respect to estate planning and the like.

The preservation of embryos and spermatozoa is now governed by statute. Currently, the Human Fertilisation and Embryology Act 1990 states that gametes may not be stored for longer than 10 years (s.14(3)). The original embargo on storage of embryos for more than five years has now been lifted: in certain circumstances, and only for the purpose of providing treatment, a similar 10-year limit can apply subject to the further consent by the couple concerned, including, where appropriate, the consent of the donor. Even so, the period of preservation must not extend beyond the 55th birthday of the provider of the female gamete.[35] Disposal of preserved embryos is, in any event, subject to the very stringent regulations as to consent that are detailed in sch. 3 in the 1990 Act. Put simply, these are as follows:

a   Para. 2(1)   Consent to the use of an embryo must specify whether it is to be used for the treatment of the person giving consent or of that person and another specified person together, for providing treatment services for other persons or for research purposes. It may specify the conditions subject to which the embryo may be so used. Effective consent – that is, a consent under the Schedule which has not been withdrawn – must be given by each person whose gametes have contributed to the embryo (para 6(3)).[36]
b   Para 2(2)   Consent to the storage of any gametes or embryos must specify the maximum period of storage (if this is less than the statutory maximum) and must state what is to be done with the gametes or embryos if the person who gave the consent dies or is unable by dint of incapacity to vary the terms of the consent or to revoke it. Again, the consent of both contributors to the embryo is required (para 8(2)).

In all cases, consent must be in writing, it must be preceded by professional counselling, it may apply generally or to a specific embryo and it may be varied or withdrawn at any time prior to the gametes or embryos being used. Special regulations as to counselling, information and consent apply if the storage period for embryos is to be extended beyond the normal maximum of five years.

I admit to finding some difficulty as to the dual consent required in the case of embryos. The regulations seem to assume that there will be agreement between the man and woman concerned and this may not always be maintained – particularly, say, in the turbulent emotional conditions of divorce.[37] The difficulties which may arise have been vividly demonstrated in the United States[38] and, while it is true that the provisions for counselling and for a statement of intent that are embodied in the 1990 Act go some way to pre-empting the problem, the fact remains that either party may modify their consent in conflicting ways. It may well be that the wording of the Act is such as to ensure that, in the event of consent to use being withdrawn unilaterally, the embryo or embryos would be destroyed,[39] but this is, at least, uncertain and, if accepted, represents an arbitrary rejection of the alternative view. The remarkable contrast between the statutory paternal rights as to the embryo and the fetus has already been noted but, while greater recognition of the father's role in parenting is, in many ways, to be welcomed, it is doubtful whether the present regulations are ideal. It seems both logical and pragmatically desirable to vest the ultimate disposal of an embryo in the person for whom it was intended: that is, the woman who was to carry it.[40] The man's consent would, then, be limited to the original preparation of the embryo, at which point he could, of course, impose his own vetoes, such as to forbid the later insertion of the embryo into another woman. While it has to be noted that, so far as is known, there have been no actions related to the disposal of preserved embryos in the United Kingdom, the difficulties of tracing the donors of both gametes has undoubtedly contributed to the unfortunate situation in which very large numbers of embryos have had to be destroyed at the end of the first five-year storage period.[41]

The Warnock Report[42] (at para. 10.11) recommended legislation to ensure that there is no right of ownership in a human embryo. While it says nothing specifically to the point, the 1990 Act eliminates any commercial trade in embryos by stipulating that no money or other benefit shall be given or received in respect of any supply of gametes or embryos unless authorised by directions (s.12(*e*)). At least two further legal issues remain in doubt: what, if any, inheritance rights has an unimplanted embryo, and what, if any, criminal offence is committed in destroying a surplus embryo?

As to the first question, it has been said, in my view rightly, that the chaos and uncertainty in estate planning which would result from allowing any inheritance rights in the *in vitro* embryo would be intolerable.[43] Even so, it is reported that an Australian court has held that an embryo thawed after its father's death could inherit once it was born, this being on the grounds that the rights of the *in vitro* embryo were comparable to those of the fetus *in utero* at the time of its father's death;[44] it is hard to imagine what effect such a ruling can have if it is allowed to stand. In the United Kingdom, the issue is partially resolved in the 1990 Act, where s.28(6)(*b*) holds that, where the sperm of a man, or any embryo the creation of which was brought about with his sperm, was used after his death, he is not to be treated as the father of the child.[45] As in the case of artificial insemination with the husband's sperm (see p. 209), this does not meet the case of the husband who is missing and is later found to have died, a scenario which would, at least, provide an interesting exercise for the forensic pathologist!

The question of criminality associated with the destruction of the *in vitro* embryo is, in my opinion, no longer a problem. All the offences detailed in s.41 of the 1990 Act, other than those of an essentially administrative nature, are concerned with the production or manipulation of embryos. They include:

a   placing in a woman a live embryo or live gametes other than those of human origin (s.3(2));

b   mixing human gametes with the live gametes of any animal (s.4(1)(*c*));

c   keeping or using an embryo after the appearance of the primitive streak; that is, later than the fourteenth day after the gametes were mixed (s.3(3)(*a*), s.3(4));

d   placing an embryo in any animal (s.3(3)(*b*));[46]

e   replacing the nucleus of a cell of an embryo with a nucleus taken from a cell of any person, embryo or subsequent development of an embryo (s.3(3)(*d*));[47]

f   bringing about the creation of or keeping or using an embryo in any way other than as a contravention of s.3(3) without holding a licence to do so;

g   storing gametes or using donor sperm for treatment in the absence of a licence (s.4(1)(*a*) and (*b*));

h   placing sperm and eggs in a woman in any circumstances specified by regulations except in pursuance of a licence.[48]

Embryocide is not mentioned, nor could it be, as it is an inevitable statutory consequence once the embryo has reached the 'warm' age of 15 days (ss.3(*a*) and 4) or once it has reached the permitted limit of its 'frozen' existence. There is no statutory recommendation as to disposal, but the Code of Practice advises that the procedure should be sensitively devised and described;[49] this is perfectly consonant with the somewhat indifferent attitude which we have seen the law adopt in respect of the pre-viable fetus. The holder of a licence to treat, store or research using embryos stands to lose his or her licence should the embryos in his or her care be submitted to unlicenced processes; the licence holder who contravenes the conditions imposed by the nature of the consent given is also liable to an action in civil law. But the criminal law limits itself to the unlawful *production* of embryos, and this is as it should be – the moral problems associated with the *disposal* of embryos arise at the time they are created.[50]

The aftermath of the Warnock Committee

The 1990 Act was founded very largely on the report of the Warnock Committee which adopted a relatively liberal stance on the many issues involved; it was, however, widely criticised at the time for its pragmatic approach, which was thought to pay too little attention to the moral problems raised. Perhaps the most contentious recommendation – which was agreed by only a 9:7 majority of the committee – was that the production of embryos for the *primary* purpose of research or experimentation was morally and practicably acceptable and, in allowing this, Parliament took the United Kingdom a stage further than any other anglophone jurisdiction in the pursuit of research. Most people will perceive a difference between making use of an unfortunate, but inevitable, by-product of a therapeutic regime, which could well be covered by the moral doctrine of 'double effect', and producing embryos while intending their destruction – a practice which must be regarded as being beyond such protection.[51]

I would include myself in that group – and that is an admission which is, to an extent, inconsistent with the views previously expressed (at p. 234) as to the status of the pre-implantation embryo. Even so, while the embryo may not be a human being attracting the rights of a human being,[52] it consists of human tissue; a similar antipathy would be expressed were it possible to manufacture inanimate human tissue for the purposes of experimentation. Granted, then, that, as the Warnock Committee said, the embryo is entitled to some protection in law (see p. 234), can one discover any moral basis, other than intuition, for the claim that, whereas research on the therapeutically 'surplus' embryo is acceptable, the production of embryos for the purpose is not, given the fact that the end result in either case is the harm of death? The answer may lie in distinguishing harm from wrong.[53] No *wrong* is done to the embryo created for the purpose of implantation; the fact that it never achieves that end is largely a matter of unfortunate chance. By contrast, the embryo that is created for the sole purpose of research and death is *wronged* from the moment it is formed. The harm done to each is the same, but the wrong done is of a different quality. Perhaps, however, our legislators preferred to adopt an unabashed utilitarian ethos; but one cannot help wondering what would have been the result had this, and other matters, been discussed in public rather than in the halls of Parliament.[54]

One last important legal question related to embryo storage concerns the problem of primogeniture: in short, does the seniority of an embryo depend upon the date and time of its fertilisation, of implantation or of birth? The Warnock Committee firmly recommended that the date and time of birth should be the determining factor (at para. 10.14); this is obviously correct and represents the current law insofar as s.3(4) of the 1990 Act disregards the time spent in storage when assessing the age of the embryo.

Other treatments of childlessness

In vitro fertilisation has been discussed as an entity in itself because, when used for the treatment of tubal insufficiency, it is that form of assisted reproduction which interferes least with the natural order of marriage and procreation. Only those who object to any form of surgical interference with nature – which would, logically, include the treatment of acute appendicitis – can object to assisting a husband and wife, or stable partners, to have a child of their own. There are, however, other causes of female infertility which cannot be surmounted by the basic process of IVF described above. All share the feature of the involvement of a third party either as a donor of gamete or zygote or as a participant in gestation of the fetus. The latter ploy is so distinct that it will be discussed separately in the chapter which follows. The former all involve the *techniques* of IVF and ET; only the components differ, and it is that which raises particular legal and moral problems and which distinguishes them from simple IVF.[55] From the genetic aspect, the least complicated variant is that of ovum donation.

Ovum donation

Just as a man may be unable to produce or mature spermatozoa, so may a woman fail to produce fertile ova. Circumvention is by means of replacement in both: through the medium of artificial insemination in the case of the male and, in the female, by ovum donation.

Obtaining ova is, however, a very different technical problem from that of obtaining spermatozoa. Effectively, ova can only be harvested through the abdominal wall. While this may be accomplished by the relatively mildly invasive technique of laparoscopy, ova can also be obtained during other abdominal invasions, of which the most practical in the present context is sterilisation by tubal occlusion. It was reported several years ago[56] that 90 per cent of women undergoing sterilisation were prepared to donate their ova for research purposes and that at least half of them would consent to their ova being used for the benefit of infertile couples – and this despite the fact that hormonal stimulation, which is often used to improve the yield of ova, causes discomfort and no little inconvenience to the donor. In addition, a number of women would be prepared to donate their eggs in return for financial or other benefit, the latter often being in the form of IVF in the private sector.[57] This procedure is widely condemned on the grounds that it is exploitive of women, the alternative view being that it is a valid expression of an adult woman's autonomous choice; the arguments for and against are very similar to those raised in relation to surrogate motherhood; the reader is referred to p. 254.

Even so, there is a serious shortage of ova available for donation. The fact that ova cannot, at present, be cryopreserved with safety (or with an acceptable success rate) lies at the heart of this because, as a result, there is an inevitable wastage of potentially therapeutic ova;[58] they can be preserved as embryos (see p. 235 above) but the generalised, as opposed to individual, use of such embryos for therapeutic purposes is limited. Paradoxically, frozen ova and the embryos derived from them have enormous potential for research into the very reasons which make them unsatisfactory as treatment agencies.

I use the term 'ovum donation' to describe the process whereby an ovum donated by an anonymous woman is fertilised *in vitro* by the semen of a man and the resultant embryo is implanted in the womb of that man's wife or partner. Subject to the limitations of experimentation, the legal and moral complications of ovum donation are then comparable to those of artificial insemination by donor, but they are not identical and are, in some ways, easier. Nature being what it is, it is sometimes not unreasonable to question the paternity of a child; no-one has, however, ever doubted the maternity of an infant,[59] other than in the contexts of hospital error, 'baby snatching' or concealed adoption; there are, therefore, even fewer good reasons for legislating as to openness concerning a child's genetic origins when he or she has been the product of ovum donation than there are in the case of one who resulted from AID. Similarly, in a patrilineal society, there is, rightly or wrongly, far less concern as to the origin of female genes than attaches to the male genetic line; not even the esoteric problems of the inheritance of titles of honour would be disturbed by ovum donation in England and Wales.[60] Once again, the Human Fertilisation and Embryology Act 1990 has clarified the legal, if not the genetic, position. By virtue of s.27(1), the woman who carries a child as a result of the placing in her of an embryo or of sperm and eggs, and no other woman, is to be treated as the mother of the child;[61] gestation and parturition are the bases of motherhood and there can be few other aspects of contrived parenthood that provoke as little contention as does ovum donation. It was, in fact, pointed out by the Warnock Committee (at para. 6.5) that ovum donation has a moral advantage over AID in that, in the former, both husband and wife contribute to the child of the family – the husband genetically and the wife through her pregnancy. Ovum donation is, of course, governed by the strict rules of consent laid down in sch. 3 of the 1990 Act, but the procedure is a matter for the woman alone. The vast majority of ovum donations and the subsequent implantation of an embryo will, however, fall to be treatments for a man and a woman together; the same process carried out in a single parent environment would be better regarded and discussed as an aspect of embryo donation.

One further aspect of ovum donation falls to be mentioned: the treatment of the post-menopausal woman who wishes to have a child. The evidence is that, while ovarian function is, by definition,

lost at the menopause, significant uterine function may be maintained; the opportunity therefore exists for relatively elderly women
to bear children conceived as a result of ovum donation. There must
be few women who would want to be pregnant when most are
thinking of retirement but, nevertheless, a case can be made out for it
being a medically acceptable option in limited circumstances – and
the British Medical Association accepts such a need in principle.[62]
Much of the opposition to the practice stems from an intuitive concern for the welfare of any resultant child; the present writer believes
that this may be a significant factor during the child's early adolescence, but that there are insufficient cases on which to justify an
evidence-based opinion. It is, however, something which must be
specifically considered when offering reproductive treatment facilities (1990 Act, s.13(5)). Otherwise, there is no doubt that the risks of
pregnancy increase with age, the 'take home baby' rate following
treatment falls with maternal age and more implanted embryos are
required to achieve an acceptable result.[63] It is probably this last
'resource' aspect which tips the scales against the practice, and the
right of the Health Authority to utilise its supply of ova in the most
efficient way has been upheld in the courts.[64] Which leads us to a
brief consideration of methods to combat the dearth of donated ova.

Improving the supply of ova   The shortfall in the number of eggs for
donation has resulted in proposals for three relatively bizarre rem-
edies: firstly, the harvesting of ova and ovarian tissue from adult
female cadavers; secondly, the use of fetal ova or, indeed, of fetal
ovarian tissue for alleviation of primary female sterility; and, thirdly,
the use of ovarian tissue derived from living donors. These three
procedures have now been considered by the Human Fertilisation
and Embryology Authority.[65]

The first raises considerable administrative as well as ethical issues. The former concern, in the main, the relationship between the
Human Fertilisation and Embryology Act 1990 and the Human Tissue Act, 1961, which controls the invasion and use of the human
body after death. Section 1(1) of the 1961 Act effectively allows the
hospital authority – as the 'person in legal possession of the body' –
to remove tissues from a dead person when that person has made a
valid legal request in life that his or her body or specified part of the
body be used after his or her death for therapeutic, educational or
research purposes. There is, however, a distinct difference between,
on the one hand, disposing of an organ which must, at some time,
die and, on the other, of donating one's genes – particularly in the
form of implanted ovarian tissue which, although such a procedure
is currently in the realm of science fiction, could result in their widespread distribution. It is, at least partly, for this reason that the HFEA

has vetoed the removal and use of ovarian tissue from females under the age of 18 who have died.[66] The Authority is less clear as regards adult women, but it seems that its intention is that consent to the donation of ovarian tissue must be specific and distinct from any 'blanket' instructions as to the use of the individual's cadaver – and this is, surely, how it should be.[67]

But what if no instructions have been given in life? Then s.1(2) of the 1961 Act states that, subject to certain restrictions, the person in lawful possession of the body, having made such reasonable enquiry as may be practicable, may authorise removal of any part from the body, provided he has no reason to believe that either the dead woman did or any of her surviving relatives does object to the body being so dealt with. This is no place to consider the many defects of the 1961 Act, but it is clear that much depends on the attitude of the delegated hospital authority. Should the distribution of one's genes be vested in the hands of a surrogate and, if so, should it depend, not on a positive consent, but on the absence of an expressed refusal? In either case, should the power to consent or refuse be limited to those in the direct genetic line? It may well be that, as the Authority says, there is no provision for proxy consent to the use of eggs in the 1990 Act but, equally, there is no exclusion as to ovarian, or testicular, tissue in the 1961 Act; it is even arguable that an egg is a tissue and it is certainly a part of the body, which is the subject of the 1961 Act, s.1, when it is within the ovary. The resolution of these questions is so complex that, in this writer's opinion at least, genetic material should be positively excluded from the provisions of the 1961 Act, s.1(2) pending a thorough overhaul of the transplant legislation.

Although there is no strictly apposite case law in point, some idea of the courts' likely approach to consent, given the current legislation, is to be found in the case of Mrs Blood, which has been discussed in the previous chapter.[68]

The Human Tissue Act, 1961 does not apply to the non-viable fetus, but the use of fetal ovarian material raises equally or more serious issues that have been noted already in Chapter 7. They can be categorised, on the one hand, as those that stem from its provision and, on the other, those associated with its use. The former derive from the fact that the provision of fetal eggs or ovarian tissue suitable for use is irrevocably bound up with therapeutic abortion; the procedure is, therefore, anathema to a minority of the population which is, perhaps, more significant in, say, the United States than in the United Kingdom.[69] Opposition is not based entirely on moral grounds; there is a tenable practical argument which points out that the existence of a neonate available for adoption offers a more realistic chance for the successful treatment of childlessness than does the harvesting of fetal ova. Nonetheless, the great bulk of the opposition to the use of fetal tissues of any sort stems from antipathy to abortion, rather than from a reasoned rejection of the therapeutic possibilities. It will be seen from p. 199 that the present writer has no great difficulty with the concept that it is right to extract some good from what many would see as a bad practice. This would not, of course, satisfy the strict moralist who would hold that *no* good can derive from a morally unacceptable premise; it is, however, possible to hold that therapeutic abortion is not unacceptable *per se*: it is its application which is objectionable to many. Even so, it could be argued that the absolute maternal discretion as to the disposal of her fetus, as expressed in Polkinghorne terms (see p. 194), should be constrained in respect of fetal ovum donation insofar as the contained genes that are likely to be replicated also belong to her parents; logically, however, the same argument could be applied to the donation of gametes of any sort. HFEA lays great stress on the potential effect on a child who is derived from a fetal egg but, to my mind, the most potent objection to the use of such eggs stems, as has been pointed out already, from the unknown effects of interfering with nature; it is more than possible that defective ova are screened naturally and discarded during adolescence: no-one knows what would be the effect of eliminating such a process of natural selection. In point of fact, as we have noted, the therapeutic use of fetal ovarian tissue or of embryos derived therefrom is, currently, illegal.[70]

HFEA has no objection to the live donation for therapeutic purposes of ovarian tissue by adults who can give the necessary consent. However, such a use is currently so futuristic as to merit no further discussion here.

Embryo donation

There may also be occasions where both the husband and the wife are infertile; the statistical occurrence would be something in the region of 15–19 per cent of infertile marriages. In these circumstances, the logical extension of the processes already described is to combine semen and ovum donation so as to produce an embryo which is implanted in the infertile woman; this procedure of embryo donation is distinguished by the feature that the resultant child is genetically unrelated to either of its parents: it is, therefore, a process which is at a moral disadvantage as compared with either AID or ovum donation. A further complication arises from the fact that the embryo to be transferred, rather than being formed *in vitro*, may be established *in vivo*; that is, in the genital tract of another woman. This process, which is generally known as uterine lavage, is, however, sufficiently distinct to be considered separately below.

Speaking medico-legally, *in vitro* embryo donation introduces no new problems *per se*: it is simply a matter of applying the questions and solutions posed by artificial insemination and ovum donation together. Thus, given the necessary conditions as to relationship and consent, the husband or partner of the recipient woman will be the legal father of the child, while the woman who has carried a child as a result of the placing of an embryo in her womb will be treated as the mother of the child. There are, however, specific moral and economic evaluations to be made. As to the former, it may well be questioned whether the process does not overstep the acceptable bounds of both nature and the concept of the family as a genetic unit, to which the answer would be that, having once accepted the principle of the treatment of childlessness, there is no real reason to distinguish between partial and total genetic replacement. Alternatively, it can be argued that embryo donation differs from adoption only insofar as, although it involves some deception, a familial relationship can be built up from the age of conception rather than of childhood – something which is, in general, likely to be an improvement. An economic counterargument of some strength could, however, be sustained on the grounds that scarce resources are being applied to a totally artificial end. This is, however, only to question whether the end justifies the means and, in the final analysis, this can only attract a subjective answer.

In vivo embryo donation, or uterine lavage, has some advantages (although there are undoubted balancing disadvantages) over the *in vitro* process. The technique involves the artificial insemination of a volunteer donor woman, 'flushing out' the resultant embryo before it has implanted and transferring it to the recipient womb. It is clear that, given insemination by the husband of the intending gestational mother, uterine lavage is also an alternative method of ovum donation as here defined. In either circumstance, uterine lavage carries its own moral and legal problems. The Warnock Committee recommended that it should not be used (at para. 7.5), but this was largely on the basis of potential injury to the donor, including that of inadvertent pregnancy. Irrespective of its future efficacy, the process can easily be seen as being so close to animal husbandry as to be one which should never be sanctioned by a licensing authority. Having said which, it is now clear that the procedure is, at least, not unlawful: the 1990 Act, sch. 3, para. 7, specifies the form of consent needed before it can be carried out. Were this not so, it could be argued that the same considerations and misgivings apply to uterine lavage as to menstrual extraction (see p. 60 above).

Gamete intrafallopian transfer

This technique (GIFT) can be used as an alternative either to *in vitro* fertilisation or to ovum or embryo donation, depending upon the origin of the gametes. It has both technical and economic advantages over the standard methods of reproductive assistance, but it also has disadvantages. GIFT using donated gametes is subject to the 1990 Act, s.4(1)(*b*) but, insofar as it does not involve the creation of an embryo outside the human body, it does not require a licence when the gametes used are those of the woman and her husband or partner (s.1(2)), which is unusual as compared with other jurisdictions, the majority of which recognise that the hazards inherent in the two techniques are very similar and that they merit equivalent control.[71]

Basically, the process consists of introducing ova and sperm directly into the Fallopian tubes. Fertilisation thus occurs in its natural situation and the chances of successful implantation are, thereby, improved.[72] Figures which suggest that the pregnancy or 'take-home baby' rates are better in GIFT than in IVF must, however, be read on the understanding that the underlying causes of the childlessness being treated are different: GIFT cannot, for instance, be used effectively when there is tubal disease. The major disadvantage of GIFT is that the fact of successful fertilisation can only be proved by the fact of pregnancy. Moreover, there is no opportunity to select the resultant embryos, a matter of some importance when assisted reproduction is being used to circumvent genetic disease.[73] Perhaps the main concern is that unlicensed clinics might be tempted to use more ova than HFEA would normally allow and that, as a result, the number of multiple pregnancies would rise; as we have seen, high-order multiple pregnancies should, whenever possible, be avoided for the benefit of both the mother and her fetuses. The results of the HFEA survey indicate, however, that such fears are very largely groundless.

Notes

1   The Church of Scotland, for example, objects to the donation of eggs or sperm by a third party since it involves the intrusion of a third party into marriage: M. Paterson, 'Fertility treatment poses quandary for Kirk' (1996), *The Scotsman*, 7 May, p. 7.

2   Although now rather dated, a good review for the lawyer is to be found in D.J. Cusine, *New Reproductive Techniques: A Legal Perspective* (1988), Aldershot: Gower, ch. 2.

3   C. Dyer, 'Selective abortions hit the headlines' (1996) 313 Brit Med J 380. There was massive media coverage of this case at the time due to the fact that the woman rejected reduction of pregnancy; all eight fetuses were born dead at 19 weeks' gestation. A measure of the public reaction is to be found in the leading article, 'The death of babies' (1996), *The Daily Telegraph*, 4 October, p. 25.

4   The results depend, to an extent, on the centre involved. The Human Fertilis-ation and Embryology Authority publish individual details in *The Patients' Guide to DI and IVF Clinics*. The national average is a live birth rate of 14.5 per cent per cycle.

5   First Report of the Voluntary Licensing Authority for Human *in vitro* Fertiliz-ation and Embryology (1986), p. 8. Ethics Committee of the American Fertility Society (1986) 46 Fertil Steril, Supp. 1. The Australian inquirers, however, found no reason to use any word other than 'embryo' .

6   For a full discussion of this topic, see the series of articles by G.H. Mooney and M.F. Drummond, 'Essentials of Health Economics' (1982) 285 Brit Med J 949 and subsequent issues. Specifically to the point, see P. Kincaid Smith, 'Ethics and *in-vitro* fertilisation' (1982) 284 Brit Med J 1287.

7   *Report of the Committee of Inquiry into Human Fertilisation and Embryology* (Dame Mary Warnock, Chairman) (1984), London: HMSO, Cmnd 9314 (hereafter the Warnock Committee) at para. 5.8.

8   For a valuable overview, see D. Giesen, 'Developing ethical public policy on reproduction and prenatal research: whose interests and what protection?' (1989) 8 Med Law 553.

9   For classic cases, see *Re Walker's Application* (1987) 3 BMLR 32; *R* v. *Cambridge Health Authority, ex p B (a minor)* (1995) 25 BMLR 5, QBD, (1995) 23 BMLR 1, CA.

10   This is a technique whereby the genetic status of an embryo can be established before implantation.

11   K. Dawson and P. Singer, 'Should fertile people have access to in vitro fertilis-ation?' (1990) 300 Brit Med J 167. For a controversial view of the IVF programme as a whole, see M.G. Wagner and P.A. St Clair, 'Are *in vitro* fertilisation and embryo transfer of benefit to all?' [1989] 2 Lancet 1027.

12   L. Edwards and A.M. Griffiths, *Family Law* (1997), Edinburgh: Sweet & Maxwell, in press, ch. 3.

13   Editorial comment, 'Too old to have a baby?' (1993) 341 *Lancet* 344.

14   M.G.R. Hull, C.F. Fleming, A.O. Hughes and A. McDermott, 'The age-related decline in female fecundity' (1996) 65 Fertil Steril 783.

15   Interestingly, the problem seems to lie in the ova rather than in the uterus; the success rate using donor eggs is unaffected by age: HFEA, *Fifth Annual Report* (1996), Table 3, p. 32.

16   *R* v. *Sheffield Health Authority, ex p Seale* (1994) 25 BMLR 1.

17   *Code of Practice* (2nd revision, 1995), para. 3.36. Some countries set a maximum age; for example, it is 40 for IVF in the Netherlands, but this is due for review and possible increase to 55: Royal Dutch Medical Association, *IVF op latere leeftijd* (1996).

18   *R* v. *Ethical Committee of St Mary's Hospital (Manchester), ex parte Harriott* [1988] 1 FLR 512.

19   Even if their function was purely advisory, hospital ethics committees *could*, in certain circumstances, be subject to judicial review.

20   The clinical pregnancy rate rises from 7.7 per cent of treatment cycles when one embryo is inserted to 24.9 when three are used: HFEA, *5th Annual Report*, Table 5(b), p. 33.

21   HFEA, *Code of Practice*, para. 7.9.

22   R.L. Berkowitz, L. Lynch, U. Chitkara *et al.*, 'Selective reduction of multifetal pregnancies in the first trimester' (1988) 318 New Engl J Med 1043.

23   For discussion, see J. Keown, 'Selective reduction of multiple pregnancy' (1987) 137 NLJ 1165; D. Brahams, 'Selective reduction of pregnancy' (1988) 85(1) Law Soc Gaz 25.

24   The section also specifically allows for selective termination; that is, the selec-tive abortion of any fetus at substantial risk of serious handicap.

25   R.L. Berkowitz, 'From twin to singleton' (1996) 313 Brit Med J 373.

26   The subject was well discussed by P.W. Howie, 'Selective reduction in multiple pregnancy' (1988) 297 Brit Med J 433.

27   Quoted in B.J. Culliton and W.K. Waterfall, 'Flowering of American bioethics' [1978] 2 Brit Med J 1270.

28   J.K. Mason, *Human Life and Medical Practice* (1988), Edinburgh: Edinburgh University Press, ch. 8.

29   My views as expressed here are not totally without support: M.C. Shea, 'Ensoulment and IVF embryos' (1987) 13 J Med Ethics 95. See also N.M. Ford, *When Did I Begin?* (1988), Cambridge: Cambridge University Press.

30   'Values from the Vatican' (1987), *The Times*, 11 March, p. 13.

31   M. Warnock, *A Question of Life* (1985), Oxford: Blackwell, p. xiii.

32   M. Warnock, 'Ethical challenges in embryo manipulation' (1992) 304 Brit Med J 1045.

33   Which, at least, eases the present situation, but which might have to be faced in the future. Many of the arguments put forward here would fail were it possible to develop the embryo to the state of a viable fetus in the laboratory.

34   The same cannot be said for ova, which cannot, as things stand, be successfully and consistently preserved.

35   The necessary circumstances are (a) where the woman being treated or her partner, if he provided the sperm, has, or is likely to develop significantly impaired fertility; (b) where the woman being treated or her partner ... carries a significant gene defect; or (c) where the woman being treated or her partner ... is, or is likely to become, prematurely and completely sterile. In the last case, storage may be allowed for more than 10 years subject to the clinical judgment of two registered practitioners. The maximum storage period cannot be extended if the woman to be treated using the embryos is aged 50 or over when the storage begins. (Human Fertilisation and Embryology (Statutory storage period for embryos) Regulations 1996 (S.I. 1996/375)).

36   Interestingly, only the consent of the woman concerned is required when an embryo is recovered by lavage (para. 7) (see p. 245).

37   To give the Warnock Committee its due, it foresaw such difficulties and opted for control of the stored embryos reverting to the Authority after a given period, but this recommendation was not accepted.

38   *Davis v. Davis* 842 SW 2d 588 (Tenn, S Ct, 1992) where not only the parents but also the judges in the various courts disagreed as to what should be done. Moreover, the woman herself changed her mind in between hearings.

39   See D. Morgan and R.G. Lee, *Blackstone's Guide to the Human Fertilisation and Embryology Act 1990* (1991), London: Blackstone Press, p. 137.

40   This is a proposal which is not unique to the writer: see A. Trounson and K. Dawson, 'Storage and disposal of embryos and gametes' (1996) 313 Brit Med J 1.

41   K.D. Hopkins, 'First batch of human embryos destroyed in UK' (1996) 348 Lancet 399, in which it is pointed out that extension of the maximum storage time to 10 years will not solve the administrative problems. The situation is criticised in Editorial comment, 'What to do with spare embryos' (1996) 347 Lancet 983.

42   M. Warnock (Chairman), *Report of the Committee of Inquiry into Human Fertilisation and Embryology* (1984), Cmnd 9314.

43   See H. Brown, M. Dent, L.M. Dyer *et al.*, 'Legal rights and issues surrounding conception, pregnancy and birth' (1986) 39 Vand L Rev 597 for discussion.

44   M. Perry, 'Judge rules frozen embryo can be heir' (1996), *The Scotsman*, 23 April, p. 11.

45   The converse problem related to the 'mother' is dealt with in s.27(1), whereby

the mother of a child is defined as the woman who has carried that child as a result of the placing in her of an embryo. A dead woman could, therefore, never be the legal mother of a child who was *in vitro* at the time of her death.

46 Section 3(3) specifies the procedures for which a licence cannot be issued.

47 Following conviction on indictment for the offences specified in (a) to (e), the person is liable to imprisonment for up to 10 years or a fine, or both; the offences listed in (f) to (h) are punishable by imprisonment for up to two years or a fine, or both; in the latter case, summary conviction carries a liability of six months' imprisonment or a statutory maximum fine, or both.

48 GIFT or gamete intrafallopian transfer is not, currently, covered by regulation, although there are good reasons why it should be.

49 Human Fertilisation and Embryology Authority, *Code of Practice* (2nd revision, 1995), para 7.25.

50 It is to be noted that Victoria, which led the way in legislating for assisted reproduction, has now followed the United Kingdom in establishing an Infertility Treatment Authority under the Infertility Treatment Act 1996: S. Cordner, 'Infertility treatment centre for Victoria, Australia' (1996) 347 Lancet 684.

51 'Double effect': so long as there is no less injurious alternative, an action is permissible where its intended good effect can be obtained only at the expense of a coincidental ill effect. The action itself must be either good or morally indifferent, the good effect must not be produced by means of the ill effect and there must be a proportionate reason for allowing the foreseen evil to occur: J.K. Mason and R.A. McCall Smith, *Butterworths Medico-Legal Encyclopaedia* (1987), London: Butterworths, p. 171.

52 For a statement of this position, see J. Harris, 'Embryos and hedgehogs: on the moral status of the embryo', in A. Dyson and J. Harris (eds), *Experiments on Embryos* (1990), London: Routledge, p. 65.

53 I have argued this at greater length in J.K. Mason and R.A. McCall Smith, *Law and Medical Ethics* (4th edn, 1994) London: Butterworths, p. 380.

54 The position may have to be amended, as the Council of Europe has agreed that the creation of human embryos for research purposes is to be prohibited: *Convention on Human Rights and Biomedicine* (1996), article 18(2). At the time of writing, the United Kingdom has not ratified the Convention.

55 The distinction accounts for the fact that there are many who would approve of IVF but would not condone techniques which involve the participation of third parties as donors.

56 I. Craft and J. Yovich, 'Implications of embryo transfer' [1979] 2 Lancet 642.

57 Although this is a worldwide phenomenon, it has been publicised particularly in Canada. See, for example, R. Harvey, 'Women trade eggs in try for baby' (1994), *Toronto Star*, 12 December, p. A1. Payment in money or benefits for the supply of gametes in the United Kingdom is subject to directions made by HFEA (1990 Act, s.12(e)); any such practices are currently frowned upon and payments of all sorts are being phased out.

58 Eggs or sperm which have been subjected to procedures which carry an actual or reasonable theoretical risk of harm to their development potential, and embryos created from them, should not be used for treatment (HFEA, *Code of Practice* (1995), para. 7.5).

59 See the classic observations of LORD SIMON in *The Ampthill Peerage* [1977] AC 547, HL at 577.

60 But, in certain circumstances, this might not be so clear in Scotland.

61 Subject, of course, to the rules of adoption (s.27(2)).

62 (1994) 308 Brit Med J 723.

63 See Editorial comment, 'Too old to have a baby?' (1993) 341 Lancet 344, and the debate, 'Should older women be offered in vitro fertilisation?', initiated by T.

Hope, G. Lockwood and M. Lockwood, 'The interests of the potential child' (1995) 310 Brit Med J 1455.

64　Note 16 above; Mrs Seale was refused infertility treatment by way of the NHS on the grounds that she was aged 37.

65　HFEA Report, *Donated Ovarian Tissue in Embryo Research and Assisted Conception* (1994).

66　Report, para. 19. The same restriction is placed on donation for embryo research although, in both cases, the policy is subject to change in the light of further information as to the motivation and effects of donation.

67　In practice, the Authority does not intend to license treatment with cadaver eggs until more is known about the psychological consequences for the recipient couple and the prospective child.

68　*R* v. *Human Fertilisation and Embryology Authority, ex parte Blood* (1997) 35 BMLR 1.

69　The use of material from natural miscarriages is highly suspect as many of these are associated with genetic defect.

70　Human Fertilisation and Embryology Act 1990, s.3A inserted by the Criminal Justice and Public Order Act 1994, s.156.

71　HFEA is currently considering the situation: HFEA, *Fourth Annual Report 1995*, p. 21.

72　A variation is known as 'ZIFT', or zygote intrafallopian transfer, where zygotes formed *in vitro* are transferred to the tubes. Although the technique is not discussed further here, there are obvious distinctions from GIFT. In particular, since it involves the formation of an embryo outside the body, it is subject to the 1990 Act in any circumstances.

73　The technique of embryo biopsy, whereby an early embryonic cell is detached and studied for genetic abnormality, is being increasingly used in association with *in vitro* fertilisation.

10 A Third Party to Marriage

The methods for the alleviation of childlessness due to female abnormality which we have discussed in the preceding chapter have involved considerable medical and technical expertise. It scarcely needs pointing out, however, that there are ways in which the infertile woman can obtain a child which involve no such competence and which society, in its role of protector of the vulnerable, seeks to control to a variable extent. Thus 'baby snatching' is everywhere a criminal offence and the worldwide laws which constrain adoption are expressly directed to preventing the purchase of infants by infertile women. Until recently, however, contractual agreements as to the bearing of children on behalf of others have either gone unnoticed or have been accepted without serious question. It is almost trite to mention that the practice was well known in biblical times; thus, we have Sarai saying to her husband, Abram: 'Have intercourse, then, with my maid; perhaps I shall have sons through her' – and Abram heeded Sarai's request.[1] Times have changed and there are few who would, today, condone blatant adultery as an acceptable means of circumventing childlessness. But adultery is not essential to assisted procreation in the modern reproductive world. Given artificial insemination, embryo donation, uterine lavage and the like, there is no technical reason why the Sarai/Hagar relationship should not be played out in a clinical, legalistic and unemotional framework.

The Warnock Committee[2] defined surrogacy as the practice whereby a woman carries a child for another with the intention that the child should be handed over after birth. This is a wide definition which covers too many possible conditions. It would, for example, include an informal antenatal agreement for adoption which would be unacceptable in the United Kingdom[3] and in most other westernized countries. 'Surrogate' motherhood differs fundamentally from adoption, in that it must involve some genetic affiliation between the 'commissioning parents' and the resulting child; even then, further distinctions are needed. These are based mainly on the genetic con-

251

tribution of the carrying mother: that is, whether or not she provides the ovum. Thus, if the receiving woman is quite unable to produce her own ova and would, at the same time, be an unsuitable subject for ovum or embryo donation, she requires a true surrogate if she is to have a child to bring up. The term 'surrogate motherhood' is, therefore, limited here to the circumstance in which a fertile woman is impregnated with the semen of the husband or partner of one who is infertile – ideally, for the reasons given above. There may, however, be times when a woman who cannot carry a child *could* provide her own ova; when impregnated, these could be implanted in another woman by the process of embryo donation; the 'surrogate' is, then, only carrying another woman's child. This concept is described in this book as 'womb leasing'. There is a third possibility: that the recipient woman who is able to provide the ovum but is unable to sustain a pregnancy has, at the same time, an infertile husband and, thus, requires the help, not only of a surrogate mother, but also of an anonymous semen donor. Such a situation provides an example of surrogacy in which the recipient parents were responsible for half the genetic make-up of the resultant child but where, in contrast to the usual procedure, the genes were of maternal origin; the circumstance must be very uncommon and the matter has recently been the subject of judicial analysis.[4]

The conditions justifying surrogate motherhood and womb leasing are, perhaps, not so rare as might be supposed.[5] This applies particularly to womb leasing, in that the conditions which contraindicate *carrying* a child include not only uterine abnormality but also general systemic disease involving, say, the cardiovascular system, the kidneys, the liver or some endocrine glands. By contrast, the ideal candidate for medically indicated surrogate motherhood must not only suffer from uterine or systemic disease, but must, also, be anovular; indeed, many such persons may exemplify the testicular feminisation syndrome (see p. 6) and are not, therefore, genetic women. Thus it will be seen that, not only are there more medical indications for womb leasing than for surrogate motherhood but, also, womb leasing is the preferred technique, in that the receiving mother is genetically related to the child she is to rear.[6] On the other side of the coin, however, surrogate motherhood requires little or no technical expertise; it may, therefore, be the better option on practical (including financial) grounds and, for this reason, is far more often used than womb leasing, a procedure which involves embryo transfer. It may well be that the techniques are used only rarely but, even so, surrogate motherhood and womb leasing have provoked very great interest among both academics and legislators: the statutory regulation of surrogacy, for example, preceded that of artificial insemination in the United Kingdom. Both, therefore, merit consideration in some detail; we will, however, use surrogate motherhood as the template for discussion on the grounds that it is by far the more representative of the two procedures.

Surrogate motherhood

The basic pattern of surrogate motherhood as here defined is that a woman, the 'surrogate',[7] agrees to carry a baby for a husband and wife (or partners) who are infertile by reason of abnormality in the wife. She is inseminated artificially by the husband's semen, gestates and hands the resulting infant back to the 'commissioning parents' or recipients. There is no technical difficulty in this process. The only unnatural element is the artificial insemination of the surrogate and, clearly, even this minor expertise is not essential.[8] Nor is it *fundamentally* a legal problem; there can be little doubt that surrogate motherhood is practised, very often by way of an altruistic sister, and, although the law, particularly as regards registration and adoption, has clearly been broken in the past, there has been no public outcry or, probably, even awareness. The furore over surrogacy which erupted in the 1980s was born of national moral indignation at the introduction of commercialism to the field of human reproduction. The main cause for any residual concern lies in the age-old questions as to how far the law should go in reflecting the public morality and to what extent it should take the lead. By and large, legislators tend to take the latter course, whereas the courts are prepared to adopt a more pragmatic attitude; this would explain the nuances of conflict which can be discerned in the history of surrogacy in the last 20 years.

It is not even certain that the public conscience is deeply concerned with private morality. The Warnock Committee (at para. 8.10) believed that it is: the objection to surrogate motherhood was thought to be that it attacked the value of the marital relationship. In fact, the opposite may well be the case and the alternative view, as suggested above, is that the public rightly came to fear the intrusion of transatlantic commercialism into family relationships. It is doubtful whether surrogate motherhood would ever have become a major issue were it not for this connection – and had it not been fanned by the press's delight in a 'human story' with sexual overtones. In point of fact, surrogate motherhood can be seen as something of a nine days' wonder; seldom can there have been an issue over which the public attitude changed from revulsion to unconcerned acceptance as easily as it did in this instance.[9] In view of the remarkable U-turn that has come about, we should look, first, at the general or basic morality of surrogacy and, second, at the socio-economic aspects and their consequences.

Moral aspects

It is important to emphasise that surrogate motherhood as defined in this chapter is concerned with the alleviation of childlessness in the wife who is medically unsuited to treatment by *in vitro* fertilisation or by ovum or embryo donation. Most will be associated with genital atresia or uterine abnormalities; others may result from previous surgical intervention. The Warnock Committee recognised the possibility of medical indications (at para. 8.2), although it did not accept the distinction that is made here between surrogate motherhood and womb leasing. The first point in favour of surrogacy is, therefore, that, given the fact that we are prepared to alleviate *some* forms of childlessness by artificial means, it is wrong to discriminate on the grounds of their causes; it has very properly been pointed out that to allow embryo donation but to prohibit surrogate motherhood is to discriminate against the woman with no adequate uterus in favour of the one with no functioning ovary.[10]

Much has been made of the indignity to which a surrogate mother is subjected, the process having been likened to the undeniably degrading practice of wet-nursing which was common in the 19th century, to which one answer would be that the true comparison with wet-nursing lies not in surrogate motherhood but in womb leasing for hedonistic rather than medical reasons (see below). It is, moreover, difficult to see why the concept of surrogate motherhood should not be attractive to the feminist movement. Women have virtually won the right to control their own reproductive destiny through abortion; the corollary should surely be that they have an equal right to use their capacity to bear children in whatever way they wish. This view has been powerfully expressed and it is, effectively, only the law governing the rights and interests of children which inhibits its development.[11] Yet society accepts the right of a mother to offer her child for adoption and even to be compensated in some ways for so doing;[12] it does not allow her simply to abandon her maternal obligations.[13] So far as the infant is concerned, the essential difference between surrogate motherhood and adoption is that the latter process is strictly controlled whereas the former, currently, is covered relatively indirectly, in that artificial insemination is governed by the Human Fertilisation and Embryology Act 1990, while a parental order (q.v. p. 259) in favour of the recipient couple can be granted only if the conditions of the Act have been met. Given that this provides satisfactory regulation of surrogacy, there seems little to choose between the two from the child's point of view; indeed, insofar as the child is returning to its biological father, the surrogacy arrangement is preferable. There is no compelling reason to suppose that surrogate motherhood introduces new parenting hazards for the child in question; rather, it is more likely that, considering the difficulties with which they are prepared to grapple, the commissioning couple will provide a peculiarly satisfactory environment for a man's child.[14]

In short, it seems that there is no major moral *principle* which would debar surrogacy absolutely; the counterarguments which are available will reduce such a claim to one of relative importance only. Despite the considerable support provided from the alternative feminist viewpoint,[15] I suggest that to speak of outlawing surrogacy in terms of preventing the exploitation of a human being is to seek to deprive that being of her autonomy; only imperative policy reasons should prevent a woman disposing of her body as she wants.[16] As an analogy, we may not *like* prostitution but we do not regard it as criminal activity; the criminal context of prostitution lies in exploiting a woman for the financial gain of another.[17] Moral suspicion of financial involvement in reproduction is greatest when advantage accrues to parties who are uninvolved in the biological sense, and it is this darker side of surrogacy which has been addressed in the Surrogacy Arrangements Act 1985. As we will see, however, the 1985 Act significantly omits to criminalise the principals in any unlawful financial transaction and the definition of a reasonable – and lawful – 'reward' for the surrogate is, at least, elastic. Despite the fact that relevant legislation is now in place in the United Kingdom, it is still worth considering the socio-economic pressures which surrogacy may provoke; we are, here, discussing principles which are unaffected by legislation that may be passed in one particular jurisdiction.[18]

The socio-economic atmosphere

Several types of woman can be envisaged as becoming surrogate mothers. There is, first, the member of the family or close personal friend who acts altruistically and regards the gift of a baby in much the same light as a satisfactory Christmas present; the combination of a determined child seeker and an outstandingly generous sister[19] cannot, however, be statistically common. Nevertheless, it may be less rare than one supposes and the same may be said of the woman who regards her blessing of fertility as something she could share with those who are less fortunate; Mrs B, who was a principal in a case brought before the Family Division of the High Court in early 1987, was such a person and was approbated by the judge.[20] Even so, it is a fact of life that the major motivation for supplying such a service will be mercenary. This raises three main questions: should a woman be allowed to receive remuneration for having a child; should an outside agency be permitted to profit from making the arrangements; and, following a rather different theme, how does any financial agreement between the parties affect the possibility of subsequent adoption or the issue of a parental order?

We have seen in Chapter 4 that preventing a mentally retarded person from exercising a right to procreate attracts adverse comment; court orders to that effect have been branded as excessive judicial interferences.[21] If that be so, it is inconsistent to oppose the exercise of that same right by a competent adult woman – on her own terms. Such a woman, it may be said, is under no obligation to become pregnant and is in no need of legal protection, but that is too simple a view. The pressures may be more subtle, but they are certainly there, not the least powerful deriving from the fact that there are relatively few persons who would fail to be impressed by the chance of earning up to £10 000 in a year for performing a natural function. In this context, it has been noted that 40 per cent of surrogate mothers in the United States before 1981 were either unemployed or in receipt of welfare benefits;[22] the economic pressures are probably greater than one would care to admit: consent to surrogacy cannot be said to be free and unfettered in all cases. Such considerations, however, should be a reason, not for prohibiting the practice but, rather, for subjecting it to suitable control.[23] In the event, the United Kingdom Parliament has chosen a somewhat indirect method by which to do so. As long as no third party is involved, there is nothing to stop the exchange of money between the recipient couple and the surrogate. Once a direct payment has been made, however, a parental order cannot be made,[24] and the payment also precludes resort to adoption.[25] Reasonable expenses – generally regarded as up to £10 000 – may, however, be given and the court may authorise payments either prospectively or retrospectively; we will see later that these provisions can be interpreted liberally.

Inevitably, the introduction of financial gain leads to the correlate of a contract and, here, Parliament has deemed that no surrogacy arrangement will be enforceable by or against any of the persons making it.[26] In my view, this is an example of 'knee-jerk' legislation. It is something of a throwback to the earliest case to attain judicial notice, in which the judge regarded 'an agreement between a couple and a girl that she should have the man's child by AID for them to keep' as being pernicious and void.[27] Such expressions of disapproval are founded, essentially, on the intuitive belief that any arrangements assisting surrogacy are *contra bonos mores*, but it is doubtful if intuition is an adequate base on which to erect an absolute ban on a practice which, at least, has its advocates.[28] The better view by far is that of the minority of the Warnock Committee who considered that arrangements should be made through a licensing agency and that, were they made outside the agency, the principals should not be criminalised.[29]

The current legislation, as expressed in the Surrogacy Arrangements Act, s.1A, does little more than accentuate the many admitted difficulties which surround the practice of surrogacy. Absent a binding agreement, the surrogate may expose the fetus to toxic and mechanical danger during gestation, she may terminate the pregnancy, she may refuse to surrender the resultant child or she may refuse to return any disbursements already made in the event of a natural or a therapeutic miscarriage.[30] When conflict arises, the odds are heavily weighted against the commissioning couple by current statutory and common law but, for their part, they could withhold agreed financial assistance or they could refuse to accept the baby. The grounds for doing so might be dishonourable as, for example, if the baby was born defective; they might be understandable if, say, there was a real doubt as to paternity[31] or if there had been deliberate gestational misbehaviour. But the precise reason would be immaterial: there can be no agreement if the agreement is unenforceable. Human nature being what it is, the probability of disagreement is very real. The cry of Sarai is exemplary: 'You are responsible for the outrage against me ... but ever since [Hagar] became aware of her pregnancy, she has been looking at me with disdain.'[32] Sarai, herself, was not above reprisals and family relationships became very strained; the modern family is unlikely to be any more immune to emotional challenge. In these circumstances, it is doubtful if the law in this particular area could be worse drafted. It would surely not be beyond the wit of man to allow of binding agreements or contracts but, at the same time, to legislate for those conditions which could *not* be imposed; it should not, for example, be contractually legal to deny to a gestating woman her right to a medically indicated termination of her pregnancy.

None of which takes into account the possibility of introducing a third party or agency into the equation. Undoubtedly, as has been already noted, there is an intuitive distaste for an agency which sets out to make a commercial profit from a woman's reproductive misfortune. But, even then, to classify such activity as wholly intolerable is to adopt a peculiarly British attitude. The medical ethos of the British over the last half-century has been directed to the concept of the distribution of health and welfare by the state. By contrast, American society, in its search for the perfection of life, is happy to allow the purchase of such commodities as a person has earned the ability to afford; equally, a person is entitled, within limitations, to earn by supplying something which is in demand and, as a result, there is no objection in principle to competent professionalism bringing the two sides of a surrogacy arrangement together. Thus there is no *universal* ethical contradiction to commercialism in surrogacy; it is a matter for the individual societal conscience. It would be difficult to find anyone in the United Kingdom who would support commercial agencies and some states of the United States are antipathetic to their activities.[33] Even so, the discourse is not entirely one-sided. The dissenting view in the Warnock Report as to the need for *some* form of intermediary has been mentioned, and favoured, already. The current situation, however, is that no such governmental support has been provided while, at the same time, the Surrogacy Arrangements Act 1985 prohibits any professional assistance in the procedure. 'Amateurism' is, therefore, a statutory requirement of legally acceptable surrogacy in the United Kingdom, and there is little doubt that the 'amateur' surrogate is at serious risk of physical, psychological and emotional injuries.[34] The interposition of a well-qualified agency could be a major factor in their prevention and it is this possibility which lies at the heart of criticism of the existing legislation in the United Kingdom.[35]

The Surrogacy Arrangements Act 1985 is, in fact, concerned only with commercialism by a third party. In essence, the Act makes it an offence for anyone to initiate or take part in any negotiations with a view to the making of a surrogacy arrangement, to offer or agree to negotiate to that end or to compile any information with a view to its use therein (s.2(1)). The offence is only committed when done on a commercial basis: that is, when any payment is at any time received in respect of the arrangement or when the act is done with a view to payment being received (s.2(3)). No offence is committed, even in a commercial situation, either by the surrogate mother or by the commissioning couple (s.2(2)).[36] It is important to note that s.2(3) includes professional advisers such as solicitors and doctors in its provisions unless they are offering their services free – and it is doubtful whether a doctor contracted to the National Health Service *can* give his services 'free'. It is believed that a solicitor can give general advice and can produce a legal document, but he cannot 'take part in negotiations': he cannot, for instance, indicate that a document as drafted is unfavourable to one side.[37] In effect, as already suggested, the Act prohibits any surrogacy arrangements other than those of the homespun type, which is the very situation that the minority of the Warnock Committee were concerned to avoid. And therein lies the paradox. We can argue that surrogate motherhood is acceptable provided that it is properly, and professionally, supervised and we deprecate legislation which limits that supervision. Yet, intuitively, we visualise that supervision in the well-known and protective environment of the solicitor's office or the doctor's surgery. The moment a lady with a degree in business management offers to coordinate surrogate selection, legal advice and medical counselling in a single package, we recoil in indignation. Would we feel the same if she were a government employee?[38]

We are left with the problem of the relationship between surrogate motherhood and adoption, a matter which underlines the concern which is so widely expressed: in adopting surrogacy, are we under-mining decades of refinement of the adoption laws and, in effect, reverting to the sale of infants? Despite the obvious similarities, there are several reasons for distinguishing surrogacy from adoption. From the societal perspective, it is evident that the surrogate is not a mother at the time she is approached; she may be under some pressure to take part in an arrangement, but she is not under the immediate economic threat of having to care for a growing child; the commis-sioning couple are *not* buying an *existing* baby. In short, surrogacy is a matter of pre-arrangement, while adoption is an after-the-fact ac-commodation. It has, in fact, been suggested that standard surrogacy can be regarded as ovum donation *in situ*, this carrying the corollary that the surrogate is simply providing a gestational service for an infant that she has never 'owned'.[39] A more telling, albeit negative, point would be that the two procedures cannot be the same, since adoption would be one way – and a distinct way which has been used in the past – of establishing the status of a child born to a surrogate mother.[40] In practice, the current law clearly distinguishes the two procedures by the introduction of the parental order in sur-rogacy cases.

Parental orders

The parental order was something of a makeshift addition to the 1990 Act when it became clear that the existing legislation failed to address the problem of surrogacy and, particularly, of womb leasing. It was clearly something of a contradiction in terms for a couple to be forced to adopt a child in order to obtain recognition of their un-doubted genetic parentage, yet, at the time, no alternative existed; moreover, while the genetic father of the child might, at the time, have had a right to be recognised as the father of an illegitimate child, no such opportunity was available to a genetic mother, for no woman other than the woman who has carried a child as a result of the placing in her of an embryo is to be treated as the mother of the resulting child.[41]

The conditions governing the making of a parental order are com-plex and derive from the Human Fertilisation and Embryology Act 1990, s.30. The main gist, however, is that the court may make an order providing for a child to be treated in law as the child of a commissioning or recipient couple, who are parties to a marriage, if the child has been carried by another woman as a result of the placing in her of an embryo or sperm and eggs or her artificial insemination and the gametes of one or both of the commissioning couple were used to bring about the creation of the embryo (s.30(1)). This is subject to certain conditions being met, *inter alia*:

a   that the application is made within six months of the birth of the child;
b   that, at the time of the application, the child's home is with the commissioning couple;
c   that both the applicants have attained the age of 18;
d   that both the father of the child, where he is not the commissioning man,[42] and the woman who carried the child have freely, and with full understanding of what is involved, agreed unconditionally to the making of the order;
e   that the woman's necessary agreement is given not less than six weeks after the birth of the child; and
f   that no money or other benefit, other than for expenses reasonably incurred, has been given or received by the commissioning couple in relation to the arrangement and the making of the order unless it has been authorised by the court.[43]

It is interesting to note the understandable anxiety on the part of the authorities to maintain the principle of the conventional family: despite the attention paid to the consent of the surrogate's partner, should there be one, only a husband and wife may apply for a parental order. Our legislators will, also, have no truck with adultery. For an order to be obtained when only the male gametes contribute to the embryo, the surrogate must have been artificially inseminated (1990 Act, s.30(1)(*a*)) which, as has been noted already, means that surrogacy is under the indirect control of the Human Fertilisation and Embryology Authority.

It will be seen that, apart from the genetic conditions, the criteria for making a parental order generally follow those for making an adoption order; indeed, the definitive regulations are, somewhat confusingly, based mainly on the Adoption Act 1976 and the Adoption (Scotland) Act 1978.[44] As a result, a number of features are introduced which are not apparent from the wording of the 1990 Act. In particular, the first consideration of the court is to be the need to safeguard and promote the welfare of the child throughout his childhood;[45] since the commissioning couple are likely to be reasonably affluent, the dice are fairly heavily loaded in favour of making an order. Similarly, the child who is the subject of a parental order is to be regarded as being the child of the commissioning couple and of no other persons; the status provisions contained in the 1990 Act, ss.27–29 are, as a result, effectively negatived. Perhaps the major innovation in the regulations is the establishment of a Parental Order Register under the control of the Registrar General, to which the children concerned will have a right of access having attained the age of 18 – a provision which is in stark contrast to the very limited rights to genetic information available in other forms of assisted reproduction. I have already expressed my misgivings as to the generally accepted 'right' of a child to delve into his or her genetic history (see p. 221); these are amplified in a case of womb leasing, where the identity of one's gestational mother must be of very limited significance to a young adult.

Thus, although the processes of surrogacy and of adoption have undoubted similarities, they are quite distinct in law and, indeed, this distinction was adopted in the Scottish case of C, Petitioner[46] (see below). This case illustrated a further significant difference between the two procedures in that, whereas the court may overrule the gestational mother who unreasonably withholds consent to an adoption order,[47] no such latitude is available in the case of a parental order. Major interest, however, must centre on the financial implications: are the barriers to the passage of money or other benefits as expressed in the Adoption Act 1976, s.57 (or Adoption (Scotland) Act 1978, s.51) and in the Human Fertilisation and Embryology Act 1990, s.30(7) the same, or are they qualitatively different? There is a statutory suggestion that they are intended to be different insofar as s.30(7) is one of the few provisions of s.30 which is allowed to stand on its own in the regulations. One might suspect that Parliament's intention was to narrow the field in the 1990 Act so as to compensate for the greater likelihood of monetary reward in the case of surrogacy; the reported decisions, however, indicate that the courts will adopt a pragmatic attitude based on the facts of the individual case.

Re an adoption application (surrogacy)[48] is arguably the most important of the relevant English decisions, in that it specifically considered the relationship between surrogacy and adoption. The circumstances were remarkable, the commissioning couple and the surrogate having been drawn together largely as a result of media coverage; there was no written consent or agreement – the arrangement was 'one of trust which was fully honoured on both sides'. The surrogate, who was motivated by a conviction that she could offer an important service to a childless couple, was impregnated naturally. A sum in recompense of £10 000 was agreed but, having been paid half of this shortly after the birth of the child, the surrogate renounced the remainder on the grounds that she had made a considerable amount of money from publishing her story. The receiving mother attended the birth and the four principals spent the next week together before the surrogate returned home, leaving the baby behind; all were, in the words of the judge, supremely happy. They were also inexperienced and, nearly two and a half years after the birth, which preceded the Surrogacy Arrangements Act 1985, the father and his wife applied for an adoption; the problem posed was simply whether any 'payment or reward' had been given so as to preclude an adoption order. The opinion of the court was that a surrogacy arrangement did not contravene the Act so long as the payments made did not include an element of profit or financial reward; the amount involved in the instant case did no more than recompense for loss of income and of amenities. The judge had, however, a second string to his bow in that, even if he were wrong as to the terms of the payments, the court had discretion to authorise recompense or reward if it saw fit;[49] he interpreted authorisation as including retrospective action and was prepared to do so, having the welfare of the child as his first consideration. The adoption order was, accordingly, made with the judge warning future childless couples that surrogacy was not a primrose path. The influential academic Michael Freeman is reported as saying: 'It is a compassionate, sensible, humane judgment – I am delighted by it – though I don't agree with the judge's interpretation of the law. It does show what a mess the interface between adoption and surrogacy is in'.[50] Despite these misgivings, it is to be noted that this decision was followed in *Re Q (parental order)*,[51] due regard having been paid to the credibility of £8250 being reasonable expenses.

The comparable Scottish case, *C, Petitioner*,[52] is more recent and the conditions provided a marked contrast. The surrogacy arrangement was conducted through an unlicensed agency and a sum of £8000 was paid in respect of loss of earnings and inconvenience; the surrogate was, however, unemployed and was clearly undertaking the task because of the money involved. Shortly after the child was born and handed to the commissioning couple, the surrogate became distressed and regretted what she had done. When the baby was a year old, the commissioning couple sought an adoption order, the alternative of a parental order being precluded by the birth mother's refusal of consent. The sheriff at first instance held that she was withholding consent to adoption unreasonably but, at the same time, refused an adoption order on the grounds that the financial arrangements constituted a serious breach of the Adoption (Scotland) Act 1978, ss. 24(2) and 51. The alternative of a custody order was granted. On appeal to the Inner House of the Court of Session, it was found that it was a parental order which had been in the mind of the commissioning couple as a means of obtaining parental rights when the child was born and it was this application that had been invalidated by the payment of £8000. The court could find no reason to suppose that the Adoption (Scotland) Act 1978 had been, simultaneously, contravened, the issue being one for the discretion of the court. An adoption order was, therefore, substituted for the custody order.[53]

The decision in *C, Petitioner* involves two separate issues. That relating to consent is reconsidered briefly at p. 265. The findings as to recompense seem to have been forced on the Court of Session by the decision of the judge at first instance. Otherwise, there was really no reason for making a somewhat contrived distinction. The precedent for retrospective authorisation of monetary payments in respect of parental orders was already confirmed in *Re Q*; whether by accident or design, the courts of England and Scotland now seem harmonised on the point. The apparently contradictory recent decisions can be reconciled under the general rule that the courts in both England and Scotland will strive to do their best for the resultant child of a surrogacy arrangement and, to this end, they will bend the rules, including the interpretation of expenses, so far as is practicable. While many would deprecate *any* mercenary nuances in a surrogacy arrangement, we should consider the financial implications of other widely approved treatments of childlessness before we condemn the passage of money between the commissioning couple and the surrogate outright. Thus, so long as IVF or other forms of embryo transfer are barely available within the National Health Service, the infertile couple that uses them are 'paying' for their child. This is not to deny that there *is* a difference between a payment to a skilled professional for constructing a pregnancy and one to a woman for supplying the means of pregnancy – but the difference is not extreme.

Thus, while the legal attitudes to surrogacy seem, by now, to have been comparatively settled, it is worth a moment's digression into history to see how this has come about.

The British cases

Although there have been occasional reports in the press of surrogacy arrangements which have not come to judicial notice, it is possible to discern some important landmarks in those which have done so.[54]

Re C (a minor),[55] the first case to receive reasonable consideration, was essentially concerned with wardship. An American couple arranged a surrogacy in England through a commercial agency. When the baby was born, the local authority, being appraised of the fact that it had been abandoned by its mother, obtained a place of safety order under the Children and Young Persons Act 1969, s.28. The inseminating father then issued a wardship summons. The court specifically regarded the ethics, morality and desirability of the arrangement as being irrelevant: the baby had been born and all that mattered was what was best for her and not how she had arrived. LATEY J found that no-one else was better equipped for the child than the commissioning couple and, accordingly, an order was made that the wardship should continue, care and control being committed to them on their undertaking to return the baby to the jurisdiction of the court should it so order; leave was given to take the baby to live outside the jurisdiction.

This case demonstrates very well the overriding concern for the interests of the child in wardship proceedings; the judge was at pains to emphasise that the natural mother did not want the baby and that her genetic father and his wife did; moreover, the latter were sensible people who would be able to answer the baby's questions when the time came; the form of registration of the birth was not, however, disclosed. The major relevance as to surrogacy agreements was that the judge specifically rejected any suggestion that the father and his wife were unsuitable as parents because they had entered into a commercial surrogate arrangement.

Re an adoption application (surrogacy)[56] has already been discussed in connection with the relationship between surrogacy and adoption and its main importance lies therein. For present purposes, it need only be noted that LATEY J's approbation of (and, indeed, enthusiasm for) what was clearly seen as a success story shines through his judgment. Even so, he went out of his way to stress that, in other cases, it might well not end up happily. In the event of the mother being unable to part with the baby, 'the trauma and turmoil then for all needs no describing' (at 832).

Precisely that situation arose in *Re P (minors)*,[57] which was heard at the same time as the adoption case. Here the surrogate was impregnated with the sperm of a professional man and went through a twin pregnancy; it was agreed that a large sum of money would be transferred. She refused to hand over the children and the case became, essentially, a matter of custody. The well-being of the twins was, therefore, the paramount consideration and, faced with a conflict of views, the judge, SIR JOHN ARNOLD, was influenced mainly by the degree of maternal bonding that had arisen. He could find 'nothing to outweigh the advantages to these children of preserving the link to the mother to whom they are bonded, and who has exercised a satisfactory degree of maternal care'.[58] At the same time, the judge had it in common with LATEY J that he saw nothing shameful either in the commissioning parents wanting a child by way of a surrogate arrangement or in the surrogate offering herself for the purpose. It must, however, have been a very unhappy relationship.[59]

The common thread uniting these apparently disparate decisions lies in the best interests of the child; this is simply applying the principles which govern all decisions in family proceedings[60] and, in doing so, the courts are implicitly accepting that surrogate motherhood is not to be condemned on policy grounds alone. The rights of individuals to seek and to provide the means for the relief of childlessness are maintained, subject, of course, to these coming within the statutory law; no British court – leaving aside the rather unusual and now irrelevant case of *A* v. *C*[61] – has sought to attach opprobrium to commissioning couples.

The problem then remains as to what it is that influences the courts in their search for the best interests of the children concerned. From the above decided cases, it would be easy to distinguish the presence of conflict as providing the judiciary with a watershed for decision making. In a material world, the financial status of a child's parents must be a powerful indicator of its best interests. Since the commissioning couple *must* be relatively affluent if they can afford the expenses of the surrogate, one can well imagine the courts' first instinct would be to place the child in their care. Yet, although the commissioning couple in *Re P (minors)* were just as well-off as were those in the other two cases, the natural father was not granted custody. The obvious conclusion would be that instinct and pragmatism will determine the outcome when there is no disagreement – a practical policy which is now given statutory effect insofar as the making of a parental order depends upon the consent of all parties. The decision in *Re P (minors)* then gives a clear indication that preference will be given to the claims of maternal bonding over those of material comfort when there is conflict; there would have to be particularly compelling reasons before the court ordered an apparently willing and effective mother to demit her parental rights to her child's genetic father.

How, then, are we to reconcile the decision in *Re P (minors)* with that in the later case of *C, Petitioner*? Does the Scottish case uncover a specific ideological difference in English and Scottish jurisprudence? One imagines not. Has there been a significant change in societal attitudes over a decade? Undoubtedly, the concept of surrogacy has become very much more acceptable but, on the other hand, support for the more vulnerable parties to a dispute has, if anything, become more marked. Can it be that the mere existence of the Human Fertilisation and Embryology Act 1990, s.30 exerts an influence? At the end of the day, the difference between the two cases may rest, not on any point of principle, but on the simple facts of each. Of these, the most significant is that, whereas the P twins had lived with their mother for six months, child X in *C, Petitioner* had joined the commissioning parents on the day of his birth and was aged 18 months at the time of the hearing. 'Bonding' was, therefore, the motivating factor in both cases and may, properly, remain so. At the same time, one can foresee difficulties for the future, in that the consent of the mother, which is essential to the granting of a parental order, must be delayed for six weeks after the birth of the child. This is likely to be a 'grey period' for a woman prone to doubt. Perhaps the most important practical condition imposed by s.30 lies in sub-section (3)(*a*), which dictates that the child be living with the commissioning parents at the time of the application; clearly, the earlier this move is effected, the easier the transition will be for all concerned.[62]

As something of an aside from the main discussion, it may be noted that the provision of a parental order has highlighted some other difficulties associated with legal and genetic parentage in surrogacy cases. In *Re Q (parental order)*,[63] the surrogate carried to term an embryo derived from the egg of the receiving mother and sperm from an anonymous donor. JOHNSON J concluded that the donor was clearly not the father by virtue of s.28(6) and, since the surrogate was unmarried, no-one was available as a father under common law principles. The judge was, further, unable to accept that the commissioning man and the surrogate were persons having treatment together for the purposes of establishing fatherhood under s.23 (3) – a possibility which was even more improbable than when the commissioning man's sperm was used. It followed that the child was fatherless,[64] and no paternal consent was required to a parental order. We can surely be said to have weaved a tangled web of deception.

The American scene

The current United Kingdom legislation related to surrogacy has been accused of being, in the one hand, too lax and, on the other, of being unduly interventionist. It may be useful to compare it with the law in other jurisdictions and, particularly, with that in the United States, where surrogacy has been practised on a wide scale for a considerable time. Inevitably, it is difficult to establish a uniform trend in a country which contains so many different cultures within its borders – and, so far as is known, the Supreme Court has not yet considered an apposite case. It has been stated that 'no State has adopted a law that specifically addresses, either affirmatively or negatively, the concept of surrogate parenting although legislation has been introduced in several legislatures'.[65] In fact, it seems that Arkansas, in legislating that the child of a single woman acting as a surrogate mother shall be the child of the intending mother,[66] is an exception to this rule. All states, however, have laws governing adoption, of which those of Michigan[67] are not only typical but were also the first to be challenged in the courts as to their relevance to surrogacy.

In brief, they prohibit offering, giving or receiving any money or other consideration in connection with the adoption of a child; the statute allows for the receipt of court-approved fees and would not, therefore, prohibit surrogate motherhood absolutely. There are, however, alternative types of statute law which might be available to inhibit the practice, including those which prohibit the transfer of rights to care and custody of a child other than by adoption.[68] As already noted, there is a school of thought which believes that a surrogacy contract is, essentially, one concerned with transfer of custody; if that were so, these statutes, which define the law in only a minority of states, would impose a powerful restraint on surrogate motherhood. Even so, it is no more certain that contracts for custody are enforceable in the majority of states that have no appropriate statute and which, therefore, depend upon the precedents of case law. Much would now depend upon the relationship of the child to the would-be custodian and on the precise method of conception, for example as between surrogate motherhood and womb leasing.[69]

The first challenge to an apparent statutory prohibition of surrogacy is to be found in *Doe v. Kelly*.[70] This case was brought in an attempt to show that the Michigan adoption statute was unconstitutional if applied to surrogacy, in that it violated the parents' rights to privacy; the court was therefore more concerned with the constitutionality of the decision to have a child than with the contractual issues involved. In the end, the State Court of Appeal, to an extent, avoided the major issues by deciding that the statute precluded the payment of a consideration while making use of the state's adoption procedures. The right to privacy in procreation was accepted, but this was distinguished from the state's compelling interest in preventing 'the evils attendant to the mix of lucre and the adoption process'. The interpretation that a surrogacy arrangement without payment would be acceptable, is, therefore, available.[71] In a later case from Kentucky,[72] the State Supreme Court, in a 5:2 decision, took a different view, holding that the surrogacy contract was one between a woman and the father of her child born out of wedlock concerning the child's custody. Consideration of the adoption laws was, therefore, irrelevant despite the fact that, in the end, the child would be adopted by the infertile wife. How much the activities of a commercial agency offended the public conscience was a matter for decision by the legislature; meantime, the courts should not cut off solutions to childlessness which were offered by science. The processes of IVF which was sanctioned by statute, and of surrogacy, which was not, were 'virtually indistinguishable from the standpoint of biological engineering'.[73]

These cases are concerned with the general principles regulating the relationship of the authorities to surrogacy arrangements in which the principals are in peaceful accord. The problems attending a conflict of interests were squarely addressed, and in a relatively novel way, in the superior court in *In re Baby M*.[74] In that case, the surrogate, who was paid $10 000 for her services, had a change of heart and absconded with her baby in defiance of a court order requiring her to surrender custody to the commissioning couple. The case had other bizarre aspects: for example, the surrogate mother claimed that the child was, in fact, that of her husband – a claim which was convincingly disproved by standard methods of paternity testing. Moreover, it was by no means clear that the adopting mother was incapable of bearing a child; it was, however, generally agreed that her decision not to become pregnant was reasonable. Once again, the economic distinction between the two parties was very evident: the surrogate was a drop-out from school married to an alcoholic, the adopting couple were solid, middle-class professional people.

The court was careful to narrow the field of controversy; the case, it was said, was to be decided on legal principle alone; 'it must neither manage morality nor temper theology'. In particular, any analogy with the adoption laws was considered irrelevant. Surrogate motherhood was unknown at the time the statutes were enacted and could not be read into them retrospectively. In any event, it was said, parents have equal rights on the birth of a baby and the father cannot 'purchase' what is already his.

The court thus confined itself to two legal principles, the concept of *parens patriae* and the law of contract. No doubts were expressed as to the latter. It was held that, once conception had occurred, the parties' rights were fixed and the contract was firm, subject only to the proviso that a contract which purported to transfer the mother's right to abortion to the father was void and unenforceable. In the instant case, the contract was valid and it had been broken by the surrogate; the only problem to be solved was that of the means of compensation, which could be either monetary or by way of application of specific performance. The former was unrealistic while the latter would replace the parties in the positions for which they had bargained. And it was here that the concept of *parens patriae* – that of the state looking after the interests of its children – applied most heavily; there were many reasons, both negative as to why the child should not be placed in the custody of her natural mother, and positive as to why she should be in the charge of her father and his wife, why the child's best interests were served by being adopted by the latter.

The outcome of this case conflicted markedly with the anticipated attitude of the court.[75] The principle of equity, or of justice and fairness to both sides, was addressed, only to be dismissed rather summarily. Moreover, the judgment rested on some doubtful propositions, including one which held that, if one has an undeniable right to procreate coitally, there is an equal right to procreate non-coitally; given the constitutional protection of the former, there is similar protection of the use of surrogacy.[76] It is equally, if not more, reasonable to maintain that there is no obligation on the state to support the obtaining of a child in any manner that is desired.

It is therefore not surprising that the ruling in *Baby M* was over-turned by the Supreme Court of New Jersey[77] – and decisively so. The surrogacy contract was invalidated as conflicting with the law and with public policy; both the termination of the surrogate mother's parental rights and the adoption of the child were voided. The court found no offence to the law in voluntary, non-commercial surrogacy, provided there was no agreement binding on the surrogate to surren-der the child. The door was left slightly ajar, in that it was specifically stated that it would be open to the legislature to alter the law so as to permit surrogacy contracts. Thus, in the end, New Jersey did not deviate from the expected pattern; whether or not the decision to grant custody rights to the genetic father and visiting rights to the natural mother was in the best interests of the unfortunate child is a matter of opinion.[78]

However, the wheel turned close to full circle in the later Califor-nian case of *Johnson* v. *Calvert*.[79] This was an instance of 'womb leasing', in which the surrogate was paid $10 000 to gestate the com-missioning couple's embryo. After six months' pregnancy, she changed her mind and, as a result, both parties filed for recognition of paren-tal rights on the birth of the child. The trial court held that a surro-gacy contract was both legal and enforceable and that the commissioning couple were the child's genetic, biological and natu-ral parents; the surrogate was seen as having no parental rights. This apparently harsh judgment was upheld on appeal and a further appeal was dismissed by the Supreme Court of California. The Su-preme Court held that, while both women concerned had statutory claims to motherhood, it was the intention of the parties when mak-ing the arrangement which decided the issue between them – and a contrast was drawn with ovum donation where the gestational mother's intention to retain and to raise the child was clear, despite her having no genetic relationship with her offspring. It was considered that surrogate contracts do not violate existing public policies as to adoption; any payments in the former are, effectively, made for services rendered and not as compensation for the transfer of parental rights. In a further set of what could be seen as *obiter* opinions, the court held by a majority that surrogacy contracts do not violate prohibitions on involuntary servitude and that they do not 'dehumanise' or exploit women, and particularly women of low economic status, the argument raised above, at p. 256, that surrogacy was no more exploitive than any other unattractive employment, was endorsed.

The decision in *Johnson* has been widely criticised and has been described as one which 'fundamentally misunderstands human re-production and ignores the biological realities of the surrogate's con-tribution'.[80] The 'blanket' nature of the ruling and its ratio have little concern for the child's 'best interests' other than to assume that these will be best served by return to the commissioning couple. Grubb, in a commentary on the case,[81] has pointed out that the surrogate's change of mind may indicate a real commitment to the child's well-being, from which it follows that each case should be judged on its own merits with the best interests of the child providing the driving force.[82]

Johnson, however, is clearly not the last American word on the matter. Only a year later, a further case came before the Californian courts[83] in which a couple's marriage broke down 18 months after the birth and acceptance by them of a child born as a result of a standard surrogate agreement, the surrogate having been impregnated with the sperm of the commissioning husband; the surrogate mother then claimed legal parenthood. The case thus differed from *Johnson* in that the commissioning woman had no genetic link with the child. As a result, the Californian Court of Appeal was able to diverge from the earlier decision of the Supreme Court and did so robustly. Presented with a congruence of genetic and gestational motherhood in the surrogate and with sterility in the commissioning woman, it held that there was no doubt as to who was the natural mother and that, as a result, the question of intent did not arise. Moreover, the Supreme Court had not enforced a surrogacy contract; it had merely found that it could be considered without contravening public policy and had done so in order to establish the intentions of the contracting parties. An application for review was later denied by the Supreme Court of California. Thus the position in America, at least on the west coast, appears to be partially clarified and is best summed up in Grubb's words: 'Infertile couples who seek surrogacy linked with IVF treatment [womb leasing] can be reasonably certain they will come out of the arrangement, come what may, as the child's parents. By contrast, couples who resort to traditional surrogacy will have no such reassurance' (at 221). Given the supposition that the doubts implicit in the last sentence will be resolved in favour of the child's best interests, this seems to be as good a solution both in equity and on genetic grounds as is likely to be found in default of specific legislation.

Prohibition of surrogacy

It will have been seen that surrogacy is at least tolerated throughout the common law countries. The only exception known to the writer is Queensland,[84] where both principals and doctors have been prosecuted for making or taking part in such arrangements. The same tolerance is to be found in the European Community, where Germany is the only country to prohibit surrogacy.[85] A contrasting example of a modern state coming to grips with permissive legislation is to be found in Israel, where alternative birthing procedures were illegal until 1996; Israel is said to be the first country to legalise the procedure other than by a process of *laissez faire*.[86] The resulting Act is, as might be anticipated, a compromise which probably satisfies no parties completely. Its main conditions are as follows:

a   the ovum must not come from the surrogate (which confines the process to womb leasing) and the sperm must come from the prospective father (which eliminates such unusual cases as *Re Q*[87]);

b   only unmarried Israeli women may surrogate, subject to special exceptions;

c   the child will be in full custody of the surrogate from the time of conception; she may have the fetus aborted or may petition the court to keep the neonate;

d   the commissioning parents must request transfer of parenthood within a week of the birth;

e   payment will be limited to expenses, including loss of time, pain, suffering and temporary loss of income;

f   all arrangements will be barred from publication without specific court approval.[88]

Innovatively – and, I believe, most importantly – any surrogate arrangements will be fully supervised by a committee consisting of physicians, a clinical psychologist, a social worker, a lawyer and a relevant clergyman.

Womb leasing

It is clear from what has already been said that womb leasing involves the production of human embryos *in vitro* and is, therefore, automatically subject to control by way of the Human Fertilisation and Embryology Act 1990. Whether or not it will be provided as a treatment service depends, however, on the interpretation of the HFEA's Code of Practice and, hence, on the approach taken by the individual licence holder.

One intuitive reaction to womb leasing could be to see it being operated simply as a matter of convenience for the commissioning couple: for instance, to avoid a pregnancy interfering with a woman's career or lifestyle. The great majority of, at least, Western states, however, have by now enacted legislation which is designed to protect a pregnant woman's rights to social support and employment protection;[89] given this, there must be very few professions where pregnancy *per se* would be positively deleterious: fashion modelling might be one such. As a result, it would be well-nigh impossible to discover any responsible body of opinion to support womb leasing on non-medical grounds and, as will be clear below, I would regard it as unsupportable.

This, however, is to see the procedure in the wrong light. The more correct view is that of the Superior Court JUDGE SORKOW in In *re Baby M*, who emphasised that there was no distinction to be made between 'infertility' on the count of inability to gestate and infertility due to, say, ovarian dysgenesis. We have already seen that there are almost certainly more women for whom womb leasing would be theoretically preferable to surrogate motherhood as a form of treatment and it certainly has the better genetic end-point;[90] by the same reasoning, the carrying mother will probably be exposed to less psychiatric trauma in surrendering an infant to which she has no genetic affiliation. Only the extensive technological requirements stand in the way of regarding womb leasing as the treatment of choice for the woman who cannot gestate.

Womb leasing does, however, cause difficulties in the application of the *mater est quam gestatio demonstrat* principle (see p. 241), now enshrined in the Human Fertilisation and Embryology Act 1990, s.27, but most of these have been eliminated by s.30; the concept of the parental order was devised, in the main, for the solution of the problem of maternity following womb leasing. On the other hand, the current regulations as to consent to such an order on the part of the 'surrogate' probably do not allow sufficiently for the genetic difference between surrogacy and womb leasing; the problem of unreasonable refusal to surrender the child is addressed below.

It is within the womb leasing context that intrafamilial arrangements are likely to be established. Two early cases, and two more recent, have caught the attention of the British press: one in South Africa and two in England where a woman carried her genetic grandchildren,[91] and one in Australia where an ovum donor's sibling carried her own niece.[92] Despite the fact that such bizarre results would be regarded as intolerable by many, the English case in 1996, at least, was approved by a hospital ethics committee. It could be argued that such arrangements must be so disruptive of the family hierarchy that it might be right to outlaw womb leasing within immediate kinship.[93] Which brings us to the question whether there should be specific legislation on the subject.

Possible legislation

It has always been a matter of surprise, at least to the present writer, that surrogate motherhood, which has been the focus of such contentious social and moral overtones, is allowed to subsist on the basis of individual court decisions no matter how well-meaning – and successful – may be the individual judges. As Brown et al.[94] have put it, 'The chaotic atmosphere of the particular method of pregnancy must be recognized and alleviated .... judges must pay more attention to the need for predictability and stability. Finally, the legislatures should act to fill this vast legal vacuum.' Admittedly, this appeal is directed to the United States, but it applies, in more muted form, to the United Kingdom, where existing legislation – in particular, the Surrogacy Arrangements Act 1985 – does much to eliminate the less attractive aspects of surrogacy. Even so, the current legislation is either of a negative or of a derivative character. The statute of 1985 falls into the former category. The remainder statutory control derives from the Human Fertilisation and Embryology Act 1990 whereby artificial insemination, and, as a result, the majority of surrogacy, is controlled while natural insemination of the surrogate is, at least, seriously discouraged by the consequent non-availability of a parental order. Public attitudes have changed and surrogacy is now seen as 'respectable' by the British Medical Association,[95] and the time could be ripe for positive legislation placing the woman who is childless by being unable to gestate on the same footing as her sisters who cannot ovulate or conceive.

This implies that the procedure should be 'medicalised'. I believe that this is essential if the moral ground is to be maintained and, although the notion has attracted criticism, it also has considerable support.[96] It is therefore suggested that surrogate motherhood should be available subject to the following conditions, which should be applied by statute. First, surrogacy arrangements should be legal only if the procedure is certified medically as being the appropriate treatment for childlessness in a woman of childbearing age who cannot or should not gestate. In keeping with other legislation in the field, it may be that this would best be certified by two medical practitioners and it might also be desirable to follow the Victorian lead[97] in the field of assisted fertility and insist on a minimum of counselling.

Second, impregnation should only be achieved by way of artificial insemination. This is needed so as to exclude the possibility of future involvement of the divorce courts on the grounds of adultery; it goes without saying that the consent of each of the commissioning couple is essential.

Third, monetary considerations should be limited to legitimate expenses and a reasonable honorarium, the expenses to be paid as incurred, but the honorarium only on completion of the agreement or contract. I can see no reason why a woman should not receive reasonable compensation for providing a service. There is, however, no way in which 'reasonable' can be defined in this context – there are very few surrogates on the Clapham omnibus. It would be a matter for the controlling authority (see below) to judge in individual cases.

Fourth, any agreement or contract must be subject to the post-natal consent of the gestatory mother. It would be difficult to justify the enforced removal of a child from its natural, and legal, mother, although we have seen in *C, Petitioner* that it is not impossible; for this reason, there is a case to be made for establishing a judicial power to declare the withholding of consent to surrender the child to be unreasonable, as is the case in adoption; it would be hard to deny that the solution of *C, Petitioner* looks very like a judicial ruse. The essential problem, as demonstrated in that case, lies in the welfare of the child and, here, a practical answer would be that no surrogate should be allowed to undertake the role unless it was agreed that she would be able to provide a satisfactory family environment in the event of her wishing to retain her baby; this, again, would be a matter for the central authority.

Finally, in order to be legal, the whole procedure must be carried out under the direction and supervision of a central authority. This is the hub of the proposals. A subject which touches so many moral and legal nerves ought not to be regulated at the level of the individual; some central direction is essential, the only problem being the form that this should take. Should it be associated with the adoption procedure or with assisted reproduction? The former approach is, in my view, unsatisfactory insofar as we have seen that there are specific distinctions to be made between adoption and surrogacy; it is also to be noted that the various adoption agencies operate independently, whereas the need is for uniformity. As to the latter possibility, Singer and Wells,[98] many years ago, advocated the creation of a State Surrogacy Board and saw this as a means of bridging the ground between surrogate motherhood for clear medical reasons and womb leasing for convenience. It is clear from what has been said that this function would not apply were my proposals to be adopted: it is, in my view, essential that lawful surrogacy be circumscribed by medical need; moreover, one shies away from establishing yet another quango[99] – especially one with such a limited remit. The most obvious solution would be to place surrogate parenting firmly within the ambit of the Human Fertilisation and Embryology Authority. The infrastructure and many of the regulations needed to do so are already in place. Incorporating surrogacy within HFEA would clearly establish the procedure as being no more than a recognised treatment for one particular form of childlessness, and the authority would be well placed to evaluate, say, the practicability of alternative forms of treatment. The authority, through its annual reports, is remarkably silent on the topic. Nevertheless, now that antagonism to surrogacy is, at least, muted, it ought to be said that the practice has evolved to the extent that the government can cease having fears of encouraging it: the medical basis is now well established and it is the concept of 'surrogacy for convenience' that is discredited. One feels that HFEA control and regularisation must come soon.

Notes

1   Genesis 16:2, *The New American Bible* (1983), Nashville: Nelson states in a footnote that Sarai's actions were all in keeping with the laws of the times.
2   M. Warnock, (Chairman), *Report of the Committee of Inquiry into Human Fertilisation and Embryology* (1984), London: HMSO, Cmnd 9314, at para. 8.1.
3   As things stand, no adoption is permissible in the United Kingdom until the child is born and is at least 19 weeks old; a mother cannot agree to the adoption of her child within six weeks of its birth (Adoption Act 1976, s.13). No matter what informal arrangement had been made, a parental order (see p. 259) would not be available because the absence of any genetic association between the receiving parents and the child.
4   The child could be made the subject of a parental order (Human Fertilisation and Embryology Act 1990, s.30(1), but, by virtue of the statute, would be, otherwise, legally fatherless: *Re Q (parental order)* [1996] 1 FLR 369 (see p. 266).
5   It is said that, in 1992, there were 43 women and couples known to be at various stages of IVF surrogacy in the United Kingdom: E. Blyth, 'Section 30 – the acceptable face of surrogacy?' (1993) 4 JSWFL 248.
6   This analysis assumes that a genetic association between the recipient mother and the child is the most important objective but, from the point of view of the parents, this may not be so. Although it is not strictly apposite to the present discussion, a study has shown that, given an enforced choice, women and their husbands are about equally divided in their preference for genetic or birth motherhood: J.G. Thornton, H.M. McNamara and I.A. Montague, 'Would you rather be a "birth" or a "genetic" mother? If so, how much?' (1994) 20 J Med Ethics 87.
7   There are good reasons for suggesting that this is a reversal of the true roles. See D. Morgan 'Surrogacy: an introductory essay', in R. Lee and D. Morgan (eds), *Birthrights* (1989), London: Routledge. But the soubriquet as used here is now very well established.
8   The infant was conceived by natural means in the case of Mrs A and Mrs B (n. 20 below): C. Dyer, 'Babies in the courts' (1987), *The Times*, 17 March, p. 15.
9   For a general review, see D.R. Bromham, 'Surrogacy: the evolution of opinion' (1992) 47 Brit J Hosp Med 767. Some unfortunate cases in the late 1990s may, however, have set off a further swing of the pendulum and the government has recently established a committee under Professor Margaret Brazier which will reconsider the law on surrogacy.
10 I. Davies, 'Contracts to bear children' (1985) 11 J Med Ethics 61.
11 The alternative feminist view, that surrogacy should be outlawed on the grounds that it degrades women, seems to be flawed as representing paternalism, if that be the right word. For discussion, see J. Mahoney, 'An essay on surrogacy and feminist thought' (1988)16 Law Med Hlth Care 81.

12   Adoption Act 1976, s.57(3).
13   Children Act 1989, s.2(9).
14   For a dissenting view, see J.G. Hogg, 'Surrogacy – nobody's child' [1991] Fam
     Law 276. The author indicates that parental orders may be there for the benefit
     of the parents, at the expense of that of the child.
15   For example, E.S. Anderson, 'Is women's labor a commodity?' (1990) 19 Philos
     Publ Affairs 71.
16   For development of this view, see L. Gostin, 'A civil liberties analysis of surro-
     gacy arrangements' (1988) 16 Law Med Hlth Care 7. A useful debate on these
     lines is to be found in S. Dodds and K. Jones, 'Surrogacy and autonomy' (1989)
     3 Bioethics 1, 35; L.M. Purdy, 'Surrogate mothering: exploitation or empower-
     ment?' (1989) 3 Bioethics 18, 40.
17   For other distinctions between prostitution and surrogacy – a false analogy
     which is frequently drawn – see A. van Niekerk and L. van Zyl, 'The ethics of
     surrogacy: women's reproductive labour' (1995) 21 J Med Ethics 345.
18   See the in-depth discussion by R. Macklin, 'Is there anything wrong with
     surrogate motherhood? An ethical analysis' (1988) 16 Law Med Hlth Care 57.
19   Or even a mother. See the views expressed in a newspaper article: D. Kennedy,
     'Surrogacy attempt by wife's mother divides experts' (1995) *The Times*, 3 July,
     p. 8. A still more recent example has been reported: S. McGinty, 'Surrogate
     mum gives birth to own grandchild' (1996) *The Sunday Times*, 8 December,
     p. 1.7. Interestingly, the 'surrogate' had passed her menopause.
20   *Re an adoption application (surrogacy)* [1987] 2 All ER 826. The distinction be-
     tween altruism and commercialism can, however, become blurred. See J. Brown
     'Ex-nun has been surrogate mother to five children' (1997 *The Scotsman*, 24
     May, p. 1.
21   For example, R. Lee and D. Morgan, 'Sterilization and mental handicap: Sap-
     ping the strength of the State?' (1988) 15 J Law & Soc 229.
22   W.J. Winslade, 'Surrogate mothers: Private right or public wrong?' (1981) 7 J
     Med Ethics 153. It has been pointed out that a similar result would probably be
     obtained were a matched sample of applications for a factory job to be ana-
     lysed: M. Freeman, 'Is surrogacy exploitative?', in S.A.M. McLean (ed.), *Legal
     Issues in Human Reproduction* (1989), Aldershot: Gower, ch. 7.
23   V.L. Payne, 'The regulation of surrogate motherhood' (1987) 17 Fam Law 178.
     The intense opposition to commercialism shown by the Supreme Court of New
     Jersey in *In re Baby M*, n. 65 below, is to be noted. See also Macklin, n. 18 above.
24   Human Fertilisation and Embryology Act 1990, s.30(7).
25   Adoption Act 1976, s.57; Adoption (Scotland) Act 1978, s.51.
26   Surrogacy Arrangements Act 1985, s.1A inserted by Human Fertilisation and
     Embryology Act 1990, s.36.
27   *A v. C* (1978) 8 Fam Law 170, reported more fully later as *A v. C* [1985] FLR 445.
     See D.C. Parker, 'Legal aspects of artificial insemination and embryo transfer'
     (1982) 12 Fam Law 103.
28   The courts should not be solely responsible for judgments that are determined
     only on the basis of morality or ethics: see LATEY J, n.20 above at 829.
29   Warnock Report, *Expression of dissent: A: Surrogacy* paras 5–6.
30   There have been at least two British cases demonstrating these problems. In
     one, the woman was thought to be acting as surrogate for two families simulta-
     neously and the police are considering a possible charge of obtaining money
     by deception: C. Dyer, 'Surrogate mother refuses to give up baby' (1997) 314
     Brit Med J 250. In the other, there were allegations that the surrogate had
     fabricated an abortion in order to keep the child: D. Kennedy, 'Minister hints at
     change in the law' (1997) *The Times*, 16 May, p. 2.
31   The somewhat unsavoury confrontation in the American case of *Malahoff* v.

Stiver was fought on just such a question (unreported, see L.B. Andrews, 'The stork market: The law of the new reproduction technologies' (1984) 70 Amer Bar Ass J 50).

32   Genesis, note 1 above, 16:5.

33   Five states are said to have passed statutes restricting commercialism: K.H. Rothenerg, 'Baby M, the surrogacy contract, and the health care professional: Unanswered questions' (1988) 16 Law Med Hlth Care 113. For a fuller analysis, see R.A. Charo, 'Legislative approaches to surrogate motherhood' (1988) 16 Law Med Hlth Care 96.

34   See Payne, n. 23 above.

35   For the supporting views of a practitioner in the field, see I. Craft, 'Surrogacy' (1992) 47 Brit J Hosp Med 728.

36   Compare, say, the Infertility (Medical Procedures) Act 1984, s.30(2)(c) (Victoria) which criminalises the surrogate mother for receiving payment or reward.

37   S. Sloman, 'Surrogacy Arrangements Act 1985' (1985) 135 NLJ 978.

38   The value of a non-profit-making coordinating organisation might be derived from the fact that a satisfactory outcome was reported in 55 out of 57 arranged surrogacies resulting in live births: Blyth, n. 5 above.

39   E. Page, 'Donation, surrogacy and adoption' (1985) 2 J Appl Philos 161 discussed by A. van Niekerk and L. van Zyl, 'Commercial surrogacy and the commodification of children: an ethical perspective' (1995) 14 Med Law 163.

40   See *Re an adoption application*, n. 20 above.

41   Later enacted in the Human Fertilisation and Embryology Act 1990, s.27. See D.B. Forrest, 'Legal rights of genetic mothers' (1990) *The Times*, 28 February, p. 15. The specific case was ultimately reported as *Re W (minors) (surrogacy)* [1991] 1 FLR 385.

42   That is, the father of the child by virtue of being the consenting husband or partner of a woman, the surrogate, who has been artificially inseminated (1990 Act, s.28).

43   In England and Wales, 'the court' is determined by the Children Act 1989, s.92(7) to (10) and Schedule 11, Part 1; the application is part of 'family proceedings'. In Scotland, 'the court' means the Court of Session or the Sheriff Court as determined by the child's domicile. In Northern Ireland, 'the court' means the High Court or the relevant county court.

44   Parental Orders (Human Fertilisation and Embryology) Regulations 1994 (S.I. 1994/2767); Parental Orders (Human Fertilisation and Embryology) (Scotland) Regulations 1994 (S.I. 1994/2804). For in-depth analysis of the Regulations, see A. Grubb, 'Surrogate arrangements and parental orders' (1995) 3 Med L Rev 204; K.McK. Norrie, 'The Parental Orders (Human Fertilisation and Embryology) (Scotland) Regulations 1994' 1995 Fam L B 13-3.

45   Likely to be altered to the whole of the child's life when the relevant sections of the Children Act 1989 are brought into force.

46   (1996) Times, 16 September.

47   Adoption Act 1976, s.16.

48   [1987] 2 All ER 826.

49   Now, Adoption Act 1976, s.57(3).

50   See C. Dyer, 'Babies in the courts' (1987) *The Times*, 13 March, p. 15.

51   [1996] 1 FLR 369.

52   Note 46 above.

53   The requirement to consider whether the making of a custody order would be more appropriate will be repealed when the Children (Scotland) Act 1995, Part III comes into force.

54   The early associated cases *Humphrys* v. *Polak* [1901] 2 KB 385 and *Kerrigan* v. *Hall* (1901) 4 F (Ct of Sess) 10 are now considered to be irrelevant.

55 *Re C (a minor)* [1985] 2 FLR 846.
56 [1987] 2 All ER 826,
57 [1987] 2 FLR 421.
58 The twins were six months old at the time. The mother was living on a social security allowance.
59 A further, uncontested case, has been reported, the main feature of which was that the judge was prepared to pre-empt the coming into force of s.30 and its associated regulations: *Re W (minors) (surrogacy)* [1991] 1 FLR 385.
60 See, now, Children Act 1989, s.1(1). Doubt has been expressed as to whether this section actually applies to surrogacy cases: J.G. Hogg, 'Surrogacy – nobody's child' [1991] Fam Law 276. The present writer is convinced that the courts would apply the section.
61 (1978) 8 Fam Law 170. See D.C. Parker, 'Legal aspects of artificial insemination and embryo transfer' (1982) 12 Fam Law 103.
62 Although Hogg, n. 60 above, questions whether the regulations are there for the benefit of the adults at the expense of that of the child.
63 Note 51 above.
64 See D. Morgan and R.G. Lee, *Blackstone's Guide to the Human Fertilisation and Embryology Act 1990* (1991), London: Blackstone Press, p. 155.
65 Per SORKOW J, *In re Baby M* 525 A 2d 1128 (NJ, 1987). See R.A. Charo, 'Legislative approaches to surrogate motherhood' (1989) 16 Law Med Hlth Care 96.
66 Arkansas Stat. Ann. 34-720-21 (Supp. 1985).
67 Michigan Comp. Laws Ann. 710.54 (1) (West Supp. 1985). Every state has comparable legislation, the differences being in the extent to which the prohibitions can be relaxed statutorily.
68 For example, California Penal Code 181 (West Supp. 1986).
69 See H. Brown, M. Dent, L.M. Dyer *et al.*, 'Legal rights and issues surrounding conception, pregnancy and birth' (1986) 39 Vand L Rev 597.
70 307 NW 2d 438 (Mich, 1981).
71 H.L. Hirsh, 'Surrogate motherhood' (1986) 5 Med Law 151.
72 *Surrogate Parenting Associates, Inc.* v. *Commonwealth of Kentucky ex rel David Armstrong* 704 SW 2d 209 (Ky, 1986).
73 But IVF in the Kentucky statute (KRS 199.590 amended 1984) is defined as being the same process as would be described here as ovum donation.
74 Note 65 above.
75 In the only known earlier case, reported by B. Cohen, 'Surrogate mothers; whose baby is it?' (1984) 10 Am J Law Med 243, such an outcome was thought to be so unlikely that the attorney for the adopting parents advised out of court settlement in favour of the surrogate. But there were, again, unusual features, not the least being that the adopting 'mother' was found to be a transsexual.
76 J.A. Robertson, 'Procreative liberty and the State's burden of proof in regulating noncoital reproduction' (1988) 16 Law Med Hlth Care 18.
77 537 A 2d 1227 (NJ, 1988).
78 For discussion, see R.P. Bezanson, 'Solomon would weep: a comment on *In the matter of Baby M* and the limits of judicial authority' (1988) 16 Law Med Hlth Care 126.
79 851 P 2d 776 (1993).
80 R.B. Oxman, 'California's experiment in surrogacy' (1993) 341 Lancet 1468.
81 A. Grubb, 'Surrogate contract: parentage' (1994) 2 Med L Rev 239.
82 A similar minority view was expressed by KENNARD J in the court's determinations.
83 *In re Marriage of Moschetta* (1994) 30 Cal Rptr 2d 893. The case is dicussed in detail by A. Grubb, 'Surrogate contract: parentage' (1995) 3 Med L Rev 219.
84 Surrogate Perenthood Act 1988 (Qd).

85 Embryonenschutzgesetz (Embryo Protection Act) 1990, s.1(1)(vii). Only the person who artificially inseminates the surrogate or who transfers an embryo to her womb is penalised with up to three years' imprisonment or an unspecified fine.

86 Which is, perhaps, only fair since it seems to have started there! – see n. 1 above.

87 Note 51 above.

88 R.H.B. Fishman, 'Surrogate motherhood becomes legal in Israel' (1996) 347 Lancet 756. The ban on standard surrogacy may result from the Jewish tradition that ethnicity is passed through the female line; equally, it may be a mechanism for controlling surrogacy by way of enforced embryo transfer.

89 For the United Kingdom, see Social Security Contributions and Benefits Act 1992, s.35; Employment Protection Act 1975, ss.34, 35.

90 Womb-leasing would, one feels, be preferable to surrogacy within the Jewish religion as 'Jewishness' is transmitted through the female line. But see Y. Ridley 'Surrogate triplets pose Jewish identity crisis' (1997) *The Sunday Times*, 8 June, p. 1.9.

91 R. Kennedy, 'Early triplets for surrogate grandmother' (1987) *The Times*, 2 October, p. 9. It is to be noted that this case arose just before the passing of the Children's Status Act 1987; it is not immediately clear what would be the position were the exercise to be repeated now. Similar 'grandparent' cases were reported in England in 1995 and 1996: see Kennedy and McGinty, n. 19 above.

92 R. Milliken, 'Woman conceives a problem' (1988) *The Independent*, 15 April, p. 12; see also *The Times*, 9 June (1988), p. 9.

93 But see Kennedy, n. 19 above, who reports that, while Baroness Warnock thought it a 'wonderful idea' to which she could see no moral objection, the fertility expert Professor Craft expressed doubts as to the arrangement – but this was largely on the basis of the gestational mother's age and the consequent risks to her.

94 Note 69 above.

95 British Medical Association, *Changing Conceptions of Motherhood – the Practice of Surrogacy in Britain* (1996), London: BMA.

96 D.R. Bromham, 'Surrogacy: the evolution of opinion' (1992) 47 Brit J Hosp Med 767. See the generally similar views expressed in the Ontario Law Reform Commission Report, *Report on Human Artificial Reproduction and Related Matters* (1985), Toronto: Queens' Printer; for discussion, see B. Knoppers and E. Sloss, 'Legislative reforms in reproductive technology' (1986) 18 Ottawa L Rev 663.

97 Infertility (Medical Procedures) Act 1984.

98 P. Singer and D. Wells, *The Reproductive Revolution* (1984), Oxford: Oxford University Press.

99 For the non-British reader: quasi-autonomous non-governmental authority.

11 Defective Neonates and Infants

The problem of the defective neonate provides an example of the cyclical nature of medical jurisprudence. When the first edition of this book appeared, selective non-treatment, including some practices which could only be described as neonaticide, was only just moving from centre stage in the theatre of medical ethics. As was remarked at the time, the rapidly evolving societal attitude to abortion, coupled with the introduction of increasingly sensitive and specific methods for intrauterine diagnosis of fetal abnormality, had reduced the number of infants born with defects very greatly. The importance of a correlative development of expertise in special infant care – and particularly in that of counselling and caring for affected parents – was also acknowledged. Since then, however, there have been a number of significant court decisions and it is now fair to say that the ground rules relating to the management of the defective neonate have been largely laid down and agreed by both the medical and legal professions. Selective non-treatment of the newborn[1] is, now, better considered under the general rubric of medical futility, a concept which has attracted much attention and, equally, debate during the last decade. It must not be forgotten, however, that not all defective babies are rejected by their parents; rather, it is everyday experience that many mothers will struggle to protect and improve the lot of their disabled children, often with astonishingly good results; any discussion of the treatment of defective newborns must be read with that important proviso in mind.

Disabled children continue to be born despite the rapid evolution of sophisticated antenatal genetic care. There are several reasons why this is so. Apart from the obvious fact that many mothers will wish to continue their pregnancy irrespective of the intrauterine diagnosis and prognosis, we have seen that not all pregnancies can be screened for all fetal defects as a routine; some chromosomal abnormalities occur in the children of young women who would be excluded from most screening programmes, and the occurrence of much

281

congenital disease, whether it be multifactorial or wholly environmental in origin, is capricious. Such congenital disease may be anatomical in nature: congenital heart disease and neural tube defects
are, perhaps, the best examples; it may be physiological: cystic fibrosis
and other precisely defined inborn areas of metabolism, including
phenylketonuria, spring to mind; it may be purely mental, which is a
feature of many chromosomal diseases, including the Fragile-X syndrome; and, of course, any of these may appear in combination. It
would be unrealistic not to admit that many defective children unwittingly impose a very serious burden on their families;[2] it is equally
sadly true that they may sap the human and economic resources of
paediatric intensive care units; and, finally, the results of treatment
may be to the apparent disadvantage of the child itself. The stark
issue is, therefore, whether such infants should be treated at all or
whether non-interference with nature is the best course for all concerned and, in particular, is in the best interests of the child. It is a
dilemma which is epitomised in the reported opinion of Professor
Campbell in 1988: 'There must be limits to intensive care if it is not to
become a new and potentially cruel form of child abuse. The decision
that an infant would be better off dead is an awesome one but one
that sometimes must be taken.'[13] In short, can such treatment be an
extreme example of futile treatment which it is wrong to provide on
both professional and ethical grounds?

The concept of medical futility

The right of the mature adult to refuse treatment is now well established, certainly in all anglophone jurisdictions. In equity, the same
right should attach to children but, within the age group with which
we are here concerned, it is clear that the patient is unable to effect a
choice.[4] Choice must, therefore, be made on the infant's behalf, the
alternative surrogates being either his or her parents assisted by their
medical advisers or the courts, who will, again, have to rely heavily
on medical opinion as to the best course of action. Thus, while such
medical opinion may not be determinative in this type of case, it
always plays a large, and probably major, role in decision making. I
suggest that this is as it should be in the case of the neonate. In the
vast majority of cases, the parents will have little or no idea of what
the future holds. They have no yardstick by which to judge the
child's quality of life which, in the circumstances envisaged, is unlikely to improve. It is only the neonatologist who can base his or her
prognosis on experience, and only the neonatologists know their
limitations. In many instances, they will appreciate that they cannot
make the patient 'better', even when this is interpreted as doing no

more than improve the child's physical status. The experienced doctor can identify futile *treatment* – that is, treatment which is not even palliative – and it is right that he should do so, and be able to withdraw further therapy when this becomes his only option.[5] It will be seen later that, since the seminal cases decided in 1981,[6] significant case law has been virtually limited to treatment or non-treatment of the infant rather than the neonate. It is suggested that, in these circumstances, the parents *have* had time to identify a benchmark and disagreements with the doctors are more likely. It is not that fewer treatment decisions are taken in respect of neonates but, rather, that they provoke far fewer arguments for the courts to settle. It follows that the ratios of judicial decisions taken in infancy can be applied with equal or greater force in the neonatal period.

The evolution of the concept

The possibility that heroic treatment of the physically defective neonate may be ill-conceived has been apparent for many years and focuses attention squarely on the problem of whether the doctor's function is to preserve life at all costs or to provide an acceptable quality of life. Almost a quarter of a century ago, we read in the *British Medical Journal*: 'The whole resources of an advanced medical service are currently deployed in the pursuit of the preservation of life. It is becoming obvious that the costs of this policy are becoming insupportable ... We must face an inescapable duty to let some patients die.'[7]

That, however, introduces a resource-based view and, if accepted, could lead the physician down a thorny path. Certainly, the allocation of scarce resources has to be considered in making treatment decisions, but it must be a secondary, rather than a basic, consideration to the clinician at the bedside. The doctor's primary concern is the welfare of the individual patient and selective treatment decisions should be made either within the framework of the 'patient's best interests' or by way of a 'substituted judgment' on behalf of the patient (see p. 299 for further discussion of the distinction). This particular aspect of paediatric medicine was first addressed by Lorber who, up to 1975, was undertaking a campaign which involved aggressive surgical treatment of cases of spina bifida.[8] A few years later, a follow-up of his work revealed such a poor quality of painful life for many of the treated children that he had greatly altered his attitude and was now advocating inactivity and non-treatment in many cases *in the interests of* the individual sufferers.[9] A similar management philosophy developed in America on much the same lines.[10]

It has been pointed out[11] that it was not so much the policy which was new but, rather, its open admission by institutions and clinicians of the highest repute; there was minimal antagonistic reaction within the rank and file of the medical profession – in fact, there was general approval. Thus, in the trial of Dr Arthur, which will be discussed more fully later, we have Dr Dunn, an expert witness, saying: 'No paediatrician takes life but we accept that allowing babies to die is in the baby's interest at times.'[12] This, then, does seem to be an area which provides a classic example of the law following, rather than moulding, public opinion when pragmatic considerations indicate that this should be so. The law on homicide by neglect has, in general, depended upon some clear, albeit antique, principles which are based on the duty of care owed to the victim of neglect. To kill a living human person intentionally is murder and, except in relation to the specific crime of infanticide (for which, see Chapter 14), the age of the victim is of no consequence. The law, however, sees an important difference between killing by positive action and killing by omission, a distinction which is of major importance in the current debate on euthanasia.[13] It is widely agreed and, indeed, it was acknowledged in *Bland*,[14] that such a distinction is morally indefensible when the primary aim in either case is the death of the subject.[15] Nevertheless, killing by omission would normally be charged only as manslaughter or as culpable homicide;[16] murder would not be charged unless there was a duty of care to the victim and the quality of that duty was extensive.[17]

And therein lies the paradox. It is hard, if not impossible, to maintain that the physician in charge of the paediatric intensive care unit does not have a special duty of care towards his neonatal patients which obliges him or her to ensure that their deaths are not due to an omission to treat. Yet it has been reported that anything up to 30 per cent of deaths in neonatal intensive care units follow the deliberate withdrawal of life support;[18] more recent analyses indicate that this may be an underestimate in the United Kingdom but, also, that similar patterns of neonatal death are to be found worldwide.[19]

Increasingly, attempts are being made to base such treatment decisions on the concept of medical futility.[20] This, however, is not as simple as appears at first sight. While it may well be true that few interventions have *no* chance of success,[21] it is reasonable to suppose that a competent doctor is able to discern when no therapeutic regime can improve the condition of his or her patient or, indeed, when the continuation of treatment in progress is doing no more than to prolong a well-nigh intolerable existence and can properly be withdrawn. This is a matter of applying clinical acumen to the individual case and there seems little need to attempt to lay down generalised criteria by way, say, of mathematical formulae[22] – the neonatologist is, again, generally capable of appreciating when the probability of treatment being useful to the individual patient approaches zero. Having said which, however, it is clear that we cannot eliminate subjectivity entirely: one man's futility can be another man's desperate endeavour. It has also been suggested that futility is not only a word which is foreign to the families of defective neonates but it is one which is unacceptable by reason of its hopelessness;[23] as a consequence, it may be that invoking the essentially medical device of futility militates against the open and frank dialogue that is essential to reaching a treatment decision that is acceptable to all parties[24] or, in other words, to achieving the proper societal response. Although I believe that the, now, universally approved practice of involving the whole health care team in non-treatment decisions in respect of defective neonates provides adequate insurance against the potential abuse of professional power,[25] it is apparent that the concept of 'futility', even if defined in purely medical terms, should not be elevated to the status of an ethical panacea. Nonetheless, it can serve as a useful benchmark when applied with circumspection and has been described as 'a psychologically tolerable way of speaking about the most difficult end of life decisions within families and our community'.[26] Perhaps most importantly, it serves to distinguish the caring doctor from the neglectful carer and, in doing so, resolves the legal difficulty, discussed above, which has evolved over the years, for it cannot be neglect to fail to establish or to withdraw treatment that is futile.

Thus it is important to re-emphasise that the principle at stake is that of *medical* futility. The decision being made relates to the medical treatment of the individual patient and it is that which is being suggested as lying easily within the province of the medical practitioner. There may well be other factors – such as the religious tenets of a child's parents – which may affect the ultimate decision but which are unrelated to the efficiency of treatment; the physician has no right to pontificate on these. I am not even persuaded that resource-based considerations form part of the spectrum of futility as defined here: these are for the macro-allocator, not for the doctor at the bedside. But the limitation of the concept of futility in this way presupposes that the condition is one for which there is, at least, a plausible line of therapy. It was a failure to appreciate this that led to a storm of protest at the prosecution of Dr Arthur for attempted murder in 1981 and, although *R* v. *Arthur*[27] has now lost any claim to being a useful precedent, it is worth a brief recapitulation for that reason alone.

The case of Dr Arthur

A vast literature was built on the *Arthur* case at the time it was heard; it has been said that there are surprisingly few substantive issues in medical ethics that it does not raise.[28] It polarised the medical profession into those who regarded the outcome as a vindication of medical autonomy in patient care[29] and those who saw it as being, at best, irrelevant.[30] The background circumstances were that an infant born with undiagnosed and apparently uncomplicated Down's syndrome was rejected by his parents. Dr Arthur concurred in this decision and wrote in the case notes: 'Parents do not wish it to survive. Nursing care only.' This instruction was understood to include non-feeding[31] and, additionally, large doses of dihydrocodeine were prescribed in order to assuage hunger pain and discomfort. The infant died at the age of 69 hours, the cause of death being certified by the coroner as 'multilobular pneumonia due to lung stasis due to dihydrocodeine poisoning in an infant with Down's syndrome'; it is to be noted that this diagnosis was reached following an intensive investigation by a forensic and a paediatric pathologist working as a team. Dr Arthur was indicted for murder but, during the course of the trial, new evidence from the paediatric pathologist was produced which indicated that the infant had not been physically healthy. The charge was reduced to one of attempted murder and the jury found Dr Arthur not guilty.

Dr Arthur was certainly not lacking powerful support for his action. We have already noted Dr Dunn (see at p. 284). In addition we have the President of the Royal College of Physicians:

> Where there is an uncomplicated Down's case and the parents do not want the child to live ... I think there are circumstances where it would be ethical to put it upon a course of management that would end in its death ... I say that with a child suffering from Down's and with a parental wish that it should not survive, it is ethical to terminate life.[32]

And the judge himself, in his charge to the jury, said, 'I imagine that you will think long and hard before deciding that doctors of the eminence we have heard ... have evolved standards which amount to committing crime.'[33] The central question raised by the case is, therefore, why, in the light of the acknowledged developments in neonatal intensive care, was Dr Arthur singled out for prosecution?

Although there is no certainty as to the motivation of the prosecuting authorities, the most logical answer lies in the 'treatability' test. Dr Arthur's patient was in no physical pain and, so far as was known at the time, required no treatment; death, it was assumed, depended upon the withholding of nourishment and of treatment for intercurrent infection. To take away such a life is to make a social, not a medical, decision – and the fact that it is taken by a doctor should have the same relevance as in the case of any member of the public;

the logic of this conclusion is immediately apparent if one transfers the decision not to feed from the hospital to the home birth situation.[34] Any confusion as to the doctor's role is dispersed once it is appreciated that there is a fundamental distinction to be drawn between physical and mental defect. The condition of the infant with, say, severe spina bifida can be assessed in the light of our own previous experience. By contrast, there is no way in which any of us can say that the life of a Down's syndrome baby is intolerable because we have no way of knowing the sensibilities of one who has been mentally handicapped since birth. Thus we have the Canadian judge, MCKENZIE J, stating:

> It is not appropriate for an external decision-maker to apply his standards of what constitutes a liveable life and exercise the right to impose death if that standard is not met in his estimation. The decision can only be made in the context of the disabled person viewing the worthwhileness or otherwise of his life in its own context as a disabled person – and in that context he would not compare his life with that of a person enjoying normal advantages. He would know nothing of a normal person's life, having never experienced it[35]

and nowhere is this more apparent than in the case of congenital mental disability.

There is little doubt that some commentators failed to appreciate this distinction in the wake of Dr Arthur's trial. In one leading article,[36] the *British Medical Journal* applauded the fact that the LIFE campaigners had lost a round in their attack on selective treatment for handicapped neonates and considered that doctors should not be deflected by Dr Arthur's experience – a statement which, in context, is meaningless in that there is *no* treatment for the mental disability of Down's syndrome. On my analysis, Dr Arthur's prosecution was logical and correct, except that the case might have been saved as a precedent had the charge been reduced, at least, to one of manslaughter; as it is, *R v. Arthur* demonstrates little more than the reluctance of a British jury to convict a doctor of attempted murder when he appears to be acting in ill-judged rather than bad faith.[37]

Futility in practice

It is clear that the great majority of decisions involving the treatment of defective neonates or young children are currently taken in private following agreement between the health caring staff and parents. Agreement may, however, be impossible and, whether it is because of the increasing attention being paid to the concept of medical futility or whether it is a matter of chance, there has recently been a spate of cases coming to court which illustrate the principles and the problems involved. It is proposed to consider a selection of these briefly.[38]

The anencephalic baby

Baby K was born in Virginia, USA with a rudimentary brain in which only the brain-stem could be said to be functioning. Consequently, she had no cerebral awareness but was able to breathe – subject to mechanical support during periods of respiratory collapse – and was fed through a gastrostomy tube. The majority of such infants die within a matter of days; Baby K survived, however, because she had been aggressively treated from birth. A conflict arose between the hospital and the child's mother. The former adopted the position that there was no obligation to provide respiratory support or other emergency medical care in the event of cardiorespiratory failure; this was on the grounds that such treatment was futile, insofar as it could not cure the anencephaly, and was medically and ethically inappropriate. The hospital also maintained that the determination of medical futility was a matter of medical judgment. The child's mother, by contrast, claimed that all life had value, no matter how limited that life was, and that God, not humans, should determine the time of death – in this case, by rendering mechanical ventilation ineffective; she also maintained that it was she, as the child's sole guardian, who had the right to decide what medical treatment was in K's best interests.[39]

From a British point of view, it is unfortunate that the case was taken through the federal courts and was, therefore, concerned largely with statutory interpretation.[40] Even so, the fact that the mother was supported at first instance and that this was confirmed on appeal came as something of a shock – and, despite the intervention of the court, Baby K died at the age of two and a half years. The case, however, raises a number of general questions, the majority of which must remain unanswered in a book of this scope.

Primarily, we have to ask to what extent must, or should, the interests of the child be subordinated to those of its parents? If we are to deny the parents the right to impose the negative religious beliefs of, say, Jehovah's Witnesses on their children (see p. 328), should we support their positive efforts to inflict what we believe to be pointless treatment in the name of religion – a question which brings us back to the definition of futility. Very few would dispute the *medical* futility of rescuing an anencephalic neonate from an episodic and potentially fatal respiratory collapse; it is, perhaps, the classic example of what has been called 'physiologic futility'.[41] The position

becomes far less clear-cut if we extend our definition of *utility* to
include the societal advantages deriving from a family's peace of mind.
This, in turn, leads us to consider the right to medical treatment: does
such a right exist and, if it does, what is its extent?[42] It has been said
that a patient's right to choose or refuse treatment is limited by the
physician's right (and duty) to practise medicine responsibly.[43] This
has the ring of a contractual, fee-paying relationship between patient
and doctor but, even within that ambience, we are still left with the
question of whether or not it is responsible medicine to take into
consideration the psychiatric trauma sustained by the parents in
such a situation. Given that this may be alleviated by continued
treatment of their child, is such treatment still to be regarded as
'futile'? It seems clear that the morality of continuation would depend upon its effect on the child. It would obviously be unethical if
there were any question of maleficence by way of extended pain or
other suffering. If, however, it could make no difference to the primary patient – as, say, to one in the anencephalic state – it might well
be possible to defend such a regime on utilitarian principles.

But what if the doctor is, effectively, a state employee, as in a
National Health Service? What, then, is the extent of the *state's obligation* to provide treatment? Clearly, this cannot be infinite but, as has
been suggested already, the limits are to be set at a political level
rather than at the bedside.

In re T (a Minor) (Wardship: Medical Treatment)[44]

The circumstances surrounding the English case of Baby T were
almost the exact opposite of those concerning the American Baby K.
Here, the child was born with biliary atresia, a condition likely to be
fatal within two and a half years in the absence of transplantation
therapy. Remedial surgery at the age of three and a half weeks resulted in no improvement, but medical opinion was unanimous in
holding that the chances of a successful transplant operation were
still good and that it was in T's best interests to undergo the operation once a suitable donor was discovered. The parents, however,
who were described as health care professionals, refused their consent. The case arose under the Children Act 1989, s.100(3) as a specific issue in respect of which the court was asked to exercise its
inherent jurisdiction; the judge at first instance found that the conduct of the parents was not that of reasonable parents and concluded
that he should override their decision and give his consent to the
operation.

When the case went to appeal, however, BUTLER-SLOSS LJ firmly
adopted the established British welfare standard and criticised the
trial judgment in that it failed to take account of the relevance of the

mother's objections in the final 'balancing exercise' (see p. 303 for further consideration of this principle). These included her deep concern as to the benefits to her son of the major invasive surgery and post-operative treatment, the dangers of long-term as well as short-term failure, the possibility of the need for further transplants, the likely length of life and the effect of all these concerns upon her son. The mother would inevitably be the primary carer through many years of continuing treatment while she believed that this course was not right for her son; the decision of the court passing back the responsibility for the parental care to the mother and expecting her to provide the necessary commitment to the child after the operation was carried out in the face of her opposition was thought to be, in itself, fraught with danger to the child. Accordingly, the Court of Appeal would not give consent to the transplant operation and preferred to leave the future treatment of the child in the hands of his devoted parents.

There are several reasons for criticising this decision, which may yet be appealed to the House of Lords, and some of these are alluded to later.[45] It is also possible to argue that this is not a case in which the principles of futility apply. Nonetheless, it does seem that the Court of Appeal, in preferring certain death to possible long-term survival, was, effectively, accepting the view of the parents that transplant therapy was futile in the prevailing circumstances. That being the case, the concept of futility was certainly not based on physiological grounds but, rather, was almost entirely a matter of social or societal reasoning. As such, it represents a significant jurisprudential advance on the purely medical considerations which have been advocated above. In point of fact, the decision seems to me to be based on doubtful premises. There are few fields in which technical advances are as rapid as they are in that of organ transplantation; I suggest that this is an instance in which the gain of a few more years of life might well have allowed time for research which could have revolutionised the quality of life and the prognosis of the infant T. This chance was noted in the judgment of ROCH LJ but was not placed in the judicial balance pan. On the other hand, it has to be admitted that many would see *Re T* as being a breakthrough case, in that it is the first court-ordered treatment decision at the level of appeal which has flatly rejected the prevailing medical consensus.

The case of Child B

The case of child B[46] provides an example of the not infrequent confusion of the problems of resource allocation with the principle of medical futility. It may be seen as lying beyond the title of this chapter insofar as the child concerned was aged 10 years at the time of the court hearing. Nonetheless, child B had been suffering from lymphoma since the age of five and the case illustrates concerns which are spread generally across the period of early childhood. Briefly, by the time of the action, B had already received two courses of chemotherapy, had undergone whole body irradiation and had received a bone marrow transplant before she suffered a further relapse. At this point, her medical carers considered that no further treatment could usefully be administered and estimated that she had a life expectancy of some six to eight weeks. Meantime, the child's father had obtained a second opinion which estimated her chances of going into remission following a third course of chemotherapy as between 10 and 20 per cent, with a similar chance of surviving a second bone marrow transplant consequent upon the success of that chemotherapy. He sought to secure funding for such treatment but the health authority, taking into account the judgment of their own clinicians, the nature of the treatment and its chances of success, declined. The father sought judicial review of the authority's decision.

In the High Court, LAWS J began his speech with the words: 'Of all human rights, most people would accord the most precious place to the right to life itself.' Inevitably, one has to question the logic of this approach. Can there be a right to life, given the fact that we must all die at some point? We cannot even say that there is an actuarial right to a given number of years of life for any such figure must, itself, depend upon a variable life expectancy. Surely, the most that can be said is that there is a right not to have one's life taken away,[47] but this can have no application in a medical setting once it is agreed that no treatment is available other than futile treatment; or, in welfare language, treatment that is contrary to the best interests of the patient. LAWS J, however, went further in regarding such a 'right to life' as being one which a public body could not infringe unless it could show a substantial objective justification on public interest grounds for so doing (at BMLR 14) and, in his view, the fact that the authority considered, on *medical grounds*, that the proposed treatment would be contrary to B's best interests did not satisfy this requirement: it failed to take into consideration the *family's* perception of her interests. The authority had, however, also submitted that the substantial expenditure on treatment with such a small prospect of success would not be an effective use of its limited resources, bearing in mind the present and future needs of other patients. To which LAWS J replied: 'where the question is whether the life of a 10-year-old child might be saved, by however slim a chance, the responsible authority must in my judgment do more than toll the bell of tight resources'. The authority had not adequately explained the priorities that had led it to decline to fund the treatment and its decision had to be retaken in the light of the court's judgment.

The Court of Appeal found, in summary, that the judge's criticism of the authority's action failed to recognise the realities of the situation. The court, per SIR THOMAS BINGHAM MR, further considered that it was reasonable to regard the proposed course of treatment as 'experimental' and, therefore, one that could properly be excluded from funding. The Master of the Rolls' further comments on funding bear repetition:

> I have no doubt that in a perfect world any treatment which a patient, or a patient's family, sought would be provided if doctors were willing to give it, no matter how much it cost, particularly when a life was potentially at stake. It would, however, in my view, be shutting one's eyes to the real world if the court were to proceed on the basis that we do live in such a world. ... Difficult and agonising judgments have to be made as to how a limited budget is best allocated ... This is not a judgment which the court can make. (at BMLR 8–9)

He went on to dissociate himself formally from the view that it would be hard to imagine a proper basis upon which the treatment could reasonably be withheld. The appeal was allowed unanimously.

The twin cases of *ex parte B* and *Re T* raise further doubts as to the precise position of the family in treatment decisions concerning infants. The significance to be attached to family preferences was at issue in both but, whereas a lack of adequate consideration was criticised at first instance but dismissed on appeal in the former, the omission to consult was founded upon in the Court of Appeal in the latter. Admittedly, the pressures from the families in the two cases were directed to different ends – the one to continuing and the other to concluding treatment – but the principles determining parental influence should still be the same. An appeal to the House of Lords in the case of *Re T* would be helpful if it did no more than establish the guidelines. As to the case of child B, there is no doubt that the arguments were complicated by the necessary linkage of clinical and financial considerations. No matter how one plays with statistics, it is difficult to see her continued treatment as being other than medically futile or experimental and it is unfortunate that the matter could not have been resolved on clinical grounds; the authority's liability for extracontractual funding, however, dictated its two-pronged argument which was, in the end, the cause of so much emotion. A final and, perhaps, marginal comment on *ex parte B* might well relate to the influence of the media in such cases. An in-depth study of the newspaper commentaries at the time[48] makes sorry reading. There may be several ways of debating treatment decisions and resource allocation, but 'shroud-waving' in the tabloid press is not the best of them. Child B was treated by way of combined public and private funding; she died 14 months after the hearing. We are, thus, still left with the question of whether the gain of a year's life as an invalid negates the concept of medical futility.

The moral ambience

It would be idle to deny that many fear the extrapolation of current attitudes to abortion to the field of neonaticide; as it was put many years ago by an American writer: 'It might be noted that most of the factors [concerning the right to privacy and the decision whether or not to terminate a pregnancy] also apply to the inconvenience of having an unwanted two-year-old ... around';[49] and, in this connection, we should remember that the so-called 'eugenic clause' to the Abortion Act 1967, s.1(1)(d), which allows for abortion on the grounds of a substantial risk that the fetus will be born defective, is clearly there for the benefit of the mother rather than that of the fetus. It is not difficult to foresee treatment decisions in respect of defective neonates being based on the interests of the mother, and there are shades of this to be found in the case of *Re T*.[50] There BUTLER-SLOSS LJ held that 'This mother and this child are one for the purpose of this unusual case and the decision of the court to consent to the operation jointly affects the mother and son and it also affects the father' (at 914); and, later: 'The prospect of forcing the devoted mother of this young baby to the consequences of this major invasive surgery lead[s] me to the conclusion, after much anxious deliberation, that it is not in the best interests of this child to give consent' (at 916) – a confusion of interests which certainly provides food for thought.

On much the same lines, a disturbingly convincing case can be made out on clinical grounds that selective neonaticide, in which the state of the infant can be seen and physically appraised, is a scientifically more acceptable way of eliminating congenital disease than is abortion, in which a decision depends, to an extent, on probabilities. Yet such a suggestion would be regarded almost universally as abhorrent. One's natural revulsion depends upon the belief that fetal rights increase with gestational age, which, when coupled with the legal protection afforded to the infant at birth, should provide sufficient grounds for making a clear moral distinction between abortion and neonaticide. The apparent certainty of this conclusion is, however, breached by the insidious encroachment of the philosophical concept of 'personhood'.

This approach to human values evolves from the early philosophy of Locke, but seems to have been introduced into medical ethics by Joseph Fletcher,[51] who proposed that, since aborting a defective fetus was effectively ending sub-human life, it was logically justifiable to apply the same reasoning to the newborn infant who was on the same level, in value and dignity, as the fetus. This philosophy was totally utilitarian: it was said that only the end makes sense of what we do. The argument was developed at about the same time with equal force by Tooley,[52] who stipulated five requirements for being a 'person' with a serious right to life which related mainly to self and self-consciousness: to have a right to life depends upon having desires to exercise that right and on an ability to envisage a future for oneself. It followed, therefore, that infanticide[53] during a time interval shortly after birth – which was left undefined – should be regarded as being morally acceptable. Glover[54] developed the argument on the lines that contraception, abortion and infanticide all reduce the amount of worthwhile life and are, accordingly, on the same level; since it cannot be said that very young babies have a desire to go on living rather than to die, it is not possible to sustain the argument that killing the infant overrides its autonomy. The more recent proponents of this school of thought include Kuhse and Singer:[55] 'the difference between [abortion] and infanticide is that abortion kills the unseen foetus in the womb while infanticide kills the newborn infant. In neither case, however, has the life of the *person* begun' (at p. 136 (1985)). And, again: 'To allow infanticide before the onset of self-awareness cannot threaten anyone who is in a position to worry about it ... Infanticide threatens none of us, for once we are aware of it, we are not infants' (at p. 138). It follows that, once the concept of 'personhood' is accepted, both the fetus and the neonate are in great and, perhaps, equal danger; although those who promote it all agree that a distinction can be made between a worthwhile life and a defective life, the arguments apply to *all* infants and children – particularly, it would seem, to the mentally handicapped child.

There are, of course, those who oppose the position. At the practical level, John Fletcher[56] distinguished between abortion and neonaticide on the grounds that the newborn is independent and has rights as a patient, that it is clearly amenable to treatment in its own right and, finally, that parental acceptance of an infant as a real person is far more developed than in the case of the fetus.[57] Others, of whom Ramsey[58] was probably the foremost example, have argued from a religious position and point, rather, to the continuum of existence from conception; personhood derives from the gift of life in the image of God. On this view, all human life is of equal value; infanticide is wrong and abortion is equally wrong. The middle ground is expressed by those such as Keyserlingk. It is comforting to read his riposte to Kuhse and Singer: '"Infanticide threatens none of us" ... Perhaps not – but it sure as hell threatens those infants!'[59] Long[60] reached the unhappy conclusion that the triumph – if there is to be one – of the Kuhse/Singer view must await merely the individual disappearance of people who think like Ramsey. The same process of attrition also threatens the medical profession; the time has now arrived when there are virtually no practising doctors who have not been trained to regard widespread abortion as a natural part of medical practice. The medical criteria for ethical neonaticide must, therefore, continue to be closely examined.

Medical indicators

It has been agreed for many years that some infants are born who would die without surgical intervention and who, in the context of pain and suffering, are better left in that situation.[61] But even such an apparently innocuous statement is open to argument. On the one hand, we have the view: 'I believe that anything, including feeding, that prolongs this nonhuman or artificial life [of the severely brain damaged child] is wrong for the child, wrong for the family and wrong for society.'[62] By contrast: 'I always found it difficult to interpret the idea that death can be in someone's best interests ... Since death will terminate his or her existence, how can one speak of there being any interest, positive or negative, arising from death?'[63]

These quotations epitomise two of the major problems which must be faced by paediatricians. The first is the near impossibility of defining the line which divides the infant who should be treated with all determination from the child who should be left to die in peace; effectively, there is no watershed telling us when an infant becomes a candidate for non-treatment and there is no consensus as to what are the conditions which make life worse than death.[64] This is, perhaps, inevitable in medicine which is practised within many and varied cultures in which each patient presents as a distinct and separate problem. Even so, it is generally desirable to have some guidelines for reference when decisions of this importance are to be taken. American commentators have defined the severely defective newborn as one who is not likely to survive without surgical and medical intervention and where the prognosis, even assuming this intervention, may be poor in terms of cognitive life and minimal functioning.[65] This, however, is of little help at the lower end of the scale of severity. The United States Child Abuse Prevention and Treatment Act 1974 Amendments of 1984 are more precise. Under these, withholding treatment is not considered to be medical neglect:

a) When the infant is chronically and irreversibly comatose;
b) When the treatment would:
   i) merely prolong dying;
   ii) not be effective in ameliorating or correcting all of the infant's life-threatening condition; or

> iii)   otherwise be futile in terms of survival of the infant;
>
> c)   [When] the treatment would be virtually futile in terms of the survival of the infant and the treatment itself under the circumstances would be inhumane.

'Inhumane' in this context is taken to mean that the treatment itself involves significant contraindications and/or significant pain and suffering for an infant highly unlikely to survive.[66] The use of the concept of futility more than a decade ago is interesting.

These regulations were drawn up at the time when selective non-treatment of neonates was the major ethical concern in medical practice. More recent guidelines have been drawn up in the form of a report by the Dutch Paediatric Association in the light of experience;[67] they merit particular attention as they may well form the template on which European Community policy is founded. Essentially, in putting the case for discontinuation of life-prolonging treatment, the report distinguishes between those infants who have no chance of survival – in which case the medical decision to withhold treatment should be taken – and those for whom treatment offers a prospect of survival but for whom there are doubts as to the quality of future life. Here the report concludes that the choice between life and death belongs to the area of responsibility of the paediatrician but, at the same time, decision making is much more difficult and is not confined to the medical profession. It is, however, only in cases where a very bad prognosis is reasonably certain that there is any debate about medical actions which prolong life. The problem, thus, remains as to how such 'reasonable' certainty is to be achieved. It is suggested that the prognosis should be evaluated in functional terms and the following questions must be asked:

a   What communicative abilities will the child have later?
b   Will the child be able to lead an independent life?
c   Will the child be continuously dependent on medical facilities?
d   Will the child suffer either mentally or physically?
e   How long is the life expectancy?

The next step is to measure the information gained against the abilities of the family to bear the burden; this can succeed only when the parents receive adequate counselling and the choice is a combined one. The report then goes on to analyse the choices available in the event of, say, severe cerebral damage. These are considered to be as follows.

a   Continue maximal intensive care and extend it if necessary. This option will be chosen when there is a good prognosis.

b Maintain the status quo – an indecisive option which is accept-able only as a temporary measure.
c Stop intensive forms of treatment – probably the best choice if it leads directly to the death of a neonate with anticipated severe handicap.
d Stop all life-prolonging measures and, if suffering occurs, give medication which will soften or even hasten death.

This last option is exemplified by the neonate who is treated in accordance with option (c), but who could, nevertheless, survive if provided with non-intensive care. It clearly allows for active, non-voluntary euthanasia, a concept which can be extended to the sev-erely handicapped neonate who survives in the absence of *any* supportive therapy. This policy is unacceptable even to a proportion of Dutch paediatricians, a fact which emphasises the near impossibil-ity of reaching a consensus in an area which is dominated by indi-vidual intuitive ethics. It would certainly be unlawful in the United Kingdom[68] and the uncertainty of the law in Holland[69] would, it is suggested, make it a difficult option even in that country: it is re-ported that a Dutch doctor who killed a three-day-old neonate with the consent of her parents was convicted of murder, the conviction being quashed only following appeal.[70]

It is dangerous to criticise a report which has been seen only in summary form. It seems, however, that Dr Arthur's regime would be subsumed within the Dutch protocol and, for the reasons already given, this cannot be acceptable. Perhaps of greater practical import-ance, the Dutch guidelines unambiguously incorporate the principle of decision making based on the anticipated quality of life of the infant and it is this which has distanced the paediatricians from many lawyers and politicians. Whether or not a similar trend is to be found in the recent relevant British cases is discussed below.

In general, all attempts to define the ethical cut-off point for with-holding or withdrawing neonatal treatment imply the need for a prognosis of very considerable disability before doing so and this indicates a strong inclination to err on the side of treatment when there is any doubt.[71] But this presupposes that it is possible to make a firm prognosis and this is, unfortunately, not always the case, par-ticularly when it is the degree of brain damage that is under consid-eration. Thus, in his very honest analysis of his results, Whitelaw[72] stated that he would not have recommended treatment in many of the defective infants which were salvaged, had he been able to pre-dict their future accurately. Moreover, the prognostic dilemmas of the very low birthweight infant still have to be addressed. On the one hand, we have the admittedly debatable statement that it is no longer acceptable to determine treatment on the basis of gestational age or birthweight,[73] and that all infants should be afforded special care; on the other, it is reported that 12 per cent of infants weighing between 500g. and 1kg. who are resuscitated and survive will remain with severe handicap.[74] This also, of course, means that 88 per cent will enjoy relatively normal lives, but it is almost impossible to forecast which infants will fall on which side of the line. A case involving such a decision has, in fact, come before the Scottish Sheriff Court.[75]

The second major obstacle to a valid assessment of the future quality of life relates specifically to those infants with mental disability, a matter which we have already touched on in relation to Dr Arthur (p. 286). The practical difficulty rests on the obvious fact that an assessment of the quality of life must be made by adult surrogates of normal mental development. A decision to end such a child's life would be based on social, not medical, criteria. – and there is the clear possibility that the child's interests might be measured in terms of the interests of its attendants. The mentally handicapped infant with additional physical defects does, however, present a special problem; at this point, it need only be said that the great majority of commentators take the view that treatment which would be given ordinarily to a mentally normal infant should not be denied to another simply because he or she is likely to be mentally handicapped.[76] The view of what constitutes ordinary treatment might, however, be modified in the latter circumstances.

The concept of the ordinary/extraordinary treatment test is often misunderstood. It is *not* a measure of the novelty or complexity of any given therapy: to discuss whether or not, say, chemotherapy *per se* is ordinary or extraordinary treatment is completely to misinterpret its meaning. The idea derives from the words of Pope Pius XII in 1957:[77]

> Man has a right and duty in case of severe illness to take the necessary steps to preserve life and health. That duty ... devolves from charity as ordained by the Creator, from social justice and even from strict law. But he is obliged at all times to employ only ordinary means ... that is to say those means which do not impose an extraordinary burden on himself or others.

It is thus clear that the measure of extraordinariness is a measure of the burden the treatment will impose particularly, but certainly not entirely, on the patient himself or herself. It is an individual test and this was accentuated by His Holiness when he qualified the distinction as being 'according to personal circumstances, the law, the times and the culture'. The principle has been accepted widely in medical circles and has even been accorded a quasi-legal authority. Its application is particularly well illustrated in the Canadian case of *Dawson*, which we have already mentioned.[78]

The case concerned the treatment of a hydrocephalic child whose shunt required replacement. The parents believed that their child had suffered sufficiently and refused permission for the operation; the matter was remitted to the courts for adjudication. The evidence presented to the Provincial Court was to the effect that the child was in a vegetative state from which there was no prospect of relief, even with treatment. Replacement surgery was, therefore, considered to be extraordinary treatment which, it was held, the parents were entitled to refuse. For administrative reasons, the Supreme Provincial Court took the case as a rehearing rather than as an appeal, and it was therefore possible to hear fresh evidence. This now indicated that there was a strong possibility that the child, rather than being moribund, would continue to live without his shunt but would, as a result, be subject to increasing physical distress. Medical evidence now held that the condition would not only be stabilised but might even be improved if the shunt was replaced. Accordingly, replacement was recognised as ordinary treatment and, as such, something which the parents could not properly refuse. It is to be noted that the decisions in *Dawson* were not contradictory; the same principle was applied equally correctly in both courts – what differed was the evidence on which the decisions were based.

Dawson greatly supports my belief that the ordinary/extraordinary test should be replaced semantically by one described as productive/non-productive, for it is the production of a 'good result', taken in its wider sense, which matters. The productive/non-productive test fits well with the concept of medical futility insofar as futile treatment can be seen simply as totally non-productive treatment; it has, in addition, an objective ring to it which is lacking in the 'best interests' and 'substituted judgment' tests which are commonly applied to surrogate decisions concerning withdrawal of treatment. The latter concept has been developed especially in American jurisprudence: the court or other surrogate is required to 'don the mental mantle of the incompetent'.[79] The 'best interests test', by contrast, is a product of the 'welfare principle' whereby the welfare of the patient assumes paramount importance; it permeates the British approach to decision making in every field involving incompetents;[80] the assessment is thus reached on the basis of what the *surrogate* thinks would be the ideal solution. Both tests are open to criticism. It has been said that the former is inapplicable in the infantile or neonatal situation as the patient can never have expressed a preference; I do not see this as an objection – there is no reason why an objective solution based on the reasonable person in the position of the patient cannot be reached on the basis of everyday human experience. The latter is unashamedly paternalistic in form and is difficult to fit into the jurisprudential concept of autonomous consent. It also produces a number of anomalies: how, for example, can it possibly be in the *best interests* of a person to die? It has been said that, at the end of the day, there is no practical difference between the two as they will always arrive at the same answer, but this is not true in the neonatal situation. Dr Arthur may have thought it was in Baby Pearson's best interests that he should die, but there is no reason to suppose that this would have been Baby Pearson's judgment.[81] The more honest approach might well be to admit that we are being led by and are forming our decisions on the basis of the productive/non-productive assessment of the available therapy.[82]

The legal position

Before reviewing the specific case law which has done so much to clarify the British position, we should look to the general provisions of the criminal law as it affects the newborn. We must, then, start with the trite observation that the deliberate killing of a reasonable creature in being is murder. Moreover, no time limit is set on this proposition. In the now famous words of DEVLIN J: 'If the act done intended to kill and did, in fact, kill, it does not matter if a life is cut short by weeks or months, it is just as much murder as if it were cut short by years'.[83] It is also to be noted that there is no such legal entity as a mitigated offence of 'mercy killing'[84] and, while the courts and the prosecuting authorities are very tolerant of the genuinely distraught parent or close relative, there is no guarantee that the court would take a similar view of medical paternalism resulting in a deliberate killing of a newborn.

More important, perhaps, is the distinction which the law makes between commission and omission. As we have already discussed, it is not easy to see any *moral* basis for the contrasting legal response to activity and passivity; a very convincing case can be made out that, given the intent, killing and letting die are on the same moral plane. The legal position is, however, quite clear. Thus we have TAYLOR LJ:

> 'The court never sanctions decisions to terminate life. That would be unlawful. There is no question of approving, even in the case of the most horrendous disability, a course aimed at terminating life or accelerating death. The court is concerned only with the circumstances in which steps should not be taken to prolong life.[85]

Accordingly, the physician may make a valid choice between treatment of disease and simple alleviation of symptoms, and the latter course may be followed in preference to maintaining a life of pain and suffering. Again, in the words of DEVLIN J: 'The doctor is entitled to relieve pain and suffering even if the measures he takes may incidentally shorten life.'[86]

This attitude to patient management is commonly justified under the philosophical doctrine of double effect, which holds that, so long as no less injurious alternative is available, an action is permissible when an intended good effect can be obtained only at the expense of a coincident, and proportionately acceptable, ill effect. Williams, however, saw no need to introduce a mainly religious concept to justify a medical practice which lies firmly within the legal doctrine of necessity: that it is better to avoid the occurrence of a major evil even if one commits a lesser criminal or tortious act in so doing.[87] It is time to consider the development of this view of selective non-treatment through decisions of the British courts.

The British cases

As has already been explained, the majority of important decisions relate to infancy rather than to the neonatal period. The principles derived can, however, be applied across the board. The first – and very influential – case is *Re B*,[88] which concerned an infant girl suffering from Down's syndrome complicated by the frequent, although relatively easily treatable, condition of intestinal obstruction. The parents refused permission for the operation, whereupon the local authority instituted wardship proceedings. Despite judicial authorisation, the surgeons concerned refused to operate in the face of parental opposition and the court order was withdrawn. The local authority then appealed and the order for operation was reinstated. The judges made some important observations when coming to their decision. Firstly, DUNN LJ clarified the therapeutic rights of the mentally handicapped neonate: 'She should,' he said, 'be put in the position of any other mongol child and given the opportunity to live an existence' (at 1425). This, however, is of collateral significance only in the present context. Of more immediate importance, we have TEMPLEMAN LJ:

> it devolves on this court ... to decide whether the life of the child is demonstrably going to be so awful that in effect the child must be condemned to die or whether the life of this child is still so imponderable that it would be wrong for her to be condemned to die ... Faced with [the] choice, I have no doubt that it is the duty of this court to decide that the child must live (at 1424).

He went on to say: 'There may be cases, I know not, of severe proved damage where the future is so certain and where the life of the child is bound to be full of pain and suffering that the court might be driven to a different conclusion', and it was this opinion which later led LORD DONALDSON MR to conclude that *Re B* either did or, at least, ought to provide a binding authority for the proposition that there is a balancing exercise to be performed in assessing the course to be adopted in the best interests of defective children.[89] Looked at in this light, and in retrospect, *Re B* was relatively easy to decide as there was virtually nothing to balance. There is no evidence at all that the life of a mentally handicapped child is, of itself, any less tolerable than is that of a normal child; to hold that such a child should be allowed to die because of that defect is simply to imply a societal evaluation that the imperfect should be eliminated.

Even so, the legal gap created by the conflicting decisions in *Arthur* and *Re B* persisted for nearly a decade before it was officially closed.[90] The process began with *Re C (a minor) (wardship: medical treatment)*,[91] which concerned a moribund infant with severe cerebral damage due to hydrocephalus. The question before the court was what to do in the event that she suffered from an infection or other illness. Should she be treated in a way that was appropriate to a non-handicapped child, as the social workers urged, or in one which was appropriate to her condition, which was the preference of the local authority? The Court of Appeal was in no doubt as to the correctness of the latter view and authorised the hospital to treat her so as to allow her life to come to an end peacefully and with dignity; there was no need beyond this to use antibiotics, intravenous therapy or nasogastric feeding and it was emphasised that the decision was based on the paramountcy of her welfare, well-being and interests. *Re B* and *Re C* lie at opposite poles of the spectrum of treatment decisions and neither was, in my view, difficult to make; indeed, it is doubtful if the latter case would have been reported had there not been a need to allay some local criticism of the hospital.

The next case, *Re J (a minor) (wardship: medical treatment)*,[92] was a harder and, accordingly, more significant judgment insofar as it concerned an infant who was subject to fits and periods of respiratory failure, but who was not dying; there was no doubt that he could be rescued in the probable event that he sustained further attacks but, at the same time, that he would die if the necessary treatment was withheld. Once again, the Court of Appeal applied a welfare test based on a balancing exercise and concluded that it would not be in the child's best interests: 'to reventilate him … in the event of his stopping breathing unless to do so seemed appropriate to the doctors treating him given the prevailing clinical situation'.

Re J is an important case in which a number of far-reaching observations were made by LORD DONALDSON MR. In the first place, he emphasised that, while there was a strong presumption in favour of the preservation of life, the person responsible for making any decision should consider it from the assumed view of the patient. The present writer, with all due respect, sees this as a confusion of the issues. The court was at pains to stress the underlying importance of the patient's 'best interests' but the Master of the Rolls is, here, undisguisedly advocating the use of substituted judgment. I further suggest that this provides by far the better standard insofar as it describes the circumstances more accurately than does the paralogistic use of the term 'best interests'. Secondly, it was held that consideration must be given to the prognosis in terms of pain and suffering not only from the disease process itself but also by way of any proposed treatment. Thirdly, it was emphasised that a decision taken in favour of death would be lawful only if death resulted as a side-effect: the concept of euthanasia was firmly rejected in favour of withholding treatment designed to prevent death from natural causes.[93]

Perhaps, then, the first impression to be gained from *Re J* is that it offers considerable latitude to doctors making *medical* decisions, and this is underlined by the opinion provided in a further case with, unfortunately, the same title.[94] In this case, which we might call *Re J (2)*, a mother attempted to enforce the intensive care of her child who had suffered severe brain damage as a result of a fall. The Court of Appeal, however, refused to entertain the suggestion that it should direct clinicians to provide treatment against their clinical judgment as to its value and reversed the order of the trial court enjoining them to do so. *Re J (2)* makes it clear that, while *consent* to treatment is essential, there is no parallel right to *demand* treatment. As the Master of the Rolls said: 'There are checks and balances' which were described later as those between consent and willingness and ability to treat (at 174). While it is not strictly to the immediate point, it is also noteworthy that the Court of Appeal simultaneously admitted the rights of the doctors to consider the utilisation of resources in general when considering the value of treatment of the individual. BALCOMBE LJ said:

> making an order which may have the effect of compelling a doctor or health authority to make available scarce resources ... to a particular child ... might require the health authority to put J on a ventilator in an intensive care unit, and thereby possibly to deny the benefit of those limited resources to a child who was much more likely than J to benefit from them (at 176).

The implication from this is that, once on intensive care, a patient cannot be removed simply on the grounds that a more deserving case has presented.

This is not to say, however, that a child cannot be removed from ventilator support when it is not considered to be in his or her interests to continue treatment. The family court has recently considered the case of a three-month-old child suffering from post-meningitic cerebral damage.[95] The child was not in a coma but had very little, if any, awareness of anything. SIR STEPHEN BROWN P put it: 'The future is, frankly, quite hopeless … There is no prospect of amelioration of her condition … It is almost a living death. It is quite clear that this little baby does not have what can really be described as an independent existence' (at 45) and, as a consequence, 'I have no doubt … that I should grant leave to the medical staff … to take the course which they recommend of discontinuing the artificial ventilation of C' (at 46). At the same time, however, the President refused to provide general guidelines for paediatricians, stating that each case must be decided on its own merits.

Re C appears to this writer to represent a considerable shift in judicial opinion. Both *Re J* and *Re J(2)* concerned omissions to interfere with the natural course of events in a child's process of dying. This is different from authorising active steps to bring about a death which would not have occurred otherwise,[96] and one wonders if this is not a significant step towards legalised active euthanasia. Is it not also possible to see in Sir Stephen's allusion to an independent existence the glimmers of recognition of the 'personhood' construct? At the very least, both *Re J* and *Re C* indicate approval of 'quality of life' decisions, and the latter suggests that, given the right circumstances, a life of appalling quality may be taken away rather than simply not preserved. As a coda, however, it might be noted that ventilation in all these cases implies ventilation of a living body. Once the child is dead by brain-stem standards, it is regarded as wholly contrary to the interests of the child – and unfair to the health carers – for his or her body to be subjected to continuing indignity; the clinicians are, then, not acting contrary to law if they disconnect the ventilator when, in their opinion, it is appropriate to do so.[97]

Finally, it may be asked how these cases affect our ideas on futile medical treatment. In fact, they tend to crystallise the essentials, even if only in a negative way. The almost enforced conclusion is that 'futility', being an absolute construct itself, can be invoked only when dealing with another absolute – in this case, death. Thus a treatment that is designed to prevent death and which fails to do so can be properly regarded as futile. Anything short of this, such as treatment designed to ameliorate pain, requires a balancing approach which, in turn, admits of *some medical* advantage. The decision as to whether such treatment should be given is, then, subject to a quality of life assessment. Physicians may be best suited to frame the choices by describing prognosis and the likely outcomes, as well as the odds for achieving them,[98] but they are not the sole arbiters and, in the end, the notion of medical futility, attractive though it may be, is of comparatively limited application as a therapeutic directive.

The American cases

It is impossible to consider the whole spectrum of American litigation in this field. A visible and uniform trend is unlikely to be found when more than 50 jurisdictions are involved. Even so, many of the decisions have been reached using jurisprudential reasoning that is different from that which has developed in the United Kingdom and a brief overview will be useful from that point of view.

Three significant decisions can be isolated as indicating the prevailing American opinion in the 1970s. In the first of these – *Houle*[99] – the decision not to treat a severely defective newborn was challenged by other hospital doctors. In authorising treatment, the court introduced the interesting concept of the 'feasibility test': the issue was not approached in terms of the prospective quality of life but, rather, as an assessment of the medical feasibility of the treatment by comparison with the almost certain risk of death if treatment was withheld. Given the fact that there was a medical need and a medically feasible response, surgery should be performed irrespective of the quality of life.

Very much the same approach was taken in *In re McNulty*,[100] when the question of repairing a heart defect in an infant afflicted with the congenital rubella syndrome was raised. The family resisted treatment at least partially on the grounds that the operation carried a mortality rate of 50–60 per cent. Again, it was held that, if there was any life-saving treatment available, it must be undertaken regardless of the quality of life that would result.

The third example – *Cicero*[101] – concerned a severe case of spina bifida. Here the court was even more determined to uphold the rights of the infant: children are not property 'whose disposition is left to parental discretion without hindrance': 'The court was not constituted to hear the cry [to terminate the lives of other people deemed physically or mentally defective]. Rather, it is our function to secure his opportunity for "life, liberty and the pursuit of happiness".' Rather significantly, in the light of later developments, considerable reliance was placed on child neglect statutes as providing authority to order treatment.

The early 1980s, however, ushered in a marked change of attitude which is exemplified in the 'Baby Doe' cases. The New York case[102] concerned a girl with multiple deformities which the parents did not wish to have treated. The court of first instance approved a guardian for the purpose of arranging for surgery, but this action was overruled on the grounds that the parents had 'elected a treatment which was within accepted medical standards'. The stay was confirmed on appeal because 'to allow any person to bypass the statutory requirements [for child care] would catapult him into the very heart of a family circle to challenge the parents' responsibility to care for their children' – and, at about this time, many decisions based on parental preferences were being taken at local institutional level.

By contrast, the earlier Indiana case[103] precipitated something of a constitutional crisis; despite this, the record has remained closed. The infant concerned suffered from Down's syndrome complicated by a tracheo-oesophageal fistula, another condition that can be corrected without great surgical difficulty. The parents refused to authorise either surgery or intravenous feeding. This resulted in intense legal activity and massive media coverage, but the baby died while efforts to involve the Supreme Court were under way. The state courts, meanwhile, upheld the decision to withhold surgery on the grounds that the value of parental autonomy outweighed the infant's right to live 'when a minimally adequate quality of life was non-existent', which is, on the face of things, a surprising assessment. The contrast with the English case of *Re B*, which was an almost identical presentation, is remarkable.

As a direct consequence, a federal regulation was promulgated applying the Rehabilitation Act 1973, s.504 (which, effectively, prohibits discrimination against handicapped persons) to the defective neonate. Further regulations imposed the display of notices drawing attention to the requirements and also established a telephone link whereby infringement could be reported to the health authorities. The constitutional legality of the rules was challenged rapidly and they were struck down in the District Court of the District of Columbia as being arbitrary and capricious.[104] The administration then produced a final set of rules that recommended the establishment of Infant Care Review Committees, authorised the posting of informational notices and provided that Child Protection Agencies should use their full authority in the investigation and judicial review of non-treatment decisions. Once again, the regulations were set aside, albeit largely on the grounds of statutory interpretation.[105]

Congress then took over, the result being the Child Abuse Amendments 1984 to the Child Abuse Prevention and Treatment Act 1974, the gist of which, having defined medical neglect, is to lay down the conditions in which withholding medically indicated treatment would not be so described (see p. 295). These rules are drawn up and promulgated on a federal basis, but are subject to implementation by the states. It is to be noted that the correction of a simple complication of Down's syndrome is not included as an exception.

The current position

We can thus see that, even if it has been reached by different paths, something of a consensus is evolving on both sides of the Atlantic as to the care of defective neonates and infants. Basically, this is determined by reference to the 'best interests' of the patient, but this formula depends, to a large extent, on agreement between the interested parties, and the overwhelming importance of a combined decision taken by the parents and their medical advisers has been emphasised repeatedly. Given the general concern to avoid recourse to the court so far as is possible, the major remaining problem is to decide whose opinion will prevail in the event of disagreement. And, here, the movement in favour of 'good medical practice' which was emerging in the United States has been reversed by *Baby K*, while the even more evident reliance on medical opinion which can be traced through the United Kingdom cases has been halted by *Re T*. The status of therapeutic decision making by parents on behalf of their children still requires analysis.

The right of parents to control their children is undisputed; the extent of that right is, however, becoming increasingly limited as the importance of children's rights is acknowledged *pari passu*. The question is discussed in greater detail in Chapter 12. As we have already argued briefly (see p. 293), it is difficult to see how there can be any parental right to harm a child, and a hardening of attitudes is to be seen in the United States case of *Guardianship of Phillip B*,[106] in which the parents were first found competent to refuse life-saving cardiac surgery for their Down's syndrome child; four years later, a second court found that parental custody had caused and would continue to cause the boy harm – by which time, unfortunately, the cardiac defect was not susceptible to repair.

In much the same way, there was no doubt that parental decision making in respect of neonatal treatment was widely accepted in the United Kingdom at the time of Dr Arthur's trial and the decision in *Re B*. Thus we have the outstanding academic lawyer, Williams, holding:

> it may also be said to be wrong to compel the parents of a severely handicapped infant to use the resources of modern medicine in order to prolong its existence when they feel that they cannot cope with it. There is a strong argument for keeping the law out of these cases ... the criminal law should stay its hand. The decision of the parents should prevail ... judges should not use the wardship procedure to supplant the parents.[107]

And from the medical establishment: 'In the absence of a clear code to which society adheres there is no justification for the courts usurping the parents' rights.'[108]

A case for caution can, however, be made out without much difficulty:

> While parents undoubtedly feel some special responsibility for all of their children, a seriously ill newborn is likely to be a financial and emotional drain on the parents and the rest of the family ... With such a substantial risk that the parents' interests will be in conflict with the child's best interest, should we still allow the parents to decide what is in the best interests of the child?[109]

In other words, parents, who will be bound to bear the brunt of their child's disability, cannot be expected to be wholly objective.[110] That being the case, the possible extreme reactions are, firstly, that parents have a right to reject their defective infant and, as a corollary, that it is for the state to provide for the future of such children. No-one would deny that states *ought* to provide better facilities for the handicapped than are generally available; but the proposition leads to the unhappy conclusion that the state itself should, then, be entitled to a share in the decision making, in which case the interests of the neonate would be even more probably compromised.

The opposing view is to deny the parents *any* rights of rejection, and this has some logic behind it. Parents cannot simply surrender their parental duties;[111] a parent who fails in his or her duty to care for a child may be, at the very least, liable to charges under the Children and Young Persons Act, 1933, s.1 or the Children and Young Persons (Scotland) Act, 1937, s.12; and any parents who opted for the death of their child in a home environment would certainly be at risk of a charge of manslaughter. In pointing out that the law protects a doctor when a parent would almost certainly be convicted of homicide, the Brahams,[112] at the same time, demonstrated the essential conceptual distinction: it is *because* the parents depend upon their medical advisers that they can make non-treatment decisions which are within the law. But, as we have seen, something of a compromise between these two extremes has been reached and decision making now depends on the widely agreed principle that the *whole* caregiving team should be in agreement before a recommendation to withdraw intensive and invasive treatment is put to the parents; in this way, parents are not being called upon to decide upon the fate of an infant; rather, they are being asked to accept or refuse a deeply considered medical opinion.

Is the physician, then, in any legal jeopardy? One would have thought not – provided he or she carries the support of the team. There was, at one time, a substantial body of opinion in both the United Kingdom and the United States which favoured some form of protective legislation. It is very doubtful whether there is now any such need, at least in the United Kingdom; the string of British cases outlined above has largely defined the doctors' position, there has been no prosecution of a paediatrician since 1981, and the unfortunate history of bureaucratic intervention as evidenced by the 'Baby Doe' cases in the United States would certainly indicate the need to pause for thought before resorting to the statute book: the statute is a blunt and rigid tool to use in such circumstances. If any legislation is indicated, it should be of an enabling, rather than a restrictive, nature. We have suggested elsewhere[113] a possible clause for inclusion in any future statute covering decisions for dying, which runs:

> In the event of positive treatment being necessary for a neonate's survival, it will not be an offence to withhold such treatment if two doctors, one of whom is a consultant paediatrician, acting in good faith and with the consent of both parents if available, decide against a treatment in the light of a reasonably clear medical prognosis which indicates that the infant's further life would be intolerable by virtue of pain or suffering or because of severe cerebral incompetence.

We believed that such wording emphasised the primacy of the neonate's interests, a concept that is central to the ethical management of the defective infant. Even so, any such legislation would have to be backed by a code of practice or guidelines. Our previously published[114] attempts in this sphere run as follows:

> If positive treatment is necessary for the infant's survival, the law should respect parental decisions not to treat their newborn when:
>   1. the decision is concurred in as being medically proper by the attending physician and by at least one other independent, qualified physician, preferably a consultant neonatologist or paediatrician;
>   2. the medical reasons for the decision not to treat (the prognosis) are entered in the medical record by the physician and are concurred in by the consultant;
>   3. the parents have been fully informed of the infant's diagnosis and prognosis with and without any reasonably available treatment; of the risks, nature and benefits of each such treatment; and of any other material facts bearing on the infant's condition and the treatment/non-treatment decision, so that they may give, or refuse, an information-based consent. The explanation and their decision should be likewise entered in the case notes and be witnessed;
>   4. the judgments required of parents and physicians have been made in good faith with the best interests of the infant as the guiding principle;
>   5. such affirmative treatment has, when necessary, continued after birth until a clear prognosis can be given with reason-

able medical certainty that the infant falls within one of the categories set out below:

a.   that death is highly probable and is expected within a reasonably short time, say one year, regardless of treatment; or

b.   that there is no reasonable possibility that the infant will be able to participate to any degree in human relationships or experiences with others requiring some interaction or response; or

c.   that treatment cannot obviate or alleviate an intolerable level of chronic pain which would make continued life-sustaining treatment inhumane.

At the end of the day, however, it is doubtful if such proposals, if put into statutory form, would do much more than confirm what is already established common law.

Feeding and hydration

The problem of whether or not a defective infant should be fed and given water is sufficiently important to merit separate consideration, particularly in the light of its being at the heart of the *Arthur* case in England and of the *Infant Doe* furore in America.

At the risk of being thought repetitive, I believe we must, again, focus on the distinction between mental and physical defect and, particularly, on the Down's syndrome baby. In my view, we have established that the uncomplicated or simply complicated Down's syndrome infant is not a morally acceptable candidate for neonaticide. This is justified deontologically by the application of the simple 'substituted judgment' test: would the child be likely to prefer to die rather than exist in its present condition? I disagree with Williams' analogy, 'If a wicked fairy told me she was about to transform me into a Down's baby and would I prefer to die, I should certainly answer yes',[115] because that would not be the judgment of the Down's baby who knows of no other existence; there is no reason to suppose that such an infant has any desire to die. The handicap of Down's syndrome does not justify failure to provide medically proven treatment; denial of treatment to a Down's baby on social grounds should not be permitted, and this must include the basic minimum of providing nourishment and fluids. I would, in fact, go further and suggest that, given that the parents would not consent to normal feeding, the health carers who persisted would be fully covered against an accusation of assault by way of the legal doctrine of necessity: the benefit to the child would clearly outweigh any technical infringement of the law.

But what of the physically defective infant who satisfies the criteria for non-treatment outlined above but does not die a natural death?

There is a strong impression that society, be it of the United Kingdom, the United States, Canada or Australia, would apply the same
criteria, at least in respect of natural feeding. The words used in the
American case of *Conroy*[116] – 'Feeding is an expression of nurturing
and caring, especially for infants and children' – would probably be
approved universally. The matter was summed up succinctly by
VINCENT J when addressing the specific issues of providing food and
water in the Australian case of *Re F*:[117]

> No parent, no doctor, no court, has any power to determine that the
> life of any child, however disabled that child may be, will be deliber-
> ately taken from it ... [the law] does not permit decisions to be made
> concerning the quality of life, nor does it enable any assessment to be
> made as to the value of any human being.

How, then, does this conclusion fit with the important decision in
Bland?[118] In that case, a young adult was in the persistent vegetative
state. The court considered that feeding and hydration constituted
medical treatment – or, at least, an integral part of medical treatment
– and that, accordingly, they could be withdrawn lawfully on the
ground that it was achieving no affirmative benefit. Effectively, however, the decision could be reached only in the particular circumstances of the case; that is, that the patient was in, or near to, the
persistent vegetative state. *Bland* is, therefore authority only for such
cases and these are likely to arise in infancy rather than the neonatal
phase. The comparable neonate is to be found in the anencephalic
where natural feeding would be impossible; I suggest that, despite
the surprising ruling in the American case of *Baby K*, it would be
unlikely in the extreme that support would be forthcoming in the
United Kingdom for *instituting* invasive feeding in an anencephalic
neonate. It follows that *Bland* does not affect one's conclusions as to
feeding and hydration of the defective neonate.

The foregoing discussion has, however, focused almost entirely on
'natural' or 'normal' feeding, and some difficulty may arise as to its
definition. The provision of nourishment can run from breastfeeding
through spoon feeding to severely invasive procedures. Setting a 'cut
off' point of 'normality' is difficult, but it is suggested that anything
involving medical expertise as opposed to skilled nursing care could
legitimately be regarded as 'abnormal'. *Bland* may be useful here, in
that it classifies such feeding as medical treatment; it can, therefore,
be provided or withdrawn on medical, rather than humanitarian,
grounds.

Passivity or activity?

There remains for consideration what is perhaps the most difficult moral question to answer in this context: given that death is the intended outcome of a non-treatment decision, would it not be better to terminate life quickly and actively, rather than to allow it to ebb away protractedly and, perhaps, painfully?

The clearest answer is, of course, that the latter may be lawful, whereas the former has been quite firmly restated as being unlawful.[119] Is there, however, any other distinction to be made? This is no place to expand on the philosophical argument that there is none provided the intention is the same in either case; this has already been touched upon at p. 300. Nonetheless, there may be a difference in *practice* which can only be justified on intuitive grounds. Campbell has expressed this: 'There is a powerful psychological distinction [between 'killing' and 'allowing to die'] which is important to the staff of intensive care units. To them, there is a big difference between not using a respirator to keep an infant of 600g alive and giving a lethal injection, although the end result is the same.'[120] Moreover, there is no doubt that the parents would appreciate the difference and, as Capron has put it in general terms: 'I never want to have to wonder whether the physician coming into the hospital room is wearing [the robes] of the healer ... or the black hood of the executioner. Trust between patient and physician is simply too important and too fragile to be subjected to this unnecessary strain.'[121]

Notes

1   Neonatologists will point out that this is a misnomer, in that the process involves taking positive clinical decisions of great significance and resolving complex problems of management. See, in particular, I. Laing, 'Withdrawing from invasive neonatal intensive care', in J.K. Mason (ed.), *Paediatric Forensic Medicine and Pathology* (1989), London: Chapman & Hall.
2   For debate, see M. Simms, 'Informed dissent: the views of some mothers of severely mentally handicapped young adults' (1986) 12 J Med Ethics 72; A. Davis, 'The view of a disabled woman' at 75.
3   Reported by T. Prentice, 'Withdrawing treatment "can be justified"' (1988), *The Times*, 21 April, p. 3.
4   The problems associated with the developing child are discussed in Chapter 12.
5   A.G.M. Campbell and H.E. McHaffie, 'Prolonging life and allowing death: infants' (1995) 21 J Med Ethics 339.
6   *Re B (a minor)* [1981] 1 WLR 1421, CA; *R v. Arthur* (1981) 12 BMLR 1.
7   E. Slater, 'Severely malformed children: wanted – a new approach' [1973] 1 Brit Med J 285.
8   J. Lorber, 'Ethical problems in the management of myelomeningocele' (1975) 10 J R Coll Physns 47.

9   J. Lorber and S.A. Salfield, 'Result of selective treatment of spina bifida cystica' (1981) 56 Arch Dis Child 822.

10 R.S. Duff and A.G.M. Campbell, 'Moral and ethical dilemmas in a special care nursery' (1973) 289 New Engl J Med 890; J.G. Robertson, 'Involuntary euthanasia of defective newborns: a legal analysis' (1974) 21 Stanford L Rev 213; M.J. Garland, 'Care of the newborn: the decision not to treat' (1977) 1 Perinat/Neonat 14.

11 T.A. Long, 'Infanticide for handicapped infants: sometimes it's a metaphysical dispute' (1988) 14 J Med Ethics 79.

12 *R v. Arthur* (1981) 12 BMLR 1 at 18. It is interesting to note that Dr Dunn has significantly refined his views over the years so as to positively exclude Down's syndrome infants from those who would be denied life-saving treatment. See P.M. Dunn, 'Appropriate care of the newborn: ethical dilemmas' (1993) 19 J Med Ethics 82.

13 For a major exposition of the English law, see *Airedale National Health Service Trust v. Bland* [1993] AC 789.

14 Note 13 above.

15 J. Rachels, 'Active and passive euthanasia' (1975) 292 New Engl J Med 78; H. Kuhse, 'A modern myth. That letting die is not the intentional causation of death' (1984) 1 J Appl Philos 21; R. Gillon, 'Euthanasia, withholding life-prolonging treatment and moral differences between killing and letting die' (1988) 14 J Med Ethics 115.

16 In the case of the death of a child, an alternative statutory charge might be available under the Children and Young Persons Act, 1933, s.1(2) or the Children and Young Persons (Scotland) Act, 1937, s.12(2).

17 *R v. Gibbins and Proctor* (1918) 13 Cr App Rep 134.

18 A. Whitelaw, 'Death as an option in neonatal intensive care' [1986] 2 Lancet 328; C.H.M. Walker, '... Officiously to keep alive' (1988) 63 Arch Dis Child 560.

19 I.M. Balfour-Lynn and R.C. Tasker, 'Futility and death in paediatric medical intensive care' (1996) 22 J Med Ethics 279.

20 See, for example, the larger part of an issue, (1992) 20 Law Med Hlth Care, in particular, R. Cranford and L. Gostin, 'Futility: a concept in search of a definition', 307; S.H. Miles, 'Medical futility', 310; A. Alpers and B. Lo, 'Futility: not just a medical issue', 327; E.R. Grant, 'Medical futility: legal and ethical aspects', 330.

21 R.D. Truog, A.S. Brett and J. Frader, 'The problem with futility' (1992) 326 New Engl J Med 1560.

22 It has been suggested, for example, that a treatment can be regarded as futile if it has been found to be useless in the last 100 cases: L.J. Schneiderman, N.S. Jecker and A.R. Jonsen, 'Medical futility: its meaning and ethical implications' (1990) 112 Ann Intern Med 949.

23 See an evaluation by parents of children with special health needs: B. Anderson and B. Hall, 'Parents' perceptions of decision making for children' (1995) 23 J Law Med & Ethics 15.

24 C. Weijer and C. Elliott, 'Pulling the plug on futility' (1995) 310 Brit Med J 683. Futility may also be used as a mechanism for positively excluding surrogates from what is seen as a purely medical concern: D.J. Murphy, 'Do-not-resuscitate orders: Time for reappraisal in long-term-care institutions' (1988) 260 J Amer Med Ass 2098.

25 See the remarks of LORD DONALDSON MR in *Re C* [1990] Fam 26 at 34.

26 Miles, n. 20 above.

27 (1981) 12 BMLR 1.

28   R. Gillon, 'An introduction to philosophical medical ethics: the Arthur case' (1985) 290 Brit Med J 1117.

29   Editorial comment, 'Paediatricians and the law' (1981) 283 Brit Med J 1280.

30   For example, D. Brahams, 'Putting *Arthur's* case in perspective' [1986] Crim LR 390.

31   Although the full transcript raises considerable doubt on the point: see 12 BMLR 1 at 8–10.

32   12 BMLR 1 at 21–22. See also the leading article 'After the trial at Leicester' [1981] 2 Lancet 1085.

33   Per FARQUHARSON J at 12 BMLR 22.

34   See M.J. Gunn and J.C. Smith, '*Arthur's* case and the right to life of a Down's syndrome child' [1985] Crim LR 705.

35   *Superintendent of Family and Child Services and Dawson* (1983) 145 DLR (3d) 610 at 620.

36   Note 29 above.

37   It appears from a recent adult case that such a jury will not, however, tolerate a positive action that is apparently designed to kill a patient. See *R* v. *Cox* (1992) 12 BMLR 38.

38   I am not including 'treatments' which involve xenotransplantation; see, for example, L.L. Hubbard, 'The Baby Fae case' (1987) 6 Med Law 385. Given the current state of the art, such endeavours are probably unlawful in the United Kingdom at the present time. For discussion, see J.K. Mason, 'Contemporary issues in organ transplantation', in S.A.M. McLean (ed.), *Contemporary Issues in Law, Medicine and Ethics* (1996), Aldershot: Dartmouth.

39   The greater part of the background information on this case is taken from the twin papers: E.J. Flannery, 'One advocate's viewpoint: conflicts and tensions in the *Baby K* case' (1995) 23 J Law Med & Ethics 7, and E.W. Clayton, 'Commentary: what is really at stake in *Baby K*?' (1995) 23 J Law Med & Ethics 13. See also M. McCarthy, 'Anencephalic baby's right to life?' (1993) 342 Lancet 919.

40   *In the matter of Baby K* 832 F Supp 1022 (ED, Va, 1993), *aff'd* 16 F 3d 590 (4th Cir, 1994).

41   Truog *et al.*, n. 21 above.

42   For detailed discussion, see D. Giesen, 'A right to health care?: a comparative perspective' (1994) 4 Health Matrix: J Law-Med 277. For specific analysis, see F.H. Miler, 'Infant resuscitation. A US/UK divide' (1994) 343 Lancet 1584.

43   J.F. Drane and J.L. Coulehan, 'The concept of futility. Patients do not have a right to demand medically useless treatment', in T.L. Beauchamp and R.M. Veatch, *Ethical Issues in Death and Dying* (1996), New Jersey: Prentice-Hall, p. 386.

44   [1997] 1 All ER 906.

45   In one analysis of the case, it was suggested that the opinion could only have been written by a woman (*Bulletin of Medical Ethics*, no. 123, November 1996, p. 7). It is to be noted, however, that concurring judgments, taking the same arguments into consideration, were delivered by two male judges. It is also reported that similar parental decisions have been taken in the field of cardiac transplantation; it is uncertain whether the court will be asked to intervene: *Bulletin of Medical Ethics*, no. 122, October 1996, p. 3.

46   *R* v. *Cambridge Health Authority, ex parte B (a minor)* (1995) 25 BMLR 5, QBD; (1995) 23 BMLR 1, CA.

47   This would seem to be the logical interpretation of the European Convention on Human Rights, art.2.

48   V.A. Entwistle, I.S. Watt, R. Bradbury and L.J. Pehl, 'Media coverage of the Child B case' (1996) 312 Brit Med J 1587.

49 J.H. Ely, 'The wages of crying wolf: a comment on *Roe* v. *Wade*' (1973) 82 Yale LJ 920.
50 Note 44 above.
51 'Indications of humanhood: a tentative profile of man' (1972) 2 Hastings Center Rep No. 5.
52 M. Tooley, 'A defense of abortion and infanticide', in J. Feinberg (ed.), *The Problem of Abortion* (1973), Belmont: Wadsworth; revising 'Abortion and infanticide' (1972) 2 Philos Publ Affairs 1.
53 The term is used in the sense of killing an infant, not of the legal definition in the Infanticide Act 1938.
54 J. Glover, *Causing Death and Saving Lives* (1977, reprinted 1986) Harmondsworth: Penguin Books, pp. 138–9.
55 H. Kuhse and P. Singer, *Should the Baby Live?* (1985), Oxford: Oxford University Press. For a précis, see H. Kuhse and P. Singer, 'For sometimes letting – and helping – die' (1986) 14 Law Med Hlth Care 149.
56 'Abortion, euthanasia, and care of defective newborns' (1975) 292 New Engl J Med 75.
57 Though this may not always be so: fetal bonding is often intense. See Duff and Campbell, n. 10 above.
58 P. Ramsey, *Ethics at the Edges of Life* (1978), Yale: Yale University Press.
59 E.W. Keyserlingk, 'Against infanticide' (1986) 14 Law Med Hlth Care 154.
60 Long, n. 11 above. For a further overview see Wells, C 'Whose baby is it?' (1988) S J Law & Soc 323.
61 Editorial comment, 'Death without concealment' (1981) 283 Brit Med J 1629.
62 A.G.M. Campbell, 'Children in a persistent vegetative state' (1984) 289 Brit Med J 1022.
63 D.D. Raphael, 'Handicapped infants: medical ethics and the law' (1988) 14 J Med Ethics 5.
64 For an early example of how different standards can be, see Z. Szawarski and A. Tulczynski, 'Treatment of defective newborns – a survey of paediatricians in Poland' (1988) 14 J Med Ethics 11, which compares their findings with those of P. Singer, H. Kuhse and C. Singer, 'The treatment of newborn infants with major handicaps. A survey of obstetricians and paediatricians in Victoria' [1983] 2 Med J Aust 274.
65 T.S. Ellis, 'Letting defective babies die: who decides?' (1982) 7 Am J Law Med 393; R.S. Shapiro, 'Medical treatment of defective newborns: an answer to the "Baby Doe" dilemma' (1983) 20 Harvard J Legis 137.
66 50 Fed Reg 14,878 (1985). For an outstanding survey of the American scene, see L. Gostin, 'A moment in human development: legal protection, ethical standards and social policy on the selective non-treatment of handicapped neonates' (1985) 11 Am J Law Med 31.
67 *Doen of Laten?* (To do or not to do?) This analysis is based on the article by Z. Versluys and R. de Leeuw, 'A Dutch report on the ethics of neonatal care' (1995) 21 J Med Ethics 14. Dr Versluys was chairman of the Association's Working Group. See also C. Versluys, 'Ethics of neonatal care' (1993) 341 Lancet 794.
68 Though whether the doctor would be prosecuted and whether a punitive sentence would be imposed in the event of conviction, say, for manslaughter is uncertain. The situation would be that of Dr Arthur (n. 12 above).
69 For a recent review, see J. Griffiths, 'Recent developments in the Netherlands concerning euthanasia and other medical behavior that shortens life' (1995) 1 Med Law Internat 347.
70 T. Sheldon, 'Dutch appeal court dismisses case against doctor' (1995) 311 Brit Med J 1322.

71   See also, for example, the Bioethics Committee, Canadian Paediatric Society, 'Treatment decisions for infants and children' (1986) 135 Canad Med Ass J 447.

72   Whitelaw, n. 18 above.

73   Walker, n. 18 above; J.G. Bissenden, 'Ethical aspects of neonatal care' (1986) 61 Arch Dis Child 639.

74   V.Y.H. Yu, 'The extremely low birthweight infant: ethical issues in treatment' (1987) 23 Aust Paediatr J 97.

75   D. Brahams, 'No obligation to resuscitate a non-viable infant' [1988] 1 Lancet 1176. The problem in many cases is one of communication: see Z. Kmietowicz, 'Premature baby was not put on ventilator' (1996) 313 Brit Med J 963.

76   B.M. Dickens, 'Withholding paediatric medical care' (1984) 62 Canad Bar Rev 196; Bioethics Committee, n. 71 above; American Academy of Pediatrics, 'Principles of treatment of disabled infants' (1984) 73 Pediatrics 559.

77   (1957) 49 *Acta Apostolicae Sedis* 1027.

78   Note 35 above.

79   Well expressed in *Superintendent of Belchertown State School* v. *Saikewicz* 370 NE 2d 64 (Mass, 1977).

80   Derived, now, from the Children Act 1989, s.1.

81   J.K. Mason, 'Master of the Balancers: non-voluntary therapy under the mantle of Lord Donaldson' [1993] Juridical Rev 115.

82   We argue the distinction more closely in J.K. Mason and G.T. Laurie, 'The management of the persistent vegetative state in the British Isles' [1996] Juridical Rev 263.

83   H. Palmer, 'Dr Adams' trial for murder' [1957] Crim LR 365.

84   See R. Leng, 'Mercy killing and the law' (1982) 132 NLJ 76.

85   In *Re J (a minor) (wardship: medical treatment)* (1990) 3 All ER 930 at 943.

86   Note 83 above. Restated with approval in *Bland*, n. 13 above.

87   G. Williams, *Textbook of Criminal Law* (2nd edn, 1983), London: Stevens, p. 581.

88   *Re B (a minor) (wardship: medical treatment)* [1981] 1 WLR 1421.

89   In *Re J*, n. 85 above.

90   A gap which was certainly not narrowed by the statement of the Attorney General following the two cases: 'I am satisfied that the law relating to murder and to attempted murder is the same now as it was before the trial; that it is the same irrespective of the age of the victim, and that it is the same irrespective of the wishes of the parents or of any other person having a duty of care to the victim. I am also satisfied that a person who has a duty of care may be guilty of murder or attempted murder by omitting to fulfil that duty, as much as by any positive act': 19 HC Official Report (6th series) written answers col. 349, 8 March 1982.

91   [1990] Fam 26.

92   [1990] 3 All ER 930.

93   In addition, the court strongly approved a policy whereby treatment decisons were taken by the health care team as a whole in cooperation with the parents, provided the choice was made solely on behalf of the child in what was believed to be his or her best interests.

94   *Re J (a minor) (wardship: medical treatment)* [1992] 2 FLR 165. Two very similar decisions have been reached in Scotland. The determination in the Fatal Accident Inquiry concerning the death of Rebecca Cassidy supported a decision not to treat an extremely low weight premature babay: see S. English, 'Doctor was right not to resuscitate "unviable" baby' (1997), *The Times*, 27 June, p. 11. In the inquiry into the death of Michelle Paul, the decision not to provide a liver transplant for a teenage girl was accepted as good medical practice: see

G. Bowditch, 'Surgeon right to refuse teenager a liver transplant' (1997), *The Times*, 23 July, p. 7.

95 *Re C (a baby)* (1996) 32 BMLR 44.
96 Baby C was thought to have a life expectancy of around two years.
97 *Re A* [1992] 3 Med LR 303. Note that the clinical autonomy of the health carers was, again, emphasised: 'The function of the court in this delicate jurisdiction is to assist by clarifying the position and not to usurp the discretion of the doctors to do what they think is best in the difficult circumstances in which they are placed' (per JOHNSON J at 305).
98 S.J. Youngner, 'Who defines futility?' (1988) 260 J Amer Med Ass 2094.
99 *Maine Medical Center* v. *Houle* (Me, 1974) Cumberland Co Sup Ct No 74-145. For the feasibility standard, see E.S. MacMillan, 'Birth defective infants: a standard for non-treatment decisions' (1978) 30 Stanford L Rev 599.
100 *In re McNulty* (1978) Mass, Probate Ct, No 1960.
101 *Re Cicero* 421 NYS 2d 965 (1979).
102 *Weber* v. *Stony Brook Hospital* 456 NE 2d 1186 (NY, 1983); followed by *United States* v. *University Hospital*, State University of New York 729 F 2d 144 (1984).
103 *Infant Doe* v. *Bloomington Hospital* (1982) Ind, Monroe Co Cir Ct, No GU 8204-004 A.
104 *American Academy of Pediatrics* v. *Heckler* 561 F Supp 395 (DDC, 1983). For some of the difficulties provoked by 'general' regulations, see *Matter of Baby F* (Ore, 1983) Coos Co Cir Ct, No J 928.
105 *Bowen* v. *American Hospital Association* 106 S Ct 2101 (1986). However, the submission on behalf of the Association for Retarded Citizens in favour of the regulations merits grave consideration. See B.R. Furrow, S.H. Johnson, T.S. Jost and R.L. Schwartz, *Bioethics: Health Care and Ethics* (1995), American Case-book Series, St Paul: West Publishing, p. 335.
106 (1979) 92 Cal App 3d 796; (1983) 139 Cal App 3d 407.
107 G. Williams, 'Life of a child' (1983), correspondence, *The Times*, 13 August.
108 Leading article, 'The right to live and the right to die' (1981) 283 Brit Med J 569.
109 Furrow *et al.*, n. 105 above, at 333.
110 For a very forthright, albeit dated, expression of this, see J. Lynn, 'Handicapped infants and their families' (1983) 11 Law Med Hlth Care 229.
111 Children Act 1989, s.2(9).
112 D. Brahams and M. Brahams, 'The Arthur case – a proposal for legislation' (1983) 9 J Med Ethics 12.
113 J.K. Mason and R.A. McCall Smith, *Law and Medical Ethics* (4th edn, 1994) London: Butterworths, p. 162. A very similar Limitation of Treatment Bill was proposed by Brahams and Brahams, n. 112 above. That, and an earlier version of our attempt, are critically discussed by M. Brazier, *Medicine, Patients and the Law* (2nd edn, 1992), Harmondsworth: Penguin Books, p. 325.
114 J.K. Mason and D.W. Meyers, 'Parental choice and selective non-treatment of deformed newborns: a view from mid-Atlantic' (1986) 12 J Med Ethics 67. It is noteworthy that these proposals are also in line with those of the Catholic Bishops' Joint Committee (England, Ireland, Scotland, Wales) on Bio-ethical Issues, *Care of the Handicapped Newborn: Parental Responsibility and Medical Responsibility* (1986), London: Catholic Media Office.
115 G. Williams, 'Down's syndrome and the duty to preserve life' (1981) 131 NLJ 1020.
116 *In re Conroy* 486 A 2d 1209 (NJ, 1985).
117 *Re F, F* v. *F* (1986) Unreported, Supreme Court of Victoria, 2 July.
118 Note 13 above.

119   In *Bland*, n. 13 above. It has to be noted, however, that the judges in that case found the distinction difficult to justify.
120   A.G.M. Campbell, 'Ethical issues in child health and disease', in J.O. Forfar (ed.), *Child Health in a Changing Society* (1988), Oxford: Oxford University Press.
121   A.M. Capron, 'Legal and ethical problems in decisions for death' (1986) 14 Law Med Hlth Care 141.

12 Consent to Treatment and Research in Children

The nature of consent to treatment

Medical treatment and medical research in children are dominated by the principle of consent, for it is consent which elides the civil or criminal consequences of a technical or a more serious assault. Even so, there are limits to the authority of consent. One cannot consent to an act which would be contrary to public policy,[1] nor can one consent to the infliction of severe injury – consent to an assault is immaterial if bodily harm is a probable outcome.[2] Surgical intervention clearly inflicts bodily harm but is exempted from the general rule, firstly, on common law grounds and, secondly, by the specific decision included in *Attorney General's Reference (No 6 of 1980)*.[3] Any such exception is, however, based on the premise that the injuries are inflicted for the benefit of the patient, and benefit may be difficult to define in, say, some types of cosmetic surgery. Indeed, every now and again the law lays down specific prohibitions, many of which concern assaults on children. The classic example lies in the Sexual Offences Act, 1956, s.6,[4] under which consent of a girl between the ages of 13 and 16 to sexual intercourse does not, save in very special circumstances, moderate an offence on the part of the man. More pertinent in relation to medical or surgical intervention are the Tattooing of Minors Act 1969, which invalidates the consent of a person under the age of 18 to tattooing, and the Prohibition of Female Circumcision Act 1985 which, *inter alia*, specifically disallows a doctor who undertakes an operation on the genitalia to take into account any beliefs of the patient as to ritual or custom.[5]

The question before us in the present context, however, is not whether consent is legal; our concern is to consider whether, given the legality of a medical or surgical treatment, the patient is *capable* of consent. Some problems associated with mental handicap have been discussed in Chapters 4 and 5; the concept of 'informed consent' has also been briefly addressed, at p. 89. Here it is proposed to look only at the particular question of the consent of minors to medical treatment. The reader is referred to Chapter 3 for additional discussion.

Consent by minors

The law has always been that anything done to a child without the consent of its parents is unlawful. Absolute parental authority over a child must, however, be a proposition related more to the 19th than to the 20th century[6] and it is one which has been steadily eroded by the courts and by statute law in recent decades.

The seminal statutory intrusion into the principle is to be found in the Family Law Reform Act 1969, s.8(1), which states that the consent of a minor who has attained the age of 16 years to medical or dental treatment which, in the absence of consent, would constitute a trespass to his person, shall be as effective as it would be if he were of full age and that, where a minor has, by virtue of this section, given an effective consent to any treatment, it shall not be necessary to obtain any consent for it from the parent or guardian. Which is perfectly clear; what the Act does *not* say, however – and as has been discussed in relation to contraception – is whether or not a minor *below* the age of 16 can give similar consent. The reason for doubt lies in s.8(3), which reads: 'Nothing in this section shall be construed as making ineffective any consent which would have been effective if this section had not been enacted' and, since the relevant conditions before the Act are undefined, the sub-section is open to interpretation. It has been widely held that it means that the common law position remains intact; that is, that the validity of consent depends upon the patient's intelligence and understanding, irrespective of his or her age.[7] This interpretation immediately poses the questions: why, if the common law position was clear, was it necessary to enact s.8(1) and why was it necessary to distinguish between the 16–18-year-old and any other understanding and intelligent minor? It is to be noted in this connection that the 1969 Act did not run to Scotland, where the situation was, and still is, covered adequately by the common law. Scots law has also clarified the position of the under-16s by way of the Age of Legal Capacity (Scotland) Act 1991. Section .2(4) creates an exception to the general rule that a contract made by a minor less than 16 years old is void. As a result, a person under the age of 16 now has legal capacity to consent on his or her own behalf to any surgical, medical or dental procedure or treatment 'where, in the opinion of a qualified medical practitioner attending him[/her], he[/she] is capable of understanding the nature and possible consequences of the procedure or treatment'. Thus, the *Gillick*[8] decision (discussed in detail in Chapter 3) is, effectively, embodied in statute in Scotland.[9]

Returning to England and s.8(3) of the 1969 Act, an alternative interpretation, to which I have always subscribed, is that the subsection preserves the rights of the parents to overrule an unjustifiable refusal of necessary treatment.[10] In fact, it will be seen that both the 1969 Act and the 1991 Act in Scotland are silent as to refusal of treatment by minors; the subject is of such significant in the context of children's rights as to merit examination in some depth.

Refusal of treatment by minors

The simplest way to settle the problem is to apply *Gillick*, so to speak, in reverse – on the grounds that a minor who is capable of consenting to treatment is equally capable of refusing it – and this is the route adopted by the great majority of commentators. To do so presupposes, first, that the *Gillick* formula, which was concerned with the narrow issue of contraception, can be extrapolated widely to include consent to treatment in general. There is no doubt that this can be, and is being, done: it is now fashionable to describe what the Americans would call a mature minor as being '*Gillick*-competent'.[11] Once this is accepted, it follows that the common law position as to the consent of minors has also been established, albeit by the narrowest of judicial margins. In summary, the general rule established by *Gillick* is that, in the event of a child wishing to exclude his or her parents from decision making, the latters' right to determine the treatment given to the former diminishes progressively until such time as the child achieves sufficient understanding and intelligence to enable him or her to understand fully what is proposed.

The second step, that of equiparating consent to and refusal of treatment is less easy to accept. Speaking, admittedly, from a minority position, I suggest that the *degree* of understanding required for valid consent to a doctor's advice is different from that needed to refuse to accept an opinion based on years of study and experience. In so saying, I do *not* deny that a child may, at times, be fully capable of a reasonable refusal of treatment – a refusal which may well be based on considerations other than medical; what I am proposing is that the *level* of required understanding may be higher in the latter than in the former circumstance. In any event, this is a stance the courts are not afraid to adopt when necessary. Thus, in *Re E (a minor)*, which concerned refusal of blood transfusion by a 15-year-old boy, WARD J held that, while the patient was of sufficient intelligence to be able to take decisions about his own well-being, he did not have a full understanding of the whole implication of what the refusal of that treatment involved,[12] and the hospital was given permission to treat him as they thought appropriate to his condition.[13]

LORD SCARMAN explained in *Gillick* that, in order to provide a competent consent, the child must have sufficient maturity to understand all that is involved, which is a very severe test insofar as children can have little insight into their adult futures. As evidenced above, the discretion of the court in wardship is certainly wide,[14] but the decisions indicate that there is a perceived need for some residual control over the minor's refusal of medical treatment despite his or her apparent *Gillick*-competence; given that the courts have retained such a role, it is reasonable to suppose that *some*, albeit minimal, responsibility should still rest with the parents. The delineation of such powers has been the subject of two controversial decisions in the Court of Appeal.

The first of these, *Re R (a minor)*,[15] concerned a 15-year-old girl who was becoming increasingly psychotic but who had rational periods during which she refused medication. She posed, essentially, three problems related to the general morality of imposed treatment, the capacity of a 15-year-old to consent to treatment and the equiparation of consent to and refusal of treatment. LORD DONALDSON emphasised that the capacity to consent will vary from child to child, according to the treatment envisaged and that, as a result, there could be no total transfer of the right to consent to or refuse treatment (at 156). He distinguished a parental right to *determine* treatment of a mature child, which Lord Scarman had discarded in *Gillick*, from a right to *consent* to treatment which persisted until the child attained the age of 18. Consent by itself created no obligation to treat and was no more than a key with which to open the door to treatment. There were, thus, two keyholders – the child and the parents – but, in the event of refusal by the child and consent by the parents, the former should be regarded as an important factor in management; conversely, parental consent in no way determined that the child should be treated, but it enabled treatment to be given lawfully. The Master of the Rolls also made it clear that consent by a competent child was equally enabling in the event of parental refusal.

LORD DONALDSON's opinion in *Re R* was subject to widespread academic criticism and was said to have driven a coach and horses through *Gillick*.[16] For reasons which have already been given, I prefer to see it as a correct statement of the law provided in the Family Law Reform Act 1969 although, R being below the age of 16, any dictum on the subject was, strictly speaking, obiter. The opinion, however, contained another thread, that of the clinical autonomy of the doctor: 'The decision whether to treat,' it was said, 'is dependent upon an exercise of [the doctor's] own professional judgment, subject only to the threshold requirement that ... he has the consent of someone who has the authority to give that consent' (at 158). At the end of the day, therefore, both parent and child may hold a key to the therapeutic door, but it is the doctor who decides whether or not it should be opened.

The second case, *Re W*,[17] concerned a minor already aged 16 who was suffering from anorexia nervosa and who refused to be transferred to a hospital providing specialist treatment for eating disorders. The court of first instance found her to be of sufficient understanding to make an informed decision but, nevertheless, ordered her removal; as she was already aged 16, she clearly came within the terms of the Family Law Reform Act 1969, s.8(1) and she appealed against the order. The case was, therefore, the first to confront s.8(3) directly as to its interpretation. The court of appeal considered that anorexia nervosa itself created a wish not to be cured. In other words, refusal of treatment was part of the disease itself and was a symptom for which the court could authorise treatment:[18] 'Where the wishes of the minor are themselves something which the doctors reasonably consider need to be treated in the minor's best interests, those wishes clearly have a much reduced significance' (at 33),

Once again, there was academic disapproval, but the alternatives available to the health care team (other than inactivity) were to wait until the child became too ill to make an autonomous decision and, then, commit her for compulsory treatment under the Mental Health Act 1983[19] or to treat her pleading necessity; both these approaches seem to be so reminiscent of the 'cat and mouse' tactics employed against the early suffragettes as to be morally unacceptable.

This time, the court was clearly at liberty to examine the Family Law Reform Act 1969 and concluded, with only minor reservations, that it does not remove the parents' common law right to consent to the treatment of a child below the age of 18; otherwise, why did the Act say it was no longer necessary to obtain the parents' consent rather than that their consent would be ineffective? The court also confirmed its earlier interpretation of s.8(3). It was further explained that the difference between the adult's undisputed right to refuse treatment and the more limited effect of refusal of treatment by a person aged 16–17 was that, in the former case, there was no-one else in a position to give consent (at 30).

It is certainly unfortunate that Lord Donaldson was clearly concerned, in the main, to protect the health carers against accusations of assault. Indeed, he went further in *Re W* by substituting the analogy of a flak jacket for that of the key he spoke of in *Re R*: the flak jacket is purely defensive equipment which does not involve even the volitional element of opening a lock.[20] Neither judgment pays any regard to the rights of children and they can, in fact, be interpreted as offending against the spirit of the Children Act 1989, s.1.[21] While there is, in my view, much good sense in Lord Donaldson's views, it would be impossible to deny that both *Re R* and *Re W* can be interpreted as being in conflict with intentions of the court in *Gillick*: the distinction of *Re W* on the grounds that, unlike *Gillick*, it was concerned with the power of the court is, at least, suspect. It may well be that any doubts will have to be resolved by a further hearing of a similar case in the House of Lords – or even by statute. It has been said that: 'It is better that any exceptions to the over-sixteen rule should be clearly defined ... with the full authority of Parliament.'[22]

Time, however, does not stand still while legislative action is considered and, as we go to press, the court has ordered the detention in a clinic – including the use, if necessary, of reasonable force – of a 16-year-old anorexic who opposed the order.[23] The case appears to be the first in which the court has taken such powers in the absence of care proceedings or without calling on the Mental Health Acts for authority. On the face of things, it seems to represent an extended use of the inherent jurisdiction of the court as retained by the Children Act 1989, s.100 (see p. 347), but it would be wrong to base discussion on a news report.

In general, however, we can say that the position in the United Kingdom is very similar to that in America. There the twin doctrines of the emancipated minor and the mature minor are well recognised in common law.[24] In the case of the former, the parents have surrendered or forfeited their duties and responsibilities and the person, in general terms, does not live at home and is self-supporting; such a person may clearly consent to medical treatment and, in some states, the doctor is entitled by statute to rely upon the patient's statement that he or she is emancipated. A mature minor, by contrast, is one who lives at home but is self-reliant and works or otherwise contributes substantially to his or her own support. The provision of treatment for a minor who appears to satisfy the law's criteria for maturity follows much the same lines as have been explained in *Gillick*, but the physician is advised to proceed with caution in so providing. The question is essentially a matter of whether or not the child can give informed consent (see p. 89).[25]

The reasonable parent

Thus far we have considered only such medical intervention as is ostensibly for the benefit of the child concerned. Conditions alter when the major benefit will accrue to some other party; the most obvious example – and one which is of particular illustrative importance because of its severity – is the *in vivo* donation of transplantable

tissue. This is, perhaps surprisingly, a considerable problem in practice. Many transplants, including, with increasing frequency, that of
bone marrow, are required during childhood; sibling donation is
often the preferred choice; and *in vivo* donation may be essential or
is, in any case, likely to produce a better result than is cadaver transplantation. The minor could, therefore, be involved frequently both
as donor and as recipient.[26]

The medico-legal difficulty in this situation is to establish the
authority of a parent to consent to donation – and there is very little
positive evidence on the point. The Family Law Reform Act 1969, s.8
is of no value as the section speaks specifically of treatment;[27] the
interpretation of s.8(3) is, therefore, irrelevant. Others have affirmed
that there is *no* authority: 'In the strict view of the law, parents and
guardians of minors cannot give consent on their behalf to any procedures which are of no particular benefit to them and which may
carry some risk of harm.'[28]

The late Master of the Rolls has, in one view, confused the issue in
saying of consent by minors:

> Organ donations are quite different and, as a matter of law, doctors
> would have to secure the consent of someone with a right to consent
> on behalf of a donor under the age of 18 or, if they relied on the
> consent of the minor himself or herself, be satisfied that the minor was
> '*Gillick*-competent' in the context of so serious a procedure which
> would not benefit the minor.[29]

He went on to say, 'This would be a highly improbable conclusion'
and, later:

> It is inconceivable that he should proceed in reliance solely upon the
> consent of an under-age patient, however '*Gillick*-competent', in the
> absence of supporting parental consent and equally inconceivable that
> he should proceed in the absence of the patient's consent. In any event
> he will need to seek the opinions of other doctors and may be well
> advised to apply to the court for guidance.

The remarks were, certainly, obiter but are highly persuasive coming
from such a source. Thus, it seems, from what has been said, that no
person in England below the age of 18 can give reliable consent to
donation of non-regenerative tissue in the absence of support from
either the parents or the court. Which would be perfectly clear had
LORD DONALDSON not put in his summary:

> A minor of any age who is *Gillick*-competent in the context of a par-
> ticular treatment has a right to consent to that treatment, which again
> cannot be overridden by those with parental responsibility, but can be

overridden by the court. Unlike the statutory right this common law right extends to the donation of blood or organs (at 35).

But it would be a brave surgeon who ignored LORD DONALDSON'S previous advice.

The whole passage, however, leads us to the concept of the 'reasonable parent'[30] who can be expected to look to the benefit to and the disadvantages for his child in the light of the benefit to others and to society in general. The reasonable parent would be able to assess these impersonal advantages against the pain and danger to his child and would be able to justify his or her decision accordingly.[31] The public interest might, indeed, provide a major plank for decision making because, as Skegg has pointed out, it could be extrapolated that the public interest would *not* be best served by considering that the donation of organs by children was something to which consent may never be given.

All of which suggests that there is a *prima facie* argument in favour of, if necessary, contriving the legality of organ donation by children, especially in the case of donation of replaceable tissue such as bone marrow, the legality of which is now virtually beyond dispute, even if by virtue only of common usage and lack of concern for the providers.[32] But the donation of non-regenerative tissue is another matter and it is noteworthy that many countries, including those with a strong cultural affinity with the United Kingdom and the United States, have evolved laws which are very restrictive of the practice. Organ donation by minors is, for example, prohibited by the Ontario Human Tissue Gift Act. In Australia, all the States rejected the recommendations of the Australian Law Reform Commission, which proposed a tightly controlled system and, as a result, it is not now lawful in Australia to remove non-regenerative material from a living child for the purposes of transplantation.[33] Brazier[34] believed that the English courts, if approached, would be far less amenable than their counterparts in America have been and there could well be a case for legislation on the matter.

An example of compromise legislation is to be found in France, where a living minor may only donate to his or her brother or sister; consent must be given by the donor's legal representative; and the procedure must be authorised by a committee composed of at least three experts, two of whom must be medical doctors, one of whom must have practised for 20 years. In the event that the minor can be consulted, refusal on his/her part must be respected in every case.

The unreasonable parent

In occasional instances, the behaviour of parents in relation to the medical treatment of their children may appear so unreasonable as to warrant paternalistic intervention by the doctor, or even recourse to the courts. Statute law is certain in imposing a duty on parents not to neglect or abandon a child in a manner likely to cause him or her unnecessary suffering or injury to health[35] – and this includes a failure to provide necessary medical treatment (s.1(2)(*a*) of the 1933 Act). Charges of murder or manslaughter may arise in the event of the death of the child. Convictions for these serious offences depend upon a duty of care being established, but there can be no doubt as to this in the case of parents and the duty may extend to a cohabiter.[36] The reluctance of the courts to convict in such circumstances is discussed in greater detail in Chapter 14, but the following quotation from *R* v. *Lowe*[37] is exemplary: 'If I omit to do something with the result that [the child] suffers injury to health which results in its death, we think that a charge of manslaughter should not be an inevitable consequence, even if the omission is deliberate' (per PHILLIMORE LJ at 709). Williams[38] regarded this as a right decision on the grounds that the low grade of duties that is imposed by a statute ought not to be translated automatically into the far more serious duties implied by the law of manslaughter – academic advice which has been followed in practice. In *R* v. *Sheppard*, a case involving neglect due to failure to provide adequate medical aid, the House of Lords held that the prosecution, to be successful, had to prove that the parents had deliberately or recklessly failed to provide that aid.[39]

Many instances of denial of what would generally be regarded as proper medical treatment derive from the religious beliefs of the parents. Sometimes these are relatively bizarre and the sects have died out. One such was the Peculiar People, whose belief in faith healing led to a number of trials for manslaughter in the late 19th century. In *R* v. *Senior*,[40] the issue turned very much on the distinction between common law and statutory manslaughter, as, indeed, it did in *Sheppard*. Senior was found guilty of the latter – and this, in passing, was despite the fact that the words '[provision of] medical aid' had been deleted in the relevant Prevention of Cruelty to Children Act, 1894. The *Senior* decision was distinguished in *Sheppard* on the grounds that the failure to give medical aid was premeditated and considered; the interesting conclusion follows that a sincerely held religious belief is not only not an excuse for disobeying the law on child protection but, also, may provide confirmation of the *mens rea* that is necessary for conviction.

The major sects whose faith involves rejection of medical treatment remaining with significant numbers of followers are the Christian Scientists and the Jehovah's Witnesses.[41] The organization of the former appears to be such that medico-legal conflict arises surprisingly seldom;[42] the latter's fundamental objection to blood transfusion, however, invites disagreement with the medical profession and, particularly, with paediatricians.

The problem has perhaps been most acute in the United States, where unconventional variations on the major religions are not uncommon.[43] The courts have, however, generally taken the view that, while an adult is free to believe in and act upon his religious beliefs, such freedom of action does not extend to exposing children to ill health or the risk of death; the state then has a compelling interest in protecting its children. This has been expressed in a number of well publicised court decisions. Thus, in *Prince* v. *Massachusetts*,[44] which was a case concerning the rights of Jehovah's Witnesses to proselytise rather than to refuse transfusion, it was said that the right to practise religion freely does not include the liberty to expose children to death. It was put even more forcibly in *Staelens* v. *Yoke*:[45] 'Parents may be free to become martyrs themselves. But it does not follow that they are free, in identical circumstances, to make martyrs of their children before they have reached the age of full and legal discretion.'

An attempt to enjoin a state statute empowering judges to authorise transfusions for children in the face of their parents' objections failed in the Supreme Court.[46] The American courts have, in fact, gone to extremes in the interests of children: for example, it was held that the state had a compelling interest in preserving the life of the mother of a seven-month-old child who would, on her death, have become a ward of the state[47] and, equally surprisingly, the transfusion of a woman has been ordered for the benefit of her fetus *in utero*.[48]

Predictably, the British courts have taken much the same line and it is to be inferred from BOOTH J in *Re R*[49] that no blame would attach to a doctor who failed to consult the parents before transfusing a child in an emergency. There is no precedent resulting in refusal of a medically indicated transfusion for a child at the request of the parents and, indeed, the only controversy has related to the procedure to be adopted by the health carers in order to acquire the almost certain authority to treat the child as necessary.[50] Thus, in *Re O*,[51] it was held that the inherent jurisdiction of the High Court was the most appropriate legal approach to a contested issue relating to emergency treatment for a child. Shortly afterwards, however, another judge of the Family Division opted for the invocation of a specific issue order under the Children Act 1989, s.8.[52] The difference is, however, largely a matter of relatively subtle interpretation of statute which is beyond the scope of this book; in point of fact, it was observed in *Re R* that the inherent jurisdiction was always available in the event of a need for a back-up. In general, it is noteworthy that the majority of Jehovah's Witnesses will support the use of any recommended medical techniques – including transfusion of blood substitutes – other than those that involve the use of blood, and the courts have stressed the need to consider the parents' views and to consult them in any other than an emergency situation; the welfare of the child must, however, remain as the paramount consideration. It has been suggested that the possibility of the transmission of AIDS or hepatitis and other less serious hazards of blood transfusion might be cited by Jehovah's Witnesses to support their religious convictions; the court in *Devon County Council* v. *S*[53] regarded such risks as minimal when balanced against the advantages of the procedure: it is extremely unlikely that they could be successfully prayed in aid in the event of criminal charges of neglect being brought against a sect member.

Having said which, it has to be noted that *Re T*[54] remains the most interesting case involving Jehovah's Witnesses in the British jurisdiction. It did, however, concern an adult and is therefore outside the terms of reference of this book. Nonetheless, T was a *young* adult and the case illustrates the importance of recognising undue parental influence on decision making by their maturing offspring. Comparison with *Re E*,[55] however, demonstrates that the courts can adopt a far more paternalistic attitude when faced with a similar situation in a minor.

Before leaving the topic of the reasonable or unreasonable parent, we should note that the courts will not always assume that the welfare of the child lies in treatment when there is a conflict of opinion. *R* v. *Cambridge Health Authority, ex parte B*[56] is a case in point which we have already discussed at p. 290. Unfortunately, it became clouded with economic and policy considerations; moreover, the highly invasive and doubtfully effective treatment for the child's leukaemia which the court refused to compel was not recommended by her *regular* medical advisers but was sought elsewhere by her parents as a last resort. A far less complicated instance is to be found in *In re T*,[57] which, again, has already been discussed in some depth. Here unanimous medical opinion was that a liver transplant was the best treatment for a four-month-old child suffering from biliary atresia; the parents did not want the child to undergo the operation. The Court of Appeal overturned the judge of first instance and declined to overrule the parental decision. BUTLER-SLOSS LJ considered the court to be unconcerned with the reasonableness of the mother's choice but, rather, it looked to the best interests of the child. To prolong life was not thought to be the sole objective of the court and, as we have seen, other factors were taken into consideration, including the mother's ability to manage the post-operative situation. Whatever one's views on the result, *In re T* it must be seen as a landmark interpretation of what constitutes the reasonable parent.

Experimental or unusual treatment

The gap between treatment of the minor and research on children is bridged by the subject of experimental treatment, a matter which becomes increasingly significant as medical technology advances ahead of legal and moral enquiry.

The consideration of a parent's right to choose an unusual or dangerous treatment for a child in defiance of medical opinion follows much the same line as that taken in respect of refusal of treatment. Again, it is convenient to look to the United States for precedents which expose some of the potential difficulties. In Massachusetts,[58] the court removed legal custody from the parents of a child suffering from leukaemia who had, on their own initiative, substituted an unorthodox regime of treatment by the biological product Laetrile and vitamins in place of chemotherapy. On the other hand, at much the same time in New York, the Court of Appeals refused to regard replacement of radiation and chemotherapy with Laetrile and nutritional therapy as constituting child neglect.[59] The cases were distinguished largely on the basis that the New York child was under the care of a physician and that there was no evidence that the disease was not responding to the unorthodox treatment; the Massachusetts case, by contrast, was regarded as one in which chemotherapy was controlling the disease and the parents had, accordingly, made an unadvised decision to deprive their child of treatment. The parents in *Hofbauer* were also said to have serious and justifiable concern about the ill-effects of radiation and chemotherapy. It is for this reason that the so-called 'Laetrile cases' are not only confusing but are also intrinsically bad examples of unusual choice of treatment; a decade ago, the side-effects of chemotherapy were greater and its effectiveness was far less than is now the case; the selection of 'comfort-care', with or without the use of a pharmacologically suspect adjunct, would have been a reasonable option.[60] One feels that the American courts would be of one mind were, say, a parent to opt for a herbal remedy rather than an antibiotic in a case of childhood meningitis; similarly, there would be no conflict were a comparable case to be brought in the United Kingdom under the Children Acts.

The outstanding experimental therapy introduced in recent years must be xenotransplantation, as exemplified by the case of 'Baby Fae'.[61] The circumstances in which a neonate with congenital heart disease was treated by transplantation of a baboon's heart seem to have been unusual and can be seen as cautionary in several respects.

Baby Fae was aged 14 days when she was given her baboon's heart; she died 17 days later. The most important issues in the present context involve not only the sufficiency of parental consent to such a procedure but also the propriety, both moral and legal, of seeking such consent. The problems are not so much those of experimentation but, rather, those of therapeutic innovation.[62] The distinction is important because, in the case of treatment, the physician is entitled to a degree of 'therapeutic privilege' in withholding information from the patient – or, in the case of an infant, from its parents – which might, if given, rebound to his or her detriment.[63] The innovative situation must, then, pose the difficult question of whether an element of investigative enthusiasm may have affected the doctor's use of this privilege. The patient's only safeguard against this possibility lies within the tort of negligence which, in this particular field, is founded on some exceptionally old cases which do not seem to have any modern counterparts.[64] It was said in *Carpenter* that 'Before the new practice can be used to shield the surgeon from the charge of malpractice it must ... have been successful in so many instances as to establish satisfactorily the propriety and safety of adopting it.' In other words, medicine must progress, but the potential benefit of a new treatment must either be easily predictable or the condition to be treated must be so severe that the added risks of pioneering are acceptable – and this, in turn, presupposes a rational or informed consent at an exceptionally high level of understanding.

Whether or not the Baby Fae case came up to these expectations has been a matter of argument. A colleague of the surgeon who performed the operation is reported as saying:

> I think that this xenograft is premature because I am not aware of any finding in the clinical literature that suggests anything but this prevailing rule – the human body will reject her baboon heart within the next week or two, and cyclosporine will not prevent it. This is not good clinical experimentation because medical science is not yet at the point we can cross the xenograft barrier.[65]

Could one say the same thing now? There are few surgical techniques that are advancing as fast as that of transplantation, and xenotransplantation offers immense resource possibilities. The constraints of speciesism probably put a limit on the use of primates,[66] but moral objections to the harvesting of non-primate material for human therapy are certainly less cogent. The effective production of transgenic pigs – or pigs adapted so as to incorporate human genetic material into their cells – is not all that far away and the use of such animals, coupled with the rapidly increasing effectiveness of immunosuppression, transforms xenotransplantation from a science fiction to near reality at least in terms of a decade or more.[67] Even so, there are vast difficulties to overcome and these are practical as well as ethical: porcine viruses could be transmitted to man, the life expectancy of a pig's heart and its effectiveness in man is currently unknown, and so on. The United Kingdom has recently decided to establish a Xenotransplantation Interim Regulatory Authority which will oversee developments in the field pending specific legislation.[68] The Nuffield Council on Bioethics has recommended that treatment by xenograft should be evaluated in adults before being used for children; one fancies that it will be some years before the appearance of a British Baby Fae.

Minors as subjects for experiment and research

It is easy to assume that children should not be used as experimental subjects until the proposed procedure has been assessed in adults or older children who are able to make their own decisions. The difficulty is that children are not merely small adults – their metabolism and response to drugs is, in many ways, markedly different. To ban all research and experimentation on immature children would, therefore, be to deprive the speciality of paediatrics of a main avenue for advancement of its expertise; this is obviously undesirable and some justifiable middle way has to be found between, at one end, the total protection of children and, at the other, their blatant exploitation as pliable subjects. Hubbard[69] has quoted Shipers to the effect:

> There should be strong reason in professional judgment for the use of immature children ... in any clinical investigation where there is no direct benefit intended for the child. However, such involvement should not be ruled out as illegal and unethical in all circumstances ... involvement should be allowed where the study has firm medical support and justification, promises important new knowledge of benefit to science and to mankind, and where there is no discernible risk involved for the child-subject.[70]

Before considering the morality of child experimentation, one has first to dispose of the legal impediments to obtaining the consent that is needed to elide a charge of battery or of negligence. We have already noted (at p. 325) the view of the Medical Research Council voiced more than thirty years ago as to parental powers, but support for this extreme view would be difficult to find today. Moreover, the Council itself went on to say: 'the reality of any purported consent which may have been obtained is a question of fact and as with an adult the evidence would, if necessary, have to show that irrespective of age the person concerned fully understood the implications to himself of the procedures to which he was consenting.[71]

It is clear from the previous discussion that the Family Law Reform Act 1969, s.8 provides neither negative nor positive precedent as to research. One is again thrown back to the common law position which is supported, very probably, by *Gillick*. This resort, however, relates only to the relatively mature child who is capable of understanding what is involved,[72] and it is self-evident that the 'understanding' required by the law would be of a high standard and at a higher level in the field of research than would be demanded for consent to treatment. Given that these conditions were satisfied, the common law would be hospitable to good research.[73] What constitutes good research is determined at primary level by Research Ethics Committees (see p. 202), one function of which is to prejudge the possible attitudes of the courts; the evaluation can be based on the harmlessness and kindness of the experiment and on its motivation and worthwhileness. The danger of justifying the means by the end through a risk/benefit ratio approach must, however, be borne very much in mind.

We are left, then, with the problem of the child who cannot understand and, accordingly, of the validity of pure parental consent.[74] Here we must again use the concept of the reasonable parent. Dworkin[75] has noted that the courts, outside wardship, have moved from the concept of the child's interests being paramount to their being of first consideration; this implies that other interests may be taken into consideration and the reasonable parent might well think that there was merit in balancing the social benefits of a trial against a minimal risk to his child. Experimentation on infants thus becomes a moral issue rather than one which is definable by law.[76]

Some years ago, the Institute of Medical Ethics published particularly detailed guidelines.[77] Recommendations and conclusions as to parents and guardians included (a) that the prime consideration in any research involving children should be that it be not against the interest of any individual child, and (b) that proxy consent to a non-therapeutic research procedure should be legally valid and ethically acceptable only when the risk of such research is no more than minimal. It was further recommended that, for consent to be valid, the consent of parents should be required for children of all ages and that the child's assent should be obtained from the age of seven upwards; non-therapeutic research should not be carried out on a child aged seven to 14 who refused assent. Particularly important recommendations for investigators included the use of Research Ethics Committees, the involvement of parents as partners to the procedure, the provision of adequate time for explanation to parents, subjects and other professionals involved and the avoidance of separating parents from their children. No financial or other reward was to be offered to parents, but small gifts could be given to the child subjects at the end of the project. In general, it was concluded that research involving children should not be undertaken unless the need was specific and there was no other route to the knowledge available; non-therapeutic research projects should not be carried out if they involve greater than minimal risk to the individual child. A minimal risk was defined by the Institute as one that involves a risk of death lower than 1:1 000 000, a risk of a major complication lower than 1:100 000 or a risk of a minor complication of less than 1:1000.[78]

While such guidelines represent what may be called the 'bottom line', the extent to which the reasonable parent can exceed the limits is likely to be a matter of opinion. The state would certainly reject the validity of consent to a manifestly hazardous procedure but, within these parameters, a balancing decision must be taken between potential risk and the public benefit. Even then, LORD DONALDSON's limitations expressed in *Re R*,[79] to the effect that parental consent does not necessarily imply action as a result, must apply; the researcher cannot proceed simply on the basis of that consent. Some formula must be found by which to include the child's interests in the equation, and this is by no means an easy task. It could be argued that the research subject *must* benefit insofar as he or she is a member of the class or group that will benefit from that research. This, however, presupposes that the answer to the relevant problem is already known: a supposition which negates the need for 'research'. An alternative is to see a moral benefit accruing to a child who takes part in an altruistic exercise designed to benefit others; there is much merit in this proposition, but it applies only to the child who can appreciate it and such a child is excluded from the present discussion. It could be suggested that the individual subject *might* benefit directly from the experiment in later years but this, and similar, attempted justifications carry with them a ring of sophistry. In the end, it seems that, provided the value of the research has been accepted by a competent Research Ethics Committee, and provided it satisfies the test of no more than minimal risk, the best justification for involving a child who has not achieved *Gillick*-competence in a research project is to view parental consent as an expression of family unity, or of the bond of trust that joins loving parents and their children. Rigid adoption of an individualistic position would prohibit any non-therapeutic research in young children, a conclusion which would be to the detriment of children as a whole.

The position of the researcher in law

It remains only to append a short note on the relatively obvious legal consequences which would follow should a researcher proceed in the absence of consent. If there were no consent at all, both criminal charges and civil actions for assault could be competent; there would be virtually no defence available should harm come to a child in the context of a non-consensual, non-therapeutic experiment. It must also be accepted that a hazardous procedure might well not be covered by an apparently valid consent which could be deemed irrelevant on public policy grounds (see p. 319).[80]

Furthermore, an action in negligence might arise[81] were the consent found to be flawed, the most likely contention being that it was based on insufficient information.[82] It is emphasised, in conclusion, that information must be particularly fully given in the case of non-therapeutic measures which, by definition, attract no 'therapeutic privilege'.[83]

Notes

1   In the adult context, see *R* v. *Brown (Anthony)* [1993] 2 All ER 75.
2   *R* v. *Donovan* [1934] 2 KB 498. For Scotland, see *Smart* v. *HM Adv* 1975 SLT 65.
3   [1981] QB 715.
4   Criminal Law (Consolidation) (Scotland) Act 1995 s.5
5   For a review, and a suggestion that the practice may still be conducted in the United Kingdom, see J.A. Black and G.D. Debelle, 'Female genital mutilation in Britain' (1995) 310 Brit Med J 1590.
6   The iniquitous case of *In re Agar-Ellis* (1883) 24 Ch D 317 was widely quoted, with profound disapproval, in *Gillick*, n. 8 below.
7   G. Dworkin, 'Law and medical experimentation: of embryos, children and others with limited legal capacity' (1987) 13 Monash U L R 189; I. Kennedy, 'Consent to treatment; the capable person', in C. Dyer (ed.), *Doctors, Patients and the Law* (1992), Oxford: Blackwell Scientific.
8   *Gillick* v. *West Norfolk and Wisbech Area Health Authority* [1985] 3 All ER 402, HL.
9   The authority of the Scottish minor is, in fact, rather wider than that of his/her English counterpart, in that consent can be given to any 'procedure', whereas the 1969 Act confines a valid consent to 'treatment'. Note also that there is no 'best interests' qualification as to the doctor's opinion (cf. Lord Fraser at p. 413). See L. Edwards, 'The right to consent and the right to refuse: more problems with minors and medical consent' [1993] Juridical Rev 52.
10 See, now, J.K. Mason and R.A. McCall Smith, *Law and Medical Ethics* (4th edn, 1994) London: Butterworths, p. 227. This view has been confirmed by LORD DONALDSON (see below) and by BALCOMBE LJ in *Re W (a minor) (medical treatment)* (1992) 9 BMLR 22 at 38.
11 A description introduced by LORD DONALDSON MR in *Re R (a minor) (wardship: medical treatment)* (1991) 7 BMLR 147 at 155.
12 (1990) 9 BMLR 1 at 6.
13 See also *South Glamorgan County Council* v. *B and W* (1992) 11 BMLR 162 where

a 15-year-old *Gillick*-competent girl was sent to a specialist adolescent unit against her wishes.

14 And it is wider than that of the parents and may be limitless: *Re W (a minor) (medical treatment)* (1992) 9 BMLR 22 per LORD DONALDSON MR at 33.

15 Note 11 above. For deeper analysis of these cases, see J.K. Mason, 'Master of the Balancers; non-voluntary therapy under the mantle of Lord Donaldson' [1993] Juridical Rev 115.

16 Kennedy, n. 7 above.

17 *Re W (a minor) (medical treatment)* (1992) 9 BMLR 22.

18 This is a ploy which the courts are quite willing to adopt. See, for example, *B v. Croydon District Health Authority* (1994) 22 BMLR 13; *Re L (Patient: Non-consensual treatment)* (1997) 35 BMLR 44.

19 Similar cases are discussed from the medical aspect by A. Elton, P. Honig, A. Bentovim and J. Simons, 'Withholding consent to lifesaving treatment: three cases' (1995) 310 Brit Med J 373.

20 A dwindling number of persons will understand that the 'flak jacket' was an item of body armour worn by bomber crews of the Second World War as protection against anti-aircraft fire.

21 See J.A. Devereux, D.P.H. Jones and D.L. Dickenson, 'Can children withhold consent to treatment?' (1993) 306 Brit Med J 1459.

22 P.N. Parkinson, 'The Gillick case – just what has it decided?' (1986) 16 Fam Law 11.

23 *Re C*, as yet unreported. See F. Gibb and J. Laurence, 'Judge orders anorexic girl to be detained' (1997), *The Times*, 13 March, p. 1.

24 For general discussion, see H.L. Hirsh, 'The law protecting children in the United States of America', in J.K. Mason (ed.), *Paediatric Forensic Medicine and Pathology* (1989), London: Chapman & Hall.

25 See D.W. Meyers, 'Parental rights and consent to medical treatment of minors', in Mason, n. 24 above.

26 Although, in practice, the use of minors as donors of non-regenerative organs is exceptionally rare. See J.K. Mason, 'Legal aspects of organ transplantation', in C. Dyer (ed.), *Doctors, Patients and the Law* (1992), London: Blackwell Scientific.

27 P.D.G. Skegg, 'Engish law relating to experimentation on children' [1977] 2 Lancet 754.

28 'Responsibility in investigations on human subjects', Report of the Medical Research Council for 1962–3 (1964), Cmnd 2382, London: HMSO.

29 *Re W (a minor) (medical treatment)*, n. 17 above per LORD DONALDSON at 31.

30 This has been suggested by P.D.G. Skegg, 'Consent to medical procedures on minors' (1973) 36 MLR 370, p. 376 and n. 44, reproduced in *Law, Ethics and Medicine* (1984), Oxford: Clarendon Press.

31 In the American case of *Strunk v. Strunk* 445 SW 2d 145 (Ky, 1969), which, admittedly, dealt with a mentally retarded adult rather than a minor, it was concluded that, in view of the close relationship between two brothers, it would be in the donor's interest that the life of his brother be saved. Skegg, n. 30 above, quotes similar unreported cases.

32 One cannot help wondering how valid is the minor donor's consent in view of the intense familial coercion which must be involved. See the exceptionally media-driven case, *R v. Cambridge Health Authority, ex parte B* (1995) 25 BMLR 5, QBD, 23 BMLR 1, CA. A useful debate is to be found in L. Delaney, S. Month, J. Savulescu and P. Browett, 'Altruism by proxy: volunteering children for bone marrow donation' (1996) 312 Brit Med J 240. A recently reported English case, involving a mentally handicapped sibling and very similar in tone to *Strunk* (n. 31 above), suggests that the courts might be prepared to stretch the concept

of the donor's 'psychological benefit' to the limit: *Re Y (adult patient) (transplant: bone marrow)* (1997) 35 BMLR 111.

33 As an example, see Human Tissue and Transplant Act 1982, ss.12,13 (W. Australia).

34 M. Brazier, *Medicine, Patients and the Law* (2nd edn, 1992), Harmondsworth: Penguin Books, p. 398.

35 Children and Young Persons Act, 1933, s.1; Children and Young Persons (Scotland) Act, 1937, s.12.

36 *R* v. *Gibbins and Proctor* (1918) 13 Cr App Rep 134.

37 [1973] 1 QB 702.

38 G. Williams, *Textbook of Criminal Law* (2nd edn, 1983), London: Stevens, p. 276.

39 *R* v. *Sheppard and another* [1980] 3 All ER 899.

40 *R* v. *Senior* [1899] 1 QB 283.

41 Born-Again Christians (see *Re S (adult: refusal of medical treatment)* (1992) 9 BMLR 69) seem to make their rules individually rather than as a sect.

42 In the United States, the Supreme Court has recently refused to review a case in which $1.5m was awarded to the father of a child whose diabetes was unsuccessfully treated by spiritual healing at the request of its mother. Significantly, however, criminal charges against the mother were dismissed in the state court. See J. Roberts, 'Religion should not put a child's health at risk' (1996) 312 Brit Med J 268.

43 For an overview, see H.L. Hirsh and H. Phifer 'The interface of medicine, religion and the law: religious objections to treatment' (1985) 4 Med Law 121.

44 321 US 158 (1944).

45 432 F supp 834 (Ill, 1980), quoting from *People ex rel Wallace* v. *Labrenz* 104 NE 2d 769 (Ill, 1952). An alternative formula has recently been stated by the Minnesota Court of Appeal: 'Although one is free to believe what one will, religious freedom ends when one's conduct offends the law by, for example, endangering a child's life'. See Roberts, n. 42 above.

46 *Jehovah's Witnesses in Washington* v. *King County Hospital Unit No 1* 88 S Ct 1260 (1968).

47 *Application of President and District of Georgetown College Inc* 331 F 2d 1000 (1964); see also *Hamilton* v. *McAuliffe* 353 A 2d 634 (Md, 1976).

48 *Raleigh Fitkin–Paul Morgan Memorial Hospital* v. *Anderson* 201 A 2d 537 (NJ, 1964).

49 *Re R (minor)* (1993) 15 BMLR 72 at 76.

50 In *Devon County Council* v. *S* (1992) 11 BMLR 105, it was not even thought necessary to call on the plaintiffs' counsel.

51 *Re O (a minor)* (1993) 19 BMLR 148.

52 *Re R,* n. 49 above. For fuller discussion, see C. Gilham, 'The dilemma of parental choice' (1993) 143 NLJ 1219.

53 Note 50 above.

54 *Re T (adult: refusal of medical treatment)* (1992) 9 BMLR 46.

55 Note 12 above.

56 Note 32 above.

57 *In re T (a minor) (wardship: medical treatment)* [1997] 1 All ER 906.

58 *Custody of a Minor* 379 NE 2d 1053 (Mass, 1978); 393 NE 2d 836 (Mass, 1979).

59 *In re Hofbauer* 393 NE 2d 1009 (NY, 1979). For discussion, see M. Swartz, 'The patient who refuses medical treatment: a dilemma for hospitals and physicians' (1985) 11 Am J Law Med 147; D.W. Meyers, *Medico-Legal Implications of Death and Dying* (1981), Rochester: Lawyers Co-operative Publishing Co, pp. 407 ff.

60 Whether a hospital should cooperate with parents who have obtained experimental treatment of doubtful value is well discussed in C. Yeoh, E. Kiely and

H. Davies, 'Unproven treatment in childhood oncology – how far should pae-diatricians co-operate?' (1994) 20 J Med Ethics 75, with commentary by J. Jackson, at 77.

61 See L.L. Bailey, S.L. Nehlsen-Cannarella, W. Concepcion and W.B. Jolley, 'Baboon-to-human cardiac xenotransplantation in a neonate' (1985) 254 J Amer Med Ass 3321; H.S. Schwartz, 'Bioethical and legal considerations in increasing the sup-ply of transplantable organs: from UAGA to "Baby Fae" ' (1985) 10 Am J Law Med 397; L.L. Hubbard, 'The Baby Fae case' (1987) 6 Med Law 385..

62 For an analysis of the distinction, see B.M. Dickens, 'What is a medical experi-ment?' (1975) 113 Canad Med Ass J 635.

63 For the seminal cases, see, in the UK, *Sidaway* v. *Bethlem Royal Hospital Gover-nors* [1985] 1 All ER 643; in the USA, *Canterbury* v. *Spence* 464 F 2d 772 (DC Cir, 1972); and in Canada, *Reibl* v. *Hughes* (1980) 114 DLR (3d) 1.

64 *Slater* v. *Baker and Stapleton* (1767) 95 Eng Rep 860 and, in the USA, *Carpenter* v. *Blake* 60 Barb 488 (NY S Ct, 1871).

65 Hubbard, n. 61 above. It was also said that no effort was made to obtain a human heart and that the option of heterotransplantation was not put to the parents who were, in fact, unmarried minors. It is difficult to believe that they understood the implications fully.

66 Nuffield Council on Bioethics, *Animal to Human Transplants* (1996), London: Nuffield Council on Bioethics, para.4.40.

67 See, for example, F.H. Bach, 'Transplanting porcine hearts to humans' (1996) 312 Brit Med J 651.

68 Advisory Group on the Ethics of Xenotransplantation (I. Kennedy, chairman), *Animal Tissue into Humans* (1996), London: Department of Health.

69 Note 61 above.

70 W.J. Shipers, 'Informed consent and the child in nontherapeutic human experi-mentation: evolution to solution' (1985) 32 Med Trial Tech Q 33.

71 Note 28 above.

72 See Skegg, n. 27 above; also J.M. Burchell, 'Non-therapeutic medical research on children' (1978) 95 Sth Afr LJ 193.

73 G. Dworkin, 'Legality of consent to non-therapeutic medical research on in-fants and young children' (1978) 53 Arch Dis Child 443; and more recently, 'Law and medical experimentation: of embryos, children and others with lim-ited capacity' (1987) 13 Monash U L R 189.

74 The Declaration of Helsinki ('Recommendations guiding medical doctors in biomedical research involving human subjects') specifically states: 'when the subject is a minor, permission from the responsible relative replaces that of the subject in accordance with national legislation' (at para I(11)).

75 Dworkin (1978) n. 73 above.

76 For an ethical overview, see R.A. McCall Smith, 'Research and experimentation involving children', in Mason, n. 24 above.

77 Institute of Medical Ethics 'Medical research with children: ethics, law and practice' (1986), Bulletin no. 14, p. 8. For discussion, see R.J. Robinson, 'Ethics Committees and research in children' (1987) 294 Brit Med J 1243.

78 More recent guidelines include those of the British Paediatric Association, *Guidelines for the Ethical Conduct of Medical Research Involving Children* (1992); the Medical Research Council, *The Ethical Conduct of Research on Children* (1991) and the Royal College of Physicians of London, *Research Involving Patients* (1996). Parental consent is obligatory – certainly in the case of children under 10 years old.

79 Note 11 above.

80 Although it is taken in a wholly different context, the European Court of Human Rights has said: '[The United Kingdom] is unquestionably entitled to

regulate the infliction of physical harm through the criminal law [even in a consensual siuation]': *Laskey, Jaggard and Brown* v. *United Kingdom* (1997) Times, 20 February.

81 See D. Giesen, 'Civil liability for new methods of treatment and experimentation: a comparative examination' (1995) 3 Med L Rev 22, which argues, correctly in my view, that the civil law makes no distinction between medical treatment and medical research.

82 The fundamental UK case, from which all other 'consent' cases (including *Sidaway*, n. 63 above) flow, is *Chatterton* v. *Gerson* [1981] 1 QB 432.

83 *Halushka* v. *University of Saskatchewan* (1966) 53 DLR (2d) 436.

13 The Protection of Young Children

There are two main aspects of the protection of children which have to be considered separately. Firstly, children must be protected against a society which may see them as a source of cheap labour or as a group who are defenceless in other ways. A review of this particular form of child abuse involves discussion of the steady improvement of industrial law since the middle of the 19th century and of the evolution of social law designed to prohibit the sexual exploitation of young people. The latter, which began with the Criminal Law Amendment Act, 1885, is still evolving; the legislation of 1978,[1] which was designed to halt the increasing trade in child pornography, has now been overtaken by the Internet.[2] But it is not this type of child abuse which is to be discussed here. We are concerned with the second problem – that is, of intrafamilial abuse, which must have existed in antiquity but which was brought into the bright light only in the 20th century.[3] The sophisticated society of the time, whether represented by the medical profession or the public at large, was unprepared to accept the concept of premeditated violence against the young by those responsible for their care until Kempe jolted the public conscience by introducing the term 'the battered baby'.[4]

The medical and sociological literature in this area has mushroomed in recent years and this helps to feed the impression that child abuse itself is increasing in similar fashion. Yet the very history of the topic suggests that we should be cautious before accepting this as fact. There are four basic ways by which any apparent increase in abuse might be explained. It could be (a) that there is a real increase in violence within the family; (b) that the definition of child abuse has been changing; (c) that there has been an increase in awareness of the problem; or (d) that there has been an increase in the reporting of cases. And, of course, all four factors may be operating together. All need examination, but a rational assessment of the first is impossible without a preliminary consideration of the others.

The definition of child abuse

The difficulty here is that one must first define the culture of which one is speaking. In Sweden, for example, the child who is chastised by its parents has a right of action for criminal assault; United Kingdom law is still clear that parents have a right to punish their children and that this includes the use of reasonable corporal punishment.[5] For this reason, *comparative* reviews of child protection are virtually meaningless and, to all intents, this chapter is confined to conditions in the United Kingdom. A further complication is inserted by the passage of time during which attitudes change within an individual culture. I recollect receiving eight strokes of the cane – for no greater offence, let it be said, than giving a sherry party to celebrate promotion in the school hierarchy – and the only parental comment was one of surprise at the leniency of the sentence; some 50 years later, a case is taken as far as the European Court of Human Rights (albeit unsuccessfully as to the immediate point) on the grounds that corporal punishment in schools is degrading and inhumane.[6] But, while the time factor may have considerable impact on the perceived incidence of child abuse, there is no doubt that the most important influence has been the gradual extension of the definition of child abuse so as to cover increasingly wide medico-legal fields.

The syndrome which Caffey first described, and which was Kempe's focus of interest, was the repetitive infliction of physical injury on children by those having a caring role.[7] This is a relatively simple concept and one which can be accommodated under the descriptive and unemotional title of repetitive non-accidental injury (NAI) in childhood. The true frequency of NAI cannot be known for certain and estimates are derived, in the main, as extrapolations from the mortality figures. It is generally believed that there are some 200–300 deaths from this cause each year in the United Kingdom, although suggestions have been made that this figure is set both too high and too low.[8] It is even harder to discover the number of non-fatal clinical cases; estimates will vary widely, depending on whether one includes only relatively severe cases with a recognisable morbidity or one extends this to include minor injuries which are discovered incidentally. But, even if figures of 5000–10 000 are accepted, the fact remains that this is a relatively small number when distributed among all general practitioners in the United Kingdom. Some doctors will never see a case, while others may recognise no more than one or two a year. The resulting inexperience is likely to result in underrecognition.

Kempe's limited concept of child abuse has, however, been extending steadily, and particularly so as to include sexual abuse. Inevitably, this focuses attention on incest, but sexual abuse of children is by no means so confined and, again, is likely to be ever more widely interpreted. It has been stated in an official publication:

> Any child below the age of consent may be deemed to have been sexually assaulted when any person, by design or neglect, involves the child in any activity of a nature which is intended to lead to the sexual arousal and gratification of that person or any other person. This definition pertains whether or not this activity involves genital contact and whether or not this is initiated by the child.[9]

By any standards, this is a wide definition which cannot be excluded as accounting for the very different concepts of the incidence of child abuse which are now prevalent.[10] It has been suggested that some one in four women and one in nine men have experienced sexual abuse before the age of 18 in the United States;[11] figures of the order of one in 10 children being abused are bandied about in the United Kingdom. A more recent source of confusion is to be found in the 'recovered memory syndrome', a concept which is widely accepted, at least in the United States and Canada. In this syndrome, the adult patient's psychiatric problems are seen as being attributable to suppression of the memories of sexual abuse in childhood. Whatever may be the merits of such a hypothesis, a retrospective action based on such abuse is, currently, virtually unavailable in England. The House of Lords has decided that sexual abuse is an assault rather than a personal injury. As a result, the special time limit, which runs for three years from the time the plaintiff knew or should have known that injuries resulted from the incident, does not apply; claims for sexual abuse must, therefore, be brought within six years of the incident in England – which, by definition, effectively eliminates reliance on the syndrome.[12]

Definitions of abuse have now spilled over into the realms of psychology and psychiatry and have established the concept of emotional abuse of children. There can be no doubt that this is a very real matter;[13] the inevitable difficulties, as with all emotional disorders, are those of interpretation, demonstration and proof. Anyone can appreciate a physical injury: a bruise can be seen, measured and described objectively in simple terms; by contrast, the extent, or even the existence, of emotional injury is subjective to the observer. The handing over of a child to the care of a hired nursemaid may appear to one psychologist as an extreme example of parental rejection; to another, it may present as an extravagant act of loving care. Granted that the child is emotionally deprived, it is likely to be hard to ascribe this with certainty to the parents and, even then, to demonstrate that it is deliberate; conflicts between parents and child psychologists can, at times, be intense and painful, for the parents may be behaving very properly according to their own lights. Finally, even when there is emotional abuse which is blatant to the skilled observer, it may be very difficult to convince a court of a situation which is intangible to the lay mind. Clearly, to incorporate emotional injury within the confines of non-accidental injury is to stretch the definition of the syndrome very significantly.

An increasing awareness

It has been very difficult for doctors *not* to become more aware of the problem of child abuse, so powerful has been the propaganda in the field since the mid-century. Even so, it is interesting to note that, only a decade ago, sexual abuse of children was regarded as being, in the main, something which occurred across the Atlantic and which was relatively novel in the United Kingdom.[14] Despite the general decline in the teaching of forensic medicine in British medical schools, there has been a real increase in tuition on child abuse in the undergraduate paediatric curriculum. A very small study undertaken in Edinburgh illustrated the importance of education.[15] Enquiries as to the prevalence of non-accidental injury in childhood were made of general practitioners, 21 of whom cooperated. What had not been anticipated was the distinction which appeared between elderly doctors and those who had qualified relatively recently. Almost all eight doctors who had qualified before 1960 denied the existence of NAI in their practices; by contrast, the 13 practitioners who had qualified since then reckoned they each saw between two and three cases a year and took an active part in their follow-up, including frequent consultations with health visitors and social workers. No differences as to the type of patient catchment could be detected in the practices as a whole. The limited nature of this inquiry is very obvious; nevertheless a strong feeling remains that a similar pattern would have emerged had other, and larger, areas of the country been included. The corollary is that, were such a study to be repeated today, all practitioners would be found to be reporting cases.

Evidence of increasing awareness of the syndrome stems from other, rather dated, sources. Thus, in South Wales,[16] the small number of children who sustained severe non-accidental injury – that is, fractures, internal injuries or intracranial haemorrhage – actually fell in the decade 1975–84. There was, however, a dramatic rise in the number of those who were moderately injured (sustaining injuries to the soft tissues only) in 1974,[17] a rise which continued until reaching a plateau in the early 1980s. The results are due to a combination of influences: firstly, the question of definition is again raised – there is an increasing acceptance of lesser injuries as falling within the spectrum of non-accidental injury – and, secondly, it can be inferred that, since 1973 or thereabouts, physicians have been increasingly aware that injuries which are described by parents as being accidental in origin may not, in fact, be so caused. The conclusion is forced that statistics derived from 25 or so years ago are unlikely to be representative of the *actual* occurrence of child abuse in the United Kingdom today.

An increase in reporting

Increased reporting is the natural consequence of widening definitions and increasing awareness. There is a tendency to concentrate on the medical profession as the main source of information, but awareness of child abuse is a property of several other groups. Social workers, health visitors, teachers, even neighbours and the children themselves, are all alerted to the existence of the problem, and all have been increasingly indoctrinated both professionally and through the communications media. Thus there may be many reasons for the increase in reports which has certainly occurred. Referrals to Scottish Reporters to the Children's Panel (see below, p. 348) on the grounds of actual or anticipated damage to children totalled 2691 in 1986 and 5110 in 1989, representing an increase of 94 per cent over three years. By contrast, referrals on these grounds actually fell from a peak of 7093 in 1991 to 6819 in 1994, which is a decease of 4 per cent over the three-year period. There is, thus, a suggestion that the relentless growth in alleged cases may be flattening out. However, action following a referral can only be taken within a legal framework and it is that which must now be considered.

The statutory protection of children

The criminal law

Violence constitutes just as much an offence within the home as it does outside. The Offences Against the Person Act, 1861 is not mitigated in a matrimonial situation,[18] and it is even less likely to be so in the case of a child; similarly, the common law of Scotland as to assault applies within the family environment. The fact that few prosecutions are raised in any other than the most serious cases of child abuse is probably due more to evidentiary difficulties than to an unwillingness on the part of the authorities. This is particularly well shown in cases of child neglect: it has been held that parents cannot be convicted of wilful neglect unless they have deliberately or recklessly failed to provide the attention needed.[19] The prosecution in *Sheppard* was founded on the Children and Young Persons Act,

1933 which stipulates a number of specific offences which can be perpetrated by an adult on a child; in addition to assaulting or neglecting a child in a manner likely to cause it unnecessary suffering or injury to health, it is an offence to leave a child exposed to an open fire (s.11) or to be drunk while in bed with a child (s.1(2)(*b*)). Very similar provisions are to be found in the Children and Young Persons (Scotland) Act, 1937 ss.12, 22, but the penalties under both often appear derisory.

Sexual abuse is criminalised mainly by the Sexual Offences Act, 1956,[20] which perpetuates the obsession of the criminal law with defloration; thus those offences which might occur within an intergenerational relationship – having intercourse with a girl below the age of 13, unlawful intercourse with a girl aged less than 16 and incest (see below) – are all characterised by intercourse *per vulvam* and exclude other forms of penile penetration.[21] However, the 1956 Act also criminalises indecent assault (ss.14 and 15), which can be committed by either sex in a homosexual or heterosexual configuration and to which a child below the age of 16 cannot consent, and also homosexual practices against boys (ss.12 and 16). Similar offences are detailed in the Criminal Law (Consolidation) (Scotland) Act 1995, and the Act also includes the commission of lewd, indecent or libidinous practices towards girls between the ages of 12 and 16 years (s.6); such practices towards children of either sex below the age of puberty (12 years for a girl and 14 for a boy) are offences at common law. The offence covers practices which fall short of indecent assault and which would include inciting a child to perform indecent acts without any assault on the part of the adult. Comparable offences in England and Wales are covered by the Indecency with Children Act, 1960 which applies when the child of either sex is aged under 14 years.

There is thus no real reason why a child should not be protected against most forms of abuse by the criminal law. But there is no certainty of conviction even in apparently flagrant cases; it is, at least, doubtful whether the near inevitable break-up of the family which follows conviction is the ideal solution in every case; and criminal prosecution in conditions which are fair to the accused is an unsatisfactory way of protecting the child. For this, we must look to family law.

Family law

The greater part of family law as related to the protection of children in England and Wales is now consolidated in the Children Act 1989.[22] Perhaps the most important change the Act imposes as compared with the first edition of this book is to limit severely the opportunities available to local authorities to evade the conditions under which children can be removed from their families which derive from statute by seeking wardship of children at risk; on the other hand, the decisions of local authorities are no longer subject to direction by the court.[23]

Compulsory care of a child in England and Wales is now subject to the grant by the court[24] of a care or supervision order (s.31). An application for an order can be made only by a local authority or an authorised person, the latter including the National Society for the Prevention of Cruelty to Children or any person or body authorised by the Secretary of State to do so. The court may only make an order if it is satisfied:

a) that the child concerned is suffering, or is likely to suffer, significant harm; and
b) that the harm, or likelihood of harm, is attributable to –
  i) the care given to the child, or likely to be given to him if the order were not made, not being what it would be reasonable to expect a parent to give to him; or
  ii) the child's being beyond parental control. (s.31(2))

No care order or supervision order may be made with respect to a child who has reached the age of 17 (or 16 in the case of a child who is married) (s.31(3)). The court has powers to make what are known as 'Section 8' orders[25] in relation to the separate field of 'family proceedings', broadly including those which relate to the arrangements to be made for children and matrimonial and domestic matters; these can be used, if apposite, in response to an application for a care or supervision order, subject to certain qualifications detailed in s.9. Perhaps the most important 'Section 8' order for the purposes of this book is the 'specific issue order', which is one giving directions for the purpose of determining a specific question which has arisen, or may arise, in connection with any aspect of parental responsibility for a child. Such an order may, for example, be appropriate when a child's health is endangered by the religious beliefs of his or her parents.[26] Finally, although the local authority's access to wardship is severely restricted by the 1989 Act,[27] the inherent jurisdiction is retained insofar as the local authority may seek its application if the court has given it leave to do so; the court will grant such leave only if the same result could not be achieved by seeking an alternative form of order or if it is likely that the child will suffer significant harm if the court's inherent jurisdiction is not exercised (s.100). It might, however, be interjected here that the Children Act does not interfere with the common law right to apply for wardship of a child; despite the availability of a 'Section 8 order' (see above), this may well be – and probably always has been – the best way to enable doctors to treat children lawfully in the face of parental opposition.[28]

The effect of a care order is that the designated local authority must keep the child in its care so long as the order remains in force. During that time, the local authority has parental responsibility for the child and may determine the extent to which a parent or guardian may share in that responsibility, subject to that being necessary in order to promote or safeguard the child's welfare. At the same time, the parents' responsibilities are not terminated and the authority cannot prevent them or the child's guardian doing what is reasonable in respect of the child's welfare.

A supervision order may require that a child submit to initial and periodic medical or psychiatric examinations or to treatment, but it is to be noted that the 1989 Act incorporates the concept of 'Gillick-competence'[29] (see p. 321) and no such requirement can be included unless the court is satisfied that, where the child has sufficient understanding to make an informed decision, he or she consents to its inclusion.[30] Appeals, which must be lodged within 14 days, against the making of or refusal of orders in the Magistrates' Courts are made to the High Court and from decisions of the county or High Court to the Court of Appeal.[31] Anyone who was party to the original hearing can appeal but, normally, fresh evidence cannot be adduced. There is no appeal from decisions as to emergency protection orders (see below).

Comparable legislation in Scotland is to be found in the Children (Scotland) Act 1995. The two factors unique to the Scottish system are, firstly, the interposition of the Reporter to the Children's Panel[32] between the courts and any other agency and, secondly, the conduct of the Children's Hearing, which is now set out in s.39 of the 1995 Act. Any person who considers a child to be at risk may inform the Reporter direct (1995 Act, s.53(2)) although the great majority of referrals will be through the police and social work departments; a significant number also derive from educational sources. There is a statutory duty on local authority staff who believe a child may be in need of compulsory measures of supervision to provide the Reporter with such information as they have been able to obtain (s.53(1)).

The Reporter's function is to inquire into the allegations. He may, as a result, take no action or he may refer the case to the local authority with the intention that it takes advantage of voluntary schemes of assistance, which would include, for example, enlisting the aid of the Royal Scottish Society for the Prevention of Cruelty to Children (RSSPCC). For any more drastic action, he must bring the case before a Children's Hearing.[33] Both the child and the 'relevant person' involved – essentially, the person with parental responsibility for the child – must attend the hearing under penalty for failure to do so. The child may be excused if it would be detrimental to his or her interests to be present but, nevertheless, the child now has a clear right to attend. Further progress of the matter depends upon the grounds for the hearing being understood and accepted. In the event of non-acceptance or of failure to understand on the part of either the child or the parents, the question is submitted to the sheriff, who can either discharge the case or, having decided that the grounds are correct, send it back for a hearing (s.65). Since a small child cannot understand, all cases involving infants are automatically considered by the sheriff.

The Reporter must call a Children's Hearing when it appears that a child may be in need of compulsory measures of supervision and this question arises when at least one of the following conditions is satisfied in respect of him or her: that the child

a   is beyond the control of any relevant person;
b   is falling into bad associations or is exposed to moral danger;
c   is likely (i) to suffer unnecessarily; or (ii) be impaired seriously in his health or development, owing to lack of parental care;
d   is a child in respect of whom any of the offences against children to which special provisions apply[34] has been committed;
e   is, or is likely, to become a member of the same household as a child in respect of whom any of the offences referred to in para (d) above has been committed;
f   is, or is likely to become, a member of the same household as a person who has committed any of the offences referred to in para (d) above;
g   is, or is likely to become, a member of the same household as a person in respect of whom an offence under ss.1–3 of the Criminal Law (Consolidation) (Scotland) Act 1995[35] has been committed by a member of that household;
h   has failed to attend school regularly without reasonable excuse;
i   has committed an offence;
j   has misused alcohol or any drug;
k   has misused a volatile substance by deliberately inhaling its vapour, other than for medicinal purposes;
l   is subject to special restrictions and his behaviour is such that special measures are necessary for his adequate supervision in his interest or the interest of others.

It is to be noted that the existence of one or more of these grounds is not proof that compulsory measures of supervision are necessary, but their absence means that there is no need for such measures. It will also be seen that the conditions indicating the need for further action are far more specific than are the comparable grounds in England and Wales.

The Children's Hearing may, of course, decide that no further measures are needed; alternatively, it may see the need for compulsory measures of supervision, in which case it will call upon the social work department to implement a supervision requirement. This may consist of a requirement to submit to such terms and conditions of supervision as the hearing sees fit to impose in relation to residence, parental contact, medical examination and the like (1995 Act, s.70). The local authority can refer the case back to the Reporter in the event that they consider the requirement to have become irrelevant; any requirement ceases when the child becomes 18 years old, and there are regulations dictating the frequent review of any orders made (1995 Act, s.73). There are, of course, statutory arrangements for appeal against any order and this is open both to the child and to its parents; an appeal against the terms of the order is to the sheriff, but it can also be made to the Court of Session on a point of law. Parents or the child concerned may also seek review of the supervision order after certain statutory time limits have passed.

The emergency protection of children

The local authority or the NSPCC in England and Wales can apply for a child assessment order which can only be granted if the court is satisfied that the applicant has reasonable cause to suspect that the child is suffering, or is likely to suffer, significant harm and that an assessment of the child's health, or of the way in which he or she has been treated, is needed in order to determine whether or not such conditions exist; the court must also be satisfied that a satisfactory assessment would not be made in the absence of an order. The court cannot make an assessment order if it believes that an emergency protection order ought to be made, but an application for an assessment order may be treated as one for an emergency protection order. Although it is, for practical reasons, very rarely used, the assessment order can be looked upon as something of a half-way house between voluntary cooperation between the local authority and the parents and the more Draconian emergency protection order. Once again, *Gillick* rules apply and a child who is of sufficient understanding to make an informed decision may refuse to submit to medical or psychiatric examination or other assessment (Children Act, 1989, s.43(8)).

An emergency protection order can be made on application by any person if there is reasonable cause to believe that a child is likely to suffer significant harm if he or she is not removed to accommodation provided by or on behalf of the applicant. Where the applicant is the local authority investigating the welfare of a child as part of its statutory duty, or where the NSPCC is making its own enquiries, an order can be made if these enquiries are being frustrated by access to the child being unreasonably refused and the applicant has reasonable cause to believe that access to the child is required as a matter of urgency. The making of an order gives the applicant parental responsibility for the child and allows for his or her removal to designated accommodation or for preventing removal from a hospital or other secure place in which he or she was accommodated at the time. Any subsequent action must be directed to safeguarding the welfare of the child (1989 Act, s.44). In conformity with the spirit of the Act, a *Gillick*-competent child can refuse to submit to any examination or assessment ordered by the court. An emergency protection order can be made initially for eight days (with due allowance for the last of those days being a public holiday) but, on application, can be extended once only for a period of seven days – and then only if the child is likely to suffer significant harm if the order is not extended. On the other side of the coin, no application for the discharge of the order can be made earlier than 72 hours after it was made. Decisions as to emergency protection orders are not subject to appeal.

Subject to stringent controls, a police constable can remove a child to suitable accommodation, or ensure that he or she remains in such accommodation, if he has reasonable cause to believe that the child would otherwise be liable to suffer significant harm (1989, Act, s.46). Among other important conditions, which include informing the child as to what is going on and ascertaining his or her wishes,[36] the constable must, as soon as practicable, ensure that the case is inquired into by an officer designated for the purpose by the Chief Constable. No child may be kept in police protection for more than 72 hours but, during that time, the designated officer may apply on behalf of the appropriate authority for an emergency protection order to be made, in which case, the time spent in police protection is included in the maximum of eight days allowed for the order.

Very similar statutory controls are imposed under the Children (Scotland) Act 1995, including the power of the sheriff to grant a child assessment order (s.55). When the sheriff is satisfied that a child is being so treated or neglected that he or she is suffering significant harm, or will suffer such harm if not removed to a place of safety, he may make a 'child protection order';[37] he may also do so when the local authority is making enquiries as to what action would be suitable. The order ceases to have effect if it is not implemented within 24 hours of its being granted (1995 Act, s. 60(1)). The order can be challenged within two working days of its implementation but, if it is not, the Reporter must convene an initial Children's Hearing on the second working day to determine whether the protection order should continue. The sheriff must make his determination within three working days of a challenge to a child protection order; at that point, he may recall the order or continue it until a full

Children's Hearing has begun.[38] Thereafter, the child's protection is arranged through the children's hearing system. Given the intricate arrangements for review either by the sheriff or by the Children's Hearing – and the limited time available before the order comes to an end – no further appeal is available in relation to the provision or otherwise of the protection order. However, the sheriff has considerable discretion and may, for example, provide directions as to the degree of parental contact permissible under the order, as may the 'second working day' hearing.

A child protection order may, amongst other things, authorise the removal of the child to a place of safety, which may include any residential establishment provided by the local authority, a police station, any hospital or surgery or any other suitable place where the occupier is willing to receive the child. Clearly, the hospital or surgery will be the most appropriate place in cases of serious physical abuse, but it is to be noted that the child's consent is required before any medical examination or treatment is provided under the Act (1995 Act, s.90). In effect, the power of a minor of sufficient understanding to consent to medical procedures in general, which is provided by the Age of Legal Capacity (Scotland) Act 1991, is specifically preserved in relation to orders made under the 1995 Act; s.90 of the latter Act does not refer overtly to refusal, but it is clear from the wording that, in this circumstance at least, consent and refusal are equiparated.[39] In either case, however, the test is that of the understanding and maturity of the child; treatment of a very young child would, therefore, be subject to parental consent until such time as an order was in force.

Finally, it is to be noted that, should it not be possible to arrange for a child protection order in an emergency, a justice of the peace may grant a comparable authorisation which ceases to have effect 12 or 24 hours later, depending on whether the child has not or has been removed to a place of safety in the meantime (s.61). Alternatively, as in England and Wales, a constable who has reason to believe that the conditions for granting a child protection order exist may remove the child to a place of safety if it is impracticable for him to obtain an order; the power to detain the child in this way is limited to 24 hours from the time he or she was removed (s.61(5) and (6)).

A child and/or any relevant person involved in a Children's Hearing can appeal against the decision within three weeks (s.51). The appeal is, at first, to the sheriff and, from there, to the sheriff principal or to the Court of Session. As noted above, however, no such appeal is available in the adjudication of an application to make a child protection order. An interesting introduction to Scots law is that the sheriff considering the appeal may substitute his own form of disposal if he disagrees with the decision of the hearing; such a disposal must, however, be one which a hearing would be empowered to impose.

The markedly different legislative formats for the protection of children developed in England and Wales and in Scotland lead to contrasts in representation of the child during the investigative process. Under the Children Act 1989, s.41, the court must appoint a guardian *ad litem* for the child concerned for the purpose of any of the proceedings specified unless it is satisfied that it is not necessary to do so. In the event that a guardian has not been appointed and that the child has sufficient understanding to instruct a solicitor and wishes to do so, the court may appoint a solicitor to represent him or her provided it appears that it would be in the child's best interests to be so represented. Informality – at least in contrast to the summary criminal court – is, however, characteristic of the Scottish children's hearing system in which legal aid is not available and no formal professional representation is involved until the appeal stage.[40] Instead, the court or hearing shall, if it is thought necessary, appoint a person (the 'safeguarder'), under the Children (Scotland) Act 1995, s.41, to safeguard the interests of the child.[41] Because the proceedings are of an emergency nature, a safeguarder cannot be appointed in relation to proceedings for child protection orders; he or she can, however, be appointed for the purposes of the hearing which must follow the expiry of the protection order. Although the Act does not specifically say so, it seems reasonable to suppose that a guardian or curator *ad litem* could be appointed at any appeal stage under much the same conditions as pertain in England; the child can also have his or her own lawyer.[42]

The shifting emphasis of the new legislation

Both the 1989 and 1995 Acts are based on the premise that children have rights as individuals and that, so far as is possible commensurate with their age, their wishes should be taken into account when questions arise as to their upbringing; the underlying purpose of the legislation has been to revise the existing law in accordance with those principles. The deliberate retreat from the system of wardship jurisdiction, which has already been noted, is important in the present context and the consequences merit a brief analysis. The court may no longer use its inherent jurisdiction so as to require a child to be placed in the care, or put under the supervision, of a local authority. Moreover, no application may be made by the local authority for any exercise of the inherent jurisdiction in respect of a child unless the authority has obtained the leave of the court – and this will only be granted if the desired result, and the welfare of the child, cannot be obtained under the statute (1989 Act, s.100(3)).[43] There is no doubt that *continuing* control of children must now be entrusted normally to local authorities, and certainly so once a care order has been made; the role of the court is then confined to responding to any further applications under the Act.[44] It also appears that the common law right of an interested party to apply for leave to institute wardship proceedings may now be subject to the proviso that the question in respect of the child could not be resolved as effectively under the Children Act.[45] Perhaps instinctively, one regrets the replacement of the experienced and impartial judge by a politically and economically restricted local authority.

Nonetheless, the writing of the 1989 legislation was already on the wall. The courts have always been wary of the dissatisfied family hoping to use wardship in order to overcome the effect of a care order. Any suggestion that the High Court could and would assume jurisdiction over the local authority was effectively dismissed as a result of the House of Lords decisions in *A* v. *Liverpool City Council* and later cases.[46] LORD SCARMAN was especially dogmatic in *In re W*; any inadequacy as to the rights of the extended family was to be found not in the powers of the local authority but in the express enactment of Parliament. Parliament has now spoken.

The legislation overtaken by the 1989 Act in England and Wales led to complaints that the party bringing the child before the, then, juvenile court was in too privileged a position as compared with the parents. It remains to be seen whether the consolidating statute has redressed the balance; those with parental responsibility must, now, be joined as respondents in relation to any application under the Act,[47] and anyone who has party status is entitled to appeal.[48] It is, however, reasonably clear that officials, say, of the NSPCC could not carry out their function unless they worked under the umbrella of confidentiality; their right to protection has been upheld in the House of Lords.[49] Some parental dissatisfaction is likely to stem from the degree of the local authority's assumption of parental rights and its corollary, the limitation of the natural parents' contact with their children in care; this is a foreseeable outcome of the dual responsibility empowered by s.33(3) of the 1989 Act. The European Court of Human Rights clearly disapproved the interference with the rights of parents to respect for their family life which was inherent in the previous legislation and regarded the process whereby decision making was vested in the local authority as being inconsistent with their parallel right to a fair trial;[50] it has been suggested that the current arrangements may still not satisfy the European Convention on Human Rights.[51] If it does nothing else, the European decision emphasises the dilemma that faces those charged with the containment of child abuse.[52]

The practical response to child abuse

The precise conditions surrounding the investigation of cases of child abuse are, to an extent, circumscribed by the way the matter comes to public notice; the major current concern in the field is to unify the processes by increasing cooperation between the agencies involved. The problems were first addressed comprehensively in the government publication, *Working Together*.[53]

The ultimate responsibility for the safety of children at risk of abuse is vested in the local authority through the Director of Social Services.[54] There are, however, a number of other agencies which may be concerned. In particular, the health authority not only is likely to be involved *de facto* through its doctors, midwives, nurses and health visitors, but also has a statutory duty to assist the local authority by virtue of the National Health Service Act 1977, s.26. Further, the education authority may be brought in insofar as teachers may well be the first to note the results of child abuse.

The powers of the health and education authorities are, however, strictly limited. Certainly, the hospital doctor will observe, treat and make a preliminary assessment of the cause of his patient's condition but he cannot, properly, do more – and, indeed, attempts to restrict child abuse within a purely medical ambience are a not uncommon form of interagency non-cooperation which is at the root of many failures in the child protection system. The general practitioner who believes that he is dealing with a case of child abuse has two courses open to him. The first can be looked on as being based on medical practice. He sees a child patient who has sustained unusual injuries; his duty to the patient is to provide the best diagnostic and therapeutic services;[55] he sends the child to hospital and he has discharged his duty within a simple doctor/patient relationship free of any medico-legal overtones. This is not evading the issue; admission to hospital has simultaneously removed the child from danger and placed him or her in the hands of those who have the best facilities for legal follow-up: it is, on all grounds, the preferred management of the case. Nonetheless, such a solution is not always open to the primary care team. While nearly all children's hospitals are sympathetic to the ideal, the injuries may be so slight that an admission cannot be justified; secondly, the parents may refuse permission for transfer to hospital. In either event, the only practical alternative available to the practitioner is that which would probably be taken in hospital, namely, referral to the social services in their capacity of an 'investigating agency' (Children Act 1989, s.47).

The vexed question of professional confidentiality in this context can now be regarded as solved. The General Medical Council has said:

> if you believe a patient to be the victim of neglect or physical or sexual abuse, and unable to give or withhold consent to disclosure, you should usually give information to an appropriate responsible person or statutory agency, in order to prevent further harm to the patient. In these and similar circumstances, you may release information without the patient's consent, but only if you consider that the patient is unable to give consent, and that the disclosure is in the patient's best interests.[56]

This is reasonably clear as regards the individual child, though it is to be noted that the GMC supports the relevance of the concept of *Gillick*-competence in an already difficult enough area: it leaves open, for example, how far the doctor can rely on the doctrine of 'therapeutic privilege' in withholding information or dispensing with consent. It also begs the question to the extent that it provides no guidance as to the doctor's duty to a child's parents: might it not be the mother who brings her child to the surgery who has the primary claim on the doctor's duty of confidence? There is much to be said in preference for the Council's previous advice:

> One such situation [where a doctor may breach confidence] may arise where a doctor believes that a patient may be the victim of abuse or neglect. In such circumstances the patient's interests are paramount and will usually require the doctor to disclose relevant information to an appropriate, responsible person or an officer of a statutory agency.[57]

It seems reasonable to suppose that the GMC would still support a doctor along these lines even though their strength has, apparently, been diluted.

The doctor might, perhaps, feel less uneasy in reporting to a charitable organisation in the form of the NSPCC (or, in Scotland, the RSSPCC). This would be acceptable as the body not only has the powers, uniquely, of an investigating agency,[58] but also, in some areas, actually undertakes the work of child protection on behalf of the social services. Thus the results (as described below) would be the same irrespective of whether the local authority or the NSPCC was contacted originally.

It must not be forgotten, however, that inflicting bodily harm on a child is a criminal as well as a social matter. A number of cases will, therefore, be reported to, or come to the notice of, the police, who may well have a different attitude to the methods and objectives of an investigation. The police are particularly likely to be involved in instances of sexual abuse, which is covered more *specifically* by statute than are other forms of child molestation;[59] it was in this field that the differences became most apparent in England in 1986 and 1987. Two opinions from that era are exemplary, the first from a clinician: 'there is growing evidence that the collection of evidence by the police and police surgeons may be damaging and that abused children do not subsequently receive advice or treatment'.[60] On the other hand, we have senior police officers testifying that: 'detectives experienced in this work were seriously doubting the validity of the paediatricians' diagnoses'.[61]

Reasons will appear below why notification to the social services is preferred, but it is to be hoped that the potential for confrontation will, by now, have abated. Even so, there is increasing evidence that the parents may be exposed to undeserved risk once child protection measures have been instigated. The societal consequences of making an error detrimental to the child, whether to the social services or to the police involved, are such as to virtually enforce a policy of 'better to be safe than sorry' and, by and large, there is less sorrow in an error which puts the parents at a disadvantage.[62] Even so, it is probably right that neither the children nor the parents should be able to bring an action for wrongful management of child protection procedures, whether this be for breach of statutory duty or in negligence. The system is multidisciplinary and to single out one or more of the agencies involved as being negligent would, it was said, be 'manifestly unfair'. LORD BROWNE-WILKINSON put it: 'To allow councils to be sued for negligence over their child protection duties would cut across the whole statutory system set up for the protection of children at risk.'[63]

Yet it is difficult to decide whether such reasons, which are, largely, an expression of impotence, are adequate to justify yet another measure which acts to the disadvantage of the parents.[64] The House of Lords, per LORD BROWNE-WILKINSON, went on to say that local authorities might adopt a more cautious and defensive approach which would prejudice those who had suffered child abuse if they were liable for damages, but this does little for the parents who are wrongfully suspected of abusing their children. It is virtually impossible to decide how often this occurs. In a study of 160 allegations of sexual abuse in Newcastle, it was found that 57 led to prosecution and that 86 per cent of these resulted in conviction.[65] This was claimed as a satisfactorily high rate of conviction in carefully chosen cases. It may well be that many actual cases of abuse were hidden in the 103 cases which were not prosecuted. This is, clearly, to be deprecated even if one balances the adverse effects on the family of a trial and its consequences against those of just punishment; nonetheless, the alternative, albeit extreme, interpretation is that 64 per cent of allegations resulted in persecution for which there is no redress.

Once a case is reported, the process follows two lines. The first is quasi-legal and depends upon the use of a combination of locally agreed arrangements and directive guidelines issued by government departments; the second is the implementation of the statutory law. The two avenues can be followed independently but, even so, they commonly converge and the first is generally a preliminary to the second.

The quasi-legal response begins with the case conference, a process which was mandated by government directive many years ago[66] and which, it has been held, should be convened before it is sought to remove a child from his or her home.[67] Precise conditions will vary from area to area, but the general principles and underlying ethos are those of a multidisciplinary approach to management; the theory is admirable but, in practice, there are few simple solutions to the problems of how 'multi' and how 'disciplinary' the conference should be: while the primary purpose is to decide whether or not the case should be registered on the child protection register (see below), the individual constituents of the conference may see their duties as conflicting with the corporate view.[68] There can be no doubt that this raises grave problems of confidentiality, a matter which is sufficiently important to ethical medicine as to deter some doctors from participating.[69] The value of the conference must be diminished thereby, but it is equally possible to accept the strength of conscience which impels others to use any received information on behalf of what they see as the best interests of the child, which must be their and society's primary concern. Even so, it is disturbing to see that the courts, apparently, will not recognise an obligation of confidence unless the material to be disclosed forms part of the court file.[70]

Current proposals envisage the police as being routinely represented while, at the same time, insisting that any police officers involved should understand the confidential nature of the proceedings. This places a heavy onus on the police representative whose primary duties might well be seen as the enforcement of the criminal law through prosecution of offenders. This should not give rise to much difficulty in practice, as both the Crown Prosecution Service in England and Wales and the Crown Office in Scotland have wide discretionary powers as to prosecution. However, the relationship between the social services department and the police remains an important factor affecting the management of cases of child abuse; it is discussed further below. It is to be noted that, irrespective of their intentions under the criminal law, the involvement of the police in the case conference may be very valuable in providing essential background information, including, say, the criminal records of the parents or other carers who are said to be involved in the abuse.

The parents are not entitled to inclusion in the conference, but importance is being increasingly attached to their involvement and they will be invited to attend such parts of it as are considered practicable. They must be informed of the result of the conference[71] and, particularly, as to whether the child's name has been placed on the child protection register; however, the generally informal nature of the conference proceedings excludes any rights of appeal against 'registration', unless the decision can be shown to be quite unreasonable.[72]

As implied above, a main function of the case conference is to decide whether or not the child's name should be included on the child protection register. This is a list maintained by the social services department, or by the NSPCC on its behalf, of children suspected of being subjected to abuse. It has no legal or evidentiary standing and is, essentially, a guide to management – both clinical and social. Thus a doctor concerned as to whether he is dealing with a case of non-accidental injury can consult the register to see if similar injuries to the child or other children have been reported in the past;[73] a health visitor who suspects violence can ascertain whether similar violence has been noted in other members of the family; and the social worker can note *ab initio* that a given family has been registered on more than one occasion and can take appropriate action. The register also ensures that the management of a child subject to protection is reviewed every six months. Needless to say, extreme care is taken to limit access to the register to those with a professional 'need to know'; a register custodian is nominated to manage it. The register is a valuable tool, particularly in the field of preventive medicine; it is designed to protect the child in the future rather than to record the past. Nevertheless, it can be a double-edged weapon if not used with discretion and if it is not seen to be so used. Everyone knows of its existence and everyone whose child is registered is informed of the fact. There will be an obvious reluctance to be involved and it is at least possible that parents will avoid seeking medical attention for their children who have been genuinely injured accidentally for fear of a misdiagnosis in favour of non-accidental injury. It is virtually certain that the advantages of the register overwhelm the potential disadvantages, but this can only be true when both registration and diagnosis are made with skill and circumspection. The use of the at-risk register is subject to judicial review.[74]

The whole quasi-legal approach to child protection is carried out under the supervisory eye of the Area Child Protection Committee, which is made up from, and is responsible to, the various agencies involved in child protection. The function of the committee is, in general, to review and to advise on interagency procedures and, particularly, to ensure a satisfactory relationship between the quasi-legal and statutory elements of child protection.

Statutory child protection in the form of care or supervision orders as described above will come into operation when the local authority's investigations have indicated that the child is otherwise likely to suffer significant harm. There is little need to add to what has already been said save, perhaps, to mention that the standard of proof in parental child abuse cases is that of the balance of probabilities with due allowance for the fact that the degree of probability required to satisfy the court must be commensurate with the gravity of the accusation.[75] It is also worth stating what is, perhaps, close to the obvious: that the risk of harm must be based on fact rather than supposition.[76] Inevitably, mistakes are made in both directions and, in the great majority of such cases, it can be assumed that the authorities were doing no less than their best. The coincidence of multiple allegations, however, tends to generate subjectivity on the part of the investigators; not only are less rational decisions then made, but the consequent publicity is greatly amplified and public opinion also becomes distorted. There have been a number of such instances in the past decade – at Cleveland in 1987, Manchester in 1990 and, in Scotland, in the Orkneys in 1991 and in Ayrshire in 1993. So many lessons are to be learned from these occurrences that it is worth briefly recapitulating some of the findings in two of them.

The Cleveland experience

The problem in Cleveland came to public notice when over 200 children were placed in care on the grounds of parental sexual abuse between May and July of 1987. The results of the consequent public inquiry have been published[77] (referred to hereafter as the Butler-Sloss Report or the 'Cleveland guidelines'); a brief overview of the conditions leading to the setting up of that inquiry is useful in demonstrating the many difficulties surrounding the management of abuse – and, particularly, of sexual abuse – of children.

In the light of protests by many parents, the local authority itself cooperated in taking out wardship summonses in respect of some children remitted to its care; the fact that wardship was continued despite the children being returned, with safeguards, to the care and control of their parents, emphasises the complexity of the situation. A number of children were diagnosed as having been sexually abused *per anum* on the basis of the presence of a reported clinical sign of reflex anal relaxation and dilatation,[78] but a second opinion concluded that there was no evidence of sexual abuse in the majority. The significance of the fact that the second observers were qualified by way of police surgeoncy will be discussed later but, for the present, it is interesting to note the hypothetical nature of the evidence on both sides. The first examiners, both paediatricians, attributed a slack anal canal to sexual penetration, for which there was no corroborative evidence; the police surgeons, by contrast, considered that the finding could be explained by the evacuation of a large stool – but, again, there was no evidence of this. One result of being forced to use such negative evidence must be that its value is assessed on the skill of the clinical experts as witnesses and the hazards of an adversarial system are, thereby, introduced to an investigation for which it is ill-suited.[79] Such observations highlight the question which has been central to the medical investigation of child abuse cases: who should be responsible for the medical examination?

By and large, the choice rests between a clinical paediatrician and a police surgeon, and the solution of that choice, before Cleveland, depends almost entirely on who raises the matter. When this is the police, there must be sympathy for the view that they will wish to deal with the physician they know and trust – the police surgeon. Social workers, by contrast, may find themselves in ideological opposition to the police. The satisfactory conclusion of a criminal case is, to the police, a successful prosecution; the desired end of a child abuse case to the social worker is a reunited family. The result may be – and was in Cleveland – a clear-cut confrontation between the paediatricians, supported by the social services, on the one hand and the police surgeons on the other.

The underlying nature of any professional conflict is easy to see and is, to an extent, understandable. Proof in the event of child care proceedings is, as we have seen, on the balance of probabilities. The clinician sees transfer of care and control as a satisfactory therapy for his child patient; he is generally unversed in the law and he is likely to see the abuser as little more than a further therapeutic responsibility. The police surgeon, on the other hand, knows that proof in the criminal court is a matter of being beyond reasonable doubt; he is fully conscious of the enormous severity of a prison sentence on a child abuser; on all counts, his opinion is likely to be more conservative and he will not, himself, entertain any reasonable doubt. It is not so much that there is a conflict between police surgeon and paediatrician as that each operates on a different conceptual plane.

Even so, discussion has, thus far, not considered the effect of different attitudes upon the child concerned. The major argument as to reaching the diagnosis of abuse, and of sexual abuse in particular, has centred on the provision of a 'second opinion'.[80] If this is required, the child may be examined twice as a routine. But, given the possibility of criminal proceedings, the defence are also likely to demand an examination of the child, and the probability increases that the 'cure' is becoming more traumatic to the child than is the 'disease'; the number of examinations *must* be limited. The clinician and the police surgeon have an input to the investigation which is of equal potential importance. There is a good case for a mandatory requirement for a dual, and simultaneous, examination of a child in any case in which its future is going to depend upon the result, and this was strongly recommended in the Cleveland guidelines. Simultaneous clinical and forensic observations may be both supportive and restraining; each expert can indicate the type of evidence which will be available to the criminal or family courts; and public conflict and, above all, damage to the child can be limited along with subjectivity on the part of the observers.[81]

For, in fact, it is difficult to separate awareness, which is highly desirable, from subjectivity, which is likely to be self-defeating. One case from Cleveland demonstrated the classical dilemma. A five-year-old girl presented with bleeding from an injury to the vulva which was said to have been sustained as she fell from a bench. By any standards, this was an unusual injury and one which might well have been due to sexual abuse; the doctor had every right to be suspicious, yet precisely similar cases have been reported in the general medical literature.[82] In another incident, three siblings were taken from bed at 10pm and were examined intimately; all three were detained in hospital and a place of safety order was obtained; following the granting of an interim care order, the magistrates refused to make a permanent order and the council then applied for wardship; the saga ended with the judge discharging the wardship summons with the comment: 'All the evidence points to this family being a normal, happy family until [the injury was seen in hospital]'. The doctor is reported to have said that he had 'become convinced that uncovering sexual abuse was the most important aspect of child health'.[83] While the sincerity of the doctor cannot be disputed, the fact remains that a change from awareness of to a determined search for child abuse almost certainly caused more damage to the health of the child than would have watchful inactivity. An experienced police surgeon has said, and has not since changed her mind, that there is no medical evidence of abuse in half the children referred to her: 'you have to take … the various factors together, rather than look at just one'.[84] This is the basis for one of the most important lessons to be derived from the Butler-Sloss Report – that no physical sign can, at the present time, be regarded as being uniquely diagnostic of child abuse alone; the medical aspects are only one element in the diagnostic process.[85]

The problem remains as to the circumstances in which a doctor should be looking for child abuse: does a routine visit to the surgery warrant such an examination? It is scarcely possible to avoid searching for and observing the signs of physical abuse or, indeed, for the signs, ephemeral though they may be, of emotional abuse; the problem area is, therefore, limited in practice to sexual abuse. The question is then whether the physician, in examining the perineum of a young child, is 'looking for signs of sexual abuse', or is performing the routine examination of a child that he was taught as a medical student.[86] The author who posed the question was convinced on the point: 'Any child that comes to my outpatient clinic … will have a full assessment that will include … a head to toe physical examination … Such a practice is normal in children's medicine, and proposals that deter doctors from assessing the whole child should be resisted.' No-one could doubt the clinical wisdom and motivation of this view. Nevertheless, it carries an element of paternalism, in that it ignores the consent issue and, accordingly, is scarcely justified in the current climate of medical ethics. There can be little or no doubt as to its truth so long as the child is brought for 'a thorough check-up'; but the same cannot be said without fear of contradiction if the surgery visit is for a specific purpose, such as the investigation of an earache. Something more than 'good medical practice' is needed before non-consensual examination of a child's genitalia can be regarded as being routinely acceptable; the Butler-Sloss Report recommended, with minor reservations, that the informed consent of the parents should be sought before a medical examination for forensic or other evidential purposes unconnected with the immediate care and treatment of the child was undertaken.

In the event, the Butler-Sloss Report did not contain many recommendations which are not inherent in the foregoing discussion; perhaps the most important conceptual emphasis lies in a strong recognition of parental rights to information and support. Many of the conclusions stress the importance of interagency cooperation and these have been expressed in the publication *Working Together*.[87] The duties and conduct of the expert witness have been very fully explained by CAZALET J;[88] it is inherent within these guidelines that the experts should cooperate for the ultimate benefit of the court and the children concerned, and this applies even in the context of criminal proceedings.[89] We can leave it to the Butler-Sloss Report to provide the summary:

> It is unacceptable that the disagreements and failure of communication of adults should be allowed to obscure the needs of children both long term and short term in so sensitive, difficult and important a field. The children had unhappy experiences which should not be allowed to happen again.

Possibly the most innovative recommendations in the Report relate to the preservation of evidence. Strong support was given to video recording or, in its absence, audio recording of interviews with children. At the very least, adequate notes should be taken; it was a failure to provide such evidence, coupled with serious defects in training, which led to trenchant criticism of the social services in the alleged 'satanic ritual' incident in Manchester in 1990.[90] That case and others[91] suggest that, in England and Wales at least, the Cleveland guidelines have acquired something of a legal status and must be followed. The same is not true in Scotland, where it has been held that the fact that the Cleveland guidelines were not followed does not automatically render the evidence obtained unreliable.[92]

Scotland: the Orkney debacle

The Orkney affair was, of course, on a very different scale from that at Cleveland. Nonetheless, it caused comparable concern and the subsequent inquiry ('The Clyde Report')[93] disclosed almost as many administrative and medical shortcomings. Briefly, seven children were removed from their family home following allegations of sexual abuse by one of them. During the months of investigation that followed, the younger children gave evidence that suggested the presence of a paedophile ring in the area. As a result, a further nine children from four families were removed from home and were accommodated in places of safety on the mainland.

The case then became something of an administrative nightmare. All but one of the parents refused to accept the grounds for referral to a Children's Hearing and, quite properly, the matter was referred to the sheriff for adjudication. The hearing had, however, decided to dispense with the children's evidence on the grounds that they could not understand the issues and the sheriff regarded this as blatantly untrue. In effect, he held that the children's panel had never put itself in a position from which it was capable of directing the Reporter to make application to the sheriff and, consequently, the applications were fundamentally flawed; the children were returned to their parents without further consideration of the evidence. The sheriff was highly critical of the Reporter, who appealed to the Court of Session.[94] The Court of Session, in turn, upheld the Reporter's appeal, holding the sheriff to be in breach of natural justice. The disastrous saga ended with the Court of Session directing that the case be reheard before a different sheriff, but with the Reporter abandoning further pursuit of the proof.

All of which might be thought to have little relevance in the present context, were it not for the fact that the Clyde Report contained no fewer than 194 recommendations resulting from criticism of every agency involved. It is impossible to summarise these adequately, but they included the need to balance the risks inherent in intervention in suspected cases of child abuse against the probable success of the legal process (para. 15.28); the importance of coordinating the work of the police and the Social Work Department (para. 15.32); the advantages of prepared guidelines, albeit advisory rather than mandatory, at both national and local levels (paras 15.55–66); the importance of keeping all parties, including the parents, well-informed as to the procedure (ch. 16); the designation of persons regarded as appropriate to conduct medical examinations which should not be carried out against the refusal of the individual child (para. 17.42); and the importance of using improved techniques for the recording of interviews and of keeping, as a minimum, a full written record of what was said and what illustrations were used. It was, however, specifically recommended that a departure from suggested guidelines should not be automatically seen as a breach of good practice (para. 17.78).

It is thus clear that much the same errors in the investigation of child sexual abuse, leading to very similar recommendations, have been found throughout the United Kingdom. The overriding need has been identified as being the maintenance of objectivity in an area which can easily become dominated by subjective emotions. The unhappy fact remains that every review of the major incidents that has been undertaken in recent years refers to precipitate action on the part of the social workers and, in particular, to a failure to evaluate the evidence and its sources. It is nowhere suggested that children should be disbelieved until proved believable; it is, however, recommended everywhere that their evidence should be carefully considered and, if possible, corroborated. The critical issue that the 'group' cases, in particular, have exposed is the need to balance concern for the children's immediate welfare against the probable long-term ill-effects of family break-up.

As a result, it is difficult to escape the conclusion that, throughout the whole spectrum of child abuse, there has been something of a swing of the pendulum, as was foreseen by the *British Medical Journal* more than a decade ago.[95] So long as this results in a fairer and more rational approach to the problems, this can only be a good thing – and it does appear to motivate the relevant sections of the Children Act 1989 and the Children (Scotland) Act 1995.

Münchhausen Syndrome by Proxy

That is, of course, not to say that vigilance should be relaxed, or that there should not be ongoing research into variations on the theme of child abuse. One such instance is the so-called 'Münchhausen syndrome by proxy'. The original syndrome referred to the fabrication of disease in adults: the proxy syndrome extends this to similar fabrication of signs and symptoms of disease in children by their mothers. It was first described in 1977,[96] but has become widely recognised only comparatively recently. In my opinion, the so-called syndrome contains a number of variants. It may be that, in some cases, the mother is seeking attention for herself; in others, she may be so convinced of her child's illness that she feels forced to produce symptoms and signs in order to attract maximum attention from the health caring professions. On the other hand, there does seem to be a group of mothers who are engaged in deliberate infanticide or child murder – intentional, repetitive smothering of children is being discovered surprisingly often,[97] as is child abuse by poisoning. Whatever the reason behind the fabrication of disease or injury, and the management of cases depends very much on their accurate classification, the children are put in double jeopardy as the health carers increase their efforts to diagnose and treat a disease that refuses to go away.

It is, of course, important to the perpetrator that the symptoms continue when the child is admitted to hospital; the opportunity for correct diagnosis by way of covert video recording is, thereby, opened up. Inevitably, this raises serious ethical problems: should doctors risk the inevitable damage to the trust on which the doctor/patient relationship is founded? Should the profession be involved in what is clearly entrapment?[98] It could be argued that such techniques are unnecessary (and, therefore, unethical) given the opportunities for separation and observation of the child that are available under the Children Acts; others would hold that covert surveillance, properly used, is a vital addition to the armamentarium of those involved in child protection.[99] The major difficulty, as we have seen throughout this discussion of child abuse, lies in the definition and application of 'proper use'.

Incest

Although instances of child sexual abuse are often associated with incest, this is by no means always the case; the two are, however, combined sufficiently often to justify a short consideration of incest in the current chapter. In distinguishing the two conditions, it is important to remember that, in the United Kingdom, incest is a tightly defined entity which consists of sexual intercourse between near kindred, laid down in England and Wales as sexual intercourse between a man and a woman he knows to be his mother, sister, daughter or grand-daughter; women over the age of 16 years can be guilty of incest in reciprocal fashion; the sibling relationship persists as to the half-blood and any relationship applies notwithstanding that it is not traced through lawful wedlock.[100]

The crime of incest is one of the most illogical on the statute book. The most obvious expression of this lies in the diversity of definition; there is, for example, no crime of incest as such in France, while the offence is wider in Scotland than in England (see below) although narrower than in the United States and Australia by virtue of the fact that the definition of sexual intercourse is wider in those jurisdictions (see Chapter 2). It is assumed that the modification of the definition of sexual intercourse, introduced in the context of rape in England and Wales by the Criminal Justice and Public Order Act 1994, s.142 (see p. 24) does not extend to incest which can, by statutory definition, be committed only in a heterosexual configuration;[101] the only reasons why buggery of a man's son should be any less offensive than intercourse with his daughter seem to lie, firstly, in the importance attached to defloration in the criminal law and, secondly, in the likely historic and anthropological association between the criminal law of incest and the family law of marriage.

Which leads to a brief consideration of the incest taboo.[102] The great majority would probably place this in the field of genetics, in that recessive deleterious genes are likely to achieve homozygous domination with progressive in-breeding. While this may be a negligible risk in respect of clear-cut monogenetic factors, it has to be admitted that the argument has greater force in respect of multifactorial traits which depend to a varying extent on the environment in which the genes operate. It does, however, seem a very unlikely basis for the *origin* of any incest taboo insofar as it would scarcely have been appreciated by separate generations of primitive peoples; moreover, it ignores the alternative and not uncommon quest for 'purity of the line' which was resolved in some cultures by selective in-breeding between siblings; and, finally, it is reiterated that incest is a matter of intercourse rather than of procreation which is covered by the marriage laws. Nevertheless, the fear of genetic dysfunction still haunts modern legislators and is expressed by the prohibition of bastard relationships in both the English and Scottish legislations.

The second major group of theoretical objections to incest concern the disruption caused to the family and to hierarchal arrangements within the family which result if incest is permitted. Such arguments, again, fail on anthropological grounds (it is by no means difficult to find cultures which are quite happy to accept confusion of the generations) and they are, to an extent, incompatible with the modern view that incest is the result of family disharmony rather than its cause. I have suggested a variation on the theme to the effect that those who were idle as to seeking sexual partners were also idle at work; the incestuous man was despised and excluded by the clan because it was one aspect of his general ineffectiveness;[103] that is, however, a relatively unresearched approach. Most serious students of the subject have now reached common ground that incest is condemned because it represents an abuse of power within the family hegemony.[104] The stronger the power is, the easier it is to abuse; hence father/daughter incest is regarded as the most unacceptable form of the crime on a worldwide basis and hence the widespread assumption that a female minor, or the most vulnerable member of the family, cannot be guilty of incest. Such a view must, of course, also incorporate intercourse between step-father and step-daughter – or, indeed, between the 'lodger' or a mother's paramour and her child – as being incestuous, for such sexual abuse is just as traumatic to the young, dependent girl as are the attentions of her natural father; it also justifies the American concept of father/son incest, which is a contradiction in terms in the United Kingdom. If this is the true basis, it follows that modern law should reflect the concept of the abuse of power, and that trend is demonstrated in Scottish legislation.

This states[105] that a man commits incest if he has intercourse with his mother, daughter, grandmother, grand-daughter, sister, aunt, niece, great-grandmother or great-grand daughter. Incest is brought into line with the Marriage (Scotland) Act 1977, insofar as a man now also commits incest in having intercourse with his adoptive mother or former adoptive mother or with his adopted daughter or former adopted daughter. Thus the forbidden relationships remain wider than those in England and, in addition, there is no age limit as to when the reverse relationships constitute a crime. Intercourse involving any other relationships cannot be incest, but two other specific offences are incorporated in the 1995 Act. The first is that of having intercourse with a step-child if that child is aged less than 21 years and has lived at any time when below the age of 18 years as a member of the same household (s.2). The more interesting innovation is the offence of a person over the age of 16 years having intercourse with a child below the age of 16 when being in a position of trust or of authority in relation to the child as a member of the same household (s.3).

Scottish legislation is, therefore, something of a compromise in that, on the one hand, it retains much of the rather wide category of incestuous relationships which was based originally on biblical texts; even so, relationships by affinity can no longer lead to incest. The genetic canard is maintained to an extent by the inclusion of illegitimate relationships but is, at the same time, partially discarded with the inclusion of adoptive relationships; the latter provision serves to emphasise the importance of the position of trust or authority which is further supported by the inclusion of the two related offences.

There is still some reason to wonder whether the crime of incest as such is still needed on the statute book and, also, to question whether intrafamilial relationships should be criminalised rather than being dealt with within the family jurisdiction. As to the first, there is good reason to suppose that public opinion strongly supports the isolation of father/daughter and mother/son sexual intimacy as something which is so repugnant – even if only for the intense measure of trust involved – that it deserves the pejorative definition of incest. There is, however, less reason to categorise other sexual relationships in the same way. By so doing, the severity of the father/daughter relationship, including the adoptive relationship, is diluted; there is no essential reason why lesser relationships should not be encompassed within the existing statutory sexual offences so long as the added element of trust or authority were reflected in sentencing; the uncle/niece relationship is a particularly apt example of a case where this might be applied. The failure of the legislation to protect young boys is noteworthy, but the omission can be excused on just such grounds: indecent assault, gross indecency and buggery are all already proscribed.

The dilemma of incest and the criminal courts still persists. A strong argument can be made that the incest laws are there, primarily, to protect young children whose best interests cannot be served either by using them as witnesses or simply by allowing them to see their fathers imprisoned through what might well be seen by them as being partly their responsibility. If we are prepared to go to so much trouble to shield children from criminal justice by way of family proceedings or children's hearings, why do we suspend the rules in the face of maximum sexual abuse? The time may well come when incest is dealt with in the first instance in the family court, where the primary aim is rehabilitation of the family, reference to the criminal court being retained as an option in the event of proof of a manifest and inexcusable abuse of power.

Notes

1 Protection of Children Act 1978; Civic Government (Scotland) Act 1982, s.52.
2 The Criminal Justice and Public Order Act 1994, s.84 amends both the Protection of Children Act 1978 and the Civic Government (Scotland) Act 1982 so as to include pseudo-photographs: that is images made by computer graphics or otherwise which appear to be photographs. See also *R* v. *Fellows, R* v. *Arnold* [1997] 2 All ER 548: computerised material was, at least, a copy of an indecent photograph.
3 The prototype paper is that of J. Caffey, 'Multiple fractures in the long bones of children suffering from chronic subdural hematoma' (1946) 56 Am J Roentgenol 163. It is to be noted that, at the time, the author believed he was dealing with a syndrome of natural disease.
4 C.H. Kempe, F.N. Silverman, B.F. Steele, W. Droegemueller and H.K. Silver, 'The battered-child syndrome' (1962) 181 J Amer Med Assoc 17.
5 *Attorney-General's Reference (No. 6 of 1980)* [1981] QB 715. But this is not to say that the social services may not be alerted: *R* v. *East Sussex County Council, ex parte R* [1991] 2 FLR 358.
6 *Campbell and Cosans* v. *United Kingdom* (1982) 4 EHRR 293. Corporal punishment is now illegal in state-run schools in Great Britain: Education (No 2) Act

1986, ss.47, 48. Not all judicial opinion is, however, happy with the situation: J. Bale, 'Judge blames EU ban on caning for juvenile crimes' (1997), *The Times*, 8 March, p. 1.

7   D.G. Gill, 'Physical abuse of children: findings and implications of a nation-wide survey' (1969) 44 Pediatrics 857.

8   A.D.M. Jackson, 'Wednesday's children: a review of child abuse' (1982) 75 J R Soc Med 83, considered the incidence to be far lower. By contrast, the *Report of the Committee on Child Health Services* (S.D.M. Court, chairman), Cmnd 6684 (1976) had previously quoted, without comment, figures from the British Paediatric Association indicating an annual mortality of 350–400.

9   Child Sexual Abuse Guidelines for Medical Practitioners, issued by the Lothian Health Board (1987).

10   Increased awareness has been adduced for the apparent escalation of sexual abuse in the USA: (W. Feldman, E. Feldman, J.T. Goodman *et al.*, 'Is childhood sexual abuse really increasing in prevalence? An analysis of the evidence' (1991) 88 Pediatrics 29.

11   D.E.H. Russell, ' The incidence and prevalence of intrafamilial and extrafamilial sexual abuse of female children' (1983) 7 Child Abuse Negl 133.

12   *Stubbings* v. *Webb* [1993] 1 All ER 322, HL.

13   For a very full exposition, see A. Gath, 'Emotional abuse of children', in J.K. Mason (ed.), *Paediatric Forensic Medicine and Pathology* (1989), London: Chapman & Hall.

14   D.P. Addy, 'Talking points in child abuse' (1985) 290 Brit Med J 259.

15   E.M. Boyter, D.W. MacLean, H.E. Zealley and J.K. Mason, 'Non-accidental injury to children: a survey of professional attitudes' (1983) 33 J R Col Gen Pract 773.

16   J. Jenkins and O.P. Gray, 'Changing incidence of non-accidental injury to children in South Glamorgan' (1987) 294 Brit Med J 1658.

17   The year in which the horrifying death of Maria Colwell was reported: T.G. Field Fisher (Chairman), *Report of the Committee of Inquiry into the Care and Supervision Provided in relation to Maria Colwell* (1974), London: HMSO.

18   *R* v. *Cutts* (1987) 17 Fam Law 311, CA.

19   *R* v. *Sheppard and another* [1981] 3 All ER 899.

20   And by the Criminal Law (Consolidation) (Scotland) Act 1995.

21   Rape in England and Wales can now be committed by a male against a male and also includes intercourse *per anum*: Sexual Offences Act, 1956, s.1 as amended by Criminal Justice and Public Order Act 1994, s.142. This extended definition does not run to Scotland at the time of writing. However, see n. 101 below for some, probably spurious, doubts as to incest.

22   For a full exposition, to which this author is greatly indebted, see J. Masson and M. Morris, *The Children Act Manual* (1992), London: Sweet & Maxwell.

23   Save as to access and emigration with which we are not concerned here.

24   The court may be the Family Proceedings Court, which is part of the Magistrates' Court, the County Court or the High Court (s.92(7)). See the Family Proceedings Courts (Children Act 1989) Rules 1991 (S.I. 1991/1395); Children (Allocation of Proceedings) Order 1991 (S.I. 1991/1677).

25   These include contact orders, which enable a person to have contact with a child, prohibited steps orders, which limit the steps parents can take without the consent of the court, and residence orders, which dictate the person with whom a child is to live.

26   For example, *Re R (a Minor) (Blood Transfusion)* [1993] 2 FCR 544. BOOTH J gives her reasons for preferring this route to an application for wardship (see n. 28 below).

27 Note that wardship as such is still available to anyone other than a local authority who could apply for it before the 1989 Act was enforced.

28 *Re O (a minor) (medical treatment)* [1993] 2 FLR 149. For discussion, see C. Gilham, 'The dilemma of parental choice' (1993) NLJ 1219; for views prior to 1989, see G. Williams, *Textbook of Criminal Law* (1983, 2nd edn), London: Stevens, p. 575.

29 *Gillick* v. *West Norfolk and Wisbech Area Health Authority* [1986] AC 112, HL. See *Re R (a minor) (wardship: medical treatment)* [1992] Fam 11 for the introduction of the term.

30 Children Act 1989, sch. 3, paras 4(4)(a), 5(5)(a). Requirements for psychiatric treatment are subject to evidence from a medical practitioner approved for the purpose under the Mental Health Act 1983, s.12 that the child's mental condition requires treatment and is susceptible to treatment.

31 For procedure, see Family Proceedings Rules 1991, r.4.22 (S I 1991/1247).

32 A Children's Panel is established for every local government area. The members are drawn from all walks of life in accordance with advice given to the Secretary of State by a Children's Panel Advisory Committee; the names of panel members are published (Schedule 1 to the 1995 Act).

33 The hearing consists of three members of the Children's Panel and must not consist wholly of men or women. The need to call a hearing derives from s.56(6) and from s.65(1) of the 1995 Act, though it is difficult to see where the distinction lies.

34 Criminal Procedure (Scotland) Act 1995, sch.1.

35 Incest and intercourse with a child by a step-parent or a person in a position of trust.

36 But he is not obliged to act on them.

37 The child protection order must terminate within eight working days of its creation, by which time it will have been reviewed at least once, either by the sheriff or by an initial Children's Hearing.

38 This must be no later than the eighth working day after the implementation of the order; otherwise, it falls (1995 Act, s.65(2)).

39 I have argued elsewhere that the *capacity* to consent to and to refuse treatment may not necessarily be the same; but this is a minority view. See J.K. Mason and R.A. McCall Smith, *Law and Medical Ethics* (4th edn, 1994), London: Butterworths, p. 229.

40 There is no reason, however, why a lawyer should not be an accompanying 'friend' (Children's Hearings (Scotland) Rules 1996 (S.I. 1996/3261, r.11(1)).

41 Essentially, this is a responsible member of the public who has been appointed and who should have received suitable training (1995 Act, s.101).

42 1995 Act, sch.4, c.40.

43 For early doubts as to the wisdom of the changes, see S. Cretney, 'Tarnishing the golden thread?' (1989), *The Times*, 25 April, p. 36.

44 *In re L (Sexual Abuse: Standard of Proof)* [1996] 1 FLR 116.

45 *Re T (a minor) (Child: Representation)* (1993) 4 All ER 518.

46 *A* v. *Liverpool City Council* [1982] AC 363; *In re W (A minor) (Wardship: Jurisdiction)* [1985] 1 AC 791; *M* v. *H and others* [1988]) 3 All ER 5, HL.

47 Family Proceedings Courts (Children Act 1989) Rules 1991 (S I 1991/1395), r.7 and sch.2.

48 Family Proceedings Rules 1991 (S I 1991/1247), r.4.22.

49 *D* v. *National Society for the Prevention of Cruelty to Children* [1978] AC 171. The proposition has not been tested in Scotland, but it is probable that the RSSPCC would be similarly protected.

50 *O* v. *United Kingdom, H* v. *same, W* v. *same, B* v. *same, R* v. *same* [1988] 2 FLR 445. See also (1988)10 EHRR 29, 74, 82, 87, 95.

51　J. Eekelaar, 'Parental responsibility for children in care' (1989) 139 NLJ 760.
52　The Scottish system has also come in for some criticism although most of this is administrative in nature: A. Finlayson, *Reporters to Children's Panels: Their Role, Function and Accountability* (1992), Edinburgh: Scottish Office. See also J. Rose, 'Procedure in Children's Hearings' 1994 SLT 137. It is arguable that the system, which was primarily set up to deal with young offenders, is ill-equipped to deal with the escalating number of child abuse cases. See L. Edwards and A.M. Griffiths, *Family Law* (1997), Edinburgh: W Green & Co, ch. 8.
53　Department of Health and Social Security and the Welsh Office, *Working Together* (1988), London: HMSO.
54　Who is responsible to the Social Services Committee established under the Local Authorities Social Services Act 1970.
55　And diagnosis can be difficult: D.M. Wheeler and C.J. Hobbs, 'Mistakes in diagnosing non-accidental injury: 10 years' experience' (1988) 296 Brit Med J 1233.
56　General Medical Council, *Guidance to Doctors: Confidentiality* (1995), para. 11.
57　General Medical Council, *Professional Conduct and Discipline: Fitness to Practise* (1993), para. 83.
58　Children Act 1989, ss. 31(9), 43(13) and 44(2).
59　For example, Sexual Offences Act, 1956; Indecency with Children Act, 1960; Criminal Law (Consolidation) (Scotland) Act 1995.
60　N.J. Wild, 'Sexual abuse of children in Leeds' (1986) 292 Brit Med J 1113.
61　I. Smith, '"Open hostility" between police and consultants' (1987), *The Times*, 14 April, p. 3.
62　For a very explicit expression of the doctor's dilemma, see Anonymous, 'Child protection: medical responsibilities' (1996) 313 Brit Med J 671 and accompanying commentaries.
63　*X and others (minors)* v. *Bedfordshire County Council, M (a minor) and another* v. *Newham London Borough Council and other appeals* [1995] 3 All ER 353, HL per LORD BROWNE-WILKINSON at 380. The arguments are succinctly analysed by L. Edwards, 'Suing local authorities for failure in statutory duty: Orkney reconsidered after *X* v. *Bedfordshire*' (1996) 1 Edin L Rev 115.
64　As SIR THOMAS BINGHAM MR said in the appeal stage of the case, 'it would require very potent considerations of public policy … to override the rule of public policy which has first claim on the loyalty of the law: that wrongs should be remedied' [1994] 4 All ER 602, CA at 619.
65　C. SanLazaro, A.M. Steele and L.J. Donaldson 'Outcome of criminal investigation into allegations of sexual abuse' (1996) 75 Arch Dis Child 149. It is interesting that none of nine alleged female abusers was prosecuted (see Chapter 14 for further discussion).
66　Originally, Department of Health and Social Security *Battered Babies* (1972) CMO 10/72, London: DHSS. See also Social Work Services Group, circ. SW 4/ 82 (NHS circ 1982 (GEN) 18), 1982.
67　*In re A and others (minors) (child abuse: guidelines)* [1991] 1 WLR 1026.
68　For a simple exposition, see Editorial comment, 'Reporting child abuse' (1996) 348 Lancet 557.
69　Although there are other reasons, such as inconvenient timing. See C. Lea-Cox and A. Hall, 'Attendance of general practitioners at child protection case conferences' (1991) 302 Brit Med J 1378.
70　*Re G (a minor) (social worker: disclosure)* (1995) 31 BMLR 175.
71　And, indeed, they must be given access to relevant reports: *R* v. *Hampshire County Council, ex parte K and another* [1990] 2 All ER 129. It is part and parcel

of the child's welfare that its parents are given every proper opportunity of having the evidence fairly tested.

72 In which case judicial review may be applicable. See the very interesting *R v. Norfolk County Council, ex parte M* [1989] 2 All ER 359 which also raised starkly the issue of confidentiality. See also *ex parte R*, n. 5 above, for a practical example.

73 Evidence of striking similarity may or may not be admissible in subsequent proceedings, depending on the nature of the similarity: *R v. P* [1991] 3 All ER 337, HL.

74 *R v. Norfolk County Council, ex parte M* , n. 72 above. It was later emphasised that this power should be used only sparingly: *R v. Harrow London Borough Council, ex parte D* [1990] 3 All ER 12, CA.

75 *Re L (minors)*, n. 44 above, confirming *In re G (a minor)* [1987] 1 WLR 1461. See also, in Scotland, *Reporter to Central Region Children's Panel v F* (1990) Scotsman, 7 November.

76 *F v. Suffolk County Council* [1981] 2 FLR 208; *In re H (minors) (sexual abuse: standard of proof)* [1996] 1 All ER 1. But the court can take pre-birth conditions into account, without waiting for the neonate to be injured: *D (a minor) v. Berkshire County Council* [1987] AC 317, HL.

77 Lord Justice Butler-Sloss (Chairman), *Report of the Inquiry into Child Abuse in Cleveland 1987* (1988), London: HMSO.

78 C.J. Hobbs and J.M. Wynne, 'Buggery in childhood – a common syndrome of child abuse' [1986] 2 Lancet 792. For a criticism of the test, see D.M. Paul, '"What really did happen to Baby Jane?" – the medical aspects of the investigation of alleged sexual abuse of children' (1986) 26 Med Sci Law 85.

79 The lesson has been well learnt and it is now recognised that the evidence of experts in such cases should be collated and presented concisely to the court: *In re C (Children Act: expert evidence)* [1995] 1 FLR 204. In general, care proceedings are not adversarial: *R v. Birmingham Juvenile Court, ex parte G, Same v. Same, ex parte R* [1988] 3 All ER 726, CA. Hearsay evidence may also be available: *In re W (minors) (wardship: evidence)* (1989) 154 JPN 363; in Scotland, *W and another v. Kennedy* 1988 SLT 583.

80 See, for example, the Ayrshire cases in 1990, discussed in *L, petitioners (No 2)* 1993 SLT1342.

81 See the authoritative document issued by the Department of Health and Social Security, *Diagnosis of Child Sexual Abuse: Guidance for Doctors* (1988), London: HMSO, s.12.

82 See R. West, A. Davies and T. Fenton, 'Accidental vulval injuries in childhood' (1989) 298 Brit Med J 1002.

83 Note 61 above.

84 R. Roberts, 'Police doctor tells of diagnostic risks' (1987), *The Times*, 10 August, p. 3.

85 Note 81 above, at paras 12.20 and 2.3.

86 R. Meadow, 'Staying cool on child abuse' (1987) 295 Brit Med J 345.

87 Note 53 above.

88 In *Re R (a minor) (experts' evidence)* [1991] 1 FLR 291.

89 Police and Criminal Evidence Act 1984, s.81.

90 In all, 20 children from six families were made wards of court on the basis of a single child's allegations. See *Rochdale Borough Council v. A and others* [1991] 2 FLR 192.

91 For example, *Re E (a minor) (child abuse: evidence)* [1991] 1 FLR 421.

92 *F v. Kennedy (No. 2)* 1993 SLT 1284 per LORD ROSS L J-C at 1287.

93 Lord Clyde, *Report of the Inquiry into the Removal of Children from Orkney in February 1991* (1992), Edinburgh: HMSO.

94 *Sloan* v. *B* 1991 SLT 527.
95 Editorial comment, 'Child abuse: the swing of the pendulum' (1981) 283 Brit Med J 170.
96 R. Meadow, 'Munchausen syndrome by proxy: the hinterland of child abuse' [1977] 2 Lancet 343.
97 Editorial comment, 'Diagnosing recurrent suffocation of children' (1992) 340 Lancet 87. The main differential diagnosis will, of course, be the natural 'cot death': R. Meadow, 'Suffocation, recurrent apnea, and sudden infant death' (1990) 117 J Pediat 351.
98 See D. Brahams, 'Video surveillance and child abuse' (1993) 342 Lancet 944.
99 See the excellent debate between, on the one hand, D.M. Foreman and C. Farsides, 'Ethical use of covert videoing techniques in detecting Munchausen syndrome by proxy' (1993) 307 Brit Med J 611 and, on the other, the response by D.P. Southall and M.P. Samuels, at 613. The greater part of the *Journal of Medical Ethics* (1996), part 1, pp. 16–32 is taken up by discussion papers which also include guidelines for surveillance.
100 Sexual Offences Act 1956, ss.10, 11.
101 R. May and J.J. McManus, in their annotation to the 1994 Act, say that s.142 'defines sexual intercourse to include anal intercourse'. My own view is that the section redefines rape rather than sexual intercourse and would not, therefore, apply to incest – or, indeed, to any sexual offence other than buggery and, now, rape in England and Wales. The 1995 Act does not define sexual intercourse in Scotland, but the annotation to s.1 (C. MacIntosh) defines it as penetration of any degree of the vagina by the penis and states that it is restricted to heterosexual intercourse.
102 I discussed this many years ago, in M. Noble and J.K. Mason, 'Incest' (1978) 4 J Med Ethics 64.
103 J.K. Mason, '1567 and all that' 1981 SLT 301.
104 See, for example, R. Card, 'Sexual relations with minors' [1975] Crim L R 380; V. Bailey and S. McCabe, 'Reforming the law of incest' [1979] Crim L R 749; T. Honoré, *Sex Law* (1978), London: Duckworth, p. 70.
105 Criminal Law (Consolidation) (Scotland) Act 1995, which incorporates the Incest and Related Offences (Scotland) Act 1986 and the Sexual Offences (Scotland) Act 1976.

14 The Killing of Children Within the Family: Filicide

This book is concerned with the family and with the medico-legal issues associated with parenting. This chapter does not, therefore, attempt to review the topic of child homicide in general; the 'stranger killing' of children and its modern extension, the serial murder, are of great sociological and psychological interest, but are outside the present remit.[1] Discussion will be limited to the killing of children by their parents (that is, filicide) extending, where necessary, so as to include those standing *in loco parentis* by affinity or association.

It might well be thought that child homicide is the logical outcome, and the common result, of child abuse as described in the preceding chapter, but this is not so. Certainly, some horrifying deaths of this type do occur. Many outrageous cases of cruelty to children, however, involve some sadistic gratification for the abuser; the death of the child removes this source of satisfaction. Moreover, given the fact that social workers have no powers of forced entry, many cases of child abuse – even of the most serious type – can remain uninvestigated for surprisingly long periods, and this despite the fact that *detection* by outside agencies is relatively frequent;[2] by contrast, there is very little prospect of successfully hiding a death which results from persistent and repetitive ill-treatment; discovery and prosecution must be anticipated, so that, in most cases of child abuse, death represents a mistake or an accident. The alleged cry of Whitaker,[3] 'Oh heck, I've done it this time', summarises the situation admirably. Thus, although it may, at times, seem bizarre to the outside observer, there is no necessary illogicality in such cases being prosecuted for and/or convicted of manslaughter rather than murder.

Paternal filicide

Since criminal cases are rarely reported unless they demonstrate a point of law, it is difficult to assess the practical results of this type of killing. By its very nature, the precipitating circumstances cannot be concealed within the home and some complicity between husband and wife – or cohabiters – is almost always assumed at first. Thereafter, however, the scales are weighted very heavily against the man, the presumption – and, often, the defence – being that the woman acted under male domination.[4] Indeed, it appears that the police will, on occasion, use the public's generally protective attitude to women so as to ensure the conviction of the man.[5] In practice, it is accepted that abusive filicide is virtually confined to the paternal element in the family (for further discussion, see p. 392). Scott's series of fatal battered baby cases,[6] for example, dealt *only* with 'fathers', of whom less than half were putative biological parents. The author commented on the fact that 95 per cent of the deceased infants had more than one significant injury and the psychiatric state of the 'fatal batterers' was interesting in this respect. Mental illness at the time of the offence was demonstrated in none of the 29 cases; by contrast, an abnormal personality – or psychopathy – was common and ranged between immaturity and aggressiveness. Scott clearly considered that leaving a child alone with an unstable father was hazardous and he pointed to the proportion of affected families in which the mother was the breadwinner and in which there was an element of role reversal. It is thus possible to see room for mitigating circumstances in paternal filicide and this is, perhaps, reflected in what appears to be, otherwise, a capricious sentencing policy. It is not possible to identify individual cases in Scott's series, but the dispositions included six life sentences and three of imprisonment for 10 years or more; the remaining 20 men received lesser sentences and these included four non-custodial dispositions. Thus, only about one-fifth of the fathers were convicted of murder and it was concluded that, even in these relatively extreme cases, both juries and judges were striving to exclude premeditation on the part of the accused. To an extent, however, much will depend upon the nature of the prosecution. It is perfectly feasible, for example, to bring a prosecution under the Children and Young Persons Act, 1933, s.1, which carries a maximum sentence of two years' imprisonment; most such cases, if fatal, would, however, be prosecuted as murder or as manslaughter *ab initio*, with or without an additional charge of child abuse.

It is impossible to decide how often repetitive non-accidental injury leads to death; a somewhat dated Australian estimate lay between 1 and 2 per cent, evolving from some 74 new cases of abuse each year.[7] The pattern, when it arises, is so characteristic of paternal filicide that d'Orban,[8] in his major study of the British scene, did not include the battered baby syndrome in his classification of maternal killings. In his paper, he defined the battering maternal filicide as one who kills on a sudden impulse characterised by loss of temper resulting from a stimulus initiated by the victim. It is true that Scott also attributed many of the paternal killings associated with repetitive injury to a final sudden outburst of temper occasioned by an immediate precipitating action or behaviour on the part of the child, and a number of cases of paternal killing arise in which there is no antecedent history of ill-treatment and which are comparable to those deaths that are so often attributed to 'accident' by mothers. Such cases can be particularly sad, as they may occur in families which have been conspicuously happy, but, at one isolated moment, circumstances have combined to make, say, the baby's crying intolerable. Occasionally, the courts have seemed to be over-harsh as a result of applying an objective test to what must, in general, be a very subjective situation. Thus, in *Ward*,[9] a man was sentenced to death for killing the 18-month-old daughter of his established partner. He averred that he shook the baby only to make her quiet and had no intention of hurting her. Since the body was concealed for nearly two years, the cause of death was uncertain; nevertheless, the sentence was confirmed on appeal on the grounds that a reasonable man would have anticipated that severe injury would result from such treatment.[10] One can, perhaps, take comfort from the fact that *Ward*'s case is more than 40 years old.

In more recent years, however, the courts have been adopting a rather more humane line. *Williams*[11] concerned the death of a three-year-old child who was beaten on the buttocks. Death was, somewhat doubtfully, attributed, *inter alia*, to fat embolism – a very uncommon cause of death in the absence of bone fracture. Looked at from a distance, it seems that the beating must have been of considerable force, yet it was regarded as a chastisement rather than an attack; a sentence of seven years' imprisonment for manslaughter was reduced on appeal to four years.

Cases of this type raise the question of mitigation by virtue of provocation. This problem was addressed in the case of *Doughty*.[12] Here a mother was ordered to bed after her confinement and the management of the neonate was left to the husband; the baby was found dead 17 days after birth, death being due to head injuries. The explanation given in defence was that, being very tired, the husband had lost his temper when the baby cried and had covered its head with cushions and knelt on them. The trial judge refused to allow the issue of provocation to be put to the jury, although the defence contended that he should have done so by reason of the Homicide Act, 1957, s.3; the appeal was taken on this point alone. The Crown put forward the 'floodgates proposition' to the effect that, if the judge's direction was held to be wrong, it opened up the possibility that an argument based on provocation could be raised in any case in which there was an allegation of baby battering ending in death. The Court of Criminal Appeal, however, held that 'reliance can be placed on the common sense of juries ... [which] will ensure that only in cases where the facts fully justified it would they be likely to hold ... that killing a crying child would be the response of a reasonable man' (at 326). The conviction for murder was quashed and a sentence of five years' imprisonment for manslaughter substituted – and it reads as if even this was imposed with some reluctance. It is therefore clear that a plea of provocation is competent in such cases and it brings the law in relation to paternal filicide closer to that which is applied to mothers and which is discussed in greater detail below.

Child neglect

The injury or killing of children by neglect within a two-parent family must, almost by definition, involve conspiracy between the cohabiters. This differs little from neglect of any vulnerable persons, including the aged, and has been remarked upon already, in Chapter 12, in relation to the withholding of medical treatment. It must, however, be distinguished from neonatal neglect or abandonment which is a condition that is, to all intents, confined to the mother alone.

As is well known, it is not easy in law to prove murder by omission. Difficulty derives, firstly, from the general premise that failure to act is inoffensive unless there is a clear duty to do so and, secondly, from the problems posed in establishing the necessary *mens rea* or intent to justify conviction for murder. The classic case of child murder by neglect is now some 80 years old and is unlikely to be copied.[13] In it, a man and woman living together were held guilty of the murder of the man's child when the woman, with the man's concurrence, withheld food from the child *intending* either its death or grievous bodily harm. The necessary elements of a duty of care – which was assumed by the woman when she cohabited with the man – and of intention were both covered. Much importance attached to the fact that the woman had been given money especially for the purpose of providing food; it was generally considered at the time that, in default of precise instructions, a woman, who was effectively the servant of her husband, had no access to food and, as a result, could not be guilty of a crime involving starvation. This defence, at least in respect of manslaughter, was laid to rest in 1959 in *Watson,*[14] in which a similar argument was led following conviction, albeit in respect of providing medical aid rather than food; the Court of Criminal Appeal had no doubts that it was false law based on conditions which had no relevance to modern-day living.

Deaths due to neglect are now ordinarily prosecuted as manslaughter or culpable homicide, but this is not to imply that a conviction for these lesser offences is all that much easier to obtain. The courts have always insisted that, for a death due to negligence to be classed as manslaughter, the negligence must be of a gross character. As WILLS J put it when stating the seminal case of *R v. Senior*:[15] 'to make out a case of manslaughter by negligence at common law, the negligence must be gross and intended including something of an evil mind' (at 285). This was, however, to be contrasted with the test when, as in the particular case, the prosecution was statutory.[16] The trial judge had held that, in such circumstances, 'if he had done anything which was apparently forbidden by statute, and in doing so had caused or accelerated the child's death, he would be guilty of manslaughter no matter what his motive or state of mind' (at 285, 290). The Crown Cases Reserved Court agreed with this and, per LORD RUSSELL CJ, defined something wilfully done as that done deliberately and intentionally. At the same time, the court applied an objective definition to neglect; that is, the omission of such steps as a reasonable parent would take; on these grounds, failure to provide medical assistance constituted wilful neglect.[17] *Senior* is, however, almost a century old and the views expressed therein have been greatly modified and partially overturned by the House of Lords. In *R v. Sheppard*,[18] the House held that there was no strict liability implied in the Children and Young Persons Act, 1933, s.1. It was up to the prosecution to prove in each case that the parents had deliberately or recklessly failed to provide the necessary aid for the child; the test was, therefore, subjective and related to the individual circumstances of each case, the concept of the reasonable man being one of civil law which should not be extended to the criminal law lightly. The decision rested on a 3:2 majority and the dissenting opinion of LORD FRASER bears repetition:

> The provisions [of the Act] are intended by Parliament for the protection of children who cannot look after themselves ... There is nothing unreasonable in their being stringent and objective. If the offence required proof that the particular parents were aware of the probable consequences of neglect, then the difficulty of proof against stupid or feckless parents would certainly be increased and so might the danger to their children ... Such a sharp change towards relaxation of the law on the subject seems appropriate only for the legislature (at 913).

Nonetheless, the majority opinion in *Sheppard* represents the current law and there can be no doubt that convictions based on simple neglect are now less easy to obtain. And one could well ask, what is wrong with that? No matter how much we may – indeed, must –

sympathise with the lot of the neglected child, is it right that people should be punished for something that is beyond their comprehension? The answer lies in improvements to the already overstretched social services: Utopia must be a wonderful place in which to live.

Other forms of child killing

There are at least two other rather non-specific forms of child killing which can be identified, the surrounding circumstances of which are relatively self-explanatory.

Multiple murder

Occasional instances occur in which a whole family is attacked, generally by the father, who is usually affected by severe manic-depressive psychosis; filicide is, in such circumstances, incidental to the main condition. A typical case, except for the fact that it was apparently dissociated from mental illness, was described in *Christie* v. *Christie*.[19] After nine months of happy marriage, the husband got up in the night and attempted to strangle his mother-in-law. The next morning, he strangled his minor sister-in-law and concealed her body; he later attempted to have sexual intercourse with a married sister-in-law. The case illustrates the sympathetic attitudes of juries to intrafamilial crises: a verdict of not proven was returned in respect of the attempted murder while, in the case of the child, the man was convicted only of culpable homicide by reason of diminished responsibility; the judge was, however, of sterner disposition and sentenced him to 12 years' imprisonment.

Rather similar occurrences may be followed by suicide, and mothers are then involved. Altruistic filicide associated with suicide, in fact, comprised the largest groupings in both maternal and paternal categories (and 38 per cent of the total cases) of Resnick's first survey of the world literature,[20] which is discussed briefly below. Wilkey's[21] more specific series contained four instances, three of which were maternally oriented; depression, with death being seen as the ultimate protection of the helpless child, is a frequent underlying factor.

Mercy killing or active euthanasia

The conditions here are, of course, different, although both types of killing are usually altruistic in intention. The victim of mercy killing is, or is suspected as being, in an intolerable situation due either to physical or mental incapacity, and the parental intention is to put the child out of its misery. It is, however, impossible to eliminate some element of self-interest on the part of the killer: parents, in many cases, will have been under great pressure in their caring roles and, while in many instances they are at the end of their tether, it could be that, fundamentally, they have simply had enough; it is this factor particularly which complicates both legal and public attitudes to child euthanasia.

The dilemma was well summed up by SLADE J in *R v. Johnson*:[22]

> I accept the fact that what you did was done without thought for yourself but out of compassion for the child ... but what you did was done after considerable premeditation ... You knew you were breaking the law and I cannot pass over a matter of that gravity ... lest other people might be tempted to think they can deal in this way with any mongol child, misformed child, or child not in possession of its faculties.

A sentence of 12 months' imprisonment was passed and, in general, judicial response to such tragedies has been very humane. Thus, in sentencing a man who had battered his autistic nine-year-old son to death to 12 months' probation, HEILBRON J thought it her 'public duty not to add to the hell' of the accused's knowledge of what he had done.[23]

Such lenient sentences are possible only when the accused can be found guilty of manslaughter or culpable homicide by reason of diminished responsibility, and there is here an evident jurisprudential difficulty: while it is true that many 'mercy killers' are suffering from an abnormality of mind, the majority are acting after deep consideration and with a marked degree of responsibility; a verdict of guilty of manslaughter is, therefore, something of a contradiction in terms, particularly if premeditation is to be used as one measure of the severity of the crime.[24] As Williams[25] said, 'The defence of diminished [responsibility] is interpreted in accordance with the morality of the case rather than as an application of psychiatric concepts' (at 693) and, again:

> The invocation of the psychiatrist and the probation officer [in the quoted case of *Price*[26]] could not have been regarded as necessary for any of the purposes for which those persons are normally used. It was merely an attempt by the judge to render workable a law that is grossly out of accord with present thought, and to maintain, as is required by his office, an appearance of official disapproval towards an act that most people nowadays would regard as a normal reaction to an impossible situation (at 694).

Unqualified approval of such a view may not come easily, particularly in the light of the distinction to be made between the mentally and the physically defective neonate discussed in Chapter 11, but it serves to reopen the question of whether 'mercy killing' should be statutorily recognised as a ground for mitigation in itself.[27] The working party of the Criminal Law Revision Committee (CLRC) recommended this change originally, it being suggested that the offence carry a maximum penalty of two years' imprisonment; but they withdrew it from their final report as being too controversial to be included in the exercise in law reform in which they were engaged.[28] Effectively, therefore, as Leng pointed out, the CLRC were fondly hoping that the connivance of the psychiatrists and judges would continue to accommodate mercy killings without the need for legislative change. This certainly operates in practice, although it is debatable whether the law should be founded on a fiction; the problem is reverted to in the discussion of infanticide.

Any supposed need for euthanasia of children should, in fact, have decreased markedly in the last three decades as a result of the combined influence of the Abortion Act 1967 and modern attitudes to selective treatment of the newborn which have been discussed in Chapter 11.[29] In addition, the availability and quality of the social services have expanded so as to give far more relief to families under stress.

Maternal filicide

There is little doubt that the major medico-legal interests attached to filicide relate to maternal killing, this being because of the unique bonding which is normally set up between mother and child. Comparative analysis of the issues is complicated by an inconsistent terminology. Infanticide in England and Wales is a tightly defined entity confined to maternal filicide in the first year of life.[30] Elsewhere, including the United States, it can have a wider meaning comparable to what would be called child homicide in the United Kingdom; it is to be noted, however, that Wilkey and his colleagues excluded deaths due to non-accidental injury from their category of infanticide. It is also unfortunate that the word 'neonaticide' has come to mean different things. As defined originally by Resnick,[31] it meant killing of the newborn infant by its mother during the first 24 hours of its life; it would thus include the English offence of concealment of birth or its Scottish equivalent, which includes an element of concealment of pregnancy.[32] The main disadvantage of Resnick's nomenclature is that it isolates what is the most common time for maternal filicide[33] from the general crime of infanticide which is, itself, statutorily defined . I prefer to reserve the term 'neonaticide' to describe euthanasia of the newborn by persons outside the family, including the infant's medical attendants.[34] Thus used, the word has no legal connotation in the United Kingdom, although it is tending to be accepted in this sense;[35] in the context of filicide, it is better to speak of early infanticide than of neonaticide. An unfortunate practical result of this semantic confusion is that it makes it very difficult to make a meaningful comparative study of child killing; I will not attempt a systematic study of national differences. The overall, and somewhat surprising, impression is that patterns have not varied greatly over the recent decades and that geography seems to make very little difference. Most series are small – the offence itself appears to be relatively uncommon – and it is difficult to distinguish between maternal and paternal filicide in some reports. In general, however, the very early American series analysed by Adelson[36] and that somewhat later of Myers,[37] the later Australian studies of Wilkey and those of d'Orban in England at much the same time provided quite remarkably similar results as to broad principles, and this applies to observations made in such contrasting circumstances as in the Far East a decade ago.[38] We have now, however, a relatively recent review on which to draw and this is discussed in some detail below.[39]

Historical aspects

O'Donovan[40] quoted Langer[41] in saying that infanticide has, from time immemorial, been the accepted procedure for disposing of sickly infants and of all such newborns as might strain the resources of the individual family or the community. While this can no longer be regarded as the case – at least in the Western world – the present attitudes to maternal filicide have evolved from this premise in a gradual fashion and, even now, are subject to change.

As O'Donovan has pointed out, this evolution results from an increasing interpretation of infanticide within a medical model. Thus the statutory provisions governing the killing of infants in the 17th century were punitive in nature and were aimed specifically at the unmarried mother.[42] Under legislation dating from 1604, a woman who concealed the death of an illegitimate child was, until 1803, presumed, in England and Wales, to have murdered it unless she could prove stillbirth; as many as 40 per cent of women so charged were hanged.[43] Infanticide within wedlock was seen in a different light and, indeed, the opportunities for disposing of a neonate were so wide that many cases must have gone undiscovered. Nevertheless, although the evidential requirements were reversed in Lord Ellenborough's Act of 1803, the offence remained one of murder until 1922, when the Infanticide Act reduced it to infanticide, punishable as manslaughter, if the killing of a newly born infant, by act or omission, was maternal in origin and if, at the time, her balance of mind was disturbed by reason of her not having fully recovered from the effects of giving birth to the child. There is a strong suspicion that the Act was, essentially, a judicial effort to avoid perverse jury verdicts and to cut out the charade of passing death sentences which were never likely to be carried out; it was thus compounded of socio-economic intent and medical reasoning.

The legislation suffered from the surprising laxity of the term 'newly born' and this caused considerable difficulty.[44] The anomaly was removed in the Infanticide Act, 1938, which is still in force and which defines the victim of infanticide as being a child under the age of 12 months; the 1938 Act further 'medicalised' the offence by including disturbed balance of the mind due to lactation consequent upon the birth of the child.

A study of the epidemiology of infanticide in the half-century since the passing of the 1938 Act has been published since the first edition of this book.[45] This shows a dramatic drop in the homicide rate for infants aged less than one year following a peak in 1945. I doubt if this represents anything more than a return to generally more normal conditions after the Second World War because, since then, the infant homicide rate has remained relatively constant at around 45 per million infants each year,[46] which accounts for some 30 cases a year. It is of passing interest that there was no obvious fall following the passage of the Abortion Act 1967 and the authors point out that the constant rate has persisted despite continuing improvements in social conditions. On the other hand, it is to be noted that the infant homicide rate has not followed the relentless increase in that of homicides as a whole.

Current jurisprudential attitudes

Whether the law requires further modernisation has been a matter of considerable debate. The attack has come from both the legal and the medical sides. From the legal aspect, it was pointed out in the Butler Report[47] that puerperal psychoses were, in fact, no different from other psychoses; it was therefore considered that infanticide could be absorbed into the jurisprudential concept of diminished responsibility[48] a place it has, in practice, always occupied in Scotland, to which the 1938 Act does not run. The medicalisation of infanticide suffered a further blow at much the same time when d'Orban,[49] in particular, emphasised that only a relatively small proportion of filicidal women were, in fact, suffering from any mental abnormality. It became increasingly obvious that the problem of infanticide, associated as it is with very great public sympathy for mothers who kill their newborn children, was being 'solved' by simply fudging the issue through the retention of discredited medical theory; both judges and juries have always been, and still are, extremely reluctant to pursue the logical legal process and, instead, will adapt their reasoning to accommodate public policy.

The practical approach to infanticide is, therefore, very comparable to that which has been discussed already in relation to mercy killing, and there are equally good reasons for doubting its jurisprudential basis. Firstly, there is the general premise that the law should not be seen to depend upon an evasion of the facts. Secondly, to do so inevitably leads to arbitrariness and, in the present context, the distinction between sympathy and perversity becomes blurred very easily. This was highlighted in *Soanes*,[50] where a mother killed her child two days after discharge from the maternity ward and at a time when she was apparently in possession of all her faculties. The judge refused to accept a negotiated plea of infanticide and insisted on her standing trial for murder; the jury found her guilty of infanticide. Even so, a sentence of three years' penal servitude was undisturbed on appeal, when LORD GODDARD CJ had this to say:

> It is impossible to say that the learned judge was not fully justified in passing a substantial sentence on a woman who thus, with apparently no excuse, deliberately killed her child; in fact, he was bound to do so ... The jury returned a verdict of guilty of infanticide although it is difficult to see on what evidence they could find that the balance of the applicant's mind was disturbed at the time as a result of her confinement.[51]

Thirdly, questions arise as to whether the law is, in fact, being fashioned by psychiatrists and whether this is something to be encouraged – or, for that matter, something that the psychiatrists themselves want.[52] Walker[53] referred to psychiatric perjury as being a harmless misinterpretation of 'disturbed balance of mind' and it is certainly true that filicidal mothers are not dangerous to the general public; it is, however, questionable whether such manifest deception is 'harmless' to the image of the legal system as a whole.

In fact, the Butler proposals to eliminate the offence of infanticide would, if adopted, probably limit the woman's defence insofar as there is, currently, no need to prove a causal relationship between mental imbalance and the homicide. Rather, the modern trend is to turn away from the medical tactics of infanticide and to revert to the socio-economic attitudes of the 19th century. The fact, as Walker has pointed out, is that psychiatrists have moved away from viewing infanticide as a crime committed in a state of mind that is attributable to physical processes peculiar to women and use it to cover stresses that result from a miscellany of social difficulties. To this end, the Criminal Law Revision Committee[54] suggested that the concept of the 'effects of giving birth or of lactation' be extended to that of 'circumstances consequent upon birth'; the object would be to extend protection to the woman suffering from environmental stresses, the most important of which include marital discord and housing difficulties. In practice, a reference to 'mental disorder' rather than to 'disturbance of the balance of the mind by reason of [giving birth or lactation]' would cover a wider spectrum of maternal stress; it is not easy to argue convincingly that 'stress' does not result in some sort of disorder or disability of the mind.[55] Such semantic juggling is, however, no more than an expression of the fact that the statutory provisions 'do not recognize legally the connection between child birth and infanticide but create it'.[56] An alternative, and perhaps preferable, approach is to follow the Canadian line and simply to legislate that it is not essential to establish that the balance of a woman's mind was specifically disturbed in order to satisfy the conditions for a conviction for infanticide.[57] A good argument can be made that, irrespective of the nomenclature, the conditions of pregnancy and childbirth do give rise to specific psychiatric abnormalities in women which should be recognised; as a corollary, the offence of infanticide should be retained and, with it, a corresponding sympathy for the perpetrator.[58]

And yet one wonders whether the warning lights should not start to flicker. There is widespread support for including children of the family other than the most recently born under the umbrella of infanticide; the Royal College of Psychiatrists has suggested that the filial 'age limit' in such circumstances should be as high as five years. The line distinguishing stress from inconvenience can be displaced very easily; and it might well be asked why a father should not be subject to the environmental stress of a new baby just as much as is a mother and, similarly, reap the benefit of ameliorating legislation. Liberalisation of the criminal law tends to be founded on very slippery slopes. It is important that we do not lose the essential balance between child protection in general and the protection of others involved in neonatal death.

Conviction and sentencing for infanticide

One of the largest reviews of infanticide in England and Wales, that of Parker and Good dealing with reported offences between 1967 and 1978, is now over 15 years old;[59] nonetheless, it demonstrated some significant trends. It showed that there was a significant fall in the number of convictions over those years even allowing for the falling birth rate, and that an average of only 8.7 women were so convicted in the six years from 1973 to 1978. Interestingly, however, there was no statistically significant change in the overall numbers of homicides of children less than one year old in which the mother would be the principal suspect. Only 'other manslaughter' – meaning manslaughter outwith the terms of the Homicide Act, 1957, s.2, which provided, for the first time in England and Wales, for a reduction of a charge of murder to one of manslaughter on the grounds of diminished responsibility – showed an increase, and the paper studied the interrelationship of these two trends.

Two possibilities were recognised. Either there had been a true decrease in maternal filicides resulting from improved post-natal care and sophisticated family planning – in which case the increase in manslaughter represented no more than part of the general increase in violent crime by women which has clearly come about – or a number of women who might have been available for a verdict of infanticide were being convicted of 'other manslaughter', a scenario which involved a presumption that some women accused of murder were convincing juries that they lacked the necessary intent. Going along with this was the parallel possibility, not discussed by Parker and Good, which presupposed that prosecutors were, in some instances, aware of the token sentences likely to be imposed following conviction for infanticide and were not prepared to see blatantly undeserving cases disposed of by way of a plea of guilty to that offence.[60] It would then be left to a jury to retain or reduce the offence charged and the punishment would then be more likely to fit the crime. Parker and Good, in fact, offered no preference as to cause, but we can get further insight from the later paper by Marks and Kumar.

Their paper confirmed the findings of Parker and Good, in that the proportion of child homicides charged and convicted as infanticide compared with those treated as murder or manslaughter has fallen very markedly since 1956; it is, however, unclear how much of this effect is attributable to the inclusion of both paternal and maternal filicides in the data presented. The figures showed very marked differences, depending on whether the homicides were within the first 24 hours of birth or later. Between 1982 and 1988, 29 of 45 mothers suspected of involvement in the former were not indicted, leaving only 16 (or 35 per cent) to face charges; by contrast, 72 per cent of 68 mothers suspected of killing their babies after the first day were charged. Of the 16 early infant homicides, 11 were charged with infanticide and five with murder; the comparable figures for the 49 'late' cases were 17 infanticides – or approximately half the proportion of the early cases – with 32 indictments for murder or manslaughter. The final verdicts in the early cases were one acquittal, 14 infanticide and 1 'section 2' manslaughter; the late cases resulted in four acquittals, 25 infanticides or lesser offences (51 per cent), 19 manslaughters and one murder (41 per cent when combined).

The problem of indictment is certainly difficult. The slight absurdity of the prosecution bringing a charge of infanticide and, as a result, being bound to bring proof of mitigation was emphasised in the early Australian and Canadian cases.[61] Even so, it was assumed in *Hutty* that it was the intention of the legislature, following passing of the Act, that a case involving the filicide of a neonate was to be presented 'not upon a charge of murder but upon a charge of infanticide'.

The even greater anomaly is that the law, having established the offence and placed it on a criminological par with manslaughter and, in some circumstances, murder,[62] then appears to use the charge as one of exoneration. In 1973,[63] it was noted that prison sentences were so rare that no sentencing policy was discernible and no recent Court of Appeal decisions were available; the case of *Scott* typifies the situation: the guilty mother was detained in prison because it was to her advantage to complete a remedial course in home economics. Subsequently, the Court of Appeal has confirmed that no custodial sentences had been imposed in 59 convictions for infanticide between 1979 and 1988 – all had been dealt with by way of probation, supervision or hospital orders and a pattern was, thereby, established.[64] Judges who attempt to alter that pattern are unlikely to persuade the Court of Appeal. In *R* v. *Lewis*,[65] a 21-year-old woman gave birth to a child she thought was stillborn and concealed it in plastic bags; she stabbed it repeatedly through the plastic when it moved. She was sentenced to 12 months' imprisonment, the sentencer believing that he had a duty to consider the needs of society and that her actions were a denial of the cardinal obligation to protect human life. The Court of Appeal agreed with the judge's sentiments, but questioned whether society required the imposition of a custodial sentence on a young woman whose responsibility was substantially impaired; the sentence was varied to one of probation with submission to psychiatric treatment.

Since only the mother can commit infanticide, fathers who kill their children are in a different category and, as is apparent from the foregoing, this is clearly to their disadvantage. Parker and Good concluded their article by speculating on the reasons why this particular group of homicides should stimulate such partisan legislation and jurisprudence and on why mental disturbance or imbalance related to childbirth should have different legal consequences from mental disturbance brought about by any other cause. They also sounded a warning by contrasting the preferential treatment given to mothers with the consequent reduction in the protection given by the law to a vulnerable section of the population – the infanticide victims. I believe, perhaps simplistically, that this is little more than a reflection of the male instinct to protect women and of a coincident distaste for punishing them. That this may be so is borne out by the work of Marks and Kumar. Irrespective of policy related to convictions for infanticide, men will be more severely punished than will women in cases of child homicide. This is so in relation to both 'section 2' manslaughter and other manslaughter which includes reduction from a charge of murder; it applies irrespective of the brutality of the killing.[66] Their observations have been confirmed by looking at the whole spectrum of homicidal death. Far more women than men who are suspected of homicide will be charged with manslaughter rather than murder: 63 per cent against 22 per cent. Following conviction, only 9 per cent of women were imprisoned in England and Wales in 1982–9 as compared with 56 per cent of men.[67] Increasing evidence indicates that severity of sentencing is a function of the sex of the perpetrator. This is not a universally popular policy. Osborne, for example, pejoratively described the legal process associated with infanticide as an example of the sexist attitude that is ingrained in the criminal law, under which women are not accorded full responsibility for their actions. Moulds[68] has expressed this in the following way:

> It is true that women do enjoy certain benefits of a chivalry factor. They are arrested, prosecuted, and sent to prison less often than are men – the benefit to them is their freedom. A major cost to them, however, is a continuation of a state of public consciousness which holds that women are less able than men and thus in need of special protective treatment. This results in extensive personal, psychological, social, economic and political damage to the democratic notions of self-determination and equality.

I prefer the view of Pollak,[69] whose research was, admittedly, open to criticism:[70] 'One of the outstanding concomitants of the existing inequalities between the sexes is chivalry and the general protective attitude of men towards women.'[71] It is by no means clear to me that respect for womanhood necessarily implies disrespect for women; the anomaly in the law, such as it is, is not a matter of the nature of women but is, rather, one of the nature of men. Perhaps it would be more useful for us to concentrate on eliminating the remaining vestiges of 19th-century thought which tended to hold small children as disposable commodities.

As something of a coda, it should be pointed out that not all jurisdictions have an Infanticide Act or its equivalent: Scotland and the United States are two which spring to mind. This may be because a statute was thought unnecessary. This is certainly true in Scotland, where the concept of diminished responsibility has been available to the defence since long before 1957.[72] It may be, however, that such a discriminatory attitude to women is not universal. In the prosecution in the United States of a British woman, Caroline Beale, who attempted to smuggle her dead baby out of that country, the presiding judge is reported as saying: 'I believe that any law that grants a blanket exemption from prosecution or punishment to those who kill their children when their children are under the age of one, is a law that is primitive and uncivilised.'[73] Ms Beale, who pleaded guilty to manslaughter, was sentenced to eight months' imprisonment, which she had already served on remand, and five years' probation with psychiatric treatment. It is said that a prison sentence is a common penalty for filicide in the United States.[74] Jackson,[75] on the other hand, suggests that the US courts generally treat infanticide suspects leniently; criticism of the investigation of the Beale case should not, in his view, have been directed at the vigour with which it was conducted but, rather, at the time it took to complete it.

Women who kill their children

The general similarity of patterns of maternal filicide irrespective of period or location has already been noted. The major British study remains that of d'Orban,[76] whose classification was based on those of Scott[77] and Resnick.[78] D'Orban recognised six causative categories of maternal filicide in an investigation of 89 women who were accused of killing or attempting to murder their children in the years 1970–75. These categories, in descending order of frequency, were as follows.

a   Battering mothers (36 cases). It is important to note that battering here is defined as filicide on a sudden impulse characterised by loss of temper provoked by a filial stimulus. There were *no* cases of deliberate cruelty of prolonged type.
b   Mentally ill mothers. There were 24 instances, the diagnosis being generally either depressive psychosis or personality disorder.
c   Neonaticide (11 cases). These were isolated on Resnick's criteria: killing or attempted killing within 24 hours of giving birth.
d   Retaliating women. Surprisingly, there were as many as nine instances in which the mother transferred her aggression from her husband to her child.
e   Unwanted children. Eight cases were separated from the neonaticide group because they lived for more than a day. Half the deaths resulted from neglect and half from active aggression; the former involved a markedly younger group of mothers.
f   There was one mercy killing.

Comparing these results with those of Resnick, there are two major differences: there were far more acutely battered children in the British series (40 per cent against 6 per cent) and there was a wide difference in the results for altruistic murder (40 per cent of Resnick's cases as opposed to a single British case). These discrepancies are probably no more than illustrative of the difficulties of definition to which attention has been drawn already. Resnick's analysis was of the world literature, involving papers in 13 languages dating from the mid-18th century; the number of sub-cultures involved and the opportunities for alteration in public attitudes are, therefore, so many as to make the series inappropriate for comparative study. Moreover, the ages of the included victims run as high as 20 years. This, of itself, is sufficient to explain the high incidence of altruistic killing; an even more important limitation is that reported cases reach the literature because of their immediate interest – they cannot be regarded as an unselected sample of the total.

We are, however, more interested in the similarities between series and, of these, the most important by far is the universal distinction which has been found between early and late infanticides. Here the significant, and previously noted, finding is that disturbance of the mind is rare in cases of early infanticide occurring within the first 24 hours of infant life. Mothers who kill their babies at this time are commonly young and unmarried; they conceal their pregnancies and conceal their victims, in whom the cause of death is most often suffocation or drowning; the infants are killed because they are unwanted, yet, so 'passive' are the mothers' personalities, that they do not seek termination of pregnancy. This last attribute may explain the anomaly already noted that liberalisation of the abortion law has not affected the occurrence of *early* infanticide.

There is evidence that filicide is very much a female crime. Some 10 per cent of all homicides are attributable to women in the United Kingdom; the proportion rises to 47 per cent when killings attributed to parents are isolated.[79] The observations of Marks and Kumar also shed some interesting light on maternal filicide. Twenty-one per cent of 213 infant homicides occurred within 24 hours of birth, and it is here, as would be expected, that the proportion of infant deaths resulting from maternal action is highest: the ratio of maternal/paternal filicides is as high as 11:1. In direct contrast, the ratio of mother to father or other suspects above this infant age is either lower than or close to 1.0. Marks and Kumar also found that, leaving aside those killed in the first 24 hours of life, younger children were still at greatest risk. This is in general agreement with an *a priori* expectation that the disturbing effect of a child on both the mother and the father would normalise with time; but one is left wondering whether the reported incidence of early maternal filicide is not artificially low and whether there are other, essentially practical, reasons why this should be so.

Early infanticide and the pathologist

The prosecution's major practical difficulty in securing a conviction lies in the assumption of stillbirth until the opposite is proved – and this may be, frankly, impossible. The simplest example is the baby delivered into the lavatory pan; such an infant may be perfectly viable in normal circumstances but will never have a chance of demonstrating this in the conditions envisaged. Moreover, live birth presupposes *total* extrusion from the mother, and it is more than probable that the neonate's feet will still be within the birth passage when its head is in the water. It is true that a charge of child destruction (see Chapter 5) could then be brought, but the hurdle of intention then becomes very hard to overcome – and rightly so, for accidental precipitate labour is not uncommon and, even in this modern age, some young mothers do not even know that they are pregnant. Similarly, intracranial haemorrhage due to head injury is a common mode of death in early infanticide, but so it is in unattended precipitate first labour, and it would be a brave pathologist who guaranteed to make the distinction accurately. Many similar examples could be given.

Perhaps the most important factor is that true infanticide – or maternal filicide – frequently results from non-wounding violence in the form of suffocative types of death.[80] Marks and Kumar's series indicates that the proportions of wounding and non-wounding violence are approximately equal in this type of case. By contrast, fathers are more than eight times more likely to kill their children by way of wounding violence (shaking, hitting, strangling, stabbing and so on) than they are, say, to smother or drown them. Isolated figures for the first 24 hours of life confirm this pattern by way of a mirror-image: only 18 per cent of 44 such deaths were associated with wounding. When one remembers that mothers are almost as likely to kill their children in the first 24 hours of life as at any other time during the first year, it becomes apparent that, whereas child murder may be easy to identify, infanticide presents a problem of almost unique complexity.

Proof of life which has existed for only a few short moments after birth must depend upon demonstration of aeration of the lungs and, easy as this may sound in theory, it is something that is often very difficult to determine satisfactorily. Spontaneous breathing within the birth canal does occur; anoxic convulsions can give rise to spurious signs of aeration; and, while it is always said that spontaneous respiration can be distinguished from attempted resuscitation, it is certainly not easy to do so in practice. These are specific examples. Overall, however, the pathologist is in greatest difficulty in the face of putrefaction of the body, which is very common in view of the frequency with which infanticidal deaths are concealed. The well-known hydrostatic test for pulmonary aeration has been subject to criticism, much of which is focused on the production of gas by putrefactive micro-organisms. While fully appreciating its limitations, I do not believe the test to be as useless as it is often portrayed,[81] but the controversy is such that it is true to say that a successful prosecution for infanticide is improbable even if there is no more than slight putrefaction – and that is so even when evidence of breathing is to be seen on microscopic examination. In short, the pathologist is often forced to diagnose stillbirth, even though he has the best of unbiased intentions;[82] as a result, an unknown number of infanticides must be excluded from the official records. The neonatal period is that which provides the greatest difficulties in the practice of forensic pathology; it is also one of the least rewarding in terms of professional satisfaction.

The cot (or crib) death problem: the sudden infant death syndrome

The peak incidence of cot death is at some 12 weeks of age and it is at this time that what Myers termed 'post-partum blues' are likely to be at their height. Suffocation is the commonest method of infanticide and the findings in both suffocation and cot death are those of anoxia; these are, themselves, variable and non-specific, particularly insofar as suffocation is that form of unnatural asphyxia which involves no regional increase in capillary pressure and thus gives rise to no localising signs. It is clear that it can be extremely difficult to determine between the two entities at a post-mortem examination; there can be few forensic pathologists who have not been confronted with at least one confession of infanticide in a case which has been diagnosed as a cot death.

This is not, however, to suggest that all such 'confessions' are genuine. Parents – and, particularly, mothers who are inadequately counselled – often have strong feelings of guilt following a cot death and it takes very little further psychiatric stress to convert these to a conviction of culpability. The combined result is that the occurrence of infanticidal suffocation is unknown and unknowable, and estimates depend very much on the unsupported impressions of individual observers. The classic case in the United Kingdom was that of Adam Bithell,[83] who became the fourth apparent cot death in a family. The coroner's pathologist, who was convinced that some 50 per cent of cot deaths were, in fact, concealed filicides, diagnosed death as being due to mechanical asphyxia, a conclusion that was accepted by the coroner; a second opinion emphasised the difficulties involved and the uncertainty of diagnosis. The inquest verdict was quashed at judicial review on the grounds that the coroner had paid insufficient regard to the more conservative view.

One most important contribution to the debate was that of Emery,[84] who pointed to the surprisingly common occurrence of cot deaths in unfavoured populations such as second aboriginal children and female Chinese infants. Emery believed that the proportion of 'cot deaths' discovered to be filicides depended on the depth of inquiry; his own estimate was of some 10 per cent in his own catchment area and between 2 per cent and 10 per cent overall. Emery's experience of cot deaths is second to none, and he has always advised and applied a thoroughly sympathetic attitude to the sudden infant death syndrome; this surprisingly high estimate of the occurrence of criminality therefore deserves serious consideration. Unfortunately, even if his assessment is correct, it does not help the pathologist to identify the individual cases in his or her practice – and this, perhaps, typifies the reasons for dissatisfaction with the medico-legal management of infanticide.

Summary

We are, then, left with the statutory crime of infanticide as one which is illogically based, often extremely difficult to prove, somewhat arbitrarily prosecuted and very rarely punished seriously. Currently, it seems to lie in a limbo of discredited tradition and it is surely time that public attitudes to maternal filicide were redefined. On the one hand, the current laxity in prosecution and sentencing could be seen as incompatible with calls for increasing protection of the very young – in which case, the concept of post-partum psychosis should be discarded. At the other extreme, early infanticide could be accepted as a logical and inevitable extension of liberal abortion legislation, a process which, as we have already noted, forms part of the philosophy of 'personhood'. Discovery of an acceptable compromise defies the efforts of academic lawmakers – but there can be few who are satisfied with the current irregularity in both the concept and the application of the law.

Notes

1   For an appraisal, see P.R. Wilson, '"Stranger" child-murder: issues relating to causes and controls' (1988) 36 Forens Sci Internat 267.
2   For an old but still useful review, see the study by P.D. Scott, 'Fatal battered baby cases' (1973) 13 Med Sci Law 197.
3   *R v. Whitaker* (1976) 63 Cr App Rep 193.
4   This may not be true in cases of particular severity. In *R v. Aston and Mason*

(1988), *The Times*, 22 December, p. 4, both man and woman received sentences of 12 years' imprisonment; equal sentences of seven years' imprisonment were also imposed in *R* v. *Hussain and Hussain*, noted in the same report.

5 See, for example, *Whitaker*, n. 3 above, when charges against the mother were dropped very early in the case, despite conflicting evidence.

6 Note 2 above.

7 I. Wilkey, J. Pearn, G. Petrie and J. Nixon, 'Neonaticide, infanticide and child homicide' (1982) 22 Med Sci Law 31.

8 P.T. d'Orban, 'Women who kill their children' (1979) 134 Br J Psychiatry 560.

9 *R* v. *Ward* (1956) 40 Cr App Rep 1.

10 Doctors should certainly know of the syndrome and there is a live campaign to educate the general public. See H. Carty and J. Ratcliffe, 'The shaken infant syndrome' (1995) 310 Brit Med J 344.

11 *R* v. *Williams* (1984) 6 Cr App Rep (S) 298.

12 *R* v. *Doughty* (1986) 83 Cr App Rep 319.

13 *R* v. *Gibbins and Proctor* (1919) 13 Cr App Rep 134.

14 *R* v. *Watson and Watson* (1959) 43 Cr App Rep 111.

15 [1899] 1 QB 283.

16 In fact, under the now repealed Prevention of Cruelty to Children Act, 1894, s.1, LORD RUSSELL CJ was not satisfied that there was not sufficient evidence also to justify a conviction at common law (at 292).

17 Failure to provide medical aid is now part of the definition of neglect: Children and Young Persons Act, 1933, s.1(2)(*a*); Children and Young Persons (Scot) Act, 1937, sch.1 as amended.

18 *R* v. *Sheppard and another* [1980] 3 All ER 899.

19 1964 SLT (Reps) 72. There are some classic examples from the United States, such as *People* v. *McQuiston* 12 Cal App 3d 584 (1970) or, for a maternal case, *State* v. *Gindorf* 512 NE 2d 770 (Ill, 1987).

20 P.J. Resnick, 'Child murder by parents: a psychiatric review of filicide' (1969) 126 Amer J Psychiat 325.

21 Wilkey *et al.*, n. 7 above.

22 (1961) 1 Med Sci Law 192.

23 *R* v. *Taylor* (1980) CLY 510, quoted by Leng, n. 27 below.

24 B.J. Mitchell, 'The gravity of murder' (1987) 137 NLJ 977.

25 G. Williams, *Textbook of Criminal Law* (2nd edn, 1983), London: Stevens.

26 *R* v. *Price* (1971) Times, 22 December.

27 For discussion, see R. Leng, 'Mercy killing and the CLRC' (1982) 132 NLJ 76.

28 14th Report of the Criminal Law Revision Committee, *Offences Against the Person* (1980), Cmnd 7844, London: HMSO. See [1980] Crim LR 331.

29 It is becoming increasingly difficult to see some 'non-treatment' decisions in the courts as other than being based on the quality of life and, hence, indistinguishable from legalised 'mercy killing'. See, for example, *Re C (a baby)* (1996) 32 BMLR 44. There is, of course, a profound difference between the home and the hospital environments.

30 Infanticide Act, 1938. The distribution of comparable legislation in the Commonwealth is patchy. This definition of infanticide is recognised in Canada. In Australia, New South Wales, Victoria and Tasmania have legislation based on that of England; the crime of infanticide exists neither in the Code States of Queensland and Western Australia, nor in South Australia and the Northern Territories – an omission that was responsible for one of the most sensational trials for child murder in recent times (*Chamberlain* v. *The Queen* (1983) 46 ALR 493 (FC); [No 2] (1983) 153 CLR 521 (HC)).

31 P.J. Resnick, 'Murder of the newborn: a psychiatric review of neonaticide' (1970) 126 Amer J Psychiat 1414.

32   Offences Against the Person Act, 1861, s.60; Concealment of Birth (Scotland) Act, 1809.
33   The most recent comprehensive review of infanticide is to be found in M.N. Marks and R. Kumar, 'Infanticide in England and Wales' (1993) 33 Med Sci Law 329.
34   J.K. Mason and R.A. McCall Smith, *Law and Medical Ethics* (4th edn, 1995) London: Butterworths, ch. 7.
35   See, for example, M. Davies, *Textbook on Medical Law* (1996), London: Blackstone Press, ch. 14.
36   L. Adelson, 'Slaughter of the innocents' (1961) 264 New Engl J Med 1345.
37   S.A. Myers, 'Maternal filicide' (1970) 120 Amer J Dis Child 534.
38   P.T.K. Cheung, 'Maternal filicide in Hong Kong 1981-85' (1986) 26 Med Sci Law 185. But the large number of 'cot deaths' (see p. 393) that occur in female infants in mainland China may give cause to wonder if there are not hidden cultural differences.
39   Marks and Kumar, n. 33 above.
40   K. O'Donovan, 'The medicalisation of infanticide' [1984] Crim LR 259.
41   W.L. Langer, 'Infanticide: a historical survey' (1974) 1 Hist Child Quart 353.
42   The same point is made in all historical surveys: for example, K.L. Moseley, 'The history of infanticide in Western society' (1986) 1 Issues Law Med 345; J.A. Osborne, 'The crime of infanticide: throwing out the baby with the bathwater' (1987) 6 Canad J Fam Law 47; M. Jackson, 'Infanticide: historical perspectives' (1996) 146 NLJ 416.
43   Jackson, n. 42 above.
44   In *R* v. *O'Donoghue* (1928) 20 Cr App Rep 132, it was held that a child aged 35 days was not newly born and that the mother who killed such a child was guilty of murder. See also the Canadian case, *R* v. *Marchello* (1951) 4 DLR 751, which precipitated a change in the Canadian law.
45   Marks and Kumar, n. 33 above.
46   Despite the comparatively small numbers, this is still four times the average for homicide of children aged more than one year.
47   *Report of the Committee on Mentally Abnormal Offenders* (Butler Report) (1975), Cmnd 6244, London: HMSO.
48   Introduced into England and Wales by the Homicide Act, 1957, s.2.
49   Note 8 above.
50   *R* v. *Soanes* (1948) 32 Cr App R 136.
51   It is fair to say that, as will be discussed later, this was probably the last time that an overtly punitive sentence was passed following conviction for infanticide. Manslaughter may, however, be a different matter, subject to the general considerations discussed at p. 388. In 1995, a 22-year-old woman, who killed her 14-month-old child and attempted suicide, was sentenced to four years' imprisonment despite being diagnosed as having an immature personality disorder: *R* v. *Leggett* [1996] 2 Cr App Rep (S) 77.
52   D. Chiswick, 'Use and abuse of psychiatric testimony' (1985) 290 Brit Med J 975.
53   N. Walker, 'Butler v. The CLRC and others' [1981] Crim LR 596.
54   Note 28 above.
55   Mental Health Act 1983, s.1(2).
56   Osborne, n. 42 above.
57   Criminal Code, s.590.
58   D. Maier-Katkin and R. Ogle, 'A rationale for infanticide laws' [1993] Crim LR 903. Support for the view is provided by R.D. Mackay, 'The consequences of killing very young children' [1993] Crim LR 21.
59   E. Parker and F. Good, 'Infanticide' (1981) 5 Human Law Behav 237.

60   The court, itself, might take that view as in *R* v. *Soanes*, n. 50 above; *R* v. *Broad* (1978) 68 Cr App Rep 281.

61   See A.A. Bartholomew and A. Bonnici, 'Infanticide: a statutory offence' [1965] 2 Med J Aust 1018, quoting *R* v. *Hutty* [1953] VR 338 and *Marchello*, n. 44 above. It is to be noted that a charge of attempted infanticide is competent: *R* v. *K A Smith* [1983] Crim LR 739. See A.J. Wilkins, 'Attempted infanticide' (1985) 146 Br J Psychiatry 206.

62   *Practice note* [1987] 3 All ER 1064; Coroners Act 1988, s.16.

63   *R* v. *Scott* [1973] Crim LR 708.

64   *R* v. *Sainsbury* [1990] Crim LR 348.

65   [1990] Crim LR 348. See also similar comments in *Sainsbury*, above.

66   The authors are clearly doubtful whether justice is thereby done and call for urgent research on the point.

67   A. Wilczynski and A. Morris, 'Parents who kill their children' [1993] Crim LR 31. Their findings seem to be confirmed by more recent work: see S. Haynes, 'Juries allow more women to walk free' (1997), *The Sunday Times*, 2 March, p. 1.7.

68   E. Moulds, 'Chivalry and paternalism: disparities of treatment in the criminal justice system', in S.K. Datesman and F.R. Scarpitti (eds), *Women, Crime and Justice* (1980) New York: Oxford University Press. For a different view, see C. Docherty, 'Female Offenders', in S.A.M. McLean and N. Burrows, *The Legal Relevance of Gender: Some Aspects of Sex-based Discrimination* (1988), London: Macmillan.

69   O. Pollak, *The Criminality of Women* (1950), Philadelphia: University of Pennsylvania Press.

70   The above quotations from Moulds and Pollak are taken from M. Eaton, *Justice for Women?* (1986), Milton Keynes: Open University Press, which takes a very critical view.

71   Pollak himself is less anti-feminist than he is often presented: 'Many male attempts to understand women have actually been attempts to rationalize men's treatment of the other sex and have frequently been nothing but self-deceptions' (*The Criminality of Women* (1961), New York: A.S. Barnes & Co, at p. 149).

72   *HM Advocate* v. *Dingwall* (1867) 5 Irv 466.

73   J. Butler and S. Hall, 'First steps to a partial recovery' (1996), *The Scotsman*, 9 March, p. 6.

74   Wilczynski and Morris, n. 67 above.

75   Note 42 above.

76   Note 8 above. This classification has been maintained in current authoritative literature. See, for example, R. Bluglass, 'Infanticide and filicide', in R. Bluglaas and P. Bowden, *Principles and Practice of Forensic Psychiatry* (1990), Edinburgh: Churchill Livingstone, ch. VII, 7.

77   Note 2 above.

78   Note 20 above.

79   Wilczynski and Morris, n. 67 above.

80   This is confirmed in a small recent study from Canada which shows some other interesting similarities – and differences – from other results discussed here: J.D. Marleau, R. Roy, L. Laporte *et al.*, 'Homicide d'enfant commis par la mère' (1995) 40 Canad J Psychiat 142.

81   For major criticism, see B. Knight, *Forensic Pathology* (1991), London: Edward Arnold, p. 409. My own views are set out in J.K. Mason, *Forensic Medicine for Lawyers* (3rd edn, 1995), London: Butterworths, p. 274.

82   Theoretically, charges could still be laid under the Offences Against the Person

Act, 1861, s.60 (concealment of birth) or under the Concealment of Birth (Scotland) Act 1809, but the technical difficulties are considerable.

83 *In the matter of an inquest into the death of Adam Bithell, deceased* (1986) 150 JP 273.

84 J.L. Emery, 'Infanticide, filicide, and cot death' (1985) 60 Arch Dis Child 505. Similar views were later expressed by R. Meadow, 'Suffocation' (1989) 298 Brit Med J 1572.

Index